1991 Which? Wi

1991 Which? Wine Guide

Edited by Andrew Jefford

Published by Consumers' Association
and Hodder & Stoughton

Which? Books are commissioned and researched by
The Association for Consumer Research and published by
Consumers' Association, 2 Marylebone Road, NW1 4DX and
Hodder & Stoughton, 47 Bedford Square, London WC1B 3DP

British Library Cataloguing in Publication Data

Which? wine guide. – 1991 –
   1. Wines. Buyers' Guides – Serials
   2. Great Britain. Wines trades.
   Directories – Serials
   641.2′2′0294

ISBN 0 340 52817 6

Cover Linda Schwab
Cover typography Dick Vine
Illustrations Sally Kindberg
Index Jill Ford

Typesetting by Page Bros (Norwich) Ltd
Printed and bound in Great Britain
by Collins, Glasgow

Acknowledgements

The Editor would like to thank Philip Atkinson, James Berry, Liz Berry,
Simon Farr, Aileen Hall, Peter Hastings, João Henriques, Rosamund
Hitchcock, Caroline Miles, Dirk van der Niepoort, Jordanis Petrides, Philip
Rowles, Stephen Skelton and especially Joanna Bregosz and Sarah Wright
for their help in the preparation of this Guide.

Contents

CONTENTS

Part III   Where to buy

Part IV   Find out more about wine

The Association for Consumer Research (parent body of Consumers' Association) has for some years declined to evaluate South African products. The Association is a founder member of the International Association for Consumer Unions, which is vigorously opposed to discrimination against any group of consumers on grounds of race, creed, gender or nationality. The Association looks forward to the change of conditions in South Africa which will allow that country to be reinstated in Consumers' Association publications.

Introduction

What is special about buying wine in Britain? Two things. One is choice. In no other country in the world will you find so many wines from so many different wine-growing regions for sale in so many country corners, small towns, quiet suburbs and city-centre boutiques. The British have always revered wine, probably because they have never produced it themselves on a wide scale; the last decade has seen reverence become passion, even familiarity. A long trading tradition has blossomed in a profusion of importers and importing: we have never had so many bottles to choose from as we do at present, and this choice looks set to extend still further as the political freedom that 1989's autumn of astonishment brought to Eastern Europe permits agricultural and commercial excellence there.

The second particularity of wine purchase in Britain is its high cost, relative to other everyday purchases and relative to wine purchase in other European Community countries. Britain is closer to Scandinavia than to Europe in its approach to the taxation of alcohol, and John Major's first budget as Chancellor in March 1990 made the prospect of common duty rates within the EC by 1992 look even more distant than it did in 1989 or 1988. We pay 83p per bottle of table wine as a direct tax on alcohol; the French pay a mere 70 centimes (about 8p) via 'transport taxes' (the *capsule-congé* system) and the Italians nothing at all. Other costs, such as 15 per cent VAT, agent's and merchant's profit, and distribution and shipping costs, conspire to make 25p's worth of wine cost at least £2.50 on British shelves. (VAT on wine is 18.6 per cent in France, but only 9 per cent in Italy for still wines; sparkling wines attract a VAT rate of 19 per cent in Italy.) This high price has, no doubt, been another contributory factor in our according wine reverence.

Combine these two particularities, and you have compelling reasons for the existence of *Which? Wine Guide*. We are here to help you get the best value you can from your wine purchases and to provide you with the guidance you need to explore wine intelligently, to the extent you wish, and in the directions you wish.

Two ends; and we offer two means to those ends. The first is the heart of our book: an A-Z listing of Britain's wine stockists, together with descriptions of their service, their range, their strengths and weaknesses. When you go into a merchant's premises, the wine world is effectively limited to the stock

9

available in that shop. It can be depressingly small or bafflingly wide. If the former, that merchant should not be in this *Guide*, unless you've stumbled on a bad branch of an otherwise good chain. If the latter, the service factor comes into play: even the most knowledgeable among us will meet areas of unfamiliarity, dark peninsulas which we can chart only with the help that shop staff are able to offer us. In either case, when you take a bottle home, you are trusting the palate of whoever owns, or buys for, that shop. This is why we set so much store by the description of stockists: they are the channel through which we all travel to meet the world's wines.

In this respect, please let us know if we've overlooked anyone, misjudged anyone, or included anyone who, you feel, does not offer an adequate service. *Which? Wine Guide* has not, to date, attracted the level of reader response of its sister publication, *The Good Food Guide*. Help us change that. Any comments at all, on any aspect of the *Guide* – but particularly on the level of service and help available from merchants, and on the quality of their wines – will be read with close attention and reflected in next year's *Guide*. Only with your help can we fulfil the *Guide*'s potential. Only in fulfilling its potential can the *Guide* be as useful as possible to you.

The second means we offer to achieve the dual end of helping you to find value for money, and to explore wine in a rational and informed manner, is more disparate than our listing of stockists but, we hope, no less useful. It takes the form of a series of preliminary features, a short guide to the wines of the world and a reference section at the end of the book containing names and addresses that may be useful in furthering your knowledge of wine.

As a theme to link this year's introductory features, we have chosen the general notion of 'understanding'. We all want value for money with our wine purchases, but what does this mean? The appreciation of wine is notoriously subjective, so can a wine ever be said with any certainty to be good or bad value for money? The Editor offers some perspectives on this elusive ideal in the first feature, to help you to decide for yourself whether a wine is good value or not.

The second feature turns to matters of practical understanding. We are all familiar with bottles of wine on shop shelves, and the growing of grapes and their vinification are well documented. But what happens between these two stages? How does wine actually get from Cloudy Bay in New Zealand to a crowded shop in Oxford Street? Wink Lorch tells the Bottle's Tale.

Do merchants understand what customers want? And do customers understand the difficulties and problems faced by merchants as they try to provide the best service they can? To find out, we thought we would ask two consumers, student Richard Marriott and International Wine and Food Society member David Latt, to write open letters to an imaginary compound merchant. Understanding, though, is a two-way process, so we also asked Simon Loftus of Adnams and Oddbins branch manager David Robertson to write to an equally compounded customer. We hope there are surprises all round.

Wine is, in almost every case, designed to accompany food, and there are few foods that are not well accompanied by some wine or other. But which foods go best with which wines, and why? Aileen Hall, editor of *Which? Wine Monthly* and food writer as well as former chief inspector for *The Good Food Guide*, deepens our understanding of this issue, one which can make enormous difference to our perception of the success of wine, and the pleasure of a meal.

Health, next, is something we all hold dear. What exactly happens inside us when we drink a glass of wine? If wine can damage health, can it also promote it? How can we enjoy wine to the full without jeopardising our health? Dr Thomas Stuttaford, Medical Correspondent to *The Times*, helps us to understand what happens once we've swallowed that mouthful of Nuits.

Under the 'Stocking Up' heading, you will find a discussion of all the different types of shops through which wines can be bought, to help you choose where you can best buy what you wish. There are also notes on storing and serving wines in this section. A cautionary tale brings Part I to a close, and clarifies what protection the law affords you as a wine consumer.

Part II of the *Guide* provides an introduction to the wines of the world, and is preceded by a master glossary containing all the terms you are likely to encounter on wine labels, or in the articles that follow. This year we've put the emphasis on accessibility, profiling tastes and types rather than individual wineries so that you can explore and discover for yourself what's good and what isn't. Our 'taste boxes' should give you at least some idea as to the type of wine you will find when the cork comes out, how best to serve the wine and what kind of foods it will accompany. We have recommended distinguished or trustworthy producers where relevant, but do remember two points in this connection. First of all, these recommended producers will not be the only people making good wines in each district: there will certainly be others, and the wines of some of these other producers will certainly be sold in this country. Secondly, even the best producers make disappointing wines from time to time, so don't assume that 'recommended' is cast in bronze. It's thrown in clay, and fired by a success or two, yet an untimely hailstorm or a spot of ill health when the racking or bottling was due can break the pattern. If a merchant whom you trust recommends a wine to you, try it, no matter how little known or even despised its producer may be. If the wine is poor, revise your opinion of your merchant, and think about going elsewhere. If it's good, stick with the wine – and the merchant.

Similar qualifications apply to the Editor's Choice, another of this year's innovations. This is a personal choice of those wines which, in the course of a year's drinking, have impressed the Editor with their concentration, style and price. They are not the year's twenty best wines, because there is no such thing as a 'best' wine. Beauty in wine, as in all things, is various and relative. The choice won't please everyone, nor is it meant to: its aim is simply to stimulate readers to try something new. Do write with comments.

That's our *Guide*. Use it; stay in touch; enjoy your wine.

1991 Which? Wine Guide awards

We have moved away from a system of regional awards to awards based on specialities. This, we hope, will allow readers to pursue enthusiasms with those well placed to further them, and will provide open fields in which merchants can compete for awards in future editions of the *Guide*. Remember that one speciality does not exclude another, and that any merchant of award-winning merits will have an enormous amount to offer even the uncommitted wine enthusiast.

Bordeaux Specialist of the Year
Jointly awarded to *Master Cellar Wine Warehouse* and *Davisons*

For quietly acquiring a huge stock, discreetly ageing it, and pricing it with restraint

Burgundy Specialist of the Year
Haynes Hanson & Clark

For a wide range of wines from top growers – and a retail licence. Runners-up *Laytons, Le Nez Rouge* and *Thos Peatling* deserve mention, for kindred virtues

Rhône Specialist of the Year
Croque-en-Bouche

For immoderate buying and remarkable hoarding abilities

Loire Specialist of the Year
Nobody Inn

For devotion to the cause. Runners up *D Byrne & Co, Raeburn Fine Wines, Lay & Wheeler* and *Adnams* deserve mention for sterling stocking

French Country Wine Specialist of the Year
Bordeaux Direct

For a decade of getting to Entraygues, Estaing, Marcillac, Montravel and everywhere else before the rest

Italian Specialist of the Year
Winecellars

For rising to the challenge few others are ready for yet, and meeting it capably and communicatively. Runners-up *Valvona & Crolla* and *The Upper Crust* deserve mention for rising to the same challenge

Spanish Specialist of the Year
La Reserva

Simply for being the best in a surprisingly large field. *Moreno Wines* and *Laymont & Shaw* are close behind

German Specialist of the Year
Wine Schoppen

For assembling a first-class list, and for giving customers much-appreciated help in exploring it

Australian Specialist of the Year
Alex Findlater

Still the antipodean list to beat – or even to match

North American Specialist of the Year
Windrush Wines

For commitment to unfashionable excellence. Runners-up *Les Amis du Vin* are no less committed, and *D Byrne & Co* is the best of the North

Supermarket of the Year
J Sainsbury

For achieving the best balance between innovation and consolidation, and for buying that is as surefooted as ever. Runners-up *Booths* and *Waitrose* deserve mention for their merchant-like approaches to supermarket wine sales

Mail-Order Merchant of the Year
Adnams

For communicative abilities that demean neither seller nor purchaser, and that respect wine's complexity; and for a range that is never less than characterful

Fine Wine Merchant of the Year
Reid Wines
For both depth and width of stock, honesty,
scrupulousness – and a retail licence. *Peter Wylie Fine
Wines* and *T&W Wines* in hot pursuit

Wine Warehouse of the Year
Ad Hoc Wine Warehouse
For the best warehouse range in Britain. *Majestic Wine
Warehouses* and *Wizard Wine Warehouses* deserve mention
for proving that many branches do not jeopardise the
warehouse deal, and *Master Cellar Wine Warehouse*
deserves mention for its classical strengths

High Street Chain of the Year
Oddbins
For combining the service of an independent, the prices
of a supermarket, the range of a mail-order specialist and
the enthusiasm of a warehouse – and putting it in the
high street

Independent Merchant of the Year
D Byrne & Co
For buying and stocking what others only dream about.
Peter Green and *The Wine House* will dazzle you, too

Service Award of the Year
Tanners
'. . . wonderful. They are helpful, they correct mistakes
uncomplainingly, they *keep their word*: if they promise,
they deliver the goods. If I had to deal with only one
commercial outfit . . . it would be Tanners.' One reader
speaks for many

Organic Merchant of the Year
Haughton Fine Wines
For taking it seriously and doing it well

En Primeur Merchant of the Year

Farr Vintners

For daring, and winning, with '89 Bordeaux. Runners-up *Nigel Baring* (long, sound service) and *Adnams* (thoughtful; not Bordeaux-obsessed) deserve mention

Wine List of the Year

John Armit Wines

For aesthetic excellence beyond what is reasonable. Runners-up *Vessel du Vin* (the photography) and *Haughton Fine Wines* (the format) deserve mention

Part I

Features

appreciation of wine

Is It Worth It?

Andrew Jefford

'A strawberry is a strawberry,' said Peter Hall, an English wine-grower, thinking out loud about why he'd chosen to grow vines in preference to anything else; 'and a dead pig is a dead pig.' He knew: he'd spent ten years as a pig farmer and loves pigs, as testified by the pig motif on the floor tiles in his kitchen and the pig-shaped weathervane over his barn outhouse. But pork is just pork, year in and year out; so Peter Hall took up wine-growing.

Wine is man's greatest agricultural challenge: no other farmed product is so supple, changeable and complex. It is the variousness of the earth and of the seasons made liquid, rendered perceptible.

And that is why, in an age when the only constraint on the source of what we consume is our desire, the purchase of wine is such a complicated affair. There can be few more baffling experiences for a consumer, no matter how well informed, than walking into a well-stocked wine merchant's premises with a £10 note and no preconceptions as to what to spend it on. The range on offer (all in uniform glass and cork), and the complications wrought by the multilingual nature of the product, combine to produce wine-buyer's vertigo, in which shelves full of bottles labelled with half-remembered names begin to spin and shuffle before the victim's eyes. Magazine articles and books devoted to the wines of the world are no help then; a chat with a friendly and competent assistant is the only lifeline. Which is why this Guide is published.

Let's suppose you get the help you need, and you take two bottles home, two bottles which you have every reason to vest high hopes in. Will you be pleased or disappointed? Will you buy those wines again, visit that shop again? Was it, after all, worth it?

This, the fundamental question for every consumer, is as relevant to the purchase of wine as it is to the purchase of a tumble drier or a three-door hatchback, though it is more difficult to answer with precision about wine than about domestic equipment or cars. Difficult, because wine is a luxury item, and luxury items are priced irrationally; difficult, too, because the appreciation of wine is subjective, therefore value for money changes constantly according to different individuals' judgments of a single wine. This short article explores four perspectives concerning wine's value for money, with the aim of helping you, if not to make every buy a bargain, at least to see through some of the mist that shrouds its purchase.

The first perspective is one that only you can provide, for it concerns your personal finances. How much is £10 to you? Is it a trifling sum, one you can spend without regard for the consequences, or does it require a glance ahead to the rest of the week's likely expenditure on food and other essentials before you can exchange it for wine? How wealthy you are is a primary determinant in establishing value for money. If £10 or even £20 is a trifling sum to you, then most wines will be, potentially, good value. All you have to do is appreciate their qualities, or note their failings. If £10 or more for a bottle of wine is affordable for a special occasion, then the same is true, though the stakes are higher: you won't be very tolerant of failings. If £10 is a lot of money, though, then few burgundies or champagnes – no matter how fine they are in absolute terms – are ever going to be good value for money compared with available alternatives. They may be better, but will rarely be twice as good, as the best alternative at half the price. We could call this perspective the Law of Lucre: the more money you have to spend, the greater the number of wines that may provide good value for money.

If your resources are limited, don't be bullied by merchants or journalists into buying top, classic wines because 'nothing else can match such-and-such' or 'so-and-so really out-performed the rest in '89': if the wine is frighteningly expensive, you can always find better value elsewhere. For many of us, any wine at over £10 or £15 a bottle offers dubious value for money, because £10 or £15 is the maximum which it is reasonable to spend, within the context of our other outgoings, on 66cl of water, 7cl of alcohol and 2cl of flavoury residues. Spend more by all means, to buy a label or taste a big name, but be aware that that's what you're doing; expect whatever you like, but don't count on value for money. Some of the wines at £25 per bottle are certainly finer than those at £8 per bottle, but by no means all; and if finer, by how much? In what way? To whom, when, and where?

This brings us to the second major perspective governing value for money in wine, which we will call the Twin Fallacy of Excellence. It should be pointed out immediately that this does not mean that excellence in wine is mythical. It isn't. Excellence in wine is very real, and always to be applauded. The twin fallacy is to assume that:

    (a) price reflects relative excellence;
    (b) 'excellence' is always what is wanted.

The prices of wines never reflect (other than coincidentally) the excellence of those wines; what they reflect is production costs plus demand (as anticipated by the producer) for his or her product. As fine wines are subject, being luxury items, to the whims of fashion and snobbery, prices may rise dizzily as the wealthy and the fashionable, in their simple-minded way, seek to impress each other with names and labels, without any regard to the excellence or otherwise of the wine they are apparently purchasing. Beware celebrity, therefore. Seek excellence in the humble and the obscure.

The second strand of the Fallacy concerns the accepted definition of excellence in the wine context, and the way in which it is established. This is generally by tasting, sometimes by one taster with the labelled bottle in front of him or her, but more reliably by a team of tasters with the bottles hidden in bags to conceal their identity (this is called blind tasting). What generally ensues is that, of – for example – 40 wines, 10 prove good, 20 average and 10 poor. In many cases, the biggest gap is between the 10 poor wines, often appearing to represent shocking value for money, and the 20 average wines. The ten good ones, most tasters will admit, are often only a tiny bit better than the top ten out of the 20 average ones. And if five are picked out as excellent from among the top ten, again it will often be by margins whisker-wide (and sometimes amid disagreement among tasters). Yet those five will be announced to the world as 'excellent', the next five 'good', and the following 20 'average' only: trenchant distinctions, boldly unfaithful to the subtle shadings and nuances, the dappling of flavour, experienced by tasters as they moved from glass to glass. This is not a fault of blind tasting, which is the best tool we have for establishing excellence in a highly subjective field; but we would do well not to put too absolute a trust in the results.

And what of those five excellent wines? They were generally deemed excellent because they were able to make a final push at the last hurdle, express a little extra depth or summon up a last, final aromatic grace. Would you notice that tiny distinction in the wine, tasted away from its peers, after a busy day at work, as the children quarrel over which television programme to watch? Would any of those present at the tasting notice it in such circumstances? You, or they, might be looking for something completely different in the wine at that point, something that might even have relegated it to 'average' at the tasting: an extra half degree of alcohol, say, combined with a marked suppleness, a very light tannic structure, that enables you not to lose your temper when the children reach the compromise of constant zapping from one programme to another. This is but one of countless examples in which 'average' may be better than 'excellent'. Another common example is when a dense, tannic wine, needing the best part of a decade in a hole under somebody's house before it becomes drinkable, is judged 'excellent' (which it will be, but isn't yet), while a wine far superior for immediate consumption (though not suitable for cellaring) is damned as 'average'. A third example common enough to merit description is the wine that tastes appealing but drinks uncomfortably or tediously. This puzzling phenomenon is often evident when comparing Californian and Australian wines with their French or Portuguese competitors. The New World wines have the kind of appealing immediacy and intensity of fruit, often with a big whack of sweet oak, that is hard to ignore or criticise at a blind tasting. Three mouthfuls bent this way and that in the mouth, and the taster is refreshed and possibly enraptured. European wines tend to be more reticent and shy about revealing their charms in three short mouthfuls: your tongue searches, but the wine seems mean and sulky, its different elements out of kilter with each other, or playing an irritating game of hide and seek with your tiring brain. Yet open the same bottles for dinner and see how the evening progresses with each. The Californian or Australian that so impressed at the tasting may soon pall, its oak seem obvious and its bright fruit have you sweating uncomfortably under the eyes. The European wine, by contrast, may open and blossom as you move on to your second glass; by the end of the bottle it will have completely captivated you with its shape, style and subtlety, and your meal will have been a feast. The New World wine was 'excellent'; the European only 'average'. Be sceptical, then, of excellence, especially when you are asked to pay a premium for it. Blind tasting laureates guarantee only that two or three slurped and spat-out mouthfuls impress within a peer group. No one has drunk the wine; no one has eaten a meal with it; no one has passed an evening with it; and these are the three things that you're about to do. The only excellence you can be certain of is the one you find for yourself.

The third perspective is called, for summary's sake, the Fallacy of the Tasting Note.

Because there has been an explosion in wine drinking in Britain, and because wine is a complex subject, it has been followed by an echoing boom in books, magazines, newspaper columns, even television programmes and radio slots about wine. These began simply enough, by telling readers about the places where their wines came from, and about the men and women who made them. The best of this writing was evocative and inspirational, though it was sometimes of little use to those who wished to know the difference between the three table wines stocked by their grocer. Now the pendulum has swung away from wine journalism which seeks to inform, stimulate and inspire towards that which seeks to quantify and evaluate. 'Buy this,' will be the conclusion, 'because it's better than that.' A praiseworthy, consumer-aiding aim, one would think, save that the objective evaluation of wine is impossible, for reasons outlined above and below. Taken to its logical conclusion, this approach, far from aiding consumers, misleads and tricks them into believing in a primitive theology of absolutes and fixed values in wines, decreed by solemn priest-tasters and acolyte-statisticians. The assumption of this hieratic role is an abuse of the consumer's trust.

The main tools of wine's theologians are some kind of points scale, and the tasting note. Awarding a wine a number of points, regardless of who is to drink it, when, where and with what, is absurd. It is a massive simplification that does little justice to the rich, fugitive complexities of that wine. The correction factors of time, place, drinker and food accompaniment will halve the scores of some wines, and double others, and leave almost none unchanged, even if the original assessment was 'correct' within the context of an individual's preferences, and in tasting (not drinking) circumstances. Scoring wines may be useful to professional wine buyers seeking to distinguish between samples, or to anyone trying to make up their mind if they like wine A more than wine B on a given occasion, but to suggest to readers and consumers that some wines really are a hundredth, or even a twentieth, better than others, absolutely and always, is misleading and deceitful.

I bought my first wine in a wooden box: a case of Château Haut-Bailly 1976, which proved highly instructive. I drank the first bottle and thought it delicious. Then I mistakenly consulted Hugh Johnson's Wine Companion, *where I discovered that the shallow, stony soil of Haut-Bailly made for problems during drought years – such as, of course, 1976, whose vintage was denounced as 'raisiny' (obviously a bad thing, even for a grape). This wrecked the next four bottles I drank: the wine tasted filthy and I was dismayed. My first punt, and I'd landed a poodle. By about bottle seven, though, it was beginning to taste quite nice again. By bottle eleven I loved it. Then Parker's* Bordeaux *came out. Haut-Bailly 1976 got a humiliating 62 points: it was old, loosely knit and diluted. I opened the final bottle with trepidation. Hey, it wasn't as bad as all that. No, quite a bit of fruit there, decent weight, and so on. Really, these wine experts ...* Julian Barnes, 'Bin End', *Decanter*, November 1989

Tasting notes, another tool of professional buyers, have assumed a talismanic value in some of today's less imaginative wine journalism. What is a tasting note? A tasting note is the hasty jottings of an individual as he or she tastes a few mouthfuls of a particular wine on a particular occasion, spits it out, and makes observations on what has been tasted. They are generally couched in jargon, for reasons of speed and ease of use for the taster. They are rarely adequate descriptions of that wine for anyone except the taster, though they may serve as a basis for such descriptions, if contextualised and reworked into evocative, accessible language. Often, however, they are printed verbatim; whole articles in magazines and periodicals are now cobbled together using this lazy and tedious shorthand. Here are some examples. *'The [wine in question] had a delicate, soft, seemingly sweet aroma, but suggestions of hidden power, and a quite dry, vaguely ungenerous flavour, but firming up at the finish.'* Or, from the same text, a wine is described as having *'a lively colour, a young, crisp, slightly dusty aroma with no indication of its age, and a firm, dry flavour, still rather hidden, but with good keeping acidity'*. Any the wiser? Compare these 'tasting notes' with a grand Johnsonian description, of old-style Chablis, say. *'It is hard but not harsh, reminds one of stones and minerals, but at the same time of green hay; actually, when it is young it looks green, which many wines are supposed to. Grand Cru Chablis tastes important, strong, almost immortal. And indeed it does last a long time; a strange and delicious sort of sour taste enters into it at ten years or so, and its golden green eye flashes meaningfully.'* (Hugh Johnson, *The World Atlas of Wine*, first revised edition, Mitchell Beazley, 1983)

A points score may mislead; an undigested tasting note generally bores and confuses. The two together reinforce the fallacy that it is possible to pass precise and absolute judgment on a wine, whereas in fact they are simply the momentary impressions of a particular palate as it sluices its way towards lunch or dinner. Regard all of them with as much scepticism as you can muster. Follow enthusiasm rather than statistics, and reserve judgment for yourself. Value for money rarely corresponds to a high score and the adoration of the magi.

The fourth and concluding perspective on wine's value for money stresses the importance of personal taste, the context in which you drink a wine, the effect of air on it, and other imponderables, so let's call it the Law of Relativity.

Two friends came to dinner. They liked port, so I poured four in advance into unlabelled decanters to give them a mini blind tasting. There was a 1966 vintage port, a 1963 colheita port, a 1984 LBV port and an undated 'portwine' from Azerbaijan which had been purchased in Poland. Each was representative of its type, the last being, for me, a luridly flavoured cocktail of blackcurrant juice and brandy. Yet one of my friends liked it most of the four, and the other placed it second after the 1966 vintage port. In the great democracy of taste, there are no rights or wrongs, only differences. If, having tried six different Côtes du Rhônes, you like the cheapest best, revel in your luck. Value for money may be easier to find than you might imagine.

We have already discovered how the excellence of blind tasting winners may not prove excellent in a less artificial setting, and the concept of context is a vitally important one in gauging a wine's true worth. For no wine is ever drunk in a vacuum: there is always a time, a place, a glass, a drinker. Variations in each play a large part when you come to answer the question 'Is it worth it?'. Poor, overfilled glasses, for example, can rob a wine of its aroma, and serving a fine red wine at too high a temperature, or a fine white one overchilled, can emasculate it in each case. Certain wines (rosés from Languedoc or Provence, for example) taste best in the region in which they were made; others (vintage port) seem better under alien skies and in alien climates. Anyone who has ever bought a case of wine will know that substantial variations in one's enjoyment of the same wine can occur according to the context in which each bottle is drunk: in summer or winter; with food or without; when feeling burdened or when feeling relaxed ... in addition to the changes the wine undergoes as it ages and matures. It is idle to pretend that presentation does not matter, and that it's only the wine in the bottle that counts: a smartly labelled wine is certainly better value for money than an indifferently labelled competitor of equal quality. A number of red wines (the young and sturdy) improve beyond recognition after they have been open a day or two, and exposed to the sometimes benevolent effects of oxygen, turning poor value for money into good value – but only if you don't drink the whole bottle on day one. The opposite is true for other reds, and for most whites.

In short, there is a shoal of factors that may disrupt the pleasure trajectory plotted for a wine by experts. This should not surprise us: wine is a living, changing thing, responding to the stimulus of a mobile environment, like all other living things. When we meet a wine, the encounter is always a new one, and its success is relative, unpredictable, almost human.

Let's summarise:
- You do not have to spend a lot of money to enjoy good or even fine wine: not all fine wines are expensive, and not all expensive wines are fine. Many are expensive because demand has

pushed prices up, and demand is often driven by fashion and snobbery.

- Excellence in wine is surprisingly difficult to define: be sure that you know what you mean by it, and that it tallies with your interlocutor's definition, before paying more for it.
- Blind tasting is useful, provided its results are not taken as absolute. They are simply the conclusions reached by a number of tasters (not drinkers) about a set of wines on a given occasion. Journalists' opinions are useful, too, provided they are not offered as absolutes, but rather as findings, always provisional. Beware the neat mark, and spurn the lazy, repetitive tasting note; follow enthusiasm and the enthusiastic.

Respect your own taste, even if it contradicts received wisdom. Remember that every time you encounter a wine, the book is rewritten, the sum of learning is increased, your own study programme is deepened. The spirit of openness and enquiry will be worth more to you than any quantity of printed matter. Listen to what wines have to say to you, even the humblest, about their corner of the earth, and your money will be well spent.

The Bottle's Tale

Wink Lorch

..one of its numbers may be snatched away..

We are taught to handle wine with respect and care. We must not shake it on the way back from the shops; if it is to be stored we must lay it down gently in a cool, dark place free from vibrations; when we finally get around to drinking it we must serve it at the right temperature and open it with the correct tools. Most wines have led such a traumatic life before reaching their final destination that they deserve good treatment to recover before being drunk.

As if the process of turning grapes into wine was not drama enough, the wine, once bottled, is handled by a dozen or more

27

people before reaching the drinker. It travels accompanied by reams of documentation, and from time to time, without warning, one of its numbers may be snatched away, never to be returned. Rumour has it that it is subject to various forms of analysis, finally ending up down the drain.

Any romantic image one might have of wine is soon destroyed when buying and shipping processes are considered. To an extent, wine is treated as any other commodity. The wine industry has its share of agents, middle-men, brokers, merchants and speculators, all trying to cut themselves a slice of the cake. And every wine-producing country or region conducts its business differently.

Take Bordeaux, for instance. One big shock that a wine lover may receive on his or her first visit to one of the shrines of wine, a top Médoc cru classé château, is that you cannot buy a souvenir bottle. Likewise, the importer of top-class Bordeaux rarely buys direct from the châteaux: usually merchants and importers must buy from a négociant.

The négociants must have agreements with the top châteaux, each of which allows them an annual allocation of wine which must be bought through another middle-man, a courtier (broker). The role of the courtier many years ago was to check that wine tasted by the négociant was the same wine that he eventually received. Today, a courtier ferries samples, conveys prices and orders and collects his commission. The négociant's role has changed, too: the traditional négociant-éleveurs hardly exist any more in Bordeaux, superseded by a new breed, the négociant-téléxistes. The négociant-éleveurs used to own large cellars under the Quai des Chartrons in Bordeaux's port area, where they matured wines in cask before it was bottled or shipped in cask. Since all self-respecting châteaux have for many years bottled their own wine, today the cellars contain vats of regional wines enjoying less lofty appellation status and some stocks of château-bottled wines.

The négociants-téléxistes have no long-standing agreements with châteaux, hold few stocks, and often live outside the city in houses equipped only with a telephone, a fax and a telex. They buy and sell top classed growths without the wine passing through their hands, behaving just as a broker might on any commodity market. However, many UK importers value the more traditional négociants, and rely on them to keep in touch with the Bordeaux gossip and to arrange appointments and tastings.

In Burgundy it is not the middle-men, but the intricate structure of the vineyards and producers that creates problems in getting wine from growers to shop shelves. Specialist Burgundy fine wine merchants buy 'parcels' of wine from numerous growers scattered in the picturesque hillsides of the Côte d'Or; every individual wine requires its own precise paperwork; and in order to reduce costs the wines from each producer are grouped together for shipping. If you have ever fantasised about importing your own wine from a few friendly vignerons, you would be wise to reconsider. The minimum shipping charge for each pick-up is usually the total price for 25 cases, likely to be upwards of £75 delivered to one London address.

This is where the freight forwarder enters the scene. Specialist freight forwarders are used instead of dealing directly with transport carriers by all but the biggest wine shippers. Specialists have the advantage of understanding the nature of the product, and the price for not using them can be high. How would you like your wine to be tainted with the smells of chemicals, machinery or even fish? Most wines are imported from Europe in trailers or containers by road, or occasionally by rail, and from the Americas and Australasia by container ships. Air freight is used to get samples to buyers quickly, or occasionally for very fine and already expensive wines where the cost (£80+ per case) adds relatively little.

Imagine that, after extensive tastings and possibly even a full laboratory analysis of samples, a UK buyer orders 25 cases of Puligny-Montrachet from a grower on the outskirts of the village of the same name in deepest Burgundy, and 25 cases of Chardonnay from Marlborough on the South Island of New Zealand. Two things happen: the producer is instructed to prepare the wine for shipment, labelling and packing it and preparing the paperwork; while the freight forwarder is alerted to collect the wine. Wines always travel accompanied by various 'birth certificates', known formally as 'accompanying documents'. Which ones depend on whether the wine is from within the European Community or without, and each one has its own bureaucratic code – T, VA1 or VA2, VI1, C10 or SAD, they all mean something to HM Customs. If the wine and the forms do not match, the wine is impounded.

The 25 cases of Puligny-Montrachet are shipped in a trailer together with other burgundies and wines from the Rhône Valley. Rather than trying to get 40-foot lorries up the lanes of Puligny-Montrachet the freight forwarder has an agent in Beaune who uses a smaller vehicle to collect all the local orders and bring them to his depot. From there, a lorry picks up all the wines and heads for Calais. Dover Customs check the paperwork – and occasionally the wine – which could mean a day's delay. The Puligny then goes either into the forwarder's bonded warehouse or travels 'under bond' (no duty paid) to the buyer's own bonded warehouse.

It all sounds simple enough, but importers will tell you a different story. A dozy grower may not have got the wine ready, or may have overlooked the paperwork; the forwarder's agent may have failed to collect the wine; the ferries may be on strike or Customs may have a 'go-slow' – just some of the possible hiccups! And the result is always the same: a wine appears on a merchant's list but not in his shops.

Shipping from New Zealand generally takes six weeks door-to-door instead of one or two for European wines. An agent in New Zealand arranges for the Marlborough Chardonnay to be picked up and delivered to Auckland where it is packed into a container ready for shipping. The cost of trailering a consignment from the South Island to Auckland in the North Island often costs as much as the sea journey to London. From Auckland the ship travels across the Pacific, through the Panama Canal (presuming no war is taking place) and into the Atlantic. The container, holding around 1,000 cases, sits on deck since wine, being inflammable, is classified as a hazardous product. At the expense of a few cases, the container can be insulated, protecting it against large temperature variations.

It is tempting to cut costs and use a lesser-known shipping company, but it can be dangerous. If the company goes bust, the ship drops anchor in the nearest port, and stays there until someone buys it. Eventually it arrives at a new, unforeseen destination where the valuable containers are immediately emptied and left to be claimed by their owners. No regard is paid to the goods in them; all, whether wine, raw meat or wool, are emptied on to the dockside.

If all goes well, the container with the Marlborough Chardonnay arrives at Tilbury, where the freight forwarder collects it to take to his depot. The paperwork, ironically, is simpler for non-EC wine than for EC wine, although it must include an Import Licence and a Certificate of Analysis. Customs Duty is paid either on entry to the UK, or later, together with Excise Duty and VAT, when the wine is released from bond.

The cost of importing the New Zealand Chardonnay is unlikely to be more than £1 per case higher than for the Puligny-Montrachet. The cost, per case, from Auckland to London for a full container is less than £2. By comparison, if a full trailer comes from one producer in Burgundy, the price is about 80p per case. The difference amounts to a mere 10p per bottle for shipping a wine halfway round the world or for bringing it across the Channel from Northern France.

By far the biggest fixed cost in every bottle of wine is Excise Duty: the tax levied by the government on it. The shipping costs and middle-men do add to the cost, but UK importers do their best to limit these obscure extras, whether they are ordering 5,000 cases of wine or only five. Next time you drink a bottle, think of all the places and people it has seen on its travels. No wonder some wines seem tired.

Wink Lorch is a freelance wine writer, editor, lecturer and wine consultant.

Letter to a Wine Merchant I

..not having much idea about what it is they're selling..

Dear Merchant,
I like wine and you have a shop full of it. Provided you take the trouble to fill your windows up with it in a reasonably attractive manner (dusty bottles and empty bottles are both a mild deterrent), I am likely to enter your shop. As a student, my resources are limited and my appearance – though less outrageous than some (the best Oxfam outlets only) – confirms my status. But I am a customer after all.

The types of merchant I most dislike are those staffed by people called Rupert. Rupert wears a tweed jacket, has a public school accent, and immediately asks me if he can help me. The translation reads: 'Look, you don't belong here, so let me show you where the Liebfraumilch is and then you can clear orff.' No, Rupert, old mate, you can't help me. Just leave me alone to nose around your shelves – I'm not going to nick anything. But if it's all overpriced claret and burgundy, as it usually is with Rupert, then I'll walk out with my fiver still in my pocket.

Slightly more liberal outlets, staffed by Rory or Alastair, sometimes take my name and address in the guise of sending me their lists. If they do send me their lists, it's appreciated: I can always dream. But if they pass their mailing sheet on to Toby or Vanessa, who invite me to attend a fine art sale whose catalogue alone costs the price of two bottles of Shiraz, then I know what I think of the famous 'service' of the independent merchant. Are these people really surprised at the success of Oddbins, staffed by wine-loving human beings rather than establishment clones, with hundreds of wines that come from somewhere other than Bordeaux or Beaune, and that tend to the underpriced rather than the overpriced? Are they really dim enough to carp at the wine press for repeatedly praising Oddbins?

Unfortunately, Oddbins is the exception rather than the rule when it comes to the nationwide high-street chains. For many of them, the description 'wine merchant' so readily bandied about is a flagrant flouting of the Trade Descriptions Act. Shelf upon shelf full of lager, spirits and cigarettes, with a couple of bog-standard Bulgarians and some dusty Bull's Blood tucked away in a corner isn't going to entice me back into the shop after the initial mistake. These shops, with their pitifully limited choice, tend to be found in the parts of towns and cities where the cheaper accommodation is also located. Someone, somewhere, is getting it wrong. This is precisely where the locals need a reliable source of cheap, good-quality wine. But perhaps 'wine merchants' can make a better profit on beer and fags. Even when you find a well-stocked high-street shop, the chances are it's the staff who turn out to be limited, chiefly by not having much idea about what it is they're selling. Why is this, dear Merchant? Anything to do with the rubbish money being paid, perhaps? Or maybe your personnel department could do with a little gingering? Whatever the cause, it's high time things were changed. There's a vast public out here already some way down the road to conversion to the joys of wine drinking and you have a duty to help speed things up.

But credit where it's due. Some high-street chains are beginning to get their acts together. Threshers is one example of how a national chain can transform itself into a reliable shop selling a range of decent quality wines from people like Duboeuf, Montana, Antinori and Penfolds among others. Sadly, I haven't been well placed to take advantage of the range of options opened up by the advent of the wine warehouse phenomenon in recent years. The standard location up a railway siding close to some derelict buildings is usually not a problem, but coming away with 12 bottles of wine generally is. Easy enough if you've got a car, perhaps; not so easy if you're on a bike (and no, I'm not going to pay for a case then take it home two at a time before you ask again), on foot or by bus. Having it delivered, of course, can wipe out the price differential. For those of us constantly struggling to make ends meet, the outlay entailed when purchasing a case at one go can be daunting, too, even though from 1991 the government reckons it's going to be willing to lend me the money in the form of student loans. We need more liberal retailing laws, I think, and in the meantime more accommodating warehouse merchants like the one I ran into in... well, perhaps I'd better not say, who helpfully let me return a few minutes after my initial visit so that we could conclude a 'private sale' of just a couple of bottles. A further disincentive to buying 12 bottles at a time is lack of adequate storage space; the temperature in my house is probably just about perfect, but the more normal centrally heated environment doesn't do wine any favours at all.

You see, dear Merchant, if I just want, and can only afford, a bottle or two at a time, the supermarkets remain my best bet. Obviously they're not searching out good wine purely for altruistic reasons, but the fact remains that the customer gets a very good deal, as excellent new wines for well under a fiver continually become available at the more progressive supermarkets such as Tesco or Sainsbury's. However, in the interests of good customer relations, what about a bit more information when one line is replaced by another? It's extremely frustrating to go into a branch in search of something specific, which you know to have been in stock previously, to find it vanished and no one with much idea about what's happened. A simple label on the relevant shelf saying 'wine x is no longer stocked at this branch because it wasn't very popular', or 'stocks of it have run out', or whatever, would leave everyone a bit less in the dark.

While we're on labelling, I wonder if I'm alone in being bored rigid with seeing 'good with meat' on the back of bottles of supermarket red wine and, equally, inevitably, 'good with white meat or fish' on the back of whites. Who writes this stuff with such monotonous regularity, and is their diet equally monotonous? I shouldn't think anyone would be too shocked if confronted by something a bit more imaginative for a change, such as 'this wine would go particularly well with lasagne or a nut roast', say. It's worth remembering that there are vegetarian customers out here, most of whom stopped eating quiche altogether when they found out the eggs are laced with bacteria.

Finally, we customers could do with a few genuine sales from you merchants. Fifty pence off some dodgy Beaujolais Nouveau that's 18 months old does not constitute a bargain in anybody's language. But if you've got '88s from Alsace itching to get on to the shelves, start selling off the '87s at half price and we can do business. Oh yes, and if you're holding any more free tastings in the near future, here's my number...

Yours sincerely,
Richard Marriott
Nottingham

Letter to a Wine Merchant II

Dear Merchant,

Many thanks for tracking down the bottles of Domaine Cauhapé
Jurançon Sec I was after, and phoning me back. Shame that it's
gone up so much. £7.25! I can't say that I'm surprised: all your
competitors were near that price already. I couldn't believe my
luck that you had been stocking it at around a fiver. Obviously the
market has finally caught up with the quality of the wine.

By chance I had overlooked a couple of bottles of the 1987. They
were sensational partnering smoked salmon the other evening.
With a little bottle age the wine takes on an almost honeyed note
behind the fruit. I shall look forward to seeing how the 1988
develops. I'll just have to drink it more sparingly now, I suppose.

I'll be in to collect the rest of the order, and pay, in the next few
days. Don't deliver. I can't guarantee when I'll be home, besides, I
like coming in for a browse. No doubt I'll add a couple of bottles –
or six.

Now there's the rub. I do wish you'd start offering storage space
(some other merchants do, after all). More and more often, I find
myself buying wine that needs 'a year or two in bottle yet'. I don't
mind tying up my non-existent life savings, but I do wish that I
had room to move at home. And I keep having visions of whole
consignments of wine spoiling, as my 1976 Châteauneuf did. What
I want is somewhere away from the central heating where my
wines can grow old gracefully. How about it? Ideally, I'd want to
be able to make mixed withdrawals. Perhaps if I put mixed cases
into store? Or is that asking too much?

Which reminds me: I need to find a home for my two boxes of
Madiran Château Montus. I do wish they could have stayed in
bond. When you suggested that I buy them in bond to overcome
my storage problem, I was delighted. Had they stayed there all
would have been nice and simple. I still don't understand why
they couldn't have been transferred to your new bonded
warehouse after the other one had gone bust. We mere mortals
know nothing of these matters and are completely in your hands.
There should be a layman's guide to wine trading. I suppose I
shouldn't complain too much. Of course, if it hadn't have been
taken from bond, then the second case of the 1985 wouldn't have
been dropped... However, it was very generous of you to do a
straight replacement with the 1986. The 1985 had sentimental
value, being the wine we were charged to bring back to you by

Alain Brumont, when we visited him on holiday. Extraordinary, the effect of dropping your name into what passed for 'conversation' (an unhappy combination of his dialect and my poor French). Suddenly, all doors were open, special samples grabbed, gifts given and his 1985 Montus thrust into our hands on pain of death for non-delivery! Ah well, we still have a case, and we were wondering what the 1986 was like (he never did reply to our letter) so we're very happy to have a case of the later vintage to compare with the earlier some time in the next 5, 10, 20 years.

In the meantime, where do we put it, please? And what do we do with the Mas de Daumas we've just bought? It looks lovely in its wooden crate, but I don't really think it can stay for ever in an obscure, unheated corner of the office. We've long wanted to buy some top-quality claret – the sort of stuff you might still be enjoying when you're 70 – but we've no where to put it. What do we do?

The perils of bad storage have been quite apparent in one or two tastings we've been to: a tragic Clos Vougeot (*every* wine badly oxidised?!) and a hilarious pre-sale affair at one of the big auction houses. (I thought claret was meant to be red.) That's put me off buying at auction – good news for you, no doubt, but in the meantime how do I get mature, quality wines without moving to a mansion and having lots of patience? I presume one has to buy the back-bottles of Musar (ludicrously underpriced) or Simone or Vignelaure from Provence that are available, but are there no other options? What would you suggest?

Perhaps we can have a chat at your next wine fair? I must say I've found those invaluable for discovering some real gems. (Who in their right mind would buy any of the atrociously labelled Mâcon La Roche Vineuse on spec?) I hope they will be a permanent feature with you. I know of nowhere else where one can taste, comparatively, half the list. I hope in future you'll be able to include some more rare back vintages (as you did with the Barolos and Barbarescos – that was extraordinary); it reminds one of what one is investing in and promotes, I think, Merchant Loyalty.

Although I buy eclectically, as you know, I find myself coming back to you time and time again. I did dabble once with one of those mail-order clubs. They were efficient enough, bar the odd change in a mixed taster case. The real problem is that you have to take on trust the description of the wine given. That only works if you know exactly *who* is describing the wine to you: one person's 'firm structure' is another's 'mouth-puckering tannin' – the difference between 'drinking now' and 'trip over it for another two years to come'! Besides, it's so impersonal. I much prefer custom-made recommendations. There's a lot you can tell by the look on someone's face when you ask for their assessment of a wine. And it certainly helps to be recognised and remembered. I must say that I was impressed by the genuine interest your staff took in the buying decisions I made, once I had explained to them the budget limitation for the International Wine and Food Society event for which I was buying. (Hence not the Jurançon.) They offered plenty of suggestions, but there was no pressure. It was quite simply helpful: descriptions of the wines, enthusiastic personal reactions (thank heavens for sales staff who actually taste the wine and know the stock) and then I was left to decide for myself. Much appreciated.

If only you were still open on Sundays, everything would be pretty well hunky-dory. Still, I suppose you must be entitled to the odd day off.

I haven't received your latest tutored tastings list yet. Is it ready? Anything on red burgundies? I've yet to be convinced that there really are some worth buying. Champagne? I love Krug, but... Does anything affordable remotely compare? Or are we back to yet more bottle age?

Let me have your thoughts about the storage. Hope to see you soon...

Yours sincerely,
David Natt
Beckenham

Letter to a Customer I

..when a lady with a poodle arrived..

Dear Customer,
It's true that when you came into the shop today it was a quiet
moment, but it was half past nine on an evening on which
Scotland were trying to beat Brazil in the World Cup. 'What do
you find to do all day?' you asked me. I seem to remember I just
laughed. I didn't really have the energy left to describe it all. But
now I'm at home, it's quiet, and I've got a glass of Aussie
Chardonnay beside me, let me see if I can remember.

The Notting Hill branch may be the biggest of all the 150
Oddbins shops up and down Britain, but that doesn't mean that
an average day doesn't have its problems. 'I rather liked that 1985
Hermitage from Chave,' the man in the blue pin-striped suit said,

soon after we opened at 10. 'Do me a case, will you?' Well, I'd love to have done him a case, but we sold out ages ago. I remember talking to the man in the suit when he came in before – about how long the wine would need to reach its best, and so on. (Obviously he couldn't wait another five years.) I mentioned that we didn't have much stock, but it can't have sunk in. At least I still had some '86 to offer him, or Guigal's '86; in the end he settled for the Chave. Everyone is delighted when we stock wines like these, but they forget that there just isn't much to go around.

Then the delivery lorry arrived, so it was time to start unloading – 20 pallets' worth. That's 1,200 cases, which is what we sell in a week, and it needs a lot of muscle to move them in and out of the shop; sadly no one's yet invented a way of emptying them straight on to the shelves. Just after we'd started, keen Mr Smith arrived for the Gaja wines for which we'd put in a special order last week. We told him they'd be here today, but that we'd ring him first. Of course they were towards the bottom of the eighteenth pallet, three-quarters of an hour on – by which time he'd had to go off to a meeting in rather a disgruntled mood. We carried on stacking the shelves as fast as possible, though it's never easy as customers will keep emptying them; we temporarily concealed the bottles of Rosso del Conte behind some Montepulciano d'Abruzzo as we did so. 'Ah *there* it is,' said the long-haired customer, reaching excitedly for the wine he'd been looking for, and two bottles of the Montepulciano crashed to the floor and broke as he extracted it. 'Sorry about that, but they weren't in the right place, you know.' 'You're right, sir, they weren't ...'

I'd almost finished mopping up when a lady with a poodle arrived, which we eventually persuaded her to leave outside. 'You know I bought such a lovely wine from you ... oh, it must have been in February, or was it before Christmas? Anyway, I had it with my sister a week or so ago, so nice it was, white, dry I think, or at least that's what my sister said, with a pretty label with a château on it. Yes, that's it, Château something. Now whatever was the other name? I'm sure it was French. One of your colleagues recommended it, said it was ever so good, and it was, too, my sister loved it. Do you think I could have another bottle?' We spent ten minutes looking at the shelves, without finding Château X. Eventually she settled for another recommendation.

Ten minutes later and we had another 'price of success' problem from a photographer parked on double yellow lines outside. 'Have you got a couple of bottles of that wine, um, whatsisname was going on about in *The Guardian* last week, it sounded great. Leathery or something. I've gotta try that, I said to Josie. I think it was red, about a fiver, something like that. What are the wardens like round here?' After about six similar queries last Saturday we'd gone out to buy the paper and found out what the wine was, so we were able to help today before he got clamped. Just. We're almost out of it now, but we're getting in extra back-up stock on the delivery next week.

I was about to check the van deliveries schedule when three girls in the middle of a hilarious afternoon in an open-topped car arrived. 'We've just got our diplomas – God knows how, you should've seen Caroline's Gâteau Saint-Honoré, it was a complete disaster!' There was some dissent from within the group about this. 'Anyway, we're going to have a party tonight. You have that champagne offer, don't you, seven for six or something? We thought we'd fill the bath with ice – do you have ice? oh good – and then fill it up with bottles of champagne, oh and we're hoping you can help out with glasses, you do loan glasses, don't you?' Yes, we do, but they must come back tomorrow and clean, as they're already booked out again tomorrow night. 'No problem – we're going to the country tomorrow. You'll have them first thing.' Fingers crossed. On second thoughts I must remember to check reserve stock levels in the morning. 'Can you do three cases of ... what is it? Caroline, do you remember Hugo's party, the one in that lighthouse? What on earth ... Ah! Veuve Clicquot, that's it, Why don't you chill them first, and then bring them over to Shepherds Bush by six or so?' Unfortunately we only have fridges, not a cold store, so chilling three cases isn't possible, as we already have two other orders in there and driving them towards Shepherds Bush at six would be the surest way I know to bring them back to room temperature. We load the glasses and champagne into the open-topped car and I suggest they rush home before the ice melts.

'Excuse me, but this wine's gone up by 30p since I was in here last week,' said the red-faced man. 'That's ridiculous. I know this isn't new stock because you had plenty here then. Looks like sharp practice to me.' I explain how on the last Sunday of every month we stocktake, changing prices where necessary on the succeeding Monday, and how French wine prices – especially for the Muscadet this customer favours – have risen steeply recently. Logistically it would be a nightmare to raise prices on new stock only, especially with the number of branches we have. After all, who would know which bottle was what price? Why not try this Sauvignon de Touraine instead? – even cheaper than the Muscadet was before, and just as good. 'No thank you, no, I know what I like, I'll pay the extra, but it still seems a bit steep to me ...'

And so the day went on. It wasn't all problems, though; one

41

customer said that her boyfriend had proposed to her after a bottle of our Château Nenin 1987 and a man from the local OAPs' club said what good value our Campo dei Fiori Chilean Cabernet was, and how he was going to buy it for his less mobile friends. And then, at the end of the day, when I was wondering if I'd be home in time to watch the highlights of the Scotland game, you arrived – and invited me to your party on Saturday. I'll come with pleasure; maybe I'll even tell you what I do all day.

Cheers,
David Robertson
Oddbins

Letter to a Customer II

Dear Customer,

Unlike all other luxuries and most necessities, wine is sold at an absurdly low margin of profit, barely sufficient to cover the merchant's costs. If a third of the price you pay represents gross profit to the wine merchant, that would be a princely mark-up by the standards of the trade. Frequently the margin is closer to 10 per cent, which must somehow cover the cost of premises and staff, fuel, light, telephone, computer and all the other expenses of running a business, including the major element of finance charges on the investment in stock. In which context it is worth remembering that a serious merchant may list a thousand different wines and will expect to hold many of these for several years, until they reach maturity.

I am not asking for sympathy, but for understanding – that what appear failings to you, the customer, are frequently heroic improvisations devised to conceal the fact that we simply cannot afford the level of personal service which you expect and we long to provide. In the complex process of delivering a mixed case of wine to your doorstep in Northumberland, assembled from the produce of twelve different growers in seven different countries of origin, there are decisions we have to take which sometimes balance perfection against economy.

An example. Glass bottles of wine are fragile, difficult to transport safely. If you subject our normal heavy-duty cartons to the mechanical sorting systems used by the Post Office (and by most carriers who guarantee next day delivery, nationwide) the probability is that between a third and half of the cases will incur breakages. I know because we've tried. There are two alternatives. One is to use very expensive polystyrene packaging for every bottle in the case; the other to employ carriers who sort the cases manually and, as a result, take slightly longer to deliver the more distant orders. We have to opt for the second choice on grounds of cost, even though this means the customer may wait an extra two or three days for delivery.

So give us time to invoice, pack and deliver your order. If there is an urgent deadline (the wine is needed for a wedding, three days hence), *let us know*, so that we can give the matter special attention. We can't pull out all the stops for every case that leaves the store but we gladly help when there is a crisis.

Clear directions are vital. Is the delivery address the same as the invoice address? Is anyone at home to receive deliveries during the day or can we leave the wine with a neighbour, or in the garden shed? A daytime telephone number is vital so that we can resolve any problems when they arise. An example. A delivery driver recently called us on his portable phone to say that he had arrived at the correct address but could get no answer from the doorbell. We telephoned the customer (who was asleep in bed upstairs) and suggested that she go down to take delivery of her order. End of problem, which could otherwise have developed into a saga of misunderstandings.

The question of substitutions often arouses unreasoning fury. We always try to telephone before making substitutions if the wine you ordered is unavailable or the price or the vintage has changed, but sometimes we cannot make contact and must decide whether to hold up your entire order pending authorisation for a vintage change (which may be an improvement, and would not be proposed by us unless thought satisfactory) or risk your wrath by delivering the substitution.

A wine may be unavailable because of poor stock control on our part, or because it has been delayed in transit by HM Customs & Excise (who sometimes spend days unpacking every case in a consignment from Italy), or because it may simply be sold out. Our supplier in Quincy, for example, is a small grower with very limited production. Our orders are rationed (he needs to keep faith with his local customers and with the top restaurants in France) and it is inevitable that the wine will run out before the annual reprint of our list. Neither we nor the grower can turn on a tap to produce more on demand. Estate-bottled wine is not a commodity in endless supply.

As importers we are at the mercy of currency fluctuations, which play havoc with our prices. If a price increase is implemented we try to notify you but, as with substitutions, that may be difficult and we have to make a decision: not to send the wine ordered or to invoice at the higher price. Either choice is likely to upset some customers.

You may see such mishaps as evidence of a conspiracy to defraud (business versus the consumer) and you may take out your wrath on a hapless invoice girl. But reducing her to tears is much less likely to achieve positive results than a cheerful explanation of the problem, an assumption that we are as concerned as you when things go wrong.

Other grievances hurled at us by irascible customers tend to focus on what many would regard as our virtues: price, my enthusiasm for Italy, the fact that we don't stock a particular brand of Liebfraumilch. 'I can buy Chablis cheaper in the supermarket,' rages a disgruntled critic. Of course you can. The supermarket buys its mass-produced Chablis very keenly and sells it as a loss leader. But ours was selected from innumerable blind tastings and comes from a young grower of exceptional dedication and competence, with well-sited vineyards near the classic heart of the region. Our Chablis costs more; it could also be very much better. The choice is yours.

And there is, after all, a huge variety to choose from, of merchants as well as wines. You may prefer Robin Yapp's purple prose to my mellifluous phrases, or Richard Wheeler's bulky list to my eclectic selection. You may like the lustre of associating with Corney & Barrow's royal customers or enjoy Bill Baker's jokes or Liz Berry's parrot*. These are all perfectly good reasons for choosing a wine merchant and it is much better that you should be happy dealing with someone of compatible temperament than get irritated by my taste in ties.

The perfect wine merchant could only exist in a world of perfect customers. In reality, we each make mistakes. But the customer is always right and we know our place.

Your humble and obedient servant to command,
Simon Loftus
Adnams Wine Merchants

* [No longer in residence at La Vigneronne – *Ed.*]

Matching Wine and Food: Logic or Magic?

Aileen Hall

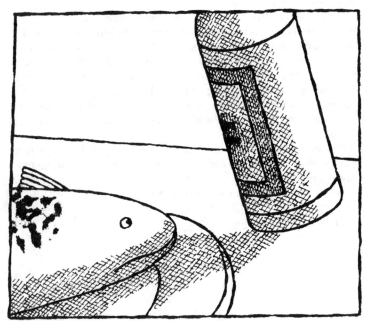

..the first precious wild salmon of the season should not have to suffer G.B.H...

'Always true to you, darling, in my fashion...'

Not so long ago, marriages of food and wine were assumed to be made in heaven, with appropriate vows of fidelity imposed on them; Muscadet would always love and cherish oysters; claret and beef would be parted only by death; Stilton would remain faithful to port and forsake all others. However, current thinking sees the relationship more as a series of one-night stands – a chance to explore food, wine and oneself, a journey which can be both fun and enlightening.

Before we get to the wine and food, let's consider you, as impresario (or marriage-broker) and participant. With you comes such a package of variables as to make this matching game seem closer to three-dimensional chess than snakes and ladders. Your personal preferences, prejudices, tastebuds, digestion, mood and general state of health all combine with other inevitable factors – the season, the climate, the atmosphere (literal and metaphorical), the place, the company and the occasion. Although this is not a new concept – 'Better is a dinner of herbs where love is, than a stalled ox and hatred therewith' (*Proverbs*) – it is one often forgotten in menu-planning.

Now that we've remembered it, we should be better prepared to accept the variability and fallibility of human arrangements: what works one day may not the next; what pleases one group of friends may bore another; what seems an inspired and original match on one occasion may, in different circumstances, leave us dismayed at its ineptitude.

Having set the complex human scene, let's turn to one of the other elements in this three-way equation, the food. Any hope of simplicity is soon dashed, for – as sure as eggs is eggs – cod, say, is much more than cod. Is it spanking fresh or elderly? Under- or over-cooked? A fillet or a steak? Boiled, grilled, fried in batter or cooked in a spicy sauce? Is it served with parsley sauce, aïoli or chips and vinegar? As salt cod, itself primitively savoury in flavour, it may acquire the additional Mediterranean complexities of oil, garlic, chillies, almonds, even tahini (sesame paste).

Whatever the food – from raw carrot sticks to cassoulet – it is worth analysing some of the aspects which will affect its relationship with wine. If you are a cook and/or a connoisseur, you are already well used to assessing a dish for saltiness, sweetness, acidity and richness (often allied to the amount of fat in the recipe, whether it is foie gras with its built-in fat, a butter-based sauce, an oily salad dressing, or sauté'd or deep-fried ingredients). Strength of flavour can come from any of these, as well as from herbs, spices and other seasonings. Gaminess in meats is worth assessing, and ignore inherent character, as in brassicas, tripe and olives, for example, at your peril. Texture is important too, whether you are serving a thin soup, an airy mousse or soufflé, a sticky oxtail stew or a crunchy salad. A little evaluation of the assertiveness, weight and style of a particular dish will pay dividends when it comes to picking a wine partner.

Similarly, when weighing up a wine as a possible partner, you need to assess its general style but also be aware of the individual qualities, many of them common to food: acidity, sweetness, fruitiness, tannin (from grape or oak barrels), concentration and length of flavour.

The next step in planning the theoretical partnership is to decide whether this is to be a marriage of equals or whether one partner should be dominant. And are you aiming for similarity or contrast? If a special, celebratory bottle is to be opened, the food should obviously play a secondary role. On the other hand, the first precious wild salmon of the season should not have to suffer GBH from an extrovert bully of a New World Chardonnay.

As to matching or contrasting wine and food, both have their virtues: an acid young white wine can be as refreshing as a squirt of lemon or vinegar with fish and chips; smoked food (fish or meat) can take either a smokey/oaky wine of similar strength of flavour (bring out that New World Chardonnay) – or something much lighter with a slight undertow of sweetness (think of the appeal of sweet relishes and chutneys with ham). On the whole, rustic dishes such as casseroles, which may involve the depth of flavour of a dozen or so ingredients married by long cooking, are best served by rather simple, forceful wines which match them in rusticity, perhaps, but contribute a contrasting simplicity to the union.

So far our matching has been all in the mind. In theory, X ought to go well with A and Y with Q. Human physiology and chemistry introduce yet another hazard: some food and wine combinations taste unexpectedly unpleasant, either initially or as an aftertaste. For example, the old rule of 'white wine with fish' may have been carved in stone by people who had had unhappy experiences with tannic red wines, either youthfully brash or oakily old, leaving a metallic taste in the mouth when drunk with white fish. Luckily, lighter, fruity reds – such as young Beaujolais or Loire Gamays – go particularly well with oily or strongly flavoured fish like mackerel and red mullet. Oysters give some wines a rotten-eggs finish, and watercress can transform, on some palates, a sedate white into a patchouli-scented raver. Asparagus, artichokes and juniper berries have also been found guilty on occasion of producing chemical or metallic aftertastes.

Enough of generalisations. Most people will be faced with a specific situation – tonight's family supper or next month's formal dinner – and have to make decisions as to how much they want to spend, how many wines they would like to serve, and what they hope the wine will contribute to the meal. With that in mind, let's consider a few meals and the wines which might go with them.

The one-bottle meal

Some experts claim that champagne is the one wine which you can serve happily throughout a meal, from aperitif to cheese: we would question whether it does much for roast lamb or a red-wine stew. Ironically, those who can afford to make the experiment could also afford a selection of different wines matched more precisely to each course.

Most of us will hope for a wine that will go well with the main course and, with luck, not too badly with one of the others. White wine is rather more flexible than red, with the additional benefit of making an easier aperitif than most reds. Australian Semillon or Semillon-Chardonnay blends have enough body, acidity and liveliness to see you through, say, as aperitif and partner to a light pâté or gentle salad as a first course, with straightforward poultry, fish, ham or salady main course. (Go carefully on the vinaigrette – a ratio of five to one for oil to acid, with wine vinegar or lemon juice rather than anything fiercer.)

Other wines to consider for a one-bottle meal include the zingy Vin de Pays des Côtes de Gascogne and the greenly acid Loire Sauvignon Blanc, both crisp and flavoursome enough to avert boredom and match a wide variety of dishes. If you enjoy Muscat flavours, consider a dry Alsace Muscat, the Portuguese João Pires Palmela White or the Spanish Torres Viña Esmeralda (a punchy blend of Muscat and Gewürztraminer). These wines, drunk young while their acidity is still lively enough to balance the heady Muscat flavours, can partner anything from salads and pâtés to vegetable casseroles and creamy, slightly sweet dishes (such as scallops in wine and cream sauce). They are particularly effective with oriental food. For something more esoteric, consider a dry or medium dry Jurançon from the Pyrenees. Made from local grapes, mainly Gros and Petit Manseng, Jurançon has a flavour concentrated enough to match fish or ham in a spicy sauce; in the medium-dry/medium-sweet version, it can take on sweet-sour flavours and even chilli-hot dishes.

If for you 'the first duty of a wine is to be red', Beaujolais is almost as flexible as a white wine. Serve it young, fresh and lightly chilled when its fruit and acidity will contrast with oily fish, coarse pâtés, roast ham, chicken or pork, sausages, cereal- or pulse-based casseroles, as well as such cheeses as Camembert and chèvre. The same fruit and acidity can match, for example, a tomato-based sauce with pasta or meat loaf, provided the tomatoes are ripe – or the sauce assisted by a pinch of sugar. If you fancy a gentler but equally accommodating wine, a light, fairly mature Pinot Noir (Hautes Côtes de Beaune, say, rather than the big guns of the Côte d'Or) would not outface simple grills or roasts, cold meats and young game.

Obviously the choice becomes simpler if only one course is involved in the match: Côtes du Rhône, Minervois or Dolcetto with appropriate casseroles; Muscadet, Soave or Chablis with many fish dishes; claret with lamb or ham; Chianti or a young Shiraz with a barbecue.

The two-bottle meal

Introduce a second bottle and you widen the possibilities and – of course – add to the complications of planning a meal to show both food and wine to advantage. It is no bad thing to remember the old maxim, 'white before red, young before old, light before heavy, dry before sweet' – even if you deliberately ignore several of the diktats. This is an appropriate place to remind you of the vital role of bread and water as palate-cleansers: have them on hand throughout the meal so that people have a chance to erase one flavour before contemplating the next.

As in our one-bottle meal, you may hope to have a wine match more than one course. If your guests enjoy sherry, serve a well-chilled fino or manzanilla as an aperitif (with a few olives or almonds) and continue with the sort of first course served in tapas bars in Spain: grilled sardines, fresh lightly pickled anchovies, spicy sausages or other cold meats, tortilla (potato or onion omelette, served cool), little meat balls in spicy tomato sauce or smoked fish or ham. The second course would need plenty of character – look to the Rhône, Rioja or Cahors, and with it a gutsy casserole (beef and pork and/or earthy beans and lentils); or perhaps even a mature Barolo capable of moving smoothly on from high game to strong cheese.

Those who are sweet-toothed and open-minded may like to begin and end a meal with the same sweet wine, with something lively in between. Fine Sauternes – or the cheaper relatives from Monbazillac and Premières Côtes de Bordeaux – provide the tangy botrytis flavour which easily flatters an unctuous pâté or modern 'sweet and savoury' salad at the beginning of the meal. In the same breath it will take in its stride cheeses as disparate as mature Gouda, Roquefort, Cheshire and chèvre, to say nothing of coping with a fruity pudding or demure cake (almonds and apricots are two flavours which flatter dessert wines). The rule with sweets and wine (*this* one worth observing) is to ensure that the pudding is less sweet than the wine: the result otherwise is a thin, sorry relic of the wine's self-confident lusciousness.

Zinfandel, made from California's only indigenous grape, has rich porty overtones which allow it to befriend Indian food, barbecues, blue cheeses and mature Cheddar (though for tandoori dishes, Gewürztraminer tastes even better). Serve it after a light and elegant white wine so that the total effect is not leaden: stay in California with a fine Rhine Riesling, perhaps, or consider the same grape from its homeland, or even a Loire Sauvignon – from basic Touraine Sauvignon to an elegant Sancerre if the food and occasion justify it.

A two-bottle meal based on white wines need not be dull. Alsace could provide, for example, a crisp and flowery Pinot Blanc to serve as aperitif and with a first course of quiche or other egg- or cheese-based dish; and a mature Tokay-Pinot Gris (wise to go for the concentration and class of a Grand Cru) which could partner game, creamy casseroles of fish, chicken, pork or veal with its own particular richness cut by tangy acidity.

Other two-bottle combinations beyond the Bordeaux and Burgundy conventions might take you Down Under for a wealth of flavoursome wines. If you opt for such European grapes as Chardonnay, Sauvignon Blanc and Cabernet, be aware that the wines made from them are likely to taste punchier than their French equivalents – no bad thing if a piquant sauce, say, needs some firm control from the accompanying glass. The grapes which Australian wine-makers have made very much their own are Semillon, a sunny and self-opinionated white, and Shiraz, the swaggering version of the Rhône's Syrah, packed with ripe fruit and, often, gamey overtones fit to challenge most strong flavours in food.

You're on your own with the three-bottle meal and beyond. The principles remain the same; the complications increase. Some people enjoy the ceremonial overtones of an array of bottles and glasses; other find it indigestible.

Blind man's bluff

The most basic matching of food and wine, and the most challenging for your guests, is a blind tasting. At its simplest, this might involve one item of food – smoked mackerel, baked beans, caviare, egg mayonnaise or whatever – and half-a-dozen bottles which you think might be appropriate partners for it. Wrap them to conceal their identity, number them to keep the records straight, and encourage everyone to taste and assess first the wines on their own, then each wine after a mouthful of the foodstuff. We can guarantee some surprises, no matter what you choose.

Try to analyse why some matches work better than others. Is it the clean acidity in the young Mosel which contrasts with the richness of the fish pâté? Does the sweetness of the baked beans overwhelm the modest Chenin Blanc? Is it the complexity of the oak-aged white Graves which makes it stand up to the mayonnaise? Is the grilled steak with shallot butter too forceful for the Bulgarian Merlot, turning it jammy on the palate? People who are good at lists (and manage to keep a diary after January 12) might like to make a chart, annotating each match according to the aspects outlined at the beginning of this piece: acidity, sweetness, saltiness, fruitiness, etc.

The mirror image of that tasting would involve choosing one interesting wine and a selection of theoretically appropriate nibbles. Does that Sancerre which tasted so good with poached turbot go equally well with its own local goats' cheese, smoked fish, asparagus, eggs?

These tastings can explore any number of themes: regional wines and specialities, for example; some of the notoriously difficult foods – grapefruit, kippers, chili, sweet-and-sour pork, Christmas pudding – as well as any dishes you particularly enjoy. You will find that whether a dish is vegetarian or not is largely irrelevant: the same aspects of weight, strength of flavour, fattiness, acidity and so on apply to them as to dishes based on meat or fish.

To whet your appetite, here are some favourite combinations enjoyed recently:

- smoked salmon with an oaked white Graves, Sémillon-based, the oak of the wine matching the smokiness of the fish, the well-balanced fruit and acidity cutting the salmon's richness, and the strengths of flavour fairly evenly matched
- casseroled hare in a sweetish sauce with a Rheingau Riesling Auslese, where the relative sweetness of the two were in harmony and the wine's underlying acidity lightened the intensity of flavour in the hare and its sauce
- demi-sec Vouvray with a Chinese meal of many dishes, not all of which flattered the wine; but it worked for several of the dim-sum, for the sweet-and-sour pork and for the chicken with almonds, the wine teasingly delicate with some dishes, complex and subtle with others, always bringing a light note to the combination
- mature goat's cheese with Coteaux du Layon, one of many pleasant surprises which showed how well a sweetish wine can

cope with strongly flavoured cheeses. In this case, the flowery, honeyed, lemony sweetness of the wine contrasted effectively with the fiercely animal flavours of the cheese

- cassoulet with Côte Rôtie, a pair of well-matched heavyweights: the wine alone seemed unnervingly forceful, mature, alcoholic, with a petrolly edge to it, but with the cassoulet, its ripe fruit became more obvious, the cassoulet's massive richness was cut, and the aftertaste was clean and appetising
- roast lamb with California Pinot Noir, a change from the traditional claret, and an inspired matching of gentle sweetness in both, with the wine's ripe fruit acting almost as a sauce
- Lebanese Château Musar with a coarse pâté, the wine (mainly Cabernet Sauvignon, the rest Cinsault and Syrah, oak-aged) aromatic and ripe, with earthy, even farmyardy, tones which complemented the strident pâté perfectly
- New Zealand Sauvignon Blanc with grilled mackerel and gooseberries, an interesting example of how the extra ripe fruitiness – in a Sauvignon from the only New World country which can make one to rival the best Sancerre – could take on not only the oily fish but also the tart sauce – both, of course, tasting of gooseberries
- Christmas cake and old tawny port, both nutty, fruity and slightly spirity, in a richly festive way.

Bon appétit for your life-time study of the magic of food and wine matching. Let us know what you like with chocolate...

Aileen Hall, editor of *Which? Wine Monthly*, has also worked on *The Good Food Guide*, for which she wrote and edited several cookery books.

Wine and Health:
a User's Primer

Dr Thomas Stuttaford

.. gait becomes rather careful ..

Wine had a ritualistic role in Ancient Greece and Rome as well as being then, as now, one of the standard commodities on the Greek and Italian larder shelf. Although it is traditionally taught that civilised British behaviour owes more to the Greek culture than the Roman, it was Bacchus rather than the Greek god Dionysus who became synonymous with drinking, and it was the spread of the Roman Empire which introduced the benefit of wine to most of the rest of Europe. The Romans even planted vineyards in Britain, and grapes grew as far north as Ely, despite its being surrounded by dank fens. The Romans cared about their wines and by AD 200 writers were comparing and contrasting different varieties as if they were contributors to an early *Which? Wine Guide*. They understood that the way in which grapes were grown, as well as wine-making processes, affected a wine's drinking qualities. The foundations of a wine culture, laid by the Romans, was built on by the monks of the Christian Church, who, by keeping the monastery cellars stocked, established the pattern of a future wine trade across Europe. Wine has never had a universally good press, though; Old and New Testament writers as well as the Romans have written on the disadvantages of excessive drinking as well as praising its virtues in moderation.

'Feeling the click'

For as long as wine has been drunk there has been an interest in its metabolism by the body, an interest stirred by the ability to see a physiological experiment being performed in everyday life as the effects of taking small, moderate or excessive amounts can be observed minutely by fellow drinkers around the dinner table or bar. Alcohol in small quantities lowers inhibitions, produces a sense of relaxation and wellbeing, and increases talkativeness so that the shy, introverted guest may suddenly blossom and not only enjoy the wine but also warm to his or her companions. The amount of alcohol required to reach this point, or as Tennessee Williams described it, 'to feel the click', varies from person to person. Women respond more quickly to smaller quantities of alcohol than men, and small, plump women need less than large muscular ones; likewise, large men tolerate alcohol more easily than their round, short brothers. As a very rough guide, one unit of alcohol increases the blood level by 15mg per 100ml in men, and by 20mg per 100ml in women. At 60mg per 100ml (four glasses of wine in a man or three in a woman) there is a chance that some drinkers will have to start weighing up the disadvantages of drinking against the advantages: speech can become slightly altered and face flushed, reaction time is slowed, gait becomes rather careful and, horror of horrors, those aspects of a person's character which are better hidden can be revealed for all to see.

Alcohol affects the mood of people differently. This is partly determined by the pervading culture: in some, aggression is expected, hence the phenomenon of the lager lout at Bournemouth, or the Assassins Club at Oxford. On the other hand in at least one cavalry regiment it was explained to new officers that it was permissible, albeit dangerous, to slip blind drunk beneath the mess table, but considered unforgivable to become over-emphatic, aggressive or rumbustious. Other regiments had different traditions and with them different patterns of drunkenness.

As the blood level of alcohol increases the changes are more marked: at 100mg per 100ml (the greater part of a bottle of wine) some evidence of lack of co-ordination shows: in most people not used to alcohol speech is becoming slurred, gait is unsteady and reaction time too slow for intricate work. Over 300mg brings the risk of coma or convulsions; over 500mg and the possibility of disaster becomes a probability. Usually death from acute intoxication occurs as a result of inhalation of vomit, for the cough and vomit reflexes have been knocked out by the alcohol; occasionally, as recently happened to a well-known journalist, the throat becomes so relaxed with the alcohol overdosage that the very lack of muscle tone causes collapse, and obstruction, of the airway, a condition inaccurately referred to by the layman as 'swallowing your own tongue', a physical impossibility.

Absorption of alcohol

Once the wine has given pleasure to the palate by passing through the mouth it reaches the stomach, where it is absorbed relatively slowly, and from there passes through the pylorus, the valve between the stomach and duodenum, into the small intestine – from where it is absorbed into the bloodstream very quickly. The speed of absorption of any given quantity of wine depends on a wide variety of factors: women absorb it more quickly than men; the absorption can be delayed by drinking and eating at the same time, particularly if there is fat in the food; and above all the strength and type of alcohol affects its rate of absorption.

If the stomach is assaulted by strong drink, neat spirits for instance, the pylorus closes, gastric emptying is delayed and the alcohol is absorbed relatively slowly, through the stomach itself. If comparatively weak solutions of alcohol, such as wine or beer, arrive at the stomach, the pylorus remains open, and the alcohol goes quickly through to the small intestines where it is rapidly absorbed. An alcohol strength of 15 to 30 per cent is the most dangerous, for example in drinks such as spirits with 'mixers', as well as vermouth, port, sherry and Madeira; they are strong enough to pack a punch, but not so strong that they close the pylorus. In consequence they are absorbed quickly, causing a rapid rise in blood alcohol levels. This phenomenon accounts for the effect a couple of glasses of sherry at the church party can have on people unused to alcohol. The effect of champagne is particularly interesting: stronger than many wines, it is also fizzy and thus seems light and airy; both palate and stomach are, as it were, kidded into believing that they are dealing with a less powerful drink than is in fact the case. The pylorus therefore remains open and the champagne is quickly absorbed. It is thought that carbonated or sparkling alcoholic drinks in general are quickly absorbed, as the fizz tends to keep the pylorus open. The paradoxically slow absorption of neat spirits can have important consequences: brandy after dinner may be slowly absorbed, and may therefore impair driving on the way home.

After absorption, alcohol spreads rapidly throughout the tissues of the body. The majority is detoxified by the liver, but five per cent is excreted unchanged through the kidneys and urine, and traces are lost through the skin and breath. In the liver, alcohol is oxidised to acetaldehyde through the action of the enzyme alcohol dehydrogenase; this ADH enzyme system is supplemented in experienced drinkers by a subsidiary one, the microsomal ethanol oxidising system; this is one of the reasons why hardened drinkers, who still have an intact liver, sober up more quickly. The rate of detoxification can vary by up to 25 per cent in people of the same size and sex, but on average the alcohol blood level is reduced by 15mg per hour; i.e. a single glass of wine takes an hour to leave your body. A man who has drunk a bottle of wine at dinner (nine units), has had two glasses of gin before (four units if poured at home) with two glasses of brandy afterwards (another four) will still have an appreciable amount of alcohol in his blood at breakfast time the next day. Similarly, a woman who has had a bottle of wine at dinner will be unfit to drive until at least five hours after the last glassful. It cannot be stressed enough that individual variation is enormous, with drinking experience, age, sex, the degree of hunger and current health all playing a part; hard and fast rules on safety are therefore impossible.

The danger level

The body's power of adaptation is as apparent in its ability to deal with increased doses of alcohol as with life at high altitudes or with heavy exercise. For many years the liver becomes increasingly proficient at detoxifying alcohol, but sooner or later, in 10 to 30 per cent of very heavy drinkers, the fatty deposits (which are almost invariably to be found in the liver of such people), give way to scarring and changes in the liver's architecture; as the healthy active tissue is replaced, and lost, the body's capacity to detoxify alcohol falls, often suddenly. Once a heavy drinker's liver has started to fail he or she becomes intoxicated very early. This was illustrated by George Brown who always said in his own defence, when charged with some alcohol-induced scrape, that he had only had a couple of drinks. I never believed him until I watched him at a political party where he was transformed from a totally sober, considerate statesman to an intemperate and loud-mouthed lout by two drinks; his liver had been sacrificed to a lifetime in politics and public life.

The hangover

Few drinkers become problem drinkers. Most remain social, sensible drinkers able to enjoy its advantages but, however careful, most have to suffer a hangover at some time. The hangover – headache, nausea, tremor, shivering and sweating – can occur for the unlucky few after as little as five units of alcohol, while in over 50 per cent of drinkers, eight to ten units will induce one; some people never suffer them. Whereas the risk of long-term damage to the body is related to the quantity of alcohol taken, and not to the type, hangovers are related to type as well as quantity. Most drinkers will have noticed that whisky, brandy, port and red wines are more likely to cause a hangover than vodka or white wine; this is because the former owe their specific taste to the presence of extracts and congeners, those substances which give 'darker' drinks their distinctive character. Although acetaldehyde contributes to a hangover, so do the breakdown products of the congeners, including methanol, which has formic acid and formaldehyde as metabolites. Any hangover is made worse by dehydration and hypoglycaemia. Alcohol is a diuretic: it increases the flow of urine so that although some cells, including brain cells, become damaged and swell, the body as a whole becomes dehydrated; hence the dry mouth and throat. The hypoglycaemia, low blood sugar, is due to the liver's glucose-producing qualities being hindered by the alcohol. Treatment of hangovers is symptomatic: soluble aspirin for the headache, alkaline mixtures for the stomach, food (if it can be tolerated) for the hypoglycaemia, and plenty of fluids for the dehydration.

A hangover is proportional to both the amount of alcohol consumed, usually greater if the alcohol content of the drink is high, and the nature of the drink. The nature of the drink is dependent on the congeners; as well as the chemicals already mentioned they include traces of minerals, vegetable residues, and anthocyanins. They are found in greater quantities in dark drinks: the darker they are, the more congeners are present. To avoid a hangover drink vodka rather than brandy, Pouilly Fumé rather than claret, a white wine from Alsace rather than a young burgundy. Maturing in wood increases the amount of congeners present, hence the morning-after notoriety of some Spanish wines. Although long-term damage caused by regular heavy drinking can occur – even in the absence of drunkenness – many, but not all, doctors feel that light to moderate intake, two to five units of alcohol a day, will not only not harm most people but in all probability will increase their lifespan. Some of these benefits may be due to alcohol's relaxing effect, but most are probably dependent on the changes found in the proportion of the high-density lipoprotein to total cholesterol in a person's blood. Modest drinkers tend to have greater proportions of their cholesterol as high-density lipoprotein. The greater the proportion of this high density lipoprotein, the less likely a person is to suffer coronary heart disease. Hence, in a review of 163 published references there is an inverse association between moderate alcohol consumption and coronary heart disease. The beneficial effects of small quantities of alcohol have been bitterly refuted by the anti-alcohol brigade: they claim that the apparent evidence showing that people who drink under two units of alcohol a day share the same mortality as those who drink six units a day, leaving those who drink between two to four units with the best prognosis, is confounded by the number of teetotallers who are ex-alcoholics, or who are diseased from other causes. Their evidence doesn't explain the evidence of several long term studies, particularly two from California. One of these projects looked into the past and present drinking habits of 87,526 female nurses. It showed that the marked reduction in coronary heart disease in moderate drinkers more than outweighed any increase from other causes. Nearer home, 1,422 male British civil servants were followed up for ten years; moderate drinkers had the lowest mortality. The very occasional person may suffer alcohol-related damage at a lower intake than this, which has prompted health authorities to recommend a weekly intake of not more than 21 units for men, and 14 units for women. As with any official advice this has to err on the side of caution and has to take into consideration the 'worst case' scenario, but for most a glass or two of wine a day may not only make us feel better but may actually be healthier.

Dr Stuttaford, formerly an MP, is medical adviser to a wide variety of firms and medical correspondent of *The Times*.

Stocking Up

Andrew Jefford

.. *swirl the wine to draw out its aromas..*

Buying wine

Wine, unlike washing-up liquid, potatoes and replacement dust bags for your vacuum cleaner, is fun to buy, and fun to sell. This may be one of the reasons why so many different companies are trying to get us to purchase so many different wines in so many different ways. Deciding where to buy can be as bewildering as choosing what to buy.

Supermarkets

For most people, supermarkets are the first choice. For low prices,
they are rivalled only by wine warehouses. For ease of purchase,
they are rivalled by no one, and for reliability, too, they lead the
field. These are all-powerful attractions, and anyone for whom
money is any sort of an object would be foolish to ignore
supermarket wine selections. They are useful, too, if you enjoy
wine in an uncomplicated way, and want to keep your enjoyment
at that level, without filling your head full of names, years,
categories and price differentials. Simply find the kind of wine
that suits you via the description on the shelf label, or on the label
on the back of the bottle. If the wine is good, stick with it, and you
can be reasonably sure that the style won't change much as long as
the supermarket runs that particular line. For more adventurous
drinkers, supermarkets offer an increasingly wide range of quality
wines from less well-known regions of the world, as well as fine
wines from classic regions – always keenly priced. Many people
enjoy the anonymity of a supermarket wine purchase: you can
quietly look at what's on offer and make up your own mind about
what you want, without having anyone trying to sell you
anything, and without it mattering one way or the other whether
you actually buy anything or not.

The disadvantages of buying wines from supermarket chains
are bound up with their advantages. In order to ensure the lowest
possible prices, most supermarkets specialise in 'own-label' or
'own-brand' wines: tailor-made, bulk-purchased selections
specific to each group, and designed for maximum appeal within
each *appellation* or price category. These may be, and often are,
sound and enjoyable wines, but they will rarely have the character
and individuality that you will find in the wines of a top estate or
virtuoso small grower within the same *appellation*. The labels of
such wines, too, often share a 'house style' which identifies the
supermarket loudly and the wines's origin softly, obscuring the
pleasure many of us take in mentally matching tastes to the distant
parts of Europe or the world in which those tastes were created.

A number of supermarkets are now moving away from the
'own-label' principle towards exclusive reliance on wines
packaged and labelled at origin. In many cases, the change is only
cosmetic: the wine inside the bottles is still the same tightly
specified blend at a much haggled-over price from the same huge
co-operative, whose label may in any case be as dull as the
supermarket's was uniform. And the virtuoso small grower still

won't make an appearance, because he can't supply the quantities that the supermarket needs in order to stock his wine in its many different branches, for at least a few months. The same qualification applies to those fine wines from classic regions: supermarkets will only consider wines available in substantial quantities (though the higher the price, the less substantial the quantity will need to be). There is, furthermore, a limit to the range that supermarkets can offer, particularly in city-centre sites where space is at a premium, and the way in which some wines appear at 'selected outlets' only is always a source of frustration. This problem is not confined to supermarkets, but it is at its most acute there. A branch of Oddbins or Victoria Wines will order up one or two bottles of a line not stocked by that branch for you from the central warehouse, but it's not always easy to find anyone in a supermarket prepared to do that for you; in most cases, you'll just have to find a bigger branch. Finally, if you are a purchaser who would like personal help and guidance in buying wine rather than relying on vaguely worded printed slips and tags, go to a wine merchant.

Wine merchants

Independents

But what sort of wine merchant? The choice here is enormous. There are two main categories of merchant: the chain and the independent. Most of the merchants listed in this Guide are independents, for the simple reason that chains get only one entry, covering all their branches; it is generally the independents, though, who will offer you most in the way of help and advice. As far as we know – but write to us if you feel it is not the case – all the independents in *Which? Wine Guide* are genuine enthusiasts who care deeply about wine, and take great pride in the range they stock. They will happily discuss these wines with you for as long as you wish, and will go to great pains to find something to please you from among their range. They are often open for long hours, and will even open specially for you at other times if you telephone through with a request. They will arrange tastings for groups, and carry out local deliveries. Many of them specialise in the wines of a particular part of the world, or in a special category of wines, such as fine and rare bottles. What most of them won't be able to offer is a huge range, nor will they be able to match the very cheapest prices. As they are scattered around the country and have no facility or even need to advertise nationally, they receive little press coverage, despite the fact that they may have pioneered the sale of a particular grower's or region's wines. Our small independents are the wine-lover's front-line infantry, unsung defenders of the special role Britain has always enjoyed as the best-informed, most appreciative wine-drinking nation in Europe. If you have a good independent in your area, and you like a personal touch when it comes to buying wine, give him or her your support.

Mail order

The larger independents do manage to serve the whole country, by offering a mail-order service. Buying wine by mail-order is in many ways an attractive method. You can take as much time as you want over making your selection, and consult as many sources as you wish in doing so; then you simply jot down your order on the merchant's printed form, enclose a cheque or a credit card number, and the merchant and carrier do the rest. Most are happy to take orders by telephone or fax, too. Mail-order specialists generally have a very large range on offer, and produce detailed and inspiring wine lists which make choosing wine a great pleasure. You can mix cases, or buy unmixed ones, or buy some of the merchant's own 'ready-mixed' selections, the last two options bringing you a modest discount. With some mail-order specialists you must buy at least one whole case; with others, you can buy as little as a single bottle. A number of mail-order merchants don't have a retail outlet, but work from home or from an office; others have one or more shops; and some national or regional chains also offer mail-order facilities.

The disadvantage of this system is that it takes time: there will usually be a two- or three-week gap between sending off your order and receiving your wine. If no one is at home during the day, taking delivery of the wine can be complicated. You see the wine for the first time only when you unpack it and, such is the power of labelling and packaging, you may be disappointed by the appearance of some bottles. Sometimes substitutions will have been made for out-of-stock wines, though you will generally have been telephoned first for your agreement as to the proposed swaps. On occasion you will receive bottles with torn or damaged labels, and very rarely bottles themselves will have been broken in transit. The merchant will help you sort out these problems, but it will take more time. A further disadvantage of mail order is that you can taste the wines only by buying them first, and you must take their descriptions on trust. Prices, finally, are high, and if you buy only a small quantity of wine, you may also have to pay a premium for delivery.

Chains

If time presses, the speediest way to buy wine is generally to make use of one of the branches of the national or local chains. These describe themselves as 'wine merchants', but often fail to live up to the description, except in its most literal sense; 'off-licence', with its connotations of discounted beer and cigarette sales, supplemented by anonymous bottles of Muscadet and Bordeaux, is more apt in many cases. This is a shame, because when chains take their role as specialist wine suppliers seriously, they can be very good indeed, as Oddbins has proved beyond all reasonable doubt. Some previously lacklustre chains have been working hard over the last two or three years to live up to their 'wine merchant' billing by improving and extending their wine ranges, smartening up their shops and ensuring that their staff at least know a little about the wine range rather than nothing at all. Others haven't; and relying on an off-licence to provide an interesting and enjoyable bottle en route to dinner with friends is still unwise.

Wine warehouses

Wine warehouses are now a familiar part of the British wine-buying scene. They originally came into being thanks to a peculiarity of the British licensing laws: if you wish to sell between one and eleven bottles of wine, you need to apply for a retail licence and be granted it, should you be thought suitable, in court; if you wish to sell twelve or more, however, fine: no problem, go ahead. (Initially there was a 'wholesale licence', but this no longer exists: see below.)

The pioneers of this form of retailing reasoned that if the public were to be persuaded to buy twelve bottles of wine at one time, they had better be offered a large choice and low prices – hence the railway-arch location and the functionalism of piles on piles of bottles and boxes from every part of the wine-growing world.

For the absolute beginner, wine warehouses can be bewildering, though they are generally staffed by some of the least stuffy and most knowledgeable of all wine sales assistants, always happy to glide you enthusiastically through their darkest canyons. Tasting facilities are usually offered, and choice of wines is always wide, bearing the warehouse hallmark of buccaneering eclecticism. Prices are never high, and are often pegged down towards bargain levels. The disadvantages of wine warehouses are the obligatory purchase of at least twelve bottles, and the fact that you need to be a car owner to take the wine away afterwards (though free local delivery is slowly becoming a standard warehouse service).

British licensing laws

Anyone can set themselves up as a wine or spirit merchant provided they sell twelve or more bottles (9 litres) of wine, or of spirits, or 20 litres of beer or cider, to every customer: for these 'wholesale' quantities, no licence is required. To sell less than twelve bottles of either wine or spirits, you will need an 'off-licence', for which you have to apply to a committee of licensing justices at the local magistrates court. Both premises and person have to be licensed. Note that any merchant who will mix in one or two bottles of spirits to make up a case of wine, or who will sell beer in under 20-litre quantities, must hold an off-licence, and this includes many 'wholesale' merchants selling on a by-the-case-only basis. In these examples (Majestic Wine Warehouses are the field leaders), the 'wholesale' aspect is company policy rather than a legal necessity – except outside the restricted licensing hours in force on a Sunday, when traders of this sort are obliged to revert to being strict wholesale operators, selling a minimum of 9 litres of wine or of spirits, or 20 of beer. Finally, if you decide to sell on a wholesale basis for yourself, remember the four categories of person the law forbids you to sell alcohol to: people believed to be under 18, people who are intoxicated, policemen or policewomen in uniform, and – rather unreasonably – people known to be prostitutes.

Buying wine *en primeur*

Independent merchants and mail-order specialists sometimes offer fine wines for sale *en primeur*, and indeed some of them specialise in this form of wine sale. At first glance, its attractions seem doubtful. Why pay for anything in advance, especially something as expensive as fine wine? You won't take delivery of it for several years, and it won't be drinkable for at least a decade. At the moment at which you are asked to pay, no one can be confident of exactly how good the wine is, nor can they be confident of how the market for the wine will evolve.

The appeal of *en primeur* purchase is that, throughout the 1980s, it proved itself to be the cheapest way to buy fine wines, particularly clarets. It is also at the *en primeur* stage that you are offered the greatest choice of these wines: high demand means that many of them subsequently disappear from the market, only reappearing many years later at auction. If you hope to make money by investment in wine, too, it is essential that you buy as early as possible. But if you don't want, or can't afford, a cellar full of classed-growth claret, plus a few cases of vintage port, top Sauternes, northern Rhône reds and burgundies, then you need not feel tempted by *en primeur* offers. If you'd like to buy just one or two bottles of such wines before they become too expensive, a number of merchants, particularly the best of the mail-order specialists, will usually offer fine wines around three or four years after the vintage in single-bottle quantities. The price for one bottle will be more than it would have been *en primeur*, but it will still be much less than when the wine is mature.

Buying en primeur: how to do it

1 Contact a number of specialists (see list below) and ask for any *en primeur* offers they may have available at present.

2 Research the wines you are interested in, discussing their qualities with the merchant (who should have tasted samples) if you need to. Compare prices for the same wine from offer to offer: they can vary by £25 per case or more. When you have decided what and how much you want to buy, pay. (Some merchants offer special payment terms and finance schemes.)

3 You should receive documents indicating your ownership of the wine in the records of the company you are dealing with. Guard these carefully until you are ready to take delivery of your wine.

4 Around two years later, you will be contacted by the merchant, asking for delivery instructions. You will have to pay shipping costs, duty, delivery charges, and VAT on everything. If you don't have storage facilities at home, arrangements can generally be made to store the wine on your behalf: remember that good storage is vital if you have any intention of reselling the wine at any point, as well as in order to get the most out of it when you eventually drink it. If you ask a merchant to store on your behalf, clarify any ambiguities, satisfy yourself that the storage conditions are sound, and guard the paperwork carefully again. Check that the wine is insured in storage. The merchant from whom you bought the wine will be able to advise you on the best moment to begin drinking it.

Recommended merchants from whom to buy *en primeur*:

Adnams, Les Amis du Vin, Averys, Nigel Baring, Berry Bros, Bibendum, Corney & Barrow, Philip Eyres, Farr Vintners, Findlater Mackie Todd, Goedhuis, Haynes Hanson & Clark, Hicks & Don, Hungerford Wine Company, Justerini & Brooks, Laytons, Lay & Wheeler, Morris & Verdin, Christopher Piper Wines, Raeburn Fine Wines, Summerlee Wines, Tanners, Willoughbys, The Wine Society, Peter Wylie, Yorkshire Fine Wines.

Buying wine at auction

Wine auctions are chiefly of use to those who wish to acquire cases of fine wines in a mature condition, or bottles of rare wines, and many of the customers at auctions are consequently wine merchants, restaurateurs or international collectors. Other, less fine wines are also sold at auction, and bargains can certainly be had, though in this case make sure that you attend the pre-sale tasting and verify the quality of the lot you intend to bid for, as the vagaries of storage and provenance can mean that the less expensive sale wines may not prove as good in the glass as they look on paper. If you are a thoroughgoing enthusiast or a collector, you will certainly want to join the sale-room habitués; if you are a consumer who just wants a bottle of something special from time to time, you will find it much easier to deal with a merchant specialising in fine wines.

Buying at auction: how to do it

1 Contact one of the auction houses, and request catalogues for forthcoming wine auctions (you will have to pay for these).

2 Read the catalogue carefully, noting the amount of wine in any lot for which you intend to bid, and noting all the extra charges you would have to pay if your bid was successful (such as shipping charges, duty, delivery charges, a buyer's premium, insurance, and VAT on everything). For example, you may want to bid for a lot containing two dozen bottles of a wine whose estimated price is £65-£80 per dozen. You decide that you may be prepared to go as high as £78 per dozen, making a total of £156. These wines are still in bond, so you will have to pay duty of £9.96 per case on them, plus £15.60 buyer's premium. The total comes to £191.52, to which 15 per cent VAT must be added, making a grand total of £220.25. Note that £78 per dozen (£6.50 per bottle) has become a real price of £110.12 per dozen (£9.18 per bottle). Delivery and insurance, from this auction house, are free (and it should be pointed out that most wine sold at auction has already had duty and VAT paid on it).

3 If possible, go to the pre-sale tasting, and taste samples of the lot or lots you intend to bid for.

4 Go to the auction, or register a postal, fax, telex or telephone order bid. If you go in person, wave your catalogue to register a bid. If you are successful, the auction staff will contact you and explain further steps, as well as asking if you wish to purchase any subsequent lots of the same wine at the same bid price. You will normally be invoiced for the wine and all further supplementary charges, and you should pay within a week of receiving the invoice. Delivery will follow.

Auction houses

Christie's

8 King Street, London SW1Y 6QT
Tel 071-581 7611
Fax 071-839 1611
Telex 916429
85 Old Brompton Road, London SW7 3LD
Tel 071-581 7611
Fax 071-584 0431
Telex 922061
56-60 Gresham Street, London EC2V 7BB
Tel 071-588 4424
Fax 071-600 1782
Telex 928637
164-166 Bath Street, Glasgow G2 4TB
Tel 041-332 8134
Fax 041-332 5759
Telex 935704

Christie's run the largest number of auctions. The King Street auctions are of finer wines; Old Brompton Road sells everyday wine as well as finer wines and bin-ends; and the City branch tends to deal in port, burgundy and claret. Catalogue subscriptions cost: (King Street) £40 a year for fine wine other than claret, £30 a year for claret; (Old Brompton Road) £30; (Glasgow) £7. Pre-sale tastings take place between 11 am and noon the day before the sale at King Street and on the day of the sale at Old Brompton Road and in the City. Advice on the market in general and on whether to sell in particular is available. Delivery from the South Kensington branch to elsewhere in the UK is charged at £4 plus VAT per case or part case, and insurance is the responsibility of the purchaser. Delivery is free from the other two addresses if the wine is paid for within 21 days. There is a 10 per cent buyer's premium. Two sales a year are held in Glasgow or Edinburgh.

Sotheby's

34-35 New Bond Street, London W1A 2AA
Tel 071-493 8080
Fax 071-409 3100
Telex 24454 SPBLONG
Summers Place, Billingshurst, West Sussex RH14 9AD
Tel (0403 78) 3933
Fax (0403 78) 5153
Telex 87210 GAVEL
Unit 5, Albion Wharf, London SW11 4AN
Tel 071-924 3287
Fax 071-924 3110
Telex 935704
(Call press office for details – 071-408 5162)

Sotheby's hold fewer auctions than Christie's. The auctions at the New Bond Street address correspond to the auctions in Christie's King Street rooms, with fine wines dominating. A wider range is sold in Sussex. Sotheby's have set up a computer-linked bidding service. Subscription to the catalogues is £31. Delivery is £4 per case or part-case, including insurance, within the UK. There is minimum consignment charge of £13 (plus VAT) per collection/delivery. There is a 10 per cent buyer's premium.

International Wine Auctions
40 Victoria Way, London SE7 7QS
Tel 081-293 4992
Fax 081-293 4925

Bigwood Auctioneers Ltd
The Old School, Tiddington, Stratford-upon-Avon, Warwickshire CV37 7AW
Tel (0789) 69415
Fax (0789) 292686

Lacy Scott
10 Risbygate Street, Bury St Edmunds, Suffolk IP33 3AA
Tel (0284) 763531
Fax (0284) 704713

Lithgow, Sons & Partners
The Auction House, Station Road, Stokesley, Middlesbrough, Cleveland TS9 7AB
Tel (0642) 710158
Fax (0642) 712641

Phillips, Son & Neil
39 Park End Street, Oxford OX1 1JD
Tel (0865) 723524
Fax (0865) 791064

Storing wine

Once you have bought your wine, how should it be stored? The great enemies of wine are light, movement and temperature variations. It follows from this that the best place for wine is somewhere dark, free from knocks or vibrations, and steady in temperature. If the temperature is a low one – anything from 5°C–12°C, say – so much the better. But a steady temperature of 15°C–18°C is preferable to one which swings during the day from 10°C–19°C and back again at night.

In practice, these conditions are generally found as low as possible and as centrally positioned as possible within any building, the classic underground wine or coal cellar being ideal.

But if you don't have a cellar, cupboards under the stairs can be suitable, as can cupboards in ground-floor rooms, particularly if the room isn't used much, and isn't heated in winter. Make sure the sun doesn't shine on the cupboard and that central heating pipes don't pass through it. Attics and top-floor rooms are not recommended storing places for wine, due to the temperature variations they experience, particularly during sunny weather.

If you don't have anywhere like this in your house or flat, and you wish to buy young fine wines to age yourself until they reach maturity, there are two options. The first one is to invest in a purpose-made wine storage unit, such as a temperature-controlled bottle cabinet, or a spiral cellar that can be excavated beneath your house or garden. The second is to make use of a merchant who offers storage facilities, or a storage or deposit company specialising in wine storage. Facilities of this sort are advertised in specialist magazines such as *Wine* or *Decanter*.

Don't worry about any of this, however, if you just want to store wine for a few months, to give it time to rest and compose before you drink it. Simply lay the wines down on their sides in any quiet place (a bedroom, for example, is likely to be quieter than a kitchen), and cover them with a blanket; or put them on their sides in a cupboard. A wine rack is helpful, as it means you can remove a bottle in any position without disturbing the others. All wines, even those that should be drunk as young as possible, benefit from a month or two's rest before their final journey.

Serving wine

It is worth serving wines carefully. If you have paid £8 or £9 for a fine bottle of claret and you stand it by a roaring fire for an hour, then serve it in recycled mustard jars, you will be wasting some of your money. Wines give of themselves most generously in appropriate glassware, served at an appropriate temperature.

Appropriate in the glass context means thin, plain glass, with a slender stem and a tulip-shaped bowl. The International Standards Organisation has designed such a glass, and it is available by mail order from the Wineglass Company, 89-91 High Street, Odell, Bedford MK43 7AS (0234) 720220. The price is £11.95 per set of six glasses, plus £2.75 post and packing, and anyone who wishes to enjoy wine to the full is strongly recommended to invest in a set. The ISO glasses are appropriate for any type of wine, though you may wish to have flutes for sparkling wines (a similar design, but with a bowl of a less bulbous tulip shape), and copita-style glasses for fortified wines (again similar to the ISO glass, except smaller). Remember not to overfill glasses, as almost all wine waiters do: one-third to one-half full is ideal. You can then swirl the wine to draw out its aromas without staining the tablecloth.

The decanting of wine serves one of three purposes. The first is to remove it from its sediment: you will need to do this only if the wine is red and old. The second is to aerate it: this can be useful if you suspect you may be drinking a wine before it's fully mature, as the aeration helps provide a little instant ageing, and can bring out aromas and soften flavours. The third is to render a wine anonymous: ideal if you want to set up a small blind tasting for your guests or yourself – though obviously you'll need someone else to do the decanting for you. Decanters, like wine glasses, are best plain rather than cut.

The classic method for decanting wines such as vintage port, which have thrown a heavy sediment, begins by standing them upright for anything between a day and a week to allow the loose sediment to drop to the bottom of the bottle. Remove the capsule and cork, and slowly begin pouring the wine into a rinsed decanter. If you wish, you may hold the wine over a candle, torch or other light source as you do this, to illuminate the wine as it passes through the bottle neck. Continue to decant the wine steadily, and at first sight of any sediment approaching the bottle neck, stop pouring. The left-overs can be used for cooking if you like, though allow the heaviest sediment to settle out first.

Everything is now ready; all that remains is for the wine to leave the glass and enter your mouth. It will still not show at its best, however, if it is at an inappropriate temperature. Do you know how cold your fridge is? Do you know how warm your living room is? If you want to get the most out of wine, it is worth finding out. No red wine, for example, should ever be served at over 20°C or 21°C, so if it's 25°C on the dining table, put the bottle in the fridge for fifteen minutes or so. Equally, no fine white wine except Sauternes should ever be served at temperatures below 8°C, so if your fridge temperature is 5°C, leave the bottle out on the table for ten minutes before pouring. As a general rule, the sweeter or lighter a white wine is, the cooler it should be; full dry white wines like most Chardonnays or Gewürztraminers are best served at 10°C–14°C. The lighter in body a red wine is, the cooler it should be, too: light reds such as Gamays from Touraine or Ardèche, or Pinot Noirs from Alsace or Germany, will show best at temperatures of 14°C–16°C. You should aim for 17°C–18°C for medium-bodied reds such as clarets or burgundies, while only the biggest Rhônes or Australian Shiraz wines come into their own at 19°C or 20°C. This may seem pettifogging and trivial, but there is no more common reason for 'good' red wines proving disappointing that their being served at too warm a temperature. You've bought this book, you've read this far: why abandon the quest at the last hurdle?

Wine and the Law

Andrew Jefford and Ashley Holmes

..he was only vaguely aware of the existence of Great Aunt Ruth..

Alan had always enjoyed wine, but over the last five years he had found himself getting more and more enthusiastic about the subject. He took to wandering studiously around his local wine warehouse, and he checked the credentials and origin of every bottle he bought, using his collection of closely printed pocketbooks. From time to time he purchased one of the wine magazines, and would make detours on his professional travels to find the 'best buys' that their tastings had recommended. But only if the bottle cost under £6 or so; Alan, who was married and had three small children, was constrained by lack of funds from building the collection in the coal cellar that he dreamed of.

He was only vaguely aware of the existence of Great Aunt Ruth, and had no idea that she had taken a keen and skilled interest in her late husband's investment portfolio before she died. Alan's surprise was considerable, therefore, when a solicitor's letter informed him that, in her will, Great Aunt Ruth had bequeathed him fifteen hundred pounds. He reasoned that, as this money was unanticipated, it could be spent on something other than necessities. Like wine.

But first he decided to go out for a splendid dinner with his wife. They went to the grand London hotel that Jill had always wanted to visit every time their wedding anniversary came around, but which they'd never been able to afford before. The surroundings and the service were wonderful, and the food was... well, rich. Alan chose Moët & Chandon 1982 to go with their saumon au fumet de champagne, and the waiter opened it with assurance and panache. It didn't taste quite as intense as Alan had hoped, somehow, but it was only as they were finishing the bottle that Alan noticed the vintage was in fact 1981. When he queried this, the waiter assured him that 1981 was a much better vintage than 1982, but that they would only be charged the same price. Alan looked at the bill when it came, and the bottle was entered as £55, rather than the £42 that Alan had expected to pay for the 1982. Another gentle query brought the news that all champagne prices had been put up the week before, but that they hadn't time to change the wine list yet. The 1981, said the waiter with a knowing smile, should really cost no less than £75. 'It's like that all over London, sir. It's crazy at the moment!' Alan had mixed feelings about all this as they walked back towards Charing Cross, but he didn't want to spoil an evening that Jill had so enjoyed.

The ability to buy more or less what he wanted lent new zest to Alan's evening readings. He ordered several mixed cases from merchants whose lists offered mail-order facilities, and after further research he bought two cases of second-growth Pauillac, a case of Sauternes, one each of Hermitage and Côte Rôtie, and a case of Mosel Auslese, all from the latest *en primeur* offers. He even tried a postal bid for a case of twenty-year-old Colares in an auction catalogue, and was surprised to find that his bid had secured the lot. And to celebrate Jill's forty-fourth birthday, he bought the bottle of beautifully labelled 1947 Gevrey-Chambertin les Cazetiers that he'd noticed two or three years ago in the 'finest and rarest' section of his local merchant's shop.

The first of the mail-order cases arrived – the one Alan had ordered over the phone using his credit card. Everything was safe and sound, though they did seem to have made two or three substitutions: one changed vintage (1987 Alsace Grand Cru Kitterlé rather than 1986), one different producer (Patriarche rather than Faiveley), while the Crozes-Hermitage from Jaboulet didn't seem to have any mention of 'Thalabert' on the label, though it was definitely a wine called Domaine de Thalabert that Alan had ordered. The price, Alan discovered when he got the credit card bill, was the same, though he noticed only after he'd paid the bill. He telephoned the company, and they said that their stock situation meant that they had had to substitute, but the substitutions (which were not on the list) cost the same.

The second mail-order case contained all the right bottles – except that one of them had broken en route, another two had badly torn labels and a child seemed to have scribbled all over the back label of a fourth. Another telephone call, and this company said that he should have taken the matter of the broken bottle up with the carrier, and that they didn't guarantee that all the labels would be in perfect condition.

The third case didn't arrive at all. A month after the cheque had been cashed, Alan's considerable patience ran out and he phoned the company, who said they would look into the matter. They sent him a letter saying that, as no one had been at Alan's house when the carriers called to deliver the wine, the driver had left it with some helpful neighbours at number 22. Number 22 was in fact five doors away, and its occupiers had never in the past enjoyed a reputation for helpful neighbourliness. They told Alan they didn't know anything about any wine, yet in their front garden, among dismembered motorcycles, an old supermarket trolley and a number of jumped-on beer cans was a burnt fragment of a box on which Alan thought he saw part of the mail-order company's name.

The 1947 burgundy was, frankly, a disappointment. It was so thin and vinegary that they could only manage a couple of mouthfuls. Alan joked valiantly about how much more successfully Jill had matured than the wine, but his heart was heavy with disappointment for her and the boeuf bourguignonne she had taken so much care over, and outrage at so much money wasted. He felt he should take the bottle back to the merchant, a friendly ex-civil servant whom he liked enormously, though he was uneasy when the merchant had quipped 'Caveat emptor' as he left the sun-filled shop.

Alan was surprised to find that he'd actually bought three cases of Colares at auction rather than one, and that the cost was so much more than he thought he had bid. It was true that he hadn't realised the wine was still in Portugal, and that he hadn't read the small print telling him that shipping, duty, customs clearance charges and VAT, as well as something called a buyer's premium (plus VAT), still had to be added. When it finally arrived, it looked as if it had been stored in a cow shed: the labels had mostly rotted away, and many of the bottles were splashed with dry mud. It tasted rather strange, too, very harsh and bitter and tannic, and Alan and Jill both got headaches every time they drank it. After three bottles they gave up, and the rest is still in the coal cellar.

Four years have now passed since Alan received his inheritance. He hopes that his Pauillac and Sauternes will soon arrive; at the moment he's trying to clear up a series of confusions with the company from whom he bought the wine, who claim that Alan has collected it from bond while Alan tries to prove that he hasn't. The fact that Alan has lost all the paperwork relating to the purchase doesn't help. He learnt with the Mosel that you have to pay shipping costs, duty, delivery costs and VAT on top of everything before you can call the wine yours, but he did that for these wines over a year ago now. He's still waiting for the Rhônes, too. The smaller company from which he bought these never replies when he writes to them, and their phone number is dead. Since Alan fell out with his local merchant over the 1947 burgundy, he's got no one to ask for advice, so he's not sure what to do next. There's still a little of Great Aunt Ruth's money left; he and Jill use it to buy Minervois and Australian Shiraz from time to time. Alan sometimes wonders where all the money went. Perhaps he should have made more of a fuss about that champagne business, those substitutions, the damaged bottles, the wine the neighbours drank, that awful burgundy, the fact that he didn't want all that Colares, let alone the headaches it brings, and that, having bought six *en primeur* cases, he's still waiting for them all to arrive. After all, the law would be on his side. Wouldn't it?

Ashley Holmes writes:
What a shame that Alan and Jill's splash-out celebration at the hotel was a disappointment. When Alan ordered a Moët & Chandon 1982, he was entitled to get just that. He should have been served with what he ordered. But since the bottle was consumed Alan's rights are weakened. All he could have done was to ask for a reduction in the bill, reflecting the difference in value between what he paid for the champagne and what a bottle of Moët & Chandon 1981 was worth.

Alan may have expected to pay £42 for the 1982, but he should have checked the price before ordering. A restaurant or hotel can charge what it likes for food and drink, but it must display a menu and a wine list either outside, or immediately inside the door. The rules about which prices must be displayed are complicated: not all items have to be listed on the menu. But if the bottle was listed at £42, or if the waiter said it would cost £42, Alan was obliged to pay only £42 rather than the £55 he was asked for. He should have deducted £13 from the bill, plus a reasonable amount of compensation (because he didn't get what he ordered), explained what he was doing and left his name and address.

He could also do something about the first mail-order cases he ordered. When a mail-order company accepts your order a legally binding contract is made. If the company fails to provide the wine you've ordered, it's in breach of contract, and you are entitled to claim compensation for any loss suffered as a direct and foreseeable result. Often companies try to wriggle out of their obligations to pay compensation by relying on their small print ('bottles are subject to availability', say). But don't be put off by this. To have any effect the small print has to be 'fair and reasonable'. If the substitute bottles in the first case were not of a similar standard and quality to those that Alan had ordered, he would be entitled to ask for a fair amount of compensation.

He was wise to pay for the first mail order case with his credit card. Payment by credit card (e.g. Access or Visa) gives you the added protection of the Consumer Credit Act, provided the goods cost over £100. If you pay with plastic, like Alan, then along with the wine merchant, the credit company is liable for breach of contract. So if the wine didn't correspond to its description in the order form, Alan may be able to claim from the seller, the credit card company or both. He won't get two lots of compensation, but he will increase his chances of getting a satisfactory settlement. He could also get his money back from the credit card company if the merchant went bust.

The damaged case is more of a problem. Alan may have some comeback against the merchant if it can be shown that the case did not leave him in perfect order, or that he failed to pack the case with reasonable skill and care. But if the bottle was damaged by the carrier in transit, Alan would have to claim from the carrier. If the case was sent by post, Alan will have to get form P58 and send it to the Head Postmaster. If he can show that the case was damaged in the post he'll be entitled to compensation set out on a sliding scale. It might have been sensible to get the case insured against accidental damage beforehand as such compensation does not always reflect the loss. As for the torn and defaced labels, Alan should take this up with the merchant. If you're paying for good quality merchandise you're entitled to receive it in good condition.

But what about the lost case? It was part of Alan's contract that the goods would be delivered to him. Obviously, if the merchant never sent the case, Alan has a claim for the money he paid. Similarly, if the contract said that the case was to be delivered to Alan's home, but was left at the wrong address, Alan would be able to claim from the carrier. But if the case was properly delivered and the obliging neighbours at Number 22 had helped themselves to his wine, Alan would have to think about suing them. He could also tell the police about the incident.

More bad luck with the 1947 burgundy! If the wine was just past its best, it was Alan's tough luck. He shouldn't be put off by the merchant's jocular warning, though. Legally, the wine should have been of 'satisfactory quality' and fit for human consumption. If it wasn't, Alan would be entitled to compensation. However, he would have to prove that the wine wasn't drinkable rather than simply not to his taste.

Alan's postal bid at auction seems to have brought him no better luck. He has got more than he bargained for, in more ways than one: three crates of wine which are fit, as far as he is concerned, only to pour down the drain. In auction sales, any implied term about satisfactory quality can be excluded by the auctioneers' small print. Alan's rights are also against the seller rather than the auctioneer. Since the seller is based in Portugal it will be very difficult for him to do anything. He should, however, have a word with the auction house – with a bit of good fortune they'll help him negotiate a settlement with the seller.

As for the 'hidden' extras, Alan will have to pay up. The shipping charges, duty, customs clearance and VAT were mentioned in the small print and he should really have read this before sending his bid so that he knew exactly what he was letting himself in for.

He will also have problems in connection with the Pauillac and Sauternes. He can sue the company for not giving him the wine since it was the seller's duty to give him the cases at the warehouse. But he'll have to prove that the firm has not surrendered the wine to him – and losing the paperwork does not help. He should write to the manager of the bonded warehouse, who should have records backing up his claim.

The same applies to the Mosel. Alan was entitled to delivery within a reasonable time. Clearly, a reasonable time has elapsed, so Alan should make 'time of the essence' and give the firm 14 days, say, to deliver. If the wine doesn't turn up he can safely consider the contract at an end and demand his money back. But he'll have to prove that he paid for the wine, so he should contact his bank and go through all his old cheque stubs for proof of payment.

Any hope for the Rhône? Not much – it seems that the firm has gone bust – which doesn't look too good for our luckless hero. Unfortunately there's little chance of recovering money from a company that has gone into liquidation. When a company goes bust there's a strict pecking order in which people get paid. Often there's not enough money to go round, and consumers who have lost money are at the bottom of the pile. If only Alan had paid on credit card he would have had the benefit of the Consumer Credit Act protection, as with the first case that he ordered.

It's a pity that Alan left it so long before wondering what to do about all his mishaps. It pays to sort things out as soon as possible. And it pays to know your rights. If in doubt, complain straightaway. If you get nowhere, think about getting advice. And let's hope that if you decide to spend a windfall on wine, you have a happier time than Alan in your tippling!

Ashley Holmes is a barrister employed by Consumers' Association as a senior consumer lawyer in the legal department.

What's in a Bottle?

James Berry, a reader from Guildford in Surrey, has studied the issue of bottle sizes, and prepared the following report for this year's Guide.

For some years, meetings, discussions and consultations have been taking place under the aegis of the European Commission to decide on the standard bottle sizes for alcoholic drinks thoughout the EC. Some progress towards achieving standardisation has now been made. The background to this issue is as follows.

Many years ago, wine traders discovered that, even to the experienced eye, it was impossible to tell the difference in outward appearance between a bottle holding 75cl and one holding 70cl. Naturally, it made commercial sense to market wine in the smaller size which meant that, for each case of 12 sold, the supplier saved 60cl of wine, or four-fifths of a 75cl bottle. Wine consumers, however, rarely appreciated that some wines were sold in 75cl bottles and some in 70cl bottles. Happily this practice – in the case of still table wines since 1 January 1989 and sparkling wines from 1 January 1991 – will end. From these dates, the standard bottle size is to be 75cl.

Fortified wines, such as port and sherry, also suffered the same fate as table wines many years ago, and sherry is still sold almost everywhere in the UK in 70cl bottles (a notable exception is the Sunday Times Wine Club's sherry, sold in 75cl bottles), whereas port finds its way variably into bottles of either 70cl or 75cl. A decision on a mandatory size for fortified wines will probably be taken within the coming year, and it seems likely that 75cl will prevail.

The fate of spirits is less satisfactory. At present, the commonest size for spirits in France is 68cl, while in Germany it tends to be 70cl. British major spirits (full-strength whisky and gin) are sold in 75cl bottles: under-strength spirit (whisky under 40%, gin, rum and vodka under 37.5%, brandy under 36%) in 70cl bottles. Before issuing a proposal for such things as standard measures, the Commission takes the views of consumer and trade associations and other interested bodies. The proposal is then put to the Council of Ministers, representing the Member States, for a decision. In the case of spirits, the UK was virtually alone in preferring 75cl to other sizes for spirits. The smaller continental bottle won the day, and from 1 January 1992, the standard size of a bottle of spirits, including gin and whisky, will be 70cl.

Part II

What to buy

wine regions

Glossary

abboccato (Italy) medium-dry

abocado (Spain) medium-dry

Abfüller (Germany) bottler

adega (Portugal) winery

alberello (Italy) a vine-training system in which individual vines are trained low, like small bushes (the equivalent of the French *en gobelet* system). Gives low yields, lots of alcohol

almacenista (Spain) a small-scale sherry stockholder

amabile (Italy) medium or medium sweet

amarone (Italy) dry passito (*q.v.*) wine from the Veneto

amontillado (Spain) an aged fino (*q.v.*) sherry on which yeast flor (*q.v.*) has ceased to grow but which continues to age oxidatively; commercial 'medium amontillados' are not made in this way, but are blended, sweetened sherries

amoroso (Spain) medium sweet style of sherry

ampelography the study of grapes and grape varieties

Amtliche Prüfungsnummer (APNr) (Germany) official test number

Anbaugebiet (Germany) growing region

annata (Italy) vintage or year of harvest

año (Spain) year; 3° año signifies bottling in the third year after the harvest

appassimento (Italy) drying of grapes to concentrate their sugars

aszú (Hungary) indicates the sweeter styles of Tokaj: *see* puttonyos

Ausbruch (Austria) dessert Prädikat wine, between Beerenauslese and Trockenbeerenauslese in terms of must weight, from nobly rotted grapes

Auslese (Germany) wine from selected ripe grapes, possibly with noble rot (*see* botrytis)

autoclave (Italy) pressure-resistant tank used to make many Italian sparkling wines (the equivalent of the French *cuve close – q.v.*)

azienda agricola (Italy) estate making wine from its own grapes

azienda vinicola (Italy) estate making wine from bought-in grapes

azienda vitivinicola (Italy) estate making wine from both its own and bought-in grapes

barrique literally 225-litre barrel of new (or nearly new) French oak in which wines are matured and sometimes fermented; now loosely used to describe any smallish (up to 500 litres) oak barrel used for the same purpose

Beerenauslese (Germany) wine from specially selected ripe berries, probably with noble rot

Bereich (Germany) region

bianco (Italy) white

blanc de blancs white wine or champagne made from white grapes only

blanc de noirs white wine or champagne made from red grapes vinified without skin contact (the juice of most red grapes is colourless; all the colouring matter is found in the skins)

blanco (Spain) white

Bocksbeutel (Germany) flagon-shaped bottle used in Franken

bodega (Spain) cellar, winery

botrytis *Botrytis cinerea*, a form of

grey rot that shrivels grapes and concentrates their sugars

botte/i (Italy) oak or chestnut barrel/s. Traditionally large

branco (Portugal) white

brut (Champagne) dry or dryish (up to 15g sugar/litre)

bual (Madeira) smokily sweet Madeira

cannellino (Italy) sweet, used only for Frascati

cantina (Italy) cellar or winery

cantina cooperativa (Italy) private co-operative winery

cantina sociale/cantine sociali (Italy) co-operative winery/ies

caratello/i (Italy) small barrel/s used for vin santo (Tuscany)

casa vinicola (Italy) wine company making wine from bought-in grapes

castas (Portugal) grape varieties

cava (Spain) champagne-method sparkling wines

cerasuolo (Italy) cherry-coloured, often light red or deep pink

chaptalisation the addition of sugar to the must to increase the final alcohol content of the wine. The EC is divided into five zones – A, B, C1, C2 and C3 – changing from north to south. The zone in which a vineyard is situated governs whether or not chaptalisation may legally take place, and if it may, the degrees of alcohol that may legally be acquired in this manner. Chaptalisation is not permitted, for example, in Mediterranean vineyard areas; it is permitted, though, in Alsace, Burgundy and England

chiaretto (Italy) light-coloured rosé; term usually applied only to wines made near Lake Garda

clarete (Portugal, Spain) light red wine

classico (Italy) heartland of a DOC zone, producing its best wines

clavelin (Jura) 62cl bottle, used for vin jaune (*q.v.*)

clos (Burgundy) vineyard site that was walled in the past, and may still be walled

CM (Champagne) coopérative manipulante (*see page 153*)

colheita (Portugal) vintage (table wine); single-vintage tawny (port)

colle/i (Italy) hill/s, theoretically larger than 'collina' but usage varies

collina/e (Italy) hill/s

Consejo Regulador (Spain) organisation overseeing and policing denominacions de origen (DOs) (*q.v.*)

consorzio (Italy) association providing quality control and promotion of an area's wines. Membership is voluntary but usually most producers join. Some have very high standards; others less so

cosecha (Spain) vintage

cream (Spain) sweet sherry

criadera (Spain) literally 'nursery'; signifies a stage in a sherry solera system (*q.v.*)

crianza, sin (Spain) without wood-ageing

crianza, vino de (Spain) basic wood-aged wine, with one year's oak-cask ageing and one year's bottle or tank ageing

cru (France) literally 'growth', meaning either a distinguished single property (as in Bordeaux) or a distinguished vineyard area (as in Beaujolais or Burgundy)

cru (Italy) wine from grapes of a single vineyard, usually of high quality. Term is in common use but not officially permitted

cru bourgeois (Bordeaux) 'bourgeois growth', indicating a wine from the bottom tier of the Médoc's secondary classification system

cru classé (Bordeaux) 'classified growth', indicating a wine from the Médoc's primary classification system, divided into five strata (premiers, deuxièmes, troisièmes, quatrièmes and cinquièmes crus classés); or from the classification systems of the Graves, Sauternes or Saint-Emilion

cru classé (Provence) domains bottling their own wines since 1953

cru grand bourgeois (Bordeaux) 'a fine bourgeois growth', indicating a wine from the middle tier of the Médoc's secondary classification system

cru grand bourgeois exceptionnel (Bordeaux) 'exceptionally fine bourgeois growth', indicating a wine from the upper tier of the Médoc's secondary classification system

crusting/crusted (Portugal) a blend of port of different years for short-term cellaring; needs decanting

cuve close a method of making sparkling wines by carrying out the second fermentation inside a sealed tank rather than in bottle. Also known as the 'tank method' and 'Charmat method'

cuvée (France) vat or tank; sometimes means a 'selected' wine, but the term has no legal status on labels

demi-sec (Champagne, Loire) sweet (up to 50g sugar/litre)

Denominación de Origen (DO) (Spain) wines of controlled origin, grape varieties and style

Denominazione di Origine Controllata (DOC) (Italy) wines of controlled origin, grape varieties and style

Denominazione di Origine Controllata e Garantita (DOCG) (Italy) wines from areas meant to be one notch above DOC zones

doce (Portugal) sweet

dolce (Italy) sweet

domaine (Burgundy) domain, meaning the totality of vineyard holdings belonging to a grower or négociant

doux (Champagne, Loire) sweet to very sweet (over 50g sugar/litre)

dulce (Spain) sweet

edelzwicker (Alsace) 'noble mixture': wine made from a mixture of grape varieties

édes (Hungary) sweet

Einzellage (Germany) single vineyard site

Eiswein (Germany) wine made from frozen grapes

elaborado (Spain) made, matured or blended (by)

éleveur (France) a merchant who buys new wine, stores it, blends it and bottles it

embotellado (Spain) bottled (by)

engarrafado (Portugal) bottled (by)

English table wine (England & Wales) all English wines, including the very best, are classed as 'table wine' by the EC

enologo (Italy) oenologist, i.e. a qualified wine-maker

enoteca (Italy) 'wine library': place to taste and buy wine; these may have wines from just one area, from all Italy and, rarely, from other countries

enotecnico (Italy) qualified wine technician

erzeugerabfüllung (Germany) estate-bottled (co-operative cellars may also use this term)

etichetta (Italy) label

extra brut (Champagne) absolutely dry (no added sugar)

extra dry (Champagne) off-dry (12-20g sugar/litre)

extra/exceptional reserve (Madeira) Madeira with a minimum age of fifteen years

fattoria (Italy) farm

fermentación en botella (Spain) transfer method (*q.v.*) used for sparkling wines

fino (Spain) light, dry sherry matured under flor (*q.v.*)

fiore (Italy) 'flower'. Best grape juice, which runs out naturally or under very light pressure

flor (Spain) a layer of yeast growing on sherry in a part-empty butt; gives fino (*q.v.*) its character

frizzante (Italy) lightly sparkling

fusto/i (Italy) oak or chestnut barrel/s

Gallo Nero (Italy) black cockerel. Symbol of the Chianti Classico Consorzio

Garantia de Origen (Spain) seal authorised by Consejos Reguladores, guaranteeing authenticity

garrafa (Portugal) bottle

garrafeira (Portugal) better-than-average table wine given longer-than-average ageing; a colheita port given bottle age as well as cask age

generoso (Portugal, Spain) fortified wine

grand cru (Alsace) named vineyard site

grand cru (Burgundy) finest category of named vineyard site

grand cru (Saint-Emilion) basic level of classification, now abandoned

grand cru classé (Bordeaux) 'fine classed growth', indicating a wine from the second level of the Saint-Emilion classification system

grand vin (Bordeaux) 'fine wine': the top wine of a Bordeaux château, blended from selected cuvées only, as opposed to the 'second wine', which is blended from less successful cuvées and perhaps the wine of younger vines, and which is generally sold at a lower price; in other regions the term is used more loosely

gran reserva (Spain) red wine aged for a minimum of two years in oak casks and three in bottle; white (or rosé) wine aged for a minimum of six months in oak casks and three and a half years in tank or bottle

granvas (Spain) tank method (*q.v.*) sparkling wine

Grosslage (Germany) collective vineyard site

halbtrocken (Germany) semi-dry

hectare metric land measurement equivalent to 2.471 acres

imbottigliato all'origine (Italy) bottled in the zone of production

imbottigliato da/a (Italy) bottled by/at

Jahrgang (Germany) vintage

joven (Spain) young

Kabinett (Germany) first category of Prädikat wine, light and delicate in style

kolektziono (Bulgaria) reserve

labrusca *see* vinifera

Landwein (Germany) country wine

Late Bottled Vintage (LBV) (Portugal) a medium-quality red port of a single year. Only 'traditional' examples need decanting

late harvest (North America) sweet wine made from grapes picked in an over-mature or botrytised condition

lieu-dit (Burgundy) named, but unclassified, vineyard site

liquoroso (Italy) wines fortified with grape alcohol

località (Italy) small locality, occasionally seen as an alternative to 'cru' (*q.v.*)

MA (Champagne) marque auxiliaire (*see page 153*)

maduro (Portugal) a term, meaning 'matured', used loosely of any non-verde (*q.v.*) white wine

malmsey/malvasia (Madeira) the most sweet and raisiny of Madeiras

malolactic fermentation a secondary, non-alcoholic 'fermentation' that converts malic acid into lactic acid and carbon dioxide. The process is accomplished by bacteria rather than yeast

manzanilla (Spain) soft fino from Sanlúcar de Barrameda

manzanilla pasada (Spain) aged manzanilla (*q.v.*)

maso (Italy) vineyard or 'cru' (*q.v.*)

meio seco (Portugal) medium dry

metodo classico (Italy) champagne-method sparkling wines

método tradicional (Spain) champagne-method sparkling wines

minösegi bor (Hungary) quality wine

mis en bouteille par (France) bottled by

mistelle France) fresh grape juice fortified with alcohol before fermentation begins; examples include the Jura's Macvin, Champagne's Ratafia and the Cognac region's Pineau des Charentes. Labelled as vin de liqueur

moelleux (France) medium sweet to sweet

mousse (France) term used to describe the effervescence in sparkling wine

muffa nobile (Italy) noble rot

naturale (Italy) natural; used to describe non-sparkling or slightly sparkling Piemontese Moscato wines with lowish alcohol

négociant (France) wholesale merchant and wine trader

NM (Champagne) négociant manipulant (*see page 153*)

noble rot *see* botrytis

non-vintage (NV) a wine or champagne made from a blend of wines of different years

normale (Italy) non-riserva; most commonly mentioned for Chianti

nouveau (Beaujolais) new wine sold from the third Thursday in November after the harvest

novello (Italy) new wine, for drinking very young, on sale from November of vintage

nuevo (Spain) new, young

Oechsle (Germany) measure of sugar in grape must

oloroso (Spain) sherry aged oxidatively rather than under flor (*q.v.*)

palo cortado (Spain) light and delicate style of oloroso (*q.v.*)

passerillage (France) the process of leaving grapes to dry and dehydrate on the vine with the eventual aim of producing a dessert wine from them

passito (Italy) dried or semi-dried grapes or wine made from them

pergola (Italy) a vine-training system in which individual vines are trained high, then at right-angles to ground. Used in north Italy, especially in Trentino and on narrow terraces

perlant (France) with a slight prickle of gas, visible on the side of the glass

pipe (Portugal) a port cask, containing between 534 litres (shipping pipe) and 630 litres (lodge pipe)

podere (Italy) small farm or plot in larger farm. Sometimes means vineyard or 'cru' (*q.v.*)

Port with an Indication of Age (Portugal) true tawny port, in four styles: 10 Years Old, 20 Years Old, 30 Years Old, over 40 Years Old

Prädikat (Germany) a category of German wine with a 'special attribute' based on natural sugar levels in must, such as Kabinett, Spätlese, Auslese, Beerenauslese, Trockenbeerenauslese or Eiswein (*qq.v.*)

premier cru (Burgundy) second highest category of named vineyard site. If no vineyard name is specified, wine made from a number of different premier cru sites

premier grand cru classé (Bordeaux) 'first fine classed growth', indicating a wine from the top level of the Saint-Emilion classification system

primeur (vin de) *see* nouveau

produttore (Italy) producer

propriétaire (France) vineyard owner

puttonyos (Hungary) in practical terms, an indication of sweetness of Tokaj Aszú wines (*q.v.*). The more puttonyos specified (3-6), the sweeter will be the Tokaj

Qualitätswein (Germany) quality wine

Qualitätswein bestimmter Anbaugebiet (QbA) (Germany) quality wine from a specific region

Qualitätswein mit Prädikat (QmP) (Germany) quality wine with a 'special attribute' (*see* Prädikat)

quinta (Portugal) farm, estate. In the port context, any style may be branded with a quinta name, but 'Single Quinta' port generally refers to a single-farm Vintage Port from a lesser year

rainwater (Madeira) a medium-dry Madeira based on the Tinta Negra Mole variety

rancio (Spain) tangy, oxidised wine

récemment dégorgé (RD) (Champagne) recently disgorged (*see page 153*)

recioto (Italy) sweet passito wine from the Veneto

récolte (France) harvest

região demarcada (Portugal) demarcated (wine) region

reserva (Portugal) better-than-average wine; slightly higher (0.5%) in alcohol than legal minimum; at least one year old

reserva (Spain) red wine aged for a minimum of one year in oak casks and two years in bottle; white (or rosé) wine aged for a minimum of six months in oak casks and one and a half years in tank or bottle

reserve (Madeira) Madeira with a minimum age of five years

réserve (France) 'reserve': this term has no legal status on labels

ripasso (Italy) Valpolicella refermented on the lees of Amarone (*q.v.*) della Valpolicella to give extra weight and richness

riserva (Italy) wines aged for longer than normal. If DOC wines are riserva, then a minimum (but variable) ageing period is laid down. Usually the best wines are held back for riserva

RM (Champagne) récoltant manipulant (*see page 153*)

rosado (Portugal, Spain) rosé

rosato (Italy) rosé

rosso (Italy) red

ruby port (Portugal) basic red port

sec (Champagne, Loire) medium dry (17g-35g of sugar per litre of wine); (other wines) dry

secco (Italy) dry

seco (Portugal, Spain) dry

second wine (Bordeaux) *see* grand vin

Sekt (Germany) sparkling wine

sélection de grains nobles (Alsace) wine made from botrytis-affected grapes (*see* botrytis) or from partially dried grapes (raisins passerillés)

sélectionné par (France) selected by

semi-seco (Spain) medium dry

sercial (Madeira) the driest Madeira, though cheap examples are rarely fully dry

sirvase frio (Spain) serve chilled

solera (Spain) sherry ageing system which, by fractional blending, produces a consistent and uniform end product

sous-marque (France) a wine sold or labelled under a secondary, possibly fictional, name

spalliera (Italy) a vine-training system in which canes are trained low on wires; good for quality

Spätlese (Germany) wine from late-picked grapes, possibly with noble rot

special reserve (Madeira) Madeira with a minimum age of ten years

spumante (Italy) sparkling

stravecchio (Italy) extra old

sulfites sulphur dioxide, present in all wines (including organic wines), used as a preservative and disinfectant

supérieur (France) higher alcohol content than usual

'(tiré) sur lie' (Loire) this should refer to a wine (generally Muscadet) bottled directly from its lees, without having been racked or filtered. The term has, though, been used in a lax fashion in recent years; grant it credence only in conjunction with an indication of domain-bottling, such as 'mis en bouteille au domaine'

superiore (Italy) wine with higher alcohol, and sometimes more age too

super-Tuscan (Italy) non-DOC wine of high quality from Tuscany

super-VDT (Italy) non-DOC wine of high quality

Süssreserve (Germany) unfermented grape juice which may be added to fully fermented wine to sweeten it; the process is known as 'back-blending'

szamorodni (Hungary) usually denotes a dry wine, though Tokaj Szamorodni is produced in both dry and sweet forms

Tafelwein (Germany) table wine

tank method *see* cuve close

tawny port (Portugal) basic light port. True wood-aged tawny ports are either marketed as colheitas (*q.v.*) or as Ports with an Indication of Age (*q.v.*)

tendone (Italy) a vine-training system in which vines are trained high. Gives better quantity than quality

tenuta (Italy) holding or farm

tinto (Portugal, Spain) red

tipicità (Italy) 'typicality': much prized and insisted on by DOC

tiré sur lie *see* sur lie

transfer method a method of making sparkling wines in which the second fermentation takes place in bottle, but the sediment produced by this process is eliminated by decanting and filtering under pressure. The wine is then rebottled

transversage (France) *see* transfer method

trocken (Germany) dry

Trockenbeerenauslese (Germany) very sweet wine from raisined grapes affected at least partially by noble rot

uva/variedad (Spain) grape variety

varietal a wine based on a single grape variety

vecchio (Italy) old

velho (Portugal) old

vendange tardive (Alsace) 'late harvest', meaning wine made from especially ripe grapes

vendemmia (Italy) vintage or year of harvest

vendimia (Spain) harvest

verde (Portugal) 'green', meaning young

verdelho (Madeira) medium-dry Madeira

viejo (muy) (Spain) old (very)

vigna (Italy) vineyard or 'cru' (*q.v.*)

vigneto (Italy) vineyard or 'cru' (*q.v.*)

viña (Spain) vineyard

vin de paille (Jura) medium-sweet wine made from grapes that have been dried in wicker trays prior to vinification

vin gris (France) pale rosé wine

vinho (Portugal) wine

vinifera (North America) a grape variety that is a member of the European *Vitis vinifera* family, as opposed to some of the other vine families (such as the native American *Vitis labrusca* family)

vinificato in bianco (Italy) juice from black grapes fermented without skin contact to make white wine

Vinimpex (Bulgaria) State Wine Board

vin jaune (Jura) dry, oxidised wine based on the low-yielding Savagnin grape and aged under a thin yeast film for at least six years; bottled in clavelins (*q.v.*) or half-bottles

vino (Spain) wine

vino da tavola (VdT) (Italy) table wine: wine that is nither DOC(G) nor liquoroso nor sparkling nor low in alcohol. Quality may be basic or exceptionally fine

vino de la tierra (Spain) country wine

vino de mesa (Spain) table wine

vino di fantasia (Italy) super-VdT

vino espumoso natural (Spain) *see* fermentación en botella

vino gasificado (Spain) carbonated wine

Vino Kontrolirano (Bulgaria) Controliran wine, made from certain grape varieties in certain DGOs (*see below*)

Vino ot Deklariran Geografski (Bulgaria) Wine of Declared Geographic Origin

vino santo (Italy) type of passito wine from Trentino

vino tipico (Italy) new category for Vino da Tavola with some regional characteristics

vin santo (Italy) type of passito wine from Tuscany and Umbria

vintage champagne champagne made from a blend of a single year, sold after at least three years' ageing

Vintage Character (Portugal) medium-quality red port. This style may cease to exist in the near future

Vintage Madeira (Madeira) the finest Madeira; declared only after 20 years' maturation

Vintage Port (Portugal) very fine port, bottled young and requiring long cellaring (8 to 40 years); needs decanting

vinifera (North America) a grape variety that is a member of the European *Vitis vinifera* family, as opposed to some of the other vine families (such as the native American *Vitis labrusca* family)

viticoltore (Italy) grape grower

viticulteur (France) wine-grower

vitivinicoltura (Italy) the whole process of wine-making, from the vineyard through to the finished wine

VQPRD (Italy) 'quality wine produced in a specified region'; EC term indicating DOC, DOCG, AOC, DO, RD and other similarly controlled quality wine categories

Weinbaudomäne (Germany) wine estate

Weingut (Germany) wine estate

Weinkellerei (Germany) wine cellar

Weissherbst (Germany) rosé

Winzergenossenschaft (Germany) growers' co-operative

Australia

Anthony Rose

'So far as I can learn, Australia is not well adapted, either by soil or climate for growing wine, and this opinion seems confirmed by the unsuccessful efforts of many years.' Just to be Devil's Advocate in case future generations should catch him out, Thomas Shaw, who wrote that remarkably unprophetic passage in the middle of the last century, included an extract from a South Australian newspaper. The anonymous journalist suggests: 'We can produce wines in all respects equal, and in some respects superior, to those of France. That the lighter wines will commend themselves to the taste of the great majority of Englishmen we have but little doubt.' It was a long time coming, but the last five years have seen a boom in the consumption of Australian wine in this country, thanks to our appreciation of what the anonymous journalist referred to as Australia's 'pure juice of the grape'.

Australia is a big country, so it may seem odd to suggest that the noise it has been making in the last five years has been out of all proportion to its size. But that's precisely what has happened. Despite the grandiose scale, Australia achieves only one-twentieth of the production of the world's biggest wine producer, Italy, most of this coming from the south-eastern corner of the country. The energy behind the explosion in the United Kingdom has been phenomenal: 94,400 cases in 1985 grew to 800,000 cases in 1988. That may sound a lot, but in fact it's a trickle – about one bottle in every hundred poured down the collective British throat. Yet through the deliciously ripe, sun-drenched flavours of its wines and the unstuffy Australian way of going about things, 'strine wine' has made an indelible contribution to our pleasure and leisure.

Technical progress in hot-climate wine-making has also been filtering through to Europe for our long-term benefit. Peter Allan Sichel of Bordeaux was in Australia in 1988 to learn about warm-climate techniques for producing wine. Why? In order to apply them to his recently acquired property in the Midi, Domaine du Réverend. There, too, at the same time, was Jean-Marc Pottiez of Skalli. Skalli, with operations in the Napa and Pope Valleys in California, has invested in a new hi-tech winery at Sète in the South of France to produce varietal wines. Other movers into the Midi are two Australian companies, Global Vineyards of Montpellier and Hardy's La Baume at Béziers. Coals to Newcastle, perhaps? But when the combination of sun, grape variety and technical know-how pays off, we consumers will be the beneficiaries. And the traffic is not just one way. Go and harvest in one of France's classic wine regions and in vineyard after vineyard you'll see an Australian wine-maker or oenology student figuring out if a concept like 'terroir' might be valid back home.

Varietal wines are the key to the difference between the wines of Australia (and the New World generally) and those of Europe, where tradition is so firmly rooted in the soil. The beauty of varietal wines has been their simplicity and immediate flavours. A Chardonnay label is easy to understand, the flavour easy to appreciate. The same goes for Semillon, Sauvignon Blanc, Rhine Riesling, Cabernet Sauvignon and Shiraz. This simplicity is partly to do with the way the Australia wine industry developed. Its origins lay in convenience of location, generally for economic reasons. The vineyards of Great Western in Victoria were developed when the gold rush fizzled out. In the Barossa Valley in South Australia, where colonies of German immigrants settled, they weren't thinking lofty thoughts about mountains and microclimates, but simply of a place in the sun to put down a few roots.

Today's table wine industry originated in the early 1950s, and for good reason. One of the great spin-offs of war technology was the capacity to cool everything down in the cellar. Thanks to the fridge, a table wine industry was born. That isn't to underestimate the quiet, pioneering contribution of cellar masters like Max Schubert on the one hand or the rather noisier evangelism of Len Evans, Max Lake, Murray Tyrrell and James Halliday on the other. Technology has been one of Australia's trump cards. With no tradition of 'terroir' or religion of soil, wine-making has, for the most part, been a cellar exercise. The technical jargon still rolls easily off the tongue. Attitudes towards wines – and expressions that go with them – are bound up with wine-making faults. A wine we might describe as 'cheesy', 'meaty', or 'yeasty' might in Australia be considered as respectively 'oxidised', 'sulphidey', or 'autolysed'. Obsession with fault has, until recently, been the Australian form of perfectionism.

But home consumption in Australia is on the wane after peaking at just over 28 bottles per head annually. Driven by the need to export, and realising that their wines can compete on the world stage, Australian wine-makers have been looking around them. Thanks to this more outward-looking attitude, it has begun to dawn that technical perfection may not be the only goal. Without good grapes, no amount of alchemy is going to help them make good wine. The search is now on for complexity, a process which involves the interaction of vineyard and cellar. While the 'pure juice of the grape' is the basis of what the consumers want, our sophisticated palates also crave complexity. Having spent so much time working in the cellar, Australia's wine-makers are now getting the dirt under their fingernails out in the vineyards to try to give us complexity.

All of a sudden, Australian wine-makers are talking about the relationship between yield and quality, recognising that perhaps a little stressing of the vine – not too much, mind you – might have an effect on quality. Plant density has therefore become important. New vineyard buzzwords are flying around like bush flies: vine stress, canopy management, clonal selection, plant density. There is a move away from the burning plains and on to the cooler hillsides in the belief that climbing higher, getting cooler, is one of the major keys to finesse. An understanding of microclimate does not necessarily mean a 180° religious conversion to an unswerving belief in the properties of the soil, but soil is now looked at with far greater respect. Slopes, altitude, exposure to the elements, not to mention drainage and water retention, are becoming major factors in the comprehension of what the vineyard might have to offer.

A new 'label integrity' scheme is currently being developed to police claims for vintage, grape variety and region of origin. Pinot Noir does exceptionally well in the Yarra Valley, for instance, Cabernet Sauvignon in Coonawarra, Rhine Riesling in the Clare Valley and Chardonnay in Padthaway. The character of the same grape variety may differ enormously according to the location of the vineyard: Hunter Semillon, for instance, in New South Wales and the cool-climate Semillon of Western Australia's Margaret River are as alike as chalk and cheese.

In tandem with the search for complexity is the general fragmentation of the industry from large scale to small-is-beautiful, in line with trading-up trends. Unlike California – where the quality pyramid is capped by the smaller boutique wineries – much of Australian quality wine has come in the past from the biggest companies, such as Penfolds, Lindemans, Orlando or Hardy's. While these big companies take care to maintain their quality image with a number of small-production, high-calibre wines, smaller wineries are now taking more of a lead, encouraged by the readiness of the Australian consumer to trade up and look for quality and individuality. As wine has gone beyond the commodity stage, investment money and professional brains have moved in. Leeuwin and, more recently, Chittering Estate in Western Australia are examples of this glamorous, high-profile look. Victoria's up-and-coming Mornington Peninsula, with its population of ex-doctors and lawyers, is smaller in scale but no less committed to quality.

Sensible marketing pitched at the correct level, led by companies like Rosemount, has helped Australia to a flying start in Britain. The momentum has slowed down in the last year, but the increasing value to Australia of its exports implies that it is quantity, not quality, that has been sacrificed. Australian wine still maintains that delicate balance between mass-market and fine-wine appeal, with value for money a key plank in the success story. Now Australia is rising to the challenge of satisfying an increasingly sophisticated wine-drinking public, already spoilt for choice, with an expansion of the range, particularly at the fine-wine level. While in some circles it has become fashionable to knock Australia as last month's flavour, a number of specialist wine merchants have given it a continuing vote of confidence. Wine lists have been expanded to cater for newcomers. And this year has seen the opening of The Australian Wine Centre in the Strand and the Peatlings Wine Centre, formerly Ostlers, in the Clerkenwell Road, with a strengthened Australian list.

The continuing success of Australian wine in Britain in the long run depends on Australia expanding our choices on a number of levels. At the most basic level, Australia can keep producing good clean, fruity value-for-money Chardonnay or Cabernet Sauvignon until it comes out of its ears. A step up the ladder puts varietal and regional blends within reach: wines have a bit of extra character and concentration to satisfy the appetites of customers prepared to pay extra for superior quality. At the highest level, Australia is starting to offer complexity without the added complications of wine- buffdom. We are beginning to see some of those great, individual wines in Britain at prices that can compete favourably with their European counterparts. From within the amorphous mass known to wine-drinkers as, simply, 'Australia', the new decade should see the dim outlines of the Australian wine map start to emerge. Colouring it in is up to us.

NEW SOUTH WALES

New South Wales is Australia's second largest wine-producing state after South Australia, producing over a quarter of the country's wine. White grape production outnumbers red by roughly three to one, with Semillon easily the biggest producer, followed by Trebbiano. In red production, Shiraz is number one, followed by Cabernet Sauvignon.

Lower Hunter Valley

Just over a couple of hours' drive beyond Sydney's jacaranda, lilac and red coral bloom, the Lower Hunter Valley's gum trees leave a smoky-blue haze on the skyline. Open-cast mining is the only blot on the landscape of this otherwise beautiful valley, which is becoming an increasingly popular tourist spot. In Australian terms, the Lower Hunter Valley is almost an extension of the big city. It is the hub of the New South Wales industry, with famous names – Rothbury, Lake's Folly, Murray Robson Wines, Lindeman's Ben Ean Winery, McWilliams, Brokenwood and Tyrrells – rubbing shoulders like properties along the Route des Châteaux in Bordeaux. The best-known and most original styles of the Lower Hunter are its Semillon and Shiraz. Rothbury, McWilliams, Tyrrells and Lindemans are all first-class exponents of Hunter Semillon, which can mature into toasty, smoky, Chablis/Riesling-like glory. Adjusting to the trend away from reds towards white wines, Chardonnay is on the increase and wineries like Petersons, Lake's Folly, Rothbury, Tyrrells and Simon Whitlam all make excellent examples. Traditional Hunter Valley Shiraz, with Lindemans as the archetypal producer, develops a meaty, gamey quality with age that aficionados call 'sweaty saddle'. The Australian critic James Halliday now suggests that 'sweaty saddle' is simply a side effect of poor wine-making, but the ageing capacity of Hunter Valley Shiraz is beyond doubt.

Hunter Valley Semillon

Type *Full-bodied dry white wine, oaked or unoaked*
Profile *When young, Semillon is clean and refreshing, with grassy and sometimes smoky aromas and flavours of lemon and honey. In maturity it develops into an intriguing, soft wine with toasty, smoked meat, Chablis-like character*
Advice *Drink within two to three years in most cases; however, the better wines of Rothbury, Lindemans and McWilliams, for instance, will develop nicely into old Hunter Semillon*

Upper Hunter Valley

A goods train running between Rosemount's winery and vineyard carries coals to Newcastle, which is where the Hunter River makes its exit into the Pacific Ocean. In this spectacular, idyllic valley, comparatively recently developed, Rosemount Estate is the dominant presence with a consistent range of quality wines produced by its talented wine-maker Philip Shaw. Top of the range is a rich, toasty Chardonnay from the flagship red-earth vineyard, Roxburgh, now being expanded to accommodate demand. Arrowfield, recently renamed Mountarrow, is a winery with potential under the direction of Simon Gilbert and the new ownership of Japanese sake producer Hokuriku.

Mudgee/The Murrumbidgee Irrigation Area/Cowra

Mudgee is a small, sometimes overlooked district north-west of Sydney, and 500 metres above sea level. Good Chardonnay is produced here from Montrose and Settlers Creek, but perhaps the real strength of the district lies in its Cabernet Sauvignon and Shiraz from producers such as Huntington Estate and, increasingly seen in Britain, the attractive organically produced reds of Gil Wahlquist's Botobolar estate. The name of Murrumbidgee Irrigation Area may be an affront to European sensibilities, but from this high-yielding mass-production area comes 15 to 20 per cent of Australia's cheap varietal cask wine, most of it respectable if unexciting in quality. De Bortoli makes good wines here including a superbly luscious botrytis-affected Semillon. Cowra is a high-yielding district from which some excellent Chardonnay comes.

VICTORIA

Victoria, Australia's third largest wine-producing state, is the southernmost of those on the mainland, and therefore well supplied with cool climate sub-regions and a plethora of small to medium-sized wineries. After a long period in the doldrums, it has re-emerged as one of Australia's most exciting regions. White grapes outnumber red by about six to one. Bulk-production Sultana and Muscat of Alexandria are the dominant varieties with Chardonnay and Rhine Riesling the main quality varieties. Shiraz just pips Cabernet Sauvignon to the post as most planted variety.

Yarra Valley

The Yarra River is so muddy that 'it runs upside down', according to James Halliday. The beautiful pastoral valley, just an hour's drive north of Melbourne, is where lawyer and wine writer Halliday has chosen to turn his critical faculties to wine-making. At Coldstream Hills, he has already demonstrated, along with his next-door neighbour Dr Bailey Carrodus of Yarra Yering, Mount Mary and St Huberts, that the cool-climate Yarra is an outstanding area for Pinot Noir and Chardonnay. Cabernet Sauvignon can be good, too, but is sometimes on the vegetal side. Moët & Chandon have chosen the Yarra for their Australian fizz operation, Domaine Chandon, which is already bubbling under nicely after a highly successful first release in 1989.

Yarra Valley and Mornington Peninsula Pinot Noir

Type *Elegant burgundian style of dry red matured in oak*
Profile *Cherry and raspberry aromas and flavours with vanilla hints of oak reminiscent of red burgundy, the best examples having a degree of ripe fruit and finesse hard to find outside Burgundy*
Advice *For drinking between two and five years upwards, the best examples being Mount Mary, Coldstream Hills, Yarra Yering, Hickinbotham, Dromana*

Geelong/Mornington Peninsula/Gippsland

Of these three coastal districts, Geelong, air-conditioned by the Indian Ocean south-west of Melbourne, has established a reputation for outstanding Pinot Noir principally through Bannockburn and the now departed Hickinbotham family. Mornington Peninsula, Australia's southernmost mainland wine district, is an up-and-coming area of small, technically conscious wine-makers, many of them ex-doctors or lawyers, including Dromana, Hickinbotham, Merricks Estate, Moorooduc and Paringa. Gippsland, east of Melbourne, is, to date, best known for its blue cheese.

Bendigo and District and Central Goulburn Valley

In Goulburn, the climate is warmer than the Yarra, and the area is home to the traditionalist Victorian vineyard Château Tahbilk as well as Tisdall and the up-and-coming Michelton winery. The old gold-mining centre of Bendigo is best known for the classy wines of Balgownie, as well as being the fizz home of Landragin and Yellowglen.

Great Western

Still in gold-mining country, the mines are now the cellars for Seppelts' Great Western, home of Australia's most consistent champagne-method sparkling wines under the direction of fizz specialist Ian McKenzie. Excellent value-for-money table and fortified wines are also produced here. Classy Shiraz comes from Mount Langhi Ghiran.

North-East Victoria

From Ned Kelly country come Australia's famous luscious fortified muscats and tokays, powerful 'stickies' akin to Malmsey Madeira and Tawny Port. In the hands of Baileys of Glenrowan, Morris, Chambers and Stanton & Killeen of Rutherglen, these wines acquire an aromatic power and concentration of flavour that has to be tasted to be believed. Wynn's Ovens Valley Shiraz also comes from nearby. A stone's throw from the hillbilly towns of Wangaratta and Yackandandah, the family company of Brown Brothers at Milawa continues to produce a wide range of reliable varietal wines, with an exciting new experimental 'kindergarten' winery and 'cold-climate' vineyard at Whitlands, Australia's highest, providing further quality potential.

Also in Victoria is the Macedon area, north-west of Melbourne (Hanging Rock and Goonawarra), the Pyrenees (Redbank and Taltarni) near Ballarat, and the high-yielding irrigation areas centred on the Murray River (home to much of the bulk production of Lindemans and Mildara).

Flood

The lingering clouds, rolling, rolling
And the settled rain, dripping, dripping
In the Eight Directions – the same dusk.
The level lands – one great river.
Wine I have, wine I have:
Idly I drink at the eastern window.
Longingly – I think of my friends,
But neither boat nor carriage comes.
T'ao Ch'ien

Liqueur Muscat

Type *Stickily sweet fortified Muscat and Tokay*
Profile *Highly aromatic with complex scents of rose petal and raisins, matched by viscously sticky and powerfully concentrated raisiny fruit. The best have the acidity to cut through their own treacly richness*
Advice *Drink on its own after a meal, or with a rich pudding or chocolate to take the edge off the wine's sweetness*

SOUTH AUSTRALIA

South Australia is the engine room of Australian wine-making, providing more than half the country's wine production. White grape varieties outnumber reds by two to one, the most important being Muscat of Alexandria, followed by Sultana and Rhine Riesling. Shiraz provides the biggest quantity of red wine, with Grenache second and Cabernet Sauvignon third. Huge quantities of bulk wine come from the Riverland area.

Barossa Valley

'Hier spricht Barossadeutsch.' The Silesian immigrant influence is still strong in this tourist showcase of a valley just outside Adelaide. Consistent wine-making with Rhine Riesling is a hallmark, but reliable Cabernet Sauvignon, Shiraz and Chardonnay come from here too. A host of good names include Basedows, Hill-Smith, Krondorf, Kaiser Stuhl, Leo Buring, Orlando, Penfolds, Peter Lehmann, Seppelt, Tollana, Wolf Blass and Yalumba.

Clare Valley

North of Adelaide, Clare Valley is a small, rather hot valley of small wine-makers like Mitchells, Geoffrey Grosset, Tim Adams, Jim Barry, Tim Knappstein and Petaluma doing particularly aromatic things with Rhine Riesling, while some of the bigger companies have plantings here too. Cabernet Sauvignon and Shiraz can also perform well here.

Clare Valley Riesling

Type *Aromatic, refreshing, full-bodied dry white wine*
Profile *Aromas of lemon and lime, with opulent dry to off-dry tropical fruit flavours of pineapple and lime, sometimes with a suggestion of toastiness and good acidity for elegance*
Advice *Good as an aperitif or with light dishes based on fish or poultry*

Coonawarra and Padthaway/Keppoch

Celebrated for its well-drained, limestone terra rossa soil, Coonawarra is Australia's most famous, highest quality wine-producing strip of dirt for premium red wines made from both Cabernet Sauvignon and Shiraz. Bowen Estate, Krondorf, Orlando, Seppelt, Rosemount, Penfolds, Wynns, Mildara, Lindemans (with Limestone Ridge and St George), Rouge Homme and Petaluma have all made names for themselves with red wines produced here, or produced elsewhere using Coonawarra grapes. At nearby Padthaway, Lindemans, Wynns, Seppelt, Orlando and Thomas Hardy grow grapes for a variety of first-rate white wines made from Chardonnay, Riesling and Sauvignon Blanc.

Adelaide Hills/Southern Vales

This densely populated district of, in the main, small-scale wine-makers is sited immediately south of Adelaide, centred on McLaren Vale and McLaren Flat, and enjoys good basic raw material for wine-making and lots of potential. Top producers include Geoff Merrill, Woodstock, Richard Hamilton, Coriole, Wirra Wirra, Hugo and Hardy's Château Reynella. The cool Adelaide Hills area south-east of Adelaide is an up-and-coming one, with high wine-making standards particularly from Henschke, Yalumba's Heggies and Pewsey Vale (white wines) and Brian Croser's Petaluma. Still further south-east, Langhorne Creek supplies big wine companies with good blending material.

WESTERN AUSTRALIA

Swan Valley/Perth Hills

The hot Swan Valley just outside Perth is dominated by Houghtons who, under the late Jack Mann, developed the biggest selling 'white burgundy' in Australia as well as an excellent premium range called Wildflower Ridge. Evans and Tate, and Sandalford, are names to look out for. From near Perth Hills north-east of Perth, a big investment in a new estate, Chittering, by fishing magnate George Kailis, has – so far at least – produced the most beautifully packaged wines in Australia.

Margaret River

The vineyards of this maritime area lie along a 56-mile coastal strip between Cape Leeuwin in the South and Cape Naturaliste in the North. First-class producers of a variety of styles from elegant Sauvignon, Semillon and Chardonnay to stylish Cabernet Sauvignon and Shiraz include Leeuwin, Cape Mentelle – bought during 1990 by Veuve Clicquot – and Vasse Felix and Moss Wood, the latter two wineries' Cabernet Sauvignon being among Australia's finest. Other good names include Cullens, Sandalford Margaret River and Sandstone.

The Lower Great Southern Area

This is a vast, rapidly developing district comprising Mount Barker, Frankland River, Denmark, Albany, The Porongurups and Manjimup/Pemberton. Quality is already good, and the potential is considerable. Plantagenet and Goundrey are names to watch.

TASMANIA

Tasmania has the coldest climate in Australia, with all its attendant advantages and disadvantages. Its tiny wine industry flourishes at present: Louis Roederer has set up a joint venture with Heemskerk to produce fizz, and Heemskerk, Moorilla Estate and Andrew Pirie's Piper's Brook all produce attractive, steely wines, with Pinot Noir from Tasmania looking promising.

REST OF AUSTRALIA

Some wines are produced in warm-climate Queensland and around Canberra. Even the Northern Territories boast one winery, Château Hornsby, at Alice Springs.

Australia: vintages

The sheer scale of Australia makes it hard to be specific about vintages: wide variations in latitude and altitude complicate the picture. You have to divest yourself of preconceptions based on European vintages because, as Oliver Mayo points out in *The Wines of Australia*: 'In Europe grapes are grown on the warm fringes of a cold continent, and in Australia they are grown on the cold margins of a hot continent.' The following vintage information should therefore be taken as the most basic of outlines. Vintages in Australia, remember, take place from January.

1990 Part of New South Wales was hit by rain at harvest time: whites are expected to be better than reds. Elsewhere the outlook is for a bumper crop of high-quality wines, with particularly good natural acidity levels thanks to a long, moderate summer suggesting wines with good structure. High production, coupled with a declining home market, should mean competitive prices. This vintage is being talked about as 'the vintage of the decade'.

1989 A variable vintage with rain, followed by heatwave and drought, followed by more rain at vintage time in almost all the major regions save Central and Northern Victoria. These conditions have tested the skill of wine-makers to the limit. Quantity is down and quality uneven.

1988 The vintage was variable in New South Wales with rain arriving on cue for the vintage. Quality was good to outstanding in the cooler regions of South-East Australia, notably Victoria and South Australia, but rather patchy in Western Australia, with quantities varying across the country. Frost and hail problems caused shortfalls in much of South Australia.

1987 Cool and dry weather throughout Australia led to lower-than-average yields in many areas. Quality was generally good to excellent, particularly in South Australia, less so in Coonawarra. There are good varietal flavours and balance and a generally elegant character.

1986 An average crop of good to outstanding wines, with many wine-makers confident that it is one of the best vintages of the decade. Acid levels benefited from cooler-than-usual weather, so Hunter Valley whites and Clare and Eden Valley Rieslings are superb. Reds are excellent too, with the accent on structure and longevity.

1985 A record crop. The weather was cool, creating full-flavoured wines with good acidity and structure, with the best quality coming from Western Australia and Coonawarra.

Other vintages 1984 was generally a cool, elegant vintage throughout Australia; 1983 a difficult year of bush fires, drought and floods, though high-quality wines emerged from the Hunter Valley. An excellent vintage in 1982, average in 1981, with 1980 superb for reds in South Australia and Victoria.

Stockists

Adnams; David Alexander; Australian Wine Centre; Averys; Barnes Wine Shop; D Byrne & Co; The Celtic Vintner; Chaplin & Son; Croque-en-Bouche; Cumbrian Cellar; Drinksmart; Alex Findlater; John Ford Wines; Fulham Road Wine Centre; Great Northern Wine Co; Peter Green; Gauntleys of Nottingham; Haughton Fine Wines; Hunter & Oliver; Lay & Wheeler; Majestic Wine Warehouses; The Nobody Inn; Oddbins; Thos Peatling (especially Peatlings Wine Centre, London EC1); La Reserva; Seckford Wines; Selfridges; Thresher; Upper Crust; Waitrose; Whitesides Wine Merchants; Windrush Wines; Wine House; Wines from Paris.

Anthony Rose was a full-time lawyer until 1986. In 1985 he won *The Observer*/Peter Dominic New Wine Writer award, becoming the wine correspondent of *The Independent* newspaper in the following year. He is also a regular contributor to *House and Garden*, *Decanter*, *Wine* magazine and *Wine & Spirit*.

Eastern Europe

Don Philpott

The political and economic changes that have taken place in Eastern Europe over the last year or so have been revolutionary. Barriers have been swept aside and trade with the West has expanded dramatically. In perhaps no other sphere can this be seen so clearly as in that of wine.

In the next three or four years Eastern Europe and the Soviet Union are set to become major exporters of wine to Britain; the first products of this new détente are already available in the high street. British drinkers are going to have to learn a new vocabulary of wine words (see the Glossary on page 83) while discovering a fascinating collection of varieties and of wine-producing regions such as Azerbaijan, Voivodina, Dobrudja and Rozova Dolina. It is not just £2-a-bottle table wine on offer, but a staggering array of quality wines, fortified wines, sherry- and port-style wines, sparkling wines and brandies.

Eastern Europe has, of course, been supplying wines to Britain for many years but the trickle could well turn into a flood before the end of the decade. There are now almost six million acres of vineyards in the Soviet Union and Eastern Europe, and plantings are continuing at a tremendous rate – at a time when the European Community is considering banning new plantings.

Exporting successes by Bulgaria and Hungary have convinced the Eastern European wine producers that much-needed foreign currency can be earned if they can produce attractive wines at keen prices, and that Britain is the key target.

Massive potential and investment

Bulgarian Cabernet Sauvignon has already become the best-selling red wine in Britain. Hungarian Tokaj is famous as one of the world's greatest sweet wines, but it is the new wines from Romania, the USSR and elsewhere which show what enormous potential Eastern Europe offers. Czechoslovakia, East Germany and Yugoslavia are all anxious to impress on foreign markets as well. Not only are there sound wines at very competitive prices, but also a growing range of high-quality alternatives which have, if anything, even more chance of success than cheap, mass-market wines because the volumes available are smaller and such wines no longer have to be priced at the lowest possible level. As a result, resources have been concentrated on planting huge acreages of the classic European varieties, although the same effort has not always gone into improving the wineries and the commercial infrastructure needed to market wine successfully.

Wine merchants and shippers in the West are clamouring to buy wines from Eastern Europe and the Soviet Union, despite the recognition that major hurdles will have to be overcome before full trading links can be established and continuity of supplies of the right quality achieved. (It took International Distillers and Vintners almost a year to receive their first consignment of Russian wines – and then only after they sent a letter to Mikhail Gorbachov appealing to him to speed things up.) Massive investment is needed throughout Eastern Europe in new wineries, bottling lines, quality control and packaging. Many of the wineries require hard currency to be able to buy better corks, and obtain professional help from the West to market their products. Labels have to be re-designed, and wine-makers and marketeers need to be able to travel to the West so they can see for themselves what they are up against.

The political changes that have swept through Eastern Europe have also swept away the monopolies of the state wine-exporting agencies. Many wineries now find themselves with a new-found freedom to market their own wines – although they have no previous experience of this. In the next year or so a number of European and American companies, in response to this need, will enter partnerships with wine producers in the East, giving producers a welcome boost. The wineries will have access to the investment capital and marketing skills they lack, while western partners will have access to a huge source of good-value wines. The consumer should profit most of all.

BULGARIA

Bulgaria has been the most successful of the wine-producing countries of Eastern Europe to date. Although it has been making wine for more than 3,000 years, it was not until the 1950s that modern viticulture was developed there. The country was surveyed to identify the best areas for specific varieties and extensive plantings of Cabernet Sauvignon, Merlot and Chardonnay followed. New wineries were built and a marketing and export organisation established. There are now more than 180,000 ha of vineyards in the country and an extensive planting and re-stocking programme is under way to cope with increasing worldwide demand. Production tops 400 million litres a year, of which more than 85 per cent is exported. Exports to Britain exceeded 1.7 million cases last year – a record total. Bulgaria is now the world's fourth largest wine exporter, and the fifth largest producer to the UK, while Suhindol Cabernet Sauvignon is Britain's best-selling red wine.

The Bulgarian range now includes more than 30 wines, from inexpensive blended wines to varietals, both classic and indigenous. Effort is being concentrated on producing quality wines of Reserve and Controliran standard, and promoting those made from the best indigenous varieties – Mavrud, Gamza and Melnik. Last year the Bulgarians launched their first Special Reserve Wines in the UK – a 1987 Khan Krum Chardonnay and a 1985 Merlot from Stambolovo – breaking through the £5 price barrier for the first time. Quantity is limited and only exceptional wines will be released, so Special Reserves may not appear every year.

Wine is produced almost everywhere in the country, apart from around Sofia, but there are specific differences between those from the north and south because of the Balkan Mountains (Stora Planina) which split the country. Wines from the north – Pleven, Pavlikeni and Suhindol, for instance – tend to be more elegant than those from the hotter south, such as Plovdiv, Asenovgrad and Haskovo, which are usually much bigger and more full-bodied. Controliran wines designate the highest quality levels. Controliran areas to watch out for are Asenovgrad, Harsovo, Preslav, Novo Selo, Oriahovitza, Sakar, Stambolovo, Svichtov and Varna.

Stambolovo Merlot Special Reserve

Profile *Lovely new oak scents and richly jammy, curranty fruit*
Advice *Try with grilled meats, especially lamb*

Svichtov Cabernet Sauvignon

Profile *Rich, intense blackcurrant fruit, easy drinking*
Advice *Good with pizzas and pasta dishes*

Damianitza Melnik

Profile *Well balanced, oaky, spicy and full of rich, ripe fruit flavours*
Advice *Try with spicy stews and stuffed vegetables*

Oriahovitza Cabernet Sauvignon

Profile *Good blackcurrant flavours, with plenty of new oak and tannin on the palate*
Advice *May be cellared for one to three years. Good with roast meats*

Plovdiv Cabernet Sauvignon

Profile *Rich, full of damson fruit and subtle oak*
Advice *May be enjoyed on its own as a party wine, or with cheese and cheese dishes*

Stockists

Ad Hoc Wine Warehouse; Bordeaux Direct; The Celtic Vintner; Drinksmart; Peter Green; Guildford Wine Market; Hunter & Oliver; Ravensbourne; Snowdonia Wine Warehouse; Villeneauve Wines; Wessex Wines; Wines of Westhorpe; Wizard Wine Warehouse.

CZECHOSLOVAKIA

Annual wine production in Czechoslovakia is about 200 million litres a year from 55,000 ha of vineyards. The Czechs consume most of this themselves, although a little has always been exported to the UK for Embassy use and special occasions. Traditionally, the wine has been blended from the fruit of whatever vines were to hand, but there are now sizeable plantings of Pinot Noir and imported whites such as Sauvignon Blanc, Traminer and Pinot Blanc. Furmint and Hárslevelü are promising local varieties, shared with neighbouring Hungary.

Cheaper Czech wines, if exported, would be competing directly with Bulgarian wines, and unlikely to win the fight, but better quality wines from Moravia have started to appear in the UK: these hold an interest of their own over and above keen prices. Other areas to watch out for are Slovakia and Bohemia.

Stockists

Bordeaux Direct; The Sunday Times Wine Club.

Give me some more wine, because life is nothing.
Fernando Pessoa

EAST GERMANY

There are extensive vineyards around Meissen in the south of East Germany, but home consumption accounts for almost all the production of this zone. The country imports wines, especially from Algeria, which it blends with its own to produce a range of sparkling wines, and trade officials believe these offer export potential because of the continuing boom in sparkling wine sales in the West. However, German unification, and incorporation into the European Community, would mean that such wines could not be sold within the EC.

HUNGARY

Hungary's wine-producing reputation in Britain has suffered in recent years, due to variable quality, but a drive to boost exports to the UK was launched in 1990, concentrating on middle-range wines.

Hungary has well over 160,000 ha of vineyards and produces about 380 million litres of wine a year. About half the production at present is exported to Eastern Bloc countries and about 30 million litres to the West, one quarter of this in bottles, the rest in bulk. The vineyard area has almost halved in the last twenty years as efforts have been concentrated on quality rather than quantity. There have been extensive plantings of western varieties, especially Chardonnay, Riesling, Traminer for white wines and Cabernet Sauvignon and Pinot Noir for reds. The local Kardarka grape makes big, gutsy reds with great potential, while the Ezerjo grape can produce classy whites, especially around Mór. Other Hungarian grapes producing varietal wines include Furmint and Hárslevelü. Among the best Hungarian wines are Cabernet Sauvignon from Vilány in the north-east of the country, Tramini from Sopron, near to the Austrian border, and fine whites from around Lake Balaton.

Tokaj comes in various sweetnesses, measured in puttonyos. The driest style of Tokaj is Szamorodni Dry; there is also an off-dry Szamorodni Sweet. The sweeter styles (3, 4, 5 or 6 puttonyos, with Aszú Essencia being still sweeter) have a complex sherry-like nose, are surprisingly fresh and clean yet lusciously sweet with soft, rich fruit flavours and a big, lingering finish. Chill lightly if you wish and serve with desserts and pastries or on their own.

Cabernet Sauvignon 1983, Vilány

Profile *Complex rich fruit, blackcurranty with a hint of sweetness*
Advice *Serve with pork, or rich vegetable dishes*

Hungarian Merlot

Profile *Tasty, soft and fruity, very easy to drink*
Advice *A top-quality party wine and good all-purpose red*

Stockists

Alba Wine Society; Belfast Wine Co; Bentalls of Kingston; Bordeaux Direct; Fortnum & Mason; Peter Green; Guildford Wine Market; La Vigneronne; Wines from Paris; Wines of Westhorpe.

ROMANIA

Romania is a country with enormous viticultural potential. It can look forward to buoyant exports once its social structure and economy are on a sound footing. There are more than 300,000 ha in the country – this figure represents a 50 per cent expansion in the last 15 years – and annual production is around 750 million litres, the largest of all the East European countries, making it the sixth largest producer in Europe. Most exports still go to the USSR and production is concentrated on sweet white wines. However new acreages have now been planted with Cabernet Sauvignon, Merlot, Pinot Noir, Chardonnay and Sauvignon Blanc with an eye on western markets. Local varieties of interest are Feteasca Alba, used for dry, sweet and sparkling whites, and Tamiioasa Romaneasca, used mainly for dessert wines.

Small quantities of Romanian wines have already been exported to the UK and a number of leading shippers and importers are at present negotiating deals which should increase supplies in 1991 and beyond. Quality production regions to look out for include Wallachia, Moldavia and Transylvania, while among the most successful wines are Cotnari, a natural white dessert wine like Tokaj, and sweet Muscal Ottonel Edelbeerenlese from Transylvania.

> *... a silent smile: that which shines in fine old wines*
> Antoine de St-Exupéry

Classic Romanian Merlot 1985

Profile *Attractive fruity aromas; soft, jammy flavours; easy to drink*
Advice *A good red wine to accompany pies and other baked dishes (including fish)*

Classic Romanian Cabernet Sauvignon 1985

Profile *Good fruit, well flavoured and balanced*
Advice *Serve with beef, lamb and cheese dishes*

Stockists
Del Monico; Drinksmart; Hunter & Oliver; Snowdonia Wine Warehouse; Ubiquitous Chip.

USSR

The scale of wine production in the Soviet Union is staggering. In the last 40 years the vineyard area has increased from 400,000 ha to well over 1.4 million ha and plantings are continuing at a rapid rate. Annual production now tops 4,000 million litres. The USSR already has the second largest area under vine after Spain, and is the world's third largest producer, after Italy and France. It is expected to lead both statistics within the next three or four years.

Apart from imported western varieties (there have been substantial plantings of Cabernet Sauvignon, Aligoté and Sauvignon Blanc), the Soviet Union has an extraordinary wealth of indigenous varieties, with more than a thousand grown in Georgia alone. The most promising of these so far (and any judgment must be provisional) are the white Rkatsiteli and Mtsvane, and the red Saperavi (this last blends well with classic Western European red varieties). Krym, planted in the Crimea, produces quite acceptable champagne-method sparkling wines. Exports from the Soviet Union to Britain have started to trickle in, notably from Moldavia and Georgia, and a growing number of UK companies are talking with producers and examining samples. Areas of most interest are Armenia, Azerbaijan, Georgia, Moldavia and the Crimea. Trade buyers have discovered a wealth of table wines, both red and white, and sparkling wines in those areas, as well as Armenian brandy, all of which have export potential. Early samples, however, have been disappointing. The first bottles of Moldavian Cabernet Sauvignon, and a Cabernet-Merlot blend, appeared during the spring of 1990. Both were from the 1984 vintage and were uninspiring. The quality of the wine and the bottles, as well as the labels, all need improving, and the price needs adjusting downwards if the wine is to stand any chance in the marketplace, even when its faults are corrected.

Cabernet Sauvignon 1984, Moldavia

Profile *About 11%, although the front label (in Russian) covers itself by describing the wine as 9-14%. Subdued old plummy fruit, slightly oxidised, very mellow*
Advice *Drink now, as it will not last for much longer*

Cabernet Sauvignon-Merlot 1984, Moldavia

Profile *Soft, obvious fruit, mellow with old wood flavours*
Advice *Treat as a curiosity. Both this wine and the Cabernet Sauvignon from Moldavia lack the character of their Bulgarian counterparts, as well as being expensive, but it must be remembered that ambitious wine-making is still in its infancy in the USSR*

Stockists
Croque-en-Bouche; Villeneuve Wines.

YUGOSLAVIA

There are more than 250,000 ha of vineyard in Yugoslavia and annual production is about 650 million litres of wine although yields have been hit in the last two or three years, reducing this figure somewhat. It is the world's tenth largest wine producer, and about 25 per cent of its production is exported. After building its exports to the West on the popular, easy-drinking white Laski Rizling (as it is now called, to distinguish it from Germany's Riesling, a different grape variety), Yugoslavia is beginning to produce some very good reds, especially from Cabernet Sauvignon, Pinor Noir and Merlot. Imported white grape varieties like Gewürztraminer, Rhine Riesling (i.e. true Riesling) and Sauvignon Blanc are producing wines which improve with each vintage. Local varieties which show promise are the white Smederevka and Zilavka.

New export laws have recently been introduced to boost exports in order to win foreign currency, desperately needed to combat chronic inflation at home. Producers are concentrating on varietals rather than blends for export. Areas capable of producing quality wines to watch out for are Dalmatia, Kosovo, Croatia, Slovenia, Serbia, Istria, Montenegro and Macedonia.

Vranac 1986

Profile *An indigenous red variety from Montenegro: big, rich and robust, ageing well*
Advice *Serve with lasagne or moussaka*

Alpi Juliani Cabernet Sauvignon

Profile *Strong and quite tannic but with rich fruit*
Advice *A good red for barbecues and grilled meats*

Cabernet Sauvignon 1986, Istria

Profile *Big, chewy, fruit wine, lots of tannin, will age well*
Advice *Serve with roast meats and braises*

Tiger Milk 1988

Profile *Late-harvested naturally sweet dessert wine, very good fruit, clean and with good balancing acidity*
Advice *Serve well chilled, and enjoy as a light-hearted summer afternoon wine*

Stockists
Bordeaux Direct; Del Monico; The Sunday Times Wine Club; Willoughbys; Wine House.

Don Philpott was consumer affairs editor with the Press Association for twenty years. He is now a freelance food and drink writer; his most recent book is about the wines of Bulgaria.

England and Wales

Andrew Jefford

..it is only feasible thanks to the fact that Britain is an island..

Viticulture in England and Wales is beyond the pale, outside the charmed latitudes of 30°N-50°N. It is only feasible thanks to the fact that Britain is an island, and therefore subject to the tempering effects of a maritime climate. Otherwise wine could no more be made at Pulham or North Elmham than it could around Warsaw, or anywhere else at a similar distance from the equator.

So it can be done. Is it a good idea, though? From the point of view of the grower, possibly not. If you make wine in the anonymity of the Bordeaux AOC zone, you may not be able to sell all of your annual harvest, and you may not be able to sell it at the price you'd like, but at least you'll have something to sell each year. No English or Welsh wine-grower enjoys this certainty. If the weather is kind (as it was in 1989), there will be plenty of ripe grapes. An average year means some grapes, though it may be necessary to keep them on the vines into November before ripenesss is achieved. But two or three times a decade the weather is unkind and the vines produce little or no fruit. 'The technical term for it is f*!*ing awful summers,' says one grower. Those who make wine for a living, with no other income-yielding activity, are often buffeted by ill-fortune to a degree beyond endurance.

From the point of view of the wine drinker, though, the making of wine in England and Wales is a good idea. Historically, it returns an activity practised during the Middle Ages to this country. The exigencies of climate mean that English growers have specialised (though not exclusively) in a range of early-ripening varieties little grown elsewhere, with profiles and tastes of their own; and the long, gentle, teasing growing season is excellent for ensuring that, when maturity is achieved, it is maturity of a complex and subtle kind. Wines grown in England and Wales very definitely possess regional character and qualities, and these are as specific to Britain as tea cosies, jumble sales and undressed lettuce.

England and Wales have around 1,000 ha under vine, though only 600 ha or so is cropping at present; even when all these vineyards are productive, it will still only be a small area, about the size of the vineyards in the Beaujolais *cru* of Brouilly. Of the ten or so grape varieties grown in more than experimental quantities, Müller-Thurgau (sometimes called Rivaner) is by far the most important, with 250 ha or so planted. The reason for its popularity is that it gives wines that are almost always pleasant to drink, with classically flowery aromas and grapey flavours, whereas some of the other varieties used exhibit smells and flavours of such singularity that their appeal is questionable. Müller has a lowly average yield in Britain (around 40 hl/ha), where it experiences disease and flowering problems; this is in contrast to the prodigious yields achieved in Germany, where it accounts for an even higher proportion of plantings than it does here. Low yields may be one of the reasons why even those Müller-Thurgaus made using *süssreserve* (unfermented grape juice, generally of non-English origin, added to round and sweeten wines before bottling) have a distinctively English quality to them, characterised by hedgerow flower aromas and slender, delicate flavours, quite distinct from their often blowsy German counterparts. German wine-growers visiting England are often enthusiastic about English Müller-Thurgaus. 'Now that,' they say, 'is how our Müller used to taste in the old days.'

Reichensteiner, a crossing of several other crossings (Müller-Thurgau x [Madeleine Angevine x Early Calabrese]), is the second most widely planted variety, with plantings approaching 100 ha. Its attractions are that it achieves better productivity and higher sugar levels than Müller-Thurgau, though its wine is often less characterful.

Seyval Blanc, planted to the same extent as Reichensteiner, is a hybrid rather than a crossing, the distinction being that a hybrid is a crossing involving *non-vinifera* plant material, whereas a 'crossing' generally involves *vinifera* plants only. (Hybrids are sometimes called inter-specific crossings.) Despite this mongrel bloodline, Seyval Blanc has been a great success in England, producing much better wines here than in its native France, its particular virtue being that it performs well in whatever style is required of it: dry, medium-dry, sparkling, even oak-aged. (It is also widely grown in the cooler parts of North America.) In its youth, it can have a characteristic smell and taste of grapefruit, but this disappears with time. Being a hybrid, it requires little disease control, and this makes it one of the most suitable varieties for English organic wine production.

Other leading varieties include Schönburger, Bacchus, Huxelrebe, Madeleine Angevine (the variety technically known as Madeleine x Angevine 7672), Kerner and Ortega, all of them crossings achieved in Germany, and all producing fruity and aromatic, sometimes highly aromatic, wines, though with very variable yields. The relative merits of each depend more on the grower's skills, and the generosity of the summer, than on the varieties themselves, though this may become less true over the next decade.

Pinot Noir is the only red grape grown to any extent in Britain, and if it is to be vinified as a red or rosé wine, it needs an exceptionally warm site and/or summer in order to ripen sufficiently to permit skin maceration without the risk of leaching out unpleasant aromas and flavours. It will, however, nearly always make good white wines here, and these can be very useful in blending. One reader, a wine-grower with a collection of over 150 vine varieties, has written to the *Guide* expressing optimism about Triomphe d'Alsace as a red grape variety for future use in the UK, and indeed one of Britain's most successful reds, Meonwara from Hampshire's Meon Valley, is based on Triomphe d'Alsace.

At present, vines are grown in such a variety of soils and sites in England and Wales, most of them selected by the pepperpot method, that it is difficult to say what and where might be the most suitable and favoured combinations. The more southerly, the better: that for sure. Greater specificity is a decade away.

Technical competence among English wine-growers is more widespread now than it has been in the past, and unsatisfactory bottles from the larger growers will be due to nature's insouciance rather than the wine-maker's. (It is still best to taste before buying in the case of the smaller producers.) English growers are beginning to move away from the German model, ease up on the use of imported *süssreserve*, and not pick early for safety's sake and then deacidify as a matter of principle; it is to be hoped that these trends will continue. Medium-dry wines sweetened with home-produced *süssreserve*, or fully fermented dry white wines, both made from grapes left on the vines for as long as it takes to achieve proper maturity: this is surely the way forward. English wines will then taste of England (and Welsh wines, of course, of Wales).

English white wine

Type *Light white wine*
Profile *Aromatic, with appealing mayflower, hedgerow scents; light, usually off dry to medium dry, with delicate, limpid, slenderly fruity flavours*
Advice *Chill; a perfect summer aperitif, and a refreshing wine to drink without food at any time*

Recommended producers

Astley; Biddenden; Breaky Bottom; Harrow; Headcorn; Lamberhurst; Meon Valley (red Meonwara); Nutbourne Manor; Sharpham; Staple St James; Tenterden; Three Choirs; Wootton.

Stockists

English Wine Centre; Fine English Wine Co; Great Western Wines; Harcourt Fine Wine; Gerard Harris; Hicks & Don; Ravensbourne; Tanners; Whitesides Wine Merchants; Willoughbys.

> *Wine is bottled poetry.*
> Robert Louis Stevenson

British wine

Any bottle of wine or 'sherry' with the word 'British' on its label is not what it seems, as you will discover if you read the small print. It is made from grapes grown and pressed anywhere but in Britain, usually in one of the hotter corners of the EC, in Cyprus, or in South Africa. The juice is concentrated, and shipped to Britain in tankers. A lot of British water is then added, and the reconstituted juice is fermented into wine. Such wines are characteristically British only in so far as they represent a triumph for business interests over consumer interests, and a victory for expediency over honesty. Always look for the the words 'English' or 'Welsh' if you want to taste the fruits of British soils. If you feel strongly about this abuse of the word 'British', write to your MP and protest.

France

Andrew Jefford

.. all the senses are viewed as a fit domain for education, culture and experiment..

France, Britain's closest neighbour, leads the wine world – not in terms of quantity, that distinction being Italy's, but in terms of quality. This position has been France's for centuries, and pre-dates most of the national boundaries that segment today's Europe. Why such dominance?

Nature made France the world's most important vine nursery.

Ask any independent expert to name the ten finest grape varieties for international use, and at least five of them will be of French origin (Cabernet Sauvignon and Chardonnay will inevitably qualify, with Pinot Noir, Syrah, Merlot, Sauvignon Blanc, Semillon and Chenin Blanc all receiving serious consideration). Nature also gave France the soils, slopes and climates to perfect their fruiting; indeed, our independent expert may well point out that one reason why France was able to breed these varieties was that viticultural conditions in much of the country were propitious enough to tease out the genetic mutations that foster excellence.

And then there is culture. It is a strange irony that Britain, notorious for being either adversarial or neglectful towards the pleasures of the senses, should neighbour France, the European country that has struggled most consistently and valiantly on behalf of those pleasures. In this respect, the Channel is as deep as the Mariana Trench, and it will take more than a tunnel to bring the two nations closer. French wines have achieved the distinction they have because few Frenchmen or Frenchwomen will willingly eat or drink anything that tastes mediocre. Every pleasure – and these in particular, being so commonplace – is up for discussion in France; its delights are dwelt upon, analysed and judged; if found wanting, improvements are immediately sought. Traditions are retained only if their results continue to please. Hours spent toiling to create fine tastes and scents are not considered lost time. The transitory and the fugitive may be accorded the status of works of art. The British are primitives by comparison, a nation of uncultured mouths and innate sensual unease. In France, no organ is regarded with more respect than the mouth, and all the senses are viewed as a fit domain for education, culture and experiment.

It has been so for centuries, and that is why the quality of French wines – all French wines, not just the very best – is so high. This does not mean that French wines are all good value for money: the fineness of the best French wines has not passed unnoticed by the world at large, and demand means that some of them, most notably champagne and burgundy, are relatively bad value for money. France's most exciting wines at the moment are her 'little' wines, her Fitous and her Menetou-Salons and her Vin de Pays d'Ocs. Oenological advances and competition from around the world have improved these wines enormously in under a decade, and many of them are now better than some of France's 'fine' wines were twenty years ago. They are reasonably priced, and they are French: subtle, balanced, shaped, expressive ... and pleasure-bringing.

French wine law

The French are proud of their wine laws, and justly so. The system was instituted in the 1930s – the Jura's Arbois was the first Appellation d'Origine Contrôlée (AOC), the decree dated 15 May 1936 – and over half a century's refinements and embellishments have left the structure proudly intact. It has the necessary consistency to impose order on chaos, but is flexible enough neither to stifle obscure but worthy local traditions nor to humiliate innovative new developments. It is a good example of the elegant systematisation that characterises French thought.

There are four tiers. At the top are the **Appellations d'Origine Contrôlée** (which may also be awarded to foodstuffs, such as Chasselas de Moissac table grapes or Crottin de Chavignol cheese). These are 'names of controlled origin'. Zones are designated, and in wine's case so are grape varieties, yields, minimum natural sugar levels in the grapes before fermentation, and other matters of detail. In some cases, obligatory tasting must take place before AOC is awarded. Further designations may be permitted in certain areas – 'Premier Cru Classé' in Bordeaux, for example, or 'Premier Cru' in Burgundy – but these must always qualify, and never replace, the basic geographical AOC.

The next tier is a transitional one: that of **Vins Délimités de Qualité Supérieure** ('demarcated wines of superior quality'). This denomination is for trainee AOCs: similar constraints concerning yield and varieties are imposed while growers have a chance to prove that they can produce wines of quality on a regular basis.

The third tier is occupied by 'country wines' – **Vins de Pays**. These come in three sizes. The biggest are regional denominations: there are only three for the whole of France (Jardin de la France, Oc and Comté Tolosan). Next come departmental denominations: every wine-producing *département* (a *département* is the approximate French equivalent of an English county) may claim one of these, provided its name does not already form part of an AOC (like Savoie, Jura or Rhône): Vin de Pays de l'Hérault, for instance. Finally come zonal denominations, covering natural areas smaller in size – in some cases, much smaller – than *départements*, and varying hugely, too, in production and market importance (Vin de Pays des Collines Rhodaniennes or, Vins de Pays des Sables du Golfe du Lion are two examples).

Wine gives courage and makes men apt for passion.
Ovid

Vins de pays are subject to fewer constraints than are AOC or VDQS wines, and quality can vary considerably. The best – often made in part or in whole with fine non-local grape varieties – are better than many AOC wines. The worst, if our merchants are doing their job, we never see, for there is such a wealth of choice that when an importer does take a chance on a new name, it's generally because he or she has found something good enough to enthuse about.

France still produces plenty of indifferent wine, and most of it is called **vin de table**, occupying the bottom of the four tiers of the quality control system. Vin de Table Français must come from France, and shouldn't poison you – but these are the limits of its guarantee. Vins de pays (regarded, officially, as a superior category of vins de table in any case) are so good, and so cheap, that nobody need have recourse to vin de table any more, save in the gravest emergencies.

ALSACE

During the last 120 years, Alsace has been German for 54 years and French for 66. It seems unlikely ever to become German again, but Germany has left its stamp. The Alsatian appellation system is serious and systematic, devoid of idiosyncrasy; the wines are almost all white; and they are sold in tall, green bottles with rather unimaginative labels, sometimes rendered indecipherable by sombre gothic lettering. Growers have names like Humbrecht, Sipp and Zimmer, and most of them live in half-timbered houses that any erring Hansel or Gretel would be delighted to come home to. Alsace is German on the outside.

On the inside, it's as French as Piaf or Chevalier. To prove it, pull the cork on a bottle of Alsace Sylvaner or Pinot Blanc. It will be dry, with attractive vanilla-edged fruit scents; it will be full, with at least 11% of alcohol; and it will accompany to perfection any piece of pork you care to roast, or fish you care to fry. The combination of aromatic interest, fundamentally dry fruit and prominent levels of alcohol is very French.

The three appellations of Alsace are AOC Alsace, AOC Alsace Grand Cru, and AOC Crémant d'Alsace. This isn't the only information the label will give you; in fact in many ways it's the least important. What really marks the difference between bottles of Alsace wine is the name of the grape variety from which each is made.

Sylvaner and Pinot Blanc account, between them, for nearly 40 per cent of the Alsace vineyard area, and these grapes provide the most inexpensive bottles of Alsace wine (which, in truth, aren't as inexpensive as we might wish: value for money in Alsace is fair, but no more). The Sylvaner, when well made, has perhaps more to offer in a softly earthy way than has Pinot Blanc, which is generally a plainly, though amply, fruity wine. (Another variety called the Auxerrois may also be used in Pinot Blanc.) Lest this should seem like damningly faint praise, the cardinal virtue of Alsace's wines – reliability – should be made plain. Poor bottles from Alsace are rare, and the general standard of quality is superior to that of every other part of France save Bordeaux, which has recently come to equal Alsace, thanks to a decade of superb weather. It is for reasons of reliability that Alsace Sylvaner and Pinot Blanc should be almost the first names you look for when surveying a restaurant wine list: their unspectacular but dependable virtues make them perfect for four people, each of whom is eating something different, in often distracting surroundings.

Riesling is considered by most Alsatians to be their finest variety: it has qualities of finesse and raciness, and its fruit a closeness of texture, that set it apart from the others – but only when well made, from modestly yielding vines in a sunny site. High yields are a problem in Alsace – a massive 100 hl/ha is permitted by the regulations – and it is hard to sustain noble Riesling raciness when the vines are being milked immodestly for all the fruit they will bear. Alsace Riesling can often taste cold and hard, too, whereas it is the full, spicy richness of other varieties that many of us find so attractive in wines from this corner of France. It is best to buy the generally pricey Riesling on recommendation, whereas other Alsace varietal wines may be bought speculatively without too much risk.

Alsace Riesling

Type *Dry white wine*
Profile *Floral, honeyed aromas which, after ageing, may become suggestive of petrol fumes or Kerosene; pure, clear, tight, sometimes chilly fruit flavours*
Advice *Drink with fish; the best improve with ageing*

Gewürztraminer is Alsace's real gift to the world, though it has become sadly fashionable to criticise this wine's 'vulgarity'. Gewürztraminer is powerfully aromatic, smelling sometimes spicy, sometimes of musky roses or ylang-ylang, sometimes of lychees, and nearly always oily and sweet. It isn't sweet to taste, though its low acidity levels and high alcohol levels give the impression of richness. If it has a failing, it is that it is square in shape, not round: good examples deliver a big block of flavour that is rarely elegant. Given that so few of Spain's or Italy's white wines can manage even a small block of flavour, and the barest whisper of aroma, this is cavilling criticism; Gewürztraminer is emphatically a reason to be grateful to this long fillet of disputed Rhineland.

Alsace Gewürztraminer

Type *Richly dry, aromatic white wine*
Profile *Powerfully perfumed; spicy, solid flavours, with high alcohol and low acidity*
Advice *Drink on its own as a conversation wine, or serve with rich and spicy foods*

Pinot Gris (also known as Tokay d'Alsace or Tokay-Pinot Gris) is Alsace's second heavyweight: it is less flamboyantly aromatic than Gewürztraminer, replacing the flower border with smoky fruit, but it is no less rich and oily on the palate. The fact that its character is more discreet than that of Gewürztraminer, and its acidity levels higher, gives it greater adaptability with food; it also ages better.

Alsace Pinot Gris

Type *Richly dry white wine*
Profile *Oily, smoky, sometimes spicy scents and flavours informing creamy fruit base*
Advice *Drink with rich food; the best improve with cellaring*

Muscat is the least widely planted of the named grape varieties used for AOC Alsace: its often cuttingly dry flavours come as a shock after the grapey, zesty perfume released by a swirl of the glass. It makes the region's best aperitif.

Pinot Noir is used to produce Alsace's red wines. They are light but attractively fruity; like all red wines from predominantly white-wine-producing regions, and whites from predominantly red-wine-producing regions, they are overpriced, due to buoyant demand from locals wanting a change from the usual.

The word **Edelzwicker** is found on labels of wine made from a mixture of the varieties cited above, plus Chasselas (though little of this variety remains in Alsace today). Two other terms may be seen on wines sold under the Alsace AOC: Vendange Tardive and **Sélection de Grains Nobles**; these categories can be claimed only for Gewürztraminer, Pinot Gris, Riesling and Muscat wines. Vendange Tardive signifies a late-harvested wine; Sélection de Grains Nobles a wine vinified from grapes affected by noble rot (botrytis), as is the case with Sauternes, or one vinified from grapes that have been sun-dried on the vine (*passerillés*). Minimum natural sugar levels are specified by law; in the case of Vendange Tardive wines, these may be completely fermented to a rich and succulent dryness, or some proportion may remain after fermentation to give a more or less sweet dessert wine. Sélection de Grains Nobles wines are nearly always sweet. Some of these wines are very fine indeed; others are dull, lack definition and concentration, and represent shockingly poor value for money. This tradition – common further down the Rhine valley in Germany – has been comparatively recently revived in Alsace, where botrytis occurs less regularly and acidity levels are lower. Many producers make such wines because fashion requires them to do so, not because this is the only way to bring out the full potential of their fruit and their vineyards. In a number of cases, this potential would have been better realised by picking the fruit a few weeks earlier, along with the rest of the harvest, and making a fine dry table wine. Buy only on firm and reliable recommendation.

Alsace now has 51 Grands Crus: fine, single vineyards, almost always in multiple ownership, the name of which may be mentioned on the label in combination with the **AOC Alsace Grand Cru**. Strangely enough, only half of these vineyards have defined edges; the other half have yet to be precisely delimited. The AOC is open only to wines made from Gewürztraminer, Pinot Gris, Muscat and Riesling, and yields must be reduced to the (still generous) level of 65 hl/ha. The first Grands Crus were distinguished as such in 1975, and most commentators judge the system a useful way of drawing the drinker's attention to the best sites of the region. Critics claim that there are too many *crus* for them all to be *grands*; that yields are still too high; and that restricting the sites to four grape varieties does a disservice to tradition (some sites, like Sonnenglanz or Zotzenberg, have always been prized for their Sylvaner, for example).

Non-Grand Cru single vineyard sites may also be mentioned on the labels of ordinary AOC Alsace wines, and when Grand Cru vineyards are planted with varieties other than the approved four, the vineyard name may still be used – but the appellation must be that of Alsace rather than Alsace Grand Cru.

Recommended Grands Crus

Brand (especially Gewürztraminer, Pinot Gris, Riesling); Furstentum (especially Gewürztraminer, Pinot Gris, Riesling); Geisberg (especially Riesling); Goldert (especially Gewürztraminer, Muscat); Kirchberg de Barr (especially Gewürztraminer); Kirchberg de Ribeauvillé (especially Riesling); Kitterlé (especially Riesling); Muenchberg (especially Gewürztraminer, Riesling); Osterberg (especially Riesling); Rangen (especially Pinot Gris); Rosacker (especially Riesling); Schlossberg (especially Riesling); Schoenenbourg (especially Muscat, Pinot Gris, Riesling).

AOC Crémant d'Alsace covers the region's champagne-method sparkling wines. These are well made, with considerable intensity of fruit. Their price is usually at least a pound or so more than the best champagne-method sparkling wines of the Loire, whose profile and quality level they share; but at five or six pounds less than champagne itself, they are still good value.

Recommended producers

Adam (especially Pinot Gris) Dopff 'Au Moulin' (especially Crémant d'Alsace, Gewürztraminer) Faller/Domaine Weinbach (especially Gewürztraminer, Riesling) Rolly Gassmann (especially Gewürztraminer, Pinot Gris, Riesling) Hugel (especially Pinot Gris, Riesling) Marc Kreydenweiss (especially Gewürztraminer); Gérard Neumeyer (especially Riesling); Domaine Ostertag (especially Riesling); Schlumberger (especially Pinot Gris, Riesling) Trimbach (especially Riesling) Cave des Vignerons de Turckheim (especially Gewürztraminer, Pinot Gris, Riesling); Willm (especially Gewürztraminer, Pinot Gris); Zind-Humbrecht (especially Pinot Gris).

No longer drink only water, but use a little wine for the sake of your stomach and your frequent ailments.
The First Letter of Paul to Timothy

Alsace: vintages

1989 A very fine harvest for every category, though also a very large one, with less reputable growers over-cropping their wines shamelessly: choose with care.

1988 A good harvest, with considerable quantities of Vendange Tardive and Sélection de Grains Nobles wines being produced. Gewürztraminer is variable.

1987 A mixed year, with some good and some disappointing wines.

1986 A mixed year, with some good wines, especially Riesling.

1985 An excellent year for all wines.

1984 A poor vintage: avoid.

1983 A fine vintage, with the best Riesling and Pinot Gris still showing well.

1982 A large crop producing wines that lack concentration: avoid.

1981 A good year of balanced wines. The best producers' best cuvées still reward.

1980 Avoid.

Stockists

James Aitken & Son; Les Amis du Vin; Bibendum; Borg Castel; Anthony Byrne; D Byrne & Co; Cadwgan; Classic Wine Warehouse; Eldridge Pope; Philip Eyres; Peter Green; Gerard Harris; Heath Street Wine Co; Hicks & Don; J E Hogg; Hopton Wines; Victor Hugo Wines; Lay & Wheeler; Morris & Verdin; Raeburn Fine Wines; Reid Wines; La Réserve; Thresher; Ubiquitous Chip; Upper Crust; La Vigneronne; Wright Wine Co; Yorkshire Fine Wines.

BEAUJOLAIS

What is your perception of beaujolais? And, more importantly, your merchant's? As likely as not, your merchant will shelve beaujolais next to (or even within) the burgundy section, and the sales pitch will urge you to buy beaujolais as 'inexpensive burgundy'. The bottles used by Beaujolais growers are identical to those used for burgundy. Wine books, for reasons of geographical convenience, append Beaujolais to Burgundy. The fiction is profitable for all.

But fiction it is. Burgundy is in northern France; Beaujolais is in southern France. The climate, soils and grape varieties of the two regions differ starkly. And so does the potential of the wine, which is why it is so misleading to describe beaujolais as 'inexpensive burgundy'. Burgundy, for all its failings, is unquestionably a fine wine; beaujolais, for all its successes, is unquestionably a country wine. It is simple, good-natured, inviting, a wine of warmth and fallibility, a wine with a human touch. But fine, sublime? Not on your nelly.

So long as you view beaujolais as the king of country wines, you should not be disappointed in it. Its price, as has been the case for several years, is at the limit of the tolerable, and the region offers few bargains. Yields are high, and over-chaptalisation is common. But good beaujolais, for those occasions when you want to drink wine by the gobletful, ward off demons and affirm your presence on the planet, has few peers, and is worth a fiver a bottle.

Beaujolais reaches you as Beaujolais Nouveau in mid-November, and as Beaujolais, Beaujolais-Villages or as one of the ten beaujolais *crus* at other times of the year. (Beaujolais Superieur is, in practical terms, the same as beaujolais, though its maximum alcohol content, nearly always exceeded, is 11° rather than 10°.)

Beaujolais Nouveau Day on the third Thursday in November is much less of a media event in Britain than it once was, and as our wine-drinking has become more sophisticated, Nouveau has slipped in our priorities. But there is nothing like new wine for heady charm, and there is no new wine to match that of beaujolais. The Gamay grape was made for this. Supermarket chains work hard to find sound Beaujolais Nouveau, and generally succeed. Drink and be merry!

Ordinary beaujolais is often disappointingly thin, as likely as not made from the leftovers that nobody wanted to buy as Nouveau. Beaujolais-Villages, on the other hand, can be excellent. The wine comes from 38 villages in the best, granite-soiled, northern part of the region, and in many cases these villages contain sites almost as propitious as those found in the named *crus*. Look out, in particular, for Beaujolais-Villages whose producer has an address in one of the *crus*, or in the villages of Jullié, Lantignié, Lancié or Quincié.

Beaujolais crus

There are ten Beaujolais *crus*. They are, from north to south, Saint-Amour, Juliénas, Chénas, Moulin-à-Vent, Fleurie, Chiroubles, Morgon, Régnié, Brouilly and Côte de Brouilly. They do produce most of the region's best wines, but remember, no matter how your merchant eulogises the depth of their fruit and assures you that after four years' storage you won't be able to tell them from Nuits, that they are still beaujolais. Even the deepest (Moulin-à-Vent, Juliénas and Morgon) are at their most exciting when young, steaming with purple fruit, and to allow a beaujolais to lose excitement is a crime against Bacchus. Similarly, if you have to pay the kind of prices for a top *cru* beaujolais that induce veneration, you will miss the point of the wine altogether, and risk disappointment. Few wines from Beaujolais emerge unshaken from close and sober scrutiny; they need drinking, and stoutly.

The lighter *crus* (Saint-Amour, Fleurie, Chiroubles, Côte de Brouilly) are not dissimilar to the best Beaujolais-Villages, though their excellence should be more consistent than can be expected of -Villages; while Brouilly, Régnié and Chénas are variable in style and quality.

Beaujolais-Villages

Type *Fruity red wine*
Profile *Bright, come-hither aromas hinting at raspberries and tar; full, fruity and vigorous tastes, with an incitement to gulp*
Advice *Drink as young as possible; chill lightly, especially in hot weather; use to restore flagging spirits*

Recommended producers

Domaine Aucoeur (Beaujolais-Villages, Morgon, Régnié); Georges Duboeuf (all appellations); Cave du Château de Chénas (Chénas, Moulin-à-Vent) Domaine des Duc (Saint-Amour); Eventail des Vignerons Producteurs (all appellations); Jean Garlon (Beaujolais); Jacky Janodet (Morgon, Moulin-à-Vent); Claude et Michelle Joubert (Beaujolais-Villages, Juliénas) Château du Moulin-à-Vent (Moulin-à-Vent); Domaine des Pillets (Régnié); Château Thivin (Brouilly, Côte de Brouilly); Château des Tours (Brouilly).

> When they came to the royal palace, they took their places on the settles and chairs, and the old man prepared a bowl of mellow wine for his guests, from a jar that had stood for ten years before the maid undid the cap and broached it. When the old king had mixed a bowl of this vintage, he poured a little out, with earnest prayers to Athene, Daughter of Zeus who wears the aegis.
> Homer *The Odyssey*

Vintage guide: Beaujolais

1989 Full, ripe wines, drinking very attractively at present.

1988 Firm, structured wines which, in the case of the *crus* and the -Villages, continue to show well.

1987 Fruity and forward: drink up.

1986 A large crop, but beginning to fade and dry now: drink up.

1985 A fine vintage. The *crus* continue to please, with complex secondary aromas now replacing the pungent primary scents of fruit.

1984 A poor vintage: avoid.

1983 The biggest *crus* (Moulin-à-Vent, Morgon, Juliénas, some Chénas) are still appealing: drink this year.

1982 Originally light and lively; now dead and gone.

Stockists

Anthony Byrne Fine Wines; D Byrne & Co; Domaine Direct; Roger Harris Wines; Victor Hugo Wines; Lay & Wheeler; Marks & Spencer; Le Nez Rouge; Christopher Piper Wines; Stapylton Fletcher; Upper Crust; Whitesides Wine Merchants; Wright Wine Co.

BORDEAUX

Bordeaux is the giant among French quality wines, and a run of magnificent vintages during the 1980s has added several inches to its already lofty stature. Its vineyard area is over 11 times the size of Burgundy's Côte d'Or; its 1989 harvest – the biggest ever for AOC wines, beating the previous records of 1986, 1985 and 1982 – was 59 times the size of that of Savoie. Even its finest estates – the so-called 'first growths' – are little monsters, each producing more than all the producers together can manage for the smaller Burgundy Grand Cru AOCs.

In only one sphere does Bordeaux fail to come across as an incredible hulk: in the glass. There, all is elegance and restraint. If only one word had to be found to describe what characterises the world's favourite red grape, Cabernet Sauvignon, when grown on its home territory, that word might be 'austerity'. The Merlot grape, in fact grown more widely than Cabernet Sauvignon in

Bordeaux, gives a richer, meatier wine, but this richness is still tempered by a sense of classical decorum, of proportion and grace.

Nowhere in Bordeaux do alcohol levels exceed 13°, whereas in Alsace you'll find plenty of Gewürztraminers weighing in at 13.5°. Nowhere in Bordeaux will you find the wild-eyed, tousle-haired, gorilla-chested kind of red wines that the Rhône valley or the Barossa valley can unleash. Bordeaux wears a suit and tie, quotes Montaigne and Montesquieu, and will never, in either aroma or taste, make any of the improper suggestions that its anarchic rival to the title of France's greatest wine, burgundy, loves to spring on unsuspecting drinkers. All this, no doubt, has much to do with the traditional warmth the British have felt for Bordeaux's wines, or 'clarets' (an anglicisation of *clairet*, meaning a light red wine). There is a temperamental affinity between the Briton, an unflamboyant, gentle and taciturn individual who feels at ease only within the familiar walls of one tradition or another, and Bordeaux, the most urbanely dependable of the world's great wines.

Bordeaux's vineyards spread out serenely to either side of the Gironde estuary, and they continue to upholster the Gironde's hinterland, formed by the lower reaches of the Garonne and the Dordogne. There are 19 basic *appellations*, some of which are sub-divided by commune or on an internal zoning basis to give a total of nearly 30 *appellations*. Not all are in use, and some are very much more important than others.

The most important area, and an AOC of consequence in its own right, is the Médoc, lying on the left bank of the Gironde estuary, and sheltered from Atlantic excesses by thousands on thousands of pine trees. The pines grow in sandy soil, while the vineyards of the Médoc are sited on gravel banks dumped by the Gironde over the course of millennia. The area is divided into Bas- (low) and Haut- (high) Médoc, both at sea level; map readers find it curious, therefore, that Bas-Médoc appears above (i.e. to the north of) Haut-Médoc, though this is logical enough should you find yourself standing in Bordeaux, to the south of both. The area is divided into six further *appellations*, in addition to that of Haut-Médoc: Saint-Estèphe, Pauillac, Moulis, Listrac, Saint-Julien and Margaux. The Haut-Médoc is Bordeaux's treasury: the famous 'classed growths' are all, bar one, situated here.

These *crus classés* comprise 61 *châteaux* (literally 'castles', though few are) in five groups, jotted down by a team of wine brokers for promotional purposes for the Paris Universal Exhibition of 1855. This list, prepared during three April days, presented by the brokers with a degree of unease, and summarising the way things stood 135 years ago, has since been cast in bronze, erected on a pedestal, and limed on by generations of pigeons with no obvious damage to its fabric. It still stands. Any wine reference book will print the full 1855 list of *crus classés*, while any of the many good books on Bordeaux will discuss the various merits of different *châteaux*. So, too, will the merchants listed below – though of course they will be keen to sell you the wines of those châteaux of which they hold substantial stocks. If you are wealthy, most classed-growth Bordeaux is fair value for money, for most of the wines are very fine and remarkably reliable, as well as very expensive. The relative prices of each château's wines reflect demand, and demand reflects excellence – with a time lag of up to five years. The key to getting good value from *cru classé* claret is therefore to discover excellence, with the help of merchants and journalists, during this five-year period before everyone else discovers it. However if you find it hard to justify spending over £10 on a bottle of wine, do not bother with *crus classés* at all; the top 'second wines' and *crus bourgeois* offer better value.

Cru Classé Médoc

Type *Fine, medium-bodied dry red wine*
Profile *Elegant, cedary aromas; expressive, harmonious flavours, sometimes suggesting blackcurrant, with a long, lean finish. Its lasting beauties are those of composition rather than impact, presence or flesh*
Advice *Follow merchant's recommendations on cellaring; do not serve at over 19°C: decant if very young or very old; serve with the best cuts of meat, plainly prepared*

Second wines

Over the last decade and a half, leading châteaux all over the Bordeaux region have begun to distinguish between different portions of their crop. The best vatsful (*cuvées*) get blended into what is known as the *grand vin*, and the *grand vin* is what is bottled and sold under the château's name. Other *cuvées* – from younger vines, for example, or from parts of the vineyard that have been less successful in a particular year for microclimatic reasons – are blended and sold as a 'second wine', usually at around half the price of the *grand vin*. This laudable development is due in considerable measure to the influence of Emile Peynaud, Bordeaux University's celebrated Professor of Oenology, now in retirement, who has always stressed the importance of this practice if châteaux wish to improve their wines and their reputations. Many second wines are good value for money: they often share the profile and style of the *grand vin*, but lack its concentration, depth and length. In practical terms, that means you can drink them this year or next rather than in a decade's time.

Recommended second wines

Château Notton (Château Brane-Cantenac); Clos du Marquis (Château Léoville-Las-Cases); Connétable Talbot (Château Talbot); L'Ermitage de Chasse-Spleen (Château Chasse-Spleen); Les Fiefs de Lagrange (Château Lagrange); Les Forts de Latour (Château Latour); Pavillon Rouge du Château Margaux (Château Margaux); Réserve de l'Amiral (Château Beychevelle) Réserve de la Comtesse (Château Pichon-Lalande); Sarget de Gruaud-Larose (Château Gruaud-Larose); Villeneuve de Cantemerle (Château Cantemerle).

Petits châteaux

The other source of good inexpensive Médoc and Haut-Médoc wines are those properties known as *petits châteaux* (literally 'little castles': the region's less celebrated wines), the best of which may be classified as *crus bourgeois* ('bourgeois growths'), *crus grands bourgeois* or *crus grands bourgeois exceptionnels*. Different requirements govern each tier of the classification – oak-ageing, for example, is required of wines of *grand bourgeois* or *grand bourgeois exceptionnel* status, though not of a *cru bourgeois* (though an ambitious *cru bourgeois* owner will use oak anyway). Despite these requirements, the differences between the best wines in each of the three categories are not great, and these wines may routinely reach *cru classé* standard (of fifth to third growth level): stylish, concentrated and often surprisingly tannic. Over-achieving *crus bourgeois* provide the best value in the Médoc. We provide a list of widely admired *crus bourgeois*, but a good Bordeaux specialist merchant will certainly be able to recommend others – as well as outstanding *petits châteaux* not classified on any tier of bourgeois growth at present.

Recommended crus bourgeois

Château d'Angludet (Margaux) Château Beausite (Saint-Estèphe) Château Chasse-Spleen (Moulis); Château Cissac (Haut-Médoc); Château Coufran (Haut-Médoc); Chateau Le Crock (Saint-Estèphe); Château Fonbadet (Pauillac); Château Fonréaud (Listrac); Château Haut-Bages-Averous (Pauillac) (also part second wine); Château Haut-Marbuzet (Saint-Estèphe); Château Labégorce-Zédé (Margaux); Château Lanessan (Haut-Médoc); Château Monbrison (Margaux); Château Les Ormes-de-Pez (Saint-Estèphe); Château de Pez (Saint-Estèphe); Château Sociando-Mallet (Haut-Médoc); Château La Tour de By (Médoc).

Graves

The city of Bordeaux lies at the southern tip of the Médoc, on the left bank of a large, moon-shaped curve of the River Garonne (Bordeaux's port was, in the past, known as the *port de la lune*, 'moonport'). South of Bordeaux, continuing on the Garonne's left bank, is the Graves.

Graves is the French word for gravel; as we might expect, its soil, particularly in the northern part of the zone in AOC Pessac-Léognan, is composed of the same gravel banks as are found in the Médoc. In the southern Graves, the soils are sandier. Cabernet Sauvignon dominates in the Médoc, and in the Graves it continues to do so, though at some Graves châteaux the Merlot begins to approach equality with the Cabernet. The red wines of the Graves are softer and earthier than those of the Médoc, though still with a fine blackcurrant ring to them. The major difference, though, between the Médoc and the Graves is that white wines, for which no *appellation* exists north of Bordeaux, appear here. These have traditionally been made with Sémillon, plus a little Sauvignon Blanc and Muscadelle; nowadays, Sauvignon Blanc increasingly plays the leading role, freshening up the rather lazy white Graves of tradition, while soft little Muscadelle is often excluded altogether. Oak is used more and more, to seductive effect. Sweet white Graves, once cheap, sulphury and found in every wine merchant's shop from Aberdeen to Truro, is now only the memory of a heavy Sunday-morning headache (inexpensive Graves Supérieur, though, can still be sweet and mischievously SO_2-laden).

The Graves, indeed, has made strides of progress as marked as any in Bordeaux in recent years, and is certainly a source of exciting and reasonably priced red and white Bordeaux in 1991. One of its châteaux, Haut-Brion (now a suburban vineyard), was the only non-Médoc property to be included in the 1855 classification, as a first growth; other Graves châteaux were selected for a classification of their own in 1953 (modified 1959), but without stratification into a hierarchy of different 'growths'.

At the south-eastern end of the Graves is another sub-district which, like Pessac-Léognan in the north-west, enjoys an AOC of its own: Cérons. Most of the wine produced here goes to market under the Graves *appellations*, but one fifth of it is made as a sweet white wine inspired by but rarely as distinguished as that of neighbouring Sauternes.

133

Recommended producers

Château Cabannieux; Château Couhins-Lurton; Domaine de Chevalier;
Domaine La Grave; Château de Fieuzal; Château Haut-Bailly; Château La
Louvière; Château Montalivet; Château Roquetaillade-la-Grange; Château
Smith-Haut-Lafitte; Château La Tour Martillac.

Sauternes and Barsac

Continuing south-east from the Graves, further up the left bank of
the River Garonne, lie Sauternes and Barsac, two separate though
similar AOCs. Here, France's greatest sweet wines are produced,
from Sémillon plus a small proportion of Sauvignon Blanc and
Muscadelle grapes affected by noble rot. The soils are a clay-gravel
mix, the landscape a pleasing one of low hills and knolls, and the
autumns long, warm and golden. Mists roll off the river in the
mornings, spreading through the vineyards in thick, indolent
waves, promoting the growth of rot in the grapes. The midday sun
sees off the mist and desiccates the grapes, whose skin and cell
structure has been broken by the lance-like botrytis spores. The
sun is as important as the mist, for it checks the rot and prevents it
damaging the fruit irreparably and spoiling its flavours. If the mist
never lifted, the harvest would be ruined. Without the mist,
though, the grapes would just shrivel to raisins, and the resulting
wines would be simply sweet, without the delicious tang brought
by partial rotting. These weather conditions are so specific as to be
unattainable year in, year out; some years are much more
successful than others in Sauternes.

Sauternes/Barsac

Type *Sweet white wine*
Profile *Aromas vary from light and lemony to lanolin-rich; flavours
vary from delicately sweet to honeyed, often with the slightly bitter
finish of botrytis; sustained acidity, high alcohol levels and complexity
of flavour prevent the sweetness from cloying, and the best weigh
deliciously heavily on the tongue*
Advice *Chill well; serve on its own or with fine, fruit-based pâtisserie.
Other classic partners include pâté de foie gras and Roquefort cheese.
The finest Sauternes may be cellared for many years; aromatic interest
and subtlety of taste grow with bottle age*

The leading châteaux of Sauternes and Barsac were classified in 1855, at the same time as those of the Médoc, into first and second growths (*premiers* and *deuxièmes crus classés*), with Château d'Yquem singled out as *premier cru classé supérieur*, the undisputed regent of the region. Differences between the wine of the two *appellations* are not pronounced; the usual generalisation confines itself to stressing richness and voluptuousness in Sauternes and honeyed elegance in Barsac, but a vintage or a wine-maker can see these traits reversed. The wines, although expensive, are good value for money, for the production process is a costly and a risky one, and yields are minute (25 hl/ha maximum; d'Yquem averages 7 hl/ha). The red and dry white wines of châteaux in the Sauternes and Barsac area are marketed under the Graves or Bordeaux AOCs.

Recommended producers

Château Bastor-Lamontagne; Château Cantegril; Château Climens; Château Coutet; Château Doisy-Daëne; Château Lafaurie-Peyraguey; Château de Malle; Château Rieussec.

Stockists

Adnams; Christchurch Fine Wines; Eldridge Pope; Master Cellar Wine Warehouse Nobody Inn; Tanners; Peter Wylie.

Between two seas

Across the River Garonne, facing Graves and Sauternes from the right bank, are six of Bordeaux's minor *appellations*: Premières Côtes de Bordeaux, Cadillac, Loupiac, Sainte-Croix-du-Mont, Côtes de Bordeaux-Saint-Macaire, and Bordeaux-Haut-Benauge. Cadillac, Loupiac and Sainte-Croix-du-Mont are sweet white wine *appellations*; as the market for these has dwindled in recent years, so has production, yet the best properties in both Loupiac and Sainte-Croix-du-Mont can produce sweet wines of complexity and finesse, offering excellent value for money. Premières Côtes de Bordeaux is a lucky dip *appellation*, a dip into the soft, ripe reds generally proving luckier than one into the sweet wines. The other two AOCs are for little-seen, unfancied whites which may be dry, medium or sweet.

The area that lies between the Garonne and the Dordogne, as they near each other to form the Gironde, is known as Entre-Deux-Mers, 'between two seas'. It is a pretty area of little valleys, green slopes, sturdy windmills – and, of course, vines, many of them with deeply lobed leaves and tightly packed bunches of white grapes. Sauvignon Blanc is much planted here and, together with some Sémillon, Muscadelle and Colombard, produces what can, at best, be some of Bordeaux's simplest, fruitiest, freshest white wines, and at worst some of its most characterless. Red wines from Entre-Deux-Mers are marketed under AOC Bordeaux. Entre-Deux-Mers-Haut-Benauge has a separate AOC for no good reason; those of Graves de Vayres and Sainte-Foy-Bordeaux to the north of Entre-Deux-Mers, on the left bank of the Dordogne, justify their existence with soft but rich reds, especially the Merlot-based wines of Graves de Vayres. The whites are less interesting, and are in general no better than those of Entre-Deux-Mers.

Recommended producers

Château Beauduc (Entre-Deux-Mers and Bordeaux Rouge); Château de Berbec (Premières Côtes de Bordeaux); Château Bonnet (Entre-Deux-Mers and Bordeaux Rouge); Château Fayan (Cadillac); Château Loubens (Sainte-Croix-du-Mont); Château Mazerolles (Entre-Deux-Mers and Bordeaux Rouge); Château de la Meulière (Premières Côtes de Bordeaux); Château de Ricaud (Loupiac); Château Thieuley (Entre-Deux-Mers and Bordeaux Rouge and Clairet).

Saint-Emilion and friends

On the right bank of the Dordogne, the quality barometer begins to rise again. Côtes de Castillon is the first right-bank *appellation* passed on a river journey from Bergerac to Bordeaux, and its supple and lively red wine hints at the splendidly vibrant and meaty clarets of the next *appellation*, Saint-Emilion. Côtes de Castillon is for red wines only, whereas Bordeaux-Côtes de Francs, to its north, is for red and white wines, with a sensationally obscure *liquoreux* version enjoying a separate AOC.

Saint-Emilion and its associated 'satellites' (Lussac-, Montagne-, Puisseguin- and Saint-Georges-Saint-Emilion), taken together, dwarf other regions of Bordeaux in terms of production: Saint-Emilion alone yields over six times as much as Saint-Julien in the Médoc. Here, as in the neighbouring *appellations* of Pomerol and Lalande-de-Pomerol, the Merlot grape dominates blends, and it results in wines of supple, spicy richness, franker and easier to enjoy than their Médocain counterparts. The very best of them, like the world's priciest wine, the almost pure-Merlot Château Pétrus from Pomerol, have such a depth of soft flesh and singing fruit that it is hard to stay seated after downing a glassful. Pomerol and Saint-Emilion produce hedonist's claret.

International appreciation of these wines has been won comparatively recently, and properties here are generally smaller and architecturally more modest than in the Médoc. For the stars, demand creates high prices. In Saint-Emilion, though, such a huge number of châteaux produce good wine that examples of quality can be found comparatively cheaply; not so, alas, in Pomerol. The only classification in this area is for the wines of Saint-Emilion, the best of which are *grands crus classés* or *premiers grands crus classés*. This classification came into force in 1986; on labels of wines of earlier vintages, the now-abandoned category of *grand cru* (without any *classé*) may be seen.

Saint-Emilion/Pomerol

Type *Medium- to full-bodied red wine*
Profile *Generous, warmly fruity aromas, sometimes suggesting the smell of roasting meat; rich, earthy flavours of ripe, sweet fruit, with a ferrous, mineral edge*
Advice *Serve with robust, classic dishes*

Recommended producers

Château des Annereaux (Lalande-de-Pomerol); Château Bel-Air (Lussac-Saint-Emilion); Château de Belcier (Côtes de Castillon); Château Le Bon Pasteur (Pomerol); Château Cadet-Piola (Saint-Emilion); Château Canon (Saint-Emilion); Clos du Clocher (Pomerol); Château Figeac (Saint-Emilion); Château de Gardegan (Côtes de Castillon); Château Gardoux (Lalande-de-Pomerol); Château Le Jurat (Saint-Emilion); Château Lagrange de Lescure (Saint-Emilion); La Grange Neuve de Figeac (Saint-Emilion); Château Latour-à-Pomerol (Pomerol); Château Moncets (Lalande-de-Pomerol); Château Nenin (Pomerol); Château Pavie (Saint-Emilion); Château Pitray (Côtes de Castillon); Château Puyguéraud (Côtes de Francs); Château Tertre-Rôteboeuf (Saint-Emilion); Château Troplong-Mondot (Saint-Emilion); Château Trottevieille (Saint-Emilion).

Hamlet in Fronsac

Four further *appellations* lie west of Saint-Emilion, still on the right bank of the Dordogne and, post-confluence, of the Gironde. Two of these – Fronsac and Côtes de Canon-Fronsac – neighbour Saint-Emilion; the other two are found beyond Saint-André de Cubzac, across the water from Margaux and Saint-Julien, around the towns of Bourg and Blaye.

The Cabernet Franc grape, having played a supporting role to Merlot in Saint-Emilion and Pomerol, and little more than a walk-on part in the Médoc and Graves, finally gets its chance to play Hamlet in Fronsac and Côtes de Canon-Fronsac. These two areas, especially the latter, are excellent sources of chunky, close-textured claret at a very reasonable price, and provide evidence from somewhere other than the Loire of how sadly undervalued the Cabernet Franc is.

Bourg and Blaye have a more complicated *appellation* system, but produce less impressive wines: the reds are sold as Côtes de Bourg (or Bourg, or Bourgais) and Premières Côtes de Blaye (or Blaye, or Blayais, if they are only 10° rather than 10.5°); whites are sold as Côtes de Blaye. The best of these are the Merlot-dominated Côtes de Bourg; when good, they can rival lesser Saint-Emilions.

Côtes de Canon-Fronsac

Type *Medium-bodied red wine*
Profile *Lively aromas combining currant scents with a suggestion of freshly cut nettle; vibrant, rounded flavours, sometimes with a slightly bitter edge*
Advice *Serve with roast and grilled meats, sausages and cheese dishes*

Recommended producers

Château Beaugérit (Côtes de Bourg); Château Canon (Canon-Fronsac); Château Canon-Moueix (Canon-Fronsac); Château Dalem (Fronsac); Château Haut-Guiraud (Côtes de Bourg); Château Haut-Sociondo (Premières Côtes de Blaye); Château Lariveau (Canon-Fronsac); Château Mazeris-Bellevue (Canon-Fronsac); Château Moulin-Haut-Laroque (Fronsac); Château La Rivière (Fronsac); Château La Vieille Curé (Fronsac); Château Villars (Fronsac).

Aspiration in the big zone

The basic *appellation* for the whole Bordeaux area is Bordeaux (Rouge or Blanc): quality in this, France's biggest AOC, varies enormously, depending on the aspirations of the merchant (or property) under whose name the wine is sold. The very best wines often originate in more exalted *appellations*, but are declassified for reasons of unworthiness, though they may be by no means unworthy in absolute terms; or hail from areas whose *appellation* is for one style of wine only, AOC Bordeaux being claimed for the other style (red wine from parts of Sauternes, or from Entre-Deux-Mers, for example). Such bargains are difficult to identify from the label alone, though merchants will usually find ways to hint at their provenance. Bordeaux Rouge from an individual, named château may be better than that from a *négociant*, but there are many exceptions to this crude rule of thumb. The recommendations of a good merchant are your surest guide. As is customary in France, Supérieur (as in AOC Bordeaux Supérieur) refers not to quality but to higher-than-usual alcohol content. Bordeaux, finally, produces some of France's best, Cabernet-based rosés, sold under the Bordeaux Clairet or Bordeaux Rosé *appellations*.

Vintage guide: Bordeaux

1989 A very good vintage; its position in the hierarchy of the 1980s is as yet undecided, but it will be somewhere in the top three. *Crus bourgeois* from Saint-Estèphe, and *petits châteaux* in general, are unusually good. An excellent year for Sauternes.

1988 A less fashionable vintage than 1989, but insiders tip it as one to watch as the top wines turn into the home straight in around 2005. Not such a good year for *petits châteaux*; very fine for Sauternes.

1987 A light, attractive year, full of simple pleasures. Most wines, even the best, are ready for drinking.

1986 A good year, but unlovely in youth. The wines are lean, and at present seem tight-lipped about their plans for the future, but their furrowed concentration bodes well. The Sauternes vintage was a magnificent one.

1985 A sensationally attractive vintage from the moment the starting gun was fired. The best from every *appellation*, save those for sweet whites, tastes irresistible, and *crus bourgeois* and *petits châteaux* have rarely been as good.

1984 The one mean vintage Bordeaux has produced in the 1980s, though the most talented wine-makers were able to produce acceptable, if unexciting, wines.

1983 A fine, classic vintage, attractively priced. Buy now, and drink the top wines from 1993. An excellent year for Sauternes.

1982 The most talked-about vintage of the 1980s, producing clarets of strange, exotic opulence. Costly but unique, with a long life ahead.

1981 A sound vintage of comfortable, tempered classicism.

1980 A light but appealing vintage. Drink up.

Previous vintages of merit 1978, 1970, 1966, 1961, 1959, 1955, 1953, 1949, 1947, 1945

Stockists

Ad Hoc; William Addison; Adnams; James Aitken; David Alexander; Les Amis du Vin; John Armit; Averys; David Baillie; Nigel Baring; Battersea; Berry Bros

& Rudd; Bibendum; Booths; G E Bromley; Butlers; D Byrne; Cadwgan; Cairns & Hickey; Chaplin & Son; Christchurch; Colombier Vins Fins; Corney & Barrow; Croque-en-Bouche; Davenport; Davisons; Direct Wine; Eldridge Pope; Ben Ellis; Philip Eyres; Farr Vintners; Findlater Mackie Todd; Friarwood; Matthew Gloag; Goedhuis; Green's; Harrods; Gerard Harris; Harveys; Haynes Hanson & Clark; Hedley Wright; Hicks & Don; J E Hogg; Hopton; House of Townend; Victor Hugo; Hungerford; Tony Jeffries; Justerini & Brooks; S H Jones; Kurtz & Chan; Lay & Wheeler; Laytons; Majestic; Marks & Spencer; Master Cellar; Morris & Verdin; Nickolls & Perks; Oddbins; Thos Peatling; Le Picoleur; Christopher Piper; Arthur Rackham; Raeburn; Reid; La Réserve; Richmond; Selfridges; Edward Sheldon; Frank Stainton; Summerlee Wines; T & W Wines; Thresher; Tanners; Turville Valley; El Vino; Waitrose; Peter Watts; Weavers; Willoughbys; Wine Growers Association; Wine House; The Wine Society; Peter Wylie; Yorkshire Fine Wines.

BURGUNDY

Red burgundy is for romantics and gamblers. Successful gamblers, and prosperous romantics: the area is a small one, and its wines are prized, so they are never cheap. But only gamblers and romantics will be able to accept the disappointment and humiliation so often inflicted by red burgundy, and judge it worthwhile to pursue the elusive ideal, the high rolling prize.

White burgundy is rather different. It is much more reliable than red burgundy, because white grapes ripen more easily than red ones in the region's marginal climate, and because Chardonnay is a more compliant variety than the ill-mannered Pinot Noir. Yet it is in even shorter supply than its red counterpart, putting still greater pressure on prices, and tempting growers to leave an extra bud or two on the vines, harvest an extra trailerful of grapes, sell three bottles in place of two, and give themselves a 33 per cent pay rise for next year. How many of those who have paid £20 for a *premier cru* Meursault question its concentration? Statistics of this sort are hard to come by, fortunately for the growers. Their markets are global and fragmented. For every merchant who declines to reorder, there are three at the door ready to buy into this or that *premier cru* to the tune of a few overpriced cases, simply to have the names on their lists. White burgundy is no surer value than red, and in many bottles, too many, the region simply lives off its reputation.

In Burgundy, as in Bordeaux, classifications are important, the difference being that here they are built into the *appellation* system, whereas in Bordeaux the classifications are complimentary to the *appellation* names. At the top of the ladder are the Grands Crus: 31 impeccably sited and immaculately soiled sites, each of which basks in the luxury of its own *appellation* (example: 'Corton/ Appellation d'Origine Contrôlée' or 'Appellation Corton Contrôlée'). It is important to be able to distinguish between Grand Cru *appellations* and village *appellations*: a list of Grands Crus is given in the box below.

Burgundy's Grands Crus

Bâtard-Montrachet (Côte de Beaune); Bienvenues-Bâtard-Montrachet (Côte de Beaune); Bonnes Mares (Côte de Nuits); Chambertin (Côte de Nuits); Chambertin-Clos de Bèze or Clos de Bèze (Côte de Nuits); Chapelle-Chambertin (Côte de Nuits); Charlemagne (Côte de Beaune); Charmes-Chambertin (Côte de Nuits); Chevalier-Montrachet (Côte de Beaune); Clos des Lambrays (Côte de Nuits); Clos de la Roche (Côte de Nuits); Clos Saint-Denis (Côte de Nuits); Clos de Tart (Côte de Nuits); Clos de Vougeot (Côte de Nuits); Corton (Côte de Beaune); Corton-Charlemagne (Côte de Beaune); Criots-Bâtard-Montrachet (Côte de Beaune); Echézeaux (Côte de Nuits); Grands Echézeaux (Côte de Nuits); Griotte-Chambertin (Côte de Nuits); Latricières-Chambertin (Côte de Nuits); Mazis-Chambertin (Côte de Nuits); Mazoyères-Chambertin (Côte de Nuits); Montrachet (Côte de Beaune); Musigny (Côte de Nuits); Richebourg (Côte de Nuits); La Romanée (Côte de Nuits); Romanée-Conti (Côte de Nuits); Romanée-Saint-Vivant (Côte de Nuits); Ruchottes-Chambertin (Côte de Nuits); La Tâche (Côte de Nuits)

On the next rung down are the Premiers Crus: vineyards of quality which may be named on the label, but only in conjunction with the village name (example: 'Aloxe-Corton Les Valozières/ Appellation Aloxe-Corton Premier Cru Contrôlée'). A wine that simply proclaims itself to be 'Premier Cru' without specifying a vineyard will be a blend of wine from different Premier Cru sites. If the legislators had ruled that only Premier Cru-classified vineyards could be named on labels, or that any Premier Cru-classified vineyard must include mention of its Premier Cru in the *appellation* formula, this category would be impossible to mistake. But other, non-Premier Cru vineyards (known as *lieux-dits*) may also be mentioned on labels, and some Premier Cru vineyards are classified as such only in part, while the unclassified portion may also go to market under the vineyard name. To distinguish between these apparent Premiers Crus and the real ones, you have to see if the vineyard name is in letters half the size of those used for the village name, or if it is in letters of the same size. If half the size, the vineyard is a *lieu-dit*; if the same size, it is a Premier Cru. There is no obligation, furthermore, to specify that the vineyard is a Premier Cru in the *appellation* formula, though vineyards are permitted inclusion in the *appellation* formula only if they are Premiers Crus; *lieux-dits* must be marketed under the village *appellation* formula. This is legislation of needless and vexing complexity, a wart on the otherwise fair face of French wine law, and it can leave even the best informed consumers confused.

On the penultimate rung of the ladder perch the village or commune wines (example: 'Aloxe-Corton/Appellation d'Origine Contrôlée' or 'Appellation Aloxe-Corton Contrôlée'); *lieux-dits* may be named, if appropriate, as described above. On the bottom rung of the ladder are the regional wines, sold under the Bourgogne Rouge, Blanc, Rosé and Clairet *appellations*. Bourgogne-Passetoutgrains is a regional wine blended from one third Pinot Noir and two thirds Gamay, while Bourgogne Ordinaire or Bourgogne Grand Ordinaire is the same as Bourgogne but with lower minimum alcohol levels and higher permitted yields – a horse, in other words, whose teeth need checking very carefully before purchase. It, too, may come in Rouge, Blanc, Rosé and Clairet guises, in theory at least. (For the Hautes Côtes, see page 146.)

Burgundy's heart is the Côte d'Or: the 'golden slope' that runs from just south of Dijon to just south-west of Chagny. The Côte d'Or is divided into two parts: the Côte de Nuits, between Dijon and Corgoloin, south of Nuits-Saint-Georges; and the Côte de Beaune, between Corgoloin and Cheilly-lès-Maranges. To the north-west of the Côte d'Or lies Chablis, almost halfway to Paris; while south of the Côte d'Or lie two regions in which the splendours of fine burgundy tail away slowly: the Côte Chalonnaise and the Mâconnais.

Chablis

Chablis is a small, hilly region clustered around the little River Serein and its tributary streams. It has long been famous for its chilly winter and spring weather – severe or untimely frosts have repeatedly deprived local growers of their livelihood – and for its flint-hearted, cutlass-edged white Chardonnay wines. The *appellation* area for Chablis has been greatly expanded in recent decades (it is now four times the size it was in 1945) and many feel that with this expansion, and in particular with increased plantings on portlandian rather than the celebrated kimmeridgian limestone, has come a dilution in Chablis' traditional character. Other factors working to blunt the edge and soften the flint in Chablis are the run of generous, sunny vintages the 1980s brought, and the internationalisation of Chardonnay: American purchasers, who take a substantial proportion of Chablis exports, like a bigger, richer, oakier style of wine than the green, nervy Chablis of old. Whatever the causes, Chablis today is less pronounced in character than it once was, though it is still inimitably and often stylishly Burgundian. Chablis has eight Grands Crus and twelve principal Premiers Crus, though the number of the latter is swollen by the use of alternative names for sub-vineyards within the main Premier Cru zones. Most of the rest of the wines are sold under the basic Chablis *appellation*, many of the vineyards previously eligible for the modest Petit Chablis *appellation* having been upgraded. Light Pinot Noir reds are produced at Irancy, Coulanges-la-Vineuse and Epineuil; and at Saint-Bris, wines based on Sauvignon Blanc have won a VDQS denomination of their own. They are fresh and lively, but less drivingly severe than Sauvignon Blancs from the Loire.

Chablis Premier Cru

Type *Medium-bodied dry white wine*
Profile *Pale in colour, with sappy, blossomy, sometimes nutty aromas and light, chalkily textured, fresh flavours*
Advice *The Chablis of the past partnered oysters; modern Chablis is better suited to crab, river fish or poached chicken*

Recommended producers (Chablis)

La Chablisienne; René Dauvissat; Joseph Drouhin; Jean Durup; Long-Depaquit; Domaine de la Maladière (Fèvre); François & Jean-Marie Raveneau.

Côte de Nuits

The Côte de Nuits devotes itself almost exclusively to the production of red wines: they outnumber whites by 100 bottles to one. With Fixin and Marsannay, the Côte opens in a solid and four-square manner; Marsannay originally won its reputation for rosés, but the *appellation* was extended to include reds in May 1987, and at present these offer some of the best value in the whole Côte d'Or.

Marsannay

Type *Medium-bodied red wine*
Profile *Deeply coloured, plentiful aromas of dung, decomposition and the closeness of animals, especially after three or four years' bottle age; lively, peppery fruit, sometimes with slightly green acidity*
Advice *Should be served at no more than 19°C; partners most meat dishes well*

Pretensions grow at Gevrey-Chambertin, and quality sometimes follows: a good Gevrey can be round and sonorous, but many are over-cropped and over-chaptalised, giving an imbalanced and thinly flavoured wine. The village of Morey-Saint-Denis is fortunate in having a number of better-than-average growers rooted within its boundaries; as a result, Morey's firm, flavoury style of red Burgundy can be found without too much difficulty, though it can rarely be paid for with concomitant ease.

The next village, Chambolle-Musigny, produces lighter wines, often magnificently aromatic, silky to the tongue, yet persistent and long. Vougeot and its celebrated Clos are notoriously unreliable: red burgundy should generally be bought on recommendation, and to find the muscular poise of the best Vougeot it is essential. Flagey-Echézeaux and Vosne-Romanée can be contemplated only by the wealthy; if luck matches means, they will be rewarded with lustrous, perfumed, vibrantly flavoured red wines. The less wealthy (relatively speaking, of course) make do with one of Nuits-Saint-Georges's martial Premiers Crus. These are worth a £5 premium over ordinary Nuits-Saint-Georges, which is often a disappointing, swag-bellied wine.

Recommended producers (Côte de Nuits)

Bruno Clair; Joseph Drouhin; Dujac; Faiveley; Bertrand de Gramont; Machard de Gramont; Labouré-Roi; Georges Lignier; Maume; Antonin Rodet; Daniel Rion; Ropiteau (Marsannay); Philippe Rossignol; Joseph Roty.

Côte de Beaune

The Côte de Beaune opens undramatically with the twin villages of Ladoix and Serrigny, but already the Côte d'Or's loftiest hill, that of Corton, is within sight. Corton's slopes are shared between the last of the red Grands Crus and the first of the white, while the lowlier vineyards are apportioned between the villages of Aloxe-Corton and Pernand-Vergelesses. Reds of power, humming with sinewy fruit flavours, continue to dominate here, as in the Côte de Nuits. The town of Beaune is not far to the south, and its harbingers are the lighter, comparatively graceful reds of Savigny-lès-Beaune and Chorey-lès-Beaune. *Négociants* dominate vineyard holdings in the great pool of barely sloping vineyards that surround Beaune itself, and they produce reliable, comfortable, though often expressionless reds, and smaller quantities of similarly bland whites, from their holdings there.

Red wines continue to eclipse whites in Pommard which, like Nuits-Saint-Georges, is a village with some fine, poised Premiers Crus and some unappealingly paunchy village wines. With Volnay, the style lightens and freshens, and expressive fruit scents and flavours provide the distinguishing features of the best wines. Monthelie, Auxey-Duresses and Saint-Romain, the last sited well off the main Côte in a small side valley, are names of modest renown, and all of these villages provide red and white burgundies of authenticity, if not grandeur, for under £10.

Meursault is a small town rather than a village; in times past, it used to produce almost as much red wine as white, but the success of the white – Burgundy's richest – has seen Pinot Noir almost completely chased from the vineyards. Blagny and Saint-Aubin to its south produce small but shapely reds (Blagny exclusively so), while Puligny-Montrachet and Chassagne-Montrachet mark a resurgence of white-wine-making. The Montrachet family of Grands Crus should represent a pinnacle of Gallic artistry with Chardonnay – tight buds of searchingly nutty, intensely fruity, almost honeyed yet lingeringly dry white wine. Some match this description; some don't; and when two bottles cost three-figure sums you may consider that anything less than a hundred per cent hit rate is not good enough.

The reds of Chassagne are not dissimilar to those of its southern neighbour Santenay: at best limpidly fruity, delicate and choice, at worst so mild-mannered and slight that you stare in disbelief at your receipt. The Côte d'Or comes to an end with the newly awarded, and as yet rarely encountered, Maranges AOC.

Meursault Premier Cru

Type *Full dry white wine*
Profile *At best buttery, toasty aromas, sometimes simply fruity; unctuous, smooth though lively flavours with sustained vinosity*
Advice *Do not over-chill; serve with fish, poultry, pork or fine vegetable dishes*

Recommended producers (Côte de Beaune)

Robert Ampeau; Adrien Belland; Simon Bize; Domaine Coche-Dury; Joseph Drouhin; Faiveley; Jean Germain; Antonin Guyon; Louis Jadot; Labouré-Roi; Michel Lafarge; Comtes Lafon; Domaine (Vincent) Leflaive; Mongeard-Mugneret; Hubert de Montille; Domaine de la Pousse d'Or; Jacques Prieur; Antonin Rodet; Etienne Sauzet; Tollot-Beaut.

Other Côte d'Or *appellations*, not specific to particular villages, include Côte de Nuits-Villages (red and white wines from five communes at each end of the Côte de Nuits only: Fixin, Brochon, Comblanchien, Corgoloin and Premeaux-Prissey), and Côte de Beaune-Villages: red wines from a total of 17 communes running the length of the Côte de Beaune. Wine from any one of these 17 villages may, if the producer wishes, have '-Côte de Beaune' appended to the village name on the label; while a wine labelled Côte de Beaune alone comes from a small area behind the town of Beaune itself. The best of the '-Villages' wines come from producers already making higher-born wines of note, as well as from Burgundy's best négociants.

Recommended Burgundy négociants

Drouhin; Faiveley; Jaffelin; Jadot; Labouré-Roi; Moillard; Rodet.

Hautes Côtes

The two areas known as the Hautes Côtes de Nuits and the Hautes Côtes de Beaune are sited to the west of the Côte d'Or, in a large and pretty zone of hills, valleys and blackcurrant bushes (this is where much of France's Crème de Cassis originates). Viticulture here had dwindled to almost nothing by the 1950s and 1960s; with resurgent demand came replanting, and the Hautes Côtes are now a leading source of simple, generally well-made red and white burgundies. This replanting process began in the Hautes Côtes de Beaune, so the vines are generally older there, meaning better depth of flavour, but good growers in either area, as well as the top cuvées of the leading producer, the co-operative Cave des Hautes Côtes, are worth following.

Recommended producers (Hautes Côtes)

Cave des Hautes Côtes; Jayer-Gilles; Jean Joliot; Michel Serveau; Thévenot-le-Brun.

Côte Chalonnaise

The Côte Chalonnaise, to the south of the Côte d'Or, is discontinuous and lacks a focal point, a local centre, a shop window: Chalon-sur-Saône, from which it takes its name, lies away to the south-east. The five villages that make up this small sub-district of Burgundy have, however, a long tradition of wine-making, much of their production in the past having been passed off under the more famous names of their northerly neighbours. The legacy of this tradition is substantial ownership by Burgundy's négociants in the Côte Chalonnaise, especially in Mercurey, Burgundy's biggest single appellation for Pinot Noir. Passing off is, however, rare today, for these wines command £7 or £8 price labels under their own names. The best of them are worth that, though as usual in Burgundy standards vary greatly and the adjective 'best' is applicable to no more than one in seven bottles. That means that six out of seven bottles offer indifferent value for money – par for Burgundy as a whole.

The northernmost village in the Côte Chalonnaise is Bouzeron, and its *appellation* specifies Aligoté as sole grape variety; Bouzeron's Pinot Noir and Chardonnay must be sold as humble Bourgogne Rouge or Blanc. Aligoté, Chardonnay's lieutenant throughout Burgundy, gives a sharp, slender style of wine with, at best, briskly lemony scents. Rully is the next village southwards, and here red and white wines are produced, as well as considerable quantities of sparkling Crémant de Bourgogne. The village's soils seem able to produce good, light but fruity examples of each genre, and Rully's name is one of the few in the whole of Burgundy worth committing to memory.

Chunky, robustly fruity but sometimes rather ungainly reds are the speciality of Mercurey and Givry, while Montagny is a white-wine-only *appellation*, with one or two of the best producers achieving nutty depth and searching intensity in their wines. The Côte Chalonnaise has no Grands Crus, but Rully, Mercurey and Givry all have Premiers Crus as well as unclassified *lieux-dits*. 'Premier Cru' on a Montagny label, though, signifies only that the wines have attained at least 11.5° of potential alcohol in natural sugar before chaptalisation – a misleading piece of legislation, and another pimple on French wine law's otherwise agreeable complexion.

Recommended producers (Côte Chalonnaise)

Cave des Vignerons de Buxy; Jean Chofflet; Domaine du Gardin; Michel Juillot; Domaine de la Renarde; Antonin Rodet; Château de la Saule; Baron Thénard; A & P de Villaine.

The Mâconnais

The Mâconnais lies south of the Côte Chalonnaise and north of Beaujolais: it is a sunny, predominantly limestone-soiled region considerably larger, though less intensively planted, than the Côte d'Or. Well over half the vineyard area is under Chardonnay vines, to give what are usually solid, generously built white burgundies, though these rarely have any great finesse or depth. The best wines are those from the *crus* of Pouilly-Fuissé, -Loché, -Vinzelles and Saint-Véran, all of which are sited in the far south of the Mâconnais: steeper slopes than elsewhere, and stony white limestone soils, join to lend the fruit a lusciousness and a richness that it does not attain further north. The Mâcon-Villages *appellation* is for whites only from just over 40 villages which, rather than producing outstanding wines, produce more than usually reliable ones; only an outstanding wine-maker can produce outstanding wines in the Mâconnais. If the wine comes exclusively from one village, that village's name may be linked with Mâcon in the *appellation* formula: three of the best are Mâcon-Charnay, Mâcon-Clessé and Mâcon-Viré. Ordinary Mâcon (it comes as a Gamay-based red and rosé as well as white) is dull. As usual, Supérieure simply indicates higher alcohol without any promise of higher quality.

Mâcon-Villages

Type *Medium-bodied dry white wine*
Profile *Sweet vanilla scents; broad, earthy flavours, buttery or smoky if the producer ages his or her wines in oak, hinting at ripe summer fruit if not; good structure and vinosity*
Advice *An amenable white-wine partner for a wide range of foods, including vegetarian dishes*

Recommended producers (Mâconnais)

Cave des Grands Crus Blancs; Cave de Lugny; Duboeuf; Château Fuissé (Vincent); Manciat-Poncet; Producteurs de Prissé; Jean Thevenet.

Burgundy vintages

1989 An early harvest, giving both red and white wines of good quality and full, ripe flavour.

1988 A fine year, producing balanced white wines and concentrated, structured red wines for cellaring.

1987 A year of average quality, producing appealing, harmonious and reasonably priced red and white wines.

1986 A fine year for white wines, and a good year for some red wines, though others are poor: taste reds before buying, or follow trustworthy recommendation.

1985 A very good year for white wines, and a fine year for red wines, which are stylishly charged with powerful, lush fruit. The best need further cellaring.

1984 A poor to average year: the best reds and whites are fresh and lively; the worst are thin and over-acid. Follow trustworthy advice, and drink soon.

1983 This year produced white wines that were full and early-maturing: drink remaining bottles soon. The red wines are inconsistent: the best, despite light colours, have power and structure, and need one or two years' cellaring; others were tainted with rot and imbalanced. Taste before you buy.

1982 A large harvest of easy-drinking wines. Drink soon.

1981 A very small crop. The best growers produced good wines, which are holding well.

1980 A good year for Côte de Nuits reds, but rather mixed elsewhere. Drink soon.

Stockists

Ad Hoc; William Addison; Adnams; Alba Wine Society; Les Amis du Vin; John Armit; Averys; Adam Bancroft; Battersea Wine Co; Berry Bros & Rudd; Bibendum; Binocular Wine; Anthony Byrne; D Byrne; Christchurch; Colombier Vins Fins; Corney & Barrow; Davisons; Direct Wine; Domaine Direct; Eldridge Pope; Ben Ellis; Farr Vintners; Findlater Mackie Todd; Friarwood; Goedhuis; Gerard Harris; Harveys; Haynes Hanson & Clarke; Hopton Wines; Hungerford Wine Co; Ingletons Wines; Justerini & Brooks; Kurtz & Chan; Lay & Wheeler; Laytons; Lea & Sandeman; Marks & Spencer; Master Cellar; Morris & Verdin; Le Nez Rouge; Thos Peatling; Christopher Piper; Arthur Rackham; Raeburn;

Reid; La Réserve; Howard Ripley; Russell & McIver; Safeway; Seckford Wines; Selfridges; Edward Sheldon; Summerlee Wines; T & W Wines; Tanners; Turville Valley Wines; Upper Crust; David Watt; Peter Watts; Weavers of Nottingham; Whiclar & Gordon; Whitesides; Willoughbys; Windrush Wines; The Wine Society; Peter Wylie; Yorkshire Fine Wines.

CHAMPAGNE

There would be a large field jostling for position in a competition to find the world's best red wine, and the title of the world's best white would be disputed by at least half a dozen contenders. The cup awarded to the world's best sparkling wine, though, would have only one name engraved on it, over and over again: Champagne. It is the undisputed sparkling wine champion of the world. To date, nowhere else has a combination of soils, climate and grape variety been found to match that of Champagne (Chardonnay, Pinot Noir and Meunier grown on chalk in a climate as chilly as those grapes will put up with). Two hundred years of tradition help, too, as do the resources provided by sales of undeflatable buoyancy.

For the world, and in particular Britain, cannot get enough champagne. *The Daily Telegraph* ran a story on champagne rationing in 1989, not on 1 April but during the summer, its intent at least half serious. Exports to Britain, champagne's largest market outside France, have risen by 150 per cent in ten years, from 9.2 million bottles in 1979 to 22.8 million bottles in 1989. No wine was better suited to the Thatcher decade of economic growth and untempered ostentation, for champagne is the ultimate status symbol, the conspicuous consumer's automatic choice. Its success here also owes much to the fact that it is the most institutionalised of wines: no other is served so often at 'official', business or wedding receptions; no other is so strictly *de rigueur* at British tribal gatherings of the Henley/Ascot ilk. On most of these occasions its symbolic presence and cachet are primary, and its aroma and taste secondary – which is why champagne's roaring success is in some ways a sad one. It is loved more for what it stands for than for what it is.

Champagne is its own AOC, and is the only one in France

relieved of the obligation to use an *appellation* formula on its labels. There are, though, two other *appellations* in the region: Coteaux Champenois (still red, white and rosé wines; villages may be mentioned on labels, with Bouzy's red being the most frequently encountered) and Rosé des Riceys, a rosé from Les Riceys in the Aube sub-zone. Only the very best years cover the ribs of these wines with any flesh at all, and they are absurdly expensive.

Most champagne is Non-Vintage (often abbreviated to NV): a blend of wines from different years. The purpose of this blending is to maintain a consistent house style from year to year – in theory; in practice, the enormous demand for champagne in recent years has meant that some producers' brands (generally known as *marques* in the champagne context) have varied in quality from bottle to bottle to an unacceptable extent, sometimes tasting fine, long and deep, but on other occasions thin and green.

Non-Vintage Brut Champagne

Type *Dry sparkling wine*
Profile *Fine-beaded bubbles; fresh, yeasty or toasty aromas; crisp, deep, nuanced flavour, sometimes with green acidity; long, vinous finish*
Advice *Chill before serving. Ideal as an aperitif; also accompanies fine, sauced fish and poultry dishes well*

Vintage Champagne

Vintage Champagnes are produced in better years, much as Vintage Ports or Madeiras are, though the quality standard in the champagne case is more variable than it is with port or madeira. Indeed Vintage Champagne is often a disappointment to consumers, who expect it – on the basis of its price – to be invariably better than Non-Vintage, whereas its chief attraction is that it is more marked in character, carrying the stamp of its year in its flavours, often for better but sometimes for worse. It should also be aged for at least three times as long as Non-Vintage's statutory one year, and this helps the best examples attain a subtle and finely balanced flavour, full of creamy finesse. The worst examples suffer from champagne's customary vice of sharp-nosed tartness and imbalance, made all the more unforgivable by dashing the hopes that £17.99 had raised, and failing to do justice to the celebratory cause for which you opened the bottle. Buy only on your merchant's firm recommendation, and try to age any vintage under six years old for a further year or two. Very old vintages, moreover, may also disappoint, this time because the wine may have lost its crisp edge and will almost certainly have seen most of its carbon dioxide leave via the cork and set off into eternity. Some people love the honeyed, gentle richness of 15- or 20-year-old champagne – but some don't. Approach it, above all, with an open mind.

The other important information a label will give you concerns sweetness. Most champagne sold in Britain is Brut – dry, broadly and practically speaking, although the regulations permit up to 15 grams of sugar per litre, and if all of that was used to 'dose' a Vintage Champagne from a year in which the fruit ripened particularly fully, the result would taste decidedly soft and round. Extra Brut – without any sweetening – guarantees absolute dryness, but be forewarned about this style's mouthstripping acidity. To move away from a dry style, look for the confusing term Extra Dry (12 to 20 grams per litre of sugar), then Sec (17 to 35 grams per litre), Demi-Sec (up to 50 grams per litre) and finally Doux – by which time the sugar blurs all trace of champagne's nerve and finesse. A Crémant champagne is one that is half as fizzy as an ordinary NV. Blanc de Blancs signifies a champagne made only from Chardonnay grapes, usually very light and fine-featured; while Blanc de Noirs signifies a champagne made only from black grapes (the white juice is pressed from the black skins soon after picking and before fermentation, thereby avoiding the extraction of any colouring matter) giving a vigorously fruity result. Rosé champagne is usually made by blending a little red wine into a lot of white to achieve a suitably pretty result, although a few are also made by controlled maceration of a proportion of Pinot Noir (or Meunier) grape skins to bleed out their colour.

Sometimes reference is made on champagne labels to disgorgement (see page 154), either in the form of a disgorging date, or as *Récemment Dégorgé* or RD (recently disgorged). Most experts counsel that such wines, which will have aged for longer than average on their lees, should be drunk as soon as possible after disgorgement in order to enjoy fully the complexity and character brought to the wine by lees ageing, without running the risk of the champagne oxidising and tiring.

If you see mention on a label of the terms Grand Cru or Premier Cru, this indicates that the champagne in question has been blended from wines sourced from the most highly prized vineyards of the region, Grand being superior to Premier; village names are also occasionally seen.

Champagne codes

Every bottle of champagne will carry, on its label, a 'matriculation number', often in small print. That number will be preceded by two letters, which will tell you whether the producer is a commercial champagne house (NM: *négociant-manipulant*), a co-operative (CM: *coopérative-manipulante*) or a small grower-producer (RM: *récoltant-manipulant*). If the two letters are MA (*marque auxiliaire*), then all you know is that the name on the label is one chosen by, in most cases, the merchant or company selling you the wine: a classic 'buyer's own brand'. The wine will, in all probability, have been bought from one of the large, high-quality champagne co-operatives, or from a house specialising in this style of sale, such as Marne et Champagne. MA may also indicate a *sous-marque* used by one of the houses or co-operatives themselves. This variety of indications means that it is the least informative of the codes.

'Prestige' champagnes (*cuvées de prestige*), finally, are wines produced by the larger houses to crown their ranges. Well-known examples include Moët & Chandon's Dom Pérignon and Roederer's Cristal. No expense is spared in their production: the fruit comes from the best vineyards, is vinified with surgical scrupulousness, the finest vats only are selected and used in the blend, and the wines are aged fully before sale. They are packaged in an eye-catching and sometimes gimmicky way, and a dizzying price is asked for them.

The prices of all champagnes have risen swiftly over the last two years: it would seem that the large houses are, after all, attempting to impose rationing on the market by pricing out its least wealthy consumers. The producers themselves would reply that they have no option: without dampening demand somehow, their stocks will be depleted and quality will suffer. So prices are rising now, and will continue to rise, being further fuelled by the breakdown in the spring of 1990 of the 30-year-old 'contract' between grape growers and champagne makers. Supermarket and 'own-label' (or BOB – Buyer's Own Brand) champagnes are crossing the £10 frontier, while well-known *marques* stride on past £15. In some cases, this means poor value for money, for champagne is not, by virtue of its name or its taste, invariably three times as good as cava or twice as good as sparkling wines from the Loire or Australia, even if it is nearly always better than these wines. But value for money is not what purchasers, individual or institutional, necessarily look for when they take champagne off the shelf. They are buying an image, a symbol: potencies for which they are prepared to pay. Until other sparkling-wine producers can build an image for their wines to match champagne's, they will have to resign themselves to looking on ruefully as champagne prices inch still further away from their own.

The champagne method

The champagne method (or *méthode champenoise*, a description outlawed from 1994 within the EC on labels other than those of champagne – where it never appears anyway) begins with rapid and delicate pressing of the grapes. The grape juice (or must) is then settled and clarified before undergoing its first fermentation. Malolactic fermentation often, but not invariably, follows: the effect of this is to reduce and soften the total acidity of the wine. The wines are blended at this stage (this process is called *assemblage*).

Once blending is complete, the wines are bottled, each bottle receiving the addition of selected yeasts, around 24 grams of sugar, and fining matter (*liqueur de tirage*). Over the next five weeks, the yeasts ferment the sugar (*prise de mousse*), producing equal quantities of alcohol and carbon dioxide as they do so: the carbon dioxide provides the bubbles in champagne. The wine then matures on the lees produced by this secondary fermentation for at least a year, or for at least three years in the case of Vintage Champagne; responsible producers will exceed these minima. This stage is called *vieillissement sur lattes, lattes* being the strips of wood used to separate the bottles as they lie stacked on top of each other. The wines acquire complexity during this period. When it is over, the sediment has to be inched slowly down into the neck of the bottle. This is sometimes carried out manually by *remuage*, the daily twisting and slight shaking of upended bottles in wooden racks (*pupitres*), and sometimes carried out mechanically. The sediment is removed by disgorgement (*dégorgement*): the neck of the bottle is frozen, the plug of ice containing the sediment removed, and the wine topped up before the bottle is corked and wired. The topping up (*dosage*) is carried out using a solution of cane sugar and wine (*liqueur d'expédition*), the amount of sugar corresponding to the desired style.

Recommended producers

Pierre Arnould; Billecart-Salmon; Château de Boursault; Deutz; Fleury; Georges Gardet; Gosset; Alfred Gratien; Henriot; Jacquesson; Lanson; Bruno Paillard; Louis Roederer; Pierre Vaudon; Georges Vesselle.

Champagne vintages

1989 A good year, producing a large quantity of fine wines; there will certainly be Vintage Champagnes from this year.

1988 An early harvest, producing wines of medium quality; there are likely to be Vintage Champagnes from this year.

1987 A large harvest of dull wines.

1986 A moderately sized harvest of sound but softish wines.

1985 A good, ripe year. Drink 1985 Vintage Champagne from 1992.

1984 A poor year.

1983 A large harvest of good wines. Drink 1983 Vintage Champagnes from 1991.

1982 A very fine harvest of early maturing wines. 1982 Vintage Champagnes are drinking well at present.

1981 A modest year. Avoid 1981 Vintage Champagne except in cases of enthusiastic and reliable recommendation.

1980 A very poor year.

Specialist stockists

Ad Hoc Wine Warehouse; Les Amis du Vin; Bentalls of Kingston; Bibendum; D Byrne & Co; Cadwgan; The Champagne House; Champagne de Villages; Classic Wine Warehouses; Eaton Elliott; Alex Findlater; Peter Green; Gerard Harris; Heath Street Wine Co; Marks & Spencer; Mitchell & Son; Nickolls & Perks; Oddbins; Arthur Rackham; La Réserve; Selfridges; T & W Wines; Tanners; Weavers of Nottingham; Willoughbys; Wright Wine Co; Yorkshire Fine Wines.

JURA AND SAVOIE

These two small, easterly pockets of vine-growing, sited on a long, green stairway of sub-alpine pasture, produce some of the most distinctive of France's wines, from some of her least well-known grape varieties. Savoie is the larger of the two, its vines covering around 1500 ha, divided up among hundreds of often small, widely scattered sites. The Jura is slightly smaller at 1400 ha, but its production is much less than Savoie's, owing to its cultivation of lower-yielding varieties. Each region produces a complete portfolio of rosé, red, white, sparkling and speciality wines. We barely see them. Why not? Our merchants tell us that they are expensive, that they are hard to sell, that they sit on the shelf and we overlook them – and they are right. The wines of the Jura, in particular, are about as unfashionable as it is possible to be.

Fashion decrees full, flavoursome, oaky whites; the Jura's are pale and interesting, proving delicately – and intentionally – oxidised on closer inspection. Fashion decrees deep reds of rippling fruit and tongue-grabbing extract, with an unmistakable varietal stamp; the Jura's are so light as to be barely red at all, and they are supple and nutty in character. We need to make a determined effort to unstrap our blinkers and suspend our disbelief if we are to appreciate these wines but, be assured, it is worth it: they possess tastes and nuances that no other part of the world can provide. Eastern France may look like an Old Curiosity Shop at present, but one day fashions may change, Californians and Australians may hurry to Arbois to learn the techniques of controlled oxidative wine-making, and we may all wonder why we ignored such originality for so long.

Jura

The Jura has four basic AOCs: Arbois, Côtes du Jura, l'Etoile and Château-Chalon. Arbois and Côtes du Jura cover the main wine-making zones, and are applicable to all the Jura's styles of wine (see below); l'Etoile and Château-Chalon are single-village *appellations*, limited, respectively, to white wines only, and *vin jaune* only.

Vin jaune (yellow wine) is the Jura's most famous, and most misunderstood, wine. Because it ages under a film of yeast mould in an ullaged cask (the casks are full to start with, and gradually lose a third of their contents over a six-year period), most commentators describe *vin jaune* as being like fino sherry. It isn't. Fino's *flor* is a thick blanket, and protects the wine from oxidisation; *vin jaune*'s film of yeast is called a *voile* (veil) and is as thin and intermittent as this name suggests, resulting in a profoundly oxidised wine. If any sherry analogy were appropriate, it would be that of amontillado.

The key to *vin jaune*'s success lies in the fact that the Savagnin, a troublesome and meagrely yielding variety, responds well to oxidisation, giving a very supple, round, velvety, yet profoundly acid wine, full of leafy forest aromas and flavours. It ages well in bottle. The worst thing to do to it is to treat it like fino, chilling it and serving it as an aperitif: it will taste strange, and seem a waste of money. *Vin jaune* should barely be chilled at all – 14°C to 16°C is ideal; it should be opened well in advance and a glassful removed to let new oxygen in; and it should be served with rich, creamy food (cockerel cooked in cream and that first glass of *vin jaune* is the traditional partner). Only then will the justification for its panther-like acidity become apparent. It is never good value for money, but with 20 hl/ha yields and six years in the making, it has to cost £15 and upwards a bottle. The *vin jaune* of the clifftop village of Château-Chalon is considered the finest and the supplest, while that of Arbois is slightly yellower and fuller.

Côtes du Jura *vin jaune* varies according to the producer. *Vin jaune* is sold in 62cl *clavelin* bottles (or ordinary half-bottles), 62cl being all that is left of a litre of new Savagnin wine after it has been through the six year ageing period. Varietal Savagnin wines are often simply would-be *vins jaunes* on which the veil of yeast never formed, aged in cask for less than six years.

Chardonnay is the other major white grape variety grown in the Jura: it can be vinified in typical Jura fashion and aged in wood (sometimes old *vin jaune* casks) to give a nutty, leafy style; or it can be vinified and stored in stainless steel to give a fruitier, more obviously varietal wine.

The Jura's red wines are based on three grape varieties, sometimes mixed, but more often vinified and sold as varietals. The first of these is the Poulsard, a variety giving beautifully light, strawberry-red wine, as pretty and delicate as alpine flowers. The commune of Pupillin has particularly favoured slopes for Poulsard, and it may add its own name to the Arbois AOC on the strength of these (though other varieties are also permitted). The Pinot Noir gives sound, cleanly fruity wines, sometimes with a vein of Santenay-like excitement. The Trousseau (identical to Portugal's Bastardo) gives the deepest, most structured red wines of the Jura, with attractive scents and flavours of cherries, plums and spice.

The region also produces some good, Chardonnay-based sparkling wines, as well as one of France's last remaining **vins de paille**. This means, literally, 'straw wine' – wine made from grapes laid out on straw mats to dry and become raisin-like. Nowadays the grapes are dried in wicker trays rather than on mats, but the principle is much the same: they taste fresh, light, not raisiny at all, about as sweet as a dessert apple.

Arbois Poulsard

Type *Light red wine*
Profile *Warmly and brightly scented, with teasing, nutty aromas; supple, peppery, refreshing flavours suggesting strawberries or redcurrants*
Advice *Chill lightly; serve with river fish, mushroom dishes, pork, lightly smoked foods*

Recommended producers
Château d'Arlay; Fruitière Vinicole d'Arbois; Henri Maire; Rolet Frères; Tissot Frères.

Stockists
Ad Hoc; Askham Wines; Belfast Wine Co; Bentalls; Croque-en-Bouche; Eaton Elliot; Gerard Harris; Nicholas; Arthur Rackhams; Frank Stainton; Tanners; Willoughbys; The Wine Society; Winecellars.

Savoie

Savoie has an *appellation* structure of comparative simplicity, modified by a range of *crus* and possible grape varieties of baffling complexity. The basic *appellation* for all wines is AOC Vin de Savoie, with Jacquère, Altesse (known locally as Roussette), Chasselas, Chardonnay and Roussanne used for whites, while Gamay, Pinot Noir and Mondeuse are used for rosés and reds. There are no fewer than 16 *crus*, though two (Sainte Marie d'Alloix and Charpignat) have no vineyards left, and another three or four produce little wine. The most important are Apremont and Abymes (Jacquère-based whites), Chautagne (Gamay-based reds) and Arbin (Mondeuse-based reds). The *cru* of Ayze is for sparkling wines only, based on the Gringet, while a speciality of the *cru* of Chignin is Chignin-Bergeron, a white based on the Roussanne grape variety (here called the Bergeron). Roussette (Altesse) also has an AOC of its own, covering a smaller area than the Vin de Savoie AOC, and with four different *crus*: Frangy, Monterminod, Marestel and Monthoux. (Chardonnay is also permitted in the Roussette de Savoie blend, but rarely used.) Finally comes Crépy (Chasselas-based whites, though the standard is not as high as in Vin de Savoie-Ripaille or -Marin) and Seyssel (fine, Roussette-based whites and good Molette-based sparkling Seyssel Mousseux).

Hidden behind all that fretwork of wine law are around four tastes. The Jacquère (Apremont and Abymes furnish the best examples) gives delicate, racy wines with hedgerow scents and lively, mineral flavours; the best Chasselas (Ripaille) is not dissimilar, though the suggestions are more of fresh white almonds and creamy, unsalted butter than anything mineral. The Roussette, by contrast, is altogether more bosomy, with an enticing summer-fruit lushness hinting at juicy pears or quince jelly, but with fresh and lively supporting acidity. The Mousseux wines of Savoie and Seyssel are better than the Jura's, and can rival lesser champagnes.

The Gamay proves surprisingly expansive in the mountain air, ripening well to provide pungent, tasty wines, with those from Chautagne, in particular, having the delicious roasted edge that this variety exhibits when it is enjoying itself. Pinot Noir is generally balanced, sound and unambitious, leaving the firework display to the Mondeuse, an unusual grape variety whose only other incarnation is as Refosco in Italy. Savoie's Mondeuse is a deep peony purple, with striking fresh-meat aromas and a richly textured, slightly ferrous flavour: an astonishingly deep and powerful wine to come from vineyards from which Mont Blanc can be seen.

Vin de Savoie-Abymes

Type *Light white wine*
Profile *Slightly* perlant; *aromas of hawthorn blossom; freshly flavoured, supple and delicate, but with a nettley edge*
Advice *Drink as soon as possible; makes a fine summer aperitif; good with trout*

Recommended producers

Pierre Boniface; Cave Coopérative de Chautagne; Jean Perrier et Fils; André et Michel Quenard; Varichon et Clerc; Le Vigneron Savoyard.

Stockists

Bentalls of Kingston; Eaton Elliot; Nicolas; Thos Peatling; Tanners.

Bugey

The Bugey region, west of Savoie, enjoys VDQS status for a range
of wines similar to those of Savoie, using the same grape varieties
with the addition of small plantings of Aligoté and Poulsard.
There are three *crus*: Manicle, Cerdon and Montagnieu. Bugey's
best are its sparkling wines and its Chardonnays, though you will
need to visit Bugey (the home of Brillat-Savarin) to find them.

LANGUEDOC-ROUSSILLON

Languedoc-Roussillon (more familiarly known as the Midi) is the
large, flat coastal stretch of southern France that curves from
Provence in the east round to the Spanish border in the south-
west. Montpellier, Béziers, Narbonne and Perpignan are the cities
of the plain, home to wine traders since Roman times;
Carcassonne commands the high ground. In this vast green
amphitheatre facing the Golfe du Lion, millions of heavy-fruiting
vines pump wine out of the dusty earth. Since the railway reached
Perpignan in the nineteenth century, Languedoc-Roussillon has
been France's table wine factory, and its port of Sète the reception
area for the heavier North African wines used to 'correct' the
overcropped and therefore light Midi products. The factory still
stands, the vines still fruit heavily, but fewer people want ordinary
table wine these days.

Consumers want quality wine, and there is no reason why
Languedoc-Roussillon should not answer this desire. Table wine
production came about because there was a huge and eager
market, and Languedoc-Roussillon's climate meant it could supply
that market reliably, which Burgundy or Orléans could not.
Adaptability is a French virtue, though, and the transition to
quality wine production is now well underway, aided by heavy
government investment. Hotter areas than this produce fine wine
in other continents, and there can be little doubt that, within a
decade, Languedoc-Roussillon will be able to offer us a mixed case
of fine wines.

The most important red-wine *appellations* at present are
Corbières, Minervois and Côtes du Roussillon. In each case,
quality varies hugely depending on the aspirations of the
producer and those of the purchasing merchant: light, Carignan-
based reds at £1.99 or £2.29 provide simple party wines, whereas

for £3.49 the same *appellation* will bring you a richly flavoured Syrah- or Mourvèdre-based wine, full of herby, tarry scents and stony fruit. The quality of the best examples from these *appellations* is now very good indeed, and paying a little extra is often well worthwhile: it buys you the finest grape varieties and the most up-to-date and ambitious wine-making (carbonic maceration, or variants on this technique, is increasingly used to provide wines of exciting fruitiness, while oak-ageing, if employed judiciously, brings complexity). In the case of Côtes du Roussillon, there is a superior Côtes du Roussillon-Villages *appellation*, with two *crus*, Caramany and Latour de France, each permitted mention of their names on labels; while the AOC of Collioure, almost on the Spanish border, provides reds of inspiring depth for Roussillon's other wine-makers to try to match. Another potentially good red-wine AOC is Fitou, composed of two enclaves within Corbières. The large Coteaux du Languedoc AOC, with its fourteen *crus* (Faugères and Saint-Chinian have recently been grafted in among these), produces red wines often lighter in style, but no less intense, than those of Roussillon or Corbières, and the same is true of VDQS Costières du Gard. Some singingly deep, fruity wines can be found among the vins de pays, where experiment with Cabernet Sauvignon and other 'noble' varieties is proving startlingly successful, the regional denomination being Vins de Pays d'Oc and the two largest departmental denominations being those of Vin de Pays de l'Aude and Vin de Pays de l'Hérault. There are a large number of zonal denominations, of which perhaps the most widely exported are the reliable Vins de Pays des Sables du Golfe du Lion, thanks to the organic endeavours of Listel.

Côtes du Roussillon

Type *Medium- to full-bodied red wine*
Profile *Deep, perfumed, smoothly flavoured and mouthfilling, with suggestions of raspberries, plums and cinnamon, sometimes oaked to toastiness*
Advice *Serve with stewed meats and stewed vegetables*

Recommended producers

Domaine Anthea (Vins de Pays d'Oc); Domaine de Baillaury (Collioure); Cuvée des Terrasses, Domergue (Minervois); Château de Gourgazaud (Minervois); Cave Coopérative des Coteaux du Haut Minervois; Château du Jau (Côtes du Roussillon); Château de Lastours (Corbières); Domaine de Lenthéric (Vins de Pays de l'Hérault); Listel (Vins de Pays des Sables du Golfe du Lion); Château de Luc (Corbières); Domaine Maris (Minervois); Vignerons de Maury (Côtes du Roussillon-Villages); Les Producteurs de Mont Tauch (Corbières and Fitou); Château de Paraza (Minervois); Château de la Rectorie (Côtes du Roussillon); Château Saint-Auriol (Corbières); Domaine Sainte-Eulalie (Minervois); Domaine Sarda-Malet (Côtes du Roussillon); Domaine de Rousseau (Minervois).

The white and rosé wines of Languedoc-Roussillon are less successful than the reds at this stage in the region's development. The technology needed to produce whites full of fruit and aromatic interest in a hot climate has not yet reached New World standards (the day may not be far off, though: last year saw the beginnings of Australian wine investment in Languedoc-Roussillon, with Hardy's purchase of the 68-ha La Baume domain near Béziers); some of the varieties planted lack potential (Bourboulenc, Clairette and Grenache Blanc are all low on both acidity and aroma); and much of the energy and effort of producers is channelled into the production of Vins Doux Naturels (VDNs): sweet, fortified wines mainly based on the Muscat family of varieties. There are four AOCs for Muscat VDNs (Muscat de Saint-Jean-de-Minervois, de Frontignan, de Mireval and de Lunel), and a further four AOCs for mixed-variety VDNs, including red grapes (Rivesaltes, Maury, Banyuls and Côtes d'Agly). Grand Roussillon is a little-used umbrella VDN *appellation*. In flavour, they vary from deliciously perfumed, honey-sweet and gardenia-rich (the Muscats of Frontignan or Lunel) to dense, mocha-edged, almost porty styles (Banyuls). *Rancio* signifies a nutty, oxidised variant.

Finally, lodged high in the Aude valley, well away from the decadent heat of the plain, is Limoux, home of one of France's oldest sparkling wines, Blanquette de Limoux. This sometimes impressive champagne-method sparkling wine is based on Mauzac, with up to 30 per cent Chenin Blanc and Chardonnay to sharpen its edge and freshen its aroma. Experts on this area, such as Tony Laithwaite and his team of Flying Winemakers, feel that Limoux may, in time, prove one of the Midi's finest still white-wine sites, too.

Recommended producers

Domaine Cazes (Muscat de Rivesaltes); Château de Jeu (Muscat de Rivesaltes); Listel (Vin du Pays des Sables du Golfe du Lion); Domaine du Mas Blanc (Banyuls); Château de la Peyrade (Muscat de Frontignan); Domaine Sigé (Muscat de St-Jean de Minervois); Domaine du Valcros (Banyuls); Société de Producteurs de Blanquette de Limoux (Blanquette de Limoux); Château de Stony (Muscat de Frontignan); Les Vignerons de Rivesaltes (Côtes du Rousillon Blanc).

Languedoc-Roussillon vintages

Buy the youngest available vintage and drink within a year. Any red wine costing over £4 may be cellared for up to five years following its harvest date.

Stockists

Ad Hoc Wine Warehouse; Adnams; Asda; Bentalls of Kingston; Bordeaux Direct; D Byrne & Co; The Celtic Vintner; Eldridge Pope; Gerard Harris; Haughton Fine Wines; Ian G Howe; Majestic Wine Warehouses; Nicolas; Oddbins; Ravensbourne; Sunday Times Wine Club; Victoria Wine; La Vigneronne; Vinceremos; Whiclar & Gordon; Willoughbys; The Wine Society; Wizard Wine Warehouses..

LOIRE VALLEY

The River Loire and its family of tributaries reach deep into France. Millennia have seen these watercourses create valley after valley, hill after hill, slope after slope: perfect vineland. Grapes share the lower half of the valley, the Garden of France, with vegetables, cereals and orchard fruits; they share the upper half, the Centre, with sheep. The lower half has schistous and tufa-based soils, and a largely temperate climate; the upper half is chalky limestone, with a continental climate of harsh winters and torrid, stormy summers. Strangely enough, though, the wines of each end resemble each other more than they do the wines of the middle portion: the middle portion has a lovely *arrière-saison*, a gilded Indian summer declining slowly into a gentle autumn. This mellow climate makes the production of sweet white wines and lengthily fermented, deeply coloured red wines possible, whereas the mouth of the Loire and the upper Loire are both famous for nervily dry, acid whites.

The very first wines of the Loire, in fact, fit none of the descriptions above. The lightly fruity Vins de Pays de l'Ardèche have a southern tang, the source of the Loire being in that *département*. Côtes du Forez, Côtes d'Auvergne, Côte Roannaise, Saint-Pourçain and Châteaumeillant: the Loire gradually leaves the south via a chain of widely scattered VDQS wines, chiefly distinguished by their high-toned and increasingly impressive Gamays.

Once past Nevers, the Loire begins to make what looks on the map like a slow left turn towards Orléans and Blois. As the river moots this change in its directional loyalties, it is gliding between the towns of Sancerre and Pouilly-sur-Loire. For the first time along its course, vines swarm over the hillsides: most of them are Sauvignon Blanc (for Sancerre, Pouilly-Fumé and, a little further west, Menetou-Salon, Quincy and Reuilly), though Pinot Noir (Sancerre Rouge and Rosé, Menetou-Salon and Reuilly Rouge) and Chasselas (Pouilly-sur-Loire) are also grown. It is the Sauvignon Blanc wines that are the most memorable and successful, with powerful aromas of crushed leaves and spring rain, and piercingly intense, dry flavours. Their only drawback is one more usual in American or Australian wines: a glass delights, but a bottle fatigues. Glasses of the red or rosé may not even delight, especially when their price is taken into account: these, like the Chasselas wines of Pouilly-sur-Loire, are ways for the locals to give themselves a rest from the exhausting pleasures of Sauvignon; we have better to choose from.

The red and white wines of Côtes de Gien (or Coteaux du Giennois), north of Sancerre and Pouilly, are light, easy and unexceptional.

Sancerre

Type *Very dry white wine*
Profile *Pungently fresh, grassy, sometimes flinty aromas; dry, searching, bony flavours, with a nettle-sharp edge*
Advice *Chill well; drink with fish or summer salads; best on day of opening*

Recommended producers

Domaine de Chatenoy (Menetou-Salon); Didier Dagueneau (Pouilly-Fumé); Masson-Blondelet (Pouilly-Fumé); Riffault (Sancerre); Jean-Max Roger (Sancerre); Guy Saget (Pouilly-Fumé and Sancerre); Vacheron (Sancerre).

The Vins de l'Orléanais, from vineyards along the river's turn, provide slight reds, whites and rosés of barely merited VDQS status, though Orléans itself, perhaps not coincidentally, produces France's best wine vinegar. Only downstream of Blois do vineyards again begin to crowd the banks of the Loire, for the Touraine group of *appellations* (Touraine, Touraine + grape variety, Touraine-Amboise, Touraine-Azay-le-Rideau, Touraine-Mesland and Touraine Mousseux). The best of these are slenderly characterful Sauvignon Blancs, and inexpensive, tasty Gamays. North of Touraine, on the Loire's masculine tributary the Loir, little Jasnières produces a tiny quantity of fine, dry Chenin Blanc; Coteaux du Vendômois and Coteaux du Loir to either side of it are less distinguished. Easterly Cheverny and Valençay can, producers willing, turn out interesting red and white wines from the Loire's usual varieties, plus one or two less usual ones such as the white Romorantin and Arbois.

The most stately and enduring wines of the Loire come from its warm, central stretch, between Tours and Angers. Here the Cabernet Franc ripens without difficulty to give glinting, ox-blood-red wines whose smell and taste are as fresh and earthy as a mixed-wood copse after a summer shower has drenched it. Seven *appellations* sanction this magic: Saint-Nicolas-de-Bourgueil, Bourgueil, Chinon, Saumur-Champigny, Saumur Rouge, Anjou-Villages and Anjou Rouge. Chinon and Bourgueil lead the pack, but the two Anjou *appellations* can provide wines as good for considerably less. The Gamay also appears as an engaging varietal in Anjou, though the wines are in every way less memorable than those based on Cabernet Franc.

Chinon

Type *Medium-bodied red wine*
Profile *Characteristic and forthcoming aromas of wet wood and damp leaves; brightly flavoured, fruity tastes, suggesting raspberries*
Advice *Serve cool (17°C max.); good with meat sautés, main-course salads, hot cheese dishes, and for refreshing summer drinking without food*

Recommended producers

Bouvet (Saumur-Champigny); Couly-Dutheil (Chinon); Pierre-Jacques Druet (Chinon and Bourgueil); Joël Gigou (Jasnières); Charles Joguet (Chinon); Lamé-Delille-Boucard (Bourgueil); Langlois-Château (Saumur Rouge, especially the Vieille Vignes); Logis de la Giraudière (Anjou); Yves Loiseau (Chinon); Domaine de Mongilet (Anjou-Villages); Domaine Richou (Anjou-Villages); François Roussier (Anjou).

For white wines, the Loire's temperamental genius, Chenin Blanc, stirs itself at this point on the river's journey. Depending on the site and the season, this late-ripening grape can produce wine in four keys. Pitched highest are the fine but austere and flint-hearted dry wines of Savennières and its two AOC *crus*, Coulée de

Serrant and La Roche aux Moines: these need a decade before they reward rather than punish the drinker. Most splendid and major are the magnificently keen-edged dessert wines of Quarts de Chaume, Bonnezeaux, Coteaux du Layon, Coteaux de l'Aubance, Montlouis, Anjou and Vouvray (in the case of the last five, look for the words *moelleux* or *doux* on the label or neck-label): these are capable of ageing to a lusciously yellow and peppery old age, and of enchanting and surprising at any time in their lives. Lively, grape-and-honey, apple-and-nut aperitif wines (any of the aforementioned in *demi-sec* incarnations); or edgy, dry wines, at best imposing and structured, at worst ruthlessly mean and acid (the same group in *sec* guise, plus Saumur Blanc), provide the two final modulations in the Chenin Blanc repertoire. In sunny years the production of the sweeter styles rises; after cloudy summers, more wines in the drier style, and more of the often fine Crémant de Loire and less consistently good Saumur Mousseux, are produced.

Vouvray Demi-Sec

Type *Medium-dry white wine*
Profile *Nutty, honeyed, waxy, and unpredictable aromas; very lively flavour, with water-fresh acidity making the wine seem drier than expected, and the sweetness seem that of a fresh grape or peach*
Advice *The perfect summer aperitif, and the liquid equivalent of a stroll in the orchard*

Recommended producers

Domaine des Baumard (Quarts de Chaume); Château de Belle Rive (Quarts de Chaume); Marc Brédif (Vouvray); Bouvet (Saumur Mousseux); Clos de Papillon (Savennières); Château des Fesles (Bonnezeaux); A Foreau (Vouvray); Gratien & Meyer (Crémant de Loire); Gaston Huet (Vouvray); Langlois-Château (Crémant de Loire); Château Moncontour (Vouvray); Dominique Moyer (Montlouis); Prince Poniatowski (Vouvray); Moulin Touchais (Anjou).

This region is also the main source of the Loire's rosé wines. Rosé d'Anjou is usually slightly sweet and carelessly made, often with what seems like a bucketful of sulphur thrown in before bottling. Slightly better are the drier rosé Cabernets of Anjou and Saumur, based on Franc and some Sauvignon, though their vice is to taste rather chilly and charmless unless the wine-maker has struggled to net all the fruit. Rosé de Loire is also dry.

To the south of this central portion of the Loire lie two satellite vineyard areas: the Vins du Thouarsais and the Vins du Haut-Poitou, both VDQS, both producing red, white and rosé wines, and Poitou some sparkling for good measure. Haut-Poitou is much the more important of the two denominations, and its varietally labelled wines are usually sound and occasionally exciting.

West of Angers lies Coteaux d'Ancenis, Muscadet and the sea. The VDQS wines of Coteaux d'Ancenis are mainly light, Gamay reds; Pinot Gris (labelled Malvoisie) is used for some of the whites, and these, interestingly, are made semi-sweet on occasion, though they are little seen in Britain. Muscadet, by contrast, is much seen, perhaps too much seen: why this often tart, bony and headache-inducing wine should enjoy the popularity it does in Britain (we drink half of all Muscadet's exports) is perplexing. Its tartness and boniness are the legacy of its cloud-ridden maritime climate and green-skinned grape variety, the Melon de Bourgogne; our headaches are the legacy of high sulphur levels and indifferent, industrial wine-making.

Three *appellations* exist: Muscadet, Muscadet des Coteaux de la Loire and Muscadet de Sèvre-et-Maine. Between 80 and 90 per cent of all Muscadet is sold under the third of these, including the top ten per cent: domain-bottled wines from good, small-scale producers. These will be *sur lie* or *tiré sur lie*: bottled straight off their fermentation lees, giving the wines an enchanting yeasty tang that makes them the wine-maker's equivalent of bread straight from the baker's oven. When drunk in their first youth, with a plateful of oysters or a bowlful of mussels, they can quicken the appetite and the senses to a remarkable degree: keen wines at keen prices. More's the pity that so many are so distant from this simple ideal.

Muscadet de Sèvre-et-Maine sur lie

Type *Light, sharp white wine*
Profile *Pale, often* perlant, *with fresh, yeasty aromas and a brisk, lemony flavour*
Advice *Drink as soon as possible and avoid old vintages; chill well. Perfect with seafood or as a bracing aperitif*

Gros Plant du Pays Nantais is usually even more challengingly acid than Muscadet is: recommended only for fish farmers with soundly enamelled teeth and robust, cream-lined digestive systems. The torrid summer of 1989, however, has made Gros Plant resemble Muscadet, and Muscadet resemble old-style Chablis, both developments being welcome.

The regional Vin de Pays denomination is that of the Jardin de la France, but as the Loire is already well-supplied with AOCs and VDQSs, the wines that sail into the world under this flag are rarely exciting or distinguished. The exceptions to this generalisation are the Chardonnay varietals, which in some cases show promise. There are thirteen departmental denominations and five zonal denominations; the departmental denominations (especially those of Loire-Atlantique, Maine-et-Loire and Indre-et-Loire) are those most likely to be seen in Britain.

Recommended producers

Donatien Bahuaud; Guy Bossard; Château de Chasseloir; Chéreau-Carré; Jacques Guindon (also Coteaux d'Ancenis); Louis Métaireau; Sauvion.

Loire Valley: vintages

1989 A splendidly sunny year, producing very fine red wines and Chenin-based whites. Sancerre and Pouilly Fumé are untypical, being less sharply vegetal and more richly fruity than usual; Muscadet is very good. It was a distinguished year for sweet, botrytis-affected wines, which have at least 50 years of life ahead of them.

1988 A very good year throughout the Loire, producing enjoyably typical wines in every *appellation*, including fine sweet wines.

1987 A poor-to-average year producing generally light wines, though there are pockets of excellence. Sancerre and Pouilly-Fumé are good, but drink up.

1986 A very good year for Sancerre and Pouilly-Fumé, though they should be dispatched as soon as possible now. Red wines are good, and are showing well at present.

1985 A very fine year for red wines, and a good year for sweet and dry Chenin whites. All other wines should now have been drunk.

1984 White wine from the best Chenin *appellations* will be worth trying, but avoid others.

1983 A fine Chenin Blanc vintage: the best dry whites are still showing well, and the sweet wines will continue to improve.

1982 Some good Chenin wines.

Earlier vintages Only sweet whites based on the Chenin Blanc, and the very finest dry Savennières, will be worth trying; they may prove exceptionally rewarding.

Stockists

Adnams; Bentalls; Bibendum; G E Bromley; Burlington; Anthony Byrne; D Byrne; Cadwgan; Croque-en-Bouche; Eaton Elliot; Eldridge Pope; Grape Ideas; Peter Green; Haynes Hanson & Clark; Heath Street; High Breck Vintners; J E Hogg; Holland Park; Hopton; Ian G Howe; Victor Hugo; Lay & Wheeler; Lorne House; Majestic; The Nobody Inn; Old Street; Thos Peatling; Christopher Piper; Raeburn; Sapsford; La Vigneronne; Vineyards Wine; Whitesides; Wines from Paris; Wines of Interest; Wright Wines Co; Yapp Brothers; Yorkshire Fine Wines.

PROVENCE AND CORSICA

Fifteen million years ago, Corsica was part of Provence: it broke away in the Miocene epoch and has been inching southwards, like a mountainous battleship, ever since. The two regions are dissimilar in almost every way today, save in respect of shared landscapes and a community of wines. Strength from the sun was the old ideal for both; flavoury authenticity from well-husbanded local varieties are the new watchwords. Provence, admittedly, has made more progress than Corsica so far, as a result of the wealth that its climate, beauty and non-insularity have attracted. In both cases, though, red wines offer the most potential; in both cases the best of these are singing with the herby, dusty, heat-drawn scents of the beautiful hillside wilderness known as *garrigue* in Provence and *maquis* in Corsica.

Provence

Most Provençal wines are not red in colour, though, but rosé: half the region's entire production is made in this way, to be consumed locally at restaurant tables set on red rocks overlooking a deep blue sea. Go to Provence and it is hard not to enjoy those rosés; bring them back to Britain and they'll seem square-shouldered, frumpy, dull as a wet bank holiday. Why this should be so is one of wine's great imponderables. The best have attractive leafy, nutty qualities, sustained fruit, and vinosity to balance their alcohol levels, which are challengingly high – thanks to the sun's generosity. Finding the best is serendipitous, because much depends on freshness: if you notice a rosé from Provence at your merchant that wasn't there last week, and if it has last year's date on the bottle, and if the weather's good, try it. Not the least of the pleasures of Provençal rosé is its colour, pitched between the faintest burnished salmon and the rose-grower's blush or soft pink; the Loire's candyfloss colours seem lurid by comparison.

Rosés are produced in all Provence's *appellations*: the large Côtes de Provence zone and its neighbouring *appellation* Coteaux d'Aix-en-Provence (which includes the sub-zone Coteaux d'Aix-en-Provence-les-Baux), as well as in the smaller and pricier *appellations* of Bandol, Cassis, Palette and Bellet. Bellet's coppery, walnut-scented rosés are perhaps the best of all, but at £7 or £8 a bottle they are hardly good value.

Provence's white wines are generally based on the Ugni Blanc, giving, here, a soft and innocuous result, a little slip of a wine. Good wine-makers manage to save some melony fruit; less talented ones produce solutions of alcohol in plant water. The best come from those smaller, pricier *appellations* again, where the Ugni Blanc is joined by more aromatic varieties like the Marsanne and the Vermentino, and even by some Sauvignon Blanc in Cassis.

Provence's finest wines are unquestionably its reds, especially those of Bandol. Grenache, Cinsault, Carignan and Syrah are all planted, but it's the Mourvèdre that most good producers favour, thanks to its ability to produce splendidly deep, leathery wines that echo the careless grandeur of the landscape. Those of Coteaux d'Aix-en-Provence and Coteaux-d'Aix-en-Provence-les-Baux can be nearly as good, especially the latter: Grenache dominates the blend of varieties to give fruitier wines than in Bandol, but the fruit is dusty, earthy and memorable. The reds of Côtes de Provence are generally lighter, at best fragrant with scents of wild thyme and rosemary and coloured with plummy fruit. Carbonic maceration is used to impressive effect for many of the reds of Provence, bringing out the fruitiness and holding unnecessary tannin at bay. Organic wine production is very well established here; the warm, dry climate makes it comparatively easy to avoid the use of anti-rot sprays and other chemical treatments, while the *douceur* of a Provençal existence appeals to the single-minded urban refugees common amongst those who adopt organic wine-growing.

This region, too, is one of France's most exciting sites outside Bordeaux for Cabernet Sauvignon, sold as a varietal under one of the vins de pays denominations, such as that of Mont Caume, as well as being used in more or less discreet proportions in the AOCs of the region (30 per cent in Côtes de Provence, for example, and up to 60 per cent in Coteaux d'Aix-en-Provence and les Baux).

Coteaux Varois is a VDQS on the rise: this denomination is likely to provide good value in the near future.

Provence has an obscure classification system. In 1953, just 23 domains in the Côtes de Provence area were bottling and marketing their own wines, and they won the right to describe themselves as crus classés. No one else has been admitted to the club subsequently, and six of the founder members have since disappeared. If you see a Côtes de Provence labelled *cru classé*, therefore, all it promises is a 37-year history of domain-bottling.

Bandol Rouge

Type *Deep red wine*
Profile *Dark in colour, with muted but appealing aromas of leather and mint; a rich, chewy texture marked by ripe tannins; and complex flavours suggesting prunes or coffee*
Advice *Good with game and roast meats; the best examples may be cellared for up to seven years from the year of harvest*

Recommended producers

Château de Crémat (Bellet); Domaine du Jas d'Esclans (Côtes de Provence); Mas de la Rouvière (Bandol); Moulin des Costes (Bandol); Château de Pampelonne (Côtes de Provence); Château Pigoudet (Coteaux d'Aix-en-Provence); Château de Pibarnon (Bandol); Domaine Richeaume (Côtes de Provence); Château Simone (Palette); Terres Blanches (Coteaux d'Aix-en-Provence-les-Baux); Domaine Tempier (Bandol); Domaine de Trévallon (Coteaux d'Aix-en-Provence-les-Baux); Domaine de Vallongue (Coteaux d'Aix-en-Provence-les-Baux); Château Vannières (Bandol); Château Vignelaure (Coteaux d'Aix-en-Provence).

Stockists

Adnams; D Byrne & Co; Bordeaux Direct; Croque-en-Bouche; Drinksmart; Gauntleys of Nottingham; Peter Green; Gerard Harris; Haughton Fine Wines; Ian G Howe; Marks & Spencer; Christopher Piper Wines; Arthur Rackhams; Safeway; Sebastopol Wines; Selfridges; Smedley Vintners; Tanners; Vessel du Vin; La Vigneronne; Villeneuve WInes; Vinceremos; Vintage Roots; Windrush Wines; Yapp Brothers.

Corsica

Corsican wine production underwent a deceptive renaissance in the 1960s and 1970s, when Carignan plantings there rocketed as 17,000 French colonists returning from Algeria tried to carry on the bulk-wine production that had been their livelihood up until then.

But the market for wine sold by alcohol content no longer existed, and a massive uprooting programme followed as swiftly as the new vineyards had appeared. Nowadays the native Corsican varieties Sciacarello and Nielluccio are promoted and prized, though Grenache, Cinsault, Mourvèdre, Syrah and the Italian Barbarossa are also permitted. Carignan is held down to a 20 per cent maximum in all Corsica's AOC wines. The results are as yet rarely distinguished, but their mid-weight, tangy fruit – with individualists liquefying in exotic hints of thyme, coffee and coriander – promise well for the future.

The Vermentino-based whites, when carefully made, can have an attractive Italianate style, with soothing aromas and flavours recalling fennel or aniseed. The basic *appellation* is that of Vin de Corse; -Figari, -Sarténe, -Porto-Vecchio, -Coteaux du Cap-Corse and -Calvi may be appended as *crus* where appropriate. The vins de pays denomination, Ile de Beauté, is so pretty that it arouses unrealistically high expectations for the wines, most of which are simple and southern. As in Provence, though, single-variety examples using France's finest grapes (enterprising Corsicans are even having a go at Pinot Noir) can be worthwhile.

As far as vintages are concerned, buy the youngest available vintage and drink as soon as possible. Any red wine costing over £4 may be cellared for up to five years after its date of harvest.

Recommended producers

Domaine de Cantone; Domaine Peraldi (Comte de Poix); Domaine de Torraccia; UVAL.

Stockists

Le Nez Rouge; Nicholas; Vessel du Vin; Willoughbys; The Wine Society; Yapp Brothers.

THE RHÔNE VALLEY

Northern Rhône

For the geographer, the first vineyards of the Côtes du Rhône are those of Switzerland's Valais, the region which acts as godparent to France's second greatest wine river as it leaves its glacial birthplace 1800m up in the Swiss Alps; Savoie's Seyssel is the first French wine to be grown on the Rhône's banks. But the wine-lover's Rhône begins south of Vienne, with a jumble of rocky terraces on the river's right bank. These terraces collectively form

Côte Rôtie, the 'roasted slope', and they get your merchant's Rhône zone off to a rousing start.

In fact, as they're among the most expensive of the Rhône's (and France's) wines, they'll probably be stationed several shelves higher than the rest, indicating their relative superiority in feet to fall should you dislodge a bottle clumsily. Syrah, with up to 20 per cent of the white variety, Viognier, gives one of its most elegant performances at Côte Rôtie, more currants and cinnamon than tar, while its makers claim a scent of violets for it. Despite its relative lightness, it still needs at least seven years' cellar time to show at its best. The Côte is divided into two parts, Côte Brune and Côte Blonde, and some leading growers produce separate *cuvées* from each (the *blonde* is thought to be lighter and faster-maturing than the *brune*). The *appellation* area has recently been extended and, as has happened in Chablis, this may lead to a loss of *appellation* character.

South from Côte Rôtie, still on the right bank, comes Saint-Joseph, a beanpole of an *appellation* producing some of the northern Rhône's most accessible and freshly fruity Syrahs. And at Condrieu, between the two, the orchidaceous world of white Rhône wines dawns with Château Grillet and Condrieu itself, two small vineyard zones planted with low-cropping, perfumed Viognier. This variety, yielding rich wines of floral grace and hauntingly peachy fruit, is the wine buff's wine *par excellence*: obscure, expensive and addictive.

By the time Tain l'Hermitage is reached, vines have crossed to the left bank, as well as continuing on the right; indeed the Rhône's second most famous – and most distinguished – *appellation*, Hermitage, is purely left-bank, soaking up every last ray of the evening sun to bring the Syrah to a thick-skinned, cricket-ball-like maturity, each grape packed with acids, tannins and sugars. Hermitage is a small *appellation*; its wines are now shockingly expensive (not so ten years ago); they need long ageing, and even a decade of patience is greeted by a dragon of a wine, roaring with fiery fruit. Crozes-Hermitage, from the lower slopes of the famous hill of Hermitage and others nearby, might be expected to offer a little less of the same for considerably less money, and the best do; the *appellation* is variable, though, and there are some green, stalky Crozes hiding like stick insects among pungent, curranty examples of the real thing.

White Hermitage and Crozes are as shy and retiring as the red versions are extrovert: based on Roussanne and Marsanne, these broad-beamed, delicately limey and indelicately pricey wines are for the well-heeled enthusiast, who gives them the time they need to open up their big, waxy blossoms. White Saint-Joseph is similar but simpler, while still Saint-Péray tends to be flat, fat and dull. Sparkling Saint-Péray is the same with bubbles.

This stretch of the northern Rhône sees the first of the ordinary Côtes du Rhône vineyards: examples from growers known for their Côte-Rôtie or Hermitage are always worth sampling, being Syrah-rich; while the Vin de Pays des Collines Rhodaniennes is one of the best in France for simple, tasty reds. Pure Syrah versions advertise the fact with 'Cépage Syrah' on the label.

The last of the major *appellations* of the northern (*septentrional*) Côtes du Rhône is Cornas, again Syrah-based, but this time even more shambling, inky and cellar-seeking than Hermitage, though finally with less intensity of fruit.

Crozes-Hermitage

Type *Medium- to full-bodied red wine*
Profile *Generous aromas, variously reminiscent of raspberries, plums, tar or stables; rich, savoury flavours, stony and full-blooded, sometimes with high tannin and acidity*
Advice *Cellar the best examples for at least five years; serve with game, guinea-fowl and rare red meats*

Recommended producers

J L Chave (Hermitage); Auguste Clape (Cornas); Emile Florentin (Saint-Joseph); E Guigal (Côte Rôtie, Condrieu, Côtes du Rhône); Jaboulet Aîné (all *appellations*, especially Crozes-Hermitage Domaine du Thalabert); Robert Jasmin (Côte Rôtie); René Rostaing (Côte Rôtie); Tardy & Ange (Crozes-Hermitage); Noël Verset (Cornas); De Vallouit (all *appellations*); Georges Vernay (Condrieu); Vidal-Fleury (all *appellations*).

Southern Rhône

Clairette de Die, a sparkling wine based on the Clairette grape variety, is generally regarded as the first of the southern (*méridional*) Rhône wines, though its position 50 kilometres east of the river sets it apart from its classmates. It comes in two guises: Clairette de Die Brut, a dry champagne-method sparkler, and Clairette de Die Tradition, a scented, sweeter and more engaging version, made by a traditional local method and with a high proportion of Muscat.

Côtes du Vivarais on the right bank of the river, and Coteaux du Tricastin on the left, raise the curtain on the southern Rhône with their light, spicy reds. Most of the Côtes du Rhône-Villages, including the majority of the 17 that are permitted to add their names to the basic *appellation*, are sited in a large, hilly semi-circle stretching away from the Rhône's left bank and exploiting the slopes of its tributaries, the Aigues and the Ouvèze. A wide range of grape varieties, dominated by the Grenache, produce red wines that can invite as tenderly as an earthenware bowl of warm, dusty plums, but which can also prove disappointingly light and soft. When you find a good example, give it your loyalty. The same is true, to a still greater extent, of Côtes du Rhône, which issues in the southern Rhône like water from a fountain. The rosés and the whites of both *appellations* are better than they used to be, but still lack the wealth of character of almost anything from the Loire.

Gigondas, among the Rhône villages, has distinguished itself sufficiently to have won its own AOC for its reds (and a few rosés): these are warm and full, but rarely as big as the name leads one to hope, and rarely as intense or memorable as a £6 price tag suggests they will be. Two other villages, Rasteau and Beaumes-de-Venise, have their own AOCs for – respectively – red, Grenache-based and white, Muscat-based vins doux naturels, of which the white (in fact it's a coppery orange) is much the better. A glass of this luxuriously perfumed, lusciously sweet wine on a warm summer's evening will leave you profoundly grateful to creation in general and to the Rhône's resourceful wine-growers in particular.

South of Orange, thousands of years of pebble-rolling by a swollen and errant Rhône has resulted in some of the most singular vineyard 'soils' in France: the *galets* of Châteauneuf-du-Pape. These large, water-rounded boulders provide an unlikely but appreciated medium for up to thirteen different grape varieties, authorised but rarely all used in this large AOC. Many different varieties, a large vineyard area, conflicting ideas about what Châteauneuf should be and how to get it that way, plus the pressures on supply exerted by a well-known name: small wonder that Châteauneuf varies from a gentle, sweet-tempered giant among wines to grape soup with alcohol. This inconsistency has, however, bred enough mistrust among wine enthusiasts to have kept prices at a reasonable level, and the best Châteauneufs are still excellent value for money. White Châteauneuf has greatly improved in the last five years, with the best growers creating lively, even blossomy wines from the palette of varieties and the large red sun freely available to them.

> *How great a thing is a single cup of wine!*
> *For it makes us tell the story of our whole lives.*
> Po Chü-I

Châteauneuf-du-Pape

Type *Deep red wine*
Profile *Warm, spicy, earthy scents and flavours making a generous and comfortable wine, sometimes slightly fiery, coarse or lacking in definition*
Advice *The best may be cellared for five to eight years; an evening wine, partnering a wide range of classic meat-based dishes; aged examples drink surprisingly well on their own*

Recommended producers

Château du Beaucastel (Châteauneuf-du-Pape); Clos des Papes (Châteauneuf-du-Pape); Cru du Coudoulet (Côtes du Rhône); Château Fortia (Châteauneuf-du-Pape); Château du Grand Moulas (Côtes du Rhône); Domaine les Pallières (Gigondas); Domaine Rabasse-Charavin (Côtes de Rhône-Villages); Domaine Raspail (Gigondas); Domaine du Vieux Télégraphe (Châteauneuf-du-Pape).

Delta wines

Across the river from Châteauneuf lie Tavel and Lirac, the two rosé-producing areas whose pink wines are traditionally declared the best in France. The biggest, perhaps, but not the best: all too often they are an angry orange-red in colour, marked by dull, rubbery fruit and over-endowed with alcohol. The reds that Lirac has turned its hand to in recent years are much better – lush fruit dusted with herbs is not hard to find in the *appellation* – and the whites are good when young.

Côtes du Ventoux and Côtes du Luberon are two recently promoted AOCs whose top estates produce fine southern French reds: the Rhône marks Ventoux, while Luberon looks more to Provence. Among the vins de pays are some equally exciting developments, with the departmental Ardèche, Bouches-du-Rhône and Vaucluse denominations, and the zonal Coteaux de l'Ardèche and Principauté d'Orange, all achieving a high standard for reds, including Syrah and Cabernet varietals. Chardonnay from the Coteaux de l'Ardèche is sound, but not assured or consistently attractive enough yet to strike fear into Australian hearts.

Recommended producers

Domaine des Anges (Côtes du Ventoux); Domaine de Grangeneuve (Coteaux du Tricastin); Pascal (Côtes du Ventoux); Domaine du Château

Saint-Roche (Lirac); Château Val-Joanis (Côtes du Luberon); La Vieille
Ferme (Côtes du Ventoux).

Stockists

*Adnams; Bibendum; G E Bromley; D Byrne & Co; Croque-en-Bouche; Farr
Vintners; Findlater Mackie Todd; Gauntleys of Nottingham; Richard Harvey;
Heath St Wine Co; J E Hogg; House of Townend; Ian G Howe; S H Jones;
Justerini & Brooks; Lay & Wheeler; Majestic Wine Warehouses; Morris &
Verdin; Oddbins; Christopher Piper Wines; Raeburn Fine Wines; Sebastopol
Wines; Tanners; Turville Valley Wines; Helen Verdcourt; Vessel du Vin; La
Vigneronne; Villeneuve Wines; Yapp Brothers.*

Rhône: vintages

1989 A very hot summer led to an early harvest – as early as
August in some places. The fruit was super-ripe, and 1989 has
produced sensational wines in some parts of the Rhône, though
quality is less even than in 1988. Where there are problems (and
the areas of light and shade will become clear over the next 12
months), these are consequent on low acidity and high extract
levels dislocating the balance of the wines. Drought has, too,
meant that some wines are a little stringy.

1988 A fine year throughout the Rhône, with Côte Rôtie,
Châteauneuf-du-Pape and the Côte du Rhône-Villages excelling
themselves. Some wines, however, are ungratefully tough, and all
of the best need cellaring.

1987 A light year, with all but the very finest wines now ready
for drinking, and some wines from elevated *appellations* proving a
disappointment: follow trustworthy recommendation. Côte Rôtie,
though, produced some fine wines.

1986 A difficult year in the Rhône, with unseasonable summer
and harvest rain causing problems of rot and dilution respectively.
Some wines are light and for early drinking; others are for the long
term. Only Châteauneuf and Gigondas reliably live up to their
appellation reputations.

1985 A fine vintage of long-lived wines. All wines costing over
£7 per bottle will need further cellaring.

1984 An unfairly dismissed vintage; the most ambitious
producers have created good wines, and the best from all
appellations continue to drink well.

1983 A fine vintage throughout the Rhône, though less
consistently so in the south than in the north.

1982 Potentially a good vintage, but high ambient temperatures during the fermentation period have given rise to some light, unbalanced wines. Follow trustworthy advice or taste before buying.

1981 A light and inconsistent vintage in the north, but good in the south. All wines are now ready.

1980 A sound vintage, with most of the wines of the top *appellations* continuing to give pleasure.

SOUTH-WESTERN FRANCE

Viticulturally, South-Western France is a pattern of islands. Most of the region's AOCs are scattered between Bordeaux and Toulouse, along slopes cut by the Rivers Garonne, Dordogne and Tarn; another handful cluster about the Adour, the Gave de Pau and the Nive, watercourses draining into the Atlantic through Bayonne. Add VDQS and Vin de Pays denominations, and you have a wine-growing archipelago, busy now after half a century or more in which many of the vineyards nearly sank without trace into the earth, together with their often distinctive grape varieties. If any part of France adequately symbolises French viticulture, with its careful nurturing of the unique potential of each vine on each hillside, then it is the South-West.

Bergerac, the Marmandais and Buzet form a convenient, and comparatively conventional, starting point for a taste-tour of the South-West. These areas have the disadvantage, or advantage (if you are irredeemably conservative) of forming a hinterland to Bordeaux, and it is only in the Marmandais that non-Bordeaux varieties like Fer and Abouriou take a turn in the blending vat with the two Cabernets and Merlot. The best of the Bordeaux lookalikes come from Buzet and Pécharmant; Bergerac, Côtes de Bergerac and Côtes de Duras are generally lighter, and it takes talented and ambitious producers to draw excitement from soils in these *appellations*. The wines of the Côtes du Marmandais play their role of country cousins to the claret grandees well.

Good rosés are produced in Bergerac, while whites are dry for Bergerac Sec, Montravel and Côtes de Duras, medium dry to sweet for Haut-Montravel and Rosette, and sweet for Monbazillac. The grape varieties used are the Bordeaux trio Sémillon, Sauvignon Blanc and Muscadelle with, in some cases, the addition of Ondenc, Chenin Blanc and Ugni Blanc. The best of these wines are the Bergeracs (look out for ambition again, generally marked by a slightly higher price). Memorable, too, are some of the medium-dry Haut-Montravels: they have none of the sharp-tongued incision of their Loire cousins, but are gentle, mellow and lightly honeyed, like dusk on the rivers in September.

Recommended producers

Cave du Cocumont (Côtes du Marmandais); Château Court-les-Mûts (Bergerac); Domaine de Haut-Pécharmant (Pécharmant); Château La Jaubertie (Bergerac); Château de Pilar (Côtes du Duras); Chateau du Tiregand (Pécharmant); Les Vignerons Réunis (Buzet); Château du Treuil de Nailhac (Monbazillac).

Witchcraft into oenology

Travel eastwards up the River Lot towards its source and you will come to a beautiful and sternly fortified bridge: Le Pont Valentré. This bridge tells you that you have reached Cahors, source of France's legendary 'black wine'. The recipe called for boiled must and buckets of brandy; most drinkers today are grateful that it remains legendary. Modern Cahors retains a fairly sombre hue; a sniff and a taste of the rich, pruney fruit of the best latter-day examples, though, confirms the evolution of witchcraft into oenology. The main grape variety used for Cahors is the Auxerrois, known elsewhere as Côt and in Bordeaux as Malbec; the result it gives when grown on the often steep slopes of the Lot valley is very different from anything urbane and Bordelais. Further up that valley, three of France's most obscure VDQS denominations are found: Vins d'Entraygues et du Fel, Vins d'Estaing and Vins de Lavilledieu. The Négrette in Lavilledieu, and the Fer in the other two denominations, seem likely to produce wines of interest in time; at present the restoration of these medieval vineyards is still incomplete.

Cahors

Type *Medium- to full-bodied red wine*
Profile *Variable aromas, reminiscent of the farmyard, of ripe plums or other red fruits, or of prunes; grippy, tangy, rustic flavours, sometimes with a marked tannic structure*
Advice *Serve with rabbit, hare, faggots or other baked, offal-based meat dishes; modern Cahors does not need long ageing*

Recommended producers (Cahors)

Château de Cayrou; Château de Chambert; Clos la Coutale; Château Saint-Didier-Parnac; Domaine Eugénie; Château de Haute-Serre; Clos de Gamot; Clos Triguedina.

Gaillac and the Côtes du Frontonnais

South of Cahors, towards the regional capital Toulouse, lie Gaillac and the Côtes du Frontonnais. Gaillac produces a wide range of wines from a wide mix of grape varieties, with Len de l'El, Sauvignon Blanc, Mauzac and Muscadelle playing a leading role in the whites, and Duras dominating the reds and roses. Sparkling and slightly sparkling wines are also produced, based on the same grape varieties as the white wines; and the region even mothers a non-*appellation* flor-aged wine (or *vin de voile*), though it is little seen away from its birthplace. All this versatility, combined with generally low prices, results in some dull simpletons, but the sparkling wines, dry whites and reds can all, producers willing, find country character on occasion.

Few Côtes du Frontonnais have surfaced in Britain yet, but one of the first to do so – Château Bellevue-la-Forêt – won such acclaim with every appearance that others are now racing in. The Négrette grape is the big attraction; nine others are allowed in the blend (to a maximum proportion of 40 per cent) but the Négrette dominates, and some producers (including Bellevue-la-Forêt) go in for pure Négrette versions. This variety is, in terms of flavour if not genetically, a soft, southern cousin to the Loire's Cabernet Franc.

Côtes du Frontonnais

Type *Medium-bodied red wine*
Profile *Brightly perfumed, with a pomade-like sheen overlying peppery, curranty scents; lively berry flavours, with a touch of tar; low in tannin, and without astringency*
Advice *Cool slightly; drink on its own, with chicken or with sausages*

Recommended producers

Château Bellevue-la-Forêt (Côtes du Frontonnais); Domaine Jean Cros (Gaillac); Château Flotis (Côtes du Frontonnais); Domaine de Labarthe; Château Larroze (Gaillac).

Gascon enterprise

Lining the River Adour as it takes the scenic route between Tarbes and Bayonne are three *appellation* zones: those of AOC Côtes de Saint-Mont, Madiran and Tursan. Madiran's boundaries count twice, the second time for Pacherenc du Vic-Bilh.

Côtes de Saint-Mont, in the heart of Gascony, produces a good range of red and white wines and a few rosés (Tannat and Fer dominate the reds and rosés; the whites are based on Arrufiac, Clairette, Courbu and the two Mansengs). Working in tandem with this *appellation* is the Vins de Pays des Côtes de Gascogne, in which the theoretically duller varieties, Ugni Blanc and Colombard, play a major role in the white wines which dominate production. Astonishingly, it is these Ugni Blanc whites which have provided the sub-region's most exciting wines in the last two or three years, demonstrating that even the humblest varieties, those habitually dismissed as characterless, can acquire nooks of aroma and crannies of flavour when the vines are well pruned and the fruit is vinified with skill and stainless steel. The Gascon precedent should give heart to Spain's Airén growers and, especially, Italy's Trebbiano producers (Ugni Blanc is the French synonym for Trebbiano).

Vin de Pays des Côtes de Gascogne Blanc

Type *Light, fruity white wine*
Profile *Attractive, fresh aromas, combining suggestions of nettle or elderflower with a heavier, citrus-oil scent; softly flavoured, but lively, singing with tangy citrus, or pineapple tastes*
Advice *Drink soon after purchase, either without food or with salads, pasta or fish. Perfect summer lunchtime wine*

Madiran is a red based on the Tannat, a grape variety that sounds as if it means business, with additions of Fer (literally 'iron', though in fact its character is more vegetal than mineral) and the two Cabernets; the wines then get over a year and a half in wood, with many producers having a go at new-wood ageing. This red rivals Cahors for the distinction of the South-West's sturdiest, the most likely to make old bones; the hessian-textured pleasures of its youth are not to everyone's taste, but if you like country hams, bean soups and are not squeamish about garlicky breath, then young Madiran may be for you. With age, the hessian turns strangely silky. Pacherenc du Vic-Bilh is a white wine made from a range of varieties, sometimes dry, sometimes less so; the best examples have blossomy fragrance and a comely, summer-fruit lushness. (Pacherenc is a dialect reference to the high training system used for the vines; Vic-Bilh are the hills in which the high training takes place.)

Madiran

Type *Medium- to full-bodied red wine*
Profile *Rich, humus-like smells; savoury, tangy flavours lurking behind a sometimes severe façade of tannin and hard fruit*
Advice *The best examples need ageing; serve with rustic, smoky food on autumn evenings*

Recommended producers

Château Aydie (Madiran); Domaine Boucassé (Madiran and Pacherenc du Vic-Bilh); Château Montus (Madiran); Domaine Laplace (Madiran); Domaine de Planterieu (Vin de Pays des Côtes de Gascogne); Producteurs de Plaimont (Côtes de Saint-Mont and Vins de Pays des Côtes de Gascogne); Domaine le Puts (Vin de Pays des Côtes de Gascogne) Domaine de Tariquet (Vin de Pays des Côtes de Gascogne).

France's final frontier

Most of the Béarn vineyards are found on the left bank of the Gave de Pau; so, too, are those of Jurançon. Béarn produces reds and rosés in the main, leaving the production of whites to Jurançon and its slightly higher, cooler sites. Béarn's reds are Tannat-based, but often with a substantial undertow from Cabernet Franc, that great freshener; they are not fine, but can be good, lively, supple, curranty. Jurançon's whites are Manseng-based (Gros Manseng dominates for the dry Jurançon Sec; Petit Manseng for the sweeter Jurançon), and this late-ripening, low-yielding variety produces attractively keen-edged results whatever the intensity of sweetness. South-east of Jurançon, deep into Basque country, lies AOC Irouléguy, French wine's last and remotest outpost: the local co-operative produces a deep, richly fruity, almost Balkan-style red based on the Tannat, from pockets of vineyard in this region of green pastures and strange speech.

The South-West is rich in vins de pays: the regional denomination is Comté Tolosan; nearly all of the *départements* have their own denominations; and there is also a small chorus of mellifluously named zonal denominations, few of which have yet reached Grantham or Glasgow. Côtes de Gascogne, described above, has provided more in the way of value than any of the others so far, but watch out for pint-sized Cahors from Coteaux de Quercy and junior Madiran from Bigorre.

Jurançon (moelleux)

Type *Sweet white wine*
Profile *Fragrant honey, vanilla and lime aromas; lush green fruit, earthy and sweet-edged, with supple, leafy textures*
Advice *Chill well; enjoy on its own or with light fruit desserts*

Recommended producers

Domaine Cauhapé (Jurançon, Béarn); Clos Guirouilh (Jurançon); Château Jolys (Jurançon); Cave Coopérative Saint-Etienne de Baïgorry (Irouléguy); Les Vignerons du Tursan (Tursan).

South-West: vintages

Buy the youngest wine available and drink as soon as possible, with the exception of Pécharmant, Cahors and Madiran, the best of which may be aged for up to seven years following the date of harvest. Jurançon (doux or moelleux) may be aged for up to ten years following the date of harvest.

Stockists

Ad Hoc Wine Warehouse; Adnams; Bibendum; Bordeaux Direct/Taste Shops; D Byrne & Co; The Celtic Vintner; Croque-en-Bouche; Drinksmart; Eaton Elliot; Fulham Road Wine Centre; Peter Green; Hicks & Don; Ian G Howe; Majestic Wine Warehouses; Marks & Spencer; Nicholas; Oddbins; Christopher Piper Wines; Arthur Rackhams; Ravensbourne; Safeway; J Sainsbury; Selfridges; Smedley Vintners; The Sunday Times Wine Club; Tanners; Tesco; Thresher; Victoria Wine; Villeneuve Wines; Vinceremos; Vintage Roots; Whiclar & Gordon; Winecellars; Wizard Wine Warehouses.

Germany and Austria

Wink Lorch

GERMANY

If only one wine style were destined to be the taste of the 1990s, what would it be like? This speculator reckons that it would be a wine to drink in moderation with food. Since the food of the decade looks like being light and tasty, though not overpowering in flavour, the chosen wine should compliment it with a light, elegant profile yet assertive flavours. This is the one style that New World wine-makers have failed to produce successfully, but it is a wine style that Germany has made for centuries. So why are its wines so often dismissed?

Germany's latitude above and below 50°N, the equivalent of Newfoundland to the west or Mongolia to the east, has always meant a struggle to produce good wines in quantity. This was one of the world's first cool-climate wine zones, and before the advent of modern technology it produced tiny quantities of stunning, world-class wines in some years, and wines best forgotten in others. Today, the quantity produced in Germany still varies greatly, but the quality is much more consistent, and contrary to popular opinion, the country produces a great variety of wines worthy of discovery. Germany's prime – and vastly undervalued – asset remains its tradition of fine Riesling wines, the best of which rank with the greatest white wines of the world.

Struggling for an image

The image of German wines is too often that of medium-sweet, cheap and, if you are lucky, cheerful white wines to drink without food. Many people turn away from German wines once they develop a liking for dry whites and reds, not realising what they are missing. It is true that medium styles are still the mainstay of German exports, but German consumers have decisively rejected these in favour of trocken (dry) or halbtrocken (semi-dry) styles. Trockens and halbtrockens are at last appearing on, and even moving off, our retailers' shelves, though many are packaged in a burgundy-shaped bottle in order to look distinctively un-German.

The most common preconception even of fine German wines is that they should be drunk on their own without food. The luscious dessert wines, which range from Auslese quality upwards and include the very special Eisweins (see below), are the lightest in the world and are indeed to be enjoyed on their own. But even fine German wines are not exclusively sweet. In every region of Germany fine quality wines are made from Riesling and other varieties, from bone-dry to medium-dry styles, often to specifications far higher than German wine law dictates, deliberately to match fine cuisine.

Wine law and a question of balance

Unlike elsewhere in the European Community, German wine law (see pages 187 and 188 for an explanation of the quality categories) virtually ignores soils and sites, putting the emphasis on individual grape quality. Germany has no hierarchy of fine wines like France's Grands Crus; instead, the different quality levels are based on the amount of sugar in the grape must. The structure of German wine law effectively means that a single vineyard may produce the lowest category of wine, Tafelwein, as well as the highest, Trockenbeerenauslese, depending on the quantity and quality of the fruit alone.

Limits on yields were introduced only in 1989, and they restrict the amount of wine sold in any particular year, rather than the amount produced. This enables growers to balance out a small harvest with a larger one. The hope is that restrictions will improve quality and increase the prices of the cheapest wines. The change is unlikely to affect the best wines since the top estates already voluntarily restrict yields.

Producing wine in Germany is all about achieving a correct balance. Acidity in a wine may be balanced by sugar and/or alcohol in addition to other flavour components, and it is this balance that is crucial to the success of German wines.

Grape varieties

Riesling forms the backbone of quality wine production in Germany. One of the world's classic varieties, it is ideally suited to growing on precipitous slopes, withstanding harsh winters, and remaining on the vine for as long as possible into a sunny autumn. Once vinified, it provides acidity for structure, balance and ageing potential, and a wealth of flavours that develop from delicate floral aromas when young to rich, honeyed, even petrolly flavours when matured. Riesling is not ideal for a grower looking for high yields, nor for one unwilling to take the risks that must be run in order to try to get the crop to ripen fully. It forms only 20 per cent of Germany's plantings, and it is left to the mediocre, high-yielding

Müller-Thurgau, a crossing developed over 100 years ago, to head the list of the most widely planted German grape varieties. Müller-Thurgau wines have pronounced floral and grapey aromas, but they tend to lack acidity and class.

Other traditional varieties include Silvaner, Gewürztraminer and Rülander (Pinot Gris), all enjoying a revival since the return to popularity of Germany's drier wines. There are also numerous grape crossings, developed specifically to deal with the harsh German climate; they do this well, but often fail in the more important task of creating exciting wines. The most successful crossings include Bacchus, Kerner and, especially, Scheurebe, whose good acidity levels and pungent flavours are winning admirers for both its sweet and dry wines.

Reds, rosés and sparklers

Plantings of black grape varieties are increasing as sales of German red wine increase on the home market. The wines will never compete with the best from France or Italy, but their light style matches the new, lighter German cuisine well. Spätburgunder (Pinot Noir) is Germany's only classic black grape variety and produces, on occasion, fine red wine and crisp, fruity rosé (Weissherbst). Of the recent crossings, the dark-coloured Dornfelder grape produces overtly fruity wines.

Germany has a large sparkling wine (*Sekt*) industry but much of it is made with imported wine. Deutscher Sekt is made only from German grapes, and its quality is improving as technology improves. As always in Germany, the best is based on Riesling grapes.

Market forces

Large producers, faced with falling exports of the medium-sweet styles, have been forced to review their product range. Some have changed their packaging to include simpler labelling; others struggle to promote drier styles. A few have made braver deviations.

Sichel (of 'Blue Nun' fame) have launched 'Sichel Novum', a dry wine so different from the standard German style that it fails to gain 'Quality Wine' approval from the authorities and is merely labelled Table Wine. Unusually for a German wine, it goes through malolactic fermentation to soften its acidity. The result is very un-Germanic and the quality is not as successful as the packaging. Deinhard have taken a different approach with their 'Heritage' range of dry wines, labelled simply with a well-known village name but no mention of vineyard. They are made from classic grapes and are of high quality, reflecting true German character, but are priced accordingly.

Co-operatives are important in Germany and, with cellars full of gleaming modern equipment, their wines should be well represented on the UK market. They are not, though, perhaps because many concentrate on drier wines to suit the German market and because, despite being well made, their wines often lack excitement.

Quality wine estates

For the right mix of tradition, innovation and excitement, one has to look to the best of Germany's estate wines. Many estates are so small that their only chance of survival is to produce wines that can sell at relatively high prices. To do this, they keep down yields in the vineyard, and use the best combination of traditional and modern methods in the winery. Many estates have stainless-steel equipment for vinification, but mature their Rieslings in the traditional old German oak *Fuder* (1000-litre casks). Some estates have experimented with new French oak *barriques*, but only a few varieties produce wines that can be successfully oak-aged. Once again, the authorities disapprove and a selection of German 'designer' table wines is appearing, much as it has in Italy.

All over Germany, individuals are banding together to improve the quality and image of their wines. The Verband Deutscher Prädikats-und Qualitätsweingüter (VDP) is a national grouping of producers that monitors the quality of its members' wines, and its eagle emblem on a German wine bottle offers an extra indication of quality. At the other end of the scale are individuals who instigate their own minimum standards and are not afraid to be innovative. Many are in the process of changing their image with artist-designed labels and unusual bottle shapes. It will take several years before we can gauge the success of these many initiatives but the signs are encouraging. Slowly, cautious UK importers are recognising the changes and are tentatively importing a range of both old and new styles from top German estates. Prices will continue to increase, but German wines still represent excellent value.

Germany's quality categories

Qualitätswein effectively occupies the bottom rung of the German quality scale, since 95 per cent of German wines are at this level or above. The categories in full are:

1 **Deutscher Tafelwein** (German table wine) From one of four named regions – Rhein-Mosel, Bayern, Oberrhein and Neckar – and from approved grape varieties. The most basic wine produced from grapes grown in Germany with a minimum ripeness level. (If the word 'Deutsch' or 'Deutscher' is missing the wine is not made from German grapes.)

2 **Deutscher Landwein** (German country wine) Regional wine equivalent to French vin de pays. The grapes must be riper than for Deutscher Tafelwein and must come from one of 15 named Landwein regions. The wine must be made in a Trocken (dry) or Halbtrocken (off-dry) style.

3 **Qualitätswein bestimmter Anbaugebiet** or **QbA** (quality wine from a specific region) Grapes must be riper than for the previous categories and come from one of 11 regions: Ahr, Mosel-Saar-Ruwer, Mittelrhein, Rheingau, Nahe, Rheinhessen, Rheinpfalz, Franken, Hessische Bergstrasse, Württemberg and Baden. The 11 quality regions are divided into 35 Bereich (districts); 150 Grosslagen (collective vineyard sites); and 2,600 Einzellagen (individual vineyard sites). A QbA wine need state only which quality region it is from; QmP wines (below) must specify the Bereich (district), or the village and vineyard.

4 **Qualitätswein mit Prädikat** or **QmP** (quality wine with a specific attribute) Grapes must have more natural sugar or ripeness at harvest than previous categories; chaptalisation is not allowed. A minimum sugar level in the grape must is set for each Prädikat, for each region and grape variety.

The Prädikats are:

- **Kabinett**: lowest in alcohol of all German wines. Generally the driest of the QmP styles
- **Spätlese**: usually from late-picked grapes, giving greater concentration and flavour
- **Auslese**: from particularly ripe grapes, occasionally affected with noble rot
- **Beerenauslese**: from selected over-ripe berries, usually affected with noble rot
- **Eiswein**: grapes must be as ripe as Beerenauslese category, but picked and pressed early on a winter morning, while still frost-frozen
- **Trockenbeerenauslese**: from grapes that have been left to shrivel and raisin on the vine to give intense concentration. Usually heavily affected with noble rot.

The quality designation denotes ripeness in the grape rather than sweetness in the finished wine – the higher the level, the riper the grapes were when picked. Kabinett, Spätlese and

occasionally Auslese levels may be sold as Trocken (dry),
Halbtrocken (semi-dry), or with residual sweetness. A grower may
pick grapes at the Spätlese level and make some wine of each style.
To achieve this, fermentation may be stopped at different times to
leave some residual sugar. Alternatively, the wine may be fully
fermented and *süssreserve* of the same origin as the wine may be
added before bottling to restore the original sweetness of the
grape juice, reducing alcohol at the same time.

Behind the German wine label

The naming of German wines deters most people from
experimenting with different styles, though the introduction of
simpler labelling is beginning to resolve this problem. German
wines give more detailed information than any other European
wines – if you can understand the way in which it is presented.
The rule of thumb is to look at the label first for region, followed by
quality designation, grape and style – ignore any mention of
village or vineyard as these may only confuse. As everywhere, the
producer's name is perhaps the most important piece of
information.

The label of a QbA or QmP wine must include:
- the region: one of the 11 specific quality regions
- quality designation, including Prädikat, if it is a QmP wine
- Amtliche Prüfungsnummer or APNr (official testing number);
  the last two digits indicate the year the wine was bottled and
  tested
- the producer's name and address
- contents and alcohol level.

The label may also include:
- more precise origin (obligatory for QmP wines). This may be a
  Bereich (district), e.g. Bereich Bernkastel, or it may be a village
  name (generally ending in '-er') with a vineyard name tagged
  on, e.g. Bernkasteler Kurfürstlay. There is no way,
  unfortunately, of telling from the label if the vineyard is a
  Grosslage (collective vineyard site) or an Einzellage (individual
  vineyard site)
- grape variety: the wine must be at least 85 per cent from the
  named variety
- vintage: the wine must be at least 85 per cent from the stated
  vintage
- style: 'Trocken' (dry) or 'Halbtrocken' (semi-dry) may be stated
  if residual sugar levels are within legal limits
- 'Erzeugerabfüllung': the word means 'estate-bottled', and is also
  used by growers' co-operatives.

Mosel-Saar-Ruwer

Some of the steepest vineyards in Germany produce its most delicate wines. They are found on the banks of the River Mosel, which cuts a tortuous path from the Luxembourg border near Trier to the point at which it joins the Rhine at Koblenz. One has only to look at the vines, supported by single stakes, clinging on to the slate-covered hillside above the village of Bernkastel, to realise why wines from the Bernkastler Doctor vineyard are legendary. Conditions like these form the viticultural extremes in which Riesling thrives, and growers in the region should be encouraged to grow no other variety.

The Mosel-Saar-Ruwer is one of Germany's larger quality regions, and it is also home to many of the bulk-production wineries. It is the ubiquitous Müller-Thurgau vine, planted in flat vineyards near the river banks, together with the indifferent viticultural practices of less-than-scrupulous wineries that have soured the taste of Mosel wine. This combination, quite legally, produces copious quantities of Piesporter Michelsberg and Bereich Bernkastel which have never been near the villages of Piesport and Bernkastel.

Fortunately Riesling is enjoying a revival, but it does need careful handling, as the grape, the cool climate and the slate soil all encourage a high level of acidity. The region is therefore not suited to producing bone dry, trocken wines, though most Mosel wines are drier than their equivalents from other regions. In many years, the grapes do not ripen sufficiently to produce wines above Kabinett level, but when they do, such as in 1983 or 1989, the sweeter styles can show striking depth of flavour and elegance.

The best wines come from the Middle Mosel region which includes famous villages such as Wehlen, Zeltingen, Bernkastel and Brauneberg. Wines from vineyards near Trier on the Saar and Ruwer tributaries compete well in the best years, showing a classic, steely quality. The VDP estates from the region, known collectively as the Grosser Ring, encourage production of Riesling wines only and vigorously promote the quality one has a right to expect from one of Germany's great wine regions.

Wine can be considered with good reason as the most healthful and the most hygienic of beverages.
Louis Pasteur

Mosel-Saar-Ruwer Riesling Kabinett

Type *Medium-dry, very light white*
Profile *Pale, often with fine bubbles; appley aromas; light in alcohol with a delicate, fruity acidity*
Advice *Age for 3-5 years; drink on its own or with delicate fish dishes*

Mosel-Saar-Ruwer Riesling Auslese

Type *Medium sweet white*
Profile *Green-golden hints; honeyed aromas; delicate sweetness balanced by crisp acidity and light peachy flavours*
Advice *The best improve for a decade or more; drink as an aperitif*

Recommended producers
Friedrich-Wilhelm Gymnasium; von Hövel; Reichsgraf von Kesselstatt; Dr Pauly-Bergweiler; J J Prüm; S A Prüm; Max Ferd Richter; C von Schubert.

Rheingau

The quality of Rieslings from the Rheingau region has served as a benchmark for this variety throughout the world. Fortunately, over 80 per cent of Rheingau vineyards are planted with Riesling, and this fruit is transformed into a range of styles ranging from steely dry wines to rare, honeyed and peachy Eisweine and Trockenbeerenauslesen. The predominantly south-facing vineyards benefit both from the protection of the forested Taunus mountains and reflected sunshine from the River Rhine. The Rheingau has a multiplicity of soil types which accounts for the range of flavours to be found in its Rieslings. It also enables the other important grape variety of the region, Spätburgunder (Pinot Noir), to grow in selected sites. The best reds are made in Assmanshausen at the northern end of the region; their pale colour but fruity character has attracted an enthusiastic following.

This is a region of historical wine-producing castles and monasteries. They include the famous Cistercian Monastery, Kloster Eberbach, which now houses the region's State winery, and Schloss Vollrads, home to Erwein Graf Matuschka von Greiffenclau, the current generation of the oldest vine-growing family in the world. A leading member of the VDP nationally, and one of the founding members of the Rheingau Charta group (see below), Graf Matuschka is a great believer in matching German wines with food, explaining that the brash flavours of New World wines often overwhelm fine cuisine, whereas the subtle German Riesling flavours complement and enhance it. The Charta Association of Rheingau producers sets high standards for its wines, which are sold in distinctive bottles embossed with the Association's 'arch' logo. They must be Riesling of QbA, Kabinett or Spätlese quality level, made in a dry to off-dry style showing classic Rheingau Riesling characteristics.

Weather permitting, Rheingau growers produce some of the best of all German Eisweine. A few rows of ripe, healthy grapes are left on the vine through to winter. If temperatures drop to -7°C for several hours, frozen grapes may be harvested and pressed while still icy to yield tiny amounts of concentrated juice – almost a grape essence. As with all Rheingau Rieslings, the ageing potential of these wines is great, due to their fine balance between high levels of acidity, sweetness and other components.

Rheingau Riesling Kabinett Halbtrocken (typical Charta Estate)

Type *Off-dry, light white*
Profile *Fruity nose developing character as wine matures; palate appears virtually dry with steely fruit flavours*
Advice *At best between 3-10 years after harvest; drink with any lightly sauced fine food, such as trout, or light meals*

Rheingau Riesling Eiswein

Type *Rare, very fine dessert wine*
Profile *Flavours of peach and apricot on nose and palate; good acidity balances luscious sweetness*
Advice *Drink on its own in order to appreciate its depth, nuances and completeness. May be cellared for many years, during which it will acquire further nuances and achieve harmony*

Recommended producers

Baron von Brentano; G Breuer (Charta member); Balthasar Ress (Charta member); Schloss Groenesteyn; Schloss Reinhartshausen; Schloss Vollrads

(Charta member); Scholl & Hillebrand (Charta member); Verwaltung der Staatsweingüter, Eltville.

Ahr, Mittelrhein and Hessische Bergstrasse

These three regions produce very little wine, and most of it is consumed in Germany. The Ahr is the northernmost wine-growing region of Germany and, surprisingly, specialises in red wine. The Mittelrhein, north of the Rheingau, and Hessische Bergstrasse to the south-east both specialise in Riesling of high quality.

Nahe

The Nahe region has a personality that is split in three ways. It has a few very steep and stony vineyard sites that produce fine and racy Rieslings, reminiscent of those of the Mosel; following the River Nahe's course to join the Rhine, it passes close to Rheinhessen where the vineyards are flatter and produce wines similar to those of its neighbour; finally, as it approaches the Rhine at Bingerbrück, the vineyards become steeper again, and drier wines are made, including Rieslings that rival those from the Rheingau on the opposite bank.

The vineyards around Nahe's central town, Bad Kreuznach, have very varied soils and aspects and are therefore planted with a range of grape varieties with, as always, Riesling reserved for the best sites. Moving upstream, Riesling from the Schlossböckelheim area offers some of the best value of all German wines. In general, though, the Nahe is such a diverse region that it does not have a clear sense of identity. That is left to the many wine estates to achieve, which the best memorably do.

Nahe Riesling Spätlese

Type *Medium-dry white*
Profile *Honeyed, fruity aromas developing the characteristic kerosene-like smell of mature Riesling after four to five years; elegant, fruity flavours with hints of honey and spice*
Advice *Best at between 3-10 years after the vintage; ideal on its own, or try with apple-based desserts*

Recommended producers

August Anheuser; Paul Anheuser; Reichsgraf von Plettenberg; Prinz zu Salm-Dalberg; Verwaltung der Staatlichen Weinbaudomänen – Niederhausen-Schlossböckelheim.

Rheinhessen

The largest of Germany's 11 quality regions, Rheinhessen has some classic vineyard sites on slopes overlooking the Rhine, but many others on flat land that produce wines of generally mediocre quality. Liebfraumilch has its home near the city of Worms in Rheinhessen, but is now produced all over the region. Almost every grape variety that exists in Germany is grown somewhere in Rheinhessen; Müller-Thurgau leads the pack, and many of the newer vine crossings are very popular here. Some, like Kerner and Huxelrebe, ripen easily to Spätlese levels in most years, and to Auslese or above in good vintages.

Riesling is also grown, however, and in good sites, such as the vineyards on the 'Rhine Terrace' above the villages of Nierstein and Oppenheim, it produces fine results. However, the traditional Rheinhessen variety is Silvaner, a grape that produces soft, dry and medium wines, and is currently winning back old friends. The local promotion board has designed a striking yellow and black label (RS) which producers may use to sell estate-bottled dry Silvaners of basic QbA level. Only the grower's name changes on the label, so recognition of the style and variety is easy.

Rheinhessen Silvaner Trocken (sold sometimes as 'RS')

Type *Dry white wine*
Profile *Light floral aromas; medium weight, with a dry but soft taste and lightly spiced fruit*
Advice *Drink on its own or with food, within three years of its vintage date*

Boys should abstain from all use of wine until their eighteenth year, for it is wrong to add fire to fire. But after forty years of age one can toast Dionysus with enthusiasm, for he gave wine to man to soften the bitterness of old age.
Plato

Rheinhessen Kerner Spätlese

Type *Medium-dry white wine*
Profile *Lightly grapey flavours; the best have sustained acidity to balance the sweet fruity flavours*
Advice *Best at between one and four years old; drink on its own, or try it with pâté or fruit desserts*

Recommended producers

Anton Balbach; Louis Guntrum; Freiherr Heyl zu Herrnsheim (some organic); Carl Koch Erben; Villa Sachsen.

Rheinpfalz

In the wines of Rheinpfalz, also known as the Palatinate, one can taste the extra sunshine and warmth enjoyed by this long strip of vineyards in the foothills of the Haardt mountains. Rieslings here are richer than elsewhere, and grapes such as Rülander (Pinot Gris) and Gewürztraminer thrive, just as they do over the French border in Alsace, to the south. There is large Liebfraumilch production in the region, as well as flavoursome wines from a range of grape crossings; altogether a great variety of styles is made. As everywhere, increasing emphasis is placed on Trockens and Halbtrockens – and in Rheinpfalz, the fashion really works. The extra ripeness achieved by the grapes provides alcohol and vinosity to balance the acidity levels, so the lack of sugar is not noticed.

Rheinpfalz is a more suitable area for red wine production than areas further north, and this is reflected in the increased plantings of black grape varieties. Wine-making is improving, too, with some growers ageing their wines for the first time in small, French oak casks. As well as Spätburgunders, which show the true sweet fruit character of the Pinot Noir grape, there are lighter reds from the Portugieser variety and succulently fruity reds from the Dornfelder.

The vineyards around Bad Dürkheim, Forst, Wachenheim and Deidesheim in the Bereich Mittelhaardt provide some of the best wines of Rheinpfalz. Top-quality Rieslings from these villages rival those from other German regions and the best estates own vineyards here. As always, it is a few wine estates that spearhead the quality drive, but several important co-operatives are producing wines of steadily improving quality.

Rheinpfalz Spätburgunder Trocken

Type *Light, dry red*
Profile *Pale colour; sweetly fruity aroma; slightly sharp, but the best are balanced by plenty of sound fruit*
Advice *Drink between two and five years; good with poultry or game dishes*

Rheinpfalz Scheurebe Spätlese Trocken

Type *Full, dry white*
Profile *Very strong, aromatic, spicy bouquet; dry, crisp with a grapefruit character; long finish*
Advice *Drink at two to five years old, on its own or with oriental food or strong cheeses*

Recommended producers
Dr von Bassermann-Jordan; Dr Bürklin-Wolf; Lingenfelder.

Franken

If you manage to find them, Franken (Franconia) wines are easy to recognise since they are all bottled in green, flagon-shaped bottles called *bocksbeutel*. The Germans tend to drink these wines themselves, because no other region can produce their full, dry earthy style, and supplies are limited. Climatically, Franken is different to the rest of Germany. It is further from the sea than any other region, and the resulting continental climate gives hotter summers but colder winters, with a higher risk of frost. These conditions limit yields, providing a natural system of quality control.

Silvaner and Müller-Thurgau grapes dominate plantings in Franken, with Riesling doing well only on particular sites like the steep Würzburger Stein (stone) vineyard in the city of Würzburg. Stoniness or earthiness describes many Franken wines, and this characteristic adds depth and complexity to the basic Silvaner and Müller-Thurgau flavours. These are excellent wines for food, generally dry, rich and flavoursome. As specialities, they are worth their high price.

Franken Müller-Thurgau Trocken

Type *Medium full, dry white*
Profile *Characteristic aromatic and flowery aroma; earthy and slightly spicy character on the palate*
Advice *Drink within one to five years of the vintage date, with fish or white meat, particularly if served in white sauce*

Recommended producers

Fürstlich Castell; Juliusspital.

Baden and Württemberg

Until recently, wines from these two southern German regions were rarely widely available in the UK. Now Baden in particular is marketing its wines here in a big way, thanks to the efforts of its vast, high-tech Central Co-operative Cellars. Much of Württemberg's production (half whites, half reds and rosés) is sold to the inhabitants of Stuttgart in the south of the region. Dry and medium-dry Rieslings and red wines from the Trollinger variety are Württemberg's dominant styles.

Baden's main wine-producing area is a band near the Black Forest, running roughly from Heidelberg down to the Swiss border at Basel following the right bank of the Rhine, opposite the Alsace region of France. It is a large region with numerous small growers, most of whom belong to local co-operatives. Kaiserstuhl and Tuniberg are the best areas, with a warm climate thanks to the shelter provided by the Vosges mountains, and volcanic and mineral-rich soils. Many grape varities are grown, with Müller-Thurgau dominating. In Baden it produces soft wines with a lightly aromatic character.

Baden's best wines come from the members of the Pinot Noir family. Spätburgunder reds benefit from the extra sunshine of the region; Weissburgunder (Pinot Blanc) and Rülander (Pinot Gris, in Baden often called Grauburgunder) ripen well and make rich and spicy dry whites which can rival those from Alsace.

> *The vine and wine are great mysteries. Alone, in the plant kingdom, the vine renders the good earth intelligible...*
> Colette

Baden Grauburgunder Spätlese Trocken

Type *Full dry white*
Profile *Distinctive, spicy bouquet; soft acidity but full, meaty flavours*
Advice *Best between two and five years after harvest; can be drunk with most meat dishes*

Recommended producers (Baden)

Badische Winzerkeller (a large co-operative supplying most generic Baden wines sold in the UK); Karl-Heinz Johner.

Recommended German producers (general)

Deinhard (basic regional wines; Heritage range; estate wines)
Sichel (single estate wines, also sold under the Sichel name)
Sekt: Deinhard Lila; Schloss Wachenheim

Germany: vintages

Every vintage in Germany produces a different range of quality categories. A good vintage for higher Prädikat wines may be less good for QbA or Kabinett wines, and vice versa. The following guide applies mainly to Riesling wines.

1989 The vintage everyone was waiting for. Very large yields created a few watery wines, but Prädikat wines of Spätlese and up, from good producers, are superb. Great potential for ageing.

1988 Very fine in the best parts of Mosel. Mostly good elsewhere, particularly for Kabinetts and Spätlese, but only small quantities available.

1987 A good vintage for Kabinetts in all areas. They will age well.

1986 A very mixed vintage. Buy on recommendation only.

1985 Good Spätlese wines from Mosel and Rheinpfalz, and to a lesser extent from the Rheingau.

1984 Best avoided.

1983 Spätlese and Auslese wines particularly good in Mosel, Nahe and Rheingau.

Older vintages worth buying: 1976, 1975, 1971.

Stockists

A & A Wines; William Addison; Adnams; James Aitken; David Baillie; Berry
Bros & Rudd; Bidendum; G E Bromley; D Byrne & Co; Wines of Interest;
D Byrne; Christchurch; Dennhöfer Wines; Eldridge Pope; Philip Eyres; Alex
Findlater; Findlater Mackie Todd; Harcourt Fine Wines; Gerard Harris; Douglas
Henn-Macrae; J E Hogg; House of Townend; Justerini & Brooks; Lay &
Wheeler; Raeburn; La Réserve; Rodgers Fine Wines; Selfridges; Frank Stainton;
Summerlee Wines; Tanners; Ubiquitous Chip; La Vigneronne; Weavers;
Whitesides; Wine Schoppen; The Wine Society.

AUSTRIA

Several major supermarkets and wine merchant chains are
stocking Austrian wines for the first time in over five years, which
must surely mean that Austria has been forgiven its former sins. A
handful of wine-makers jeopardised the future of the whole
Austrian wine industry (and did some harm to Germany too) in
the mid 1980s by using illegal additives (specifically diethylene
glycol) in their wines. However, after the fight to clear its name,
Austria has begun to acquire a reputation for wine quality that it
never managed to achieve in the past, even before the diethylene
glycol scandal.

Austria offers crisp and spicy dry white wines which have more
weight than those of Germany, and which make a welcome change
from the 'international' white wine taste of classic grape varieties.
The other string to its bow are its rich dessert wines, which offer
the best quality/price ratio of any dessert wines available
anywhere. Comparisons with Germany are often made, but the
taste of Austrian wines is quite different: Austrian wine regions
enjoy a warmer climate; the country has several indigenous
grapes; and the wine-making techniques are unlike those of
Germany in many cases.

Label terms

Austrian law categorises wines in a similar way to German wine
law, and mostly uses the same terms on the labels. The main
difference is that higher minimum must-weights are required for
each quality category. For easy identification, all quality wines
have a red and white band over the capsule of the bottle. The term
'Ausbruch' is an additional Austrian Prädikat which comes
between Beerenauslese and Trockenbeerenauslese and is used
particularly in the village of Rust, in Burgenland, for sweet wines
from dried but not raisined grapes with noble rot. 'Trocken' and

'Halb-Trocken' are used as in Germany for dry and semi-dry wines, but both styles are drier than Germany's equivalents. Austria's warmer climate provides softer, less acidic wines that do not require residual sweetness to achieve a pleasant balance.

Regional variations

Austria's vineyards lie in the eastern part of the country, bordering Czechoslovakia, Hungary and Yugoslavia. From north to south, the four main wine-growing regions are Lower Austria, Vienna, Burgenland and Styria, and between them they offer the drinker a wide range of styles.

The largest region, Lower Austria, is famed for its dry white wines, grown on the banks of the Danube and its tributaries. As throughout the country, Austria's own Grüner Veltliner grape is the most popular variety. It comes into its own in the beautiful Wachau district. The neighbouring Kamptal-Donauland district produces fine Rhine Rieslings, particularly those produced near the town of Krems, whose wine production is dominated by an excellent co-operative. Often achieving the Prädikat of Spätlese, Krems Rieslings may be broad, but are steely and can age well. Lower Austria's other districts include the Weinviertel, Austria's largest and most varied wine district.

Vienna is one of the few major European cities that gives its name to a wine region – Austria's smallest. It is famous for its *Heurigen* (wine bars); owing to their popularity, few of its white wines leave the area (those that do are mainly Grüner Veltliner). South of Vienna is Burgenland, Austria's second largest region, dominated by the Neusiedlersee, a large and shallow lake which provides a warm, damp microclimate that encourages noble rot on local vineyards almost every autumn. Austria's famous dessert wines are produced in Burgenland from a variety of local grapes.

The small, southerly region of Styria enjoys a Mediterranean climate, and specialises in pungent whites including Muskateller, and rosés, fashionable in Vienna, named *Schilcher*.

New trends and old originalities

In an attempt to woo both their own consumers and the export market, many producers have experimented with a number of French grape varieties, often given *barrique*-ageing. The very best have made high quality wines, with prices to match. However, Austria's strength lies in its own grape varieties. Rhine Rieslings (labelled simply Riesling) are always worth trying, as are those based on the Neuburger or Bouvier varieties, and in particular, the spicy Grüner Veltliner wines. Austria's unusual light and fruity reds are worth a try, too; the Zweigelt and Blaufränkisch varieties are the most popular. It pays to be adventurous with Austrian wines, for at present prices, you can hardly lose.

Grüner Veltliner Trocken

Type *Dry white*
Profile *Pale colour; peppery nose; soft but fresh acidity, rounded fruit with spicy flavours*
Advice *Drink within two years of vintage. This is a versatile wine which can be enjoyed with or without food*

Ruster Beerenauslese

Type *Dessert wine*
Profile *Dark, golden colour; honeyed, peachy aromas; sweet and rich with a faintly raisiny character*
Advice *This wine is too rich for most food. Drink from five years from the vintage onwards – good years last well*

Recommended producers

Burgenländischer Winzerverband; Winzer Krems; Lenz Moser; Fritz Salomon; Schlumberger (sparkling wines); Georg Stiegelmar (classy French styles); Alexander Unger.

Austria: vintages

As elsewhere in Europe, 1989 was an excellent vintage for Austria. Grüner Veltliner wines should generally be drunk as young as possible. The better Rieslings may be aged for several years. Particularly good years for dessert wines from Burgenland have been 1986, 1983, 1981, 1979, 1976, 1971 and 1969.

Stockists

Alba Wine Society; Raeburn Fine Wines; A L Vose; The Wine Schoppen.

Wink Lorch is a freelance wine writer, editor, lecturer and wine consultant.

Italy

Maureen Ashley MW

.. Italian wines are wines of the heart, not the head ..

Mention the wines of Italy and the first word that comes to mind is exciting. The wines are as exciting, and excitingly varied, as the country itself. And, just as in Tuscany the Tuscan scenery seems the most stupendous but in Abruzzo it is the Abruzzese scenery that is of incomparable splendour, so anyone who spends a bit of time investigating the wines of any one area will soon find themselves becoming an evangelist on that area's behalf.

For the excitement of Italy is not the quiet satisfaction of seeing slight but successful changes of emphasis and small refinements to what is basically a stable wine scene, it is the great whoops of joy at finding a country of awe-inspiring potential, where anything is possible; where, despite innumerable years of tradition, everything – accepted ideas as well as new theories – has been thrown into the melting pot, stirred well and poured out again; where every producer is doing whatever he or she can to nurture and fulfil a wine's potential. It is the thrill of discovering, year by year, completely new tastes and flavours in wines both new and traditional, from grapes both new (which can also mean old but newly rediscovered) and traditional. And it is the elation at seeing what was, until a year or so ago, a pretty chaotic jumble of producers begin to act with new-found professionalism, maturity of approach and confidence.

Finding your way around

One of the most frequent criticisms of Italian wines is that they are hard to understand. The complaint is not so much about the tastes of the wines as their birthright: a hotchpotch of regions, districts, communes, vineyards, vine varieties, estate names, producers' names, traditional names and invented names.

It is true that there *are* a lot of names to grapple with, but no more than for several other wine countries. The fact is that wine is made all over Italy, not just in half a dozen or so discrete wine regions, so it is less easy to latch onto geographical 'grab-handles' and proceed from there. But, in essence, Italian wine nomenclature is no more complicated than any other – indeed, it is much more straightforward than some.

Proof of the pudding

Remember the uninviting looking bottle of Italian wine on a shop shelf? No more. No Italian wine dares show its face these days unless dressed in *alta moda* with designer label and often tall, heavy, dark glass designer bottle too. Bottle manufacturers specialising in customised moulds have never had it so good. And as for label designers, they have been raised to new prominence: the well-informed vineyard visitor now has to ask not only who owns the estate and who makes the wine and who is the consultant oenologist, but also who designs the label, too!

There's no doubt that the instinctive Italian talent for design has created some remarkably beautiful and elegantly turned-out bottles. But beware. It is not only the top wines that have had their qualities reflected in head-turning labels. Image is all-important to Italians and many have realised the value-added effect of dressing up mediocre wine in smart wrappings. Enjoy the presentation by all means, but don't be fooled by it; it is the wine inside that counts.

New grapes for old

Or, perhaps more currently, old grapes for new. When you take into account the great variety of conditions in which grapes grow – latitudes stretching from Austria to Africa and altitudes ranging from sea level to over a thousand metres high, not to mention all manner of local weather and soil conditions – the fact that Italy has an unbelievable wealth of grape varieties is hardly surprising. For the moment, though, only a hundred or so are of any real importance. And practically every area has at least one variety which it can claim as its own. Often these are strictly local; either they thrive only under specific conditions, or nobody has ever really felt the need to plant them further afield. (Why should they, when the neighbours have their own varieties to tinker with?)

Other grape varieties, though, have such irresistible charms (the most important of which, historically, has been reliable, high yields) that they are now found far away from their original homeland – Barbera being the case in point. Of the few traditional varieties diffused throughout the entire country (Malvasia and Moscato are the classic examples here), most have been so changed by adaptation to their surroundings that, for instance, the Malvasia found in Friuli in the North-East now bears not much more than a passing resemblance to that found on Sicily's Aeolian Islands.

The two most 'Italian' of varieties are probably red Sangiovese and white Trebbiano, both from north-central Italy and both widespread there, as well as further afield. Trebbiano is planted in practically every nook and cranny of the country; only in the extreme North-West and extreme North-East has it failed to penetrate. Its chief use, apart from the capacity to produce prodigious yields if the grower so wishes, is in toning down overly assertive flavours from other varieties. But out of the maelstrom of experimentation have come one or two folk starting to show that the neutral Trebbiano (known as the Ugni Blanc in France) is capable of much more when cultivated with respect. Sangiovese is found less ubiquitously, having strayed without Trebbiano's confidence from its north-eastern heartland.

Although, in contrast to Trebbiano, it is evidently capable of producing top-notch wine, the situation is complicated by the seeming ease with which different clones have developed, some vastly superior to others.

The only other grapes you can be sure to find throughout Italy are those polyglot varieties, Cabernet Sauvignon and Chardonnay. Although both have been around in the North-East for the past 150 years, with evidence of Cabernet plantings in Tuscany much earlier than that, these varieties 'arrived' in Italy with a great hoo-ha during the 1980s. Both wowed producers only not with the user-friendly style that has made them probably the most sought-after varieties worldwide, but also with their modishness – and Italians are nothing if not slavish followers of fashion.

True, both can turn out fabulous wines in Italy, and true, making the most of them stimulated many producers to develop new wine-making skills, but when practically everyone had to have a plot of Cabernet, Chardonnay, or both, and when prime sites for high-quality native varieties were uprooted for the newcomers, it all got a bit too much.

The tide has now turned and the fascination of new flavours is being diverted into maximising the potential of the local varieties and, more excitingly, repropagating and experimenting with indigenous, lesser known, and sometimes almost extinct grapes.

If this trend continues, it can only result in still more exciting wines with unique tastes, and will ensure that Italy has a plethora of wines with unfamiliar flavours to intrigue us when terminal boredom with Cabernet and Chardonnay (from wherever in the world) sets in at last.

Large wood and small

It is well known that ageing potentially good wines in small new (newish) oak barrels can add an extra dimension to their flavour. It is probably less well known just how easily oak can dominate the taste of a wine, and there is no easy formula for determining which wines it will and will not suit. Italy has traditionally used large, old barrels (called *botti*) made mainly of Yugoslav oak and it is only relatively recently that '*barrique* fever' has swept the country. This word describes the classic 225-litre French oak Bordeaux barrel, but in Italy '*barrique*' tends to be used generically for all casks holding up to 500 litres or so.

The fashion for new oak has been one of the most pervasive in the past few years, prompted mainly, one supposes, by the seductiveness of rounded, vanillic, oaky flavours after years of more angular wines. The fact that Italy's most influential wine writer has been one of its strongest proponents cannot fail to have had its effect, either.

Without doubt a sojourn in new French *barriques* has helped some wines excel, when made from hard-pruned vines, giving enough stuffing and concentration to withstand the oak overlay. Wines from the Sangiovese and Barbera varieties are two cases that immediately spring to mind, as well as the new Cabernet Sauvignon and Chardonnay plantings. Too many wines, though, have had their character subsumed by the oak and even more have had the oaking done with an over-enthusiastic hand, creating a product needing longer to mature than the base wine can stand. The prices asked for these wines have been correspondingly over-enthusiastic, too.

There has been talk of the turning of the *barrique* tide for a couple of years now, without noticeable effect. Certainly a growing number of producers have begun to comment that, although the *barrique* can make wines more beguiling it also makes them all taste more similar; as it rounds off their angles, so it rounds down their individual characteristics. But for the graceful retreat from such a powerful trend, a face-saving excuse was needed. At last it has been found: 'We only did it to satisfy the American taste.'

Wine laws

(For the basic wine classification system, see opposite.)

Much has been said and written about Italy's wine laws, most of it condemnatory or at least patronising. Part of the criticism stems from the unrealistic expectation that once a set of rules exists Italians will mutely follow them; other complaints, equally out of tune with the Italian mentality, centre on the legislation's inability to keep up with developments on the Italian wine scene.

The realities of the situation are threefold. First, if DOC classifications are regarded as a snapshot of the state of the traditional Italian wine scene at any particular time, and all implications of quality are removed from their interpretation, the system more or less does what it sets out to do. Secondly, with the rapid evolution of new and improved wine styles in Italy it would be impossible for any classification system, however sophisticated, to keep pace, unless the criteria for inclusion in any particular DOC (or whatever system replaced it) became so slack that DOC on a label would give even the most informed drinker no indication of what sort of wine the bottle contained. It must be remembered, too, that Italian bureaucracy is not the fastest or most efficient in the world, to put it mildly.

Perhaps more importantly, though, the Italians do care about their wine law and are increasingly sensitive to the criticisms of it, both within the country and abroad. A major revision of the act that promulgated the wine law (known to Italians as 'the 930'), is in process. This revision is stimulating a lot of sensible, clear-headed, open discussion, full of positive suggestions and with a large number of worthy, knowledgeable and intelligent people taking part in the debate. There is a clear feeling that if the law *is* going to be revised, then this time they had better get it right and come up with something that will be adhered to in Italy, and respected both there and worldwide. With the country's new-found professionalism, they might just succeed.

Classification of Italian wines

You will end up with the most helpful appreciation of what the various categories signify if you regard them as style guides rather than qualitative groupings.

The backbone of the Italian wine classification system is DOC, Denominazione di Origine Controllata. Over 230 wines have gained DOC status since its inception in 1963 and the number continues to grow steadily. DOC, like equivalent categories in other EC countries, specifies production zones, grape varieties, maximum yields, minimum alcohol, minimum ageing periods and so on. Unlike its European counterparts, though, each DOC has to be lobbied for by local growers (and politicians), and the criteria laid down must be based on 'local tradition and practice'. This means that modern, innovative wines are eliminated from the DOC remit. It also has the somewhat uncomfortable result that where local traditions and practices had resulted in mediocre wines, such mediocrity became sanctioned by law.

An additional category, currently encompassing a few wines only, is DOCG (Denominazione di Origine Controllata e Garantita). Theoretically a 'superior' band, DOCs get promoted to DOCG, lock, stock and barrel: there has been no attempt to use the 'G' to segregate the best wines of any DOC zone. Since the more recent DOCG advancees are a mixed bunch, by no means representing the elite of Italian viticulture, it is not worth paying much attention to whether a wine's denomination includes the 'G' or not.

Wines not eligible for DOC status have no other category but vino da tavola, originally earmarked for the simplest quaffers, although there is a subsidiary grouping, known as IG, standing for Vino da Tavola ad Indicazione Geografica, in which the non-traditional wines sit. IG wines have restricted zones of origin and more informative labelling than straight vini da tavola. They are not, however, the Italian equivalent of vin de pays. That slot is reserved for vino tipico; vino tipico legislation, however, is still little past draft stage, despite ten years of official musings on the subject.

High quality, new-style, non-DOC Italian wines are often, but quite unofficially, called 'Super Vini da Tavola' to distinguish them from the normal, everyday kind. And in Tuscany, the epicentre of the new wave movement, the term 'Super-Tuscan' has been coined instead. All these wines will have been given some name or title, called a *nome di fantasia*, to distinguish them from the herd. Thus, for Signor X's special wine, grown in area Y from grape variety Z, all you have recall is its *nome di fantasia* (and the vintage).

There is as yet no official classification of vineyards, nor is there likely to be in the foreseeable future. There is, though, a growing tendency to separate out the production of particularly prized, or potentially prized, sites, and bottle it separately. The term in common usage for these single vineyard wines is *cru*, but as French protectionism has vetoed legal recognition of the term on Italian labels, a variety of other indicators, many of them drawn from local dialects, has been spawned. *Vigna* and *vigneto* are the most common but *podere*, *ronco*, *bricco*, *località*, *capitel*, *maso*, *sori* and others may be found.

Higher prices inevitable

There is no getting away from it: in 1991 Italian wine is going to cost you more than in 1990, and there is little likelihood of a return to prices of the 'good old days' of the 1980s. There are several causes for this, all interlinked.

The first is that for many years the vast majority of Italian wines were underpriced, giving producers margins so tight that there was little room for manoeuvre and every incentive to cut corners. As the nation changed its outlook from quantity to quality, increases were smaller than they might have been, since producers' traditional fears of losing sales to their rivals, and importers' urgings that we, the consumers, wouldn't be prepared to pay more for our wines, conspired to keep them to a minimum. So wines continued to be sold unrealistically cheaply. Remember that the greatest step towards heightened quality has been made by producers restricting yields. Yet if yields drop by a third, prices must increase by a half for income to stay the same (ignoring the small effect of fewer bottles, corks, etc.). Then came the excellent but small 1988 vintage producing some remarkably fine wines but putting pressure on supply. That of 1989 was nothing like as good, but created an acute shortfall, as quantity was again down and the only way really good wine could be produced in the great majority of cases was by being ruthlessly selective and rejecting a significant proportion of grapes. Grape prices soared.

At this point, wine price increases could be contained no longer and so many producers took the occasion, more or less thrust on them, for a thorough review of pricing policy to ensure at least an adequate return on costs in the future. At the same time, it has to be said, there have been more than a few producers taking advantage of the situation. Their wine is better than it used to be, true, but not all that much better. What has greatly improved is the presentation: the bottle and label. The price has risen, therefore, more to meet the image than in reflection of the wine itself.

There are also more than a few good quality producers who have realised, for the first time, that they have a product for which people are prepared to pay. With their pricing they are, to a certain extent, flexing their muscles and learning, by trial and error, just how much their wine really is worth. Where price hikes have been excessive there is little doubt they will settle down in the next few years. We may, understandably, moan and groan about such increases but the truth is that we have recently been drinking most good Italian wines too cheaply. It couldn't last.

The taste of Italy

It is impossible to sum up the taste of Italian wine, as it would to ascribe a taste to encapsulate all of France. The variations in climate, site and especially grape varieties can make this task difficult within a region, let alone given huge variables in latitude and altitude. Nevertheless, generalising wildly, if there is a thread linking the wines of the country, it is one of restrained, understated whites and of powerful, invigorating reds with firm acidity and a savoury tang.

Italian whites can seem to lack flavour for those coming to them from, for example, the big, brash tastes of oaky, New World Chardonnay. But then a curry eater might say the same about the flesh of a simply cooked trout. There is usually plenty of flavour to be found in Italian whites, often with nutty or mineral salt tones over a gentle, creamy base with a characteristic lightly bitter finish which leaves the mouth clean. All is contained and subtle; the wines allure gently and pervasively rather than impressing loudly. The more time you take over an Italian white, the more you find in it – at least if you buy something a bit better than basic, that is.

Reds often have the aromas of an Italian delicatessen about

them: they can be meaty, smoky, herby, spicy, even garlicky. Tea, coffee or chocolate won't be out of place as analogies either. Sometimes fruit is not the dominant characteristic; it can be hidden under a welter of other sensations. In others, there is a variable explosion of vibrant fruitiness – cherries for some wines, plums or prunes for others, raspberries from time to time, redcurrants, and so on. Italian reds are enlivening; even those from the warmest areas have a characteristic streak of integral acidity. When this combines with high tannin they can seem pretty astringent, until drunk – as they would always be in Italy – with food, when their flavours will leap into perspective. This acidity is the wines' life-blood; the Italian-tuned palate can find even the smartest of other wines lifeless and dull by comparison.

Italy also has some of the world's most undervalued rosés, from light-as-a-whisper almost-whites to succulent near-reds.

Italian wines are rarely the thing for those who want to appreciate wine: they are for those who prefer to revel in it. They are exciting, not refined; they stimulate conversation not critical appraisal; they attack the emotions far more than the intellect. When the quality is good, you may love them or hate them but you'll rarely be indifferent to them.

In short, Italian wines are wines of the heart, not the head.

THE NORTH-WEST

Piemonte, Valle d'Aosta, Liguria

North-west Italy is a land of contradictions, where the most austere, slow-developing, serious of reds sit happily with the lightest, most frivolous of whites; where the most avant-garde of producers live next door to the most stolidly traditional; where the most honest and finely crafted of wines are made just a short hop from enormous, any-wine-will-do bottling establishments; and where the angular lines of the Langhe hills, home to Barolo and Barbaresco, often appear soft under the pervasive mists.

For most wine folk north-west Italy means Barolo and Barbaresco – or at least the south-eastern quarter of Piemonte that is home to them. Home, too, to other wines made from Nebbiolo, as well as red Dolcetto and Barbera, white Moscato, Cortese (di Gavi), Arneis and less well diffused varietals such as Grignolino, Freisa, Brachetto and Favorita. The wines of northern Piemonte – Carema, Erbaluce di Caluso, Caluso Passito, Gattinara, Ghemme et al – are less easy to come by and often less consistent in quality. Valle d'Aosta, in the extreme North-West, has a plethora of wine styles and names, most of academic interest only unless you happen to be motoring through the region. Liguria, on the other hand, after generations of ignoring the world beyond its narrow riviera, is starting to export white Vermentino and Pigato, and red Ormeasco (Dolcetto) and Rossese under the umbrella name Riviera Ligure di Ponente.

Nebbiolo is the heart and soul of north-west Italy, maybe even the soul of the entire country. It is one of those rare beasts, a red variety that can produce wines of almost infinite complexity without the assistance of any other grape. It is also the variety that stirs more passions than any other; its aficionados, who become almost ecstatic at its austere brilliance, scarcely outnumber those who find little to commend in its astringent sulkiness. A genius can be hard to live with.

The genius of Nebbiolo expresses itself best in wines from the twin zones of Barolo and Barbaresco, whose harsh, seemingly unyielding exterior layers slowly give way to an intriguing nugget of fruit. This may be light as raspberries and violets or rich as prunes and chocolate. Modern styles may be more fruit-forward, but the shell of tannin and acid should still be there. Nebbiolo d'Alba and Roero are usually more accessible while Nebbiolo delle Langhe is the most common IG for experimental wines – so anything can result.

Dolcetto is the perfect counterpoint to Nebbiolo and is often drunk before it at a meal. It is bright-toned, bright-tasting and just packed with enchanting berry-like fruit. A few producers age their Dolcetto; it is usually at its most striking, though, within a year or two of the vintage. The grape comes from several zones of south-east Piemonte, and the wine's name will specify which: Dolcetto d'Alba (often the most reliable), Dolcetto d'Asti and so on.

Barbera, similarly differentiated by origin, is more muscular, with much more forceful, almost shockingly invigorating acidity – more cranberries than redcurrants, say, although both these fruits get a look in. Barbera d'Alba is seen most often and has greater heft than the more typical Barbera d'Asti, leaving Barbera del Monferrato to satisfy those searching for Barbera in a lighter, more frolicsome mould.

Sadly underrated, all too easily dismissed, the feather-light, grapily sweet wines based on Moscato are a unique gift to Piemonte. From nowhere else is Moscato so ethereally delicate, whether made fully sparkling or with barely a prickle. The wines are easy on the head, too, since they are often as low in alcohol as they can get away with without losing the right to be called wine. Along the same lines but pink, more strawberry-like and often a little sweeter is the too infrequently seen Brachetto d'Acqui.

Gavi, made from the Cortese grape and occasionally called Cortese di Gavi, is the complete opposite: often overrated and with far more attention paid to it than it merits. Goodness knows how, but it managed to become that dangerous entity, a high fashion wine – and its price rose to meet the challenge. It is all too easy to be disappointed with Gavi, especially if you forget that Italians rate restraint in their whites. If you buy from the better estates, though, and are prepared to allow the wine to work on you slowly and subtly, you may begin to understand what all the fuss is about. By no stretch of the imagination, however, could Gavi be rated as value for money. Gavi di Gavi implies superiority, but technically signifies only that the grapes have been grown in the commune of Gavi (just part of the DOC zone).

Arneis has recently become the wonder-wine of Piemonte. Newly DOC, with grape prices having soared almost beyond affordability, it is in great demand, despite mutterings that many Arneis wines seem to have more personality than the none-too-characterful grape can provide.

Recommended producers

Barola and/or Barbaresco Altare; Ceretto; Clerico; Aldo Conterno; Giacomo Conterno; Paolo Cordero di Montezemolo; Cortese; Fontanafredda (especially *crus*); Gaja; Bruno Giacosa; Marchesi di Gresy; Mascarello; Oddero; Pio Cesare; Produttori del Barbaresco; Prunotto; Ratti; Scarpa; Scavino; Sebaste; Vajra; Vietti; Voerzio.
Nebbiolo d'Alba As Barolo/Barbaresco.
Dolcetto d'Alba Altare; Castello di Neive; Clerico; Aldo Conterno; Giacomo Conterno; Paolo Cordero de Montezemolo; Gaja; Bruno Giacosa; Mascarello; Prunotto; Ratti; Vajra; Vietti; Voerzio; Viticoltori dell'Acquese; Fontanafredda 'Cru' La Lepre.
Dolcetto d'Acqui Viticoltori dell'Acquese.
Barbera d'Alba Giacomo Bologna; Castello di Neive; Pio Cesare; Clerico, Aldo Conterno; Giacomo Conterno; Duca d'Asti; Gaja; Bruno Giacosa; Mascarello; Prunotto; Ratti; Rivetti; Scarpa; Vajra; Vietti.
Barbera d'Asti Bologna; Cascina Castlet; Duca d'Asti.
Asti Spumante Arione; Duca d'Asti; Fontanafredda; Vallebelbo; Vignaioli di Santo Stefano.
Moscato d'Asti Ascheri; Bologna; Dogliotti; Rivetti; Vietti; Vignaioli di Santo Stefano.
Brachetto d'Acqui Bologna; Viticoltori dell'Acquese; Scarpa.
Gavi La Scolca; La Giustiniana; Castello di Tassarolo; La Battistina; La Chiara.
Roero Arneis Castello di Neive, Deltetto, Malvirà

Where there is no wine, love perishes, and everything else that is pleasant to man.
Euripides

Barolo, Barbaresco

Type *Full red wines, Barbaresco being slightly less full than Barolo*
Profile *Complex, suggesting some or all of violets, tar, truffles, raspberries, prunes, liquorice, chocolate, meat stock, earth and smoke, but can be austere or astringent, especially when young*
Advice *Have patience! Be prepared to keep the better vintages for up to ten years or more. Drink with fully flavoured foods*

Dolcetto

Type *Medium to full-bodied fruity red*
Profile *Ripe berry fruit, perfectly dry, firm, fruity acidity, lowish tannin, plenty of punch*
Advice *Drink with food: the younger the wine is the better*

Barbera

Type *Full (Barbera d'Alba), medium (Barbera d'Asti) or light (Barbera del Monferrato) red*
Profile *Dominant acidity, cranberry, redcurrant, plums and plum-skin flavours, low tannin*
Advice *Needs quite rich food; wines from the better vintages, and barrique-aged wines, may be cellared*

Moscato

Type *Very light, delicate, sweet white, may be fully sparkling (Asti Spumante, Moscato d'Asti Spumante), semi-sparkling or almost still (Moscato Naturale d'Asti), low in alcohol*
Profile *Grapey, musky, with hints of roses and apples*
Advice *The younger the better. Buy from stores with a quick turnover and drink immediately, either on its own or with fruit or rich desserts*

Gavi

Type *Dry white*
Profile *Steely-firm, creamy, with nut kernel, apple, honey and lemon hints*
Advice *Rest for a few months before drinking, unless bought in a mature state. A fine aperitif, and good with light dishes*

Arneis

Type *Dry white*
Profile *Subtle, sometimes quite aromatic, at other times weightier and nuttier, often with flavours of ripe pears*
Advice *A useful, flexible wine, but no longer good value*

THE CENTRAL NORTH

Lombardia, western edge of Emilia-Romagna

Lombardia is a strange, uncoordinated region as far as wine is concerned. Much of the terrain is flat, lying along the alluvial, often fog-bound plain of the massive Po river valley and more suited to rice, poplar trees and maize than vineyards; at least, that is, where the enormous urban sprawl of Milan and its surroundings hasn't blotted out agriculture altogether. But wherever the land turns hilly and rises above the fogs and stifling, humid summer heat it has been capitalised upon for viticulture, ensuring that those industrialists don't go thirsty! There is little, though, in common between the wines of each outcrop.

Just a small part of Lombardia, in its extreme west, dips south of the Po valley and hits the hills of Pavia, forming the zone of Oltrepò Pavese. Oltrepò Pavese is contiguous with the zone of Colli Piacentini in the neighbouring region of Emilia-Romagna and the wines are not dissimilar in style, so it makes sense to discuss the two areas together. The wines are generally lightish, with the emphasis, deliberately, on drinkability and ease of partnership with a wide variety of foods rather than on creating sparks in their own right. The local taste is for wines with a bit of a bubble, reds as well as whites, although producers have been persuaded to eliminate this fizz for us. Most wines are varietals, with Barbera, Bonarda and Pinot Nero leading the reds (only in Colli Piacentini is a highly successful Barbero/Bonarda blend called Gutturnio found), while Malvasia, Ortrugo (Colli Piacentini), Moscato, Riesling Italico, and Riesling Renano (Oltrepò Pavese) head the whites. Oltrepò Pavese is also one of Italy's most important centres for sparkling wine, far too much of which ends up anonymously in major brands.

The north of Lombardia climbs up into sub-alpine terrain, unsuitable for viticulture except where the east-west-flowing River Adda creates a special microclimate permitting Nebbiolo to ripen for the Valtellina wines. At their best they are supremely elegant forms of Nebbiolo; at their worst they are unripe, dull and rapidly oxidising. Sassella, Grumello, Inferno and Valgella are particularly evocatively named sub-districts of the Valtellina Superiore.

East from Milan towards Brescia is a welcome range of lowish hills, giving birth to Franciacorta. Franciacorta red is, on paper, a weird animal indeed, being made from Piemonte's Barbera and Nebbiolo and Friuli's Cabernet Franc and Merlot. Much as the modernists in the area are trying to eliminate the Piemonte half of the blend, the originality of Franciacorta depends upon that part's rawness and bite to complement the rounder, softer flavours of the 'French' grapes. There's no traditionalist-modernist conflict with Franciacorta Bianco: it is a flinty mix of Pinot Blanc and Chardonnay, rarely less than pleasant, sometimes quite classy. Franciacorta Spumante (from the same varieties) is heading for fame and fortune, though: while not consciously attempting to imitate the master, on a good day it could give all but the best champagnes a run for their money.

Next door, Valcalepio, with its Merlot/Cabernet reds and Pinot Bianco/Pinot Grigio whites, has a few good producers turning out proficient, enjoyable wines which have more the taste of north Italy than the international taste about them – thank goodness.

Lugana, in the extreme south-east of Lombardia, on lovely undulating territory south of Lake Garda, is one of the few yawn-free wines made from Trebbiano, primarily, one assumes, because the local clone, Trebbiano di Lugana, has miraculously developed elements that give *taste*. Still, however, understated and delicately creamy-nutty with a gently bitter end, it has more in common with its neighbours in the Veneto than with other Lombardian wines.

Recommended producers

Oltrepò Pavese Fugazza.
Colli Piacentini Fugazza.
Gutturnio Fugazza; Romagnoli; Zerioli.
Valtellina Negri; Enologica Valtellinese.
Franciacorta Rosso/Franciacorta Bianco Bellavista; Ca' del Bosco (atypical; French-style; expensive); Cavalleri.
Franciacorta Spumante Bellavista; Ca' del Bosco.
Valcalepio La Cornasella.
Lugana Ca' dei Frati; Zenato.

> *Back in my home I drink a cup of wine*
> *And need not fear the greed of the evening wind.*
> Lu Yu

Gutturnio

Type *Medium-weight, lively red*
Profile *Lively, zippy acidity yet rounded, cherry and chocolate flavours*
Advice *Well worth tracking down, best when youngish, good with rich or lighter foods*

Franciacorta Rosso

Type *Medium-weight, refined red*
Profile *Supple, rounded, grassy overtones, slight meat-stock character, firm backbone, unique and distinctive*
Advice *Best with lighter dishes; can be drunk young or aged*

Franciacorta Spumante

Type *Top-quality, dry sparkling wine*
Profile *Refined, grassy, salty, creamy, yeasty, long*
Advice *Treat like champagne*

Lugana

Type *Soft, light, dry white*
Profile *Floral, walnuts, apple bite, touch of orange peel*
Advice *Drink cool and young*

THE NORTH-EAST

Eastern Veneto, Friuli-Venezia-Giulia, Trentino-Alto Adige

North-eastern of Italy is the land of single varietals, and a seemingly profligate number of them, too. It is quite understandable why this should be so in Trentino-Alto Adige, but less clear in the rest of the North-East. The viticultural parts of Trentino and Alto Adige, which lead up to the Brenner Pass and the Austrian border, form, for the most part, the sides of a giant rift valley, that of the River Adige. Grapes can grow anywhere from the valley floor to – in the most extreme cases, where sites enjoy maximum sun exposure and wind shelter – 1000 metres or so. As the altitude increases and the temperature correspondingly drops, different grape varieties find suitable conditions. A number of these varietals are what we would consider to be German (Riesling Renano, Sylvaner, Müller-Thurgau, for example), while Gewürztraminer, also widely grown, is believed to have originated here, in the Alto Adige village of Tramin. Others are considered 'French' by outsiders: Cabernet Franc and Sauvignon, Merlot, Pinot Bianco, Grigio and Nero and so on, despite having been in north-east Italy long enough to have gone native. The rest of Italy is represented by Moscato and Malvasia. There are five indigenous varieties: light, cheerful, red Schiava; big, chunky red Lagrein (which demonstrates its versatility by making a delicate rosé too); firm red Teroldego, found only in north Trentino; cheerful red Marzemino, only from Trentino's south; and white, love-it-or-hate-it Nosiola, belonging just to Trentino, but not widespread even there. The summer climate is surprisingly hot by day but very cold by night with the result that all these varieties develop intense aromas and very pure varietal characteristics – as long as their producers are disciplined enough to restrict yields firmly.

The reputation of the northern, Alto Adige, half of the region is based on its whites, despite their being too intensely aromatic, in the main part, for Italian tastes. Yet production of reds outstrips whites by almost four to one. In Trentino, the honours are more evenly divided and much more sparkling wine is made, some of it of very high quality. Otherwise there are few viticultural differences between the two parts of the region: the Adige valley is narrower in Alto Adige, where the bordering mountains are higher; there's more warmth, by contrast, for reliable ripening in Trentino. The most important difference between the two sub-regions is cultural, not viticultural: a majority of Alto Atesini are of Austrian descent and persist in considering themselves 'Süd Tirolen' – you will see many bilingual or German-only wine labels. The Trentini, on the other hand, are contentedly Italian.

Apart from the occasional Germanic clutter, label nomenclature is generally simple, giving just the name of the sub-region and the grape variety. Teroldego has its own DOC, Teroldego Rotaliano. There are also a few other separate DOCs, usually to cope with blends or with districts straddling the Trentino/Alto Adige border; Santa Maddalena (mainly Schiava, just outside Bolzano), Lago di Caldaro (mainly Schiava, grown near and not-so-near the eponymous lake in both sub-regions), Terlano (a white blend or a varietal from western Alto Adige) and Valdadige (red and white blends produced throughout the Adige valley).

If Trentino-Alto Adige is Austrian Italy, Friuli-Venezia-Giulia is Yugoslav Italy. The reason why so many varieties have arrived in the region probably has much to do with its strategic position on the 'crossroads of Europe', where the major traditional north-south and east-west trading (and warfaring) routes intersect. In addition, its people are remarkably steady, studious yet forward-thinking folk and are always ready to increase the range of varietals they feel their region can support.

Friuli (as it is usually called) certainly doesn't have Trentino-Alto Adige's altitudes, much of the region being flat with only one long ridge of hills in its extreme east. If it isn't the height that helps the 'cool climate' varieties thrive, it is the rain – Appennine peaks excepted, this is Italy's wettest area – and the cold *bora* wind that can send temperatures plummeting within minutes. Friuli's reputation is high, most notably for its white wines – which can attain an amazing intensity of long-lasting flavour, without growing big and bulky, and without losing their classic Italian restraint. As is the case with Bordeaux, this reputation has been achieved by comparatively few top wines, in Friuli's case those coming from the hilly eastern strip of Collio and Colli Orientali del Friuli. These two zones lie next to each other and are best regarded as one, the border between them being a political (provincial) one, rather than a viticultural one.

Beyond these zones, in the predominantly flatter terrain of Grave del Friuli (to be fair it undulates gently) whites can be surprisingly good if yields are ruthlessly contained. Among native varieties the white Ribolla tends to be looked down on locally, so too few put the requisite effort into maximising its intriguing lemon-cream character and subtle but lingering presence. They are prouder of Verduzzo, which can vary from a thin, acidic dry white to a luscious, florally honeyed, non-cloying sweet gem; and Picolit, which despite naturally low yields and correspondingly high prices, can be a delicate, entrancing dessert wine. Native reds include the widely planted Refosco and the fabulous, punchy, brambly Schioppettino. The Grave del Friuli vineyards extend right to Friuli's western border; in fact they go beyond it into Veneto, where they become Lison-Pramaggiore and, west again, crossing the Piave river, Piave. Here, in Lison-Pramaggiore at least, the reason for a large clutch of varietals seems to be no more than fashion: just Tocai, Merlot and Cabernet were the essence of the zone until very recently.

In Piave, flat as the proverbial pancake (this is the back yard of Venice), the motive for maintaining a nurseryful of varieties is even less clear, although, surprisingly enough, high quality wines can result. This is especially true in the case of the indigenous Raboso, as long as – the usual bleat – producers keep their yields right down.

A glass of wine in Venice means something light and fizzy – Prosecco, from the zone based around the towns of Conegliano and Valdobbiadene, north of Piave. This area is the exception to the multi-varietal rule. There is just Prosecco, made still, semi-sparkling or fully sparkling, grown on the flat or in the hills around endless small, war-torn villages, each with its bell tower like a mini copy of the one in St Mark's Square. If you like sparkling wine to be a serious affair, don't even look at Prosecco. But if sometimes you want something that's fun to drink, that's just like an easy-drinking white, but with bubbles in, Prosecco's your wine. (NB: Wine labelled Trevenezie or Triveneto can come from more or less any variety grown more or less anywhere in eastern Veneto, Trentino and Friuli.)

Recommended producers

Alto Adige Lageder; Tiefenbrunner; CS Colterenzio; Viticoltori Alto-Adige.
Trentino Fedrigotti (Cabernet Merlot); Gaierhof (Chardonnay); Guerrieri-Gonzaga (Cabernet); Pojer & Sandri; Zeni.
Trentino Spumante Ferrari.
Lago di Caldaro Lageder; Schloss Schwandburg; Tiefenbrunner.
Santa Maddalena Lageder.
Teroldego Rotaliano Zeni.
Collio Jermann; Schiopetto; Borgo Conventi; Ca' Ronesca; Gradnik; Russiz Superiore.
Colli Orientali Dri; Volpe Pasini.
Grave del Friuli Collavini.
Piave Rechsteiner.
Prosecco Carpené Malvolti.

Schiava

Type *Lightweight red*
Profile *Sweet-sour, strawberry yoghurt and bacon flavours, tastes better than it sounds!*
Advice *Summer or picnic quaffer*

Lagrein Scuro/Lagrein Dunkel

Type *Solid, dark red*
Profile *Fruit sometimes does not taste fully ripe, fruit flavours mingling with rich chocolate, gaining complexity as the wine matures*
Advice *Drink young or wait four or five years. Good with rich or heavy foods*

Lagrein Rosato/Lagrein Kretzer

Type *Light-coloured, mid-weight rosé*
Profile *Firm, strawberry and plum fruitiness, clean bitter finish*
Advice *Drink young or youngish, chilled*

Teroldego Rotaliano

Type *Mid-full, dark red*
Profile *Grassy, plums and redcurrants, strong liquorice tone with allspice, peppery*
Advice *Drink young and fruity or wait at least four years*

Marzemino

Type *Light, fresh, gluggable red*
Profile *'Italian Beaujolais' with riper, more redcurranty fruit*
Advice *Drink young or youngish, possibly slightly chilled in summer*

Refosco

Type *Firm, mid-weight red*
Profile *Tangy, tarry, mixed berry fruits, very dry, salty, bitter finish*
Advice *Needs food, but choose a dish that is neither too heavy nor too rich*

Piave Raboso

Type *Chunky, mid-full red*
Profile *Sweet-sour fruit, herby, earthy, tannic*
Advice *Drink as soon as tannin subsides, from two years on*

Prosecco di Conegliano

Type *Light, cheerful, still or sparkling white*
Profile *Soft, apply-milky, touch of spice. Not a yeasty sparkler – like still wine with bubbles. Refreshing*
Advice *Drink, chilled, at any time*

WEST AND CENTRAL VENETO

With an extensive coastline along Lake Garda, remarkable, beautiful cities like Venice and Verona, and an incomparable wealth of Palladian villas, it is not surprising that the Veneto has no shortage of tourists to bolster its local economy. It has no shortage of wine, either, and it has seemed in recent years as if its wine producers had taken their cue from the worst aspects of their sister industry: they were far more concerned with filling as many mouths as possible with happy juice than with the quality of the stuff they were purveying. It even reached the stage where producers in Soave and Valpolicella, with wines already dilute from over-high yields, were asking for their DOC yield limits to be increased further.

Thankfully, commonsense has prevailed over greed and in the 'big three' zones of western Veneto, Soave, Valpolicella and Bardolino, strung out in a line westwards towards Lake Garda, even the giants are desperately trying to regain credibility by paying a bit more attention to their basic quality levels. Trying, too, to win respect by means of *crus*, Super Vini da Tavola, new wave varietals, *barrique*-ageing – every trick in the book.

For straightforward Soave and Valpolicella, the advice remains much as it always has been: stick to the better producers and always go for Classico wines; only with Classico are you sure the grapes come from hill slopes, and without hillside vineyards there is little hope for anything worthy of interest. One novelty worth investigating, however, is La Poja, made solely from Corvina, and an unprecedented opportunity to see what Valpolicella's major variety is capable of when unblended.

Valpolicella made from *passito* (semi-dried) grapes is quite a different beast: a big, strapping wine, so mouth-filling and full of oomph that it makes you wonder how a wine can assume such Jekyll and Hyde behaviour. When dry it is called Amarone; Recioto when sweet – and for an easy-on-the-head alternative to port, the latter is hard to beat. To find a halfway house between Jekyll and Hyde, the advice is to search out a *ripasso* Valpolicella: it combines the drinkability of Valpolicella with some of the weight and richness of Amarone. '*Ripasso*' signifies a Valpolicella refermented on the lees of Amarone. The problem is that the term has failed to acquire legal recognition and so it will never be seen on a label; some producers sell their *ripasso* wines as vini da tavola anyway, so you're none the wiser (but see our recommendations below). There's a Recioto di Soave too, just as revelatory as the Valpolicella version compared with normal Soave: it is a gently sweet, floral gem.

Bardolino is doubly fortunate in that most of its vineyards, Classico or not, are on sloping terrain, and as they are right by Lake Garda, that vast mass of water creates a sunnier, more benign microclimate. Bardolino is usually best young and fresh; it can lose fruit and life all too quickly when any but the real experts make it. Some of the zippiest come from the southern, non-Classico, part of the zone. Buying Classico wines, therefore, is not as essential as for Soave and Valpolicella. Bardolino also hides a delightful surprise under its denomination, but one as different from Amarone as you could imagine: Bardolino Chiaretto is a pale rosé mainly from the south of the zone – dry, gentle and elegant. If only there weren't so much anti-rosé prejudice around it might be more readily available. The same southern part of Bardolino is home to Bianco di Custoza, a Soave-like wine made more interesting by judicious amounts of the more characterful Tocai, Cortese, Malvasia and Riesling Italico added to the normal Garganega/ Trebbiano blend. Gambellara, on the other hand, contiguous with the Soave zone to its east, is so Soave-like that it hardly merits a separate denomination.

Further east again, in central Veneto, lies the one-producer zone of Breganze. Without Fausto Maculan, who has single-handedly raised the area to deserved prominence with a supremely professional range of modernist wines (see recommendations below), Breganze would be as much an also-ran zone as the Colli Euganei and Colli Berici – hardly names that trip off any tongues save those of the locals. Mind you, if someone could be persuaded to import the excellent range of Colli Berici varietals from Villa dal Ferro-Lazzarini things might change.

Recommended producers

Valpolicella Classico Boscaini; Guerrieri-Rizzardi; Masi; Tedeschi; Zenato.
Ripasso Valpolicella Allegrini; Jago from Bolla; Le Cane from Boscaini; Le Ragose; Quintarelli; Castelli d'Illasi from Santi; Serègo Alighieri; also the Vini da Tavola Campo Fiorin from Masi and Capitel San Rocco from Tedeschi.
La Poja Allegrini.
Amarone della Valpolicella Allegrini; Le Ragose; Masi (*crus*); Quintarelli; Serègo Alighieri; Tedeschi.
Soave Classico Anselmi; Pieropan; Prà; Vigneto di Monteforte from Santi.
Recioto di Soave Pieropan.
Bardolino Young styles from Le Vigne di San Pietro, Fraterna Portalupi; briefly aged styles from Boscaini, Masi (La Vegrona), Guerrieri-Rizzardi.
Bardolino Chiaretto Le Vigne di San Pietro; Fraterna Portalupi.
Bianco di Custoza Le Vigne di San Pietro; Tedeschi; Zenato.
Breganze Maculan; especially Breganze di Breganze (mainly Tocai); Prato di Canzio (mainly Chardonnay); Palazzotto and Fratta (both Cabernet Sauvignon); Torcolato (*passito* from mainly Vespaiolo); also Ferrata (Chardonnay, Cabernet Sauvignon) Super Vini da Tavola.

Soave Classico

Type *Dry white wine*
Profile *Gentle, cream and apples, hint of blanched almonds, more almondy aftertaste with some bitterness. Best wines have aroma and peachy fruit. Ordinary wines are light and neutral*
Advice *Drink youngest available. Well worth spending a little more to buy the top wines*

Valpolicella Classico

Type *Light to mid-weight red,* ripasso *styles mid to full*
Profile *Bitter cherries, anything from white-hearts to wine-drenched morellos; smoky, leathery notes dominate the fuller, less youthful wines; life-saving acidity, moderate tannin levels*
Advice *Drink either young and perky, or after two or three years. Serve with rich but not overly heavy food*

Amarone della Valpolicella

Type *Full red*
Profile *Seems sweet initially, but as it passes through the mouth it gets progressively drier up until the strongly dry and bitter finish. Concentrated, porty, plummy cherries*
Advice *Wait for a special occasion in the cooler months. Serve after the main course is over, give yourself plenty of time to savour the wine and let its magic work on you*

Bardolino Chiaretto

Type *Light, elegant, very pale rosé*
Profile *Strawberry and ripe cherry fruit backed by apple-like crispness*
Advice *Drink as young as possible, on its own or with light foods. Highly recommended*

If all be true that I do think
There are five reasons why we should drink;
Good wine – a friend – or being dry –
Or lest we should be by and by –
Or any other reason why.
Latin saying, versified by Henry Aldrich

Bianco di Custoza

Type *Dry, lightish white*
Profile *Hints of peaches, greengages, hazelnuts and almonds enliven a gentle creamy base*
Advice *Drink the youngest wine available, cool, with or without food*

EMILIA-ROMAGNA

(For the north-western corner of Emilia-Romagna, see under Lombardia)

The Po river valley may well be a godsend to Italy's agricultural ambitions, but it puts a real dampener on most viticultural aspirations along its path. Nowhere is this seen more graphically than in Emilia-Romagna, with its intensive fruit cultivation, famed Parmesan cheese and vast dairy production, renowned Parma ham, salami and other cured meat products, yet little really tempting in the way of wine. Indeed, if there were an award for the most flagrantly false advertising claim, it would be the banner *'Emilia-Romagna: dove si mangia bene – e si beve meglio'* ('Emilia-Romagna: where you eat well – and drink better'). The only variety that seems to do well in the Po's alluvial plains – humid, flat, often pea-soup foggy, stifling in summer, freezing in winter – is Lambrusco. High-yielding, spatially and quantitatively, made by huge companies full of equipment to tame a naturally unpredictable wine into the most predictable in Italy, who dare cry 'not fair' when Lambrusco is called 'soda pop' or 'cherryade' and given scant regard? And that's despite the fact that this lowish-alcohol, sweetish 'cherryade' can slip down a treat, while the less sweetish stuff matches rich salami like few other wines (except Oltrepò Pavese-Colli Piacentini Bonarda and Barbera) can. Commercial Lambrusco developed from the natural tendency of fermentations here to block in winter and sometimes to restart in spring, giving a more-or-less fizzy, more-or-less sweet, more-or-less low-alcohol wine. It is not a marketing department's creation. Indeed, when made seriously, meaning making the most of its natural characteristics without turning it into something it is not, and when tasted without inbuilt prejudices, Lambrusco really shows itself worthy of respect.

Between Bologna, the centre of the region, and the Adriatic coast, three sprawling DOCs cover vast swathes of terrain, some of it in the Apennine foothills and therefore theoretically quite promising, although too much is flat. Albana di Romagna, Sangiovese di Romagna and Trebbiano di Romagna are rarely worth searching out, though, and often not worth spending money on even when they are staring you in the face. One of only two reliably good estates, Fattoria Paradiso, has repropagated a few almost-extinct grapes which are worth trying, especially the big, ripe, comforting, sit-in-front-of-the-fire-and-forget-your-woes Barbarossa. Otherwise, there is only the outcrop of low hills behind Bologna, the Colli Bolognesi, with its flurry of 'French' and 'German' varieties to inspire interest – of an occasional sort.

Recommended producers

Serious Lambrusco Cavicchioli.
Albana di Romagna Fattoria Paradiso.
Sangiovese from Romagna Fattoria Paradiso, Castelluccio.
Colli Bolognesi Terre Rosse.

Lambrusco

Type *Light, sweetish, fizzy red*
Profile *Lowish alcohol, cherry-like, dry finish*
Advice *Forget your prejudices, treat as a fun drink; try with salami; also try drier types of Lambrusco when available*

Barbarossa

Type *Full, ripe red*
Profile *Plummy, blackcurranty, spicy, fruit-packed, tannic, mouth-filling*
Advice *Save for cold winter nights, with full-flavoured foods*

CENTRAL EAST

Marche, Abruzzo, Molise

A journey south from Rimini through central Adriatic Italy brings continuing change. From the calm, rural tranquillity of the Marche, with the warm beige of its soil and the bright green of its plant life, only intermittently vine-charged, through the dazzling, multi-coloured splendour of the wild, mountainous Abruzzo to hot, underpopulated Molise, northern Italy gradually turns into the South. The change is reflected by the red grape varieties grown. The Sangiovese of the northern Marche soon finds conditions too warm and needs to be blended with increasing proportions of the Montepulciano that starts making its appearance in wines such as Rosso Conero and Rosso Piceno. Rosso Piceno Superiore, by the way, comes from a restricted area round Ascoli Piceno and is therefore equivalent to a Classico sub-denomination; it is much better than the *normale*.

Once the Abruzzo border is crossed, Sangiovese is eliminated almost entirely and Montepulciano holds sway unchallenged until, in Molise, conditions get too southern for even that rugged variety and it gradually diminishes in favour of Aglianico, *the* great red grape of the South. For example, in Molise's Biferno DOC, Aglianico has a minority presence, although its best producer and the region's leading estate (Di Majo Norante) also makes a 100 per cent Aglianico, which shows off the grape's glories sumptuously.

The white varieties of the central east reveal different facets of the area. Middle Italy is Trebbiano's stronghold, yet despite incursions on all sides, the Marche heartland has remained immune to its invasion and has kept faith with its own Verdicchio, most notably from the area behind Jesi (dei Castelli di Jesi) and Matelica. As an ideal fish-accompanying wine in an area with a long coastline and correspondingly high fish consumption (boosted by the appetites of summer visitors) Verdicchio may not have been ousted because it has always remained economically viable.

Abruzzo (whose narrower coastal strip draws few visitors, and whose inland heart is fortified by meat-eating) abandoned its own white varieties to Trebbiano almost entirely during the lemming-like drive for bulk sales in the 1960s and 1970s – more's the pity. Trebbiano here is rarely better than average, whereas Bombino Bianco (confusingly called Trebbiano d'Abruzzo in the region) could have given Abruzzo some really fine, suitable vinestocks to work with in the more enlightened and knowledgeable 1990s, had it not been uprooted almost entirely. The picture is much the same in Molise, except that Di Majo Norante is working very hard and successfully with some salvaged Bombino Bianco, as he is with Falanghina, a superb southern white variety.

Recommended producers

Verdicchio dei Castelli di Jesi Fratelli Bucci; Colle del Sole and Il Pallio from Monte Schiavo; Casal di Serra from Umani Ronchi (Le Moie from Fazi-Battaglia is similar but vino da tavola).
Rosso Cònero Marchetti; San Lorenzo from Umani Ronchi.
Montepulciano d'Abruzzo Valentini; Barone Cornacchia; Camillo

Montori; Illumati; Orsetto Oro from Casel Thaulero; Colle Secco from
CS Tollo.
Trebbiano d'Abruzzo Camillo Montori; Valentini (Bombino Bianco).
Biferno Di Majo Norante (all wines of Di Majo Norante are
recommended).

Verdicchio dei Castelli di Jesi

Type *Mid-weight, dry white*
Profile *Excellent, firm acidity, clean and crisp, salty, minerally, maybe
a touch metallic; best examples much richer, with lemon and hazelnuts*
Advice *Go for* crus; *drink with fish and seafood to maximise pleasure*

Montepulciano d'Abruzzo

Type *Rich, full, deeply coloured red*
Profile *Dominant fruit, bramble, blackberry, sweet cranberry,
peppery, spicy; good producers and good years give much weight and
tannin; rescued by acidity*
Advice *Keep if you can; go for the best you can afford; drink with
fully flavoured dishes*

Tuscany

Tuscany is the cultural heart of Italy – and these days its
viticultural heart, too. Nowhere is experimentation and
innovation so commonplace; nowhere is there such a crowd of
quality-driven producers; nowhere is the average quality level of
wine so high and the continuing improvements so marked year by
year.

Tuscany's own heart is Chianti and Chianti's heart is Chianti
Classico; rather like the inside of a Russian doll, Chianti Classico
acts as a microcosm of all the aspects, good or ill, that make up the
dynamics of modern-day vinous Italy. The quality of Chianti
(Classico or not) depends on the Sangiovese variety, yet the laws
insist on at least a minimal percentage of Canaiolo and the white
Trebbiano and Malvasia. Some producers stick to the law but
make a 100 per cent Sangiovese too, a Super-Tuscan, to which they
give a *nome di fantasia*. Others refuse to compromise the quality of
their Chianti, make it from 100 per cent Sangiovese and to hell
with the legal niceties.

Then there's the influence of Cabernet Sauvignon. It has been
swimmingly successful in Tuscany, especially in Chianti Classico,

retaining its easily recognisable voice but picking up a wonderfully attractive, strong Tuscan accent. Some like its softening, rounding effect on Chianti and use it to the full as their permitted allowance of 'up to ten per cent other varieties'. Others, like it as they may, feel that Chianti should be Chianti and made only with classic varieties. They can always tinker with a Super-Tuscan from a Sangiovese-Cabernet mix to capitalise on the remarkable affinity these two grapes have for each other, or they may turn out a mainly Cabernet Super-Tuscan, or both, each with its own *nome di fantasia* of course. Confusing? Of course not. It is just a case of deciding which estates' Chiantis you like, irrespective of the grape mix, and remembering one or two *nomi di fantasia* per estate. In fact, it is rather like keeping abreast of Bordeaux: there is no need to know which claret has what percentage of Merlot, but it does help to remember which second wine belongs to which château and whether it is from young vines, de-selected wines or both.

Although Chianti Classico, lying between Florence and Siena, is archetypal Chianti and is usually the most satisfyingly full and round, it isn't necessarily *always* the best. Chianti Rufina, north-east of Florence, with a different microclimate and higher vineyards, produces wines of terrific structure, good acidity and superb longevity. Each of the other Chianti sub-districts has its own characteristics, too, which will become more evident with time, as producers get closer to reaching their zones' potential. West of Florence, the Carmignano zone was the forbear of 'Cabernetised Chianti'. A dollop of Cabernet is compulsory here in the otherwise Chianti-like blend; apart from ensuring an incomparably balanced, elegant wine, this equivalent upholds the long tradition of Cabernet in the area: it was brought by the Medici. A young-drinking version is also made, called Barco Reale.

Well south of Chianti are the twin zones of Brunello di Montalcino and Vino Nobile di Montepulciano (nothing to do with the Montepulciano grape), both on large, high, hilly outcrops, the former a little to the west of the latter and on a more massive lump of upland. Brunello, from a clone of Sangiovese of the same name, is rightfully regarded as one of Italy's most important wines; intense, long-lived and a superb expression of the power and class of pure Sangiovese. Vino Nobile, on the other hand, is only just beginning to produce wines to match its reputation, despite the advantage of its own good Sangiovese clone, Prugnolo. Both Brunello and Vino Nobile have come under attack for being wood-aged over-long prior to bottling; unjustifiably, since it is not the ageing per se which is at fault but careless ageing of inappropriate wines. Since both areas can now make lesser-aged DOC wines, Rosso di Montalcino and Rosso di Montepulciano respectively, the full ageing should in future be reserved for the wines that can take it. And those not admiring the final effect have the option of younger, zippier wines to get their noses into.

Sangiovese's influence extends right down to the south of the region (and beyond into Lazio). Yet another clone, Morellino, grows on the hills behind Grosseto in the Maremma, where folk used to retreat during the summer months to escape the malarial swamps – before they were cleared by Mussolini. For a cheery, vibrant, mouthwateringly drinkable version of Sangiovese, Morellino di Scansano takes a lot of beating.

Tuscany has never had anything like such good results with its whites as its reds. Mind you, the basic material, Trebbiano and Malvasia, hasn't made life easy, which is one reason why Chardonnay has been adopted with such glee. Just like Cabernet, it has kept its basic character, but picked up a bit of Tuscan personality along the way, which gives it great appeal. Some is *barrique*'d (and quite a bit of that over-*barrique*'d, but they'll learn); some sees no wood at all. Both styles work.

More traditionally, there is Vernaccia planted around the small town of San Gimignano. The resultant wine, Vernaccia di San Gimignano, can be clean, crisp and personality-less or fat, broad and oily. Fortunately, these days it generally manages to make the best of both worlds, with freshness but weight and character as well.

Recommended producers

Chianti Classico Badia a Coltibuono; Capannelle; Castellare; Castell'in Villa; Castello dei Rampolla; Castello di Ama; Castello di Cacchiano; Castello di Querceto; Castello di San Polo in Rosso; Castello di Volpaia; Castello Vicchiomaggio; Fattoria di Vistarenni; Fattoria di Felsina; Fontodi; Isole e Olena; Lamole; Monsanto; Montagliari; Monte Vertine; Pagliarese; Riecine; San Felice; Vecchio Terre di Montefili; Villa Cafaggio.
Chianti Rufina Selvapiana; Frescobaldi (Montesodi; Nipozzano).
Sangiovese Super-Tuscans Montagliari (Brunesco di San Lorenzo); Isole e Olena (Cepparello); Castello di San Polo in Rosso (Centinaia); Castello di Volpaia (Coltassala); Poliziano (Elegia); Fontodi (Flaccianello); Fattoria di Felsina (Fontalloro); Monte Vertine (Le Pergole Torte); Altesino (Palazzo Altesi); Badia e Coltibuono (Sangioveto); Vinattieri Rosso; Monte Vertine's Il Sodaccio and Castellare's I Sodi di San Niccolò have small amounts of other (non-Cabernet) grapes but are still highly recommendable.
Sangiovese-Cabernet Super-Tuscans Altesino (Alte d'Astesi); Castello di Volpaia (Balifico); Caparzo (Ca' del Pazzo); Avignonesi (Grifi); Castello dei Rampolla (Sammarco); Antinori (Tignanello); San Felice (Vigorello).

Cabernet Super-Tuscans Sassicaia; Solaia; Ornellaia; Tavernelle; Ghiaie della Furba.

Carmignano Tenuta di Capezzana.

Brunello di Montalcino Altesino; Tenuta Caparzo; Col d'Orcia Lisini; Villa Banfi.

Rosso di Montalcino As Brunello.

Vino Nobile di Montepulciano Avignonesi; Boscarelli; Poliziano; Carletti della Giovanpaola.

Rosso di Montepulciano As Vino Nobile.

Morellino di Scansano Banti; Le Pupille.

Trebbiano-based whites Tremisse from Tenuta di Capezzana.

Chardonnay – wood-free Tenuta di Capezzana.

Chardonnay – *barrique*'d La Grance from Tenuta Caparzi; I Sistri from Fattoria di Felsina.

Vernaccia di San Gimignano Teruzzi e Puthod.

Chianti Classico

Type *Mid-weight red*
Profile *Plums, with a bit of cherry and raspberry; spice, tea, pepper; seemingly infinite variations on the theme*
Advice *Drink* normale *versions young and fruity: they are pasta wines par excellence;* riserva *is best at four years plus, with mid- or full-flavoured foods*

Chianti Rufina

Type *Mid-weight red*
Profile *As Classico, but with greater firmness, acidity, longevity*
Advice *Often good value*

Carmignano

Type *Mid-weight, elegant red*
Profile *Chianti-like base, but rounder, riper, gentler, often better balance*
Advice *Versatile with foods; drinks well throughout its life; highly recommended*

Brunello di Montalcino

Type *Powerful, classy red*
Profile *Powerful pruney fruit, but powerful tannin and structure too; hints of cinnamon and other spices*
Advice *Long-lived, special occasion wine, justifiably expensive*

Vino Nobile di Montepulciano

Type *Mid- to full, firm red*
Profile *Like a halfway house between Chianti and Brunello, but with denser fruit, more plumminess and less astringency than either*
Advice *Be prepared for either a pleasant surprise or a disappointment; recent vintages are becoming more reliable*

Vernaccia di San Gimignano

Type *Mid-weight, dry white*
Profile *Tangy, creamy, nutty; occasionally reminiscent of Chardonnay with saltiness*
Advice *Drink all but the best wines young*

CENTRAL ITALY

Umbria and Lazio

Both Umbria and Lazio can claim in their own way to be the centre of Italy. Umbria is Italy's only region completely surrounded by other parts of the country. It calls itself 'the green heart of Italy'. Lazio, just south of Umbria, is geographically central, lying mid-way between the Alps and the south of Sicily, and administratively central, being home to Rome. Neither, though, can seriously challenge Tuscany's pre-eminence as Italy's heartland in wine terms.

Much wine from Umbria is conspicuously forgettable; names such as Colli del Trasimeno, Colli Altotiberini, Colli Perugini are not absent from wine merchants' lists by chance. Not all is cheerless, though, in the seemingly remote, deeply rolling hills of Umbria. Orvieto, in the south-west of the region and with some of its vineyards overlapping into Lazio, has long been one of Italy's best-known wines. Now, with larger amounts of the newly lauded Grechetto finding their way into the blend and the Trebbiano proportion constantly being trimmed, an increasing amount of Orvieto is proving rewarding to drink, which the innocuous swill of yore rarely was. The *secco* (dry) version is still the most widely available. Most of what used to be called *abboccato* (medium dry) is now labelled *amabile* (medium sweet). The wine hasn't become any sweeter; the change has been necessary to satisfy the EC. Umbria's reputation has also been salvaged by the much-admired Sangiovese-based reds and Trebbiano-based whites coming from the tiny area of Torgiano, just south of Perugia. Virtually a one-estate denomination, Torgiano is almost synonymous with the name of the producer Lungarotti. To the company's standard bearers, red Rubesco and white Torre di Giano (both brand names), have been added a wide range of other wines, including *cru* Monticchio Rubesco Riserva and *cru* Il Pino Terre di Giano Riserva, as well as Super Vini da Tavola Cabernet Sauvignon di Miralduolo, Vigna i Palazzi (Chardonnay), the highly rated San Giorgio (Sangiovese-Cabernet) and others. Lungarotti's wines aren't what they were, though. Either that, or an increasing number of ever-improving wines from elsewhere has overtaken them for quality. Reliable, yes; enjoyable, probably; but one of Italy's leading estates? Sadly no longer. If they weren't so poorly known, Umbria's reputation could be happily based instead on the wines of Montefalco in the region's centre. Red, and mainly Sangiovese, they are lifted out of also-ran status by a dollop of the wondrous Sagrantino in the blend. So powerfully flavoured is this grape that just a small percentage addition makes all the difference. Sagrantino reveals its super-star status to the full in the very small amounts of pure Sagrantino di Montefalco made. Rich and fruit-sozzled as the wine is, it gives the sensation that it ought to be sweet – as indeed some of it proves to be. A small percentage is made as a *passito* (from semi-dried grapes) concentrating its rich, ripe, spicy, almost shockingly berry-fruited explosion of flavour.

Lazio is predominantly a white-wine region; the reds, usually based on Sangiovese or the local Cesanese, sometimes on Merlot, still have considerable improvements to achieve. In effect, Lazio is more than a white-wine region, it is a one-wine region – Frascati. To be fair, this is either Frascati itself or a Frascati-like wine, for example Marino or Velletri, made from the same vine varieties but from other parts of the vast semi-circular ridge of hills south and west of the city. This portrait of Lazio does, however, ignore the now quite reasonable Est! Est!! Est!!! from the north of the region. Improved it may be, but the wine still doesn't match the fame of the legend surrounding its name.

Frascati has come in for some pretty scathing comment in its time – and not without justification. Its grape mix of Trebbiano (good for neutrality) and Malvasia (good for premature oxidation) is disastrous in careless hands and since Frascati has been seen by most as a commodity wine, many of the hands have been duly careless. Once lumbered with the 'best avoided' image, most wines have a hard job shrugging it off. Frascati is no exception, despite the fact that a vastly increased amount of it is now at least decent in quality, with several wines proving real eye-openers. It is worth re-trying not just one Frascati but several as there are stylistic variations as distinct as the qualitative ones. The grapes used may be 100 per cent Trebbiano, giving a steely-metallic, lean, crisp wine; 100 per cent Malvasia di Candia, giving a very soft, creamy wine; or any balance of the two. Malvasia del Lazio can also be added, giving greater definition of flavour. It is theoretically present up to only 30 per cent, but those who like it prefer to bend the law rather than compromise their wine. Casal Pilozzo, a new, top-quality vino da tavola made solely from Malvasia del Lazio, explains more eloquently than words why quality-conscious producers are such staunch supporters of the grape.

Recommended producers

Orvieto Bigi; especially *crus* Torricella (*secco*) and Orzalume (*amabile*); Barberani; Decugnano dei Barbi; Barbi; Antinori; Il Palazzone.
Torgiano Lungarotti.
(Sagrantino di) Montefalco Adanti.
Frascati Colli di Catone (especially Colle Gaio *cru*); Fontana Candida *cru* Santa Teresa; Zandotti.
Casal Pilozzi Colle di Catone.
Est! Est!! Est!!! CS di Montefiascone.

Orvieto

Type *Dry (secco) or medium dry (amabile) white, very occasionally sweet from noble rot*
Profile *(dry version) Gentle base, sometimes very creamy, at other times more steely, highlighted with walnuts and other nuts plus green fruits (greengages, pears, apples)*
Advice *Worth going for the better and* cru *versions. These will keep a year or two; drink others within the year*

Sagrantino di Montefalco

Type *Rich, full red, either dry(ish) or* passito *and sweetish (abboccato)*
Profile *Plums, prunes, cherries, and numerous berry fruits with liquorice and touch of Marmite. Good supporting structure*
Advice *Hard to find, little produced, but well worth tracking down. Not an everyday wine, though*

Frascati

Type *Dry* (secco), *medium dry* (amabile) *or very occasionally sweetish* (cannellino) *soft white*
Profile *Swings between crisp, light and metallic-steely to broad, round and nutty. Can have flavours of apricots, apples, buttermilk and cashews*
Advice *Styles vary greatly. Shop around and stick to whatever suits you. Drink young. Makes a very adaptable food partner*

Campania

Until very recently the wines of Campania, the region surrounding Naples, could have been summarised in no more than a paragraph. At last, though, the frenzy of activity which has seen the appearance of so many stunning wines further north is starting to attract enthusiastic reviews in Campania too. It may seem surprising that a torridly southern Mediterranean region could turn out anything of great quality. The 'Mediterranean' part of Campania, though, is only along the coast. The hinterland is high, mountainous and notorious among Italians for the inclemency of its weather. Winters are hard, cold, wet and wind-battered. Snow is common as late in the year as April. The province of Avellino, containing some of the highest of these lands, is so plagued by rains that it is uncompromisingly known as the piss-pot of Italy. Of course, when the sun does shine, it is quite powerful, but even then the altitude keeps the temperatures well down. The region was, historically, one of Italy's most important for wine and, thankfully, most developments have been with the noble grapes traditional to the area since the time of the Greeks: white Falanghina, Greco and Fiano; red Aglianico and Piedirosso.

Apart from the large quantities of mainly touristy wine from Capri, Ischia and Vesuvio (Lacrima Christi del), the centre of Campanian viticulture has been in the miserably cold and damp mountains of the province of Avellino, east of Naples. This has been a one-estate monopoly with the three major wines of Greco di Tufo, Fiano di Avellino and Taurasi all being produced almost exclusively by the large, competent family firm of Mastroberardino. In the past few years, however, an increasing number of *vignerons* previously selling their grapes to Mastroberardino have stopped doing so and have started to make their own wine. Few have yet reached the level which we might expect them to with time, and even fewer are exporting. However, the quality and the potential of the wines they are creating shows that we have been far too complacent in accepting Mastroberardino's versions as copybook.

Solopaca, further north-west in Benevento, is in one sense a typical southern DOC with its predominant grape varieties being Sangiovese (for the red) and Trebbiano (for the white) – a mix determined by misguided 1970s quantity-led thinking. The classic varieties (Greco, Aglianico, Piedirosso etc.) give wines of much greater character, prompting a strange sort of Super Vini da Tavola situation where the 'innovative' wines are really the more traditional. Also in Benevento, Falanghina and Piedirosso are beginning to show their paces as varietals in the enclave of Sant'Agato dei Goti.

Much more exciting, though, have been the advances made down near the coast in the north of Campania – the zone of Falernum, one of the most famous of all ancient wines. Endless researches, historical as well as viticultural, and endless political battles have resulted in the re-emergence of up-dated Falernum as Falerno. It is made from 100 per cent Falanghina (the white) and Aglianico with some Piedirosso (the red). Nobody can say with certainty that these wines, apart from the addition of modern wine-making know-how, are just like the ancient Falernum used to be, but they are as close as anyone can get from what little the documents reveal. Similarly famous locally, but a wine of less widespread renown, is Cecubo, and this too has been brought back to life, produced mainly from Piedirosso with smaller quantities of other local ancient varieties.

Recommended producers

Greco di Tufo Mastroberardino especially *cru* Vignadangelo.
Fiano di Avellino Mastroberardino especially *cru* Vignadora.
Taurasi Mastroberardino.
Solopaca Vinicola Ocone.
Falanghina di Sant'Agata dei Goti Mustilli.
Piedirosso di Sant'Agata dei Goti Mustilli.
Falerno Villa Matilde.
Cecubo Villa Matilde.

Greco di Tufo

Type *Full, dry white*
Profile *Smoky, minerally, firm; weight and shape more impressive than flavours*
Advice *Wait a year before drinking; needs food*

Fiano di Avellino

Type *Mid-weight dry white*
Profile *Restrained but concentrated, orange flowers, peach, kiwi, broad beans, salt; develops richness with age*
Advice *Ages well; may not impress at first tasting; perseverance well worth while*

Taurasi

Type *Full, slow-maturing red*
Profile *Can be distressingly like sour milk when too young; develops complex coffee and damson tones with age*
Advice *Be patient; drink with none-too-rich foods*

Palermo Bianco

Type *Dry white*
Profile *Herby, nettly, chalky, angelica, marzipan, raspberries, roses, slight vanilla and almonds, milky end, kept tight by good acidity*
Advice *Drink on its own or with food*

Falerno Rosso

Type *Mid-weight red*
Profile *Cinnamon and Worcestershire sauce notes, the wine's fruit is raw and strawberry-like when young, richer and sweeter when matured; develops weight and complexity*
Advice *Needs mid-weight food. Riservas need several years to develop*

THE SOUTH

Puglia, Basilicata, Calabria

Much of Puglia, Italy's heel, is flat and theoretically unpromising terrain for quality wine. It has been one of the major regions producing 'cutting wine' – heavy, alcoholic stuff for bumping up the feebler efforts of further north (including areas beyond the Italian border). It is also geographically remote from much of the rest of the country. It is hardly surprising, therefore, that the flames of the vinous revolution have been slow in spreading to Puglian wine-makers and setting them alight. Despite numerous wine names and a flurry of DOC zones, the region breaks down into three major areas: the north, exemplified by San Severo, where Montepulciano (and even Sangiovese) still make an appearance, but where grapes more suited to the climate, such as Uva di Troia, are increasingly taking over; the centre, exemplified by Castel del Monte, which is firmly Uva di Troia territory; and the south, currently the most promising part, where the powerful, dark, bitter grape Negro Amaro holds sway (apart from the area around Manduria, south of Taranto, which is the home of Primitivo). Reds are, in general, far more important than whites. Apart from Locorotondo (predominantly from the little-known Verdeca variety), widely regarded as the best white around, and new-wave oddities such as Chardonnay-based Preludio, whites are very much in the background.

The southern Puglian reds come from the true heel, the Salento Peninsula, and benefit from a double cooling effect from the sea on both east and west. Whether Salice Salentino is better or worse than Brindisi, the exquisitely named Squinzano or any other Salento wines is still impossible to judge as the vast variation in producers' standards quite overwhelms any zonal effect. The huge, tannic wines of the Negro Amaro need, and usually get, a touch of Malvasia Nera to soften them and give them perfume. They also mature slowly and far too many examples oxidise first. Nonetheless, the potential is without doubt there.

Basilicata, the instep of Italy, is remote, poor and comparatively backward. Yet in wine terms it appears more advanced and more forward-thinking than Puglia. Certainly, there is not such a plethora of seemingly identical wines to consider. Indeed, there is only one worth worrying about, Aglianico del Vulture. Promisingly, the grape is Aglianico, one of the South's best. Just as beneficially, the grapes are grown on the east (cool) face of the extinct volcano, Monte Vulture, at 200 to 650 metres high, gaining the advantage of altitude. A new generation of wine-makers is beginning to take over from their parents here. As they change entrenched ideas and uncover the wine's full potential, Aglianico del Vulture, already quite highly regarded, should really set sparks flying.

Calabria, the toe of Italy, probably has far greater potential for good wine than is at present apparent. Much of the region is narrow, with sea on both sides; there is plenty of high-altitude land, attenuating the summer heat; the predominant grape varieties (white Greco and red Gaglioppo) are indigenous to the area and well suited to its conditions. But the Calabrians tend to be reserved people, not much given to collaboration and none too open to new ideas. Even if the region were reverberating with innovation (which it isn't), it would be unlikely that the Calabrians would be falling over backwards to tell us about it. Despite sweet white delights like Greco di Bianco (Bianco is the name of the area) and Mantonico di Bianco, the sole banner-wavers in the UK for Calabria are the wines of Cirò, sturdy beasts all, be they red, white or rosé. Still, at least Cirò's chief producer, Librandi, is outward-looking and communicative, and is taking major steps to improve his wines.

Recommended producers

Locorotondo CS di Locorotondo.
Preludio Torrebianco.
Salice Salentino, Brindisi Cosimo Taurino.
Aglianico del Vulture Fratelli d'Angelo; Paternoster.
Cirò Librandi.

Aglianico del Vulture

Type *Full, tannic red*
Profile *Intense, spicy, earthy, smoky, complex*
Advice *Drink with fully flavoured or rich food*

Cirò Rosso

Type *Full, warm red*
Profile *Older wines may be stewy; newer examples have better cherry-like fruit, pepper, spice and chocolate*
Advice *Buy newer wines and wait for them to mature*

Sicily

Sicily is quite different from the rest of Italy – and not just geographically and culturally. Its most influential wine producers have more or less ignored the DOC system and have plumped for what appear to be brands. Regaleali, Rapitalà, Terre di Ginestra, Donnafugata and so on may well come from clearly defined vineyards, but the names are estate names or created names. Corvo, the best-known Sicilian name of all, is not even harnessed to a geographical location: grapes are bought from various different sites on the island. Not that any of this matters; the guarantee, as always, is the name of the estate and the wines are made unencumbered by any DOC constraints. Indeed, it could be said that Sicily foreshadowed the appearance of other regions'

Super Vini da Tavola. It is also well ahead of the rest of the South, so much so that it is impossible to consider its wines in the same context.

The island is larger than it appears – 230 miles from east to west – and 'the plains of Sicily' is a misnomer. The only significant areas of flat land are behind Catania in the east (used for citrus cultivation) and around Marsala in the west. Sicily is also predominantly a producer of simple, light, delicate whites. If you find this strange, believing that white wines need cool climates, bear in mind that not only are many vines cultivated in the hills, where conditions are considerably cooler than along the coast, but that Sicilian white grape varieties, for example Catarratto and Inzolia, are grown only on the island, are specially adapted to its conditions and, indeed, would have great difficulty ripening further north. The amount of aroma, crisp 'cool climate' fruit and slim elegance that Catarratto can achieve grown at 900 metres (in the hills behind Palermo by Terre di Ginestra) would astound anyone still locked into the 'southern, hot sweaty whites' line of thinking on Sicily.

Reds, although theoretically better from the east of the island where a few DOCs do exist to mould their styles, are more reliably enjoyable from the same leading companies, mostly based in the centre and west, who have achieved such revelatory results with their whites. Up until a year or so ago many of these reds tended to be lightish and jammy but the last three vintages have seen tremendous developments in handling and vinification techniques and the varieties, Nero d'Avola, Nerello Mascalese, Frappato and Perricone, have responded magnificently. In the east, even the red wines from Etna – actually grown on the sides of the volcano, enjoying the quadruple advantage of high altitude, cool, east-facing slopes, volcanic soil and legendary reputation – have yet to make their mark, despite the amount of interest being shown locally. The only eastern red as yet worth getting excited about is an intense, vibrant Cerasuolo di Vittoria from a small estate called COS. Encouragingly, COS appears to be inspiring other producers to follow its lead so that there is hope that the usually dull, over-oxidised wines from this corner of south-east Sicily may start to disappear. (Cerasuolo, by the way, means cherry coloured.)

The soul of Sicily is not in its red and white wines, though, however impressive they may be. It is where the sun is used to full effect on the millennia-old varieties of Moscato and Malvasia to give wonderful, sweet, *passito* wines. Moscato is most at home on Pantelleria, a small island to the south-west of Sicily, towards Tunisia; Malvasia performs at its best on the Aeolian Islands off

Sicily's north-east coast. Both are uniquely flavoured, full of personality, sweet without cloying, and they carry forward a length of tradition unparalleled anywhere else.

Marsala, on the other hand, may be Sicily's best-known wine but it has been so abused, first by the British who fortified it so that it would 'travel', then by the Marsala producers who compromised its quality and turned it into a cheap commodity product, that it has lost nearly all links with its tradition. Marco De Bartoli's unfortified Vecchio Samperi is a laudable attempt to turn back the clock; if Marsala was as good as this 250 years ago our loss has been great indeed. Still, it is possible to make impressive Marsala, in both traditional and modern styles, even with the now-obligatory fortification. Shame that De Bartoli is the only one who still does.

Recommended producers

Corvo Duca Enrico; Bianco di Valguarnera.
Rapitalà
Regaleali Rosso del Conte; Nozze d'Oro.
Donnafugata Vigna di Gabri.
Terre di Ginestra
Cellaro
Cerasuolo di Vittoria COS.
Moscato di Pantelleria Marco De Bartoli.
Malvasia delle Lipari Carlo Hauner.
Vecchio Samperi Marco De Bartoli.
Traditional Marsala Marco De Bartoli's Il Marsala Superiore.
Modern Masala Marco De Bartoli's La Miccia.

Moscato di Pantelleria

Type *Delicately sweet or richly* (passito) *sweet white wine*
Profile (passito *version): grapey, raisiny, toffee and fudge, oaky hints. (Non-*passito *version): fresher, more floral, still full and grapey*
Advice *Drink with desserts, almond biscuits or on its own*

Malvasia delle Lipari

Type *Richly sweet wine*
Profile *Bright orange, apricots and Marmite*
Advice *Unusual, may not appeal at first, but give it a chance!*

Ordinary Marsala

Type *Sweetish, intense fortified wine*
Profile *Reminiscent of Bovril and cassata ice-cream*
Advice *Not worth forsaking other fortifieds for*

Vecchio Samperi

Type *Dry, intense, unfortified, but with the shape and weight of a fortified wine*
Profile *Reminiscent of fine amontillado sherry but with chestnut, caramel and orange peel flavours*
Advice *Drink as an aperitif, after meals with cheese, nuts or chocolate or as a digestif*

Sardinia

Sardinian wine producers have absorbed the modern ethos in a big way. Traditional Sardinian wines, big, alcoholic and often sweet, have all but disappeared as the huge preponderance of co-operatives, well equipped with all vinifying mod cons, have turned the previously thumping, heavy wines into clean, light, palatable, easy-drinking charmers. There are few wines, though, that go past the cheerful quaffer stage. Whether red from the wonderfully light and gluggable Monica variety or the marginally less frivolous Cannonau (Grenache), or white from Vermentino, Torbato or Nuragus, there is little available from the island that you could really call serious.

The serious side of Sardinia lies in what is left of the sweet-and-stickies that used to dominate production. There are abundant plantings of the Malvasia and Moscato ideally suited to this style of wine but few results even begin to approach the standards of Sicily. It takes a one-off, called Anghelu Ruju, made from *passito* Grenache grapes, to reveal just how luscious Sardinian dessert wines can be.

Recommended producers (for all Sardinian wines)
Cantina Sociale di Dolianova
Sella & Mosca.

> *Give me some more wine, because life is nothing.*
> Fernando Pessoa

Anghelu Ruju

Type *Sweet*, passito *dessert wine*
Profile *Nutty, caramel, toffee, sticky*
Advice *Drink with very rich desserts, nuts or ice-cream*

Stockists

Adnams; James Aitken & Son; H Allen Smith; Bibendum; Booths; D Byrne & Co; Cadwgan; Cantina Augusto; Cumbrian Cellar; Eaton Elliot; Ben Ellis & Associates; John Ford Wines; Peter Green; Heath Street Wine Co; Millevini; Oddbins; Reid Wines; J Sainsbury; Selfridges; Tanners; Tesco; Upper Crust;Valvona & Crolla; Vessel du Vin; La Vigneronne; Waitrose; Windrush Wines; Wine Growers Association; Wine House; Wine Cellars.

Maureen Ashley is a freelance writer specialising in Italian wine.

New Zealand

Andrew Jefford

New Zealand has been through a long incubation as a wine-growing country. The first vineyards were planted by Samuel Marsden in 1819, and the first wines were made by James Busby, a British-born viticulturalist and oenophile, who had already pioneered viticulture in New South Wales. An Australian wine-maker working for the government of Victoria was loaned in 1895 to New Zealand to gauge the suitability of its different regions for wine-growing, and this man, Romeo Bragato, reported in glowing terms to the country's politicians. No one, sadly, was minded to pay him any attention. The country was beginning to flirt with prohibition, and it continued its ambiguous embrace for half a century; only since the 1960s, for example, has New Zealand decided that its citizens are responsible enough to drink wine with their restaurant meals if they wish. This generally lukewarm approach to the world's second oldest drink held back development; it was the country's enthusiastic Dalmatian immigrants and others that kept production going, but they were trying to produce the kind of hearty reds that western Yugoslavia yields, but for which New Zealand had little aptitude. Alternatives to these were sweetish, Liebfraumilch-style whites and some uninspired fortified wines.

The change came in the 1960s and 1970s, when a growing national confidence about wine found its reflection in the increasingly widespread planting of the best French and German varieties to replace the raggle-taggle assortment found in vineyards until then. Unfortunately Müller-Thurgau soon outnumbered other new varieties: investors thought that this was the best route to commercial success. This bulk-wine path proved a false start, and bankruptcies and uprooting followed. Even today, with quality wine production well established, the total area under vine is very small: less than a twentieth of California's plantings.

Yet those other classic varieties worked well from the moment they were taken out of their boxes, some of them sensationally well. Most sensational of all was Sauvignon Blanc, and every year that passes reinforces New Zealand's claims to joint world leadership with this variety. Blind tastings, indeed, suggest outright leadership, with Sauvignon Blanc from Cloudy Bay and Te Mata inching ahead of the best from Sancerre and Pouilly-Fumé as often as these events are arranged. In some ways, Sauvignon

Blanc is the ideal variety with which the New World can trounce the Old, for even in France it never acquires great subtlety, never really gets beyond the triumphant expression of varietal characteristics. At this stage, Sauvignon Blancs from the Marlborough area of New Zealand's South Island, and the Hawkes Bay area of its North Island, seem to express themselves with more emerald exuberance than any rivals, and when varietal characteristics are this appealing, who needs subtlety? Those of us who fear that this super-reliable source of super-value wine might dry up – or double in price overnight – will be relieved to hear that the 1990 harvest of Sauvignon Blanc was 55.5 per cent up on 1989, thanks to new plantings reaching maturity. The quality of the 1990 harvest, moreover, is very good.

New Zealand Sauvignon Blanc

Type *Dry white wine*
Profile *Powerfully aromatic, variously reminiscent of blackcurrant leaf, cut grass, nettles, gooseberries or asparagus; keen, intensely fruity flavours but with softer acidity than French equivalents*
Advice *Drink as young as possible for maximum vivacity; accompanies fish, vegetables and light meats well, but is also good on its own*

New Zealand's greatest success may be its Sauvignon Blanc, but this is not its only success. Chardonnay is grown in New Zealand, particularly on the warmer North Island in the Gisborne and Hawkes Bay areas, and there it dons its favoured Antipodean outfit – raffia hula skirt and flower necklace – to come undulating out of the bottle with appealing tropical fruit scents and flavours, sometimes oaked into toastiness or smokiness. New Zealand's long white clouds are responsible for more restraint in this performance than elsewhere, and further experience with the variety seems likely to enable New Zealand's growers to build levels of complexity into the wines more successfully than those working under brighter and bluer skies will manage.

Chenin Blanc, Rhine Riesling, Semillon, Gewürztraminer (locally Traminer) and even the much-abused Müller-Thurgau can all produce excitement in New Zealand, with Gewürztraminer and Riesling both performing well when botrytis-affected and late-harvested to make dessert wines. There is no doubt at all about New Zealand's first-class potential as a white-wine producer: it is as if Alsace was fattened up, broken into two and dropped into the South Pacific.

With red wines, New Zealand's success has been less uniform. Cabernet Sauvignon is, of course, there: the best are lean and fit, though nearly always with a grassy cast and highish acidity, both factors reminding drinkers more of the Loire than of Bordeaux. Cabernet-Merlot blends, though, can be very successful, the succulence of the Merlot seeming to coax the Cabernet into behaving more generously than it does in isolation. The world hopes for great things from New Zealand's Pinot Noir, but the burden of proof remains in the wine-growers' vats for the moment; while Pinotage, a Pinot Noir-Cinsault crossing, produces eccentric, rather graceless but intriguing and concentrated wines. Once New Zealand can get the grass clippings out of its Cabernet, it seems likely that this will be the variety, alone or in blends, that it will succeed best with.

New Zealand Cabernet Sauvignon

Type *Medium-bodied red wine*
Profile *Pungent, generally with minty, grass-like and vegetal aromas; light, lively flavours with sustained acidity, sometimes oaked, and often with a bitter-edged, mineral finish*
Advice *Serve with liver, kidneys and lamb dishes*

Recommended producers

Sauvignon Blanc Cloudy Bay; Cooks; Delegats; Hunters; Montana; Te Mata.
Chardonnay Delegats; Vidal; Villa Maria
Cabernet Sauvignon and Cabernet-Merlot Stonyridge; Te Mata; Vidal; Villa Maria
Late-Harvest Rhine Riesling Redwood Valley.

Stockists

Ad Hoc; James Aitken; Alba Wine Society; Barnes Wine Shop; Bentalls; Booths; G E Bromley; Cadwgan; City Wine; Cumbrian Cellar; Ben Ellis; Alex Findlater; John Ford; Fulham Road Wine Centre; Peter Green; Guildford Wine Market; Haughton; Hopton Wines; House of Townend; Kiwifruits; Lay & Wheeler; Lea & Sandeman; Master Cellar; The Nobody Inn; Oddbins; La Reserva; Selfridges; Snowdonia Wine Warehouse; Thresher; Ubiquitous Chip; Upper Crust; Victoria Wine; Whiteside; Willoughbys; Yorkshire Fine Wines.

North America

Stephen Brook

Grapes have been grown commercially in North America for over a century and a half, but only in the last twenty years has the United States taken its place among the great wine-making countries of the world. Prohibition dealt a terrible blow to the development of sophisticated wine-making across the face of America, but producers have certainly been making up for lost time ever since. Every year dozens of new wineries spring up in regions such as the Napa and Sonoma Valleys and in newer wine-making areas such as Texas.

Unlike European wine-makers, fettered by volumes of regulations and appellation restrictions, American wine-makers have a free hand. In some parts of California a rudimentary appellation system is developing to enhance the reputation of favoured regions. That is more the exception than the rule. The great majority of wineries and wine-makers may plant the grapes they please in the areas they please, and make the wines much as they please. Of course, the best wineries impose their own discipline when it comes to yields and soils, but freedom of action remains virtually complete. This means that the American wine industry is far less restricted and less predictable than the European, but also means that, without the tradition of centuries based on exact knowledge of climate and soil and grape variety, serious mistakes can be made. The Burgundians have had a millennium to establish the best sites for Pinot Noir; the Californians have had twenty years. What is astonishing, given the essentially experimental nature of American wine-making, is how very high the average quality is.

One word sums up the character of the best American wines: generosity. The climate is far less fickle than in most parts of Europe, and grapes ripen fully in almost all years. There are differences between vintages, to be sure, but they are less pronounced than in Europe. In Washington's Columbia Valley, despite the northerly latitude, growers can depend on hot dry summers every year; only in the more mountainous regions of northern California are rain and hail and fog more likely to cause problems. So even inexpensive American wines tend to be fruity, rich in flavour, and accessible relatively young. The best of them, like their European counterparts, are likely to be tannic, well structured and long-lived, but will probably be more attractive in their youth.

Technically, the standards of American wine-making are as high as anywhere in the world. The majority of wine-makers have been university-trained, usually at the University of California's Davis campus. They have access to costly equipment, such as temperature-controlled fermentation tanks, centrifuges, and filtration machinery, which makes it difficult not to produce clean and attractive wines. The disadvantage of all this technical competence is that there is little room for individuality and innovation. There has been a tendency to make wine according to formulae based on the most prestigious European models. Chardonnay, for example, is almost invariably barrel-fermented and aged in French oak. Nothing wrong with that, of course, but without the nuances of soil and microclimate that govern the character of white Burgundy, there has been a nagging worry that an awful lot of American, and especially Californian, wines are becoming indistinguishable.

The best American wine-makers are aware of this. Far more attention is being paid to vineyard sites and microclimates, and to vineyard management, than previously. Despite the wizardry of Davis-trained wine-makers, there is a growing recognition that not enough emphasis has been placed on the quality and character of the grapes themselves. There is a reluctance to persist in clinical wine-making of the kind that cleans and filters all the life and flavour out of a wine; there is a greater willingness to let the grapes speak, as it were, for themselves.

Not all the news is good. One depressing feature of American wine-making is indeed the growing uniformity of the product. The cost of good land and top-quality grapes, not to mention the cost of equipment such as new French barrels, means that almost every West Coast winery is focusing its attention on fashionable Chardonnay and Cabernet, for these varieties assure it of a high price. Varieties such as Riesling, Gewürztraminer, Sauvignon Blanc, and the wonderful Zinfandel, are consequently becoming harder to find, as more and more wineries cease to make them.

The Cabernets, once so rich and opulent and, one has to say it, obvious, are becoming more subtle, as wine-makers emulate the classic Bordeaux blends by incorporating Merlot, Cabernet Franc and even Petit Verdot into their wines. The awkward term 'Meritage' has been coined to identify such wines as a genre. Since they are in vogue at present, they tend to be highly priced and are often far from competitive with their French models. Many varietal Merlots are of outstanding quality.

Despite the ubiquity of Burgundian and Bordeaux styles, there are signs that even Americans are beginning to experience 'Chardonnay burn-out' and are trying other grapes with other flavours. In Sonoma Valley, especially, Zinfandel is undergoing something of a revival, and throughout California serious, and increasingly successful, attempts are being made to produce top-quality Pinot Noir. Some of the Rhône varieties, such as Syrah, Mourvèdre and Viognier, and some of the best Italian varieties, such as Sangiovese and Nebbiolo, are being planted and vinified. The quantities are commercially negligible, but there is a distinct and welcome movement towards diversification. Wine consumers who love the rich berry flavours of Zinfandel – like port without the spirit – should welcome the tentative revival this variety has been enjoying, while the craze for the very insipid and commercial White Zinfandel is mercifully on the wane.

North Americans have also discovered something that Europeans have known since time immemorial: that wine is best enjoyed alongside good food. Consequently, many Californian wines have been slimmed down so that they complement rather than overpower fine cooking. This trend has been welcomed in some circles, and deplored in others, as many wines have lost that characteristic American generosity of flavour and now appear mean and lean by contrast with their forbears. Although there are many who mourn the passing of burly, blockbuster, full-flavoured, rich wines, the majority of drinkers appear to welcome the more elegant and less alcoholic wines now being fashioned.

American wines have never been cheap in Britain, although some acceptable commercial wines from Gallo, Mondavi and Masson are inexpensive. On the other hand, prices have been stable for many years, and many older vintages still to be found on merchants' shelves are remarkably good value for mature wines. Prices in California especially have been soaring, and they are bound to rise in Britain, too. Whether any but a small handful of American wines are worth more than £15 per bottle is questionable.

The earth goes drinking water,
The trees drink through their roots,
The scattered sea drinks the wind,
And the sun drinks the waves;
The sun is blue from the moon,
Everything drinks, above and below;
Why then should we not drink?
Ronsard

American wine labels

American labels have the distinct advantage, for Britons, of being in English. Consumers are solemnly warned that wine contains 'sulfites' – sulphur dioxide – as do, of course, all wines. From 1989 onwards, American labels must carry a battery of solemn warnings, directed chiefly at pregnant women. Some bottles carry back labels that give copious technical information primarily of interest to wine writers, but it is better to have too much information than too little. Wine labels are also becoming more verbose as producers begin to specify appellations and single vineyards.

The description of sweet (late harvest) wines can be baffling. Select Late Harvest usually corresponds to the German Beerenauslese, and Special Select Late Harvest to Trockenbeerenauslese. Older bottles may carry phrases such as Individual Dried Bunch Selected, which have no legal force, but indicate how the grapes were picked. In general, the more words, the richer and costlier the wine.

CALIFORNIA

Napa Valley

Napa, a long narrow valley north of San Francisco, is the most illustrious of American regions. On the valley floor the soil is quite rich and the climate hot, giving powerful, full-flavoured wines. Greater complexity is to be found on the slopes of the mountains on either side of the valley, the so-called benchlands, and some vineyards are dry-farmed (i.e. not irrigated – unusual in America) at heights of 2,000 feet, giving low yields but often very high quality and intense varietal flavours. Northern Napa is the hottest part of the valley, and in the increasingly important Carneros region in southern Napa the relatively cool climate favours the production of elegant Chardonnay and Pinot Noir. Carneros is not the only sub-region to be elevated to appellation status. Areas such as Stag's Leap and Howell Mountain have been identified as sources of superb Cabernet Sauvignon.

Just as there is more variety of soil and climate in Napa Valley than many consumers imagine, so too is there an almost alarming proliferation of wineries, now numbering hundreds. They range from the tiniest boutique installations, producing no more than

5,000 cases annually, to giants of the industry such as Beaulieu and Beringer, churning out well over a million cases every year. In Napa small is not necessarily beautiful, and large is not necessarily dull. The enormous Mondavi winery has long been a pioneer in California, experimenting tirelessly with vineyard management and every conceivable nuance of barrel-ageing. Mondavi is typical of many wineries, by no means small, that continue to make high quality wines in considerable quantities and at reasonable prices.

Recommended producers

Acacia; Clos du Val; Cuvaison; Duckhorn; Dunn; Far Niente; Frog's Leap; Grgich Hills; Heitz; Mayacamas; Mondavi; Newton; Phelps; Saintsbury; Stag's Leap Wine Cellars; Vichon; ZD.

Sonoma Valley

Sonoma is roughly parallel to Napa, but one mountain range closer to the Pacific Ocean. Whereas Napa is relatively compact, Sonoma sprawls, and the considerable variations in climate within the valley make summary dangerous. Some appellations, such as Russian River, are well suited to the now unfashionable Germanic varieties of Riesling and Gewürztraminer. Autumn fogs often bring botrytis, and the nobly rotten grapes can produce sumptuous Late Harvest dessert wines. Further north, in Dry Creek Valley, Cabernet, Chardonnay and Zinfandel thrive.

Although there are large wineries in Sonoma – Kenwood and Chateau St-Jean are good examples – the region is dominated by medium-sized wineries such as Clos du Bois, Simi and Iron Horse, offering a good range of well-made wines at reasonable prices. Sonoma, because it is spread out, is less prone to invasions of tourists than is Napa, and prices tend to be slightly lower.

Recommended producers

Carmenet; Chateau St-Jean; Clos du Bois; Glen Ellen; Iron Horse; Matanzas Creek; Simi; Sonoma-Cutrer; Mark West.

Other regions

A combination of local grape-growing traditions and the astronomical cost of vineyard land in fashionable Napa and Sonoma have led to the establishment of a number of wineries in more distant parts of the state.

Some sixty miles north-east of Napa is Lake County, a somewhat bleak region suitable for cooler climate varieties like Sauvignon Blanc. In Lake County, Kendall-Jackson is a large winery producing wines of impeccable quality, much as Mondavi does in Napa. Mendocino County lies north of Sonoma and close to the ocean. Although the northernmost wine region of California, Mendocino is generally hot, and is the source of grapes for large commercial wineries such as Fetzer and Parducci.

The enormous variation in styles and grape varieties makes it hard to define the character of wines from mountainous Santa Cruz, just south of San Francisco. In the Santa Cruz hills you will encounter rich, sweet Rieslings, some of California's finest Zinfandels, great Chardonnay and Pinot Noir, and an adventurous series of Rhône varietals, notably from the Bonny Doon winery. Further south, halfway to Los Angeles, are the equally diverse regions of Arroyo Seco (where Jekel makes an impressive range of reasonably priced wines), Paso Robles (best known for Zinfandel), Edna Valley (an increasingly important source of Pinot Noir and Chardonnay), and Santa Ynez (dominated by the Firestone winery, which offers some of the best value for money in California).

Recommended producers

Calera; Chalone; Edna Valley Vineyards; Fetzer; Firestone; Jekel; Quady; Ridge.

Vintages

California There is a common misconception that vintages in California are somehow uniform. This is far from the truth. Although there is less vintage variation than in northern Europe, each region, indeed each sub-region, has its own microclimate and there can be significant differences.

The late 1970s, especially 1976 and 1978, produced some magnificent Napa Cabernets. 1980 and 1981 were good rather than great in Napa, but 1982 and 1983 decidedly problematic for both whites and reds. 1984, a very hot year, gave lush, forward Cabernets for early consumption. 1985, 1986 and 1987 were all excellent, especially 1985. The 1987 whites were very fine; a small crop for reds and whites. 1988 gave a small crop of average reds and very good whites. The 1989 vintage was wrecked in Napa and Sonoma by torrential rains. Rot was widespread and the best wineries will have rejected much of the crop. Buyer beware, especially with Chardonnay.

Oregon For Pinot Noir, 1981 was mediocre, 1982 and 1983 average, 1984 mediocre, 1985 very good, 1986 good, and 1987 very good. 1988 gave a small but concentrated crop.

Washington Most vintages of the 1980s have been very good, and 1983 and 1985 were outstanding. 1986 and 1987 have lower acidity than usual, but 1988 should be excellent.

OREGON

If California, with its different soils, climatic variations and eagerness to experiment can be bewildering for the wine drinker, Oregon presents no such problems. This north-western state has built a firm reputation for, above all, Pinot Noir. It is in the Willamette Valley, just south of Portland, that the majority of Oregon's wineries have been established over the last two decades. Although shielded from the ocean by the Coastal Range, the region receives a good deal of rainfall, often at unwelcome times such as the early autumn. Some years in Oregon can be close to a wash-out, but in good years the grapes produce wines of a distinctly Burgundian style, not unlike Beaune in their delicately flavoury character. Since production is relatively small, and vintages can be erratic, demand usually exceeds supply and the wines are far from cheap. Oregon also produces good if light white wines, such as Chardonnay and the decreasingly popular Riesling.

WASHINGTON

To the north of Oregon lies Washington, a state quite distinct in its viticulture. The vineyards lie far from the coast on the eastern side of the Cascade mountains. The rain clouds that Oregonians find so exasperating have lost most of their moisture by the time they reach the Columbia and Yakima Valleys of Washington. Indeed, these areas are officially designated as semi-arid and irrigation is usually necessary to ensure proper ripening of the grapes. The climate is predictable, with very hot, dry summer days and cool nights. The summer days are longer than in California, and this lengthy, even growing season gives fruit that is invariably ripe but never with the lush, overblown character of Californian grapes. Washington is thus well suited to the growing of white grapes such as Riesling and Chardonnay.

The sweet late harvest wines, usually from Riesling or Chenin Blanc, are among the most delicious in America. Sauvignon Blanc and Semillon are also grown successfully here, giving wines of high acidity and remarkable longevity. Washington is also establishing a high reputation for Cabernet Sauvignon and, especially, Merlot. Because the grapes tend to be high in acidity, the red wines can be ungainly in their youth and usually need four or more years in bottle before they begin showing at their best. As the best producers come to understand their grapes better and learn how to match their vinification and ageing methods to the fruit, there is a strong possibility that in time the Washington reds will exhibit far more of the classic Bordeaux character than their richer, more opulent counterparts from California.

Recommended producers

Arbor Crest; Blackwood Canyon; Chateau Ste Michelle and Columbia Crest; Chinook; Columbia; Hogue; Salishan; Snoqualmie; Stewart.

THE REST OF AMERICA

The West Coast is not the only part of north America where viticulture and wine-making flourish. From Texas to Long Island, from Idaho to Canada's Ontario, from British Columbia to Missouri, there are dozens of wineries, many of them still producing non-*vinifera* wines from grape varieties such as Chelois, Concord and Seibel, which rarely find favour outside their zones of production. Although more *vinifera* grapes are being made into wine in these lesser regions, very few are available in Britain. There are some clean, attractive wines from Texas, and reasonably priced Canadian Chardonnay from Ontario (mainly from the Niagara district), but they do not make one gasp with wonder.

Stockists

Adnams; Les Amis du Vin; Askham Wines; Averys; David Baillie Vintners; Barnes Wine Shop; Bibendum; Bottoms Up; D Byrne & Co; Croque-en-Bouche; Eaton Elliot; Guildford Wine Market; Haynes Hanson & Clark; Heath Street Wine Co; Douglas Henn-Macrae; Hilbre Wine Co; Morris & Verdin; Oddbins; Thos Peatling; Le Picoleur; Reid Wines; Selfridges; Stapylton Fletcher; T & W Wines; La Vigneronne; Villeneuve Wines; Wessex Wines; Whitesides Wine Merchants; Windrush Wines; Wine House; Winecellars; Yorkshire Fine Wines.

Stephen Brook is the author of a number of travel books, most recently *The Double Eagle* and *Winner Takes All: A Season in Israel*, as well as *Liquid Gold: Dessert Wines of the World*. He also contributes a regular column to *Vogue*.

Portugal

Andrew Jefford

.. over half of the world's cork comes from Portugal..

There are at least two good reasons why wine drinkers across the world should feel grateful to this dreamy, wave-washed country at the far western end of Europe. One reason is generally lying in the wastepaper basket as you enjoy your Chardonnay or Shiraz, but without it, the wine would not be as good as it is. Over half of the world's cork comes from Portugal, punched from sections of the inner bark of an oak tree, *Quercus suber*.

The second reason is wine with brandy in it. Madeira and port are two of the world's three great fortified wines (the trio is completed by Spain's sherry), and they evolved from a creative partnership between Portuguese grape varieties, soils and climates, and the interference of British merchants. The waves had a hand in the matter, too: they brought the British and took away the wine and, in the case of Madeira, the journey across the sea improved the cargo so startlingly that it changed production methods altogether.

A third, more recent reason to be grateful to the Portuguese is the arrival of their table wines in British shops. At present these are less consistently excellent than the fortified wines, but their potential is as great. They are inexpensive, with flavours all of their own, and 1991 is an exciting time to set about exploring them.

Approaches to Portugal

What do you admire in a red wine? If it is the slightly rough edge normally described as 'honest'; if it is the wealth of nuances wines acquire with age; if it is the animal, farmyard aromas most famously possessed by middle-aged burgundy; if it is the readiness to partner a wide range of foods; and if it is concentration of flavour, then you will find much to explore in Portugal. Stay away if you are looking for vibrant fruit and sweet oakiness, or if you want low-tannin, low-acid reds to drink without food; for these New Worldly virtues have yet to make an impact on the Old World country from which so many explorers set sail.

How do you like your white wines? Portugal offers a choice of two styles. One is all mouthwatering sharpness and slenderness, made from the fruit of tendril-crazy vines that romp up trees and cascade over gardens filled with giraffe-necked cabbages: these are the vinhos verdes (green wines) of northern Portugal. The second style is less easy to define. Portugal's non-verde white wines (*maduros*) are generally broad and full, though they may have surprisingly keen acidity. They are usually low in the fresh, fruity aromas and flavours of young white wines that have been protected from oxygen for most of their lives. Instead, they have the dappled, nutty, honeyed flavours of white wines in mid-life, with leafy, vegetal aromas appearing as the wine unfolds in your mouth. Sometimes – when they have been exposed to too much oxygen – they taste tired and flat, though this failing may be less apparent when they are served with food than when drunk on their own.

The middle way

And then there are the rosés, most of them called either Mateus or Lancers. These wines, which account for half of Portugal's annual wine exports, illustrate two of the less dreamy aspects of the Portuguese scene. The first is the commercial potential of branded wines appealing to 'international' tastes: not too dry, not too sweet, not too red, not too white, not too still, not too fizzy. But always reliable: a decent wine in a pretty bottle. The second is the way in which Portugal, with its wealth of fine, native grape varieties and its deeply entrenched but unrefined wine culture, provides the perfect springboard for skilled wine-makers to experiment and innovate. Mateus Rosé is a mass-produced example of such innovation (pink wines are not traditional in Portugal); more interesting and less 'industrial' creations are those issuing from the wine workshop of Australian Peter Bright at João Pires.

Indeed, wine-making innovation, and the production of branded wines, are both sanctioned in one of the purest Portuguese traditions: that of the *garrafeira*. This term is used of a red wine matured for at least two years before bottling and at least one afterwards (in the case of white wines, for at least six months before bottling and least six afterwards). It must have half a degree more alcohol than the minimum requirement, and it may be blended from wines sourced from anywhere in Portugal – providing the result is of 'outstanding quality'. (It may also come from a single region.) It is through their *garrafeiras* that the merchant-producers who have traditionally dominated Portuguese wine production have proved their worth to customers, and they are still among Portugal's most convincing successes.

In addition to these often inter-regional wines, Portugal is now giving birth to a wide range of wines from demarcated regions (see Portugal's Wine Laws, opposite), and it is in these that the fascination of the future lies. Most of them have barely left the maternity unit, but when they eventually totter into our shops we should extend them an indulgent welcome. It seems certain that this wine-loving nation (the Portuguese were, until recently, the world's largest per capita consumers) will eventually produce wines to equal the world's best, and when they do so, it will be by matching the right variety to the right patch of soil, under propitious skies.

Portugal's wine laws

Portugal's wine laws are two-tiered. The first tier is occupied by eleven Regiãos Demarcadas (Demarcated Regions): Vinho Verde, Douro (table wine), Douro (port), Bairrada, Dão, Colares, Bucelas, Carcavelos, Setúbal, Algarve and Madeira. Each of these regions is supervised by a regulatory body which issues the *selo de garantia* (control slip) you will find pasted over the neck of the bottle and under its capsule.

The second tier is occupied by 25 newly demarcated regions enjoying Indicação de Proveniência Regulamentada (Regulated Indication of Origin); it is intended that these regions will eventually become Regiãos Demarcadas. Few wines from these regions are seen yet on export markets; those that do leave Portugal include examples from Arruda, Palmela, Torres Vedras and Reguengos de Monsaraz, and these names will be mentioned on labels. *Selos de garantia* are not issued.

The decrees governing both RDs and IPRs specify, in addition to regional boundaries, recommended grape varieties, minimum alcohol content, maximum yield and minimum ageing requirements.

THE NORTH

Minho

The Minho provides a picture of what all wine-making used to be like. Vines are grown everywhere: no garden or field is complete without a fringe of tree- or pergola-trained vines. Grapes are everybody's everyday crop, and many of them become rough home-made wine to wash down a year's supply of dried cod and fried pork. Most of these 'green wines' are red; they are sharp as an axe and as refreshing as a cold bath.

Some years ago the larger producers perceived, correctly, that red wines with virtues of this complexion would not be popular on export markets, so what we get are white vinhos verdes, many of them finished with a prickle of gas and a pinch of grape sugar. They are sold in flask-shaped, clear glass bottles with romantic labels, and are a safe enough bet if you're looking for a light (alcohol level is generally around 9 per cent), brightly flavoured white wine. But for more authentic and adventurous tastes go for one of the better wines produced from named, single estates.

These will often be from single grape varieties – two of the best are the perfumed Loureiro and the concentrated, richly flavoured Alvarinho. Always look for last year's date on the label, and drink the wine soon. (Many vinhos verdes are non-vintage, in which case buy from an outlet with a high turnover.) Every passing month sees a little trace of excitement leave the wine to make a mysterious journey back to Portugal – for recycling in next year's vinho verde.

Vinho verde

Type *Light white wine, sometimes slightly sparkling, dry to off-dry*
Profile *Slender, refreshing, flavours of apple and lime*
Advice *Drink soon after buying, chill, good picnic wine*

Recommended producers

Chello (Sogrape); Gazela (Sogrape); Paço de Cardido (João Pires); Paço de Teixeró (Montez Champalimaud); Solar das Bouças.

Douro Litoral, Trás-os-Montes e Alto Douro

Most of the province of Douro Litoral (Coastal Douro) is vinho verde country (see above), and much of the province of Trás-os-Montes e Alto Douro (literally Across-the-Mountains and the High Douro) is port country (see below). But such is Portuguese enthusiasm for the vine that this sector produces both red and white wines that elude either category; they go to market under the Douro Região Demarcada. The best are red.

Once upon a time, port was a dry table wine: deep, dark, leathery, known to eighteenth-century topers as 'blackstrap'. Evolution has given us a sweet, fortified wine under port's name, but blackstrap is still available: it is called Barca Velha or Reserva Especial, and is made by the port producer Ferreira (also labelled Ferreirinha). Barca Velha is produced in the finest years, Reserva Especial in the others. These are some of Portugal's most profound and sonorous red wines; but they are also some of its most expensive and sought-after, and they are therefore exceptions to Portugal's excellent value-for-money rule. Better value may be had from the wines of the Douro estates Quinta do Côtto and Quinta da Pacheca, the former being marked by new oak and the latter by a little Cabernet Sauvignon.

Many of the Douro's cheaper red wines are surprisingly light, even delicate, perhaps because they were made from grapes that weren't quite up to the mark for port; the whites are soft and vegetal.

Douro red

Type *Deep red wine (expensive); medium-bodied to light red wine (inexpensive)*
Profile *Rich, rounded fruit; flavours of plums, blackberries, sometimes herbs*
Advice *Expensive examples may be cellared, and make fine dinner-party wines; inexpensive examples make good everyday reds for food*

Recommended producers

Red; Barca Velha (Ferreira/Ferreirinha); Grande Escolha (Quinta do Côtto); Lello (Borges & Irmão); Quinta do Côtto (Montez Champalimaud); Quinta da Pacheca; Reserva Especial (Ferreira/Ferreirinha).
White Planalto (Sogrape).

THE CENTRE

Beira Litoral, Beira Alta, Beira Baixa

Portugal's two best-known red table wine regions, Bairrada and Dão, are found in Beira, a large area occupying the northern part of central Portugal. Bairrada lies near the coast, north of Coimbra; Dão is further inland, south of Viseu. Both areas produce mostly red wines.

The differences between them are those of soil (clay in Bairrada, granite and schist in Dão) and grape variety. For the Bairrada reds, at least 50 per cent Baga must be used, and 90 per cent is usual; while a wide range of varieties are used for Dão reds, with Touriga Nacional and Bastardo both important. A mix of varieties is used for the whites of both regions, too, with Maria Gomes (alias Fernão Pires) dominating in Bairrada and Encruzado in Dão. The potential for differentiation between the two regions' wines, however, is blurred by traditional vinification, with its emphasis on tannin at the expense of fruit, and by traditional production methods, which decree a minimum ageing period before bottling of 18 months in both cases. (*Garrafeiras* must have at least two years of vat or cask ageing, and one in bottle.) The result is that the reds of Dão and Bairrada can resemble each other in stony-faced, hard-nosed charmlessness.

Not all the wines are ugly thugs, however; the best Dão has complex aromas of dusty, perfumed plums, sometimes qualified by a goaty note, while its tannin and astringency will be meshed in with rich, solid fruit. The best Bairrada will be rather zingier than Dão ever is, with berry aromas and flavours and a full, meaty taste. The best white wines of Dão are lovely examples of the leafy, honeyed, almost oily Portuguese style; while those of Bairrada tend to be sharper and crisper, more internationally acceptable but less interesting and characterful.

Dão red

Type *Full red wine*
Profile *At best rich, peppery, tight, tough; can be greenly astringent*
Advice *Drink with rich food*

Bairrada red

Type *Full red wine*
Profile *At best vibrantly fruity, meaty; can be acidic, ungenerous*
Advice *Drink with rich food*

Recommended producers

Dão red Asda Dão; Borges & Irmão; Grão Vasco (Sogrape); Porta dos Cavaleiros (Caves São João); Terras Altas (José Maria da Fonseca Successores).
Dão white Conde de Santar; Grão Vasco (Sogrape); Terras Altas (José Maria da Fonseca Successores).
Bairrada red Adega Cooperativa de Cantanhede; Borges & Irmão; Caves Aliança; Frei João (Caves São João); Luis Pato.

Estremadura (Oeste), Ribatejo, Setúbal

This area, which includes Lisbon and much of the River Tejo's basin, occupies the south-western part of central Portugal. It is the country's hub, and provides much of the musculature, if not the heart itself, of Portugal's viticulture. The majority of the 25 new IPRs are in this area, and four of the eleven established Regiãos Demarcadas are found here, too: Colares, Bucelas, Carcavelos and Setúbal.

This is a strange quartet. Colares, produced from sprawling (and ungrafted) vines buried deeply in sand, is as near as wine can get to ink. Little is produced, and it needs two decades in a dark cellar before it begins to open its fiercely clenched teeth. To the non-Portuguese, Colares at any age is as much penance as pleasure. Bucelas is a buttery, lemony white of modest distinction, while Carcavelos is all but extinct: the last of the line is an indifferent fortified wine based on a rag-bag of varieties. Manuel Bulhosa's Quinta de Santa Rita, however, looks set to revive the RD once its early production has acquired the necessary five years' cask maturation.

Setúbal, however, has long flourished – in the capable hands of José Maria da Fonseca Successores. This, too, is a fortified wine, produced from seventy per cent Moscatel. Five months' maceration of the grape skins produces beautifully aromatic dessert wines, grapey-sweet when young or raisin-rich after twenty years in wooden casks.

The best of the region's other wines, from areas still finding their regional identity, are all soloists, some of them virtuoso. In Estremadura, for example, Quinta da Abrigada produces elegantly aromatic, closely textured wines with a characteristically Portuguese finish that seems unpalatably austere and bitter without food, but rich and deep between mouthfuls of beef. The young wines of the Adega Cooperativa de Arruda dos Vinhos are light, skippingly fruity: a complete contrast. In Ribatejo, the best of the wines at present are merchants' *garrafeiras*, full of complicated, close-harmony flavours such as those of Romeira (Caves Velhas) and Carvalho, Ribeiro and Ferreira, though one estate – the Casa Agricola de Dom Luís de Margaride – produces a characterful range from vineyards near Almeirim (an IPR). A single grape variety, Periquita, generally lurks behind all of these wines, wearing masks of synonymy: Castelhão Francês, João de Santarém, Mortágua, Trincadeira Preta.

On the Setúbal peninsula, meanwhile, two companies compete with each other and, as they do so, produce at least half of Portugal's finest table wines. José Maria da Fonseca Successores' Periquita, Quinta de Camarate and Pasmados (all red) are its local offerings, all fine reds in a decidedly Portuguese mould: resinous, animal scents herald sinewy flavours. (Pasmados is the deepest.) João Pires' range is more innovative, as one would expect from a Portuguese company with an Australian wine-maker: it includes an almost-dry Muscat (Palmela Branco), a Cabernet-Merlot blend (Quinta da Bacalhôa) and an oak-aged Chardonnay (Cova da Ursa). Yet Peter Bright is a thinking Australian, not a dogmatic Cab-Chard internationalist, and his most exciting wines are those founded on imaginative use of Portuguese varieties: the charmingly fruity Quinta de Santa Amaro (Periquita-Merlot), the oak-aged Meia Pipa (Periquita-Cabernet), and two whites based on the Fernão Pires variety: dry, oaky Catarina and a sweet Late Harvest wine.

Recommended producers

Adega Cooperativa de Arruda dos Vinhos; Carvalho, Ribeiro & Ferreira (garrafeira); José Maria da Fonseca Successores (Pasmados, Periquita, Quinta de Camarate, Setúbal); Dom Hermano (Luís de Margaride); João Pires (Catarina, Cova de Ursa, Late-Harvest Fernão Pires, Meia Pipa, Palmela Branco, Quinta da Bacalhôa, Quinta de Santa Amaro); Quinta da Abrigada; Romeira (Caves Velhas, garrafeira).

THE SOUTH

Alto Alentejo, Baixo Alentejo, Algarve

Of these three traditional provinces, the Algarve is the only one with Região Demarcada status – yet its (mainly red) wines are inconsistent and of indifferent quality, saleable thanks only to tourist thirst; while the Alentejo produces splendid reds and attractively soft, leafy whites. The reward for this huge, parched, cork-forested hinterland is five of the new IPRs: Portalegre, Borba, Redondo, Reguengos de Monsaraz and Vidigueira. These are names to watch for during the coming years.

The Alentejo has traditionally provided rich pickings for large companies looking to assemble a fine *garrafeira* blend, and Portugal's two pacesetters – Fonseca Successores and Pires – both produce Alentejo reds that show what the draw was. Fonseca's wine, Tinto Velho, comes from the Rosado Fernandes estate, and is made and matured in beautiful clay amphoras (*talhas*). These (or some very like them) are illustrated on the label of Pires' Tinto da Anfora – which is aged in chestnut and oak casks, not clay pots at all; one of the dreamier forms of rivalry.

[at Thomas Povy's house]
. . . But still, above all these things, he bid me go down into his wine-cellar, where upon several shelves there stood bottles of all sorts of wine, new and old, with labells pasted upon each bottle, and in the order and plenty as I never saw books in a bookseller's shop...
Samuel Pepys 19.1.1663

Alentejo red

Type *Full red wine*
Profile *Sweet, dusty fruit aromas and rich, full flavours; lusher than Dão or Bairrada*
Advice *Drink with stews and braises*

Recommended producers

Alentejo red Tinto da Anfora (João Pires); Tinto Velho (J M da Fonseca Successores).
Alentejo white Herdade de Santa Marta (João Pires).

Stockists

James Aitken; Alba Wine Society; H Allen Smith; Belfast Wine Co; Bentalls; Bibendum; Bottoms Up; D Byrne & Co; City Wines; Peter Dominic; John Ford; Grape Ideas; Peter Green; Grilli; Heath Street Wine Co; Victor Hugo; Hunter & Oliver; Oddbins; Ravensbourne; La Reserva; J Sainsbury; Tanners; Tesco; Topsham Wines; Wine House; Winecellars; Wines of Interest.

Portugal (table wines): vintages

Vinho verde should be drunk as soon as possible. 1989 was an excellent year, and should still be good; avoid the poor 1988 and older vintages.

Excellent years for Douro, Dão and Bairrada were 1989, 1985, 1983 and 1980; while 1988 and 1982 were good. 1987 was good in the Douro, but less so in Dão and Bairrada. 1986, 1984 and 1981 were light years.

For the rest of Portugal, 1989, 1988, 1983, 1982 and 1980 vary from good to excellent. 1987, 1986, 1984 and 1981 were light to average years.

Remember that wine-making standards in Portugal are still variable when compared, for example, with those of Australia; if you find a bad bottle from a good vintage, this will be why.

PORT

Port is the sweet fortified wine, generally red in colour, that comes from the rockily schistous valley of the Douro in Northern Portugal. It is fortified with brandy when its fermentation is part-complete; the brandy stops the fermentation, and the wealth of natural grape sugar remaining in the wine furnishes its sweetness.

As in the case of the world's two other great fortified wines, sherry and Madeira, the complexities of manufacture, storing and blending, and traditional markets in Northern Europe and Scandinavia, have meant that the trade in port is divided among a relatively small number of merchant-producers or shippers. Some of these are British in origin, some Portuguese, and one or two are Dutch or German. The fact that the wines are fortified and blended means that large variations in quality on a year-to-year basis should not occur; and the fact that there are a small number of important shippers means that quality variations between them should not be as marked as between table wine producers, for example. So far, so simple. Life is then made difficult by the range of styles of port on offer, and the confusing nomenclature these styles have acquired down the years, as well as by the lack of control exercised over the verbiage that appears on labels (it is almost axiomatic that the more adjectives found on a port label – usually of the 'finest', 'old', 'choice' and 'special' ilk, often with a 'very' or two thrown in for luck – the less good will be the port in the bottle).

Basic styles

Basic port is generally called either Ruby or Tawny: Ruby is a little darker and fruitier, made from red grapes only; Tawny is a little lighter and softer, and is often made from a mixture of red and white grapes. There should be a fundamental difference between the two styles, which we will come to in a moment, but there isn't. They are both young, simple ports, without vintage dates or the need for decanting.

Tastes begin to get more interesting with the next two categories, Vintage Character and Late Bottled Vintage (LBV). Neither, let it be stressed, is Vintage Port; it would be more accurate to describe both as superior ruby ports, deep in colour and rich in peppery fruit. One of the pair, Late Bottled Vintage, carries a vintage date, but such dates can safely be ignored: the greatest differences in quality occur from shipper to shipper, rather than from year to year, and the 'house standard' that each shipper fixes for its LBV is maintained consistently from harvest to harvest. Some shippers specialise in one style, and some in another; there is even a third way to sell port of this type and quality level, which is by building a 'premium brand', such as Graham's Six Grapes or Fonseca's Bin 27. Some of the best Late

Bottled Vintage Ports (particularly those of Warre and Smith Woodhouse, dubbed 'traditional' by their makers) need decanting, but most ports of this quality level do not.

Late Bottled Vintage

Type *Rich, fortified dessert wine*
Profile *Plentiful aromas, sometimes reminiscent of dry hay or tea leaves; rich flavours of ripe fruit and pepper*
Advice *Serve after dinner, on its own or with fruit, nuts or cheese*

Recommended producers
LBV Fonseca; Graham; Niepoort; Ramos-Pinto; Smith-Woodhouse; Taylor; Warre.
Vintage Character Churchill.

Crusting Port

Continuing along this branch of the port family, quality-wise, we come next to Crusting Port (sometimes Crusted Port): a blend bottled young enough to mature in bottle and throw a 'crust' – a thick deposit of sediment – as it does so. (If any port deserves to be called 'Vintage Character', it is Crusting Port.) The style carries a bottling date, though the wine will be a blend of ports of different years; as with LBV, quality should not vary greatly from bottling to bottling. Crusting Port is always deeply fruity, sometimes jammy; it will never have the depth of Vintage Port, but can show you a little of its bright plumage.

Vintage Port

The loftiest spots on the branch are occupied by true Vintage Port. First comes 'Single Quinta' or 'Quinta' port, while the position of supreme elevation is occupied by Vintage Port, often the most plainly labelled wine in a shipper's entire range. Most Single Quinta ports on the British market are Vintage Ports from less successful years, their components generally (though not always) being sourced from a single *quinta* (farm) – the best one that a shipper owns or has access to. Quinta names are also, although more rarely, used for other ports, such as Crusting Port or Aged Tawny Port. Furthermore a number of individual quinta owners in the Douro now produce and export a full range of ports, all of which will bear the name of the relevant quinta. (Check the label carefully if you are unsure as to what you are buying: in every case, the style of port should be clearly indicated.)

Vintage Ports are from the most successful years only, and are blended from the finest wines of a number of different quintas. They are 'declared' to the world between two and three years after the vintage, following which they are put on sale for the first time. Both Vintage and Single Quinta Vintage Ports need long ageing and eventual decanting off their heavy sediment (the black glass used by shippers for these styles proves remarkably unhelpful at this point). After ten years, only the most lily-livered Quinta Vintage will be bright and clear, though most will be drinkable; any self-respecting Vintage Port will still be an opaque blackberry-purple after a decade in the world, finally clearing between its fifteenth and twentieth birthdays. The very best vintages (1945, 1963, 1977) are (or will be) at their peak between twenty-five and fifty years after the grapes were picked.

Vintage Port

Type *Powerful, fortified dessert wine*
Profile *Plentiful aromas and flavours, reminiscent of blackcurrants and blackberries, dried grass, roasted meat, pepper, tar and, with age, chocolate and coffee, voluptuously textured and impressively concentrated*
Advice *Cellar until at least ten years old; decant carefully. The perfect after-dinner wine. Drink on its own, or with nuts or cheese (Stilton is traditional, but a fine Cheddar makes a less obtrusive, more flattering partner). Tobacco smoke impoverishes every aspect of port save its power to intoxicate*

Port: vintages

1989 A very hot summer, producing exciting ports. Possibly a vintage year.

1987 A few shippers declared this vintage; most didn't. It will be a very good year, though, for Single Quinta ports.

1985 A good and universally declared vintage year, with most shippers producing sumptuously fruity ports for the mid- to long-term.

1983 A split declaration, with those declaring producing fine, tight Vintage Port for the long term.

1982 A split declaration; the declarers have produced lush, rounded Vintage Ports already drinking well.

1980 An underrated vintage, with Vintage Ports that still look excitingly immature in 1990.

1977 The greatest vintage of the last two decades, beginning to drink attractively now, but with a long life ahead.

1975 A light vintage.

1970 A sound, solid and satisfying vintage.

1966 A fine vintage, at its peak now.

1963 A very fine vintage, providing superb if expensive bottles of port at present and for the next two decades.

Recommended producers

Cálem; Churchill; Dow; Fonseca; Gould Campbell; Graham; Niepoort; Quinta do Noval; Sandeman; Smith Woodhouse;Taylor; Warre.

Tawny Port

So far, only one side of the port family has been described: the glass branch. All the ports above are richly coloured, full of power and fruit, the result of having spent most of their lives either stored in huge casks or in glass bottles – protected from oxygen, in either case. The other branch of the family are the wood ports, more generally known as tawnies.

True tawny port goes to market under a variety of names, but the one it never uses is 'Tawny Port' – which, as described above, is a young blended wine of light style. No young port can ever be tawny, in fact, for 'tawny' refers to the colour a port turns to as it ages in wooden lodge pipes (casks of between 580 and 630 litres) over a period of years.

There are two main types of tawny port: vintage-dated, known as Colheita (*colheita* being the Portuguese word for 'harvest'); and 'Ports with an Indication of Age', the recognised indications (in English) being 10 Years Old, 20 Years Old, 30 Years Old and Over 40 Years Old. These are styles rather than actual or even average ages.

Colheita Ports cannot be bottled and sold before the seventh year after the harvest, and most of the shippers who specialise in this type of tawny wait for considerably longer than seven years, and bottle slowly, cask by cask, over decades, meaning that it is possible to buy some very old ports in this way. (Be careful, though, not to confuse these ports, as the manager of one of the Duty-Free Shops at Heathrow Airport did in 1990, with Vintage Port. If in doubt, relate the vintage date to the bottling date: two or three years' difference for Vintage Port; seven or more years' difference for Colheita.)

Colheita Ports can be among the finest and lightest of all tawnies, perfectly exemplifying the aromatic finesse and silky nuance of taste which distinguishes this branch of the family. (Garrafeira Ports are a sub-division of the Colheita style, though only one or two shippers produce them: they are Colheitas that have received bottle age in addition to cask age.) Ports with an Indication of Age can be very fine, too: comparison of the four age brackets reveals a gentle increase in intensity and nuttiness. The younger tawnies, particularly the 10 Years Old, respond well to chilling in the summer.

Colheita Port

Type *Smooth, fortified dessert wine*
Profile *Rich, harmonious scents, sometimes nutty, sometimes mintily fresh, with delicate, silky, beautifully composed flavours and a lingering finish*
Advice *Chill lightly if you like; serve either after or between meals, especially in the summer. Tawnies make pleasant sipping wines for the afternoon*

Recommended producers

Barros Almeida; Croft; Cockburn; Feist; Ferreira; Hutcheson; Niepoort; Martinez; Poças Junior; Ramos-Pinto; Warre.

White port

White port is made in exactly the same way as red port, except that white grapes are used. While the fierce heat of the Douro is ideally suited to the production of powerfully fruity red ports, it has an ennervating effect on white grapes, which lose acidity but are unable to compensate, as red ports do, with extracts and tannins. White ports therefore tend to be strong and sweet but bland in flavour, and to seem like an unashamedly simple and rapid way to get drunk. Some of them even smell like the first whiff of dentist's gas, and this anaesthetic effect is intensified when ingested, as most are, on an empty stomach. Some shippers have tried producing lighter, drier versions, but even the driest are still glycerine-rich and almondy rather than sabre-edged and lemony, while the lighter ones seem curiously hollow and empty. White port is the world's biggest, bustiest aperitif: that's its distinction; therein lies its appeal.

Recommended producers

Churchill; Cockburn; Delaforce; Fonseca; Kopke; Niepoort.

Port stockists

Berry Bros & Rudd; Bin Ends; Booths; G E Bromley; Butlers Wine Cellar; D Byrne & Co; Davisons; Farr Vintners; Fine Vintage Wines; Grape Ideas; Guildford Wine Market; Harrods; Harveys; J E Hogg; Hopton Wines; Tony Jeffries Wines; S H Jones; Justerini & Brooks; Kurtz & Chan; Lay & Wheeler; Master Cellar Wine Warehouse; Nickolls & Perks; Oddbins; Old Street Wine Co; Selfridges; Snowdonia Wine Warehouse; T & W Wines; Tanners; Turville Valley Wines; Valvona & Crolla; Weavers of Nottingham; Willoughbys; Wines of Interest; Wright Wine Co; Peter Wylie Fine Wines; Yorkshire Fine Wines.

MADEIRA

Madeira is extraordinary. It is an island where, it would seem, no island has the right to be – lost in the middle of an ocean. It has a climate in which almost anything, from bananas to Christmas trees, can be grown. And its wine is made under the most trying circumstances, using fruit from a patchwork of tiny vineyards fermented to different stages before being fortified, then 'cooked' in one of two ways. Cheaper Madeiras undergo heat treatment (*estufagem*) in huge sealed vats: a quick way of simulating long hot ageing. High-quality Madeiras are aged in attics, where they are exposed to the kind of heat that leaves flies panting, and receive the kind of oxidisation that would put most wines out for the count. What does this treatment produce? Not the wine gravy that you might expect but the world's longest-lived, most intensely flavoured wine: Vintage Madeira.

Vintage Port is 'declared' between two and three years after the harvest, at a time when the date and the excitement of the summer are still fresh in people's minds, and after 10 or 15 years the wines are drinking well. Vintage Madeira is only declared 20 years after its harvest, and needs at least 50 years' maturation to get into its stride, making it an antiquary's wine – and frighteningly expensive, too, though it is one of the few wines in the world that can be said with any objectivity to be worth a £50 price tag. Production costs account for almost all of this; demand is minute and fashionability zero.

Further comparison with port is instructive. A well-made LBV or Crusting Port may not be a fine wine, but it will certainly be an exciting one, full of pepper and fire and lush, black fruit. In Madeira's case, the equivalent of LBV or Crusting Port – the 5-year-old Reserve or even the 10-year-old Special Reserve – all too often lack any of the reeking, savage intensity that makes the finest Madeiras so exciting. Instead, they are sweetly commercial, mincing wines, trying not to offend anyone (good Sercial, at the very least, should always be cheesily offensive) and all too often ending by pleasing no one.

There are signs, though, that improvements may be on the way. The island's slumbering giant, the Madeira Wine Company, has stirred itself recently: the Symington group (a major force in port's renaissance, owner of Dow, Graham, Warre, Smith Woodhouse, Gould Campbell and Quarles Harris) has acquired around half its shares. The Symington family are likely to revitalise the MWC, which in turn may ginger its competitors; the Symingtons also know how to market traditional, fortified wines skilfully and effectively, and may therefore succeed in persuading the world to look again at the treasure island it has ignored for so long.

The main distinction between types of Madeira is drawn according to the principal grape variety (85 per cent) from which each is made. Sercial should be the driest, although many Sercials are enfeebled by sweetening; a good dry Sercial will have a cheesy, farmyard aroma, sometimes with pretty floral touches, and an austere apple-and-nut flavour. Verdelho, the unimpressive Rainwater (a style, not a grape variety) and the uncommon

Terrantez are all medium dry, the best Verdelho being honed to the kind of knife-edge balance between sweetness and acidity that the Chenin Blanc achieves in the Loire and the Riesling in the Mosel, with lovely apricot and walnut flavours. Bual and Malmsey are both dessert wines, the former being buttery and smoky-rich, the latter more luscious still, with a raisiny sweetness. High levels of acidity in both cases (and in all Madeiras) stop the wines cloying, and the best examples of both will have layer on layer of complex flavour triggers to engage the mouth and challenge the mind.

Vintage Madeiras are almost the only ones on which you will see a date: all should be very distinguished wines. You will also see dates (often nineteenth-century ones) linked to the word 'Solera' on some Madeiras: these will be fine wines aged in small-scale, island-sized solera systems (see the sherry section under Spain), the date referring to the establishment of the solera rather than to the contents of the bottle. Madeira soleras were accidentally outlawed following Portugal's entry into the EC; they are permitted again now, but the new rules governing their establishment and running are so bizarre that almost no shipper is still making them, and at least one shipper is under the impression that they are still banned. The upshot is that we will not see much of these wines in future, some of which are as good as vintage wines. Try them while you can.

Extra (or Exceptional) Reserve Madeiras are sometimes seen, though this category is not approved by the Madeira Wine Institute: they are fifteen-year-old wines. Special Reserve wines are ten years old, and Reserve five years old: these ages are minima. Madeiras without any of these qualifications will be at least three years old, and those whose label does not specify any of the varieties mentioned above will be based on the Tinta Negra Mole, Madeira's all-purpose red grape, also responsible for making up the 15 per cent balance in the named varietals. (Only Vintage Madeira may be assumed to be made solely from the named variety.) Madeiras are traditionally stored standing rather than lying, and once opened, they last well: a month or two may pass before their quality begins to decline. Madeira needs no food accompaniment, but if you feel the need to drink wine with soup, then Sercial or Verdelho make a sound choice.

Recommended producers

Rather than recommend individual producers, each of whom makes both good and bad Madeira and many of whom form part of the Madeira Wine Company, we advise, exceptionally, that readers buy the most expensive example they are able to afford, and judge Madeira (and the producer or brand) on the merits of such a wine. Vintage and solera Madeiras are very expensive; even so, they are unlikely to disappoint. They are wines that can only be sipped, and may be left and returned to, in astonishment, over an extended period.

Stockists

Farr Vintners; Fine Vintage Wines; Peter Green; Nickolls and Perks; Turville Valley Wines; La Vigneronne; Wines of Interest.

South America

Rosemary George MW

CHILE

There's no doubt that Chile is a viticultural paradise. Thanks to her natural frontiers – the Andes, the Pacific Ocean, the Atacama Desert and Antarctica – the country is phylloxera-free, for not even the most intrepid louse can cross such barriers. Historical chance also helped in that European vines were brought to Chile just a few years before phylloxera had crossed the Atlantic from North America. Today, strict quarantine measures are maintained for imported vines. This means that all Chile's vines are ungrafted, making for stronger, healthier and longer living plants.

The climate, too, is perfect. There is very little rainfall, so the vineyards are dependent upon irrigation water from the melted snows of the Andes. The supply of this water can be regulated at will, which in the past led to overly high yields. However, there is now a move amongst the more conscientious producers towards reducing irrigation, especially in the month or so immediately before the vintage, and yields are falling to more modest proportions. Lack of rainfall also avoids problems with rot. Indeed, many of the other viticultural hazards that beset the vineyards of Europe are non-existent here. Temperatures are not too extreme, for the heat of summer is moderated by cool winds from the mountains and sea breezes from the Pacific Ocean. The seawater is brought by currents from the Antarctic: you have to be hardy to swim at the seaside resort of Viña del Mar and even a paddle is an invigorating experience. These conditions mean that the potential for organic viticulture is tremendous, but it is as yet unrealised. For the moment Chile prides herself simply on her ungrafted vines.

The vineyards of Chile are concentrated in the Central Valley. In fact, it is more of a narrow plateau, 70 kilometres at its widest, between two mountain ranges: the Andes, which dominates the skyline, and the very much lower Coastal Range. The Central Valley is crossed by several rivers, the Aconcagua to the north of the capital, Santiago, and to the south, the Maipo, Maule and Cachapaol, amongst others. In summer these broad rivers are reduced to the merest trickles of water in wide beds of pebbles. Most of the large wineries are close to Santiago, mainly for reasons of convenience. However there is a growing interest in vineyards further south where the climate is cooler, with a little more rain. Miguel Torres (see below) is based in Curicó, two hundred kilometres from Santiago, as is the San Pedro winery.

The basis of a system of denominations exists, splitting the country into four broad zones, namely Maipo, Rapel, Maule and Bío-Bío. These in turn are divided into thirty-one sub-denominations, such as Aconcagua, Lontué, Curicó, and so on. These names may appear on labels, but for the moment there is no legal obligation to use them. Other terms such as 'Gran Viño' or 'Reserva' are almost meaningless, indicating more the producer's perception of his wine than anything else.

It is the grape variety and producer's name on the label that determine the quality of a Chilean wine. The grape varieties are principally the classic ones of France. Cabernet Sauvignon dominates red wines, with some Merlot and the occasional drop of Malbec, while Chardonnay leads the field for white wines, with Sauvignon Blanc close behind, sometimes blended with Semillon. The more adventurous Torres range includes Gewürztraminer and Riesling.

Chilean wine production is dominated by a few large wineries, which may or may not own vineyards. With a couple of exceptions, they buy most of their grapes from a multitude of small farmers. As yet there are none of the tiny 'boutique' wineries that you find elsewhere in the New World, particularly in California. Foreign interest is developing in Chile, notably with the purchase by the Rothschilds of Château Lafite of a fifty per cent share in the wine producer Los Vascos. Domecq has an interest in Undurraga and the Franciscan vineyards from Napa have invested heavily in Errazuriz Panquehue. Other investors are arriving from Spain, Bordeaux and Australia. In Britain, supermarkets have gone hunting for 'own-label' Chilean wines, and Sainsburys, the Co-op and Tesco are among those who have come back with creditable examples.

The wine-making trendsetter in Chile is Miguel Torres, of Penedés fame (see Spain). He brought his European experience and spirit of innovation here in 1979, planted vineyards and built a winery. He was the first to practise cool, temperature-controlled fermentations for white wines, and the first to introduce new 225-litre *barriques* of French oak for maturing his reds. These may be commonplace in Europe, but in Chile, where the wine was usually left in large oak barrels to oxidise gently for several years, they were viewed as revolutionary. Ten years on, Torres' example has been followed by virtually every serious Chilean winery eager to make the transition from catering for a safe domestic market to meeting the challenge of broader international demand.

Therein lies Chile's problem. She has been hailed as the successor to Australia and the next discovery for the world's fine wine explorers. Yet such accolades are unfair at this stage, asking too much from a country that is still learning, mastering techniques with new oak, blending, skin contact and so on. The traditional taste within Chile was for rather tired, oxidised wines that had been subjected to long periods of barrel-ageing, and these wines are leaving the scene only slowly. Chile has yet to create an individual flavour of her own. What California has done with Zinfandel, and Australia with Semillon and Shiraz, Chile has yet to do with one of her own range of grape varieties.

However, there is no doubt that Chile has much to offer. Interest in her wines has grown significantly, and so have sales to the UK – with virtually a tenfold increase in the last two years, from 20,000 cases in 1987 to nearly 200,000 in 1989. Almost all the major Chilean producers now export their wines to Britain. Cabernet Sauvignon (see the taste box) offers the most exciting and individual flavours, and the best value for money. So far prices remain stable, and are unlikely to increase suddenly. White wines based on Chardonnay and Sauvignon Blanc are improving quite dramatically; the oxidised styles are being replaced by fresh, grapey flavours. As for Merlot, try the one produced by Santa Helena. Progress is being made with Chardonnay, but it can taste a little overoaked and clumsily buttery. Sauvignon Blanc can still resemble rather boring white Bordeaux, but the wines of some producers are getting better, notably those of Undurraga, Canepa and Torres. Look out for other wines in the Torres range, including a delicious rosé.

Chilean Cabernet Sauvignon

Type *Full red wine*
Profile *Usually shows good varietal character, with flavours of blackcurrant, ripe fruit, eucalyptus, sometimes tempered by new oak, and balanced with tannin*
Advice *Drink with food; treat like a young claret. Vintages are unimportant, but the wines will age for a few years, the exact length of time depending on whether they resemble a basic house claret or something better, like a cru bourgeois*

Recommended producers

Concha y Toro; Cousiño Macul; Errazuriz Panquehue (pronounced eh *rah* zooriz pan *kay* way), especially Don Maximiano Cabernet; Santa Helena Selección del Directorio; Santa Rita; Torres; Undurraga; Los Vascos.

Stockists

Battersea Wine Co; Bin Ends; Bordeaux Direct; Bottoms Up; D Byrne; Cadwgan; Celtic Vintner; City Wines; Cumbrian Cellar; Peter Dominic; Philip Eyres; Grape Ideas; Peter Green; Guildford Wine Market; Hedley Wright; Hunter & Oliver; Majestic; Moreno Wines; Arthur Rackham; Ravensbourne; La Reserva; Snowdonia Wine; Stapylton Fletcher; The Sunday Times Wine Club; Tanners; Victoria Wine; Peter Watts.

The sorbitol affair

Sadly, it has come to light during 1990 that Chile has blotted her copybook. The red wines of a handful of producers have been found to contain sorbitol. It is not harmful or toxic in any way; it occurs naturally in sweet wines like Sauternes and Trockenbeernauslese styles, but it certainly should not be added to red wine. Its addition was presumably intended to soften the effects of hard tannins and make the affected wines taste supple and mellow, as the prime culprit, Santa Rita's Medalla Real, does. All the offending wines have been withdrawn from the market, and any imported since January 1990 contain less than the approved level of sorbitol.

ARGENTINA

There are signs that Argentinian wines may be regaining social acceptance in Britain once again, as political differences between the two countries become resolved. Over the next year or so, more wines are set to appear on our shelves.

Argentina is the world's fifth largest wine-producing country. Like Chile, the main wine regions of Argentina depend upon the valleys of the Andes. The westerly province of Mendoza is most important, with some 180,000 ha of vines. Most of the large wine producers are here, around the city of Mendoza or close to San Rafael, further south. As in Chile, irrigation is essential, for the vineyards are planted in what would otherwise be desert scrubland. Unlike Chile, however, there is phylloxera on this side of the Andes, but the insect cannot thrive in the sandy soil conditions so the vines are largely ungrafted. Although Mendoza lies at the same latitude as Santiago, the climate is much hotter as there is no ocean to provide a tempering effect, and temperatures reach 40° or more in the summer months. The even warmer regions of La Rioja and San Juan to the north of Mendoza are known for heady sherry-style wines based on Muscat and Pedro Ximénez, for the home market. Altogether elsewhere, some 900 kilometres to the south of Mendoza, the Rio Negro region of northern Patagonia offers potential, with varieties like Cabernet Sauvignon, Merlot and Semillon planted.

However, the major discovery of a visit to South America during 1989 by various Masters of Wine was Torrontés, a white grape variety that – we were told – is a mutation of Malvoisie, brought from the Canaries in the 1550s. It may have something to do with the Terrantez of Madeira; it is also widespread in Galicia. It is grown most successfully in the province of Salta, some 1,100 kilometres north of Mendoza. Contrary to what one might expect in the southern hemisphere, the climate here is cooler than in Mendoza, as the vineyards are planted on the foothills of the Andes at 1,700 metres or more. The resulting temperate climate makes for a delicately aromatic wine, not unlike a dry Muscat from the South of France.

The main grape variety of Argentina is the red Criolla, which, like the very similar Pais of Chile, is grown almost exclusively for the domestic market. Efforts for the export market are concentrated on Malbeck (spelt with the final 'k', here, for some reason) which has been described as the Zinfandel of Argentina. Like the Zinfandel, its flavour does vary greatly according to how it is vinified, though it doesn't have quite the same range of tastes found in Zinfandel. There is growing interest in Cabernet Sauvignon and Merlot, and white varieties such as Chardonnay and Riesling, but these still represent a tiny drop in the ocean of Argentinian wine: there are just 100 ha of Chardonnay, 150 of Riesling and 2,000 of Chenin Blanc, out of a total vineyard area of 300,000 hectares.

Argentina has further to go than Chile along the road of experimentation. Her cellars are largely full of old, large oak barrels, but *barriques* are beginning to appear, along with stainless steel vats. For the moment, there is no system of appellations. However, any provenance on a label is generally reliable insofar as grape variety and region are concerned, as the distances between regions are so great that blending between them is impractical. What Argentina most definitely needs is some control over yields, for the idea that quantity equals quality still prevails.

Argentinian Torrontés

Type *Light white wine*
Profile *Very similar to a dry Muscat from the South of France, with a flowery, perfumed nose and dry, pithy, orange fruit on the palate*
Advice *Drink on its own or with food*

Recommended producers
Bodegas Esmeralda (Cabernet Sauvignon and Saint Felicien, a Cabernet/Merlot blend); Etchart (Torrontés); Trapiche's Andean range

Stockists
Bottoms Up; City Wines; Peter Dominic; John Ford; Grape Ideas; Peter Green; Guildford Wine; Hicks & Don; Hunter & Oliver; Majestic; Victoria Wine; Peter Watts; Wessex Wines.

BRAZIL

Italian immigrants were responsible for the development of Brazilian viticulture in the middle of the nineteenth century. They brought grape varieties like Trebbiano (Ugni Blanc) and Italian Riesling, but found them difficult to grow in the intensely humid climate of the provinces of Rio Grande do Sul, in the south of the country, where they settled. Hybrids and non-vinifera varieties proved a much easier option. However, over the last fifteen years or so, there has been a move back towards European varieties, although there are still only 5,000 ha of these, as opposed to 35,000 ha of vines like the hybrid Isabella and the *labrusca* Concorde.

Most of the wines produced in Brazil are sold on the domestic market, though investment by international companies like Rémy Martin, Heublein, Moët & Chandon and so on suggests that this may not always be the case. Indeed, Brazilian wines are beginning to appear in Britain. Palomas Vineyards, sited in the extreme south of the country almost on the Uruguay border, has the advantage of a drier climate than in the rest of the Rio Grande do Sul province. Palomas makes a range of varietals in what is claimed to be one of the most modern wineries of South America. Some are more successful than others: the best are Chenin Blanc, Chardonnay, Merlot and Cabernet Sauvignon.

There are numerous small grape farmers in Brazil, practising the promiscuous cultivation once common in Europe, in which a hotchpotch of different grapes – Chardonnay, Gewürztraminer, Muscat, Cabernet, Merlot, and so on – are grown muddled together with other crops. Most of the grapes are vinified in co-operatives, and the better of these are slowly modernising their methods. Small new American and French oak casks are seen alongside great vats of Brazilian wood. Vintages are insignificant here, and the wines do not need ageing. Wine laws are non-existent. In general, there is less emphasis on varietal wines than elsewhere in South America. Castel Chatelet, a newcomer to the UK, makes an immensely quaffable red based on one-third Merlot and two-thirds Cabernet Franc, with an attractive soft berry fruit flavour.

Recommended producers

Castel Chatelet; Palomas.

Stockists

Bottoms Up; Hunter & Oliver; Victoria Wine; A L Vose; Peter Watts Wines; The Wine Schoppen.

PERU

One lone winery represents the wine production of Peru. Tacama is situated high up in the foothills of the Andes, which compensates for its otherwise torrid proximity to the equator. Four of its wines are exported to Britain, namely Blanco des Blancos, Gran Blanco, Gran Tinto and Gran Tinto Riserva Especial. Malbeck and Cabernet dominate the two reds, while the whites are based upon a mixture of Chenin, Ugni Blanc, Semillon and Sauvignon, with even a little Malbeck in the Gran Blanco. They are not great, but are good enough to provide a talking point.

Stockists

Bottoms Up; Hunter & Oliver; Vinceremos.

Rosemary George discovered the delights of South America on a three-week trip to that continent in 1989 with fellow Masters of Wine. She is author of books on Chablis, French country wines, and Chianti and the wines of Tuscany.

Spain

Andrew Jefford

*.. the sun, first of all:
there is too much of it..*

The red-earthed vineyard slopes gently upwards to a ridge. It is
sometime between midday and two or three in the afternoon; a
time, here, of silence and stillness and retreat. The sun burns
down out of an empty sky. There is a small whitewashed building
up on the ridge, above the low vines, and next to it, between the
shafts of a cart, stands a donkey. The creature is motionless; its
head is lowered. From this perspective, down among the vines,

the building, the donkey and its cart are in silhouette. One comment only suggests itself, and it is a musical one: a guitar chord, played with drama and deliberation.

Let's dissect this scene, for it has much to tell us about Spanish viticulture. The sun, first of all: there is too much of it, and it is too fierce to produce the subtle wines prized throughout Europe. The vines, like the donkey, tolerate the heat, but they don't enjoy it; they turn it straight into sugar, wine-makers turn the sugar into alcohol, and all too often that's the end of the story. Then there's the gentle slope: Spain has far more vineyards than any other European country, and nearly half of them lie in the great plains of New Castile. 'Vines love an open hill,' wrote Virgil in the last century BC, and they still do: the *côtes* and *collines* familiar to us from French *appellation* names testify to the fact. A gentle slope is better than no slope, but no slope is what too many Spanish vineyards have.

The low vines, next: widely spaced, poorly tended, their fruit often sweetly insipid if eaten instead of pippy and unpalatable as fine wine grapes should be. Spain has been unlucky in its native grape varieties. Airén, Parellada, Macabeo, Palomino and Xarel-lo among the whites, and Bobal, Garnacha, Jaen and Monastrell among the reds: these are varieties that, if skilfully vinified or subject to fortification, can produce exciting wines, but rarely do. Only the red Tempranillo is considered a national treasure, with an international career ahead of it. Spanish wine-growers have little to compare with the well-explored nursery of French varieties, or the underexplored cache of varieties that Portugal has been lucky enough to discover in her back garden.

It's hard to ignore the long-suffering donkey: Spain's wine growers are among the poorest, least well equipped in Europe, and poverty, notoriously, is a trap. Finally comes the guitar chord, reminding us of the strength of long centuries of tradition. Where tradition involves the notion of striving for quality, as in Burgundy, Bordeaux or the playing of Paco de Lucia, then it acts as a spur to excellence; where tradition simply means subsistence from the vine and a dogged adherence to the methods of the fathers and the grandfathers, then it becomes more like a ball and chain. Good wines can be produced from unpromisingly arid plains, as Australia has proved; but Australia has the advantage of precious few traditions. Spain has begun to file off the ball and chain and refashion it into spurs, but the work will take decades.

Spanish strategies

How can we get the most out of Spanish wine? To a large extent, that depends on the hard work of British importers and merchants. Are they prepared to spend long and probably fruitless hours on the road, searching for the concentration and character that are so hard to find in Spanish wines? Or do they just fill up their lists and shelves with easy options – bland, forgettable whites and vaguely juicy reds – relying on low prices to turn the stock over? At the moment, our pick of Spain's memorable wines would barely fill a couple of cases; aside from the sterling work of specialists like La Reserva, the suspicion must be that our merchants are not doing their job. How many are prepared to take on a fine Montilla, even if it would cost over £3? How many trouble to stock Priorato, a leading contender for the title of Spain's most characterful red? How many have an offering from Galicia, especially a white from some of the good local varieties the region shares with Portugal? The wines of Miguel Torres are good, but Spain does not begin and end at Vilafranca del Penedés, as some merchants would have us believe.

Spain's wine laws

Spain has worked industriously at her wine laws since 1926, the year in which Rioja became the first **Denominación de Origen** (controlled name). There are now 35 of these, together with two regions classified as transitional Denominaciones Específicas, and the Denominación regulations specify geographical origin (where relevant: some DOs, such as Cava, are non-geographical); the grape varieties that can be used; maximum yields; and basic quality standards, though in this instance 'quality' can at best be defined as 'absence of faults'. An awareness that DO includes a lot of wines whose quality is basic has prompted consideration of a superior **Denominación de Origen Calificada** (DOCa); so far none has been awarded, but if such a scheme were to come into existence, it would be likely to single out the wines of distinguished producers within existing DOs rather than creating a third tier of regional denominations. The EC is at present resisting such a development.

Meanwhile, a training ground for would-be DO aspirants is the category of **Vinos de la Tierra** (country wines), working to constraints similar to those imposed for DO, but less rigorously applied (only 60 per cent of the wine has to come from the specified grape varieties, for example). DOs are policed by Consejos Reguladores, and these organisations authorise the seals that appear on front or back labels.

THE NORTH-WEST

Galicia, Old Castile

In a world in which geographical boundaries were decided by logic rather than history, Galicia would be the most northerly province of Portugal. Logic will serve the wine drinker as a better guide than history to the character of this region's wines: whites are the most interesting, with fresh fruit aromas and flavours marked by lively acidity; they are not dissimilar to Portugal's Vinhos Verdes, from further south. Galician viticulture, however, is less well organised than Portuguese, and the considerable potential of these wines, particularly those made from the Albariño grape (Portugal's Alvarinho), is as yet unrealised. DO Rías Baixas and DO Ribeiro are the two main viticultural regions; light, fragrant and keenly flavoured red wines are produced in addition to the whites, though red varieties are increasingly being pulled up and replaced by white. The wines of Valle de Monterrey (a Vino de la Tierra) are darker and stronger than other Galician reds.

Most of Spain is a huge plain cut into two by the Cordillera Carpetovetónica mountain chain and the northern part, with Valladolid at its centre, is Old Castile. Unlike the southern part (New Castile – see below), this half of the plain is not a wine factory; instead there are a few pockets where wines are grown, but what emerges from these pockets is newly minted, weighty and appealing: golden guineas when compared to the tired currency in circulation further south.

The inspiration has come from Bodegas Vega Sicilia, whose owner planted Cabernet Sauvignon, Merlot and Malbec over a century ago, and whose wine-makers have, ever since, blended the fruit of these Bordeaux varieties with a type of Tempranillo called, locally, Tinto Fino or Tinto del Pais. Low yields produce a huge wine which is locked away in wood for up to a decade, and will last in bottle for half a century: Unico. This is Spain's grandest wine. The two Valbuena wines also produced by Vega Sicilia are younger and a mite softer. Fame means high prices and questionable value for money, and the same applies to Alejandro Fernandez's newly fêted Tinto Pesquera, made from Tinto Fino with a little Garnacha. Both lie in the Ribera del Duero: a Denominación to watch. Other local producers offer more reasonably priced wines; the quality of these was initially inconsistent, but is now improving rapidly.

South-west of Ribera del Duero lie the two adjacent Denominaciones of Toro and Rueda, and these names promise, for the moment, some of Spain's most exciting wines and keenest prices. In Toro, red wines from another Tempranillo variant, Tinto de Toro, together with more or less Garnacha softening, quicken the pulse: if you can't afford Châteauneuf-du-Pape any more, but hanker after something huge, shambling and alcoholic, Toro will provide. White Toro, from Malvasía, has strange, rather catty aromas and a characterful, vegetal flavour. Much better are the whites of Rueda, based on the local variety Verdejo: these are fresh, flowery wines with lively apple flavours, sometimes oak-aged to give a softer, fuller flavour. Rueda Superior guarantees at least 75 per cent Verdejo (the other varieties used are the neutral Palomino, the slightly more characterful Macabeo, known locally as Viura, and the aromatic Sauvignon Blanc).

West of León, the new DO of El Bierzo will eventually export lively, bitter-edged reds from the Mencia grape (also grown in Galicia), while the best of León's own wines (from three Vinos de la Tierra to the south of the city) are channelled through a large *bodega* known as VILE (Vinos de León), often as table wines with no indication of origin.

Ribera del Duero Red

Type *Deep red wine*
Profile *Exciting, complex, sometimes herbal aromas precede dense, balanced flavours; wine for sipping*
Advice *Rest for at least six months and cellar if wished; decant; serve with game or roast meats*

> . . . he did now mightily commend some new sort of wine lately found out,
> called Navarre wine, which I tasted and is, I think, good wine.
> Samuel Pepys 10.2.1669

Toro Red

Type *Deep red wine*
Profile *Massive and alcoholic; scents of cinnamon; richly but softly tannic with hot, stony fruit*
Advice *May be cellared; decant up to eight hours before serving; serve with stews*

Recommended producers
Ribera del Duero Alejandro Fernandez (Pesquera); Mauro; Perez Pascuas (Viña Pedrosa); Vega Sicilia.
Toro Bodegas Fariñas.
Rueda Marqués de Griñon; Marqués de Riscal.

THE NORTH-EAST

Vascongadas, Navarra, Aragón, Catalonia

Spain's best wines begin life here, and it comes as no surprise to find that this is the coolest and hilliest quarter of the country.

Vascongadas is the administrative name for Spain's Basque region, and it produces no wines of its own. The point at which it meets with Old Castile and Navarra, however, is called La Rioja: once exotic syllables that, during the 1970s, became synonymous in Britain with inexpensive red wines full of satisfyingly oaky fruit. The upper reaches of the Ebro thread their way through this undulating, pastel-tinted landscape, while in the distance, on all sides, glower the mountains. They look menacing; in fact, like a crusty bachelor uncle, they are secretly protective, shielding Rioja from the chilly winds and rains that buffet Bilbao to the north, and from the furnace-like heat and frenzied storms that harrow Castile to the south.

Rioja
The reason why Rioja is Spain's leading table wine is that it has a century-old tradition of producing fine wines for export. Demand came, during the nineteenth century, from a mildew- and later phylloxera-afflicted France; in the twentieth century it has come from northern Europe, Scandinavia and America. These exports were initially routed through Bordeaux, only 300 kilometres to the north-east, and the Bordeaux way of doing things – in particular the ageing of the wines in small oak casks (the 225-litre *barrique*) – greatly influenced Riojan thinking. When the wine matured in

those small casks was produced from the high-quality Tempranillo, Graciano and Mazuela (Cariñena) varieties, grown in the generally temperate climate and pebbly clay soils of the region, then everything came good, business boomed, and the word 'Rioja' grew appealingly familiar to foreign ears. The wine was rich, tasty and elegant; the oakiness was seductive; and the price was irresistible.

Of late, however, Rioja seems to have lost its way. Partly, this is because other wine regions of the world have found their way so impressively: everything that had us reaching for Rioja in supermarkets in 1980 has us reaching for Australian Cabernet or Shiraz in 1990. Partly, too, it is because the best Riojas have risen in price thanks to worldwide demand, and the less expensive are so obviously less good. Partly, finally, because the use of oak seems to be on the decrease in Rioja: wines labelled *sin crianza* (meaning 'without any [wood] ageing'), once seldom seen on export markets, are now increasingly common, and even the barrel-aged styles (*crianza, reserva* and *gran reserva*) seem to be less overtly oaky than a decade ago. Close observers of the Rioja scene point out that this is a consequence of expansion in the region during the 1970s; as the new bodegas all used new wood, our initial impression of the wines was of something rather oakier than tradition warranted. Balanced oak is what has always been sought, and that is what today's Riojas offer us.

Among white Riojas, however, the retreat from tradition is beyond question: cold-fermented, neutral, cleanly fruity whites are the order of the day. They have all the character of the stainless-steel vats in which they pass their pre-bottle lives, and they could come from anywhere in Spain, France or Italy. The excellence of those white Riojas produced by the one *bodega* that has absolutely resisted this trend – Marqués de Murrieta – serves only to underline our loss. CVNE's Blanco Seco Reserva and Monopole are less uncomprisingly rich, but console nonetheless. So, too, do Rioja's often soundly fruity rosés, based on the Garnacha grape.

Up, and having set my neighbour, Mr. Hudson, wine cooper, at work drawing out a tierce of wine for the sending of some of it to my wife, I abroad, only taking notice of what a condition it hath pleased God to bring me that at this time I have two tierces of Claret, two quarter casks of Canary, and a smaller vessel of Sack; a vessel of Tent, another of Malaga, and another of white wine, all in my wine cellar together; which, I believe, none of my friends of my name now alive ever had of his owne at one time.
Samuel Pepys 7.7.1665

Rioja Reserva Red

Type *Medium-bodied red wine*
Profile *Comfortable, warm, vanilla-oak aromas; supple, balanced flavours*
Advice *Easy, adaptable yet elegant reds for a wide range of occasions; you do not need to cellar the wines, which are sold when ready to drink, but the best will improve further with more bottle age. This is true to a still greater extent with Gran Reservas*

Recommended producers

Red Rioja Campo Viejo; Contino; CVNE; Marqués de Murrieta; Remelluri (single-estate Rioja); La Rioja Alta; Bodegas Riojanas
White Rioja CVNE; Marqués de Murrieta.

Stockists

Arriba Kettle; Cadwgan; The Celtic Vintner; Tony Jeffries Wines; Mitchells; La Reserva; Wine House.

Navarra and Aragón

Navarra's vineyards, like its market gardens and fruit orchards, are well tended. One day Navarra will produced fine wines – but not yet. We have to wait until the Garnacha vines that at present dominate plantings have been replaced, as they will be, by Tempranillo, Graciano, Catalonia's Cariñena (here called Mazuela) – or even Cabernet Sauvignon. Until then, Navarra's reds (even the grandest Gran Reservas) will continue to be light, easy, raspberry-flavoured, sometimes softly oaky, but never deep or demanding. The government-sponsored research is advanced; the ban on replanting Garnacha is in force; we just need patience. As in Rioja, Garnacha-based roses from Navarra can be very good.

Aragón has four DOs so far, as well as a junior team of *vinos de la tierra*. Cariñena is not, unfortunately, an important grape variety in the DO of Cariñena; Garnacha again spreads itself through the vineyards, thanks to its ability to cope with big heat, and it does the same in DO Campo de Borja to the north and DO Catalayud to the west. As in Navarra, more Tempranillo may bring more character. The fourth DO, Somontano, is the highest and coolest, and it is Aragón's best bet for future glory, producing fresh red wines from the local variety Moristel, as well as deeper reds from

Tempranillo and Cabernet Sauvignon. Whites from Corisa based on Chardonnay and Gewürztraminer are encouraging, too.

Recommended producers

Navarra Bodegas Julián Chivite; Señorio de Sarria; Ochoa.
Aragón Cooperativa Somontano de Sobrarbe; Corisa (Viñas del Vero).

Catalonia

Catalonia is Spain's California: it is the one part of the country where financial resources are matched by industriousness and innovation, where a range of different climatic regimes can be found in close proximity, and where the 'implied drinker' for many producers is not a Spaniard but a Briton, a German, a New Yorker or a Venezuelan.

Cava is the engine of the Catalan wine industry, and it is a powerful one: this region is home to the world's biggest producer of champagne-method sparkling wines, Freixenet. Cava can come from anywhere in Spain, as the DO is non-geographical; in practice, 99.5 per cent comes from Catalonia, and almost all of that from Penedés. The DO governs sparkling wines produced by secondary fermentation in bottle (*méthode champenoise/método tradicional*), with at least nine months' ageing on their secondary fermentation lees. Most Cava is based on Macabeo (Viura), Parellada and Xarel-lo grape varieties, with Monastrell and Garnacha Tinta being used for the rosés. Chardonnay is playing an increasingly important role, with pure Chardonnay Cavas now available from Raimat, Mont-Marçal and Codorníu; Chardonnay/ Pinot Noir blends are undergoing trials, with promising results.

Cava is much better value than Champagne; indeed, in value-for-money terms, it is unmatched by any other sparkling wine in the world, save perhaps those of Australia. Its weak suits are finesse, depth and an illustrious image; if these are what you look for in sparkling wines, and if you're prepared to pay for them, stick to Champagne. Many of us, however, settle gratefully for Cava's soft and flowery foam.

It is thus that, across frivolous humanity,
Wine unrolls a dazzling seam of gold;
In men's throats it sings its exploits
And rules by gift, as true kings do.
Baudelaire

Cava

Type *Champagne-method sparkling wines*
Profile *Flowery, honeyed aromas; soft, fresh and lemony flavours; gentle acidity*
Advice *Drink within six months of purchase*

Recommended producers

Castellblanch; Codorníu; Freixenet; Cavas Hill; Loxarel; Mont-Marçal; Parxet; Raimat.

Penedés and other DOs

Catalonia's geographically defined DOs are Ampurdán-Costa Brava, Alalla, Penedés, Tarragona, Conca de Barbera, Costers del Segre, Priorato and Terra Alta. Penedés is the most important area, thanks to the widely described, praised and retailed wines of Miguel Torres and his son Miguel Torres. The only question mark hovering above these successful, if inelegantly labelled, wines concerns their Spanish specificity: the character of many of them is dominated by aromatic, non-Spanish varieties and, while they speak volumes about Miguel Torres Junior's wine-making virtuosity, they remain largely silent about the regional character of Penedés, the taste of its earth and the smell of its rain. This criticism is least applicable to the Tempranillo-based Coronas (Gran Coronas has a Cabernet Sauvignon component) and the Garnacha/Cariñena-based Tres Torres, both tangy, sapid and southern. A number of Cava producers, and a wealthy American restaurateur called Jean León, join Torres in producing exciting wines within the loose confines of the Penedés DO.

Of the other Catalan DOs, Costers del Segre is important as it provides a Denominación for the wines of Raimat to take with them to market, and Priorato because it is one of Spain's great originals. Raimat is an enormous (3,000 ha) agricultural estate owned by the Raventos family, whose fortune has been made through its involvement with the Cava giant Codorníu. Raimat produces sound red and white wines from both imported and native varieties that, as in the case of Torres and León, say more about skilful international wine-making and the engineering of fruit flavour than they say about Spain.

Priorato, on the other hand, is as Spanish as Don Quixote, and about as well suited to the modern world as that slender and high-minded knight was to his own. Two Garnacha variants (Garnacha

Tinta and Peluda) and Cariñena dig their roots deep into slaty rock; after a summer of harsh daytime heat and chilly nights, they yield tiny quantities of deeply coloured, highly alcoholic (13.75 is the minimum), concentrated and sometimes astringent wines.

Torres Gran Coronas

Type *Medium-bodied red wine*
Profile *Balanced aromas combining gentle oak and perfumed fruit; silky textures; flavours of ripe currants and mint*
Advice *An impressive yet accessible red wine; does not need food, though it accompanies many dishes well*

Recommended producers

Ramon Baladá (Penedés); Cavas Hill (Penedés); Jean León (Penedés); De Muller (Priorato); Raimat (Costers del Segre); Cellers de Scala Dei (Priorato); Miguel Torres (Penedés).

THE CENTRE

Valencia, Murcia, New Castile, Extremadura

These four regions, forming a broad belt across central southern Spain, produce most of Spain's wine. The quality of the wines produced in Valencia and Murcia (the Levante) is modest; that of New Castile (La Mancha) is indifferent; that of DO-less Extremadura is poor. These are the wine regions that keep Spain's Minister of Agriculture awake at night.

The DOs of the Levante are Valencia and Utiel-Requena in the north, and Alicante, Yecla, Almansa and Jumilla in the south. The best that Valencia and Utiel-Requena can manage at present are pleasant but anodyne whites and light reds, as well as some inexpensive, raisiny Moscatels. Alicante and Yecla produce bulk wines, and struggle to stop their names sinking from sight. Almansa is beginning to produce red wines of depth and interest from Monastrell and the red-fleshed Garnacha Tintorera, locally known as Alicante, while the Tempranillo-based 'Marius' produced by Bodegas Piqueras also suggests an exciting future for this DO. Jumilla, however, is well advanced in the production of dark, concentrated and pleasingly austere reds from low-yielding

Monastrell vines, planted in parched, stony, ochre earth. Drought and phylloxera are troubling the region at present.

DO La Mancha, sited in the arid plain of New Castile, is Europe's largest *appellation*, yet 90 per cent of La Mancha's production comes from outside the DO area. The region is hugely productive, yet yields are among the lowest in Europe. It is hot as a desert, yet its wines are white. La Mancha, the King Kong of the European wine scene, can surprise.

Its grape variety is the Airén, a tough, healthy vine producing thick-skinned grapes and strong, neutral wines. Modern vinification techniques succeed in giving them faint scents of almond or melon and a cleanly fruity taste, but they really only acquire interest after distillation and a few years in the brandy soleras of Jerez. Red wines, based on Tempranillo (locally Cencibel) are better, with a little depth and some plummy character. The same applies to the wines of Valdepeñas, almost an enclave within the southern part of La Mancha; here, some of the reds are oak-aged into fragrant silkiness. The Marqués de Griñon's irrigated Cabernet Sauvignon plantations near Toledo prove (after oak-ageing in Rueda) that while La Mancha may not be able to achieve greatness on its own, it is perfectly happy to have greatness thrust upon it. These dark, stony, dense red table wines are among Spain's best.

Recommended producers

Vinícola de Castilla/Castillo de Alhambra (La Mancha, non-DO); Marqués de Griñon (Vino de Mesa Tinto de Toledo); Bodegas Los Llanos (Valdepeñas); Bodegas Piqueras (Almansa); Bodegas Félix Solis (Valdepeñas).

Vintage guide: table wines

Spain's climate is a reliable one; the annual variations that do occur tend to affect size of crop more than quality, and it is very rare in Spain for fruit to fail to ripen properly. Yet every year is still different: the highs and lows may be closer together than elsewhere, but they exist nonetheless.

1989 Good, though quantities were reduced in the Levante, Penedés and, especially, Ribera del Duero.

1988 An extraordinary year: mildew took much of the crop. The disease is rare in Spain, and wine-growers do not routinely spray against it as their French or German counterparts do. The harvest, though much reduced, was good to very good in quality.

1987 Very good over most of Spain, though only moderate to good in Ribera del Duero.

1986 A year of moderate to good quality.

1985 Good, and very good in Penedés.

1984 A moderate year in Ribera del Duero and Rioja, but good in Navarra and Penedés.

1983 Good throughout Spain.

1982 An excellent year in Ribera del Duero, Rioja and Navarra, and good elsewhere.

1981 An excellent year in Navarra, and good to very good elsewhere.

1980 A moderate year, and lesser wines should be drunk soon.

THE SOUTH

Sherry

Spain's greatest wine comes from Andalucia. There are casks in Jerez de la Frontera whose contents make the achievements of Riojan tradition and Catalan innovation seem like a child's thirst-quenchers: burnished walnut in colour, aromatic enough to perfume a room, so powerfully flavoured as to suggest an elixir of life. Sherry is this great wine; its polyglot DO is Jerez-Xérès-Sherry; it is grown, made and blended in a small triangle facing the Atlantic ocean on Spain's 'coast of light' (Costa de la Luz).

All sherry is based on the neutral Palomino grape variety, though sweeter wines based on Moscatel or Pedro Ximénez are sometimes added to it. There's nothing neutral about sherry, though; the reason for this is that what happens to the wine after it is made is, in this case, more important than the wine itself. A transfiguration takes place, through two agencies. One is a yeasty mould; the other is oxygen.

After the base Palomino wine has finished fermentation, it is divided into two groups: that which is going to be aged under a blanket of yeast, and that which is going to be aged in casks, sometimes outside, where oxygen can penetrate the wine over a period of years. The first group is fortified lightly, to 15%, and run into casks which are incompletely filled; the soft and creamy yeast layer (*flor*) soon forms, from spores present in the air of the Jerez region. The second group is fortified to just under 18%.

Both groups are aged – for age is, quite literally, of the essence – in the solera system. The mathematics of soleras are complicated, but the principle is simple: large stocks of casks of one style of sherry are accumulated, divided into groups of different ages.

When the time comes to bottle and sell wine, this is done by emptying a small part of all the casks of the oldest group. These casks are topped up from those of the next oldest group, and so on back to the youngest group, which is topped up with new wine. The system's effect is to mix all the component wines very thoroughly yet very gradually, giving a consistent end product.

The yeast-aged wines are known as finos, and they are the lightest of the family. Manzanilla is a particularly light, soft and fresh type of fino from the Atlantic seaside town of Sanlúcar de Barrameda. After a decade or so, the *flor* runs out of nutrients to feed on in the wine, and disappears. (This concerns only the oldest part of the solera: that part 'refreshed' by wines whose average age is eight or nine years.) The fino carries on ageing, but it is subject now to direct oxidisation: the result is amontillado. Those wines that were fortified to 18% and aged oxidatively from the start are known as olorosos, while palos cortados also belong to this group: they are a light, graceful form of oloroso.

And all, without exception, are dry. If you want to taste sherry at its most commandingly authentic, look for the word 'dry' (*seco*) on the bottle, particularly in the case of amontillado and oloroso. Another key word is 'old' (*viejo* or *muy viejo*): the very best sherries will be much older than you would imagine, but for obvious reasons vintage dates cannot be used on solera-aged wines (some shippers specify average ages). And if you see the word 'British' on the label, back away: it is not sherry at all, but an imitation product fermented in the British Isles from concentrated grape juice imported from anywhere with a suitable surplus.

The word *almacenista* on a bottle will signify a sherry purchased from a small stockholder (or *almacenista*), almost invariably by the company of Emilio Lustau. It will be an unblended sherry, bottled from the one purchased cask. That cask may, for example, be one of a solera of only three casks (in which case the label will say $\frac{1}{3}$), thirty three casks ($\frac{1}{33}$) or even a hundred and thirty three casks ($\frac{1}{333}$). The sherry may be in any of the traditional styles, realised in what is generally a light, choice and fine-drawn manner. The packaging of Lustau's Almacenista range is superb: every sherry shipper should contemplate one of these elegant bottles and inwardly digest its lessons. A fine wine needs to be well dressed; too often sherry fails to draw attention to its fineness, looking dowdy rather than dashing.

Most sherries sold in Britain are sweetened: medium, cream, pale cream and brown are among them, while a pure Pedro Ximénez marks the final frontier for anyone claiming to possess a sweet tooth. The best sweetened sherries are found within the oloroso group, for only old oloroso has the depth and aromatic strength to balance out rich, concentrated grape sugars; amontillado and fino, and to a lesser extent palo cortado, all suffer an attenuation of their pungency and character with sweetening.

Fino Sherry

Type *Light, dry sherry*
Profile *Pungent, fresh aroma; clean, sharp, biting flavour, yet low to very low acidity*
Advice *Chill well; drink soon after purchase; ideal accompaniment to fish and seafood dishes, Chinese food and highly seasoned food*

Dry Amontillado Sherry

Type *Fine, dry sherry*
Profile *Fragrant, fruit aromas; intense, persistent flavours, suggesting apricot, apple or penicillin mould*
Advice *Perfect aperitif, also good with cheese dishes*

Dry Oloroso Sherry

Type *Dark, dry sherry*
Profile *Woody, rancid, nutty aromas; richly dry, austere yet lively flavours, suggesting walnuts*
Advice *Good aperitif; perfect restorative for any hour of day or night*

Sweetened Oloroso Sherry

Type *Rich dessert sherry*
Profile *Creamy, floral and fruit aromas; luscious, harmonious flavours, with many flavour notes and allusions*
Advice *Sip with dessert, or in place of dessert. Buy the more expensive examples: they are still relatively cheap, and their superb quality means that they are excellent value for money*

Recommended producers

Manzanilla La Gitana (Hidalgo); La Goya (Delgado Zuleta); La Guita (Hijos de Rainera Pérez Marin); Solear (Barbadillo).
Fino La Ina (Domecq); Don Zoilo (Diez Merito); Pando (Williams & Humbert); Puerto Fino (John William Burdon); Quinta (Osborne); San Patricio (Garvey); Tio Pepe (Gonzalez Byass); Inocente (Valdespino).
Amontillado Amontillado del Duque (Gonzalez Byass); Coliseo (Valdespino); Don Tomás (Valdespino); Dry Sack (slightly sweetened; Williams & Humbert); Fino Imperial (Diez Hermanos); Napoleon

(Hidalgo); Principe (Barbadillo); 51-1a (Domecq); Tio Guillermo (Garvey).
Palo Cortado Croft; Garvey.
Dry Oloroso Apostoles (slightly sweetened; Gonzalez Byass); Bailen
(Osborne); Don Gonzalo (Valdespino); Dos Cortados (Williams &
Humbert); Rio Viejo (Domecq); Victoria Regina (Diez Hermanos).
Sweet Oloroso Matusalem (Gonzalez Byass); Royal Corregidor
(Sandeman); Solera 1842 (Valdespino).
All styles Lustau Almacenista range.

Stockists

*Arriba Kettle; Barnes Wine Shop; D Byrne; Cunbrian Cellar; Alex Findlater;
Fortnum & Mason; Peter Green; Gerard Harris; Harrods; Harveys; J E Hogg;
Oddbins; Old Street Wine Co; Le Picoleur; Premier Wine Warehouse; La
Réserve; J Sainsbury; Selfridges; La Vigneronne; Weavers; Wine House; The
Wine Society.*

Montilla-Moriles

Sherry has fallen on hard times of late: sales have been sinking
throughout most of the 1980s. What is happening is that the region
is shedding its skin. The old days of huge bulk sales are shuffling
to an end, along with many of bulk sherry's undemanding,
slipper-shod drinkers; the new era, in which sherry comes to be
accepted and enjoyed as one of the world's great wines, on a par
with the finest wines of Bordeaux, Burgundy, Piedmont or
Coonawarra, is just beginning. The transition is proving
uncomfortable for some producers, but the quality of the best
sherries is a sure guarantee of the future.

If only Andalucia's other wine producers could enjoy that
certainty. Condado de Huelva, for example, used to help Jerez
producers fill their bulk wine orders; now it produces its own
modest sherry-style wines, some bland, cool-fermented whites,
and lorry-load on lorry-load of early strawberries.

Montilla-Moriles has, potentially, a lot more to offer: the best of
its unfortified and fortified sherry styles (based on Pedro Ximénez
rather than Palomino) have a character of their own, often marked
by floral delicacy and peachy fruit that can be most appealing. But
our merchants don't seem to make the effort to find them: for
reasons connected with Customs & Excise duty bands rather than
the stimulation of the taste buds, we are lumbered with Montillas
whose chief attraction is a favourable alcohol:price ratio. If you do
find an expensive Montilla (or, better still, Moriles), try it; it will
probably be very good.

Málaga

And so, finally, to Málaga. Like Italy's Marsala, Málaga is a nineteenth-century nobleman living out the twentieth in greatly reduced circumstances. The Málaga range of intensely sweet, fortified, almost black dessert wines, based on the Pedro Ximénez grape (here called Pedro Ximén), is as far out of fashion as the whalebone corset. Lack of custom has inevitably led to a deterioration in quality, consequent in this case on the arrival of the Airén (Lairén) to repace the lower-yielding PX. In contrast to the Morilla-Moriles situation, however, we get the best, rather than the basic, Málaga: Scholtz Hermanos's Lagrima Deliciosa and Solera 1885. Equally good is Lopez Hermanos's pale golden Moscatel de Málaga, with its wonderfully heady floral aromas and stylish, perfumed sweetness. These wines deserve our support, and merit our enthusiasm.

Recommended producers

Carbonell (Montilla-Moriles); Lopez Hermanos (Málaga); Scholtz Hermanos (Málaga).

Stockists of all Spanish wines

A & A Wines; Ad Hoc Wine Warehouse; Alba Wine Society; H Allen Smith; Belfast Wine Co; Bottle & Basket; D Byrne & Co; The Celtic Vintner; Chaplin & Son; John Ford Wines; Fullers; Peter Green; Hunter & Oliver; Laymont & Shaw; Master Cellar Wine Warehouse; Mi Casa; Mitchells; Moreno Wines; Arthur Rackham; La Reserva; Sherborne Vintners; Tanners; Ubiquitous Chip; La Vigneronne; Wine House.

The Rest of Europe

Andrew Jefford

SWITZERLAND

Beneath Switzerland's high alpine pastureland lie vineyards. The country is an important wine producer, with 1400 ha planted and an annual total of around a million hectolitres – more than Savoie, Jura and the Côte d'Or combined. Half of this total comes from the vineyards of the upper Rhône, east of Lake Geneva: the Valais region, which has light, stony soils, low rainfall and enjoys surprisingly warm summer and autumn weather. Most of the Valais wines are red, chief among them being Dôle, a Pinot Noir/ Gamay blend with the former variety accounting for at least 50 per cent. The two main whites are Fendant (based on Chasselas) and Johannisberg (based on Sylvaner).

A further quarter of Switzerland's wines come from other cantons of this western, French-speaking part of the country (Suisse Romande), chiefly the Vaud, Geneva and Neuchâtel zones. Some of Switzerland's finest white wines are found in the Vaud, whose vineyards carpet the northern shore of Lake Geneva. This is a region of *crus*, different villages producing a range of white Chasselas-based wines whose subtle shadowshifts of flavour go some way to restoring the tarnished reputation of this grape variety. Lavaux, Epesses, Dézaley and Féchy are among the best. Red wines are either Pinot Noir or Gamay varietals, or a blend of the two, known here as Salvagnin.

Geneva produces richer, fruitier reds and whites than most other parts of Switzerland: Chasselas (here called Perlan) acquires an almost Alsatian style, while the Gamays from this zone are pungent and full of tangy fruit. Neuchâtel is the source of the Swiss Pinot Noir rosé known as Oeil de Perdrix ('partridge's eye'), though the name is also used in the Vaud and Valais.

Throughout the rest of Switzerland, wine is produced in small pockets only – though there are many of these sewn into countless valley sides. White wines are generally Müller-Thurgau varietals – appropriately enough, since the canton of Thurgau was the home of the breeder of this mysterious crossing, Dr Müller. Its mystery is that no one is really sure of what was crossed with what to achieve it, though the variety is known in Switzerland, confidently enough, as Riesling-Sylvaner. For red wines, Pinot Noir is used throughout the large, German-speaking Ostschweiz, and Merlot in Italian-speaking Ticino. Good vintages can produce persuasively aromatic, ripely fruity examples.

Most Swiss wines are drunk by the Swiss, just as most English wines are drunk by the English. The Swiss pay a high price for their wines, so we have to, too, and never higher than in London's Swiss Centre. Other stockists offer better value – relatively speaking.

Stockists

Bentalls; Eldridge Pope; Peter Green; Gerard Harris; La Réserve; Swiss Centre; Tanners.

LUXEMBOURG

Luxembourg's vineyards are those of the upper Mosel. Müller-Thurgau (here, as in England on occasion, called Rivaner) is the most widely planted variety; Riesling, Gewürztraminer and Pinot Gris are among the other varieties grown. The wines can be pleasant and lightly aromatic, but rarely achieve the distinction of Germany's fine wines.

Stockists

Eldridge Pope; Gerard Harris; Lorne House Vintners.

GREECE

The world's wine drinkers have much to thank Greece for. Even if this was not wine's birthplace (Azerbaijan is thought more likely, while the Egyptians practised systematic viticulture before the Greeks), it still acted as primary school to the unruly young drink throughout its formative years. Wine is mentioned almost as often as sea in Homer's *Odyssey* (written in the eighth century BC), and the two are linked forever in one of the most famous metaphors in world literature. Any wine drinker with a sense of history should pause over retsina: it is the closest we can come to a taste of the Ancient world. The flavouring of retsina with Aleppo pine resin harks back to the sealing of amphoras with the same substance: the practice, like the Parthenon, still stands. Retsina is one of the most versatile and appealing of the world's simple wines, and – thanks to its domestic and international popularity – Greece's most reliably good.

Retsina aside, Greek viticulture lay in decorative ruins until twenty years or so ago. The dessert Muscats of the Aegean island of Samos and the sweet red Mavrodaphne of Patras, in the northern Peloponnese, were both well preserved, but almost nothing else was. Since then, Greek table and quality wines (especially red) have set off on a journey of restoration and recovery, and there is now a widening range of exciting wines to choose from. At this stage, producers' names are the ones to look for, rather than regional appellations (though a system of these exists). Boutari's Grande Reserve is a good example of what can be achieved: the 1984 has complex and harmonious secondary aromas with suggestions of leather or dried leaf, a light yet firm tannic structure, and stylish vegetal or dark fruit flavours with a bitter finishing edge. Its natural partner of comparison would be a Barbaresco.

Recommended producers

Achaia Clauss; Boutari; Cambas; Cosmetatos (Gentilini); Domaine Porto Carras; Kourtaki; Tsantalis.

Stockists

James Aitken & Son; Bibendum; Booths; G E Bromley; Cumbrian Cellar; Drinksmart; Peter Green; The Nobody Inn; Selfridges; Tanners; Whitesides Wine Merchants; The Wine Schoppen.

CYPRUS

The Cypriot wine industry – industry is an accurate description in this case – has experienced a succession of setbacks in the last decade, and the bulk wine production that the island relied on since gaining independence is rapidly becoming historical. The present is a time of transition, as the larger manufacturers that dominate the Cypriot wine scene, Keo and Sodap, attempt to produce the wines of character that Western European consumers increasingly look for, and that Cyprus has the potential to yield. These may be with us before long, while the quality of the island's best-known traditional wine, the raisin-sweet Commandaria may simultaneously begin to move back towards the levels that reputation suggests it once achieved.

For the moment, though, Cyprus's most reliable wines are its table wine brands, such as Amathus, Arsinoe and the varietal Palomino (white), and Kykko, Olympus, Afames or Othello (red).

Stockists

G E Bromley; Cumbrian Cellar; Weavers of Nottingham; Whitesides Wine Merchants.

TURKEY

Over a thousand grape varieties are found in Turkey, and the land under vine is enormous – more than in Australia, Portugal, Germany and Austria collectively. Yet there is little demand for fermentation vats, fining earth or bottling lines: ninety-seven per cent of the grape crop is consumed as grapes or as dried fruit. Turks are Muslims, though the state is a secular one, and the three per cent that does get vinified is rarely successful: a teetotal domestic market is a poor inducement to quality wine production. There are no consistently recommendable Turkish wines.

The Rest of the World

Andrew Jefford

CHINA AND JAPAN

Wine is produced in both China and Japan. Japan's is good, but it stays in Japan; China's is not, and is widely exported. The overseas help that China has received in developing her wine industry does not seem to have helped much; there is usually rumour of something good just around the corner, but this particular corner keeps retreating up the street. (Tsingtao Riesling and Chardonnay, recently arrived in Britain, have been received with qualified enthusiasm.) The Chinese wines sold in Soho's supermarkets are the most bizarrely flavoured and uniformly faulty of any available anywhere in Britain and, after 4 June 1989, few pioneer purchasers can have much heart for further experiment.

Stockists
Croque-en-Bouche.

INDIA

India's best wine, and her only wine of reliable quality, is a champagne-method sparkler produced in the state of Maharashtra and called, intriguingly, Omar Khayyam (who was a wine-loving Iranian mathematician-poet). Piper Heidsieck helped to ensure that it is as good as it is, and it offers further proof that the Ugni Blanc (combined here with a little Chardonnay) can produce wines of excitement in the most unexpected places. It was initially expensive, but its price has been held or even lowered while champagne's has romped up higher and higher, and it now offers good value for money. It has unusual, slightly rustic scents and a crisp flavour of medium depth.

Stockists
Adnams; Oddbins; Vinceremos; Waitrose.

ISRAEL

After an early start in the modern era, thanks to the nineteenth-century efforts of Baron Edmond de Rothschild in Ottoman Palestine, wine production in this small strip at the far eastern end of the Mediterranean settled comfortably into the rut of sweet kosher reds and whites to satisfy Jewish family needs, and there it remained after Israel came into being in 1948. For most of the country's short history, farmers and agricultural kibbutz members have had more pressing concerns than that of fine-wine production. In recent years, under Californian influence, this situation has changed, and Israel has begun to produce gastronomically exciting as well as religiously acceptable wines. The best of these come from the cool of the Golan Heights, grown in vineyards within mortar distance of the burnt-out remains of Syrian tanks (Gamla and Yarden reds and whites from the Golan Heights Winery), but the traditional base of the Israeli wine industry south of Haifa (Carmel) and in the Galilee area (Galil) also produces good top-of-the-line Cabernet Sauvignon (Carmel Wines). The Ben Ami red (Askalon Wines) is a soundly fruity Cabernet Sauvignon-Carignan blend. Kosher strictures require that the wines are pasteurised to remove any trace of leaven (yeast), but this seems to be no bar to excellence.

Stockists

Amazing Grapes; Cumbrian Cellar; Del Monico; John Ford Wines; Grape Ideas; Harrods; Hunter & Oliver; La Reserva; Selfridges; Tesco; Victoria Wines.

LEBANON

Just as Indian wine at present means Omar Khayyam, so Lebanese wine means Château Musar. The fact that Serge Hochar has been able to carry on producing wine at all through a decade and a half of ferocious civil war is astonishing, and all the more so because his best vineyards are in the Bekaa Valley. His 1989 vintage he describes as 'my little miracle ... it was picked under shelling, transported to the winery under shelling, and fermented under shelling'. When, furthermore, he produces wine under these circumstances which can be described as 'fine' without any charity or indulgence whatsoever, then his achievement is a great one. The grapes used are Cabernet Sauvignon, Cinsault and Syrah and the vineyards are sited high (1,000 metres), giving slower ripening than the Lebanon's hot climate would normally permit. They mature in bottle very well indeed, and remain sweetly fruity, ripe and rich for up to twenty years, acquiring more aromatic finesse and suppleness of texture as they do so.

Stockists

Barnes Wine Shop; Châteaux Wines; Peter Dominic; Fine Vintage Wines; John Ford Wines; Gauntleys of Nottingham; Grape Ideas; Peter Green; Hunter & Oliver; Le Picoleur; Upper Crust.

AFRICA

Algeria, Morocco and Tunisia are the world's leading Muslim wine-producing countries, thanks to the lingering French and Spanish influences of the colonial era and secular post-independence governments. Algeria's red Coteaux de Mascara and de Tlemcen, Tunisia's sweet Muscats and red Mornag, and Morocco's red Tarik, Sidi Brahim and rosé Gris de Boulaouane all offer good value for money, as do other parcels of wine that the larger importers and merchants chance upon from time to time. Whether anything better will come out of North Africa seems doubtful without an increase in wine-drinking by the peoples of these countries.

Elsewhere in Africa, wine is produced in Egypt, Kenya, Ethiopia, Zimbabwe and South Africa. Zimbabwe's wines show promise; for South Africa, see the boxed note at the front of the Guide.

Stockists

Algeria *Peter Dominic; Grape Ideas; Peter Green.*
Morocco *Victoria Wines; Welbeck Wines.*
Tunisia *Selfridges.*
Zimbabwe *Croque-en-Bouche; Cumbrian Cellar; Peter Green; Guildford Wine Market; Vinceremos; Wessex Wines.*

Part III

Where to buy

wine merchants

Symbols

⃝ Denotes generally low prices and/or a large range of modestly priced wines.

⃝ A merchant given this symbol offers exceptionally good service. We rely on readers' reports in allocating service symbols; this means that there may be merchants offering first-class service without the symbol, because such distinction has gone unreported. Readers, please report!

⃝ A merchant picked out by this symbol stocks a choice of organic wines and, in some cases, makes a speciality of organic wine sales.

⃝ A merchant picked out by this symbol stocks a variety of wines in bottles of different sizes, such as half-bottles, magnums, and so on.

⃝ A merchant picked out by this symbol stocks a wide range of wines, not necessarily in terms of worldwide coverage but in terms of depth and balance, offering the customer extensive choice in any wine style.

Best buys
These are, in most cases, the Editor's choice of three out of a range of ten wines selected by the merchant in question as being distinguished in terms of value for money, or offering very fine quality regardless of price.

Editor's choice

The following wines constitute a personal selection by the Editor of bottles that meet some, or all, of three interconnected criteria: an attractive price, better-than-average concentration of flavour, and an impressive, characterful style. Every effort has been made to confirm with suppliers that these wines will continue to be available throughout the twelve months that follow publication; in some cases, of course, the vintage will change. Highest and lowest prices at the time of going to press have been cited; these may increase during the life of the book.

Aperitif wines

Lindauer, Montana, New Zealand

Lowest price: £6.45 at *Barnes Wine Shop*
Highest price: £7 at *Harrods*
Other stockists include *Oddbins; Christopher Piper Wines; Victoria Wine*

Angas Brut Rosé, Yalumba (S Smith & Co), South Australia

Lowest price: £4.89 at *Wizard Wine Warehouses*
Highest price: £6.05 at *Les Amis du Vin*
Other stockists include *Asda; Bottoms Up; Celtic Vintner; Davisons; Fullers; Great Northern Wine Company; Half Yard Wines; Hunter & Oliver; Nobody Inn; Oddbins; Victoria Wine; Waitrose; Whitesides; Wine Growers Association*

Castellblanch Rosado Cava

Lowest price: £4.49 at *Booths*
Highest price: £5.75 at *Woodhouse Wines*
Other stockists include *Direct Wine Shipments; Peter Dominic; Peter Green; Richmond Wine Warehouse; J Sainsbury; Vineyards Wine Warehouse; The Wine House*

There are few more uplifting aperitifs than a sparkling wine. This is partly because of the pop! as the cork leaves the bottle, which seems to draw a firm line between everything that happened before (work) and everything that happens afterwards (pleasure); and it is partly because bubbles have a particularly stimulating effect on the palate, reinforcing the cleansing action that we use aperitifs to achieve.

This year is very definitely the year to try an alternative to champagne – even the champagne producers would concur here, so long as we don't take matters too far, as they are hoping to be able to build up stocks again with their new pricing régime. Here, then, are three alternatives.

The first – Lindauer, a sparkling wine from New Zealand produced by Montana – comes closest to mimicking the real thing. It is made from Pinot Noir and Chardonnay and spends two years maturing on its bottle-fermentation lees. It has creamy, flowery aromas, freshened with hints of apple, and its flavour is rich, vinous and yeastily acidic. 'It tastes of sick,' was what my brother and I agreed years ago when we first tried champagne; and we would say the same about Lindauer had our vocabulary not changed in the interim. Its concentration is good, and its sparkle is more persistent, and more finely beaded, than the other two alternatives.

They are both rosés – probably the area in which champagne's crown sits least firmly on its head. One is Angas Brut Rosé, an Australian sparkler. Its coppery salmon colour is appealing; the sparkle moves fairly rapidly through the wine, however, and the aromas lack a firm, clear profile: they are vaguely fruity, fresh and clean. The flavour, however, is firm and convincing, with a fine apricot-skin character. It is a deep, long and finally nutty sparkling wine, and its depth and full-bodied dryness would, if you wish, take it beyond the aperitif stage and into partnership with a first course or two: a little fish mousse, for example, or a lightly dressed avocado.

The other is a rosé cava – that of Castellblanch. It has an attractive strawberry-pink colour with a faint coppery hue; an adequate and moderately persistent mousse; fresh fruit scents and a pretty peach-and-nut flavour. It isn't completely dry, but then nor is the much-admired Laurent Perrier Brut champagne. Dry white cava often suffers in comparison with its champagne counterpart because of a general softness, floweriness and lack of vinous bite, but in the case of rosé these failings become virtues. Prettiness is all, and this is a very pretty sparkling wine.

Principe, Amontillado Seco, Balbaina Alta, António Barbadillo

Lowest price: £8.61 at *Alex Findlater*
Highest price: £10.50 at *Harrods*
Other stockists include *Barnes Wine Shop; Bin Ends; Fortnum & Mason; Fulham Road Wine Centre; Matthew Gloag; Hicks and Don; Hollingsworth of York; Laymont & Shaw; La Reserva*

Rosado cava may make the most charming of summer aperitifs, but a fine dry amontillado is unbeatable in winter for its palate-rousing and limb-warming effects. Principe is an authentic amontillado – in other words an old fino sherry on which the flor has died, and you may find ghostly reference to the yeasty, bread-like flor taste in its flavours. What makes Principe particularly choice and delicate is the fact that the fino was manzanilla, the lightest and softest of its kind; this amontillado is born in the Sanlúcar bodegas of António Barbadillo. Pale walnut in colour with amber-gold glints, it has a powerful and pungent aroma, classically tangy, yet harmonious and delicate withal. On the palate it is light, slender and fresh compared with the more raspingly oxidised Jerez amontillados. Its intensity of flavour makes it perfect for cleansing and stimulating the taste-buds as well as engaging the mind for treats in store at table.

Aperitif wines (continued)

Moscato Seco 1988, João Pires, Palmela Region

Lowest price: £3.99 at *Oddbins*
Highest price: £6.20 at *Yorkshire Fine Wines*
Other stockists include *William Addison;, Ad Hoc Wine Warehouse; Adnams; James Aitken; H Allen Smith; Barnes Wine Shop; Augustus Barnett; D Byrne & Co; City Wines; Connolly's; County Wines of Hagley; Croque-en-Bouche; Davenport; Davisons; Del Monico; Drinksmart; Eaton Elliot; Ben Ellis; Gauntleys of Nottingham; Matthew Gloag; Grape Ideas; Great Northern Wine Company; Peter Green; Gerard Harris; Harrods; Hicks & Don; Hopton; Hungerford Wine Company; Tony Jeffries; S H Jones; Majestic Wine Warehouses; Master Cellar Wine Warehouse; Moffat Wine Shop; Moreno; Nobody Inn; Premier Wine Warehouse; Arthur Rackham; Ravensbourne Wine Company; La Reserva; J Sainsbury; Sainsbury Bros; Selfridges; Sherborne Vintners; Snowdonia Wine Warehouse; Topsham Wines; Ubiquitous Chip; Victoria Wine; Vintage Wines; Helen Verdcourt; Whitesides; Whittalls; Willoughbys; Wine Schoppen; Wines from Paris; Wizard Wine Warehouses*

A third classic aperitif, in addition to sparkling and fortified wines, is white wine. Something with plenty of aroma to web the senses is ideal, and British taste – unlike French – is for a more or less dry wine. This unfortified Moscatel, from the Portuguese company João Pires, is ideal in each respect. It is full of the fresh, grapey scents of its variety, here overlayed with a pretty geranium-edged sweetness. In flavour the wine is lively, light and refreshing, dry to off-dry, very much in the Portuguese verde tradition, despite its origins in the Palmela region of Southern Portugal at the hands of an Australian wine-maker. The Moscatel character is comparatively muted on the palate, which suggests the flavour of a Cox's apple rather than anything notably grape-like or raisiny. It leaves the mouth fresh, clean and ready for food. Of all the wines listed in this selection, this is the one you should have least difficulty finding: it is very widely stocked.

White wines for first courses or light meals

Puerto Fino 'Superior Dry' John William Burdon

Lowest price: £4.50 at *Half Yard Wines*
Highest price: £6.45 at *Harrods*
Other stockists include *D Byrne & Co; Philip Eyres; Oddbins (half-bottles); La Reserva; Selfridges; Waitrose (half-bottles); The Wine House*

It is extraordinary to reflect how long the British have been drinking dry sherry before meals, without ever realising how good it can be with meals. There is, in my view, no single better all-purpose wine-with-food than chilled fino sherry. Its adaptability is the consequence of its high alcoholic strength, which means it can pitch in resourcefully against the spiciest, sauciest opposition; while its clean, pungent, but finally unassertive flavour provides the perfect line of counterpoint for almost any food taste. This particular fino comes from Puerto de Santa Maria, the least well-known of the three sherry towns. Like Sanlúcar (home to Manzanilla) it is sited on the coast, where flor grows more thickly on fino than it does in the inland bodegas of Jerez. Some Puerto fino has a flowery quality to its aroma; this one, though, is primarily fresh and yeasty, with a soft, pure flor flavour and a faintly gingery finish. It will partner almost any fish course you choose to name, and is particularly useful with 'everyday' food like fish fingers, grilled chicken or, in vegan households, broad beans stewed with tomato in olive oil. It will even set to with fish and chips, if you refrain from vinegary folly. Remember that all fino belongs in the fridge, not the sideboard, and should be finished with a week or two of opening.

Montana Sauvignon Blanc 1989, Marlborough, New Zealand

Lowest price: £4.29 at *J E Hogg*
Highest price: £6.51 at *Yorkshire Fine Wines*
Other stockists include *Les Amis du Vin; James Aitken; Barnes Wine Shop; Augustus Barnett; Belfast Wine Company; Bottoms Up; G E Bromley; D Byrne; Cachet Wines; Chaplin & Son; Davisons; Drinksmart; Fullers; Peter Green; Guildford Wine Market; Harrods; Hedley Wright; Hunter & Oliver; London Wine; Master Cellar Wine Warehouse; Ravensbourne Wine Company; Safeway; Seckford; Selfridges; Tanners; Tesco; Thresher/Wine Rack; Unwins; Victoria Wine; Villeneuve; Whiclar & Gordon; Whitesides; Willoughbys*

White wines for first courses or light meals (continued)

Is there any reader who hasn't tried this wine, or one like it? Since their first arrival here a few years ago, New Zealand's Sauvignon Blancs have been ceaselessly trumpeted by anyone who can find an old wine crate to stand on, and they are now widely stocked up and down Britain. Statistically, however, we know that there are many who have still to take their first invigorating sniff of the fresh, grassily pungent aroma and extraordinarily lively, vegetal flavours: a mouthful of springtime. If that includes you, delay no longer: Montana's benchmark example is widely available and not expensive. Sauvignon Blanc, of course, is the famous grape of the Loire's 'central' vineyards: Sancerre, Pouilly-Fumé and others. The acidity in New Zealand's Sauvignons is less tongue-curling than in France's, and the wines are hence less assertive at table; all that herbaceousness takes them beyond a simple fish scenario into partnership with salads and light vegetarian dishes, as well as with first-course dishes of dressed seafood or vegetables (providing the dressing is not too acid).

Breaky Bottom Seyval Blanc 1989 and Müller-Thurgau 1989, Northease, East Sussex, England

Lowest price: £5.20 at *Breaky Bottom farm gate*
Highest price: £5.99 at *English Wine Centre*
Other stockists include *Fine English Wine Company (Seyval Blanc only); Great Western Wines; Half Yard Wines; Harcourt Fine Wines (Müller-Thurgau only)*

1989, as you probably remember, was a lovely summer in Britain. There were water shortages, as there always are in this improvident country when summer actually justifies its name. Fine wines were produced in England and Wales, and here are two of the best. Both are produced by Peter Hall at Breaky Bottom Vineyard, near Lewes in East Sussex. Through a professional assignment, I have known them since they were grapes on the vine, and feel sure of their qualities. Both are available from Breaky Bottom (0273 476427) as well as through the merchants listed above.

The first is based on the Seyval Blanc grape, and the second on Müller-Thurgau. The Seyval Blanc is the more striking and austere of the two, filled with powerful elderflower and nettlebed aromas, and clean, sappy, grapefruit-edged flavours. The Müller-Thurgau, by contrast, seems much fruitier and sweeter in aroma, singing out with a fresh, hawthorn purity of scent that is typically English, and most appealing: the countryside, bottled. On the palate the wine is more supple and less cutting than the Seyval, full of gentle apple or sherbet flavours. The extraordinary fruitiness that characterises many English wines of 1989 is also present, filling out their structure and providing fine, palpable textures.

As both wines are dry, they accompany food well. At Breaky Bottom, the Hall family favour generous country salads, with cold cuts of home-farmed lamb, and the wines accompany these splendidly. Roast pork and river fish (the wild trout fished for, and written about so memorably, by Peter's father John Inglis Hall in his *Fishing A Highland Stream*) would also jump at the chance of a liaison with Breaky Bottom 1989. Both wines, by the way, will keep well, improving and deepening as they do so.

La Blaque 1989, Coteaux de Pierrevert, SCI Châteauneuf du Pierrevert

Victoria Wine: £3.29

Pierrevert is a large and rather disparate VDQS region situated in the high Provençal hinterland, towards the south-west corner of the Alpes de Haute Provence *département*. The height of the vineyards makes the area a suitable one for white-wine production, and this wine (based on the Marsanne, Roussanne and Clairette grape varieties) is proof of that suitability.

It is pale and bright, with complex, fine-drawn scents, characterised by floral, vegetal and fruit notes. There is something of the blossomy freshness of a wine from a mountain region (Savoie, for example) in the aroma, rather than the heavy-lidded inveiglements of a Rhône white or the softly nutty chit-chat of one from lower Provence. In taste, the wine is balanced and shapely, with flavours that hint at sherbet to begin with, but later grow rich and full, suggesting pear or nectarine. Despite the sense of amplitude, there is a gracefulness and a restraint in the wine that makes it ideal with light, vegetable-based dishes or poached, sauced poultry. It would be a good white for a cold buffet, too.

Red wines for first courses or light meals

Sicilian Vino da Tavola Rosso di Menfi 1987, Cantina Settesoli, Menfi

Lowest price: £2.29 at *William Addison*
Highest price: £3.06 at *A & A Wines*
Other stockists include *J E Hogg; Marks & Spencer; William Rush (Rosso Bonera); Valvona & Crolla*

Sicily, like Southern France, has a great future as a wine-producing region, one that it is only just at the beginning of realising. Some of the white wines produced there are startlingly good, though they lean heavily on technology and only lightly on the character of the local grape varieties. This balance is reversed in the case of the best red wines of the island: in them, the local grapes (Perricone and Nero d'Avola) speak with clarity. There is something savage and unbridled in the flavours they yield, and the most impressive example of this is the Rosso del Conte of Regaleali, stocked by *Oddbins* and *Ad Hoc Wine Warehouse*. That wine, in addition to being expensive, may not be to everyone's taste: it is uncompromisingly primitive and grand, closely modelled on the one by means of which Homer's Ulysses defeated the one-eyed giant Polyphemus on the slopes of Etna.

Try this one, stocked by *Marks & Spencer* and a few others, to see if you like the taste of Sicilian reds. It is made from the two varieties mentioned above, and the bitter-edged, mineral violence of the grapes is tempered and shaped by a lovely, juicy fruitiness. Scents of warm, stony fruit, with a faintly tarry edge, as well as first-rate label design (*Marks & Spencer*), make it an extremely attractive wine, ideal for adventurous, home-made pizzas, or pasta dishes with garlic-heavy, tomato-charged sauces. It would also be good with steaks cooked rapidly and ferociously, leaving them charred on the outside and bleeding in the centre. The wine's concentration makes it excellent value for money. If it is to your taste, move on to Rosso del Conte for a subsequent indulgence.

Romanian Classic Pinot Noir 1984, Dealul Mare region, Valea Călugărească Winery

Lowest price: £2.40 at *Ubiquitous Chip*
Highest price: £2.99 at *Hunter & Oliver*
Other stockists include *Booths; Bottoms Up; Chaplin & Son; Co-op; Del Monico; Peter Dominic; Drinksmart; Peter Green; Gerard Harris; London Wine; Mitchells Wine Merchants; Thos Peatling; Selfridges; Snowdonia Wine Warehouse; Supergrape; Wizard Wine Warehouses*

Over the last year, this simple wine has brought me as much pleasure as any. It didn't show particularly well on the one occasion when I encountered it at a blind tasting; it's not typical or characteristic of the Pinot Noir grape; but it drinks superbly. The 1984 vintage, the importers say, will run out during the life of this book, and will be replaced by the 1986 vintage: whether it will be as good is difficult to judge, for experience of Eastern European wines shows that a changed vintage can alter the whole physiognomy of a wine. But let's hope the blenders manage to make a match.

A bright mid-scarlet colour is matched by lively, fruity aromas – raspberries or cherries by way of analogy, for those who enjoy analogies, with a kind of minty freshness. On the palate – especially after the wine has had air through it, either by being decanted, or by being partly drunk and resumed later – the fruit is exuberant, shapely, superbly jaunty. In everything except the minutiae of its flavour it is more Beaujolais than most Beaujolais. This is a wine for sausages and hams, for stews and pies; a wine to cheer insipid autumn evenings. It would also be a good wine to try if you have never greatly enjoyed red wines, finding them on the whole too bitter and harsh. This is easy, friendly and welcoming.

Saumur Rouge Vieilles Vignes 1987, Langlois-Château

Lowest price: £5.59 at *D Byrne & Co*
Highest price: £6.49 at *Barnes Wine Shop and Grogblossom*
Other stockists include *Booths; Bottle & Basket*

The red wines of the Loire, based on the Cabernet Franc grape variety, are unusual and under-appreciated. They are light to medium-bodied, with invitingly fresh aromas that always remind me of the smell of water-soaked or rain-dampened wood; but for which more objective and accessible analogies might be redcurrants, raspberries or slightly underripe plums. They are best served cool, and have vibrant, fruity flavours with a refreshingly hard, tonic edge, as if every glassful contained an iron supplement. This example, produced from 35-year-old vines

Red wines for first courses or light meals (continued)

(*vieilles vignes*), is typical in every way, with a deep, curranty purity of flavour and graceful, silky textures. It makes a perfect red match for crisply grilled bacon, for lamb cutlets, for liver or for kidneys – and don't forget to give it 15-30 minutes in the refrigerator before drinking on a warm day.

Full-bodied white wines for main courses

Rioja Blanco (various vintages), Marqués de Murrieta

Lowest price: £6.59 at *Peter Dominic and Victoria Wine*
Highest price: £9.25 at *Harrods*
Other stockists include *Ad Hoc Wine Warehouse; Adnams; David Alexander; Les Amis du Vin; Arriba Kettle; Asda; Averys; Booths; Bottoms Up; Burlington Wines; Cadwgan; Chaplin & Son; Croque-en-Bouche; Davisons; John Ford Wines; Fortnum & Mason; Fullers; Gauntleys of Nottingham; Great Northern Wine Company; Peter Green; Harrods; Heath Street Wines; Hilbre; J E Hogg; Tony Jeffries; Justerini & Brooks; Lay & Wheeler; Laymont & Shaw; Master Cellar Wine Warehouse; Moreno; Nobody Inn; Pavilion; Le Picoleur; Premier Wine Warehouse; Raeburn Fine Wines; La Reserva; Edward Sheldon; T&W Wines; Tanners; Unwins; Upper Crust; La Vigneronne; Weavers of Nottingham; Whitesides; Willoughbys; Winecellars; The Wine House*

This wine is headmistress of the old school of white Rioja – the school that, rather than cold-fermenting and ageing in stainless steel to give a fresh, fruity but finally anodyne result, prefers to put all its pupils through a minimum of two years' cask-ageing to produce rich, boldly drawn characters which cut a dash in the world. Marqués de Murrieta Blanco has always been made in that way, and always will be – hurrah! It is a bright straw yellow in colour, with an aroma both lemony fresh and oakily statuesque: a comely and entrancing combination. On the palate, it is full and lemony once again, balanced and poised, with the oakiness perfectly reconciled to the vibrant fruit. In food combinations, the lemon edge proves sharper than you'd think, and this wine is well up to the challenge posed, for example, by fat fish like sardines or fresh herrings. At the same time the wine's breadth and amplitude will pitch it on terms of equality with many meats, and with meaty fish like fresh tuna or swordfish – which, grilled, make perhaps its ideal partner. It is widely stocked, and ages well, which is why you will find a number of different vintages on sale. The highest and lowest prices are quoted for the 1985 vintage, the one most widely stocked at present.

Full-bodied white wines for
main courses (continued)

Würzburger Stein Silvaner Kabinett 1989, Juliusspital, Franconia

Summerlee Wines £6.44

Wines from Franken (Franconia) have not been widely seen in Britain in the past. It was not a wine region that needed to export, as home sales have always been buoyant; and the wine it produced did not match the average Briton's notion of what fine German wine was like, that notion being based on Rheingau or Mosel Riesling Auslese from a sunny autumn that had spent five or ten years acquiring bottle age in a cool, damp cellar.

With the Trocken Revolution (the great upsurge in dry wine-making that has taken place in Germany over the last decade) all this has changed. Franconia's Bavarian (continental) climate and gastronomic traditions mean that most of its wines, even Spätlesen and Auslesen, have always been dry, albeit richly so on occasion. Growers from the Mosel and the Saar are not finding it easy to produce satisfactorily fleshed Trocken wines; for Franconians, it's a doddle.

This wine comes from one of Franconia's most famous estates, the Juliusspital, and from one of its most famous vineyards, the Stein vineyard at Würzburg. (Indeed, you may sometimes hear the generic term Steinwein used to refer to all Franconian wines.) It is made from the Silvaner grape variety. Pale lemon yellow in colour, it has a lovely vanilla-earthy aroma, sweet yet fresh, with a little sappy core to lend it depth and distinction. On the palate, it is full, broad, firm, almost spicy, with the clean, chunky fruit that proves so elusive in other German Trocken wines. There is a faint hint of grapefruit-like bitterness in the finish. It is very definitely a wine for food, as its virtues are solid but unshowy, those of a partner rather than a soloist. It is good with fish, but perhaps better with chicken and veal adventurously sauced, or with buttered, dill-sprinkled potatoes, or with stewed cabbage seasoned with strips of ham. And it is hard not to enjoy the distinctive flagon-shaped Bocksbeutel in which it is packaged.

Côtes du Roussillon Blanc 1988, 'Arnaud de Villeneuve', Les Vignerons de Rivesaltes

Victoria Wine £4.19

This extraordinary wine is an exciting pointer to the future. It comes from Roussillon – a sun-roasted area normally thought suitable only for big, fiery reds and fortified vins doux naturels – and is based on the Macabeo and Malvoisie grape varieties, neither of which is greatly prized by the wine-growing world's avant-garde. It has been aged in new oak casks. The resulting wine, ten years ago, would have been at best a strange curiosity, at worst a misguided attempt at silk-purse manufacture using a pile of pig's ears.

During the last decade, though, aspirations, technology and, most importantly, understanding of vineyard and winery requirements for fine-wine-making have all increased dramatically in France, and elsewhere in Europe. The result is that wines made from unfancied grapes in little-admired areas may taste better than many 'classical' wines at double or even triple the price. This one does.

It is big, broad and mouth-filling. It has a hauntingly waxy, limeflower aroma with a strange, lush pepperiness also tingling the nostrils. The flavours are deep, and on the palate, too, there is a peculiar blend of tallow-like weight and sweet, leafy freshness, with mellow greengage fruit a further suggestion. The textures are soft and supple, rounded off to a nutty, peppery finish. The overall impression is of a lush, sumptuous and original wine – there is nothing ostensibly oaky about it, nor is there anything remotely Chardonnay-like, or Sauvignon-like, or Sémillon-like. It is only itself.

Match it with food, and you'll see its presence and stature come to the fore. It is excellent with Chinese food; excellent with pork served in a sherry-based sauce; excellent, too, with chicken, and with grand fish dishes. When I first encountered it in a blind tasting, it seemed bizarre and eccentric, without immediate, evident attractions. It is only in drinking – and, if possible, in drinking over a two- or three-day period, for it improves on contact with air – that it communicates and convinces.

Full-bodied red wines for main courses

Toro Gran Colegiata Tinto de Crianza (various vintages), Bodegas Fariña

Lowest price: £3.49 at *Booths*
Highest price: £6.78 at *Findlater Mackie Todd*
Other stockists include *Ad Hoc Wine Warehouse; Bottle & Basket;
G E Bromley; Burlington Wines; Eldridge Pope; John Ford Wines; Fulham Road
Wine Centre; Great Northern Wine Company; Hadleigh Wine Cellars; Gerard
Harris; Richard Harvey; Hungerford Wine Company; Lay & Wheeler; Lorne
House Vintners; James Nicholson; Oddbins; Thos Peatling; Premier Wine
Warehouse; Ubiquitous Chip; The Upper Crust; Wine Emporium*

'Massive' is an adjective that might spring to mind when you first
sip this wine; sip a second time and you might add
'mountainous'. It is a handsome blood-red in colour, with
complex, forthcoming aromas almost reminiscent of those of port.
Dry tea leaves and blackcurrants are two of the hints you may
catch in the aroma; it also has a leathery or even a goaty closeness
hovering about the glass.

Sip the wine on its own, and you will feel tannins gripping at
your tongue like a Velcro fastener; drink it with the rich food
partner it merits (a beef or game stew, say) and the tannins
disappear, making the wine seem supple. This is often true of ripe
tannins, as opposed to the green, unripe kind exhibited, for
example, by northern-grown red wines after a cool summer. The
flavours are big, powerful ones, full of fiery fruit flavour (cherries
and chocolate are both hinted at), with a salty finish. The wine's
concentration makes it superb value for money. There are few
better bargains in Britain at present for those who court power in
the glass.

Penfold's Koonunga Hill Shiraz-Cabernet 1987, South Australia

Lowest price: £4.25 at *Oddbins*
Highest price: £7.25 at *Fortnum & Mason*
Other stockists include *Australian Wine Centre; D Byrne & Co; Chaplin & Son; Rodney Densem; Alex Findlater; Richard Granger; J E Hogg; Hunter & Oliver; Justerini & Brooks; Majestic Wine Warehouses; Oddbins; Sainsbury Bros; Sebastopol; Selfridges; Thresher; La Vigneronne; Vineyards Wine Warehouse; Whitesides; The Wine House* Also available from *Marks & Spencer* as 'Shiraz-Cabernet'.

Few wines are as typical of the rich yet velvety pleasures of the Australian red as Penfold's Koonunga Hill. It is deeply coloured, sweetly and seductively oaky in aroma, with an undertow that hints at eucalyptus or spice. The taste is initially salty on the tongue, then opens up with beautifully rich, berry-round fruit flavours, balanced and textured all the way to a lingeringly silky finish. Like many of the best Australian wines, it is technically hard to fault – though it may be equally difficult to ascribe it precise regional or varietal characteristics. Its satisfying depth of flavour combined with sustained, ripe acidity make it a good choice with richly sauced meats, braises and luscious pasta dishes like lasagne or cannelloni. Its charms are pure, simple, universal.

Château Ventenac Rouge 1989, Cabardès, Alain Maurel

Majestic Wine Warehouses: £2.89

This is a wine full of life. A splash of purple-red in the glass, with bubblingly fruity aromas, the kind described as 'primary' (because they appear in early youth) by oenologists and technicians. When you read this, the aromas may have disappeared for a while; if so, they'll be back before long in 'secondary' form, hinting at something like resin or woodsmoke rather than squashed blackcurrants. This change in the character of aromas is what spending time in bottle does to most red wines; the finer the wine, the longer the process takes.

The flavour at present is full of primary violence and energy, and this may also quieten during the life of this book. Château Ventenac Rouge is mostly made from Merlot, with smaller additions of Cabernet Sauvignon and Grenache, yet despite being composed of 90 per cent Bordeaux grape varieties its character is wholly southern: stony and harsh in flavour, yet with soft, ripe tannins, leaving an overall impression of tanginess and liveliness. Try it with bacon hocks, black pudding, ribs, sausages and wild mushroom stews.

Full-bodied red wines for
main courses (continued)

Domaine Richeaume (various vintages), Côtes de Provence, Cabernet Sauvignon (organic), Henning Hoesch

Lowest price: £6.65 at *Lorne House Vintners*
Highest price: £8.69 at *Vinceremos*
Other stockists include *Sebastopol; Yapp Brothers*

I want to recommend an organic wine. 'Organic' is more than usually difficult to define in the wine context; despite this, the ideal seems an admirable one, and those who work within an established prescriptive framework are to be encouraged. A Yale-educated German, growing wine not far from Aix-en-Provence, is one such, and this Cabernet Sauvignon is one of his red wines. He also produces a pure Syrah, as well as a Cuvée Tradition based on Grenache, Cinsault and Syrah. All are good. The prescriptive framework is that of the French Terre et Vie association.

Organic red wines often seem to have an engaging frankness to them, with big, pungent aromas, deep flavours and close-grained textures. Whether this is due to the spirit of non-interference in which they are made, or simply to autosuggestion on the part of the drinker, is hard to say. This wine (the 1988 from Vinceremos is the vintage this description is based on) has a fine earthy smell, and over it perfumed fruit: very straightforward, limpid and serene. In taste the fruit is still more prominent: grippy and powerful, but rich and ripe, too. The flavours have a Cabernet austerity to them, but this Bordeaux phrasing is given a Provençal twang; in place of urbanity there is something rugged, ruffled and *garrigue*-like, and the finish is almost bitter. The wine goes well with herb-perfumed meats, with olive oil-fried or butter-fried potatoes, and with peppers stuffed with highly seasoned and colourful fillings.

Grande Escolha 1985, Quinta do Côtto, Douro

Lowest price: £6.99 at *Oddbins*
Highest price: £9.50 at *Nicolas*
Other stockists include *Adnams; Berry Bros & Rudd; Bibendum; Eaton Elliot; Alex Findlater; Peter Green; Tanners; Wines from Paris*

Most wine drinkers are familar with port and Madeira, but many have still to try their first Portuguese wine – just as a number of merchants in this *Guide*, including some surprisingly distinguished ones, have still to stock their first Portuguese wine. Here is one of the most expensive available. I haven't chosen it for its expense, of course, but because it illustrates a little of the table-wine potential of this remarkable country. If any region is eventually to rival Bordeaux in the production of medium-bodied red wines of complexity, refinement and discretion, I would wager it will be a second strip of Europe's western seaboard: Portugal. Quinta do Côtto's 1985 Grande Escolha provides a little evidence.

For, despite its purely Portuguese grape varieties, this is a most clarety wine. In colour it is a deep, limpid, almost opaque purple; an early adult, in wine terms. The aromas are complex and distinguished, sonorous, sweet-edged, with a hint of cinnamon spice and a kind of cedary or resinous quality informing the whole.

It is a deeply flavoured wine, but not a heavy one. It has the tight grip of many good Portuguese reds, but none of the malevolent stalkiness of its harshest ones. The balance is superb, with carefully measured, fine-drawn acids and savoury depth to match the firm but graceful bone structure. Above all there is complexity: this is a wine that repays attentive drinking. Its sober distinction of flavour is best matched by a simple food partner: roast meat with a butter sauce, for example, or cheese on toast. With food, the fruity side of the wine's character emerges as a resonant allusion to blackcurrants. It is as fine as some clarets at twice the price, and will age further if wished. Indeed the 1985 at present needs decanting for aeration, or drinking slowly over a three-day period: the oxygen provides a gentle loosening and opening that adds to its pleasures. This is unquestionably a fine wine in the purest European tradition of subtlety, understatement and nuance.

Sweet wines for dessert or afterwards

Neusiedlersee Beerenauslese 1988, Cuvée Bouvier-Pinot Gris-Pinot Blanc, Lenz Moser, Austria, half-bottle

Asda £4.99; La Vigneronne £5.59

One of the chief delights we have missed following the diethylene glycol scandal of 1985 and the subsequent – and largely unjustified – disappearance of Austrian wines from our shop shelves has been the wonderful dessert wines produced by this country. They are inexpensive, thanks to the fact that a particular part of Austria, Burgenland, is able to produce them on a regular, wide-scale basis. Sunny autumns and the Neusiedlersee – an enormous, reed-fringed, 350 square-kilometre pond – provide perfect weather conditions for the formation of botrytis or for the *passerillage* (raising) of grapes to make sweet wines. Here is an example.

It is made from a trio of grape varieties: Pinot Blanc and Pinot Gris, together with the less distinguished, early ripening Bouvier. It is a full buttercup yellow, with beautifully rich, sweet, voluptuous aromas, both honeyed and buttery, like a kind of supercharged Meursault; yet there is also a limey freshness there, lifting this lanolin weight. Occasionally journalists have a go at using the word 'sexy' about a wine, but without defining what is meant; if it means an aroma or flavour that draws you helplessly and grindingly into the glass, then this qualifies.

I was initially going to recommend the '84 version of this wine, based on the same varieties minus the Pinot Blanc and now fully mature, but the importers told me it was about to finish and would be replaced by the 1988, whose aromas are described above. The flavours of the 1988 need more time to evolve: at the moment sweetness is all, which is typical of fine young dessert wines, but a year or two is needed to draw the acids into profile and allow the wine time to acquire the complexity it needs to lend the sugars interest. Give it this time, if you can. If you can't, you'll find its mouth-filling, tangy sweetness a great pleasure in any case. And if you bump into some of the 1984, enjoy its maturity: fresh as an apple; clean as a nut.

Fruit tarts make the best food accompaniments to classic sweet wines of this sort; be aware that the sweeter the tart, the dryer the wine will seem. Cheeses can be surprisingly successful with dessert wines, though this success is difficult to predict. Enjoying the wine in place of dessert is another alternative, as is calling on it to refresh a summer afternoon.

A Vintage Port

I wanted to recommend a Vintage Port to conclude this section, but settling on one proved more difficult than I had anticipated.

Fine vintages of 1970 and earlier are now very expensive: £30 and upwards. 1975 is also expensive now – probably more so than its quality warrants. 1977 is very fine, and is beginning to drink well, but it's a great, collectable vintage with decades of life ahead of it . . . thus expensive again. That leaves us the vintages of the 1980s.

The best of those so far declared are 1983 and 1985, but both – even for those, like me, who enjoy drinking young Vintage Port for its fire and its fury – are too young yet to tackle. The field narrows again to 1980 and 1982.

1980 is certainly the better of the two vintages, and also the more consistent of the pair. It drinks well now, though the aromas will, in most cases, improve with another four or five years' cellaring. For a long time it was undervalued – in the autumn of 1988 Warre's very fine 1980 could have been bought for the equivalent of £10.79 per bottle from *Bibendum* (in case quantities), and in August 1989 Taylor 1980 was available from *Nigel Baring* (also by the case) at the equivalent of £13.93 per bottle. By now, however, stockists have in general caught up with the wines' quality. In looking through merchants' lists I have found good 1980 Vintage Ports for under £17 from *Bin Ends; Booths; Burlington Wines; D Byrne & Co; Cairns & Hickey; Fine Vintage Wines; J E Hogg; Master Cellar Wine Warehouse; Le Nez Rouge; Old Street Wine Company; Oddbins; Thos Peatling; C J Rookes; Valvona & Crolla and Woodhouse Wines*, while the port bargain of the year is available on the Channel Islands, where *Victor Hugo Wines* lists Offley's 1980 at £8.75. In general, note that individual merchants often offer cheaper prices for Vintage Ports than large chains and supermarkets (where 1980s cost around £20); note also that many merchants are obscure about what Vintage Port they do and don't hold, and about how much they want you to pay for it. Press them for this information. The best 1980s – tight, penetrating, full of dark brambly fruit – are those of Warre, Taylor, Graham, Quarles Harris, Dow, Niepoort, Offley and Smith Woodhouse. Fonseca is disappointingly light for a house with as fine a reputation as it has, while Royal Oporto's 1980 should be avoided.

1982 is a horse with a different skin. Aromatically, the best 1982s are full of charm, with rounded, lush, cherry scents, sometimes with a fat brazil-nut quality that certain tasters consider a fault, but that I prefer to regard as simply unusual and enticing. They are much softer than diehard traditionalists consider acceptable; put them next to most LBVs or even Crusting Ports, though, and their vintage structure will be evident. The positive aspect of this softness is, again, charm, and the best 1982s have it in plenty. They dance around the mouth, waltz off down the throat, and leave a sweet little song on the tongue. Not to be scorned! Especially not at under £14 for Sandeman (*J E Hogg; London Wine*), Martinez (*Davenport*), Offley (*Victor Hugo; Burlington Wines; Oddbins; Thos Peatling*) or Cálem's Quinta da Foz (*Oddbins*). The other top-quality 1982 is from Niepoort, but this producer's ports are still difficult to find in Britain – a shame, as quality is very good throughout the range. Churchill's 1982 is the most widely stocked (generally at £13 to £15), and was the first Vintage Port produced by this new house (run by the Graham family, who no longer have an interest in the Graham *marque*). Aromatically it is slightly loose and jammy, and this impression continues into the initial flavour; later it tightens and acquires some tarry, berry-like definition, and it has the characteristic supple, dancing roundness of its year. Delaforce, Croft, Royal Oporto and Noval seem to have produced the least successful 1982s.

The classic accompaniment to Vintage Port is Stilton cheese. My own opinion is that a fine, hard, non-blue cheese, like top-quality Cheddar or Double Gloucester, is better; nuts (brazils, hazelnuts, almonds) are also very fine. Vintage Port is remarkably good with summer fruit, too, like strawberries, cherries or figs: it has the dimensions of power and sweetness to match the often wine-busting explosion of flavour found in fresh fruit.

Who's where

This is a gazetteer of individual wine stockists listed in the Guide. See also the directory of chains and supermarkets on page 334.

London

E2
Balls Brothers 357

EC1
Cantina Augusto 393
Corney & Barrow 406
Old Street Wine
   Company 521

EC2
Corney & Barrow 406
Pavilion Wine
   Company 525

EC3
Russell & McIver 548

EC4
Corney & Barrow 406
El Vino Co 595

N1
The Market 620

N2
Grogblossom 452

N6
Bottle and Basket 378

N7
Le Nez Rouge 512

N21
Howard Ripley 543

NW1
Nigel Baring 359
Bibendum 369
Laytons 491

NW3
Heath Street Wine Co
   465
La Réserve 541
Madeleine Trehearne
   Partners 578

NW4
Amazing Grapes 346

NW6
Fine Vintage Wines
   433
Grape Ideas 446
Grogblossom 452

NW10
Wine Growers
   Association 612

NW11
Grogblossom 452

SE1
Davys of London 414
Green's 450
Kurtz & Chan Wines
   487
Mayor Sworder & Co
   501
Russell & McIver 548

SE10
Ravensbourne Wine
   Co 537
Wines Galore 623

SE11
Alex Findlater 430

SW1
Berry Bros & Rudd
   366
Farr Vintners 427
Harrods 459
Jeroboams 483
Justerini & Brooks 485
Morris & Verdin 508
Pimlico Dozen 528
André Simon 561

SW3
Nicolas 515
La Réserve 541

SW5
Nicolas 515

SW6
Friarwood 436
The Fulham Road
   Wine Centre 437
Harbottle Wines 470
Haynes Hanson &
   Clark 464
Premier Wine
   Warehouse 530
La Réserve 541

SW7
Jeroboams 483
La Vigneronne 590

SW9
Ad Hoc Wine
   Warehouse 338

SW10
Lea & Sandeman
   Company 492
London Wine 495

SW11
The Battersea Wine
   Company 363
Goedhuis & Co 443

SW12
Benson Fine Wines
   365

SW13
Barnes Wine Shop 359

SW17
Cork Talk 528

SW18
Cork Talk 528
Supergrape 570
Winecellars 620

SW19
Findlater Mackie Todd
   431

W1
H Allen Smith 345
Les Amis du Vin 346
Adam Bancroft
   Associates 358
Fortnum & Mason 435
Harcourt Fine Wine
   455
Nicolas 515
Selfridges 558
André Simon 561

W2
The Champagne
   House 396
Moreno Wines 507
Le Picoleur 527, 541

W5
Côte d'Or Wines 408

W6
Haynes Hanson &
   Clark 464

W8
Nicolas 515

W9
Les Amis du Vin 346
Moreno Wines 507

W11
John Armit Wines 348
Corney & Barrow 406
Holland Park Wine Co
   473
Nicolas 515

WC1
H Allen Smith 345
Domaine Direct 418

WC2
The Australian Wine
   Centre 353
Kiwifruits 487

England

Avon

Bath
Sainsbury Bros 550

Bristol
Averys of Bristol 354
John Harvey & Sons
   460
Reid Wines 539

Bedfordshire

Luton
Smedley Vintners 562

Berkshire

Ascot
Marske Mill House
   500

Hungerford
Hungerford Wine
   Company 478

Maidenhead
David Alexander 344
Helen Verdcourt
   Wines 586

Pangbourne
Col G P Pease 470

Reading
Bordeaux Direct 375
Great Western Wines
   448
Sunday Times Wine
   Club 568
Vintage Roots 596

Buckinghamshire

Amersham
Philip Eyres Wine
   Merchant 426

Aston Clinton
Gerard Harris 457

Gerrards Cross
William Rush 546

Great Missenden
Turville Valley Wines
   579

High Wycombe
Organic Wine
   Company 522

Cambridgeshire

Cambridge
Barwell & Jones 362

Ramsey
Anthony Byrne Fine
   Wines 388

Cheshire

Alderley Edge
Eaton Elliot
   Winebrokers 421

Altrincham
Cadwgan Fine Wine
   Merchants 390

Chester
Classic Wine
   Warehouses 402
George Dutton 608

Nantwich
Rodney Densem
   Wines 416
Haughton Fine Wines
   463

Northwich
Sandiway Wine Co
   554

Stockport
Millevini 503

Wilmslow
Willoughbys 608

Cornwall

St Austell
Del Monico's 414

Truro
Laymont & Shaw 490

Cumbria

Carlisle
B H Wines 368

Cockermouth
Garrards Wine
   Merchants 439

Grange-over-Sands
A L Vose 597

Kendal
Frank E Stainton 564

Penrith
Cumbrian Cellar 411

Derbyshire

Burton on Trent
Colombier Vins Fins
404

Buxton
Mi Casa Wines 502
Pugsons Food and
Wine 531

Devon

Bideford
Balls Brothers 357

Cullompton
Peter Wylie Fine
Wines 629

Exeter
David Baillie Vintners
356
The Nobody Inn 517
Topsham Wines 577

Ottery St Mary
Christopher Piper
Wines 529

Dorset

Blandford Forum
Woodhouse Wines
627

Bridport
Wessex Wines 602

Christchurch
Christchurch Fine
Wine Co 399

Sherborne
Sherborne Vintners
560

Wareham
Richard Harvey Wines
462

Essex

Coggeshall
Peter Watts Wines 600

Colchester
Lay & Wheeler 488

Maldon
Ingletons Wines 481

Gloucestershire

Cirencester
Windrush Wines 610

Winchcombe
Winchcombe Wine
Merchants 609

Greater Manchester

Manchester
Binocular Wine 372
Cadwgan 390
Willoughbys 608

Oldham
Willoughbys 608

Hampshire

Basingstoke
Berry Bros & Rudd
366

Bordon
High Breck Vintners
470

Southampton
Liquid Gifts 494

Hereford & Worcester

Evesham
Arriba Kettle 349

Kidderminster
Hopton Wines 474
Wine Schoppen 616

Malvern Wells
Croque-en-Bouche 410

Tenbury Wells
Hopton Wines 474

Hertfordshire

Bishop's Stortford
Hedley Wright 466

Harpenden
Harpenden Wines 456

Stevenage
The Wine Society 617

Ware
Sapsford Wines 554

Kent

Canterbury
Whiclar & Gordon 603

Maidstone
Douglas Henn-Macrae
467
Stapylton Fletcher 566

Staplehurst
A O L Grilli Wines
452

Lancashire

Carnforth
Vessel du Vin 587

Clitheroe
D Byrne & Co 388
Whitesides Wine
Merchants 606

Preston
Borg Castel 377

Leicestershire

Ashby-de-la-Zouch
Davenport & Son 412

Coalville
R T Wines 616

Leicester
G E Bromley 382
Drinksmart 420

Lincolnshire

Grimsby
Lincolnshire Wine Co
522

Spalding
G E Bromley 382

Merseyside

Liverpool
Thomas Baty 608
Hilbre Wine
Company 471

Norfolk

Beeston St Lawrence
Sir Ronald Preston 470

Dereham
Hicks & Don 469

Harleston
Barwell & Jones 362

Norwich
Adnams 339
Barwell & Jones 362
City Wines 400

Thetford
T & W Wines 580

Weston Longville
Roger Harris 458

Northampton-
shire

Brackley
Farthinghoe Fine
Wine and Food 428

Earls Barton
Summerlee Wines 567

Kettering
Ferrers le Mesurier
429

Northampton
Tony Jeffries Wines
482

Nottinghamshire

Newark
Askham Wines 352
Ian G Howe 476

Nottingham
Gauntleys of
Nottingham 441
Weavers of
Nottingham 601

Oxfordshire

Banbury
S H Jones 484

Blewbury
Sebastopol Wines 556

Oxford
Fine Vintage Wines
433
Grape Ideas Wine
Warehouse 446

Shropshire

Bridgnorth
Tanners Wines 571

Newport
William Addison
(Newport) 337

Shrewsbury
Tanners Wines 571

Somerset

Taunton
Châteaux Wines 398

Yeovil
Abbey Cellars 336

Staffordshire

Marchington
Wines of Westhorpe
625

Suffolk

Halesworth
Alex Findlater 430

Ipswich
Barwell & Jones 362
Burlington Wines 384
Champagne de
Villages 394
Hadleigh Wines 454
Seckford Wines 557
Wines of Interest 624

Newmarket
Corney & Barrow 406

Southwold
Adnams Wine
Merchants 339

Woodbridge
Barwell & Jones 362

Surrey

Betchworth
Ben Ellis and
Associates 424

Cranleigh
A & A Wines 335
Lorne House Vintners
496

Croydon
Master Cellar Wine
Warehouse 500

Dorking
Whiclar & Gordon
Wines 603

East Horsley
The Upper Crust 583

Guildford
Guildford Wine
Market 453

**Kingston upon
Thames**
Bentalls of Kingston
365
Vessel du Vin 587

Richmond
Richmond Wine
Warehouse 542

Wallington
The Wine House 613

Sussex (East)

Alfriston
English Wine Centre 425

Brighton
The Butlers Wine Cellar 386

Hailsham
Michelham Country Foods 425

Hove
John Ford Wines 434

Lewes
Half Yard Wines 455

Sussex (West)

Ashington
Vineyards Wine Warehouse 594

Chichester
Pallant Wines 524
Arthur Purchase & Son 533

East Grinstead
K F Butler 511

Worthing
Chaplin & Son 397

Tyne & Wear

Newcastle upon Tyne
Dennhöfer Wines 415
Richard Granger 445

Warwickshire

Atherstone
David Watt Fine Wines 413

Shipston-on-Stour
Edward Sheldon 559

Stratford upon Avon
C A Rookes 545

Warwick
The Broad Street Wine Co 381

West Midlands

Birmingham
Connolly's 405
Vinature 592

Lye
Greenwood & Co 514

Stourbridge
County Wines of Hagley 409
Nickolls & Perks 514

Sutton Coldfield
Jacqueline's Wines 482

Walsall
Whittalls Wines 607

Wiltshire

Mere
Yapp Brothers 630

Salisbury
Nadder Wine Company 510

Westbury
Hicks & Don 469

Yorkshire (North)

Oswaldkirk
Patrick Toone 371

Skipton
Wright Wine Co 628

York
Cachet Wines 389
Fine English Wine Company 433
Hollingsworth of York 474
Yorkshire Fine Wines Company 631

Yorkshire (South)

Barnsley
Rodgers Fine Wines 544

Rotherham
Bin Ends 371

Sheffield
Barrels & Bottles 616
Mitchells Wine Merchants 505
The Wine Schoppen 616

Yorkshire (West)

Huddersfield
Pennine Wines 616
La Reserva Wines 540

Leeds
Cairns & Hickey 392
Great Northern Wine Company 447

Ossett
Vinceremos Wines 593

Wetherby
Pagendam Pratt 511

Channel Islands

Jersey
Victor Hugo Wines 477

N. Ireland

Belfast
Belfast Wine Co 364
Direct Wine Shipments 417

Crossgar
James Nicholson Wine Merchant 513

Republic of Ireland

Dublin
Mitchell & Son 504

Scotland

Aberdeen
Wine Raks 615

Ayr
Whighams of Ayr 604

Coldstream
Alba Wine Society 342

Dundee
James Aitken & Son 341

Edinburgh
Peter Green 449
J E Hogg 472
Justerini & Brooks 485
Raeburn Fine Wines
and Foods 535
Valvona & Crolla 585
Whighams of Ayr 604
The Wine Emporium 611
Wines from Paris 622

Elgin
Gordon & MacPhail 444

Glasgow
Ubiquitous Chip
Wine Shop 581

Moffat
Moffat Wine Shop 506

Peebles
Villeneuve Wines 591

Perth
Matthew Gloag & Son 442

Wales

Hawarden
Ashley Scott 555

Llandudno
Snowdonia Wine
Warehouse 563

Swansea
The Celtic Vintner 393

Welshpool
Tanners Wines 571

CHAINS AND SUPERMARKETS

Space does not permit us to list the addresses of all the branches of each chain, but details at the head of the entry include the address and telephone number of the company's head office, from whom you will be able to find out your nearest branch.

Asda 350
Augustus Barnett 360
Blayneys 373
Booths 374
Bottoms Up 379
Budgen 383
Co-op 403
Davisons 413
Peter Dominic 419
Eldridge Pope 422

Fullers 438
Hunter & Oliver 479
Majestic Wine
    Warehouses 497
Marks & Spencer 498
Morrisons 509
Oddbins 518
Thos Peatling 526
Arthur Rackhams 534
Safeway 549

J Sainsbury 551
Tesco 572
Threshers and Wine
    Rack 575
J Townend & Sons 577
Unwins 582
Victoria Wine 588
Waitrose 598
Wizard Wine
    Warehouses 626

A & A Wines ☞

Smithbrook Kilns, nr Cranleigh, Surrey GU6 8JJ *Tel* (0483) 274666

Case sales only **Open** Mon–Fri 9.30–5.30; Sat 10–2 **Closed** Sun, public holidays **Credit cards** Access, Visa; personal and business accounts
Discounts 5% on 5+ cases **Delivery** Free in Surrey and Sussex (min 1 case) and Hampshire, Kent, Berkshire and Greater London (min 5 cases); elsewhere negotiable; mail order available **Glass hire** Free with any case order
Tastings and talks Spring tasting in May, autumn tasting in October; to groups on request **Cellarage** Not available

The two As are both Andrews, Bickerton and Connor, and their clearly written list has continued to expand away from its Spanish core during the last year. This has not been at the expense of Spain, though: Riojas from nine bodegas are matched by wines from Penedés, León, La Mancha, Valdepeñas, Valladolid, Ampurdan-Costa Brava and Utiel Requena. The German section is distinguished by a range of seven different bottles from Baden as well as Paul Anhauser's Nahe wines; the selection from France is perhaps less innovative, with clarets (especially three vintages from Château Cissac) looking the most reliably enjoyable. Gisselbrecht's Alsace pair, and the Domaine Saint-André Côtes de Gascogne, both offer good white-wine value, and would be worth mixing in to your case. Expansion in Italy follows the well-trodden Piedmont-Veneto-Tuscany path; 'WATCH THIS SPACE!', we are instructed, so we hope some of Italy's more unusual wines will begin to fill it during the next twelve months. There are small collections of interest from Chile and Portugal; while the two As must be almost the only people in England to consider Australian wines 'over-expensive'. The line of least resistance has very definitely been followed for America, with two Gallos and a blush Zin, and only Churchill's Crusted offers any interest from the rather disappointing range of ports. Smithbrook Kilns, a former brickworks, is the starting point (perhaps not literally) for wine tours every year, and bi-annual tastings are organised. A very friendly and personal service is claimed; if you can vouch for this, or if you think the claim is unjustified, please drop us a line (you will find forms at the back of the book).

Best buys

Alberto Tinto 1987, Bodegas Hijos de Alberto Gutierrez (Valladolid), £2.75
Château Cissac 1985, Haut-Médoc, £11.66
Ediger Elzhofberg Riesling Spätlese 1982 (oak-aged), Landenburg (Mosel), £6.15

Abbey Cellars

The Abbey, Preston Road, Yeovil, Somerset   *Tel* (0935) 76228
BA21 3AR

Case sales only   Open Tue–Fri 11.30–6; Sat 10–3   **Closed** Mon, Sun, public
holidays   **Credit cards** Access, Visa; business accounts   **Discounts** Available (min
1 case)   **Delivery** Free within 20-mile radius of Yeovil (min 1 case); otherwise 1–5
cases £5 per case, 6–9 cases £3 per case, 10+ cases £2 per case; mail order
available   **Glass hire** Free   **Tastings and talks** Tastings held 2 times a year
(spring and autumn); tasting organised in London twice a year; to groups on
request   **Cellarage** Charge negotiable

Abbey Cellars claims to be the only wine warehouse in the
Yeovil area. In comparison with most of its kind, the list is
minute, yet effort is evident in the selection, and one could
think of a reason – other than price or convenience – for almost
every wine to be there.

'Almost', because the Italian and German sections have the
look of convenience rather than diligence about them. Spain and
Portugal, by contrast, show how you can reduce two huge wine-
producing countries to a selection of eight bottles and still
reflect a little of the diversity and excellence of their source
regions. Australia and New Zealand have elbowed their way on
to the list successfully, and so have Argentina and Chile. France,
meanwhile, dominates, with clarets, Rhônes, and French country
wines looking most appealing.

It would be good to see this list expand during the next
twelve months: Andrew Mangles' experience with Caves de la
Madeleine, London Wine and Justerini & Brooks means that he
will be no stranger to wine's wider horizons, and would
presumably be ready to expand if customer interest and
financing allow. The present list would be a sound basis on
which to build.

Best buys

Gamay de Touraine 1989, H Marionnet, £3.99
Vin de Pays des Côtes de Gascogne Rouge 1988, Domaine de
Mathalin, £3.10
Plantagenet Shiraz 1985, Mount Barket, Western Australia, £6.90

We have tried to make the *1991 Which? Wine Guide* as comprehensive
as possible, but we should love to hear from you about any other wine
merchants you feel deserve an entry, or your comments on existing
entries. Write to us either by letter or using the report forms supplied
at the back of the book.

COMPLETELY FREE OFFER
expert, up-to-the-minute advice on buying and enjoying wine FREE for 3 months.

Take advantage of this free trial offer to see for yourself how Which? Wine Monthly gives you the facts, including:

★ results of blind tastings, where to buy and what to pay

★ up-to-the-minute information on stockists offering wines of particularly good value

★ profiles of leading figures in the wine trade

★ our recommended red and white "wines of the month"

★ consumer check: a tasting of 20 wines bought anonymously from a particular merchant each month

★ a monthly recipe using wine as an ingredient

Which? Wine Monthly is yours to try out free without any obligation. Accept our offer and we'll send you the next 3 issues free. Planned reports include:

★ Best sweet unfortified wines for under £10.00

★ Amontillado sherry

★ Non-French sparkling wines

The next 3 issues — FREE

Whether you're a connoisseur or a casual drinker buying the occasional bottle, you'll find Which? Wine Monthly a helpful, practical newsletter ... one you'll rely on month after month for up-to-the-minute news and buying advice. When you take up this free offer we'll send you the next 3 issues of Which? Wine Monthly as they are published.

NO
STAMP
REQUIRED

Which? Wine Monthly
Consumers' Association
FREEPOST
Hertford X
SG14 1YB

Try Which? Wine Monthly FREE for 3 months, and see for yourself how it gives you the facts.

The publishers of Which? Wine Guide 1991 present a highly informative companion newsletter, designed to give you the most up-to-date advice on buying wine — including news of special bargains, prices and availability — the results of blind tastings and the latest news and views from the wine world.

Accept this remarkable offer and you'll receive the next 3 issues ABSOLUTELY FREE and WITHOUT COMMITMENT.

See overleaf for further details.

▲ DETACH ALONG PERFORATION ▲

HOW TO CLAIM YOUR **FREE** ISSUES

To receive Which? Wine Monthly FREE for 3 months, just complete and return the direct debiting mandate on the coupon below. We will send you the next three issues of Which? Wine Monthly as they appear. If you do not wish to continue receiving Which? Wine Monthly, you can cancel your subscription by writing to us — and your direct debiting mandate by writing to your bank — before payment is due on 1st March 1991. You can keep everything you have received, and it won't have cost you a penny.

If you want to go on receiving Which? Wine Monthly, you don't need to do anything more. Your subscription will bring you Which? Wine Monthly each month for £4.75 a quarter, until you cancel your mandate or we advise you of a change in the price of your subscription. If there should be any change in the price of your subscription at any time we would advise you at least six weeks in advance. This gives you time to tell us if you do not wish to continue your subscription, and to cancel your direct debiting mandate. You are, of course, free to do this at anytime. To accept this offer, just complete the coupon and post it — you don't even need a stamp. So why not post it off now?

OFFER EXPIRES 31st DECEMBER 1990

Consumers' Association
Castlemead, Gascoyne Way,
Hertford X SG14 1LH.

WHICH? WINE MONTHLY

I would like to accept this free offer. Please send me the next 3 months' issues of Which? Wine Monthly as they appear. I understand that I am under no obligation — if I do not wish to continue with Which? Wine Monthly after the free trial. I can cancel my order before payment is due on 1st March 1991. But if I decide to continue, I need do nothing — my subscription will bring me Which? Wine Monthly each month for the current price of £4.75 a quarter, payable by Direct Debit.

FREE TRIAL ACCEPTANCE

Direct Debiting Mandate.

I/We authorise you until further notice in writing to charge to my/our account with you on or immediately after 1st March 1991 and quarterly thereafter unspecified amounts which may be debited thereto at the instance of Consumers' Association by Direct Debit.

Date of first payment, on or within the calendar month from 1st March 1991.

Signed	Date
Bank Account in the name of	Bank Account Number
Name and address of your bank in BLOCK LETTERS PLEASE	Your name and address in BLOCK LETTERS PLEASE
TO _____	Mr/Mrs/Miss/Ms _____

Banks may decline to accept instructions to charge direct debits to certain types of account other than current accounts.

Originator's Ref. No. 992338   WX91A

William Addison (Newport)

Head office and the warehouse

The Warehouse, Village Farm, Lilleshall,
Newport, Shropshire TF10 9HB

Tel (0952) 670200
(24-hour answering
service (0952) 670300)

67 High Street, Newport, Shropshire
TF10 7AU

Tel (0952) 810627

Open Mon–Sat 9–5 **Closed** Sun, public holidays **Credit cards** Visa; personal
and business accounts **Discounts** Available **Delivery** Free in Shropshire and
Staffordshire (min 1 case); otherwise at cost; mail order available **Glass hire** Free
with wine order **Tastings and talks** To groups on request **Cellarage** £3.45 per
case per year

We asked every merchant considered for inclusion in this year's
Guide an important question: 'What do you offer that none of
your competitors do?' John Horton, Managing Director of
Addison of Newport, gave no reply. Was this simply honesty,
an admission that Addison of Newport offers nothing that its
competitors don't already offer? Was it reticence, unbecoming in
a merchant? Or was it media fatigue?

Whatever the answer, we decided to include Addison of
Newport, because you may find yourself wineless in Newport
one day; and because the company's full list contains over 600
wines and spirits, which by anyone's standards provides good
choice. Seventy-two half-bottles are also worth knowing about.
The key area is France, with big ranges of claret, Sauternes and
Burgundy, tailing off as you trail around the regions. Vintage
Port and champagne are both well-upholstered areas, and the
German section would reward exploration. Wines from other
parts of the world are in general unadventurously bought,
though there's nothing wrong with safety as a buying policy:
Mondavi, Torres and Brown Brothers are all first-class wine-
makers. We would very much like to hear from readers in the
Shropshire and Staffordshire area about their impressions of the
service offered by Addison.

Best buys

Bordeaux Sélection 1988, Pierre Coste, £3.99
Guntrum Riesling 1986, Louis Guntrum, Nahe, £3.29
Cadre Noir Saumur Brut (sparkling), £5.15

Which? Wine Guide does not accept payment for inclusion, and there is
no sponsorship or advertising.

Ad Hoc Wine Warehouse

363 Clapham Road, London SW9 9BT   *Tel* 071-274 7433

Open Mon–Fri 9–7.30; Sat 10–7.30; Sun 11–3 **Closed** Public holidays
Credit cards Access, Visa; personal and business accounts **Discounts** 5% on 6
mixed cases **Delivery** Free in London area (min 1 case); otherwise 1 case £5, 2–5
cases £3, 5+ cases £2 **Glass hire** Free with wine purchase
Tastings and talks Various promotional tastings; to groups on request held in-
store **Cellarage** Not available

East-West relations have undergone some spectacular
modifications since the last issue of this *Guide* was prepared. A
very small wave in a very big sea washed over Ad Hoc Wine
Warehouse between Stockwell and Clapham, with its takeover
by the Bulgarian Vintners Company. There has been no massive
Balkanisation on the Clapham Road; outwardly and inwardly
things look much as before (unprepossessing and impressive,
respectively). The Bulgarian selection, however, has gone into
overdrive, with a wide range of country, varietal, reserve and
controliran wines available here. Londoners wishing to keep up
to date with what Eastern Europe's most dynamic and well-
organised wine producers are up to would do well to look into
Ad Hoc from time to time. Slot Ivo Papasov or Trio Bulgarka
into the Walkman, and stroll on in.

It would be doing Ad Hoc a great injustice to suggest that
Bulgaria was the only reason for stopping by, though. There are
over 1100 wines in these well-organised and neatly laid-out
premises, and the selection is always stimulating. The fine range
of Bordeaux and Burgundies should keep the Clapham punters
happy, while an excellent Italian selection might persuade
Wandsworth-bound North Londoners that they don't really
need to go all the way to Winecellars. This Italian range, it is
worth noting, is strong on enthusiastic traditional producers
trying hard within DOC, rather than being top-heavy with
pretentious and often overpriced vini da tavola, packaged in
bottles better suited to braining burglars than to pouring wine
from. Germany is relatively disappointing – though the
selection is still better than many offer, with Mosels from S A
Prum and Maximin Grünhauser in the Mosel, Johner in Baden
and Louis Guntrum in the Rheinhessen. Spain is another
strength with good Riojas, just about everything from Torres in
Penedés, seasoned by Cavas Hill and Jean León, and bits and
pieces from elsewhere; Portugal is solid behind. There are
interludes and divertissements from Chile, Greece and a trio of
Musars from the Lebanon, before the New World opens up long
and loud as Saturday night in Stockwell. French country wines
seem to have been worked at, too: there's a Pécharmant, a
Monbazillac, a Saint-Saturnin, an Irouléguy and a pair from

Arbois, as well as the expected Buzets, Bandols and Bergeracs. Sparkling wines do not disappoint, though ports, Madeiras and sherries do. Prices throughout tally with Ad Hoc's aim of 'equalling the supermarkets on price and beating them on range', and that's an attractive combination. An increased number of promotions and tastings are planned for this year.

Best buys

Bulgarian Cabernet Sauvignon 1985, Melnik Region, £2.45
Montepulciano d'Abruzzo 1988, Umani Ronchi, £3.39
Château l'Enclos 1988, Bordeaux Sauvignon Blanc, £3.49

Adnams Wine Merchants

Mail order

The Crown, High Street, Southwold, Suffolk IP18 6DP	*Tel* (0502) 724222

Shops

The Cellar & Kitchen Store, Victoria Street, Southwold, Suffolk IP18 6DP	*Tel* (0502) 724222
The Grapevine, Cellar & Kitchen Store, 109 Unthank Road, Norwich, Norfolk NR2 2PE	*Tel* (0603) 613998

Open (The Crown) Mon–Fri 9–5 (mail order); (Cellar & Kitchen Store) Mon–Sat 10–6 (Southwold), 9–9 (Norwich) **Closed** Sun, public holidays
Credit cards Access, Visa; personal and business accounts **Discounts** 5% on 1 case **Delivery** Free on UK mainland (min 2 cases); otherwise at cost; mail order available **Glass hire** Free with 1-case order **Tastings and talks** Up to 30 wines always available for tasting in Southwold store and 8–10 in Norwich; annual tasting in May to launch catalogue; annual tasting in Norwich held in autumn; to groups on request **Cellarage** £3.50 per case per year

---

Adnams offers its customers a very wide range of wines, from the finest of the fine to the simplest of the simple; it publishes (the verb is not excessive) a superb list; it makes offers of all sorts, including attractive *en primeur* and worthwhile bin-end sales; its core mail-order business is complemented by three shops, a very superior pub (The Crown) and now a hotel (The Swan). All this, though, would not single it out in the way it is singled out in the minds of most of its customers. What does?

The answer is a middle-aged man with an earring: Simon Loftus. It is Loftus who has built Adnams as we know it; and Adnams as we know it is the only merchant in the country that succeeds in turning a vision of wine-making as one of the more beautiful and profound human endeavours into a successful commercial operation. Some share the vision, but are less successful commercially; others are first-rate traders, but the vision is blurred, obscure or parochial. Only Adnams, and Loftus, bring the two together seamlessly.

What does this mean in practice? The lists, to begin with, have always aspired to be more than sales documents, with their discussions of wine and food, their recipes, their often moving black-and-white photographs, their celebrations of growers, wine-makers, and Adnams' own Suffolk workers. The 1990 list contains an essay on oak by 'man of parts' Mel Knox, as well as Simon Loftus' own characteristically unorthodox approach to the 'organic wine' question: he has drawn up a Loftus declaration (which he admits is imperfect) of what 'organic' might mean in the wine context, has shown it to all of his growers, and got those whose practices correspond to the declaration to sign it, as 'a first step'. Loftus is a fine writer by anyone's standards (read *A Pike in the Basement*, fragments from the Loftus life story, to prove this to yourself), and the quality of his commentary on the wines listed is another reason for setting aside an evening to browse through the list.

The wine buying, jointly handled by Simon Loftus and Alistair Marshall, is always stimulating. 'We only sell what we would like to drink ourselves,' says Marshall, as a statement of fact rather than a boast. This can mean disappointing bottles from Adnams, if your own tastes don't happen to coincide with what Marshall or Loftus consider to be fine burgundy or classic Chenin Blanc – though it can also mean wonderful discoveries and eye-openers. At times, there seems to be a kind of wilful unconventionality about the buying; it may appear to you to prize unusual and bizarre flavours above the soft, supple and classic. This is reflected in Simon Loftus' own John-the-Baptist-style interventions on matters like the greediness of producers' opening prices after fine vintages, or the simplifying judgments passed by merchants and commentators on the character of those vintages. It is also reflected in Adnams' own pricing policy: you can often get bargains here for out-and-out classics and big names, which Loftus nobly refuses to make a killing with; less widely fêted wines rated highly by the team are, though, priced accordingly, out of a sense of natural justice.

Yet we would still recommend Adnams unhesitatingly for anyone for whom wine is a passion, for you will find that passion reflected here amid the many, many wines on offer. No area of the world is ignored except Eastern Europe; and even amid Bulgarian and Romanian absences you will find one of the country's biggest presences of Tokaj. There are loving selections of German, Italian and Australian wine to match the fine top-to-bottom French range. There's even a new comment this year for retsina! And lest you should be put off by our remarks about the unusual and the bizarre, know that Adnams will give you a full refund on any wine returned within a month for whatever reason – including the reason that you just don't like the taste.

Best buys

Côtes du Rhône 1989, Château du Grand Moulas, £3.95
Vin de Pays des Côtes de Thongue 1989, Domaine Comte de Margon, £3.20
Jasnières Clos Saint-Jacques 1986, Joël Gigou, £7.20

James Aitken & Son

---

53 Perth Road, Dundee DD1 4HY   *Tel* (0382) 21197

Open Mon–Fri 8.30–5.45; Sat 8.30–5 **Closed** Sun, public holidays
Credit cards None accepted; personal and business accounts **Discounts** 5% on 1
case **Delivery** Free in city of Dundee; mail order available **Glass hire** Free with
appropriate order **Tastings and talks** To groups on request **Cellarage** Free for
wines purchased from premises

'Grocers and Wine Merchants' is how James Aitken & Son, founded in 1874, describe themselves. The present Aitken, in fact, is John – and Son is Bryan; the description, though, remains accurate, with 'high quality groceries' occupying the front of the shop and wine the rest.

This merchant is a deal more adventurous than most of the old-established merchants rooted in doughty Scottish towns. Whereas they seem to get by on an almost unvarying diet of claret, Aitken's customers are clearly an adaptable and curious crowd, ready to abandon themselves to the risky pleasures of the Rhône (all Jaboulet, but nothing wrong with that), Australia (Rosemount, Brown Brothers and Hill-Smith), even Italy (three pages, with a lot of help from Antinori) . The selection from New Zealand is better than that offered by many of the pillars of the British wine trading establishment, and the same is true of the small but very well chosen Portuguese range; while the Greek selection (nine reds and six whites) is one of the very best of any merchant in the *Guide*. There is a good range of real German wines from devoted growers, and under the Alsace rubric you get the works from Dopff et Irion. The Loire, Beaujolais, Champagne and the French regions do not disappoint; only Burgundy looks a little thin on the shelves, perhaps due to an understandable reluctance on the part of canny shoppers to part with more notes than they need to.

And claret? 'Bordeaux is the region,' comes the confession, 'which is nearest to the wine-drinking heart of James Aitken & Son.' There is no shortage of claret here, ladies and gentlemen: 50 to choose from including 15 1985s starting at £4.69.

'We are constantly tasting (and drinking) wines from our stock which gives authority to our recommendations,' says John Aitken; that is a fit practice and credible statement. We cannot, however, agree that 'Prices in Vintage Port are so volatile that we ask interested customers to contact us for a quotation.' This is humbug; champagne prices might reasonably be described as volatile at present, but Vintage Port prices are no more volatile than those of any wine of equivalent standing, and there is no reason to be coy about pricing them. The Aitkens are by no means the only merchants at fault here, but it is a small blot on an otherwise excellent copybook.

Best buys

Château Fourcas-Hosten 1985, Listrac, £10.49
Coteaux du Giennois 1989, Domaine Balland-Chapuis, £6.05
Señorio de los Llanos 1978, Gran Reserva, Valdepeñas, £5.05

Alba Wine Society

Mail order
Leet Street, Coldstream, Borders TD12 4BJ   *Tel* (0890) 3166

Case sales only   **Open** Mon–Fri 8–5; Sat 9–12; public holidays 9–5   **Closed** Sun, Chr Day, Boxing Day, Jan 1 & 2   **Credit cards** Access, Visa; personal and business accounts   **Discounts** 3% on 5 cases   **Delivery** Free delivery (min 5 cases); otherwise £4.50 per case; £3 to the islands   **Glass hire** Free with 2-case order   **Tastings and talks** Regular tastings throughout Scotland; monthly tastings at Bond in Coldstream; to groups on request   **Cellarage** £2 per case per year (£10 min charge)

We should make it clear on behalf of The Alba Wine Society that it is not a specialist North Italian wine merchant – in fact a single Barolo Reserva from Borgogno is the only Piemontese on the list. 'As you might be aware,' an earlier list pointed out, 'the word "Alba" is our Pictish forefathers' name for Scotland.' This, therefore, is a Pictish mail-order wine society, and its list has a sobriety and elegance reminiscent of another mail-order wine society well established among the Angles, Saxons and Jutes in Albion.

It's a wide-ranging and well-written list – though it does turn loose-leaf after it's been opened a few times – and the selection is balanced and satisfying. The Loire, Rhône and Alsace regions are by no means eclipsed by the Pictish thirst for claret, and Burgundy, too, keeps its end up. This is the kind of tasting note to send a wine marching out of the warehouse: 'Father and son oversee this immaculate operation. Thirty per cent new oak is used every year and his wines, all red, are aged for over 18 months. He uses the Pinot Fin, a clone of the Pinot Noir, in his vineyards and the average age of his vines is over 40 years giving depth and concentration to his wine. If I was not so honest I would charge double for this wine (tasted blind you would think it a Pommard).' In fact, it's an Hautes Côtes de

Beaune (Domaine Garaudet) at £5.60 . . . and the only Pommard on the list is at £16.30.

The Spanish section is good: David Foxton has resisted the easy and familiar options, exploring instead the Penedés wines of René Barbier, the Jumilla wines of Bodegas Bleda and the Navarra wines of Bodegas Ochoa. Riojas from CVNE are as consistently good as any in the region. Portugal is present and promising – the buttery white Quinta do Côtto is not often seen in Britain – while Germany presents a distinguished roll-call of names, both those of growers and of vineyards. Alba even pushed south this year to promote itself and fine German wine at the Gateshead Garden Festival via a vineyard-cum-courtyard exhibit.

There may not be much from around the town of Alba in the Italian selection, but there are some fine Tuscan wines as well as Tedeschi's superb Amarone. American wines include three from Texas and examples from six Californian wineries, while from south of the equator Scots are offered four Chilean wines. Australia is represented by a wide range from the Brown Brothers, whose wines are sound but perhaps less exciting than some; choice from New Zealand, though, is better than average. The Alba Wine Society is one of the best merchants in the *Guide* for Austrian wines at present, with a really worthwhile range on offer at a time when this unlucky wine-producing nation needs more confidence than it is currently getting from retailers. Tokaj is supported with the same courage. All the office staff are 'forced to drink a new wine daily', while all the sales staff are Wine & Spirit Education Trust Diploma holders, so you are assured of either informed or entertaining advice. We'll leave the last word to the candid Mr Foxton: 'As the buyer I can honestly say that I am in love with 85 per cent of our wines. The other 15 per cent are there by demand.'

Best buys

The Society's Mosel ('a downgraded Riesling Kabinett from Louis Guntrum'), £2.80
Château de l'Estagnol 1985, Côtes du Rhône, £4.90
Ochoa Blanco 1988, Navarra, £3.35

Best buys – in most cases, these are the Editor's choice of three out of a range of ten wines selected by the merchant in question as being distinguished in terms of value for money, or offering very fine quality regardless of price.

David Alexander

69 Queen Street, Maidenhead, Berkshire   *Tel* (0628) 30295
SL6 1LT

Open Mon 10–7; Tue–Thur 10–8.30; Fri–Sat 10–9; Sun 12–2 **Closed** Public
holidays **Credit cards** Access, Diners Club, Visa; personal and business
accounts **Discounts** 5% for 1 case **Delivery** Free in Maidenhead and M4
corridor to West London (min £25 order); otherwise at cost; mail order available
Glass hire Free with order **Tastings and talks** In-store tastings once every three
months; to groups on request **Cellarage** Available (charges subject to quantity)

This wine shop in Maidenhead's Queen Street has the kind of
look about it that sets the wine enthusiast's pulse racing. It is
packed with bottles – if there was some way of displaying wine
on the ceiling, owner David Wright would certainly take
advantage of it – yet everything is neat and well ordered, with
every bottle priced individually, and the various sections clearly
differentiated and flagged. The finest wines are all stored
horizontally in racks, and old claret box-ends are used to add
atmosphere and tone. Free delivery all the way into West
London is more than most of the neighbourhood's shops would
provide. The same is true of a sortie into *en primeur* selling with
the '89 Bordeaux – at prices marginally cheaper than
Bibendum's, to make a comparison, though Bibendum offered a
larger range.

One list is produced each year, but to keep track of new
arrivals (and rapid departures) David Wright now produces a
quarterly newscard. The New World is an area of particular
endeavour (Argentina, Oregon, Washington and Idaho as well
as California, Chile, Australia and New Zealand), but this does
not mean the Old one is ignored, and Burgundy, Germany and
Italy are being further researched at present. Clarets,
champagnes and French country wines are already very good.
Should you grow tired of all these interesting wines, which
seems unlikely, there are plenty of exotic beers, ciders and
spirits, including that mescal with the worm in (£16.80). There
are few more spectacular ways for drinkers to confirm machismo
than by chewing up mescal-pickled agave worms, though
gastronomically the invertebrate is uninteresting.

Best buys

Undurraga Cabernet Sauvignon Reserva 1985, Chile, £4.99
Domaine de Perras 1988, Vin de Pays des Côtes de Gascogne
(white), £3.60
Hunters Sauvignon Blanc 1989, New Zealand, £7.50

H Allen Smith

24–25 Scala Street, London W1P 1LU   *Tel* 071-637 4767
56 Lamb's Conduit Street, London   *Tel* 071-405 3106
WC1N 3LW

Open Mon–Fri 9.30–6.30; Sat 10–1 **Closed** Sun, public holidays
Credit cards Access, Diners Club, American Express, Visa; personal and business
accounts **Discounts** Negotiable **Delivery** Free in central London (min 1 case)
and outer London (min 3 cases); otherwise 1 case £7.50, 2–5 cases £4.50 per case,
6–10 cases £3 per case; mail order available **Glass hire** Free with 1-case order
Tastings and talks Four in-store tastings annually; to groups on request
Cellarage £7.50 per case per year

H Allen Smith has shed another branch this year (the Heath
Street outlet in Hampstead, which passed into the La Réserve
group, *q.v.*). Buyer Finola Ryan tells us that the French listings
are increasing, with an emphasis on 'bin-end fine clarets' and
'quality burgundy' – which will not come cheap. Italy has
always been a reason for making one's way to Scala Street or
Lamb's Conduit Street, especially the Alto Adige wines of
Tiefenbrunner, Aldo Conterno's Barolo and the organic wines of
Castello di San Polo; the South Australian wines of Norman's
are scheduled to arrive here before long, bringing 'more quality
and value to our range', and Coopers Creek from New Zealand
is another addition since the last list.

Iberia seems to have been untouched, with Spanish and
excellent Portuguese selections (including half a dozen wines
from J M da Fonseca Successores) that merit the detour when
you're visiting Dillons, University friends or Bloomsbury
publishers (the parent company is 'Viniberia Ltd', a synonym
for leading Iberian shippers Ehrmanns). You may be tempted by
the sherries of Williams & Humbert – try the superb oloroso/
palo cortado Dos Cortados and the good fino Pando. Could we
ask customers to monitor further changes at H Allen Smith on
our behalf?

Best buys

Marqués de Griñon 1985, Vino de Mesa Tinto de Toledo, £7.85
Château de Putille 1988, Anjou Blanc Sec, £3.50
Coopers Creek Sauvignon Blanc 1989, New Zealand, £6.40

> *It is well to remember that there are five reasons for drinking: the arrival of*
> *a friend; one's present or future thirst; the excellence of the wine; or any*
> *other reason.*
> Latin saying

Amazing Grapes

94 Brent Street, Hendon, London NW4 2ES   *Tel* 081-202 2631

Open Mon–Wed, Fri 9.30–6; Thur 9.30–7; Sun, public holidays 10–2 **Closed** Sat
Credit cards Access, Visa; personal and business accounts **Discounts** 5–10% on 1
case **Delivery** Free in the UK (min 1 case); elsewhere approximately £5.70 per
case; mail order available **Glass hire** Available with charge
Tastings and talks To groups on request **Cellarage** Not available

Neil Isaacson's Amazing Grapes specialises in kosher wines and
spirits. The range is wider than you might think, with Chablis,
Sancerre, Vouvray, Alsace Gewürztraminer and Champagne
among those that join the extensive range from Israel (Gamla,
Golan, Yarden, Carmel and Eliaz). All have been produced
under rabbinical supervision, with Beth Din de Paris,
Strasbourg's Rav Seckbach, Rabbi G M Garelik of Milan and the
Orthodox Rabbinate of Budapest among the kosher guarantors.
The prices quoted below are for wines included in a mixed case,
but sales are also made by the bottle (at, presumably, slightly
higher prices).

Best buys

Carmel Cabernet Sauvignon 1986, Dan region, Israel, £4.45
Yarden Cabernet Sauvignon (White Harvest) 1987 (a blush
wine), Galilee region, Israel, £5.27
Yarden Cabernet Sauvignon 1985, Golan Heights, Israel, £11.94

Les Amis du Vin

(Mail order only)
19 Charlotte Street, London W1P 1HB   *Tel* 071-636 4020
Shops
The Winery, 4 Clifton Road, London W9 1SS   *Tel* 071-286 6475
Les Amis du Vin, 51 Chiltern Street, London   *Tel* 071-487 3419
W1M 1HQ

Open Mon–Fri 10.30–8.30 (W9), 10.30–7 (W1); Sat 10–6.30 (W9), 10.30–5 (W1)
Closed Sun, public holidays **Credit cards** All accepted; personal and business
accounts **Discounts** 5% per bottle, 10% per case and 12% for 10-case orders for
wine club members; 5% per case for non-club members **Delivery** Free on UK
mainland (min 2 cases or £75 order); otherwise £5; mail order available from 19
Charlotte Street **Glass hire** Free with wine purchase
Tastings and talks Monthly tastings through Les Amis du Vin Wine Club; to
groups on request **Cellarage** £4.80 per case per year

There's rather a complicated story behind this merchant's entry,
particularly for anyone who's been mentally or literally away
from the wine scene for three or four years, so let's get the
record straight before we start on the list. Les Amis du Vin now
belongs to Trusthouse Forte, and so does the old-established

Christopher & Co., sometime Royal Warrant holders and 'Wine Merchants since the Great Fire of London (Established 1666)'. The two are now merged, with Les Amis proving to have the dominant genes as far as naming and identity are concerned. Running in tandem with Les Amis/Christopher is Geoffrey Roberts Associates (also THF-owned) specialising, as it has always done, in Britain's leading portfolio of Californian wines (and some good-lookers from Australia, too). Geoffrey Roberts sells on a wholesale basis to the trade, but Les Amis/ Christopher draws, sensibly, on its riches to offer a superb New World, and especially Californian, range. Anyone can buy from Les Amis, either through its mail-order operation (by the case, mixing permitted) or in its two retail shops. However £15 brings you life membership of the Les Amis du Vin Club, which in turn brings you mailings and *en primeur* offers, but more importantly discounts from both the shops and the mail-order list.

And so to the list. It's good; sometimes very good. Very good for California, as already mentioned: Mark West, Joseph Phelps, Dry Creek, Monticello, Edna Valley, Trefethen, Firestone, Iron Horse, Heitz, Vichon, Sanford, Ridge, Schramsberg, Lohr, Mondavi, Clos du Bois, Acacia, Chateau St Jean and others: there's enough there to keep any expatriate San Franciscan happy. Many of the wineries are given succinct and useful margin notes profiling their history and wine-making; prices fall consistently within the £5 to £15 range, which is fair value for money (particularly if you are an expatriate San Franciscan). The Australia and New Zealand selections provide hot competition on the quality front combined with more attractive prices. The list bides a while at Chile on the way back to the Old World, which is mostly French.

Spain and Germany have small sections; Portugal, sadly, does not. Italy is rather larger, thanks to everything Tuscan from Frescobaldi and a few good things from others elsewhere (like d'Angelo's Aglianico del Vulture and Borgogno's antiquarian Barolos). France has both depth and breadth, with a good range of country wines, Willm's fine Alsace offerings, four different Sancerres heading up some good Vouvrays from downriver, and the sort of Burgundy, Bordeaux and champagne range that W1 expects. (The Morey-St Denis vin gris from Dujac sounds intriguing: anyone tried it?) Dow's dominance among the Vintage Ports, and Valdespino's among the sherries, are the penultimate attractions; a range of 50 to 70 half-bottles represents Les Amis' final appeal. Reports would be welcome on all aspects of the services provided.

Best buys

Delegat's Sauvignon Blanc 1989, New Zealand, £5.46

Cabernet Sauvignon 1987, Pewsey Vale (Yalumba), South Australia, £5.95

Calera, Pinot Noir 1987, Jensen Vineyard, San Benito, California, £13.54

John Armit Wines

WINE LIST OF THE YEAR **·1991·**

---

190 Kensington Park Road, London W11 2ES · · · · · · · · · *Tel* 071-727 6846

Case sales only **Open** Mon–Fri 9–5.30 **Closed** Sat, Sun, public holidays **Credit cards** None accepted; personal and business accounts **Discounts** Not available **Delivery** Free for 3+ cases; otherwise £5 per case; mail order available **Glass hire** Not available **Tastings and talks** Tastings held 2–3 times annually; to groups on request **Cellarage** £4 per case (inc insurance)

There must be more than a handful of readers who, in addition to collecting wines, enjoy collecting wine lists. If you are one of them, in no circumstances omit to obtain a copy of John Armit's: it may not have the classicism of Adnams, nor the Bacchanalian enthusiasm of Yapp's, nor the sturdy seriousness of Tanner's, but it licks them all for style and sensuality. Stephen Bartlett's 'Wine Series' paintings, beautifully reproduced at A4 size and in full colour, will make this list impossible to throw away, though you might well like to have them framed and hung all around your dining room. John Armit's own reflectively autobiographical notes, and a tailpiece by Bruce Palling of *The Independent*, are further pleasures.

As a merchant, John Armit's speciality is in helping customers to build wine portfolios, either for drinking or for investment purposes. Sales are by the case, and cases are unmixed, so you'll need to have a couple of hundred pounds to begin shopping here with any seriousness. Bordeaux and Burgundy look mouthwateringly good; if you want to spend £1,000 on wines from these two areas, then this would be one of the many good places to come and do it. *En primeur* offers are made. The large selection of the wines of the Domaine de la Romanée-Conti doubtless provides good investor-appeal. Other areas are small but beautiful, and there is evident enthusiasm and commitment to the Ribera del Duero wines of Alejandro Fernandez (Tinto Pesquera). A sound portfolio (for drinkers, if not for investors) should, though, surely include something from Germany and Italy? Prices are neither low nor high: going to Adnams rather than Armit for your Tinto Pesquera '86 and Hermitage La Chapelle '86 will save you £6.40 on a £325 spend, but Armit undercuts Adnams for a case of Jaboulet's Crozes-Hermitage Domaine de Thalabert '86 by £11.80 at the time of writing.

Best buys

Château St-Georges Côte Pavie 1982 (St-Emilion), (case) £135
Groth Sauvignon Blanc 1989 (Napa Valley), (case) £76
Rully Raborcé 1987, Olivier Leflaive, (case) £79

Arriba Kettle

Mail order

Buckle Street, Honeybourne, Nr Evesham,	*Tel* (0386) 833024
Hereford & Worcester WR11 5QB	(24-hour telephone
	answering service)

Case sales only **Open** 24-hour telephone answering service **Credit cards** None accepted; business accounts **Discounts** From £1.50 on 3 cases to £2.75 on 11+ cases; £1 per case collected **Delivery** Free on UK mainland (min 2 cases) **Glass hire** Free with order in West Midlands and north Cotswolds **Tastings and talks** For mail order customers in November held in Birmingham and north Cotswolds; to groups on request **Cellarage** Not available

The difficulty of selling fine Spanish wines has seen a continued broadening of Arriba Kettle's list during the last year, and the non-Spanish-speaking arrivals include, logically enough, a domain-bottled Muscadet sur lie (Domaine des Genaudières) and a range of New Zealand whites from Babich. Light, pungent whites of this kind complement the list's Spanish strengths, which tend to be red, smooth and oaky. With the wines of over a dozen bodegas to chose from, no Rioja enthusiast should leave Barry Kettle's number undialled.

There are wines from Navarra, Penedés and Valdepeñas, too, though it would be good to see these sections expanded, and perhaps one or two of Spain's other regions explored. It is strange to find a Spanish specialist without anything from the Ribera del Duero, Toro, Rueda, Jumilla, Priorato . . . Architect Barry Kettle should be instinctively aware of the need for proportion and harmony in list-building.

The Mont Marçal cavas, though, are among Spain's best, while the three almacenista sherries, sourced through Lustau, repay attentive drinking. Osborne's Fino Quinta (£5.94) deserves to be better known in this country: it is softer in style than some of its rivals, perhaps due to Puerto rather than Jerez ageing, yet is full and long.

Best buys

Rioja Artadi Tinto 1989 Cosecheros Alavesas, £3.89
Mont Marçal Brut Cava, £6.20
Aniversario 1981 Bodegas Julián Chivite Navarra, £7.83

Asda

Head office
Asda House, South Bank, Great Wilson
Street, Leeds, West Yorkshire LS11 5AD
Approximately 200 branches nationwide

Tel (0532) 435435

Open (Generally) Mon–Sat 9–8; Sun (Scotland only) 9–8 **Closed** Sun (except
Scotland), public holidays (vary from store to store) **Credit cards** Access, Visa
Discounts, Delivery, Glass hire Not available **Tastings and talks** Regular in-store
tastings generally on the standard Asda brand range **Cellarage** Not available

It has been very hard to ignore Asda's wine range in the last
year or two, for the simple reason that it is the most eye-
catching one in Britain. Asda, as part of an effort to improve its
image and presence in the South, entrusted its own-label range
to the design group Lewis Moberly – the same team responsible
for putting Emilio Lustau's Almacenista sherries into their
present, elegantly innovative bottles. The result has been
startling: wine labels that go far beyond anything that any
supermarket or chain has ever dared to do before in originality
and freshness. Each wine is plundered for any possible
symbolic resonance it might have, and this in turn is made
graphic. Some of the results are puzzling (what on earth does
Freud's *Interpretation of Dreams* have to do with British Sherry?);
some fail through being over-designed (the Saint-Véran label is
graphically inspiring, but far too dark and sombre for a white
wine); others, though, are memorably successful. Andrzej
Klimowski's elegant collage for a Blanc de Blancs table wine; the
embossed restraint of the Saint-Emilion label; the elegant grace
of the Beaujolais 'jazz sketch' label; a little square of fierce, vine-
spiked heat at the centre of the Côtes du Roussillon label; or the
terrace-inspired grandeur of the red Douro design: these labels
should be treasured by any collector. The visual 'country code'
at the bottom of each is a clever idea, too.

The wines in the bottles haven't always been up to the
standard of the design, but this is due to the strength of the
latter rather than any significant weakness in the former. Most
importantly, the label refit indicated Asda's desire to be taken
seriously as a wine retailer, and it was no accident that the
range of both own-label wines and fine wines improved
markedly at around the time the new uniforms were introduced.
Buyer Antonia Hadfield (who engineered the changes within
the bottles) has since moved on from Asda, and the team is now
headed by ex-Sainsburys' worker Philip Clive, whose task is
presumably to build on progress to date. The last year has seen
61 Gateway shops come into the Asda fold, bringing the total at
time of writing to 198. Not all of these stores stock wines from

the Fine Wine list; all, though, should stock wines from the main (predominantly own-label) list.

The own-label list is very strong in French country wines, and the fact that there are more white wines than red from the Bordeaux area indicates prevailing British tastes. Two interesting new arrivals are a Chardonnay sourced from the Jura, and Asda's Organic Claret (the beautifully labelled Château Vieux Gorget), which joins Guy Bossard's Organic Muscadet. The buying is less adventurous outside France for this range, but Asda keeps its head respectably above water through Spain and Portugal, with some promising stirrings in Italy, too (try the Ca' Donini Pinot Grigio and the Alto Adige Chardonnay). Sparkling wines are strong here, too, with Asda's exclusive Australian Pinot Noir/Chardonnay Brut 1983 looking remarkably like a gauntlet of some sort.

If you're lucky enough to have an Asda with a Fine Wine section near you, make the most of it: the range and the prices are good. The main difficulty is paying for it, as wines from this section often seem to cause inordinate delays at the checkouts while unpronounceable names are painstakingly matched to product codes by supervisors, the product code being the only way of communicating with the till. There are seven champagnes, including Bollinger, Krug and Dom Pérignon; some good clarets, including 'second wines' from Châteaux Lascombes, Gruaud-Larose, Talbot and Margaux; and an excellent range of dessert wines, including the bargain Cuvée Henri Peyrottes Muscat, Domaine de Coyeux's Muscat de Beaumes de Venise, Château de Berbec from Premières Côtes de Bordeaux, Château Filhot 1985 from Sauternes and Château Monbazillac from Monbazillac, Quady's Essensia from California, Domaine Touchais's 1979 Coteaux du Layon, Lenz Moser's fine Beerenauslese 1984/1988 and Campbells Rutherglen Liqueur Muscat. A most appealing collection, especially as four half-bottles are included. Those who don't yet know Franciacorta should try that from within the Italian section, while both colours of Murrieta Rioja from Spain are worth pursuing. Asda makes an effort to offer fine German wines, with nine at Kabinett to Beerenauslese level, while Australia, America, New Zealand and Chile are mostly populated by old friends of the Rosemount/Mondavi type. For as long as it lasts, Asda brings Cloudy Bay Sauvignon to the people, and Château Musar 1980 is available here at under £5 at the time of writing. Asda's wines are more than just a set of pretty labels.

See page 306 for an explanation of the symbols used in the *Guide*.

Best buys

Cava, Asda, £4.25
Côtes Frontonnais, Asda, £2.99
Organic Claret 1988, Château Vieux Georget, Bordeaux, £3.49

Askham Wines

Office

Askham, via Newark, Nottinghamshire   *Tel* (077 783) 659
NG22 0RP

Case sales only   Open (Customers are advised to make an appointment before
calling) Mon–Fri 9–6; Sat 9–12 **Closed** Sun, public holidays **Credit cards** None
accepted; personal and business accounts **Discounts** 5% on 5+ cases (by
arrangement) **Delivery** Free on mainland UK (min 1 case); mail order available
Glass hire Free with 1-case order **Tastings and talks** To groups on request
Cellarage Not available

Preparatory school headmaster Andrew Brownridge doubles as a
wine merchant, in the main providing businesses, universities
and public authorities with 'articulate, approachable and
realistic' advice about wine, but also providing refreshment for
private buyers 'jaded/mesmerised and otherwise disaffected by
supermarkets'. We have had good reports of the service from
customers.

The list (number 10 – one per year) is short, but attractively
and clearly designed, and the wines are well selected. The notes
are both articulate and approachable. Where quality and price
famously meet, as in the Alsace wines of the Cave Vinicole de
Turckheim, Jaboulet's Thalabert, Beaucastel's Châteauneuf or
Caves São João's Bairrada, then Mr Brownridge will list. But he
also lists on the basis of personal enthusiasm, as is the case
with the four Côtes de Jura wines (which include a 1964 vin
jaune at £16.29), or the brace from Idaho (Rose Creek). There are
good clarets, and the overall balance between fine wine and
inexpensive wine is well drawn, given that the list is not a large
one.

Jaded of Nottinghamshire, dial Askham 659.

Best buys

Château de Belcier 1985, Côtes de Castillon, £4.46
Hautes Côtes de Nuits 1986, Domaine Michel Gros, £8.93
Côtes de Jura Savagnin 1986, Sylvie & Luc Boilley, £5.94

> *Wine is bottled poetry.*
> Robert Louis Stevenson

The Australian Wine Centre

'Down Under', South Australia House,   *Tel* 071-925 0751
50 Strand, London WC2N 5LW   *Tel* 071-839 9021

Open Mon–Fri 10–7; Sat 10–4 **Closed** Sun, public holidays
Credit cards Access, Visa; business accounts **Discounts** 5% on 1 case
Delivery Free on UK mainland (min £75 order); otherwise £3.50 per case; mail
order available **Glass hire** Free with 1-case order **Tastings and talks** Tastings
on the first Thursday of every month; Great Australian Wine Tastings held
annually for members of The Australian Wine Club **Cellarage** Not available

If you've always wondered what happens in the rooms that lie
hidden under London's streets, the sort of places that illuminate
wet winter evenings from beneath the feet of hurrying
pedestrians, through thick pebble glass, then a visit to The
Australian Wine Centre will provide one answer. To get there,
you need to take a small side passage off the south side of the
Strand, go through the door in the wall, and walk down, under.
You'll soon find yourself in a well-lit, spacious room containing
over 300 different Australian wines, and often a handful of
Australians in animated discussion, too.

One of them will probably be the Centre's Director Craig
Smith, more quietly spoken than many of his compatriots, who
came to Britain for six months in 1974 and is still looking for his
missing return ticket. Having founded Putney's Drunken Mouse
in 1983 and watched the small rodent become ever more
intoxicated as Australian wine sales boomed in Britain, he
decided that a central London location would be best for
specialised Australian sales. The Mouse has therefore been
drowned in a butt of Campbells Old Rutherglen Muscat during
the summer – though its name lives on as a company; the
Putney premises, meanwhile, have been Oddbinned. In
addition to offering, on a retail basis, a wide range from big
producers (Penfolds, Seppelts) as well as small (Lake's Folly,
Geoff Merrill), the Centre is also home to The Australian Wine
Club, a service for mail-order customers (though you don't have
to join to order), bringing you newsletters, special offers and the
chance to come to an annual London tasting. Mail order is
basically for mainland Britain, but Australians are well known
for having a go at almost anything and they've managed to get
cases from the Strand to Ghana, with Australian deliveries also
generally no problem. (Presumably the wines are sourced there,
rather than being sent round the world a second time.)

Our only criticism of the Centre so far would be that mail-
order customers might well appreciate a slightly more
informative list. Craig Smith can explain the differences
between 50 or so Chardonnays or Cabernet Sauvignons to
callers, given time, but if you're sitting in your armchair in

deepest Cumbria some printed style indications would be useful. As it is, you'll need to have Jane MacQuitty's *Mitchell Beazley Pocket Guide* with you to begin to make sense of it all. But Australian wine most definitely needs a specialist merchant in Britain, and probably two or three; the Centre under the Strand is a good start.

Best buys

Houghton Supreme Dry White 1988, Western Australia, £4.99
Tyrrells Long Flat Red 1987, New South Wales, £4.79
Cyril Henschke Cabernet Sauvignon 1986, South Australia, £10.99

Averys of Bristol

7 Park Street, Bristol, Avon BS1 5NG   *Tel* (0272) 214141

Open Mon–Fri 9–6; Sat 9–5 **Closed** Sun, public holidays **Credit cards** Access, Visa; personal and business accounts **Discounts** Available **Delivery** Free on UK mainland (min 1 case within 5-mile radius of Bristol, 2 cases elsewhere); otherwise £5.50 for under 2 cases; £5 per case for Isle of Wight, Orkney and Shetland, £12.50 to Northern Ireland and Isle of Man; mail order available **Glass hire** Free with £15+ order (with refundable deposit) **Tastings and talks** Annual tasting in main cellars; regional tastings through Averys Bin Club; to groups on request **Cellarage** £2.50 per case or part-case per year or part year

---

Averys 1990 Wine List is printed on slightly thinner paper than was its 1989 counterpart, but this is still one of the country's weightiest, grandest and most sober. A sense of tradition (the company is gearing up for its 200th anniversary in 1993) comes across strongly from everything that passes through the Averys franking machine, and while this doubtless helps to sell the fine range of clarets and burgundies, it perhaps does less justice to Averys' innovative New World buying, which began a lot earlier than most and continues to offer much of interest.

The list opens with fortified wines, and the chief appeal here is to madeira enthusiasts: this is one of the few places in the country with a real choice of Madeiras, including vintage and old solera wines, nearly all from Cossart Gordon. Excellent; bravo; let's all start saving. Ports are good, too, but Averys is one of those merchants which suddenly comes over all coy about pricing its vintage ports in the main list, even the most recent. What an absurd tradition this is! Why should customers have to make special requests for the price of Gould Campbell 1983, when Averys is perfectly prepared to price its Cossart Gordon Bastardo 1875 (£147.34), its Remoissenet Chambertin-Clos de Bèze 1970 (£35.28) or its magnums of Lafite 1970 (£230.14)? We advise customers to reward this obfuscation by buying vintage ports elsewhere, and we would be interested to hear of any justification for this practice. If there does prove to be a good reason for it, we will let readers know in this space next year.

Clarets are as extensively listed at Averys as one would expect, while the range of burgundies is unusually large, though the majority of these are single-sourced, from Remoissenet, for whom Averys is UK agent. Wines from the rest of France are sound rather than exciting, and when looking through this section you will notice that Averys is a merchant with almost nothing bar table wines (and Niersteiner Gutes Domtal) at under £3.50. Indolence is the only excuse for buying Plaimont's Côtes de Saint-Mont here at £3.41 when almost any supermarket or chain will knock 80p off that price for you. No; come to Averys for finer wines that you can't necessarily get anywhere else, like the madeiras, clarets and burgundies already described; or the smaller producers' Australian wines, Nobilo's New Zealand wines, a wide range from California, and wines from Inniskillin at Niagara (a range of six, including an ice wine, something that Canada might be expected to show a vocation for). The neatly labelled wines of Undurraga, two Cabernets and a Sauvignon Blanc, represent Chile.

Averys' Bin Club is one of the country's leading continuous purchasing schemes: you pay a certain amount each month and your credit is used to furnish you with everyday drinking wines, *en primeur* wines for future drinking, or fine wines for investment – or all three, if you wish. Regional tastings are held for Bin Club members. Averys is also a distinguished fine wine merchant with some of the best stocks of old burgundy in Britain; there is a separate 'Fine Wines and Oddments' list (and, yes, the vintage ports are priced there). Bin End and Special Offer lists are also produced. With a staff that includes two Masters of Wine, five Wine & Spirit Education Trust Full Diplomas, three part Diplomas and 5 Higher Certificate holders, advice should be good in Park Street.

Best buys

Undurraga Cabernet Sauvignon 1987, Chile, £3.71
Nobilo Marlborough Sauvignon Blanc 1989, New Zealand, £6.64
Rouge Homme Chardonnay 1987, South Australia, £10.11

Find the best new wine bargains all year round with our newsletter, *Which? Wine Monthly*, available for just £19 a year from: Dept WG91, Consumers' Association, Freepost, Hertford SG14 1YB – no stamp is needed if posted within the UK. (Price valid until 31.12.90.)

David Baillie Vintners ☞

At the Sign of the Lucky Horseshoe,   *Tel* (0392) 221345
86 Longbrook Street, Exeter, Devon EX4 6AP

Open Tue–Fri 10–7; Mon, Sat 9–6 **Closed** Sun, public holidays
Credit cards Access, Visa; personal and business accounts **Discounts** Available
Delivery Free on UK mainland (min 2 cases); otherwise at cost; mail order
available **Glass hire** Free with order **Tastings and talks** To groups on request
Cellarage £3 per case per year

At the Sign of the Lucky Horseshoe you will find a large range
of wines from most of the world's viticultural regions, Eastern
Europe excepted. In general, the selections are balanced, with no
obvious enthusiasms eclipsing areas that have failed to arouse
proprietorial interest; an exception to this general rule is Spain,
sketched into the list rather hesitantly, and Portugal, where one
bottle of Vinho Verde looks lonely and inadequate representing
its country. 'It is a sad reflection on the wine-appreciating
public that there is still so much lack of adventure to try
pastures new,' lament Kenneth Baillie Christie and David
Sommerfelt, presumably referring to their three Washington
State wineries' offerings, Château Musar from the Lebanon or
the single Chilean wine listed; it would, in fact, be good to see
a little more new pasture from Iberia. Surely someone in Exeter
would be prepared to take a turn with some wonderful old
garrafeira?

Claret obviously goes down a treat in the South-West, and
this is a good address to note if, like us, you are besotted with
1985: there's a selection of nearly 30 to chose from, ranging from
two Côtes de Blayes up to Latour. We should also draw your
attention to stronger-than-usual support for dry white Bordeaux,
an exciting growth area at present (it's the quality rather than
the quantity that's growing). A fine collection of Burgundy
growers meet under the Sign, and you could have great fun
exploring their offerings – if you're in the market for wine at
between £10 and £20 per bottle, which is what the majority of
these cost. Chablis from Lamblin can be explored for less; only
the Grands Crus rise above £10. Growers of modest renown
mingle with celebrities in the Rhône and Loire sections, and
Alsace wines 'from the cellars of the Baron de Hoen in
Beblenheim' (a puzzling circumlocution which the list fails to
clarify) are not widely seen elsewhere. Caution is the
watchword among French country wines, with the tried and
trusted Cuvée Madame Claude Parmentier from Fitou and three
of Jean Cros' Gaillac wines heading the short line-up.

There are around three dozen worthwhile German wines
including one Trocken (sensibly enough from Franken) and
three Halbtrockens, with Friedrich Wilhelm Gymnasium, von

Hövel and Doktors Thanisch and Bürklin-Wolf among the growers. An attempt has been made to reach most parts of Italy, with some good growers and some average ones, depending on the vocation allotted to the wine. Veneto wines come from Bertani, and we would question whether they 'are, almost unquestionably, the best of their region'. Let's just settle for 'good'. Washington State wines outnumber California's, and Australian wines outnumber both – though not by much. The two 1982 Vintage Ports, at £12.75 and £14.07, are worth their price – buy a historic bottle of Churchill's first vintage for this Christmas or next.

Best buys

Montagny 1988, Bernard Michel, £7.05
Hunter's Pinot Noir 1988 (New Zealand), £8.27
Château Pique-Caillou 1985, Graves, £7.78

Balls Brothers

Balls Brothers Wine Centre, 313 Cambridge Heath Road, London E2 9LQ	*Tel* 071-739 6466
The Wine Centre, Wickham & Co, New Road, Bideford, North Devon EX39 2AQ	*Tel* (02374) 73292

Open Mon–Sat 10–6 **Closed** Sun, public holidays **Credit cards** Access, Visa **Discounts** Not available **Delivery** Free on UK mainland (min 2 cases); mail order available **Glass hire** Free with 2-case order **Tastings and talks** Annual tasting in the City for customers; tastings for groups of 20+ by arrangement **Cellarage** Not available

This is one of a number of merchants who, in response to the question 'What do you offer that none of your competitors do?', was unable to furnish us with any reply. Perhaps this was honesty on Richard Balls' part since, bearing in mind that this book is a guide to drinking wine at home, Balls Brothers' main claim to fame is ten City of London wine bars and restaurants. It does have a retail 'Wine Centre' in Bethnal Green, however, and there you can chose from the wines that you might expect roaring brokers to slake their thirsts with: claret, chiefly, with reliable if unexceptional back-up from other parts of France and, more discreetly, Italy and Germany. The rest of the world gets a walk-on part, though there is a deal of Vintage Port there waiting for big winter moments. Those clarets (you'll get a choice of 60 or so) are well selected and reasonably priced, though it's a shame that Balls Brothers are reduced to just one 1982 already. Compare this with the foresight of Gerard Harris or Master Cellar Wine Warehouse. The list, to its credit, is very clearly laid out, and the terms of sale are also expressed with commendable clarity; this is something that Balls Brothers offer that not all of their competitors do. Whether it's a reason for buying there or not is another matter . . .

Best buys

Château de Brondeau 1986, Bordeaux Supérieur, £4.60
Côtes du Rhône, Château du Grand Moulas 1988, £4.15
Saint-Julien non-vintage (wine from young vines at Château Ducru-Beaucaillou), £5.95

Adam Bancroft Associates

Gresham House, 4–7 Great Pulteney Street,   *Tel* 071-434 9919
London W1R 3DF

Case sales only   **Open** Mon–Fri 9.30–6   **Closed** Sat, Sun, public holidays
Credit cards None accepted; personal and business accounts   **Discounts** Not
available   **Delivery** Free within London (min 1 case) and within UK (min 3 cases);
otherwise 2 cases £8.62, 1 case £6.32; mail order available   **Glass hire** Free with
1-case order   **Tastings and talks** Two annual tastings for customers; to groups on
request   **Cellarage** £3.45 per case per year

Master of Wine Adam Bancroft runs a tidy and well-researched list of exclusively French wines. Most of these are, furthermore, exclusive to his list: he finds them, imports them, and sells them to retail customers, restaurants and hotels.

Sales are by the case only, though cases may be mixed, with free London delivery for all orders and free nationwide delivery for orders of more than three cases. List prices are ex-VAT. Customers are invited to two annual tastings, and *en primeur* offers are made from time to time, as they were with 1988 Burgundies.

Burgundy is the biggest strength of the list. Adam Bancroft has looked hard around the less well-known villages such as Marsannay, Comblanchien, Ladoix and Santenay: the result is perhaps 20 different Côte d'Or wines at under £10, with another 10 or so at under £15 – a considerable achievement for 1990. Chablis, the Mâconnais and Beaujolais put up a good supporting act, and the Loire and Champagne provide drinks for the interval. For the rest of France, look elsewhere. This is a merchant for those for whom appellation character is more important than a fashionable grower's name.

Best buys

Sauvignon de Touraine 1989, Alain Marcadet, £3.96
Côte de Nuits-Villages 1987, Daniel Chopin-Groffier, £7.76
Saint-Véran 1988, Domaine des Deux Roches, £6.15

Nigel Baring

20D Ranston Street, London NW1 6SY   *Tel* 071-724 0836

Case sales only **Open** Mon–Fri 9–6 **Closed** Sat, Sun, public holidays
Credit cards None accepted; personal and business accounts **Discounts** 2.5% on
minimum quantity of £5,000 **Delivery** £1 per case in London (min £7), £3 per
case outside London (min £10); free within London (min 5 cases); mail order
available **Glass hire** Not available **Tastings and talks** By invitation to clients; to
groups on request **Cellarage** £5 per case per year

If you are interested in buying Bordeaux *en primeur* – or in
catching up with the *en primeur* vintages of a few years ago that
you missed at the time – then you should get in touch with
Nigel Baring. He is one of the top half-dozen specialists in this
field, and a number of the wines that he offers are cheaper than
any other source, with almost no prices exceeding the general
market level for that vintage. Split payment terms, monthly
payments on a cellar-building scheme, a guaranteed allocation
scheme, and cellarage are some of the facilities available. There
is no shop and no fancy list, which presumably helps to keep
overheads down. Twenty-two years of experience shows
through, however, in the informative mailing sheets and
vintage/market assessments. Bordeaux (Sauternes included) is
very definitely the core of the Baring business, but there are also
expeditions into Burgundy, the Rhône and the Douro valley (for
Vintage Port).

Best buys

Fine Bordeaux and *en primeur* sales in general

Barnes Wine Shop

51 Barnes High Street, London SW13 9LN   *Tel* 081-878 8643

Open Mon–Sat 9.30–8.30; Sun 12–2 **Closed** Public holidays
Credit cards Access, Visa; personal and business accounts **Discounts** 5% on 1
mixed case **Delivery** Free locally (min 2 cases); elsewhere at cost; mail order
available **Glass hire** Free with 1-case order **Tastings and talks** Regular in-store
tasting; Barnes Wine Festival; to groups on request **Cellarage** £6 per case per
year

Ex-policeman Francis Murray's neighbourhood wine shop is
exemplary in almost every respect. Anyone contemplating
opening a shop for themselves would do well to come on a
study visit to Barnes, to look, admire and reflect. The order,
appointment, selection and service all maintain the very highest
standards.

  One of the shop's greatest assets, though, may prove difficult
to replicate elsewhere: the services of consultant James Rogers,

widely considered one of Britain's leading tasters. It is his Baba-like nose and whisker-trimmed palate that ensures the extraordinary exactitude and economy of the shop's range. The list isn't full of heroic failures and valiant mis-hits which might make attractive bin-ends in four years' time; it's full of clever purchases to suit every palate, all impeccably timed to ride on the winds of current interest, to explore the parts that other merchants don't dare fumble for, to entice, intrigue and convince. A top-class 2,000-wine list is not hard to achieve, finance permitting; a top-class 200-wine list, though, requires rare qualities of astuteness and judgment.

The balance between the classical and the new is very well struck. Australia, California, New Zealand, Italy and Burgundy are singled out as areas of strength by Francis Murray, but there isn't much in it, and French country wines, sherry, sweet wines of all sorts and from all over, and six vintages of Musar (including '80 and '78 in magnums, and '61 in halves), also deserve mention. Things change all the time here, which is another big draw; so is the range of half-bottles; so is the clever Barnes Wine Code, which matches up wine styles with food partners at a glance (if your brain is wired up in the correct way). Tastings are organised, *en primeur* offers are made, and discounted periods and sales are featured from time to time. It is a most attractive package, and anyone within bottle-lugging distance of Barnes should make the effort to come and see why there are laurels all over the front door.

Best buys

Les Hauts de Bergelle 1989, Côtes de Saint-Mont, £4.25
Stambolovo Merlot Reserve 1983, Bulgaria, £3.49
Edna Valley, Chardonnay 1988, San Luis Obispo, California, £11.95

Augustus Barnett

Head office
3 The Maltings, Wetmore Road, Burton-on-Trent, Staffordshire DE14 1SE   *Tel* (0283) 512550
Approximately 600 branches nationwide

Open Varies from store to store; most outlets open Mon–Sat 10–10; Sun, public holidays 12–2, 7–9 **Closed** Chr Day **Credit cards** Access, American Express, Visa; personal and business accounts **Discounts** 5% on 1 case **Delivery** Free locally from selected outlets **Glass hire** Free with large orders **Tastings and talks, Cellarage** Not available

---

Augustus Barnett is one of the monsters of the British wine scene, with over 600 branches the length and breadth of the country. Once upon a time, this name was synonymous with a skirmishing, buccaneering approach to wine retailing; more recently, under the ownership of big brewers Bass, it acquired the kind of somnolent off-licence booze-and-fag profile that stuns the wine enthusiast at fifty paces. Evidence of Peter Carr's (MW) three-year stint as Purchasing Manager is visible if you are lucky enough to live near one of the branches that has been designated as a 'wine' shop (as opposed to the two-thirds majority, which are either 'standard', 'local' or 'convenience' shops). We can't say more, as our invitation for Augustus Barnett to communicate something of the company philosophy was ignored; indeed, we have learned this much only by means of a third party. The monster has barely stirred yet. If you are one of the lucky readers with a 'wine' shop near you, you'll find some good French country wines and a memorable selection from northern Italy (try the Valpolicella Classico and Campo Fiorin from Masi, any of the Lageder wines, the Barolo from Fontanafredda, and the Chianti, Brunello and Rosso di Montalcino from Villa Banfi). None of the short Spanish list is likely to disappoint; favour the more expensive Portuguese wines (which are still relatively cheap, and good value for money, especially Periquita and Tinto da Anfora); Australia, New Zealand and Chile are sound, too. The Tokaj Aszú 5 puttonyos is a fine wine at a remarkably low price, and you might like to reward Augustus's temerity by trying one of the Israeli, Lebanese or Greek wines. In-store promotions can save you money from time to time, but tasting before you buy is still a light year or two away.

Best buys

Côtes de la Malpère VDQS, no vintage or producer specified, (red), £2.59
Vin de Pays des Côtes de Gascogne 1989, Colombard, Les Producteurs Plaimont (white), £2.89
Kouros Patras, 1987, Greece (white), £3.35

In writing the entries for merchants included in the *Guide*, the Editor relies on readers' reports, particularly when it comes to the awarding of service symbols. We are concerned that good service may not always be adequately recompensed at present, so please write and let us know whenever you feel you have received particularly good service (or, of course, if you feel the service you have received has been inadequate in any way). Use the forms at the back of the book, or write on a separate sheet of paper if you prefer. Our Freepost facility means that no stamp is required.

Barwell & Jones

Head office
24 Fore Street, Ipswich, Suffolk IP4 1JU   *Tel* (0473) 232322
Off-licences
118 Sprowston Road, Norwich, Norfolk   *Tel* (0603) 484966
NR3 4QH
70 Trumpington Street, Cambridge,   *Tel* (0223) 354431
Cambridgeshire CB2 1RJ
3 Redenhall Road, Harleston, Norfolk   *Tel* (0379) 852243
IP20 9EN
The Cross Inn, 2 Church Street, Woodbridge,   *Tel* (03943) 3288
Suffolk IP12 1DH
94 Rushmere Road, Ipswich, Suffolk   *Tel* (0473) 727426
IP4 4JLA

Open Hours vary from branch to branch   **Credit cards** Access, Visa; personal and
business accounts   **Discounts** Quantity discounts available   **Delivery** Free
locally; elsewhere charges negotiable; mail order available   **Glass hire** Free with
case order   **Tastings and talks** To groups on request by arrangement with
individual managers   **Cellarage** Not available

Nearly all of Barwell & Jones' sales are to other traders; the list
is resolutely wholesale, with a minimum order of five cases, and
prices only quoted for unmixed cases on an ex-VAT basis. This
would normally make an entry in the *Guide* inappropriate; but
Barwell & Jones do have a small group of retail shops in East
Anglia, drawing on the range offered to the trade. They would
be worth visiting for a sound claret range, the Alsace wines of
Pierre Sparr, the Côtes du Roussillons of Domaine Sarda-Malet,
the Bunan Cabernet Sauvignon Vin de Pays de Mont Caume,
Guerrieri-Rizzardi's organic range from the Veneto (olive oil
included), Burmester's underrated and rarely seen ports, and
Osborne's fine sherries. If you are a Barwell & Jones customer,
we would very much like to hear your impressions of their shop
or shops, and the service and range you are offered there.

Best buys

Bardolino Classico Superiore 1988, Guerrieri-Rizzardi, £4.19
Fino Quinta, Osborne, £5
Montecillo Viña Monty Gran Reserva Rioja 1981, £6.78

Wine in bag-in-box ages and spoils quicker than in bottle. If you buy
boxes, buy and drink up one box before you buy the next. Boxes in
the storecupboard will lose their freshness. Used or unopened, a wine
box will keep better if you store it tap downwards, keeping wine, not
air, in the valve.

The Battersea Wine Company ☞

4 Battersea Rise, London SW11 1ED   *Tel* 081-924 3631

Open Mon 5–9; Tue–Fri 12–9; Sat 10.30–9; Sun 12–3 **Closed** Public holidays
Credit cards Access, Visa; personal and business accounts **Discounts** Up to 10%
on 1 case (may be mixed) **Delivery** Free in Battersea, Clapham, Fulham, Chelsea
and City; elsewhere charges negotiable **Glass hire** Free with 1-case order
Tastings and talks Theme tastings every 1–2 months; 10 week basic wine
appreciation course; to groups on request **Cellarage** Not available

After 32 years in the wine trade, including a spell as cellar
manager for The Wine Society, Michael Gould has chosen
Battersea as the setting for a retail operation with free local
delivery, on the same day if necessary. 'Local' seems to be
defined psychologically rather than geographically, as the City
qualifies – along with Battersea, Clapham, Fulham and Chelsea.
    The list is full of the wisdom of the years, not in terms of
long-winded comment (there is none of any degree of
windedness, though advice is freely available in the shop), but
in the producers' names that appear on it, and in the sense of
balance between different sections. The main emphasis is on
France and its classic wines, but every other country where top
quality wines are produced is represented by something sound
and sage. Germany, however, is pared to the bone, with just six
bottles and three producers. The 'wholesome quality, clean ripe
fruit and lovely balance' of Chilean wines have won them, by
contrast, a particularly lengthy listing here, and you should
certainly pay Mr Gould a visit if these sentiments strike a chord
with you. Dry sherries, claret and burgundy provide other
reasons for dropping by. If you're in Battersea on a budget, be
warned that there's little under £4 here.

Best buys

Viña Carmen Gran Reserva Cabernet Sauvignon 1987, Chile,
£7.30
Château Saint-Jacques 1985, Bordeaux Supérieur, £6.50
Gamay d'Auvergne 1987, Coteaux d'Auvergne, La Cave des
Coteaux, £3.75

Thomas Baty & Sons

See Willoughbys.

Cellarage is generally provided at the rates quoted only when the
wines have been bought from the merchant concerned.

Belfast Wine Co

130 Stranmillis Road, Belfast BT9 5DT *Tel* (0232) 381 760

Open Mon–Sat 9.30–9 **Closed** Sun, public holidays **Credit cards** Access, Visa;
personal and business accounts **Discounts** Available **Delivery** Free in Greater
Belfast; mail order available **Glass hire** Free with 1-case order
Tastings and talks Tastings approximately every 3 weeks by invitation; to groups
on request **Cellarage** £5 per case per year

The Belfast Wine Company stocks a medium-sized range of
wines, interesting and unusual, and the one report we have had
suggests that service is enthusiastic and helpful. Could other
Belfast readers help colour the picture?

The list is ex-VAT and quotes only the case price, while for
retail customers a 'wine bulletin' is produced from time to time.
Even if you are a retail customer, it is worth asking for a copy of
the list as it contains a lot of producer information, tasting
indications and food suggestions, and only occasionally goes
over the top. '"Royal, Imperial, and Pontifical" (Frédéric Mistral)
We will never praise enough this "Black Prince" or "Prince of
Blood", which concentrates every possible quality of a great red
wine. A purple to garnet red colour shifting towards an intense
body, fleshy and with a strong structure – could one ask for
more?' Possibly not, especially at under £9. It's not Latour; it's
not Chambertin; it's Comte De Lauze's Châteauneuf-du-Pape.
In addition to this and six other Rhônes you'll find a substratum
of claret here, with some good French country wines; and a
satisfactory contribution from Spain, including six different
wines from Masía Bach. Château Tahbilk and Plantagenet from
Australia are worth pursuing and these have been joined of late
by three wines from Leo Buring in South Australia; there are
also some Italian over-achievers, though strangely enough the
emphasis seems to be on whites rather than the generally more
successful reds. We hear there is a 'knowledgeable' French
manager in charge called Gilles Crozet, while the owner's son,
memorably named Jazz Mooney, is also 'actively involved'.
More reports please.

Best buys

Spanna 1985, Dessilani (red), £3.99
Rueda 1988, Castillo la Vieja (white), £4.25
Château du Coureau 1986, Graves (red), £5.65

> *Wine gives courage and makes men apt for passion.*
> Ovid

Benson Fine Wines

96 Ramsden Road, London SW12 8QZ *Tel* 081-673 4439

Open Mon–Fri 10–5 **Closed** Sat, Sun, public holidays **Credit cards** None accepted; personal and business accounts **Discounts** Not available **Delivery** Free in London; elsewhere at cost; mail order available **Glass hire** Not available **Tastings and talks** To groups on request; Wine & Dine Society **Cellarage** Not available

Clare Benson's Fine Wine business has one of the smaller lists of its type; as usual, the emphasis is on Burgundy and Bordeaux. Most have been tasted, and notes are supplied, though these are of little descriptive use: 'Quite amazing', 'Stunning', 'Fantastic', 'Exceptional', 'Magnificent' and 'Superb' leave us, frankly, none the wiser about the character of the wines. The list also includes 'obscure' items, like the circa 1920 Jerez Especial Para Enfermos ('especially for the Infirm'), and a number of collectors' corkscrews.

Best buys

Terrantez 1792, Madeira, £345
Moulin Touchais 1947, Loire, £51.75
Chambertin 1923, Deshayes (French bottled), £46

Bentalls of Kingston

Wood Street, Kingston upon Thames, Surrey *Tel* 081-546 1001
KT1 1TX

Open Mon, Wed–Fri 9–5.30; Tue 9.30–6; Sat 9–6 **Closed** Sun, public holidays (except Good Friday and 1 Jan) **Credit cards** Access, Bentalls Privilege Chargecard, American Express, Visa; personal and business accounts **Discounts** 5% on 1 case **Delivery** Free within 10-mile radius of Kingston (min £10 order); elsewhere at cost; mail order available **Glass hire** Free **Tastings and talks** Bentalls Wine Fair in May and November; in-store tastings every Saturday; specialist tastings every last Saturday in the month; to groups on request **Cellarage** Not available

At around the time that these words are being processed, the Wine Department within Bentalls of Kingston is moving to a new area which will provide space for an extra 80 or so wines, so what is already a worthwhile and well-chosen list looks set to expand further during the coming twelve months. In addition to in-store tastings every Saturday and specialist tastings on the last Saturday of every month, Bentalls hold a bi-annual Wine Fair when approximately 100 wines go on show – that's pretty energetic for a local department store, and well worth taking advantage of.

Buyer Andrew Willy has obviously not forgotten the lessons of his six years with Oddbins, for the list is full of the exciting and the undervalued. The wide range of Tokaj and seven sherries from Valdespino certainly qualify on both grounds, while the sumptuous champagnes and classed-growth clarets simply excite. Bentalls hosts 'The Yapp Selection', which brings the wines of Thouarsais and Bellet to the lower reaches of the Thames, as well as better-known names like Hermitage/Chave or Sancerre/Vatan. The wines from the Jura, Savoie, Switzerland and Luxembourg reveal an unfettered purchasing palate, and the Portuguese section is excellent – as always, when merchants actually bother to research what this greatly undervalued country has to offer. Australia and New Zealand, Spain, Italy, Germany (what do we have to do to get merchants to list German producers' names as well as all the other information?) and Burgundy are all well chosen, and the Loire, combining Willy and Yapp, is first-rate.

At present, given the constraints of available space, this is a medium-depth list that we feel it would be hard to better. Prices aren't rock bottom, but there is plenty of value to be had by exploring the more unusual options. Kingstonians have every reason for buying their wines at Bentalls.

Best buys

Fitou 1986, Terre Natale, £3.79
Redondo Garrafeira 1982, Alentejo (Portugal), £5.99
Don Gonzalo, Valdespino, Old Dry Oloroso Sherry, £6.99

Berkmann Wine Cellars

See Le Nez Rouge.

Berry Bros & Rudd

3 St James's Street, London SW1A 1EG	*Tel* 071-839 9033
	Tel (answering machine 071-930 1888)
The Wine Shop, Houndmills, Basingstoke, Hampshire RG21 2YB	*Tel* (0256) 23566

Open Mon–Fri 9.30–5 (London), 9–5 (Basingstoke); Sat 9–1 (Basingstoke)
Closed Sat (London – except in December), Sun, public holidays
Credit cards Access, Diners Club, Visa; personal and business accounts
Discounts 3% on 2 cases minimum, 5% on 5–9 cases; 7.5% on 10+ cases
Delivery Free on UK mainland (min 1 case); £1.25 per case for Northern Ireland; charges for Scottish islands, Isle of Man and overseas at available on request; mail order available **Glass hire** Hire charge of £1.15 per dozen together with wine order **Tastings and talks** Tastings in June and November for account customers at the Basingstoke cellars; tastings held in-store for customers on request or by invitation; tastings held for City and West End customers, also other tastings held around the country by invitation **Cellarage** £3.73 per case per year

Berry Bros & Rudd's St James's shop is probably not yet one of London's leading tourist attractions, but it should be. The shop front itself is unmistakeable: it appears to have been daubed with black sealing wax about a century ago, and this wax has slowly melted on hot summer days ever since without ever quite sliding off onto the pavement. Step inside, and you will find yourself in a bare-floored room containing two desks (one high), a table scattered with books and decanters, a sideboard filled with old bottles, and most noticeably a huge pair of scales with weights in one side and a chair in the other. These were originally for tea and coffee (Berry's also traded in such things), but they have mostly been used for weighing important personages such as the portly Georgians whose portraits line the walls; this was a kind of community service for the beau monde in the age before bathroom scales. The weights were entered in leather-bound 'weighing books', which you may examine during your visit (the last time we were there we managed to find a general who weighed under nine stones). The whole room slopes downwards towards the scales, as if the floorboards had given up the unequal struggle to support all the distinguished bottoms that have lowered themselves onto the stool.

But it is, though you may be forgiven for having forgotten the fact, a wine merchant. You will be politely asked what you would like, and here you have two options. You can either discuss some requirement or other – a good red wine under £10 for drinking tonight, for example, or a fine Auslese for next Sunday afternoon on the lawn – or you can sit awhile and browse through the enchanting little list while you settle on your choice. Once your mind is made up, you convey your instruction to the suited assistant, who will walk down through the hole in the floor to the cellar to prepare your order. You, meanwhile, sit quietly, watching people arrive and leave through hinged panels in the walls, and listening to the slow ticking of the clock (which disappointingly tells the correct time). The heavy-goods vehicles roaring by outside are the only reminder of the twentieth century.

That's the 'Berry experience', as it might be called if it took place in some museum or other, and everyone should savour it at least once in a wine-buying life. The list provides plenty of choice, especially from the classic regions, and whatever your appearance you will be treated politely and courteously. But don't expect to be able to browse through shelf on shelf of bottles, don't expect the lowest prices, and don't go there in a hurry. In exchange for the relinquishment of these things, you may enjoy a breath of fresh history.

For the record, we should note Berry Bros' Bordeaux *en primeur* offers (not cheap, but only the crumbling of the social order would threaten eventual delivery of the wine), a programme of special offers and customer tastings, and an excellent delivery service.

Best buys

Domaine de Tholomies 1986, Minervois, £3.78
Château Sainte-Michelle Fumé Blanc 1985, Washington State, £5.65
Château Léoville-Barton 1983, Saint-Julien, £16.95

B H Wines

Boustead Hill House, Boustead Hill, Burgh-by-Sands, Carlisle, Cumbria CA5 6AA   *Tel* (0228 76) 711

Case sales only   Open 'All reasonable hours', but advisable to phone before calling   **Credit cards** None accepted   **Discounts** Not available   **Delivery** Free within Carlisle/North Cumbria area (min 1 case) and outside this area for larger orders; otherwise by negotiation   **Glass hire** Free with 1-case order
Tastings and talks Free tastings twice yearly; participate in 'Wine at the Sands' – Carlisle's wine tasting society; weekly evening classes at Newcastle-upon-Tyne University and in Cumbria; to groups on request   **Cellarage** Not available

B H Wines claims to be Britain's remotest wine merchant: it is sited in a lovely Georgian house on the most north-westerly road in England, facing Scotland across the Solway Firth. Croquet-playing customers are welcome to a breezy game on the lawn, after which you can descend to the stone cellars (below sea level, as it happens), look at the massed banks of bottles in terracotta pipes, make your selection, and drink a toast to the first editor of this *Guide*, Jancis Robinson, whose home village this is. Mail-order facilities are available if the remoteness defeats you.

The selection is a cosmopolitan one, Richard and Linda Neville aiming for between one and five examples of the best of what each wine-producing region or country can offer. It is not a huge range, but it is so well balanced that it would be misleading to select special areas of strength or weakness. The notes reveal that Boustead Hill House is not so remote as to prevent the wine media reaching it, for there is barely a wine not garlanded with some magazine accolade, commendation, medal, award or selection (though it should be noted in passing that *Which? Wine Guide* does not permit wine merchants to use its name for advertising purposes). The list has been compiled with obvious enthusiasm; prices are as low as one could reasonably expect on the edge of the Solway Firth; the business is open at 'all reasonable hours'; an emergency delivery service is provided; there are free tastings and a wine society . . . The Nevilles appear to serve their customers well.

Best buys

Château Peyros 1983, Madiran, £4.49
Tramini 1979, Badacsonyi region (Hungary), £2.99
San Leonardo 1983, Guerrieri Gonzago (Trentino), £10.29

Bibendum

113 Regent's Park Road, London NW1 8UR   *Tel* 071-722 5577

Case sales only   **Open** Mon–Sat 10–8   **Closed** Sun, public holidays
Credit cards Access, American Express, Visa; personal and business accounts
Discounts Negotiable   **Delivery** Free within London postal districts (min 1 mixed case) and elsewhere (min 5 cases); elsewhere £4.95 per consignment; mail order available   **Glass hire** Free with 1 mixed case order   **Tastings and talks** In-depth tasting held in tasting room by invitation approximately 6 times a year; monthly special featured areas; to groups on request   **Cellarage** £4.82 per case per year (inc insurance)

On a previous page you will find the entry for Berry Bros & Rudd: a merchant of religiously guarded tradition, into its third century of trading. In summer 1990, Bibendum was precisely eight years old, yet in that short time it has succeeded in making itself – like Berrys, though in a very different way – something of a benchmark for wine trading in Britain's capital city. What's the attraction?

It would be tempting to suggest that, matching Berry Bros' irresistible fogey-appeal, Bibendum has all the attributes a yuppie yearns for in his or her wine merchant: it is smart, fast and talked-about. Smart it certainly is, with elegance and clarity characterising the half-warehouse, half-town-house headquarters at Primrose Hill, as well as the first-rate list; any merchant wishing to improve the appearance and the informativeness of his/her own list would do well to study Bibendum's as a model of the genre. Smart, too, was the Fulham Road outlet beneath the Conran Shop in Michelin House, though it is there no longer – a shame, as it means the opportunity to buy single bottles from Bibendum has gone, Regent's Park Road being 12-bottle sales or more only.

Fast? Well, you don't get much faster than a free same day delivery service (where required) within London postal districts; and it is typical of Bibendum that, while it is by no means the only merchant offering free London delivery, it is almost the only one who succeeds in communicating the message and making it the prime draw that it should be. Simon Farr has always been pretty fast, too, at sniffing out and stocking the new classics: Bibendum can certainly claim to have ridden the Rhône wave from the surf side, and the list is full of exciting things from Oregon, Portugal, California, Australia and Italy, as well as sound Bordeaux, Burgundy and German wines.

Talked-about, finally. There are really only two reasons why anyone should talk about their wine merchant in enthusiastic terms to anyone else: the first is sound buying across the range, and the second is an excellent service. Bibendum has managed to achieve both over the last eight years, and of course it has won the company friends and customers who couldn't remotely be described as yuppies. These are the classic wine-mercantile virtues, universally appreciated.

We should also add that there is completeness in what Bibendum offers: it is a leading *en primeur* player, particularly for fine Rhône wines but also for Burgundy, Bordeaux and almost anything else en primeurable. Make sure you ask for a copy of the Fine Wine Supplement to the main list; this isn't a roster of tottering octogenarian Chambertin, but a list of fine wines in early maturity or immaturity, including the last two or three *en primeur* vintages (at present market prices) for those who missed the boat when originally launched. Very handy, that: these wines tend to disappear from other merchants' lists between the *en primeur* moment and the moment when they surface at around six or seven years old, costing £20 each. There is always a good selection of sample bottles open at Regent's Park Road, and large and enthusiastically attended customer tastings are organised. Cellar planning, cellar valuations and a buying and selling service for customers are available. Bibendum doesn't compete hard on price; we'd say it was softly competitive. And by intelligent use of the *en primeur* offers you can end up with fine wine bargains. There is little reason for London wine enthusiasts not to have Bibendum's list and phone number to hand.

Best buys

Domaine de Valescure 1987, Vin de Pays du Gard (red and white), £3.15
Alsace Sylvaner 1988, Rolly Gassmann, £5.42
Clos du Clocher 1987, Pomerol, £10.55

Most wine merchants will hire out glasses free of charge, provided they are collected and returned clean, and that you are buying enough wine to fill them! In most cases, it's first come, first served, so get your order in early to ensure supply.

Bin Ends

Toone House & Cellars, 83–85 Badsley Moor Lane, Rotherham, South Yorkshire S65 2PH	*Tel* (0709) 367771
Associated outlet (By the case only) Patrick Toone Personal Wine Merchant, Pavilion House, Oswaldkirk, York, North Yorkshire YO6 5XZ	*Tel* (04393) 504

Open (Bin Ends) Mon–Fri 9.30–5.30; Sat 9.30–12.30 **Closed** Sun, public holidays **Credit cards** Access, Visa; personal and business accounts **Discounts** 5% on 1 unmixed case, 7.5% on 3+ mixed cases (for still wines only) **Delivery** Free in Derbyshire, Lincolnshire and Yorkshire (min 1 case); otherwise at cost **Glass hire** Free with 1-case order **Tastings and talks** Various tastings held thoughout the year; to groups on request **Cellarage** £3 per case per year

An engaging mural of two jolly cellar workers apparently stealing wine from the *patron*'s casks at midnight brightens the exterior of Bin Ends, while inside, the medium-sized range of mainly fine wines is attractively displayed.

The citizens of Rotherham appear to have conservative tastes, if this list mirrors them accurately, for Bordeaux, Burgundy, Sherry, Port and Madeira are the areas of evident strength. The Bordeaux selection is soundly chosen, so price should be your chief guide there; in Burgundy, follow Faiveley; while Garvey and Barbadillo provide a range of sherries in which paying a little more money brings a lot more intensity. Ports from Fonseca and Kopke provide an instructive contrast with each other: the former are built in the thunderously deep British style, while the latter show how well Portuguese elegance and delicacy can work (though Kopke's LBV 1981 seems bizarrely overpriced at £12.95 – a few lines below you will find Quarles Harris's vintage 1980 for only a pound more, and Kopke's own fine 1977 colheita actually costs less – £9.95). Basic Madeiras come from Blandy – try the Verdelho (£6.95); while Henriques & Henriques Reserva Sercial may, if the list description is accurate, be worth every penny of the £22 asked for it. See if you can get a taste first; bottles of Madeira can stay opened without deterioration for some time, so there is no reason why this should not be possible.

Other areas contain wines of interest, particularly the flurry of appealing Chileans and the antique Barolo from Borgogno (price on application). The champagne selection has been much improved during the last year. Pride is taken in providing a personal service and one reader has written telling us of how a faulty bottle was immediately and unquestioningly replaced, which suggests the integrity that we look for in preparing the *Guide*.

Best buys

Château de Terrefort Quancard 1985, Bordeaux Supérieur, £6.50
Sancerre Clos de Chêne Marchand 1988, Sylvain Bailly, £7.35
Nuits-Saint-Georges Premier Cru Clos de la Maréchale 1983,
Faiveley, £17.95

Binocular Wine

Not a shop
28 Catterick Road, Didsbury, Manchester   *Tel* 061-434 2465
M20 0HJ

Case sales only   **Open** Telephone orders only (during holidays an answering
machine is provided – all calls are returned to confirm orders)   **Credit cards** None
accepted   **Discounts** Possible   **Delivery** Free within 10-mile radius of Didsbury
and in Greater Manchester (min 1 case) and elsewhere (min 10 cases); otherwise
£1.80 per case; Scotland, Northern Ireland and Cornwall subject to quotations
Glass hire Free with 1-case order   **Tastings and talks** Approximately monthly
tastings held in the local Fine Arts Gallery; to groups on request   **Cellarage** £2.20
per case per year

Stan Gallon's Binocular Wine 'started as a result of many years'
long-distance lorry driving'. You won't find a lot of British wine
merchants able to claim that. The company letterhead shows
some stylish Egyptian pyramids – a lorry driver's mirage,
presumably, for you can rest assured that there are no Egyptian
wines on the list. 'The wines are mainly from a s-t-r-e-t-c-h-e-d
Burgundy,' says Stan, 'encompassing the area between the south
Rhône and Chablis.' And the Binocular bit – we're guessing
here – perhaps refers to Stan's working relationship with Jean-
Pierre Renard, a wine writer and teacher living in Echevronne
in the Hautes Côtes de Beaune.

The range of wines is small, and much as Stan describes it –
stretched of late all the way over to Muscadet, too. We would
say that this is a good phone number to dial if you want to put
together a case of inexpensive burgundies (most are under or
around £10) with one or two bottles from elsewhere, and you'd
like to discuss your purchases with a friendly enthusiast who
knows most of the growers and all the wines well. Try not to
phone during Old Trafford Test Matches, though, or you might
end up with the answering machine.

Best buys

Givry 'Sous La Roche' 1987, Sarrazin, £6.27
Chablis 1988, Michel Barat, £7.50
Fixin Premier Cru Clos de la Perrière 1986, Philippe Joliet,
£13.38

Blayneys Wine Merchants

Head office
Riverside Road, Southwick, Sunderland,   *Tel* 091-548 4488
Tyne & Wear SR5 3JW
224 branches and 5 Blayney Extra Stores in the North

Open Generally Mon–Sat 10–10; Sun, public holidays 12–2, 7–9.30 **Closed** Chr
Day **Credit cards** Access, American Express, Visa; personal and business
accounts **Discounts** 5% on 1 case **Delivery** Free from selected branches by
arrangement (min 1 case) **Glass hire** Free with wine order
Tastings and talks Occasional in-store tastings; to groups on request
Cellarage Not available

Blayneys, based in Sunderland, has a large number of shops
scattered across northern England. As usual with large chains,
the range carried will vary considerably depending on how
Blayneys view the potential wine demand in any given area.
The full list, though, does seem to lack excitement, so residents
of even the most favoured areas may need to top up once in a
while from other retailers.

There is no printed list for customers to refer to, just a
computer print-out. Computers up and down the country seem
to hate printing more than one line of information, so when you
let them loose on wine lists the usual result is a dearth of
producers' names; they will also ruthlessly chop off any other
information that takes them beyond the requisite number of
characters. The Blayney computer is no exception to this rule.
Even without producers' names, we can see that the French and
Bulgarian sections are more-or-less adequate (if everything
listed was stocked), but the ranges from other countries look to
be of doubtful interest. Germany, in addition to the usual Blue
Nuns and Black Towers, offers a Dry Fisherman, Father Rhine
and The Bishop of Riesling; we catch sight of a Wehlener
Sonnenuhr Kabinett '87 or a Graacher Himmelreich Something
'86, but we have no idea whose. In Italy the Negarine
Valpolicella would be worth trying, especially if it's the Classico,
and the Montepulciano d'Abruzzo is usually good, though again
there is no hint as to who has put this one together. The
Australian and Californian selections are sensationally
unimaginative, considering what is now available, though all
the wines stocked are sound and good value for money.

What do you think of the range and service offered by your
Blayneys? Write and tell us.

Best buys

Viña Albali Reserva 1984, Valdepeñas, £2.99
Domaine de Grandchamp 1988, Bergerac, £4.09
Château de Beaucastel 1985, Châteauneuf-du-Pape, £9.09

Booths

Head office
4–6 Fishergate, Preston, Lancashire PR1 3LJ   *Tel* (0772) 51701
20 branches in Cumbria and Lancashire

Open Mon–Sat 9–5 **Closed** Sun, public holidays **Credit cards** Access, Visa
Discounts Not available **Delivery** Free on UK mainland (min 5 cases); mail order
available **Glass hire** Free **Tastings and talks** Occasional in-store tastings; to
groups on request (maximum 50 people) **Cellarage** Not available

Booths proves that South-East England doesn't have a monopoly
on the good things in life. 'High Class Supermarkets, Tea and
Coffee Blenders, Wine and Spirit Merchants' is how these
northern grocers describe themselves, and their ample list of
wines certainly qualifies the final third of the self-portrait. As
with all supermarkets and chains, not every wine is stocked by
every branch, so if you read about a bottle that you'd like to try
but that your local branch doesn't stock, be persistent in finding
someone who will order it for you, or phone the head office and
ask for the wine to be sent to your shop. And, as always, let us
know how easy or difficult this process is.

There is an awful lot of good claret secreted away somewhere
near Preston – and it's not just youngsters, either. Gruaud
Larose 1961 would make a lovely 30th birthday treat for
someone, while other Booth-favoured châteaux include
Cantemerle ('78 and '85), de Fieuzal ('81, '84 and '85),
Hanteillan ('85 and '86), Lynch-Bages ('79, '81 and '84),
Montrose ('70, '78 and '86), Prieuré Lichine ('75, '82, '83, '84
and '85), Palmer ('70 and '87) . . . well, you get the idea. The
list goes on and on. Burgundy isn't quite so impressive, but
there are still plenty of appellations and producers to choose
from. Guigal, Chapoutier and Château de Beaucastel make the
Rhône sparkle, while Loire and Alsace wines, and those from
the South of France, impress by their quality rather than by
their number.

Italy has been the subject of some adventurous buying, with
Jermann's Vintage Tunina, Barolo from one of the Conterno
brothers (the computer can't tell us which), and Pieropan's
Recioto di Soave all surely raising eyebrows, and spirits, in
Kendal. There's less of a sense of adventure with Germany,
Spain and California, but some good wines are on offer
nevertheless. Try the Viña Marcos from Chivite in Navarra, and
the Marius Reserva from the little-known Almansa DO: at £2.99
each, both are very good value. Australia and New Zealand
receive enthusiastic endorsement from Edwin Booth, wine
buyer and a member of the founding family's fifth generation,
though we are surprised to see only one straight Sauvignon
Blanc among an NZ range of 12 wines. You won't come across

Wagner's New York State Seyval Blanc often, wherever you live in Britain, and a fine selection of port brings Booths' offering to a classic close. This is a range that would really reward close inspection. Prices for the finer wines are always realistic and often very attractive, while the cheaper wines match up to better-known supermarket price standards without any difficulty at all. We have heard good reports of the service in at least one branch, and would like to hear more.

Best buys

Château de Malle 1986, Sauternes, £7.99
Marius Reserva Tinto 1982, Almansa, £2.99
Château de Fieuzal 1981, Graves, £10.79

Bordeaux Direct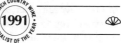

Mail order
New Aquitaine House, Paddock Road,   *Tel* (0734) 481718
Reading, Berkshire RG4 0JY   (enquiries)
     Tel (0734) 471144 (orders)
6 Bordeaux Direct shops in or near Reading, Ashtead, Woking, Beaconsfield, Windsor and Bushey

Open 7 days a week (answering service outside office hours); Shops: Mon–Fri 9–5.30 (Reading); Mon–Wed, Fri 10.30–7, Thur 10.30–8; Sat 9–6
Credit cards Access, Diners Club, American Express, Visa; business accounts
Discounts Available   **Delivery** Free nationally excluding Channel Islands (min £50 order); mail order available   **Glass hire** Free with 1-case order
Tastings and talks Regular tastings in shops; to groups on request   **Cellarage** Not available

---

The rather sober-sounding parent company Direct Wines (Windsor) Ltd has produced three offspring down the years: Bordeaux Direct is the eldest, the Sunday Times Wine Club (*q.v.*) is the middle child, while the infant of the family is the Wine Options continuous buying scheme, run in conjunction with Barclaycard. Taken together, these three make up one of Britain's most important merchant groups, with an annual turnover of around £5 million.

Of the three, Bordeaux Direct is the most innovative and exciting. Most of its sales are by mail order, though there are also six Bordeaux Direct shops and a very small trade sales department. Mail-order customers have the option, if they wish, to take part in a continuous buying scheme called Four Seasons (which brings you an unmixed case every quarter), as well as a 'club-class service' called Première. For an annual fee of £12.50 and the commitment to buy at least two cases per year you are offered 'up to twelve' free tasting bottles every twelve months. If you know you enjoy Bordeaux Direct's wines, that sounds like a very good deal – though we would invite customers to write and tell us how well the system works.

Bordeaux Direct is also the operation that most closely reflects founder Tony Laithwaite's unconventional aims and style as a merchant. He aims to scour any wine-producing zone that other merchants have ignored to find the kind of fruity, appealing and supple wines that he has always sold, wines of impact and character, and this aim is combined – of late – with an innovative approach to sourcing that involves either making the wines yourself or interfering as much as is permitted in their production. The style, meanwhile, is that of a natural direct marketeer, someone who manages to make every mailing (and there are plenty of them) sound like a personal tape-recording from an irrepressible enthusiast. The company receives little media coverage, partly because it has never sought it, and partly because, being a predominantly mail-order operation selling wines that are almost all exclusives, its range is about as low-profile to non-customers as it is possible to be. It would be good to see Bordeaux Direct begin to communicate with the communicators as well as it communicates with its customers.

For the fact is that much of what Bordeaux Direct does is highly newsworthy. Laithwaite's 'Great Wine Trek' of several years ago (a world wine tour by mixed case) fell into that class, and so does the 'Flying Winemakers' initiative that at present helps fill mailing envelopes with exclamation marks and mixed cases with exciting wines. The idea is that Australian winemakers are parachuted in to Aude, Limoux, Chile, wherever Tony Laithwaite thinks the locals will tolerate the intrusion; they then get the pick of the local fruit, vinify it in the way they want, use new oak if they feel like it, and produce wines which cause a stir locally and waltz off with wine fair medals. Another good story is the Côtes de Castillon Château la Clarière Laithwaite which, as the name suggests...

There is no list as such; just a kind of merry-go-round in which new and ever more exotic animals appear as fast as others scamper off into oblivion; a monthly 'wine index' helps you keep track of what's what. The really strong area here has always been French country wines – over the last decade, Bordeaux Direct has consistently been Britain's most innovative and catholic buyer from this area, hence the award – but Chile, Eastern Europe and Northern Spain also provide much of interest. Prices can be high; because the wines are exclusive, and because they are all excellently packaged, you may not notice this. And it's hard not to enjoy the salesmanship. For anyone who likes something a bit different from *The Times* obituaries at breakfast, or for those resolutely armchair-bound when it comes to wine-buying, Bordeaux Direct provides a lot of fun and pleasure.

Best buys

Domaine de Coussergues 1989, Mourvèdre (vin de pays), £4.49
Montravel Sec Sec Sec 1989, Montravel Sec AOC, Sémillon, £4.85
Vinavius oak-aged Chardonnay (Flying Winemakers) 1989,
Domaine de Coussergues, Vin de Pays des Côtes de Thongue,
£6.99

Borg Castel

Samlesbury Mill, Goosefoot Lane,   *Tel* (025 485) 2128
Samlesbury Bottoms, Preston, Lancashire
PR5 0RN

Open Mon–Wed, Fri 10–5; Thur 7–9.30 (wine tasting); Sat possible; 1st Sun of
each month 12–4   **Closed** Sun except as above, some public holidays, 3rd and 4th
week in January, 1 week in July   **Credit cards** None accepted; personal and
business accounts   **Discounts** Available (minimum 6 cases)   **Delivery** Free
within 30-mile radius (min 1 case); elsewhere at cost; mail order available
Glass hire Free with case order   **Tastings and talks** Two annual tastings by
invitation; to groups on request on premises (30–50 people)   **Cellarage** 75p per
case per year

With a name like this, you'd expect a list of mainly German
wines, perhaps with a bottle or two of Swedish vodka tucked
away at the back. In fact Heather and Paul Hart seem to be as
much francophile as anything, with the majority of the wines on
both the 'retail' list and the 'fine wine' list coming from France.
Germany, though, is second in importance; there is a little flurry
of interest from Spain, but nothing much from anywhere else.
Ports feature the elegantly labelled Ramos Pinto wines,
supplemented by one or two bottles from the Symington stable
(Dow and Smith Woodhouse). Prices throughout are reasonable.
    The list is not a long one, but within France and Germany
there is plenty to chose from. Bordeaux is perhaps more
interesting than Burgundy, where the stock has been mainly
sourced from négociants. This is a good place to come for Alsace
wines, not in terms of variety of producers, but because there
are twelve different wines from the region's best cooperative,
that of Turckheim (consistently misspelled on the list). The
Rhône and Loire have something over a dozen bottles each; try
the Entrefaux Crozes-Hermitage and Gaston Huet's Clos de
Bourg Demi Sec Vouvray. There are four Loire sparkling wines
to experiment with, too. Much of the German section,
disappointingly, comes from a sole merchant, Drathen, rather
than the single estates and growers that generally provide this
country's finest wines.

Best buys

Château de Belcier 1985, Côtes de Castillon, £5.06
Alsace Tokay-Pinot Gris 1988, Cave Tradition Turckheim, £4.74
Bouvet Cuvée Mlle Ladubay, Saumur (sparkling wine), £5.97

Bottle and Basket   ◑ ➽ 𝖎

15 Highgate High Street, London N6 5JT   *Tel* 081-341 7018

Open Mon–Fri, public holidays 11–3, 5–9; Sat 11–9; Sun, religious holidays 12–3,
7–9 **Closed** Chr Day **Credit cards** Access, Visa **Discounts** 5% on 1 case
Delivery Free locally (min 1 mixed case); elsewhere not available **Glass hire** Free
with reasonable order **Tastings and talks** Weekly in-store tastings
Cellarage Not available

Paul Kelly, Administrative Partner at Bottle and Basket, points
out to us that last year's description of it as a 'small shop' is not
really accurate. It is true that, although the shop front on the
street seems no bigger than most, the selling area inside is
substantial, and best use of this is made with tightly packed,
neatly ordered shelves full of bottles up to giraffe's-head level.
There is also a bank of wine racks in the centre of the shop,
where fine wines wait, flat on their backs, for the drinker in
their lives. The shop has extensive cellars where good stocks of
most lines are held, so if you find something you like at the
B & B, it's unlikely that you'll return the next day to find it all
sold out.

The range is wide – around 600 wines in all. Over a sixth of
these are Spanish, which is hardly surprising as the founder
and executive partner, Fernando Munoz, is an expatriate
madrileño. Work in the restaurant trade brought him here, and
wine now keeps him here, although the lunch hours indicate
that he has certainly resisted going native. Amid the usual
Torresiana, you'll find interesting wines from the Ribera del
Duero, Toro, Navarra and La Mancha areas, and enough Rioja to
brighten a month of wet Sundays.

It would not be realistic to expect the whole of Highgate to be
hispanophile in its drinking, and Champagne, Bordeaux and
even Burgundy are well stocked. Italy, too, with Pio Cesare's Il
Nebbio and Dolcetto d'Alba looking appealing at £5.80, while
Tollo's Montepulciano d'Abruzzo is, as usual, the bargain at
£2.47. The list ranges up to Sassicaia 1986, at £28.03 (those three
pence intrigue – they suggest a consistent pricing formula is
followed throughout). During the life of this *Guide*, Fernando
Munoz and Paul Kelly expect to increase the number of organic
wines they stock still further, as this is something Highgate
drinkers do ask for at present, while the rising prices of

European wines will probably mean new arrivals from Australia and New Zealand.

If you're a North Londoner and you don't know this shop, do drop in sometime – we think you'll find it worthwhile, with plenty of interest at fair prices. As always, let us know if you disagree, though.

Best buys

Montepulciano d'Abruzzo 1987, Tollo, £2.47
Renmano Chairman's Selection Sauvignon Blanc, South Australia, £4.14
Château le Barradis 1983, Monbazillac (organic dessert wine), £6.61

Bottoms Up

Head office
Astra House, Edinburgh Way, Harlow, Essex   *Tel* (0279) 453408
CM20 2BE
70 branches nationwide

Open Mon–Sat 10–10; Sun, public holidays 12–2, 7–10 (excluding Scotland)
Closed Sun (Scotland only), Chr Day, 1 Jan   **Credit cards** Access, American Express, Grand Metropolitan Shareholders Card, Visa; personal and business accounts   **Discounts** 5% on 1 mixed case   **Delivery** Free local to stores
Glass hire Free   **Tastings and talks** Tastings held in-store monthly; managers may give talks to local groups with tastings in most cases   **Cellarage** Not available

Bottoms Up is trying; there can be no doubt about that. The problem is that the results to date have been so mixed that it seems to be trying customers' patience rather than impressing their palates. Explanations below; first, a little background.

Bottoms Up is a member of 'The Dominic Group': in other words, it belongs to the same multi-national company (Grand Metropolitan) that owns the Peter Dominic and Hunter & Oliver group of shops. For a number of years, Bottoms Up was just Peter Dominic with bells on – open for longer, bigger shops, but no real range or profile to call its own. 'What a waste,' you might say, and justly. Eventually that same thought occurred to its owners.

The result is the new, 'stand-alone', dynamic and interesting Bottoms Up; that's the aim. (Indeed, it's the aim of each member of the Dominic group at present.) A number of shops have been refurbished, and the best outlets certainly look good now. Last year came a promising range of unusual South American wines, and commendably Bottoms Up made big efforts to go out and sell them, with local leafleting, window displays and similar stratagems. This year, amid great fanfare, came Russian wines. Their arrival coincided with Issue 1 of 'The List', a new broadsheet-style, strangely Oddbins-like publication, containing 'all the latest news and prices from Bottoms Up Wine Superstores'. 'THE RUSSIANS HAVE ARRIVED!' customers were told in big black capital letters. A cheery Cossack was pictured throwing open a window. 'Glasnost brings remarkable new wines.'

You can probably guess the rest. There were only two remarkable things about them: their lamentable quality, and their high price. Something, somewhere along the line, went horribly wrong. Were these really the wines the buyers had ordered? If they weren't, shouldn't they have been sent back? At the very least, shouldn't somebody have cancelled all the hype when it became obvious that the wines weren't going to match up to it? And if they were the wines the buyers had ordered, well . . .

We don't want to make too much of this, partly because it would not be fair to stress one very public failure and omit to mention a number of quieter successes, and partly because the last thing we would like to see is the Grand Met barons timidly deciding to abort imagination and endeavour at Bottoms Up and return the chain to its previously comatose state. We hope, for both Bottoms Up and Russian wine in Britain, that the lessons of spring 1990 will be learned and that everyone concerned will be galvanised into getting it right next time.

And so to those quieter successes. South America, for example: the Mexican, Brazilian and Peruvian wines you can buy here are not geared up to challenge France yet, but they're well worth sampling, while Chile and Argentina's wines are certainly ready to climb into the ring with plucky Fitous or Rhônes or Bordeaux Supérieurs. North America is widely stocked, too; Bottoms Up gave Britons their first chance to make the acquaintance of Charbono (a grape variety rather than the remains of a barbecue) with Inglenook's inky version. Australia, New Zealand and Portugal (four different garrafeiras) look as if they might be about to lurch off down untrodden paths, while Germany, Italy and Spain are sound rather than exciting, and could do with a dusting down. Why aren't fortified wines (and spirits, come to that) printed on the list?

The French selection looks best in the country regions, and there is surely great potential for further bold buying here. There are some good Loire and Bordeaux wines, and we are pleased to see that the Cave Vinicole de Turckheim has chased away those dreary Laugel wines from Alsace that Bottoms Up used to stock. Standards in Alsace are so high that there is no excuse for anyone to stock anything that isn't enjoyable, at the very least. Greece, Israel, Algeria and the Lebanon are all on the shelves: Bottoms Up is certainly trying.

Best buys

Caves Velhas Garrafeira 1978, Ribatejo (Portugal), £4.89
Alsace Sylvaner 1987, Cave Vinicole de Turckheim, £3.99
Chilean Cabernet Sauvignon, Santa Rita 120, £3.99

The Broad Street Wine Co

The Holloway, Market Place, Warwick,   *Tel* (0926) 493951
Warwickshire CV34 4SJ

Case sales only   **Open** Mon–Fri 9–6; Sat 9–1   **Closed** Sun, public holidays
Credit cards Access, Visa; personal and business accounts   **Discounts** 5% on 6
mixed cases   **Delivery** Free in UK (min 6 cases); otherwise 1 case £7, 2 cases £3.50
per case, 3 cases £2.33 per case, 4 cases £1.75 per case, 5 cases £1.40 per case; mail
order available   **Glass hire** Free with 1-case order   **Tastings and talks** To groups
on request   **Cellarage** Not available

The Warwick-based Broad Street Wine Company are wholesalers, most of whose business is with the trade. However, their range is so choice and particular, and their specialities so attractive, that members of the public very sensibly buy direct from them when the need arises.

If, for example, you love Cognac, but you're beginning to wish you could try something a little different from the familiar brands, then the need for you to contact Russel and Gillian Hobbs is very definitely arising. Page one of the list is devoted to 44 Cognacs that can only be described as fabulous: vintage (from 1838), early landed, limited edition. Prices start at £37.35 (note that this part of the list is ex-VAT); producers range from Hine (especially for the early landed Cognacs), through Hennessy, Delamain and Exshaw to Cognacs identified only by the name of the restaurant from whose cellars they were originally salvaged. Page two dazzles you with vintage Armagnac, and page three with vintage Calvados, scorchers all. 'Order any assorted 12 bottles of vintage brandy to qualify for a free brandy cabinet,' it says at the bottom. There'd be no problem in choosing 12, but there won't be much change from £750 . . .

The wines are eccentrically chosen. Perhaps one should expect this from a merchant whose avowed aim is 'to abolish mediocrity'. The biggest range appears under the imprimatur of French chef Georges Blanc, whose fastidious palate doubtless keeps mediocrity at bay. The Blanc-labelled wines include Beaujolais, Mâcon, Burgundy, Rhône, a champagne and two table wines. Drouhin is stocked to the tune of 13 wines; there are seven scented Alsatians from the trusty Cave Vinicole at Turckheim, Château Peyros from Madiran, and Cloudy Bay, Cape Mentelle, Rouge Homme and Château Xanadu from the ends of the earth. Corsican wines from the charming Comte de Poix (Domaine Peraldi) are good but expensive. There is a long bin-end list, mainly burgundian in substance. Sales are on a case-only basis, brandies aside; there you must purchase two bottles. Mail order is available, but carriage charges are high. Unless, of course, you are going for the 12 assorted bottles of vintage brandy (and free brandy cabinet), in which case delivery is free. That's decided you, hasn't it?

Best buys

Rouge Homme 1984, Cabernet-Shiraz, Coonawarra, £5.24
Rully Blanc 1988, Joseph Drouhin, £9.89
Château Peyros 1985, Madiran, £5.23

G E Bromley

London Street, Leicester, Leicestershire LE5 3RH	*Tel* (0533) 768471
271 Leicester Road, Wigston Fields, Leicestershire LE8 1JW	*Tel* (0533) 882057
J H Measures & Sons, The Crescent, Spalding, Lincolnshire PE11 1AF	*Tel* (0775) 722676

Open (Leicester) Mon–Thur 8.30–1, 2.15–5.15; Fri 8.30–5.15; Sat 8.30–12; (Wigston) Mon–Sat 10–1, 5–10; Sun 12–1.30, 7–10; (Spalding) Mon–Sat 9–6
Closed Sun (Leicester and Spalding); most public holidays **Credit cards** Access, Visa; personal and business accounts **Discounts** 2.5% on 5 cases, 5% on 12+ cases **Delivery** Free in Lincoln, Leicester, Boston, Holbeach, Peterborough, Wellingborough, Rugby, Nuneaton, Ashby, Derby, Nottingham and Newark (min 3 cases); otherwise at cost; mail order available **Glass hire** Free with 1-case order **Tastings and talks** Major autumn tasting; to groups on request (min 20 people) **Cellarage** £2.50 per case per year (excluding insurance)

There's nothing very stylish or drum-banging about G E Bromley as a wine merchant; in fact director P Baines is desperately modest about what the company has to offer. So we had better be drum-banging on Bromley's behalf.

The fact is that an attractive and extensive selection of wines is sold at reasonable prices on a retail (single-bottle) basis. If you are prepared to buy on a by-the-case basis (mixing is allowed), then you qualify for the 'Cellar Door' prices; these are not a great deal lower, but the difference would add up to at least a pound or two per case. The list helpfully begins by dividing all the wines up into styles, so, for example, if you are interested only in medium dry whites you can see exactly what is on offer. The notes are straightforwardly written and quietly illuminating. Every wine, including the German ones, has its producer's name beside it, and there are many merchants in this *Guide* who fail that particular test. We suspect that G E Bromley is rather a good place to go to buy wine, though we invite confirmation (or contradiction) of this from readers.

The Bordeaux selection is attractive, particularly along *petit château* lines: you could buy any one of Gressier-Grand-Poujeaux 1979, Cissac, d'Angludet or Labégorce-Zédé 1985, or Chasse-Spleen, d'Angludet or Cissac 1986 for around £10 to £12 here at time of writing, with properties from Côtes de Bourg and Côtes de Castillon at around £5. Burgundy is less extensive, though what's there is good, and most of it costs under £10. Try Chofflet's 1985 Givry at £7.32 for size. The Rhône range *chez* Bromley is larger than the Burgundy range, as it happens, and is full of old friends with names like Jaboulet, Ryckwaert, Perrin, Chapoutier, Guigal and Brunier. The rest of France is again grower-led, with the Blancks dominating in Alsace, Touchais and Château de Tracy looking tempting in the Loire, and with some good French country wines of the Domaine Sainte-Eulalie ilk. Germany and Spain are both sympathetically and lengthily listed; Italy perhaps a little less so, though there are some fine wines from Pio Cesare and Tiefenbrunner among others. Australia and New Zealand seem to have made more of a splash in Leicester than California does; while Chile and Bulgaria are present in the strength that their price/quality ratio merits. The vintage ports, like everything else, are very reasonably priced: Sandeman 1982 at £14.10 is a bargain that readers are advised to take advantage of, with a view to Christmas 1992.

Best buys

Côtes du Rhône 1988, Château du Grand Moulas, £3.86
Maximin Grünhauser Abtsberg Riesling Kabinett 1985, von Schubert (Ruwer), £7.59
Gran Colegiata 1985, Toro, Bodegas Fariña, £4.69

Now the late fruits are in.
Now moves the leaf-starred year
Down, in the sun's decline.
Stoop. Have no fear.
Glance at the burdened tree:
Dark is the grape's wild skin.
Dance, limbs, be free.
Bring the bright clusters here
And crush them into wine.
Excerpt from 'For a Wine Festival' Vernon Watkins

Budgen ☁

Head office
PO Box 9, Stonefield Way, Ruislip, *Tel* 081-422 3422
Middlesex HA4 0JR
Approximately 90 branches

Open Generally Mon–Fri 8–8 or 9–6; Sat 8–6 or 9–6 **Closed** Sun, public holidays
(may vary from store to store) **Credit cards** Access, Visa; personal and business
accounts **Discounts, Delivery, Glass hire** Not available
Tastings and talks Tastings organised every 2–3 months with a tasting agency;
wine buyer will do talks to groups on request **Cellarage** Not available

As supermarket chains go, Budgens' profile is a fairly low one,
and the last year has seen the sale of 51 stores to 'Betta', a
'convenience store chain', though Budgens will continue to
source all their products including wine where relevant.
Budgens itself does not have a particularly exciting wine list,
but it does at least deserve to be called a wine list, something
that cannot be said of all of its competitors' offerings.

The German and Italian sections are dull and plonk-washed;
the small range from Australia, New Zealand and Chile is well
chosen and the wines are all worth trying; Spain brings us a
supplementary 'best buy' in the guise of Viña Albali 1984 from
Valdepeñas at £2.99; and the French connection holds good on
most fronts, with some worthwhile country wines, Alsace from
Gisselbrecht, carefully chosen Loire wines, and tasty,
inexpensive clarets. Budgens Own Claret, blended by Peter
Sichel, offers particularly good value, along with other petits
châteaux.

Best buys

Vouvray 1985, Cuvée Sélecte (grower not specified but wine
very highly rated by buyer Sarah King), £4.09
Budgens Claret, £2.85
Domaine des Hauts Sanziers 1989, Saumur Blanc, £3.99

In writing the entries for merchants included in the *Guide*, the Editor
relies on readers' reports, particularly when it comes to the awarding
of service symbols. We are concerned that good service may not
always be adequately recompensed at present, so please write and let
us know whenever you feel you have received particularly good
service (or, of course, if you feel the service you have received has
been inadequate in any way). Use the forms at the back of the book,
or write on a separate sheet of paper if you prefer. Our Freepost
facility means that no stamp is required.

Burlington Wines ☞

46 Burlington Road, Ipswich, Suffolk IP1 2HS   *Tel* (0473) 250242
Associated outlets
Wines of Interest
Hadleigh Wine Cellars

Case sales only   Open Mon–Fri 9–6; Sat 9–1   **Closed** Sun, public holidays
Credit cards None accepted; personal and business accounts   **Discounts** 5% on
orders of £250   **Delivery** Free in City of London, Ipswich and central Norwich;
otherwise London £1.50 per case (min £3) and elsewhere 1–2 cases £6.50, 3–5 cases
£8.50, 6 cases free; mail order available   **Glass hire** Free with suitable order
Tastings and talks Through Wines of Interest; to groups on request
Cellarage £2.50 per case per year (in bond only)

A lot seems to have been happening of late at 46 Burlington
Road, where Burlington Wines and its parent company Wines of
Interest operate from. The latest development is a proposed
link-up with Hadleigh Wine Cellars of Bury St Edmunds, which
is scheduled to come into the Wines of Interest fold in
September. Hadleigh will continue to trade as before, but from
Ipswich rather than Bury.

Burlington's proprietor Tim Voelcker (who has come to rest in
the wine trade after a dazzling number of careers, including that
of publisher, Outward Bound instructor, steelworks training
officer and brewery executive) has assembled a medium-sized
collection of wines . . . well, of interest: the name is justified.
There isn't much sense of system about the list, and no very
clear direction to the buying; what there is, instead, is a pot-
pourri of bottles to catch the imagination, and the prices are
generally competitive enough to appeal to the other hemisphere
of the brain, where the accounts department is lodged. We'll
spatter a few droppable names at you, much as the list does:
Anjou Rouge from Clos de la Coulaine; Mas de Daumas Gassac
and Clape's Cornas as well as Jaboulet's sensational 1985
Thalabert; plenty from Fonseca and Pires in Portugal; Pesquera
as well as the less well-known Yllera from Ribera del Duero; a
fine range of sweet whites, with Etienne Brana's Jurançon
Vendange Tardive, Tijou's Coteaux du Layon-Chaume, Huet's
Moelleux Vouvray le Haut Lieu, Bourdin's Anjou Blanc, and
Châteaux Nairac, Lafaurie-Peyraguey, Climens and Doisy-
Dubroca from Sauternes all rubbing shoulders with Mick
Morris's Old Liqueur Muscat; top-flight Alsace from Rolly
Gassmann and Schlumberger; two dozen serious Germans; a
bargain-hunter's collection of Vintage Ports from the untrendier
type of house; and some fine old solera and vintage Madeiras
from Cossart Gordon and Henriques & Henriques.

Traditionalists should know that clarets remain fair, though
Rausan-Ségla's marvellous return-to-form 1986 at last spring's

attractive price has all gone now (or has it? we couldn't find it on the list, yet Tim Voelcker suggests that he might still have some); Burgundy, meanwhile, is improved. Mr Voelcker is the sort of merchant who will buy up one-off parcels of interesting things with sediment in, like Patrick Javillier's Clos du Cromin 1984 or some old Terres Blanches, and these are always worth trying. An *en primeur* offer of '89 claret was made, and tastings are organised in both Ipswich and Norwich. Nine out of ten, in sum, for energy, enthusiasm and interest; but around half marks only for organisation and presentation.

Best buys

Selaks, Sauvignon Blanc 1989, New Zealand, £7.75
Gran Toc Tinto 1983, Cavas Hill (red wine), Penedés, £5.95
Vintage Port 1983, Gould Campbell, £13.95

The Butlers Wine Cellar

247 Queens Park Road, Brighton, East Sussex   *Tel* (0273) 698724
BN2 2XJ

Open Tue–Fri 9–5.30; Sat 9–1 **Closed** Mon, Sun, public holidays
Credit cards Access, Visa; personal and business accounts **Discounts** Not available **Delivery** Free within 15-mile radius (min 1 case); elsewhere at cost (3+ cases free); mail order available **Glass hire** Free with 1-case order
Tastings and talks, **Cellarage** Not available

Geoffrey and Gillian Butler's oddbottle shop is very popular with readers. The range is in perpetual motion, with bottles constantly arriving and leaving – 'often at below auction prices', according to the owner. We hear excellent reports of the service and quality of the advice given, and feel secure in recommending this as a place for readers to go to buy a bottle for a special occasion. But don't think that it's fine wines only; there are plenty of bottles in stock at under £10, and always a number at under £5, too. The list is strongest in the wines of classic regions, for the straightforward reason that these last the longest and are therefore most likely to move around in the trading circle. Nothing, though, is excluded on principle, and the list as we write includes wines from Chile, Australia, Portugal (the wax-sealed Valpacos Reserva 1980 from Tras-os-Montes at £3.95 sounds like just the sort of thing one would hope to discover here), Italy and – not common, this – four different vintages of the Szamorodni Dry Tokaj back to 1969. Wine enthusiasts stepping into The Butlers Wine Cellar must feel all of the excitement and anticipation of a bibliophile pushing open the bell-sprung door to a well-loved second-hand bookshop.

Best buys

Consult Geoffrey and Gillian Butler

Anthony Byrne Fine Wines ⟨D⟩ ⟨⟩

88 High Street, Ramsey, Cambridgeshire	*Tel* (0487) 814555
PE17 1BS	

Open Mon–Sat 9–5.30 **Closed** Sun, public holidays **Credit cards** Access, Visa;
personal and business accounts **Discounts** 5% on mixed cases, 10% on unmixed
cases **Delivery** Free in UK (min 2 cases); otherwise £2.50 within 150-mile radius
of Ramsey and £6.50 beyond (for orders under 2 cases); mail order available
Glass hire Free with 1-case order **Tastings and talks** Wines regularly available
in-store; to groups on request **Cellarage** £3 per case per year or part year

Anthony Byrne is a leading trade wholesaler whose terms of
sale, and whose range, are sufficiently attractive to ordinary
consumers to warrant inclusion in the *Guide*. When you are
looking at the list, though, remember to note the most
expensive of the quoted prices, which will be for single bottles
(or bottles in mixed cases), and add VAT afterwards to arrive at
the true price. The list is not very consumer-friendly, and we
would like to hear from readers who have used Anthony Byrne
as to how easy they found it.

The glamorous lures are an enormous range of Beaujolais and
Burgundy, and Alsace wines from Zind-Humbrecht. Most (or is
it all? – the list is rather terse) of the Beaujolais is sourced from
Georges Duboeuf, who is pictured on the cover of the list sitting
next to an enormous, foaming vat and looking very glum
indeed, for some unfathomable reason. Few people in Beaujolais
have as much cause to smile as Monsieur Duboeuf. The
Burgundy comes from Domaines Armand Rousseau, Georges
Clerget, Dujac, Arnoux, Tollot Beaut, Pousse d'Or, Etienne
Sauzet, Jean Grivot, Gagnard Delagrange and a host of others:
the great, the good, the lauded. It's plentiful, too, lending
probability to John Moss-Blundell's claim that you'll find 'a
wider choice of Burgundy growers than at possibly any other
merchant'. Add the magnificent Zind-Humbrecht wines, a
lovely selection from the Loire, Cuvaison from California, some
nifty clarets, Guigal from the Rhône, and Masi, Anselmi and
Maculan from Italy, and the result is the kind of merchant that
the most name-obsessed customer would be happy shopping
from. Funds permitting.

> Why not club together with friends to enjoy volume discounts and
> free delivery?

Best buys

Alsace Gewürztraminer 1987, Heimbourg, Domaine Zind-Humbrecht, £8.11
Bonnezeaux la Chapelle 1988, Château de Fesles, £14.51
Alsace Tokay-Pinot Gris 1988, Clos Jebsal, Domaine Zind-Humbrecht, £12.14

D Byrne & Co

12 King Street, Clitheroe, Lancashire
BB7 2EP

Tel (0200) 23152

Open Mon, Tue, Wed, Sat 9–6; Thur, Fri 9–8 **Closed** Sun, Easter holidays
Credit cards None accepted; personal and business accounts **Discounts** £1 on
mixed case, £1.20 on unmixed case, 5% on orders over £250 **Delivery** Free within
50-mile radius of Clitheroe (min 1 case); otherwise £4 for 1 case, £3.50 per case for
2 cases, 3 cases free; mail order available **Glass hire** Free with 1-case order
Tastings and talks One week annual tasting in September/October; to groups on
request **Cellarage** Free

This is a brilliant wine merchant. In an atmospheric rabbit
warren of cellar rooms, lit by unshaded bulbs and signposted by
small notices drawing the browser's attention to particularly
favoured bottles, punctuated by 'Please mind your HEAD'
notices, you will find enough wine of quality to keep you
drinking happily for years. Prices are good to very good,
delivery is free for 50 miles around for a case or more, and if
you tire of wine there is a fine range of malt whisky to divert
yourself with. Clitheroe is lucky enough to have had D Byrne &
Co for over a hundred years now; let's hope the firm is good for
another hundred.

Is this the best range of sherry in the country? It's almost
certainly the widest. Duke of Wellington, John William Burdon,
Valdespino, José de Soto, Garvey, Don Zoilo, Pemartin,
Gonzalez Byass, Lustau and almacenista friends, Domecq,
Harvey and Croft – they're all here, and not just to the tune of a
bottle or two, either: there are ten different Garvey sherries and
nearly as many from Gonzalez Byass, with choice for the others
as well. Port and Madeira suffer in comparison, though in
absolute terms the range is much wider than at most
competitors.

The wines of almost every country have been bought and
stocked with what appears to be unbridled enthusiasm:
Portugal and Bulgaria, New Zealand and Spain and Italy . . .
More or less every Chilean wine ever exported to Britain is
sitting underneath King Street, and we're not sure where else in
Lancashire you can compare five Californian Pinot Noirs or four
Zinfandels. The delicate splendours of fine German wines are

embraced with the same zest as legions of sun-tanned, barrel-chested Australians; every corner of France save Corsica and Savoie has been ransacked for wines of interest. The Alsace and Loire sections can only be qualified as 'very fine', there are seventeen different Châteauneufs with other Rhônes to match, wonderful burgundies from both top growers and top négociants, and reams of claret – laid out in a kind of underground ziggurat, constructed from the famous wooden cases in which fine Bordeaux reaches its customers. Inspiring.

This year sees D Byrne & Co take its stock to 'the old postal sorting office across the road', with a view to building up the wholesale side of the business; at the same time, the company intends to 'reorganise and improve the display area in our existing cellars'. Not *too* much reorganisation, please! Can Lancastrians monitor these developments on our behalf?

'Choice, quality, expertise, old-fashioned civility, browsing without the pressure to buy, reliable and flexible delivery service – perhaps we shouldn't be in business in the 1990s?' asks partner Michael Byrne. A rhetorical question, of course.

Best buys

Château Léoville-Barton 1985, Saint-Julien, half-bottle, £7.89
Rosemount Show Reserve Gewürztraminer 1988, New South Wales, £6.95
Château Musar 1982, Gaston Hochar, Lebanon, £4.99

Cachet Wines ☞

Lysander Close, Clifton Moor, York, North   *Tel* (0904) 690090
Yorkshire YO3 8XB

Case sales only   **Open** Mon–Fri 9–5.30; Sat 9–1   **Closed** Sun, public holidays **Credit cards** None accepted; personal and business accounts   **Discounts** Not available   **Delivery** Free in Yorkshire and Derbyshire (min 1 mixed case); elsewhere at cost   **Glass hire** Free   **Tastings and talks** Eight annual tastings held at restaurants; to groups on request   **Cellarage** £3.50 per case per year

---

You won't find a huge range of wines here, but some of the producers stocked by Terry Herbert and Graham Coverdale make it worth putting in an appearance at Clifton Moor. A mixed case should include a bottle of Georges Gardet Champagne, some of the Producteurs Plaimont's attractive white Vin de Pays des Côtes de Gascogne and red Côtes de Saint-Mont, a bottle from the Willy Gisselbrecht Alsace range (there are ten to choose from), one or two clarets (1986 seems to be preferred to 1985), a treat or two from the Burgundy selection where a choice of good small growers is offered (Sauzet, Colin, Senard, Trapet and Mongeard-Mugneret should not disappoint), some bottles from the Rhône-Provence axis (Cru du Coudoulet and Château Val-Joanis are likely to provide the best value), and one or two of the fine Vins de Pays des Côtes de Thongue of Domaine Deshenrys. France is the heart of the matter here, as the company name suggests, but there are five well-chosen New Zealand whites, too, including the terrific Late Harvest Rhine Riesling of Hermann and Agnes Seifried at Redwood Valley, together with some reliable Californians and Australians. Italy, Spain, Portugal and Germany are pared to the bone.

Cachet has a number of restaurant-owning clients, and this means that a good selection of half-bottles is available. Are you a customer? If so, write and let us have your impressions of the range and service.

Best buys

Château Puycarpin 1986, Côtes de Castillon, £4.59
Clos Ferdinand 1989, Vin de Pays des Côtes de Thongue, Domaine Deshenrys, £3.25
Late Harvest Rhine Riesling 1986, Redwood Valley Estate, New Zealand (half-bottle), £5.75

Cadwgan Fine Wine Merchants

152A Ashley Road, Hale, Altrincham, Cheshire WA15 9SA	*Tel* 061-928 0357
55 Spring Gardens, Manchester M2 2BZ	*Tel* 061-236 6547

Open Mon–Fri 11–8; Sat 10–8 **Closed** Sun, public holidays
Credit cards Access, Visa; personal and business accounts **Discounts** 5% on 1 case; quantity discounts by negotiation **Delivery** Free within 10-mile radius (min 1 case); elsewhere at cost; mail order available **Glass hire** Free within 1-case order **Tastings and talks** Regular in-store tastings, regular monthly dinners; to groups on request **Cellarage** Negotiable

Cadwgan (not as unpronounceable as it looks – cadoogan: the Welsh for 'Cadogan') is the middle name of Adelaide Williams, and when she and her husband Peter decided to open a wine shop in Hale, they took it as an eye-catching and lip-twisting trading title. There are now two Cadwgans: the original one, and a second branch in Manchester, run by the Williams' son Paul; more are planned. The Manchester shop is one of the most stylishly appointed in this *Guide*; the kind of place to be seen shopping, as well as to shop.

And there's plenty on the list to shop for. Champagnes are extensively stocked, with those of L Aubry (a grower in Jouy-lès-Reims) supplying the 'house' range, and others from De Castellane, Pol Roger, Roederer, Bollinger, Pommery, Laurent Perrier and Krug providing some variously extravagant options.

Alsace is another speciality: Cadwgan claim that 20 per cent of their sales are of Alsace wines, and this is a figure that will have other merchants spluttering into their claret, the prevailing opinion being that Alsace wines are 'hard to sell'. Alsace is represented on the list by portfolios from the Turckheim co-operative and Dopff & Irion, giving a choice of 21 different wines.

The Loire is extensively listed, and we applaud the fact that sweet wines are given their due alongside dry wines; there is a fine range of antiques from Moulin Touchais, with more recent collectables from Baumard and others. The Rhône range is perhaps marginally less distinguished (though the seven whites have connoisseur-appeal), while French country wines have been explored with comparative restraint – except in the case of Gaillac, where the wines of Jean Cros/Château Larroze are embraced wholeheartedly. Bordeaux and Burgundy are enthusiastically listed, though the same names recur perhaps more often than one would wish in Burgundy (Vallet) and Beaujolais (Dépagneux). Both bottle good wines, but variety spices wine purchase as it does everything else, and these areas could be a little spicier.

Outside the French compound, Spain, Italy and Germany enjoy unusual parity with one another (merchants normally find themselves taking sides at this point). Spain and Germany are mainly stocked with classics (the Riojas of Murrieta and CVNE, the modern classics of Torres, Deinhard's Heritage selection), while the avant-garde get a larger slice of the shelving in Italy, though not at the expense of top producers working within traditional DOCs. Portuguese wines, by contrast, are a joke: one 'Vinho Verdi'. Cadwgan can do better than this, surely? There is a good port range, true enough (with sherry to match), but Portugal has much more to offer than just port. In the New World, meanwhile, New Zealand and Chile command almost as much enthusiasm as California and Australia, and all four countries get the chance to show their mettle.

Cadwgan organise the annual Cheshire Summer Wine Festival, a lively event attracting around 3,000 visitors each year. It is the place to be seen toping: we have been sent a photograph of MP Sir Fergus Montgomery trying a dram of Sheep Dip, and very pleased with it he looks, too.

Best buys

Montepulciano d'Abruzzo 1987, Cornacchia, £4.55
Alsace Tokay-Pinot Gris 1989, Cave des Vignerons de
Turckheim, £4.75
Château du Grand Moueys 1986, Premières Côtes de Bordeaux
(red), £4.55

Cairns & Hickey

17 Blenheim Terrace, Woodhouse Lane,   *Tel* (0532) 459501
Leeds, West Yorkshire LS2 9HN

Open Mon–Fri 9–6; Sat 9–1; extended hours at Christmas **Closed** Sun, public
holidays **Credit cards** Access, Visa; personal and business accounts
Discounts 5% on wine only (min 1 case) **Delivery** Free within 25-mile radius of
Leeds; elsewhere at cost; mail order available **Glass hire** Free with suitable wine
order **Tastings and talks** Beaujolais Nouveau tasting in November; to groups on
request **Cellarage** £2.50 per case per year

Managing Director Ernest Cairns completes his fortieth year as a
wine merchant this year, and he claims he entered the wine
trade 'more by accident than design – but once in, it's difficult
to get out!' The list seems to have kept up with the changes the
years have brought reasonably well, and you will find wines
from Australia and New Zealand, Chile and California here –
though not many of them. What Leeds wants, if this list is
anything to go by, is plenty of claret, supplemented by
moderate ranges of other French wines, German and Italian
wines for parties, and Spanish wines for a change. Yorkshire
stoicism doubtless allows customers to take the rather alarming
spelling found in the list in their stride. For special occasions,
there is a fine wine bin-end list which includes, intriguingly, a
large number of 1961 Bordeaux *petits châteaux*. We invite Cairns
& Hickey customers to write to us to confirm the 'friendly,
personal service and expert advice' the list proposes, and to give
us their views on the range offered.

Best buys

Domaine de la Hilaire 1989, Vin de Pays des Côtes de Gascogne
(white), £3.15
Mesoners de Castilla 1985, Ribera del Duero, £6.45
Blenheim Claret 1986, Bordeaux, £3.55

Prices were current in summer 1990 to the best of our knowledge but
can only be a rough indication of prices throughout 1991.

Cantina Augusto

91–95 Clerkenwell Road, London EC1R 5BX   *Tel* 071-242 3246

Open Mon–Thur 9–6; Fri 9–6.30; Sat mornings in Dec   **Closed** Sat (except as
above), Sun, public holidays   **Credit cards** Access, Visa; personal and business
accounts   **Discounts** Approximately 10% on 1 case   **Delivery** Free in London
(min £100 order), £3 charge for orders £50–£100; £5 charge for orders under £50;
mail order available   **Glass hire** Free with order (deposit required)
Tastings and talks Regular promotional tastings; to groups on request
Cellarage Not available

This is an enterprising local merchant who tries, wherever
possible, to import wines directly, leading to a varied list full of
little-known producers. If you have a research interest in Italian
wines, you might well want to consider an expedition to
Clerkenwell, as Italy is very definitely the key strength here. For
enthusiastic and adventurous locals, there is plenty, too, from
Spain, Portugal and France, while the range of liqueurs suggests
a sweet-toothed following in EC1. There aren't many places in
London where you get a choice of three amaros: the Sicilian
Averna (£10.25) is the best of these. Regular special offers are
made and tastings are held; you can even buy vintage port here
en primeur. Mr Squillario is thorough and conscientious, proud
of his wines, and keen to help you discover them.

Best buys

Barolo 1983 Riserva, Borgogno, £5.70
Pinot Grigio del Podere Dei Lupi 1988, Angoris, £6.20
Tinto Penedés 1982, Jaume Serra, £4.80

The Celtic Vintner

73 Derwen Fawr Road, Sketty, Swansea,   *Tel* (0792) 206661
West Glamorgan SA2 8DR

Case sales only   Open Mon–Fri 8.30–6; Sat by arrangement   **Closed** Sun, public
holidays   **Credit cards** Access; personal and business accounts
Discounts Negotiable for quantity discounts   **Delivery** Free in south and south-
west Wales (min 5 cases unless on regular delivery run); elsewhere at cost
Glass hire Available with charge   **Tastings and talks** Large annual tasting in
Swansea; to groups on request   **Cellarage** Possible

The 'Celtic Vintner Crew: Brian, Margaret, Clare and (not
forgetting) Stan our delivery man' continue to issue thorough,
informative and extensively annotated lists. Wine-loving fellow
Celts would do well to write or phone for a copy, as it contains
much of interest; by dint of description and explanation, it
succeeds in arousing your curiosity about wines that might
otherwise be dismissed for a variety of reasons. How many
readers know the leading Welsh vineyard, John Bevan's Croffta,

has been twinned with Garvey's San Patricio vineyard? We also learn that Croffta is Germanic in style, that the vineyard is sited near the Royal Mint, and that both wine and wine-grower 'are great adverts for the warmth and friendship of Wales'. All incitements to try a bottle that you might otherwise have glided by, unthinkingly.

The list is very well balanced, with stirring male-voice crescendos in Bulgaria, Australia and French country wines. There is also an extensive range of CVNE's excellent Riojas, René Barbier to compare with Torres in Penedés, Mondavi to prove Californian value and reliability, some choice growers' and négociants' burgundies, and a comely selection of Graves and Saint-Emilion clarets. Ports from Niepoort, Churchill and Warre make an intelligent collection, for the house styles and specialisms of each provide ideal grounds for comparison. The selection of half-bottles here is distinguished: there are 50 and rising. Only the Italian page, which at present plays pretty safe with everything except Frescobaldi's Tuscans, looks as if it could do with some polishing.

The purchasing system contains one or two catches: case sales only, but cases can be mixed – though mixed cases may not include wines unasterisked on the list (a small minority). If you want delivery, you may have to pay a surcharge for under four cases, unless you find yourself 'on a regular run'. If in doubt, talk to Brian Johnson, and he'll be happy to explain the details to you.

Best buys

Domaine de Perras 1989, Vin de Pays des Côtes de Gascogne (white), £3.11

Domaine Berthoumieu 1987, Cuvée Charles de Baatz, Madiran, £6.04

Bourgogne Pinot Noir 1987, Domaine Parent, £6.67

Champagne de Villages ☞

9 Fore Street, Ipswich, Suffolk IP4 1JW   *Tel* (0473) 256922

Open Mon–Fri 9–5.30; Sat 9.30–5 **Closed** Sun, public holidays
Credit cards Access, Visa; personal and business accounts **Discounts** Available
Delivery Free within 20-mile radius of Ipswich (min 1 case) and outside the area
(min 5 cases); otherwise £7 per case; mail order available **Glass hire** Free with
1-case order **Tastings and talks** Wine Circle meets every eight weeks for tutored
tastings; to groups on request **Cellarage** £4 per case per year

---

Ten years ago, shop fitter Tony Westbrook began Champagne de Villages as a hobby, selling a range of just eight growers' champagnes to the festively inclined of Ipswich. The festivities went well; the business grew; in 1984 Mike Rogers, the present general manager, joined Tony Westbrook. And the list has, during the decade, expanded away from its foaming wellspring; it now goes as far as New Zealand in wine terms, and includes delicacies such as wild hare pâté and saucisses au foie de Périgord, locally produced garlic and chive mustard relish, and Cuban cigars.

Not that the champagne growers have been abandoned: eight are still there, though we don't know if they are the original octad. Prices are all well above £10 now, of course; in fact they crossed that threshold in 1989. These are artisan's champagnes, discreetly dosed and traditionally made (all the rosés, for example, are produced by controlled maceration or *saignée*, as opposed to the blending in of red wine that is practised by most of the big houses). The list provides plenty of information to help you choose between them, and there is red and white Coteaux Champenois, Rosé des Riceys, Ratafia and Marc de Champagne for the moment when you decide that you can't take another bubble.

There is also, of course, the rest of the list. This has a 'fine' feel to it; not much under a fiver, therefore, with Bordeaux and Burgundy both looking pretty glossy and grand. Elsewhere the 'growers' principle has been followed where possible; and where not, distinguished mercantile names (like Trimbach and Chapoutier) have been courted. The end result cannot be described as thorough or complete in a Lay & Wheeler-like way, but the range is choice and stimulating.

The Fore Street shop looks good, as you would expect from the boss's c.v., though the sun presents a challenge to the stock that we hope the owners will overcome. There is, finally, a Wine Circle with a modest £5 annual membership fee, bringing you the opportunity to attend bi-monthly tutored tastings of around eight to ten wines.

Best buys

Georges Lilbert 1982 Champagne, Brut, Grand Cru (pure Chardonnay), £15.95
Château Bourdieu la Valade 1986, Fronsac, £6.95
Pierre Arnould Rosé Champagne, Grand Cru (pure Pinot Noir), £14.95

Most wine merchants will supply wine for parties on a sale or return basis.

The Champagne House

Office only
15 Dawson Place, London W2 4TH   *Tel* 071-221 5538

Case sales only   **Open** Mon–Thur by appointment only   **Closed** Fri, Sat, Sun,
public holidays, Sept and early Jan   **Credit cards** None accepted
Discounts Negotiable (min 3 cases)   **Delivery** Free in Kensington, Chelsea,
Westminster, City of London (min 1 case); elsewhere at cost; mail order available
Glass hire Not available   **Tastings and talks** Not generally available
Cellarage Not available

If The Champagne House evokes an image of, say, a Georgian
shop in an elegant terrace within which corks are always flying,
in which the froth never settles in the glass, and outside which
the Bentleys are double-parked, think again. There is no shop,
just an office (callers by appointment only). Tastings are offered,
but only 'on a very exclusive basis'. Champagne is certainly the
speciality; but the business is run by Richard Freeman and his
wife with what appears from the outside to be a chilling
seriousness much at odds with the popular image of the
product.

Seriousness; and, to be fair, professionalism. Evident is a
complete commitment to finding champagnes of quality, and the
list is one of the most prodigiously informative we have seen. In
fact, 'list' is a misnomer: wines for sale are listed on only 3
pages out of 88, and the rest of it is a first-class, sparely written
introduction to the subject and the producers. The range of
'quality non-vintage' champagnes is probably the most exciting
area, with a choice of 22 at between £12.60 and £19.12 (though
Richard Freeman warns that prices will have risen during 1990).
Smaller, high-quality producers such as Adam-Garnotel (Extra
Quality Brut £12.60), Albert Le Brun (Cuvée Réservée £12.75)
and the small co-operative of Paul Goerg (Blanc de Blancs
£13.25) share the limelight with the likes of Roederer (Brut
Premier £17.98) and Bollinger (Special Cuvée £18.80). Albert Le
Brun's Carte Blanche (£10.50) is the bargain; the sting is that
you have to buy at least three cases of it at a time. For the rest,
you have to buy at least one case, and mixing is only permitted
to the tune of six bottles of this and six of that, unless you go
for The Champagne House Non-Vintage Tasting Case (contents
unspecified, though you will be told as you order: £175). This
seems rather discouraging for those who would like to
experiment through the whole range, especially given the high
cost of each bottle. There are fourteen or more vintage
champagnes (£16.40–£33.52), and just under a dozen 'Cuvées de
Prestige', tactfully named 'Specialities' (£35.68–£86.88).

A specialist serving specialists is what The Champagne House
is and, it would seem, likes to be. If you are a champagne

enthusiast, get in touch. Be warned, though, that your specialist credentials may be subject to scrutiny: 'The policy of the company is to provide the best possible service to known and established customers. It is not always our wish to do business with those who come without introduction, although exceptions are frequently made if the customers are seriously interested in the subject.'

Best buys

We usually ask merchants to select a range of ten potential best buys for us to choose from, on the basis that each merchant best knows his or her strengths. 'We are not prepared to attempt an analysis of our list in this way,' says Richard Freeman. 'Each champagne is chosen for quality and value; that is the purpose of our business.'

Chaplin & Son   ☞

---

35 Rowlands Road, Worthing, West Sussex   *Tel* (0903) 35888
BN11 3JJ

Open Mon–Thur, Sat 8.45–1.15, 2.15–5.30; Fri 8.45–6   **Closed** Sun, public holidays   **Credit cards** Access, Visa; business accounts   **Discounts** 5% on 1 mixed case   **Delivery** Free within 7-mile radius (min 1 case); otherwise at cost; mail order available   **Glass hire** Free with appropriate case order
Tastings and talks Occasional in-store tastings; to groups on request
Cellarage Not available

'We're really a little bit of London on the South Coast,' says Tony Chaplin MW, 'adapting the crazes of the capital to the realities of West Sussex.' From the outside, at least, this traditionally fronted corner shop seems a far cry from the designer-led convulsions of London's trendier wine shops – though inside, the last year has brought a refit. If West Sussex reality plays a reassuring role in enticing the customer through the door, then it's London buying that keeps him or her there, with a medium-sized range of wine and spirits in which the New World gets to play many of the best tunes.

Certain producers in each area seem to provide exactly what Tony Chaplin or his customers want, and are rewarded with fidelity across a range: Penfolds in the Australian section, Torres in Penedés, Loron in Beaujolais and Rodet in Burgundy, Pascal for Rhône wines. If these are names that chime with you, here is the place to find them – in octaves. Other strengths for this old-established family company are clarets at under £10, and choice within Washington State, New Zealand and Romania. Nearby Nutbourne Manor's wines are stocked, and a taste-tour through the five varietals on offer would be well worth making.

Italy, Germany, Spain (Torres and Rioja excepted) and Portugal are all rather disappointing, with growers of distinction getting lost on the way to Rowlands Road. This may well reflect the fact that wholesale, hotel-owning customers – a previously unimportant part of the business that Tony Chaplin has expanded greatly in recent years – find it difficult to sell wines whose story needs to be told, as opposed to those whose story is already familiar. However, if you have a favourite garrafeira or super vino da tavola and Worthing is where you'd like to buy it, Tony Chaplin offers 'to supply any wine currently shipped to the UK by anyone if humanly possible'. Would someone like to test this offer for us?

Best buys

Gaillac Rouge Gamay 1989, Domaine Jean Cros, £4.09
Columbia Crest Sauvignon Blanc 1986, Washington State, £5.29
Romanian Classic Cabernet Sauvignon 1985, £2.59

Châteaux Wines

Not a shop
11 Church Street, Bishop's Lydeard,   *Tel* (0454) 613959
Taunton, Somerset TA4 3AT

Case sales only   Open Mon–Fri 9–5.30; Sat most mornings until 12.30
Closed Sun, public holidays   **Credit cards** Access, Visa; personal and business accounts   **Discounts** Negotiable   **Delivery** Free on UK mainland (min 1 case); mail order available   **Glass hire** Not available   **Tastings and talks** Annual tasting in November held in London; to groups on request   **Cellarage** £4 per case or part-case per year for wines purchased from premises

Châteaux Wines is a small and very personal operation run from home near Taunton by David and Cheryl Miller. Small; yet a free UK mainland delivery service is offered (in principle for unmixed cases only), and an annual tasting is held each autumn in London. If you become a member of the 'Cellar Club' you will receive a quarterly selection case, with a postcard prior to dispatch informing you of the selection and giving you the option of preferring something else from the list if you wish. And personal: David Miller's commitment to what he calls the Real Wine Trade is evident in every page of the list, and photographs of the beaming proprietor in a variety of disguises, reproduced throughout the list, will enable you to put a face to the voice on the telephone.

David Miller has managed to get a lot of wine out of Robert Ampeau in Meursault (including Volnay, Beaune, Pommard and Savigny as well as Meursault), and this is certainly a reason for contacting Church Street. Other reasons would include four vintages of Château Musar, and big ranges from Rosemount in Australia, Clos du Val in California and Laurent-Perrier in Champagne. Fifteen clarets, four unassignable Alsace wines, Chablis from Simmonet-Febvre and Beaujolais from the Eventail brings the list more or less full circle, and lays Châteaux Wines open to charges of idiosyncrasy in its range. Whether enthusiasm is adequate recompense is for you to decide; let us know your conclusions.

Best buys

Auxey-Duresses Premier Cru Les Ecusseaux 1982, Robert Ampeau, £13.50
Château Musar 1982, Serge Hochar, Lebanon, £5.57
Juliénas 'Les Envaux' 1989, Domaine André Pelletier, £5.70

Christchurch Fine Wine Co ➾

1–3 Vine Lane, High Street, Christchurch, *Tel* (0202) 473255
Dorset BH23 1AE

Open Mon–Sat 10–5 **Closed** Sun **Credit cards** Access, Visa **Discounts** 5% on 1 case; 5% off all purchases for club members **Delivery** Free in Bournemouth area (min 1 case); otherwise £5 per case; mail order available **Glass hire** Free with 1-case order **Tastings and talks** Monthly club tastings; to groups on request **Cellarage** £2.50 per case per year

The shopping mall promised in last year's *Guide* is still in preparation, but by the autumn John Carter hopes that it will have been installed in front of his old coach house. Telephone before making a special visit during the week to check that this has happened.

Visitors to Vine Lane will find a wide selection of France's best, and Christchurch is a good place to go for celebration bottles. Bordeaux and Burgundy are both well represented. The claret emphasis is on old favourites, such as Châteaux Gruaud-Larose, La Lagune and Cantemerle, each threaded through several vintages. It is seldom that one sees a range of Sauternes from 12 different châteaux, from d'Yquem 1966 (£114.35) to Filhot 1983 (£19.65). Burgundy, here, is founded on *négociant* selections: those of Prosper Maufoux (and Maufoux's *sous-marque* Marcel Amance) for reds, and Louis Latour for whites, while there is a fine range of the beautifully labelled Hospices de Beaune wines. The Loire and Rhône are both strengths, thanks to a close working relationship with Robin Yapp.

It is heartening to see nearly 40 German wines listed, and there are treasures to be unearthed by those patient enough to pick their way through the thicket of German nomenclature. The classically made Wegeler-Deinhard estates' wines recur throughout the selection, albeit spelled in three different ways on the list. Maybe the three Savoie wines indicate a more adventurous buying policy for the future – the Domaine de l'Idylle's lush red Mondeuse from the *cru* of Arbin (£5.60) certainly shows that France can still surprise.

For £5, you can join the Christchurch Fine Wine Club. As it brings you a five per cent discount off list prices, a monthly newsletter, the opportunity to attend tastings, and is refundable against a case purchase, there seems little reason for regular customers not to do so.

Best buys

Wehlener Sonnenuhr 1983 Riesling Spätlese (Wegeler-Deinhard), £12.60
Château Capendu Grande Réserve 1986 Corbières (Granel), £3.95
Auxey-Duresses Blanc 1985 (Amance), £9.80

Christopher & Co

See Les Amis du Vin.

City Wines

Administration and warehouse
35 St Benedict Street, Norwich, Norfolk   *Tel* (0603) 617967/619246
NR2 4PF
Shops
305 Aylsham Road, Norwich, Norfolk   *Tel* (0603) 405705
NR3 2RY
221 Queens Road, Norwich, Norfolk   *Tel* (0603) 660741
NR1 3AE

Open Mon, Tue 12–3, 4–9; Wed–Sat (Aylsham Road) 10–10, (Queens Road and St Benedict Street) 9–9; Sun and public holidays 12–2, 7–9 **Credit cards** Access, American Express, Visa; personal and business accounts **Discounts** 5% on 1 mixed case **Delivery** Free in Norwich (min 1 case); elsewhere at cost; mail order available **Glass hire** Free with case order **Tastings and talks** City Wines annual winefair; to local groups on request **Cellarage** Not available

If its last list was anything to go by, City Wines is aiming to become the most informal wine merchant in Britain. Gone was the two-colour elegance of the previous year's edition; gone, too, were the old photos, the prints and woodcuts, and the decoratively splodgy maps. But there were double the number of jokes.

Closer inspection revealed that that was all that had doubled; most of the wine ranges were considerably contracted. Whatever happened to that wonderful range of Portuguese wines, quite possibly the largest in the UK? Cut back to just six wines, that's what, and all of them widely available elswhere; terrible news. Spain, too, has suffered erosion, with the three Toro wines being sadly missed and Murrieta's white, too, carried off in the wind. We turned to Australia and the story was the same again: forty-three wines axed back to seventeen, with no trace of the Yarra Yering championed so proudly by City Wines of old. Even New Zealand was hit, during a year when most merchants have doubled their ranges: City Wines' avant-garde dozen in 1988 had become an unexceptional eight by the end of 1989. What's going on?

'We still have extensive ranges from all the great and fashionable wine regions of the world, however we have also done a bit of back to the roots stuff. Not just playing Aswad on the CD player at St Benedicts but making big efforts to find and provide more products like cheerful, tasty, affordable Vin de Pays, Organic wines and Beers, Champagne (don't laugh . . .) priced within reach of more people, Low Alcohol Wines and Beers, good reliable House Wines, and in general making every effort to provide a service that is relaxed, friendly and above all APPROACHABLE.' Something rings a little hollow here. There were more French country wines in the old list, and there were more Champagnes, too. There was nothing unaffordable about all those Portuguese wines, or the larger Spanish range, or the larger antipodean range (even including Yarra Yering); and we don't imagine that service was ever unapproachable in St Benedicts. What seems to have happened is that a terrific, exciting list has become one that's only just a notch above average – even if it does have more jokes. We hope the trend is reversible.

There are still plenty of good bottles available from City Wines – half a dozen from almost everywhere, let's say; and if this list slid across our desks out of the blue it would be enough to take the company well into the middle of the top 200 British merchants. But there is a sense of excellence abandoned, of capitulation to those who still think that litres of Liebfraumilch and Vin du Patron Blanc represent Germany and France adequately, of a reluctance to take the struggle for horizon-expansion further. Perhaps it was hard to persuade the citizens of Norwich to buy Luis Pato's Bairrada or Paço dos Infantes from Alentejo (last year's first recommended 'Best Buy'); but was it too hard? What do the customers think? If you're an old City Wines hand, write to us with your opinion of the changes.

See the back of the Guide if you would like to help the Wine Development Board with their Wine in Pubs campaign.

Best buys

Domaine du Puget 1986, Vin de Pays de l'Aude, Cabernet
Sauvignon, £3.29
Domaine d'Ormesson 1988, Vin de Pays d'Oc (white), £4.29
Château Hanteillan 1985, Haut-Médoc, £7.49

Classic Wine Warehouses ☞

Unit A2, Stadium Industrial Estate, Sealand   *Tel* (0244) 390444
Road, Chester, Cheshire CH1 4LU

Open Mon–Fri 8–6; Sat 9–5 **Closed** Sun, public holidays **Credit cards** Access,
Diners Club, American Express, Visa; personal and business accounts
Discounts Negotiable **Delivery** Free in Cheshire, Lancashire, Merseyside,
N Wales, Manchester, Shropshire and Lake District (min 1 case); elsewhere at cost;
mail order available **Glass hire** Free **Tastings and talks** Monthly in-store
tastings; large annual tasting held at hotel; to groups on request **Cellarage** Free

'Importers, Consultants, Wine & Spirit Merchants' is how
Classic Wine Warehouses Ltd. describes itself, and the result is
something of a compendium of all the ways that wine can be
sold. At heart, this company is an importer selling on to other
traders; that is where most of its business comes from, and that
is why the list is ex-VAT, with different prices depending on
whether you buy more or fewer than 20 cases. But it also has a
retail licence and can therefore be assumed to sell single bottles,
or multiples thereof, to personal callers if wished; its final hat is
that of wine warehouse, the mid-sized range and industrial-
estate location helping it look the part in this respect.

'Champagne is very much our speciality,' says Managing
Director John Lennon, and he claims to offer the 'cheapest
prices for Champagne nationwide'. This claim would be difficult
to verify; what is certain is that a reasonably wide range is on
offer here, though not as wide as at some of the champagne
specialists listed in the *Guide*. The claret range, by contrast, is
small; there is rather more burgundy than claret, indeed, most
of it from Drouhin, and Hugel dominates Alsace and Alphonse
Segurat the Rhône in the same way. Outside France, CVNE
Rioja, Fontanafredda's Italian wines, the Bulgarian and (red)
Yugoslav selections, Wolf Blass and Rosemount from Australia,
and four Stoneleigh Vineyard wines from the Corban Estate in
New Zealand's Marlborough area would provide the most
rewarding purchases. We hope to hear from customers of
Classic Wine Warehouses as to how 'user friendly' Unit A2 of
Chester's Stadium Industrial Estate is for the non-trade buyer.

See page 306 for an explanation of the symbols used in the *Guide*.

Best buys

Alsace Sylvaner 1988, Hugel, £4.69
Viña Real 1986, CVNE, Rioja, £4.45
Stoneleigh Vineyard Sauvignon Blanc 1989, Corbans Estate, New
Zealand, £7.41

Co-op ☞

CRS Head Office, National Office,   *Tel* 061-832 8152
29 Dantzic Street, Manchester M4 4BA
Trading under Leo's (91 outlets), Market Fresh (53 outlets) and Stop &
Shop (260 outlets)

Open Generally Mon–Sat 8–8; some public holidays   **Closed** Sun, Chr period
Credit cards None accepted; personal and business accounts   **Discounts**,
Delivery, Glass hire Not available   **Tastings and talks** Regular in-store tastings
Cellarage Not available

We know from letters that one of the biggest grievances that
customers nurse concerning wine purchase from supermarkets
is that not all stores stock all lines – so a wine that we may
recommend here from the central list may be unavailable in
your local branch, much to your annoyance. This problem seems
to be particularly acute with the Co-op.

The fact is that there are good wines on the Co-op main list –
but how many outlets stock them? Some of them have been
there for several years, yet the Editor's nearest branch of the Co-
op only ever seemed to have an array of Rougemont Castle,
Concorde, assorted British sherries, Lohengrin Liebfraumilch
and St Marcus sweet until it finally shut its doors for good last
year. We will run through some of the better wines stocked by
the Co-op below, but do please write and tell us how much
success you have in finding them.

Eastern Europe, of course, is an excellent source of
inexpensive, fruity red wines, and the two from Romania are
well worth trying (Cabernet Sauvignon and, especially, Pinot
Noir – see Editor's Choice). Try the Merlot from Hungary, and
the two Cabernet Sauvignons from Bulgaria, especially the
'Mountain' version. You might like to compare that with the
Cabernet Sauvignon Vin de Pays d'Oc (producer not mentioned
on list – but it may well be sold under the Co-op's own Pierre
Chaumont label anyway, like most of the French country wines).
The Co-op used to have a good red Anjou Villages, but that
seems to have disappeared from the list; in a very different
style, see what you think of the Domaine du Bousquet Côtes du
Roussillon Villages. Other reds worth a look include (probably)
the producer-less Montepulciano d'Abruzzo from Italy, Raimat
Abadía from Spain, the Jacobs Creek Dry Red from Australia,

the Curico Valley Cabernet Sauvignon from Chile and the Pinot Noir/Cabernet Sauvignon blend from Cooks in New Zealand. You can even get Château Cissac 1982 and 1984 at some shops. 1982 is the better year, but will cost more, though we don't know how much: the list sent to us didn't include prices.

It's harder to find white wines to recommend on the list, but this problem is by no means limited to the Co-op; inexpensive white wines of quality are in general hard to come by. The Alsace Pinot Blanc and Gewürztraminer have both been good in the past, and Jadot's Mâcon-Villages should not disappoint, either, though none can really be called inexpensive. There's a good basic Chablis from Chanson in some shops, and the same goes for a Chardonnay from Orlando to join the recommendable Jacobs Creek Dry White. Gallo's Californian Sauvignon Blanc is worth trying. The Co-op itself sets great store by its white Vin de Pays du Jardin de la France, and also tells us the Anjou Blanc is good, though we have no idea how dry/sweet the wine is – it should inform you on the bottle.

To your Co-ops, and report!

Best buys

Classic Romanian Pinot Noir 1986, £2.39
Jacobs Creek Dry Red (Orlando), South Australia, £3.29
Orlando Chardonnay 1989, South Australia, £4.59

Colombier Vins Fins ☞

Ryder Close, Cadeley Hill Industrial Estate,   *Tel* (0530) 412350/412349
Swadlincote, Burton on Trent, Derbyshire
DE11 9EU

Case sales only **Open** Mon–Fri 8.30–5; Sat on request **Closed** Sun, public holidays **Credit cards** None accepted; personal and business accounts **Discounts** 5% on 10 cases **Delivery** Free in Leicester, Birmingham, Nottingham, Northampton, Peterborough and Derby (min 3 cases); elsewhere at cost **Glass hire** Free with 3-case order **Tastings and talks** 3 major tastings in cellars; annual major tasting; to private customers on request **Cellarage** £4.37 per case per year

Colombier Vins Fins offers a medium-sized range almost exclusively from Europe, distinguished by the wines of a number of small growers that Jéhu Attias has sought out in France and Italy. Colombier is the agent for many of these; and although half of trade is with the general public, the ex-VAT nature of the list still makes it look as if it is primarily a tool for selling on in the trade. If you are a Colombier regular, report back to us on your impressions of the service for by-the-case consumers.

If you're new to Colombier, don't be put off by the Vins Fins part of the name: you'll find plenty here that costs under £10, and nearly everything is from the fine vintages of the 1980s. Claret and burgundy are present in force (especially Chablis and the Mâconnais: Colombier are also *négociant-eleveurs* at Charnay-les-Mâcon), while the Rhône and the Loire offer adequate choice. The rest of France is ignored, and it would be nice to see the *vins fins* of the Midi and the South-West putting in an appearance in future. Germany brings the list up to scratch again, but it's only with Italy that excitement reappears, with Rubini's Friuli wines, Casal Bordino's Abruzzo range, and a small choice of growers from Piedmont, Tuscany, Lombardy and the Marches. If you have a taste for vintage Armagnac, and a fat wallet, then you'll find a sensational range of no fewer than 32 different vintages from 1893 to 1962 here (£333.50 to £35.65). These are all from the same grower, Michel Faure, another Colombier agency.

Best buys

Montepulciano d'Abruzzo 1988, Casal Bordino, £2.90
Château Panet 1983, Saint-Emilion Grand Cru, £7.07
Pinot Bianco Riserva 1988, Colli Orientali del Friuli, Rubini, £7.50

Connolly's

110 Edmund Street, Birmingham, W Midlands B3 2ES

Tel 021-236 9269

Open Mon–Fri 9–5.30; Sat 9–3 **Closed** Sun, public holidays
Credit cards Access, American Express, Visa; personal and business accounts
Discounts 5% on 1 case; quantity discounts by agreement **Delivery** Free in Birmingham (min 1 case); otherwise at cost; mail order available **Glass hire** Free with order **Tastings and talks** Two major annual tastings; monthly tutored tastings; to groups on request **Cellarage** Not available

---

Connolly's returns to the *Guide* this year after an absence of several years. The company's 'Book of Bacchus' is not the largest list to be found in the Midlands, and it is certainly not the cheapest, but it is cheerfully written ('Yes, just as you thought it was safe to go back into the water, the phantom scribbler returns with more wince-inducing doggerel to keep you entertained') – and it contains some very sound wines. We are told that, over the last year, 'our most significant step has been to venture on to the Continent, order book in hand, to buy direct from properties rather than from London-based shippers'. There is, as yet, little evidence of this in the list, so we would ask readers to monitor changes at Edmund Street on our behalf.

Tutored tastings were also initiated during the spring of 1990.

Why, in 1991, would you shop at Connolly's? There are good clarets from 1983, 1985 and 1986; and we hope that Chris Connolly won't give up taking Faiveley burgundies from a well-known London-based shipper, as they would be missed. You may acquire wines from the Domaine de la Romanée-Conti here, though finance may require leverage. The Rhône, Alsace and Loire are sound, if restricted. Deinhard's superbly packaged Heritage range may woo you back to German wines, and it is possible, should you turn up at the right time of year, to buy Cloudy Bay's Sauvignon Blanc here. Coldstream Hill's Pinot Noir and Cape Mentelle's Cabernet Sauvignon are further pulls. Spain and Portugal are short and safe, while Italy is dangerously short. There is plenty of champagne of the grander sort, and a good selection of vintage port, though there seems no good reason why this should all be 'price on application'. Doesn't a request for a list constitute an application?

Best buys

Cloudy Bay Sauvignon Blanc 1989, New Zealand, £8.05
Saint-Joseph 1987, Bernard Gripa, £7.60
Bourgogne Rouge 1985, Château de Chamilly, £6.11

Corney & Barrow

12 Helmet Row, London EC1V 3QJ	*Tel* 071-251 4051
118 Moorgate, London EC2M 6UR	*Tel* 071-628 2898
44–45 Cannon Street, London EC4N 6JJ	*Tel* 071-248 1700
194 Kensington Park Road, London W11 2ES	*Tel* 071-221 5122
Belvoir House, High Street, Newmarket, Suffolk CB8 8OH	*Tel* (0638) 662068

Open Mon–Fri 9–7 (City); Mon–Sat 10.30–8.30 (Kensington); Mon–Sat 8.30–5.30 (Suffolk) **Closed** Sat (City), Sun, public holidays **Credit cards** Access, Visa; personal and business accounts **Discounts** Available **Delivery** Free within M25 (min 2+ cases) and outside M25 (min 3+ cases); mail order available **Glass hire** Free (charged then credited on return) **Tastings and talks** Quarterly tastings by invitation; regular wine course; to groups on request **Cellarage** £4.60 per case per year

---

You can buy Liebfraumilch from Corney & Barrow, but it is an unusual distraction in a grand list full of grand wine. Grandly priced; and before we go any further we should say what has doubtless been said before – that Corney & Barrow's system of listing wine prices is, for the ordinary (non-business) customer, misleading and confusing. Two prices are given: a single bottle ex-VAT price, and a case price including VAT. There might be some justification for this if the VAT hat was on the other head, as business customers might well be expected to buy by the case and private customers by the bottle. Alternatively, give four prices: bottle and case ex-VAT, and bottle and case including VAT. But to do it in the way Corney & Barrow does (and they have done it like that for years) looks rather as if they wish to lull private customers into thinking that the wines are less expensive than they are. Which, by and large, is very expensive.

However, when one of your chief roles in life is purveyor of Pétrus to the nation, perhaps this doesn't matter too much. Pétrus receives the support of a wide range of other fine clarets; particularly noteworthy is the Moueix portfolio of *petits châteaux* and the page devoted to Fronsac and Canon-Fronsac. Excellent value, by and large, even after the VAT has been added. There is also a good span from the other Moueix big guns – Trotanoy, La Fleur Pétrus, Latour à Pomerol and, in Saint-Emilion, Magdelaine – so if you have acquired the taste for rich, seductive Merlot-based claret, Corney & Barrow should be your target merchant. Remember this around *en primeur* time, too, as you discover that everyone else has almost instantly sold out of their Pomerol allocations. Médoc lovers will also find Mouton, Cheval Blanc, Latour, Pichon Lalande, Margaux – all that sort of thing.

Burgundy is as starry: the featured growers are Vincent Leflaive, Thierry Matrot, Domaine Dujac, Joseph Roty, Domaine Trapet, Marquis d'Angerville and Hubert de Montille, and Olivier Leflaive Frères is the upper-crust négociant. If you are able to buy wines at £20 per bottle, you will find much to reward experiment here.

After Burgundy, the list rather drops away, though there's plenty of Hermitage La Chapelle, fine Sauternes, Sassicaia and Tignanello, Penfolds Grange '82 and Cloudy Bay to keep the name-happy contented. Simi and Stag's Leap represent California, Santa Helena slakes for Chile, and Thanisch, Ress, Bürklin-Wolf, Prüm, Müller and von Schubert furnish most of the German wines. There is a battery of Vintage Port, though strangely enough, 1982 and 1983 are absent. 1985 is there in plenty, by contrast, and all the ports are priced – Averys and others take note.

The list is impeccably produced and full of information. When it sticks to matters like maturity and wine styles, it is very useful. There is a tendency to ramble, though: 'For those of you who know (and I myself was told), a sheet anchor is a useful thing, for it represents a second, even final line of defence, when your main cable parts in stormy weather. It was this irrelevant thought and as it happened, confusion of metaphor, which came to me in the passenger seat of a Ferrari BB512 being worked at some velocity around Castle Combe's rather erratically surfaced race track.' Hmm. Scarcely more enlightening is this preamble to the table wine range. 'The elections in Greece last summer were a reasonable example of how uneasy the mixing of business and pleasure can be, but Adam Brett-Smith [C&B's MD] is owed a greater debt than this moral one for it was here he first took a peculiar liking to chilled red wine which was easily transferred to London during our own Grecian Summer.' Come on, chaps. A 'total commitment to service and top quality in all areas' should include getting your printed thoughts straight.

Best buys

Domaine du Puget 1988, Cabernet Sauvignon, Vin de Pays de l'Aude, £3.34
Pokolbin Chardonnay 1989, Hungerford Hill, New South Wales, £6.90
Santa Helena Cabernet-Malbec 1987, Chile, £3.45

Côte d'Or Wines

88 Pitshanger Lane, London W5 1QX   *Tel* 081-998 0144

Open Mon–Sat 9.30–6 (open in evenings whenever possible)   **Closed** Sun, public holidays   **Credit cards** Access, Visa; personal and business accounts
Discounts 5% on 1 case (may be mixed)   **Delivery** Free locally and within M25 radius and all south-east England (min 1 case); mail order available
Glass hire Free   **Tastings and talks** Wines available for tasting on Saturdays; to groups on request   **Cellarage** £2.50 per case per year

---

Gavin Whitmee's neatly organised neighbourhood wine shop is very popular with Ealing locals, and we understand the service provided by Mr Whitmee is first-rate. The list is not long, nor – despite the name – does it specialise in burgundy. A little of everything seems to be the aim, both in terms of sourcing and in terms of a balance between the expensive and the inexpensive, the young and the old. Great care is taken to keep the wines in good condition, with all of them stored in racks. This would be a good place to go if you have a price and a taste in mind, but would like someone else to fit a bottle to it. And if there's a wine you know you like but you can't find it anywhere, Gavin Whitmee will try and get it for you.

Best buys

Seaview Fumé Blanc 1985, South Australia, £4.95
Garcia de Velasco Cream Sherry (an unusual recommendation, but ask Mr Whitmee about it . . .), £2.95
Château de Belcier 1985, Côtes de Castillon, £4.95

County Wines of Hagley

2 The Mews, Hagley Hall, Stourbridge, West   *Tel* (0562) 882346
Midlands DY9 9LG

Open Mon–Fri 9–5.30; Sat 10–5 **Closed** Sun, public holidays
Credit cards Access, Visa; personal and business accounts **Discounts** 5% on 1
case; larger discounts negotiable **Delivery** Free for all West Midlands post codes
and Hereford & Worcester (min 1 mixed case); otherwise £5.95 per consignment;
mail order available **Glass hire** Free **Tastings and talks** Monthly programme of
tastings; 2–3 tutored formal tastings per year; to groups on request
Cellarage £4.50 per case per year

A first appearance in the *Guide* for County Wines of Hagley,
whose retail premises are sited in the converted stables of a
West Midlands stately home, Hagley Hall. Hanging baskets and
window boxes will draw you in, and a short but sound selection
of the world's wines will keep you there; while the two-feet-
thick walls keep the wines at a steady temperature, in ideal
conditions, until you take them away. Mike Hodgetts and his
team offer a wide range of services to customers: since 1987 this
has included running *The Birmingham Post* Wine Club which, in
addition to supplying a mail-order service, also organises wine
tastings and gourmet meals (in Hagley Hall, on occasion).

White burgundy from Joseph Drouhin (try the Rully 1988 at
£9.95), Chilean wines from Santa Helena, and ports from Dow
and Warre are all good. For a Christmas treat, try these two port
shippers' 1979 single quinta Vintage Ports, Quinta da
Cavadinha and Quinta do Bomfim (both at £15.90, though the
price may have risen by Christmas), or half-bottles of Dow's 10,
20 and 30 Years Old tawnies. For next year, though, it would be
nice to see a bigger, broader list, with less reliance on single,
exclusive suppliers and a little more determination to find the
very best wine for every slot on the list. And, of course,
producers' names for Italy and Germany. More readers' reports,
please, too.

Best buys

Domaine de la Hilaire 1989, Vin de Pays des Côtes de Gascogne
(white), £3.69
Domaine de Lalande Cabernet Sauvignon 1988, Vin de Pays
d'Oc, £3.69
Barbadillo Solear, Manzanilla Pasada (half-bottle), £3.45

If your favourite wine merchant is not in this section, write and tell us
about him or her. There are report forms at the back of the book.

Croque-en-Bouche

221 Wells Road, Malvern Wells, Hereford &   *Tel* (0684) 565612
Worcester WR14 4HF

Case sales only   Open Any reasonable time, by arrangement
Credit cards Access, Visa   **Discounts** 5% on 4+ cases, cash & collect
Delivery Free locally (min 2 cases); elsewhere approximately £4; mail order
available   **Glass hire, Tastings and talks** Not available   **Cellarage** Short term
only, which is free

This list bids fair to be the most extraordinary you will read
about in this book. There are 900 wines lying in Robin and
Marion Jones's cool cellars in Worcestershire: that's within only
a hundred or so of the range offered by Lay & Wheeler,
generally considered to be one of the largest in the country. And
Croque-en-Bouche is a restaurant. If you are taken with the
wine you have drunk with dinner, you can take away more
with you – in case quantities, or as part of a mixed case, for
between £3 and £6 less than the very reasonable wine list price.
Or you can use Croque-en-Bouche as a merchant pure and
simple, by arranging in advance to turn up 'at any reasonable
time', or by taking advantage of mail-order facilities (though if
you live in another part of the country you'll need to spend over
£350, or order more than six cases, to avoid comparatively heavy
carriage costs of £4 per case with a minimum charge of £10).

In fact, there are so many wines on offer that they can't all be
crammed into one list. So there are two: one for reds, and one
for whites, rosés, ports, brandies and liqueurs; £2 is charged for
the pair. The wines are ordered according to a country-by-
country system, then divided into sweetness categories. All are
annotated, the notes quite clearly based on intelligent tasting of
the wines, and various key categories are used to provide what
must often be a bemused set of diners with pointers: 'Good
Value', 'Recommended' or 'Great Wine-making'.

Robin Jones is a wine enthusiast of great resource who has
given free rein to his passions, and the result is a glowing
collection that never fails to excite. The Rhône is the key area:
Croque-en-Bouche's extravagant selection is unrivalled in the
UK, especially in terms of mature wines. There are 39 different
Côte Rôties alone on the April 1990 list, with a promise of 56 in
the cellar! All the classic areas of France are present in force and,
as so often, an enthusiasm for red Rhône is matched by one for
white Loire, particularly medium sweet and sweet wines based
on the Chenin Blanc. Nothing, though, is omitted; nothing
ignored. There are wines from Canada, Argentina, China. There
are eighteen different eaux-de-vie from Alsace, twelve different
marcs, eight different Californian dessert wines, three different
Vega Sicilia Unicos, and one wine each from the Crimea and

from Zimbabwe. The sense of a splendid cornucopia is overwhelming, and you come away tipsy just from glancing through the pages on which all these wines are enumerated.

And the prices? Low for a wine list; high for a wine merchant. But where else are you going to get six vintages of Jasmin's Côte Rôtie, four of Chave's Hermitage, and a choice of ten Guigals?

Best buys

Côte Rôtie Brune & Blonde 1984, Guigal, £11.90
Vouvray, Le Haut Lieu 1971, Huet (half-bottle), £9.40
Côtes du Rhône 1987, Clape, £5.90

Cumbrian Cellar

1 St Andrew's Square, Penrith, Cumbria   *Tel* (0768) 63664
CA11 7AN

Open Mon–Sat 9–5.30   **Closed** Sun, Chr Day, Boxing Day, Good Friday
Credit cards Access, Visa; personal and business accounts   **Discounts** 5% on 1 mixed case   **Delivery** Free in Cumbria (min 1 case); elsewhere at cost; mail order available   **Glass hire** Free with 1-case order   **Tastings and talks** To groups on request   **Cellarage** £3.45 per case per year

---

Ex-RAF navigator Kenneth Gear came down to earth in Penrith, and became a partner in the Cumbrian Cellar (now ten years old) in 1982, 'as a challenge'. It is a challenge he seems to have risen to, and the impeccably neat labelling and shelving reflects a lifetime spent finding the way in enclosed spaces.

The range is a stimulating one, with 44 Italian wines and 26 Australian wines providing the most obvious specialities. The emphasis in both sections is on the larger, value-for-money producers. There are a number of esoteric lines, including Flame Lily from Zimbabwe, five English wines, two from Russia, a big Greek and Cypriot range, and wines from Texas, Washington and Oregon. Fortified wines receive sterling support in this damp corner of Britain, and there is an outstanding sherry section. It is matched by good ports, as well as by Liqueur Muscats from Australia and Greece, VDN Muscats from Frontignan, and Rivesaltes and Beaumes de Venise.

With only one bottle at over £10 in the Burgundy section you'd be right in assuming that it's anything but Côte d'Or; mostly Mâcon and Beaujolais, in fact. Bordeaux, too, has been stocked with an eye to economy; this optic explains the commendable wealth of country wines. Deinhard's beautifully packaged Heritage range provides much of the German interest; the Spanish wines are Rioja-centred, while Portugal is rather overlooked. Service, one reader tells us, is 'friendly and helpful'.

The Cumbrian Cellar would be a good place to visit if you'd like to try some unusual wines without loosing sight of too many ten-pound notes.

Best buys

Boutari Grande Reserve 1981, Greece (red), £4.99
Cerasuolo, Montepulciano d'Abruzzo 1986, Rosato, Illuminati, £4.65
Tio Diego Dry Amontillado, Valdespino, £6.75

Davenport & Son

The Courtyard, 52 Market Street, Ashby-de-la-Zouch, Leicestershire LE6 5AN   *Tel* (0530) 412827

Open Mon–Sat 8.30–5 **Closed** Sun, public holidays **Credit cards** Access, Visa; personal and business accounts **Discounts** 5% on 1 case **Delivery** Free in Midlands (min 1 bottle); elsewhere at cost; mail order available for business and company gifts **Glass hire** Free with wine order **Tastings and talks** Weekly tastings for customers; to groups on request **Cellarage** £1.35 per case per year

---

Davenports of Ashby-de-la-Zouch claims to be the oldest wine merchant in Leicestershire, and bases its claim on a criminal act. 'Thomas Davenport was convicted and fined 20 shillings in 1645 for selling wines to the King's forces at Ashby.' Nearly all of its business is now to the trade, but it does hold a retail licence and the cover of the list shows an attractive shop front; presumably by-the-bottle customers are also encouraged. If you are a Davenport's retail customer, write and give us your impression of the range and service.

The heart of the list is claret-coloured, and there is a wide range of the vintages of the 1980s on offer, though these are only priced on the (ex-VAT) list, in most cases, up to 1983. The others are 'for laying down' and 'price on application', these last three words being those we least like to see in a wine list; they are unhelpful and unnecessary. There are some pursue-able burgundies from Javillier, Dufouleur and Pousse d'Or, while Duboeuf gets most of the Mâconnais and Beaujolais to himself. Outside these classic areas, what we might call the 'Duboeuf principle' operates: the tried and trusted supplier is followed. Hence the presence of Antinori, Torres, Rosemount, Tyrrell and Khan Krum Chardonnay. There's a satisfactory range of recent Vintage Ports, and a few of the less expensive styles, but no tawny at all. We suspect that the range could do with a little gingering from someone with the initiative of the convicted Thomas Davenport.

Best buys

Chianti Classico Riserva 1983, Antinori, £7.16
Dão 1981, Grão Vasco, £4.09
Vintage Port 1982, Martinez, £13.88

Davisons Wine Merchants

Head office
7 Aberdeen Road, Croydon, Surrey CR0 1EQ   *Tel* 081-681 3222
Approx 80 branches in London and Home Counties

Open (Generally) Mon–Sat 10–2, 5–10; Sun 12–2, 7–9   **Credit cards** Access, Visa;
personal and business accounts   **Discounts** 8.5% on 1 mixed case   **Delivery** Free
locally (min 1 case); mail order available through Master Cellar Wine Warehouse
Glass hire Free   **Tastings and talks** Regular tastings at selected shops
Cellarage Not available

How much 1988 *en primeur* claret did you buy? Michael Davies
bought 12,000 cases of it – and he thinks he'll probably do the
same with the 1989s. It's a family tradition, you see; as
Managing Director of Davisons, Michael Davies has a reputation
to feed. If you want good claret, ordinary or extraordinary,
classed or unclassed, immature or fully mature, at very fair
prices, Davisons (or Master Cellar Wine Warehouse, *q.v.*) has for
many years been a quietly distinguished option open to you.
The selection is superb. No branch will have the full range, of
course, so ask for the list and give it a good going over at home
– then get the branch manager to order up whatever you want.
The same applies to Vintage Port, which Davisons also buy
exclusively *en primeur* to age themselves. The result is, again, an
excellent selection, realistically priced. Burgundy is another area
of strength: here, Davisons take the trouble to put together a list
of growers' wines, rather than buying out of négociants'
portfolios: Grivot, Pousse d'Or, Machard de Gramont, Morey,
Dufouleur and Burguet are some of those that can be reached
through the list. Traditional tastes are well catered for by
Davisons.

And unconventional tastes? Well, there's plenty to choose
from in Australia, though here it is the big boys that dominate
what's on offer. (Big Australians have, and merit, a better
reputation than big Burgundians.) California and Chile are
restricted; while off Europe's beaten tracks the Spanish,
Portuguese, Italian and German selections are all passable rather
than accomplished. One Barolo and no Barbaresco; nothing in
the garrafeira line from Portugal; a degree of timidity in listing
the more uncompromising German wines rather than those that
form the country's large, soft underbelly . . . champagne and

France's regional wines, though, are up to scratch, if no more.
Claret's the thing here: revel in it.

Best buys

Domaine de Limbardie Merlot 1989, Vin de Pays des Coteaux de
Murveil, £3.25
Lacoste-Borie 1985, Pauillac (second wine of Château Grand-
Puy-Lacoste), £8.75
Domaine de l'Eglise 1985, Pomerol, £13.95

Davys of London

151 Borough High Street, London SE1 1HR   *Tel* 071-407 1484
See Wines Galore.

Del Monico's

23 South Street, St Austell, Cornwall   *Tel* (0726) 73593
PL25 5BH

Open Mon 10–6; Tue–Fri 10–8; Sat 9–6 **Closed** Sun, some public holidays
Credit cards Access, Visa; personal and business accounts **Discounts** 5% on 1
case **Delivery** Free within 20-mile radius of St Austell (min 1 case); elsewhere
charges negotiable **Glass hire** Free **Tastings and talks** To groups on request
Cellarage Not available

Since the publication of last year's *Guide*, David Del Monico has
sold his Cornish 'Emporium' to husband-and-wife team Pat and
Tony Lawes. This ex-Davisons pair intend to carry on the
business as before, apart from 'sweeping aside a little dust to
make way for new lines', much as Gerry's in Old Compton
Street carries on the Del Monico Soho tradition.

There isn't much, in terms of wine types, that you won't find
on these neatly stacked and labelled shelves, and the new wine
regions of the world are obviously viewed sympathetically here.
But classic wines are not ignored, either: the balance is right;
the limits are those of shop space. Producers' names do not
always find their way on to the list, as the *Guide* noted last year;
however as no mail-order service is offered and the great
majority of customers are passing browsers (or browsing
passers), such omissions are forgiveable. Lines of particular
interest include the full range of Gaillacs from Jean Cros
(including the prestige Château Larroze range), white Regaleali
from Sicily, Israel's Gamla Cabernet Sauvignon and a good
range of Romanian and Yugoslavian wines. The fact that
Château La Tour Saint-Bonnet 1982 costs £5.95 while Mouton
Cadet 1986 costs £6.25 is a sobering illustration of the power of
brand names.

Best buys

Château La Tour Saint-Bonnet 1982, Médoc, £5.95
Columbia Chardonnay 1988, Washington State, £5.99
Campo Viejo Reserva Rioja 1983, £5.15

Dennhöfer Wines

47 Bath Lane, Newcastle upon Tyne, Tyne   *Tel* 091-232 7342
Wear NE4 5SP

Open Mon–Fri 9–5.30; Sat 9–1   **Closed** Sun, public holidays   **Credit cards** All
accepted; personal and business accounts   **Discounts** 5–10% (min 1 case)
Delivery Free in North-East (min 1 case); elsewhere at cost; mail order available
Glass hire Free with 1-case order   **Tastings and talks** Monthly tastings in
conjunction with Blackgate Restaurant; to groups on request   **Cellarage** Free

Dennhöfer is a name that suggests one European wine-
producing country in particular and, sure enough, German wine
was the starting point for this friendly Newcastle merchant.
Thirty or so German wines remain on the Dennhöfer list, but
they have now been joined by rather more than that from
France, with expansion presently in progress – under ex-
Oddbins and Majestic worker Tessa Ing, who looks after buying
and marketing – in the Italian, Spanish and Antipodean ranges.
The summer monthly 'Kitchen and Cellar' news bulletin, which
ties in special offers with wine and food tastings at Newcastle's
Blackgate restaurant, suggests that expanding one's waistline as
Dennhöfer expands its list would be fun. Can readers confirm?
   The list isn't long as yet, but among the wines on it that merit
experimental purchase are the white burgundies of Patrick
Javillier, the 1985 clarets, many of the German wines, the Rosso
di Montalcino from Frescobaldi's Campo ai Sassi, the Montecillo
Riojas and Priorato from Masia Barril, and Nobilo's New
Zealand wines. Fonseca's ports are rich and sturdy examples of
their kind. Dennhöfer Wines offer attractive delivery facilities,
and make something of a speciality of company and personal
gifts, distributed nationwide, at Christmas.

Best buys

Erbacher Steinmorgen Riesling Kabinett 1988,
Winzergenossenschaft Erbach, Rheingau, £5.62
Nobilo Gewürztraminer 1988 (New Zealand), £7.68
Barolo Riserva 1978, Kiola, £8.77

Which? Wine Guide does not accept payment for inclusion, and there is
no sponsorship or advertising.

Rodney Densem Wines

Office
Stapeley Bank, London Road, Nantwich,   *Tel* (0270) 623665
Cheshire CW5 7JW   (for both addresses)
Retail
4 Pillory Street, Nantwich, Cheshire
CW5 5BB

Open Mon–Tue 10–6; Wed 9–1; Thur–Fri 9–6; Sat 9–5.30   **Closed** Sun, public
holidays   **Credit cards** Access, Visa; personal and business accounts
Discounts 5% on 1 case of mixed wine   **Delivery** Free within 25-mile radius (min
1 case); elsewhere approximately £5 per case; mail order available   **Glass hire** Free
with 1-case order   **Tastings and talks** Approximately 6 tastings annually; to
groups on request   **Cellarage** Not available

This long, thin shop in Nantwich's Pillory Street is run by
Margie Densem, while her husband Rodney operates a
wholesale and trade sales business from their home in London
Road. The shop is attractively laid-out and lit, with all the wines
clearly labelled and priced. Upstairs there is a tasting room, and
regular customers attend after-hours tastings here by invitation
about six times per year.

The range available from the shop is wide, approaching 1,000
wines. The balance between pricier wines from the classic areas
of France, and more inexpensive wines from elsewhere in
Europe and the New World, is well struck; French country
wines are not neglected either. Burgundies from Drouhin and
Jaffelin (Jaffelin being Drouhin-owned) are present in force, and
are less likely to disappoint than most from this small fillet of
French countryside. Rodney Densem made an *en primeur* offer of
Drouhin's '88s during spring 1989. There is also a major
Champagne contingent.

Alsace wines from Hugel and Willm are among the region's
best, while the Cauhapé wines from Jurançon are not cheap, but
show the startling potential lying buried in the French
countryside. Other threads to be traced through the shelves
follow quality and reliability: Pascal in the Rhône, Torres in
Penedés and Chile, Guntrum in Germany, Penfolds and Brown
Brothers in Australia; but more unusual wines motor in from
time to time on an occasional, special-offer or bin-end basis.
The shop has no list as such, but an ex-VAT wholesale list is
available, and everything that appears on the wholesale sheets
can be bought from the shop on a retail basis.

For merchants who sell a minimum of twelve bottles, we say 'Case
sales only' in the details at the head of an entry.

Best buys

Niersteiner Findling Scheurebe Spätlese 1986, Guntrum, Rheinhessen, £5.95
Berberana Reserva Rioja 1983, £6.30
Santenay Premier Cru 1985, Drouhin (red), £12.50

Direct Wine Shipments

5/7 Corporation Square, Belfast, Co Antrim BT1 3AJ	*Tel* (0232) 238700/243906
Associated outlet	
Duncairn Wines, 555 Antrim Road, Belfast, Co Antrim BT15 3BU	*Tel* (0232) 370694

Open Mon–Fri 9.30–5.30; Sat 10–5 **Closed** Sun, public holidays
Credit cards Access, Visa; personal and business accounts **Discounts** 5% on
½–1 unmixed case **Delivery** Free in Greater Belfast and certain areas in Northern
Ireland (min 2 cases); otherwise at cost **Glass hire** Not available
Tastings and talks Two 6 week courses annually; to groups on request
Cellarage Free with purchase

Direct Wine Shipments has, it claims, the largest range of wines in Ireland; some 700 to 800, filling a 150-year-old warehouse in Belfast's docklands. It holds the Northern Ireland agency for most of these wines, which means that you may find them elsewhere in the province, but you shouldn't find them cheaper. Staff training is a priority, and customer training scarcely less so: through DWS you can join six-week Wine Education Courses, and attend tastings tutored by the likes of Johnny Hugel and Marc Chapoutier. *En primeur* offers (of Rhônes, Burgundies and clarets) are made, at prices very much in line with those of London-based specialists.

The buying policy reflected in the wine list seems to be to target 'the good producer', and then bring over almost everything he or she has to offer: very much an agency philosophy. Chapoutier in the Rhône, Langlois-Château in the Loire, Hugel in Alsace, Bollinger in Champagne, Bürklin-Wolf in Rheinpfalz, Pio Cesare in Piedmont, Marqués de Cáceres in Rioja, Torres in Penedés, Caves Aliança in Portugal and Santa Rita in Chile all get this loyal treatment. The result adds up to well under 700 wines, so presumably the warehouse is full of bin-ends and other vinous sundries to make up the balance; it would be good to have confirmation of this from wine-loving Ulsterpersons. (In fact it would be good to hear from wine-loving Ulsterpersons about almost anything germane to the *Guide*.) The string of quotations – a few memorable, many dull – that festoon the list lend your purchases authority.

Best buys

Santa Rita 120 Cabernet Sauvignon 1987, Chile, £3.95
Moulin-à-Vent 1988, Domaine Diochon, £6.89
Alsace Gewürztraminer 1983, 'Jubilee', Réserve Personnelle,
Hugel, £10.95

Domaine Direct ☞

29 Wilmington Square, London WC1X 0EG   *Tel* 071-837 3521
(answering service)
Tel 071-837 1142

Case sales only **Open** Mon–Fri 8–6 **Closed** Sat, Sun, public holidays
Credit cards None accepted; personal and business accounts **Discounts** Not
available **Delivery** Free in central London (min 1 case) and on UK mainland (min
3 cases); otherwise 1 case £6.90, 2 cases £9.20; mail order available
Glass hire Free **Tastings and talks** Two annual tastings for private customers;
Annual Harvest preceded by Burgundy theme tasting; to groups on request
private customers; to groups on request **Cellarage** £5.75 per case per year (inc
receiving, insurance and outward delivery to London)

Domaine Direct means Burgundy, though as usual Burgundy is
understood to include Chablis, the Côte Chalonnaise, the
Mâconnais and Beaujolais. And note 'Domaine': it means
growers only, here, and the best of them; négociants are not
even considered for listing. The lack of a retail licence (or the
policy to sell only on wholesale terms) should simultaneously be
registered, for it signifies that every visit here will be costly.
You wouldn't really want to leave 29 Wilmington Square
without having bought at least something from the likes of
Tollot-Beaut, Domaine de la Pousse d'Or, Etienne Sauzet,
Georges Roumier or Armand Rousseau; by the time you've
mixed twelve bottles, though, you will be looking at a bill of
over £100 unless you have sewn the case together very carefully.
Prices on the list exclude VAT; this, plus the large range of half-
bottles and glassware, suggests that most of Domaine Direct's
customers are probably the capital's smarter restaurants.

There is plenty of choice at under £10 a bottle, provided you
don't mind sticking to Beaujolais (the range has been expanded
during the last year), the Mâconnais and the Côte Chalonnaise,
with Chablis of below Premier Cru level. The glories of the list,
though, are its Côte d'Or growers, so we would recommend
saving up for a one-off, red-letter visit, discussing what's
available with Hilary Gibbs or Simon Taylor-Gill, going for the
best, and hanging the cost.

If you already know your heart belongs to Burgundy, and you
can afford a monthly standing order of between £50 and £150,
then the Domaine Direct Cellar Account provides a first-class
cellar-building facility. Côte d'Or Burgundy is offered *en primeur*

here, too: from Tollot-Beaut and Pousse d'Or for the 1988 vintage, for example. Serious punters should take advantage of this when the lauded vintages come around; there's scarcely a drop of 1985 left on the list now, and the same will doubtless be true of 1988 come 1993. 'Southern Burgundy' (i.e. the rest) is also offered *en primeur*.

Best buys

Bourgogne 1986, René Bourgeon, £6.04
Montagny Premier Cru Les Coères 1988, Bernard Michel, £7.99
Corton-Bressandes 1987, Tollot-Beaut, £20.13

Peter Dominic

Head office
Astra House, Edinburgh Way, Harlow, Essex   *Tel* (0279) 451145
CM20 2BE
Approx 600 outlets nationwide

Open Varies from store to store; majority open 7 days a week, Mon–Sat 9–6; Sun, public holidays 12–2, 7–10 (excluding Scotland)   **Closed** Chr Day, 1 Jan
Credit cards Access, American Express, Grand Metropolitan Shareholders Card, Visa; personal and business accounts   **Discounts** 5% (min 1 mixed case of light wine)   **Delivery** Free locally to store (min 1 case)   **Glass hire** Free with order
Tastings and talks Selected tastings at the larger outlets and for all new shop openings; to groups on request   **Cellarage** Not available

Peter Dominic, with 600 shops in England, Wales and Scotland, is the most important of the three members of the Grand Metropolitan-owned, but now independently operating, Dominic group. (The other two members are Bottoms Up and Hunter & Oliver.) We know from readers' reports that Peter Dominic branches are often valued in towns where there are few or no alternative sources of wine, or where there is an old-established independent merchant whose range is rather more classical than Dominic's – as well as being considerably more expensive. However, where there is a wide choice of alternative merchants to patronise, then Peter Dominic seems to have little cutting edge, little clear profile or appeal beyond the mute offering of a sound, medium-length range. Its lack of dynamism suggests that the company is at present in a transitional phase, and it certainly seems to lack the sense of direction so evident at the moment at its great rival, Victoria Wine.

But let's imagine you are on the way to dinner with a friend, and the only wine shop you can find open in which to buy him or her a bottle is a Peter Dominic. (Let's also imagine that this is a Peter Dominic that carries the full range.) If you're after a budget red (under £3.50 equals 'budget' nowadays), then Bulgaria, Romania, some of the Portuguese and Spanish wines, the French country wines (don't scorn the Anjou Rouge) or Algeria's Coteaux de Tlemcen would all provide acceptable drinking. The six Portuguese reds, in particular, are most commendable (two are over £3.50, by the way), and if Dominic can be said to have an area of strength, then it would be Iberia. Whites in this price range are more difficult, as always: the Bulgarians and the three Gallos (one an off-white) would provide best value.

Up the ante to £7.50 and you bring in modest ranges of Australian and Chilean wines, some quality Loire wines like Le Master de Donatien Muscadet or the Clos des Victoires Quincy, Wolfburger's sound if unexciting Alsace wines, the deadly dull Bellicard Tavel that Dominic has stocked for years and, among the reds, some good, unpretentious Rioja as well as the beloved Musar. If price is immaterial, it's only really claret and champagne that are likely to part you from your money, though there is nothing outstanding about the selection in either case. Italy, Germany, Burgundy and Beaujolais, the Rhône and the *petit château* end of Bordeaux all look as if they are overdue for a spring clean.

These are exciting times in the world of wine, and it's a shame that this is not reflected in the range offered by a chain as important as this one. Seagram's ownership of Oddbins has proved that it's possible to be part of a large conglomerate yet still maintain a free-wheeling, incisive and audience-pleasing profile, so the Dominic group have everything to play for. Perhaps next year will bring better news.

Best buys

Serradayres 1980, Portugal, £3.59
Marqués de Murrieta 1984, Rioja (white), £6.59
Château Musar 1982, Lebanon, £6.35

Drinksmart

Bull Head Street, Wigston, Leicester,   *Tel* (0533) 881122
Leicestershire LE8 1PA

Open Mon–Thur 10–8; Fri, Sat 9–8; public holidays 10–6 **Closed** Sun, Chr Day, 1 Jan, Good Friday **Credit cards** Access, Visa **Discounts** Available **Delivery** Not available **Glass hire** Free **Tastings and talks** Tastings every Friday and Saturday; to groups on request **Cellarage** Not available

---

Drinksmart is an interesting amalgam of hypermarket and wine warehouse, and anyone living within striking distance of Leicester would be well advised to make for Bull Head Street. The range on offer is extensive, and the prices extremely attractive.

From the outside, Drinksmart looks like a classic wine warehouse, and the piles of wine cases inside sustain the impression. Yet you can buy a single bottle here if you wish, and if you want case discounts on the already keen prices, you can generally find these on cases of six wines rather than twelve. Stepping out beyond wine you'll find yourself entering the land of beer, spirits, cider, and then a dreamworld of cherryade, Diet Pepsi, Vimto, Tizer and the rest – a 'drinks superstore', as the publicity materials proclaim.

Don't expect a fancy list, nor a mail-order or delivery service. They've piled it high and are selling it cheap, and it's up to you to come and cart it away. There is a dedicated tasting area, however, with themed tastings organised every Friday and Saturday, so you can sample some of the stock before committing yourself.

When it comes to purchase, you'll find a good selection of clarets with sensible support for the Cordier range of châteaux; an extensive roam through French country wines; lots of German wine (though you may pay in disappointment for the cheapest – aim for £4+ purchases here); plenty to choose from in Italy and Spain, while Portugal is improving; and excellent Australian, Bulgarian and Romanian sections. Every popular brand in the business is here too, of course, should you retain a soft spot for some of those. For party planners, it must be one of the most useful addresses in the country.

Best buys

Château Caraguilhes 1988, Corbières, £3.59
Château Roquetaillade-la-Grange Blanc 1986/7, Graves, £4.95
João Pires Branco Moscato, 1988 (Portugal), £4.49

Eaton Elliot Winebrokers

15 London Road, Alderley Edge, Cheshire   *Tel* (0625) 582354
SK9 7JT

Open Mon–Wed 9–6.30; Thur, Fri 9–8; Sat 9–5 **Closed** Sun, public holidays
Credit cards All accepted; personal and business accounts **Discounts** 5% on 1
case **Delivery** Free within 25-mile radius of Alderley Edge (min 1 case);
elsewhere at cost; mail order available **Glass hire** Free **Tastings and talks** At
least 12 formal tastings annually; to groups on request **Cellarage** £3.50 per case
per year

Eaton Elliot – whose shop has been refurbished and extended during the last year – has an excellent list of France's more unusual wines balanced by a good selection from other countries. South-West France is a particular favourite here, and Château Peyros from Madiran, Château de Chambert from

Cahors and Domaine Cauhapé from Béarn/Jurançon would
provide an excellent introduction to what this corner of France
has to offer. This is no less true of the two Corsican wines of
Domaine Peraldi, of the two wines from Pierre Boniface in
Savoie, and of the beautifully labelled and packaged Jura wines
of Château d'Arlay. There is a good Loire selection, including
six red wines and three rosés; Bordeaux and Burgundy, by
contrast, are not stocked to any great extent, though there is a
choice of at least half a dozen wines from each. They are viewed
as regional French wines like any others at Eaton Elliot.

Italy (the Centre and the North rather than the South and the
Islands) seems to inspire more enthusiasm on Alderley Edge
than does Spain, Portugal or Germany, though a small selection
here does not necessarily mean a dull one. The three Portuguese
reds, for example, are the Grão Vasco Dão Garrafeira, Luis
Pato's Bairrada and Quinta do Côtto's Grande Escolha, each well
able to express the wine-growing potential of their native land.
The New World is not overlooked, either: there are wines from
New York State, Long Island, Washington, Oregon, Argentina
and Chile as well as from Australia (mainly Rosemount), New
Zealand (Coopers Creek and Cloudy Bay) and California
(Beckstoffer and Sutter Home). Champagne, finally, is in good
supply. We are confident that even the most blasé of our readers
would find something to reawaken his or her appetite for
novelty in this stimulating selection.

Best buys

Château Peyros 1986, Madiran, £5.65
Château d'Arlay Corail 1986, Côtes du Jura, £6.95
Roussette de Savoie 1989, Pierre Boniface, £4.95

Eldridge Pope

Head office

Weymouth Avenue, Dorchester, Dorset   *Tel* (0305) 251251
DT1 1QT

9 branches (Dorchester, Shaftesbury, Sherborne, Wareham, Westbourne,
Weymouth, Wincanton, Winchester and The Poole Wine Centre) and 4
Wine Libraries (London, Exeter and Bristol)

Open Generally Mon–Sat 9–1, 2–5.30 (varying half-days); (Reynier in London and
Exeter) Mon–Fri 11–6.30; (Exeter) Sat 11–6.30; (Bristol) Mon–Fri 9.30–6.30
Closed Sat (Reynier, London and Bristol), Sun, public holidays
Credit cards Access, Visa; personal and business accounts   **Discounts** 5% on
mixed or full cases   **Delivery** Free within 20-mile radius of Dorchester (min £35
order) and UK mainland (min 4 cases or £100 order); otherwise 2–3 cases £6.50 per
order, 1 case or part case £3.60; mail order available   **Glass hire** Available with
wine order   **Tastings and talks** Occasional in-store tastings; regular tutored
tastings; to groups on request   **Cellarage** £2.50 per case per year

Under the Eldridge Pope banner are two different styles of operation, and two different names. Eldridge Pope retail shops, first of all, sell wines drawn from the master list on a by-the-bottle basis. These have been joined during the last year by 'Britain's First Drive-In Wine Centre' in Poole, on the site of an old Dorset & Hants Bus Company depot. You don't actually drive around the shelves with your window open, hauling in bottles of what you fancy; it's more of a wine warehouse with covered parking. The Dorchester shop has recently been upgraded to a Wine Centre, too, though Driving In is not possible there.

The other name, and the other style of operation, is J B Reynier Wine Libraries, sited in Bristol, Exeter, London EC3 and London SW1. Again, the wines come from the master list, but this time the shops double as lunch-time wine bars, and you can buy wines from the list to taste and try with your lunch at shelf prices – a very good idea. Of course, you can simply use the Libraries as retail shops if you wish. All the Libraries are open in the evenings for pre-arranged tutored tastings.

And what of the master list? Great store is set by the generic wines labelled as The Chairman's Rather Wordy This or That: The Chairman's Elegantly Dry Champagne, for example, or The Chairman's Classic Flavoursome Red Burgundy. The Chairman's Exceedingly Old and Rare Cognac Grande Fine Champagne has a hand-printed label, and no wonder, with all those words looking for somewhere to sit down. 'Outstanding quality and value for money' is claimed for these wines, and Eldridge Pope are happy to let you judge them on the basis of this range of seven.

However, the list is so extensive that you would need an iron will to leave it at that. Bordeaux and burgundies are lengthily listed, full of both quality and variety; prices are higher than some competitors for the Bordeaux 1985s, but the 1983s and 1982s seem comparatively good value, and in general market patterns are followed. A real effort has been made to find a burgundy range at under £10 as well as over £10, for which credit is due; indeed, this is one of the best merchants in the *Guide* for inexpensive Burgundy. The Loire and Alsace are both more extensively listed here than at many competitors, with a lovely selection of old Moulin Touchais wines. The net has been cast far and wide through the French regions, and again the selection is good. Eldridge Pope's customers are largely francophile, we suspect.

Schloss Vollrads and its Charta confrères dominate the fine range of German wines, while much that is classical in Italy, too, is gathered together in the Dorset fold. The rest of the world has yet to make much of an impression on the Chairman, though Luxembourg and Switzerland, strangely enough, will fill almost a case apiece at EP. Special and *en primeur* offers are made from time to time, too – it's all most heartening from a brewer.

Best buys

Savennières 1988, Clos du Papillon, Baumard, £5.64
Tuilerie du Bosc Rouge 1988, Côtes de Saint-Mont (oak-aged), £3.45
Vin de Pays de Franche-Comté Chardonnay 1988, Guillaume, £4.77

Ben Ellis and Associates

The Harvesters, Lawrence Lane, Buckland, Betchworth, Surrey RH3 7BE	*Tel* (073 784) 4866/2160 (with answering machine)

Case sales only Open 'All hours' – 24-hour answering machine
Credit cards None accepted; personal and business accounts **Discounts** Not available **Delivery** Free in Surrey and central London (min 5 cases); otherwise £2.30 per case; mail order available **Glass hire** Free with 2-case order
Tastings and talks Two regular 3-day tastings in spring and autumn in Surrey; two regular 1-day tastings in spring and autumn in central London; to groups on request **Cellarage** £3.45 per case per year

---

Ben Ellis and Associates is a small, shopless, wholesale wine merchant based in Surrey. Its habitually low profile (advertisement is disdained) received a hoick when Mark Pardoe – the Associate – won the Madame Bollinger Medal in 1990, awarded to the most successful candidate in the tasting papers of the previous year's Master of Wine exams. The company deserves to be better known, and this distinction is as appropriate a way as any for the word to be spread.

The list is beautifully organised, crystal clear in its presentation of information and thorough in its discussion of each region and most growers. Perhaps a little less bold type would make it easier on the eye, but this is a suggested refinement rather than a criticism. The balance between Old World and New; classic wines and innovative wines; and – to a lesser extent – expensive wines and cheaper wines is admirably struck. Bordeaux, Burgundy and Italy perhaps offer more list depth than other regions and countries, but there are one or two good bottles from almost everywhere. The names that we recognise inspire confidence in those that we don't, and there is a sense that everything is done here most scrupulously, and with great attention to detail.

Eleven ready-mixed cases are offered, as well as lists of particularly strongly recommended wines within different price brackets. Bi-annual tastings are organised for customers. We feel that anyone who likes good wine, or is reasonably well off, but doesn't have time to research the subject for him or herself, could entrust their buying to Ben Ellis and Associates with the greatest confidence. The company is equally attractive for armchair browsers, and for anyone who enjoys personal service as they purchase wine.

Best buys

Château du Pavillon 1985, Canon-Fronsac, £6.19
Saint-Véran 1988, Les Terres Noires, Jean-Luc Terrier, £6.65
Valpolicella Classico 1985, La Grola, Allegrini, £6.80

English Wine Centre

Drusillas Roundabout, Alfriston, East Sussex   *Tel* (0323) 870532/870164
BN26 5QS
Associated outlet
Michelham Country Foods, Michelham   *Tel* (0323) 440161
Priory, Upper Dicker, Hailsham, East Sussex
BN27 3QS

Open (English Wine Centre off-licence) Mon–Sat 10–5; Sun, public holidays 12–5 **Closed** Christmas Day, Boxing Day, 1 Jan **Credit cards** Access, Visa; personal and business accounts **Discounts** Available (min 1 case) **Delivery** Free within 20-mile radius; (min 1 case); elsewhere at cost; mail order available **Glass hire** Free with 1-case order **Tastings and talks** Always min of 3 wines available in-store; tastings of new releases of English wine; Beaujolais Nouveau open day; to groups on request **Cellarage** Limited

In addition to organising the English wine festival every autumn, The English Wine Centre also acts as a retailer and wholesaler of the wines of just over 20 English growers, most of them based in Sussex and Kent, but with examples from Hampshire, Gloucestershire, Norfolk, Suffolk, Essex and the Isle of Wight. A number of the pacesetters for English viticulture are stocked here, and the list includes a paragraph or so describing each vineyard and its medal-winning record. A visit to anywhere with an address like Drusillas Roundabout is worth making, and you will always find at least three bottles open for tasting when you arrive. As the 1989s reach the Roundabout, the journey becomes even more worthwhile.

Best buys

Breaky Bottom Seyval Blanc 1989, Sussex, £5.99
Downers Müller-Thurgau 1986, Sussex, £4.75
Berwick Glebe Reichensteiner/Müller-Thurgau 1987, Sussex, £5.40

Philip Eyres Wine Merchant

In association with Gregory Bowden & Florence Pike

The Cellars, Coleshill, Amersham,
Buckinghamshire HP7 0LS

Tel (0494) 433823
(enquiries)
Tel (0494) 432402
(The Cellars)

Case sales only **Open** Personal callers by appointment; telephone enquiries during office hours Mon–Fri 8–10, Sat, Sun 9–10 **Closed** Public holidays and during annual holiday **Credit cards** None accepted; personal and business accounts **Discounts** Not available **Delivery** Free within surrounding areas together with central London and other parts of London by mutual agreement (min 1 case); otherwise 1–3 cases charged flat fee of £5; mail order available **Glass hire** Free with 1-case order **Tastings and talks** Tastings given at various locations **Cellarage** £3.75 per case per year; held in Berkhamsted

---

Philip Eyres and Associates moves into its second year of trading with the same combination of careful buying, assiduous service and reasonable pricing structure that characterised its first. (For those who missed last year's *Guide*, Philip Eyres said farewell to his two middle names, Henry Townsend, as the merchant business which traded under these became part of Findlater Mackie Todd; he was joined in his new enterprise by Gregory Bowden, and Florence Pike of Gerard Harris. This year has seen the addition of a third Associate, Barney Wilson.)

Philip Eyres was one of the pioneers of *en primeur* claret selling in Britain, the first vintage he offered in this way being the 1966 (at prices which would have us chuckling today). He was at it again with the 1989 vintage, opening earlier than many merchants and with some of the most competitive prices of the year. Other *en primeur* offers are made, notably of German wines, and the special offers circulated to customers are usually rather more interesting than simply the 'Twelve Fresh Whites For Summer Drinking' type of thing. Last year, for example, an offer was made of a mixed case of 1981 clarets, this being a forgotten vintage if ever there was one; the line-up included Margaux, Cheval Blanc, La Mission Haut Brion, Palmer, Pichon Lalande, Domaine du Chevalier and Talbot, and the price was £278.

Lest you think that special offers of this sort mean that it's strictly fine wines only here, we should point out that one could mix at least one case from the list with wines under £5, and many of the wines listed are under £10. The range is wide and of medium length (expansion is in progress), with claret, burgundy, Alsace, Germany, Spanish reds, Australia and Chile being listed most thoroughly. This, we note, is a merchant with the patience to list all the label information for his German wines, and with the enthusiasm to taste and annotate each; neither is common. The same scrupulousness and effort is evident throughout the list, and in the service provided, and this is a merchant we feel able to recommend firmly.

Best buys

Ockfener Scharzberg Riesling Qualitätswein 1988, Friedrich Wilhelm Gymnasium, Saar, £4.10
Alsace Auxerrois 1988, Rolly Gassmann, £6.30
Faugères 1986, oak-aged, Gilbert Alquier, £5.65

Farr Vintners

Mainly mail order
19 Sussex Street, London SW1V 4RR   *Tel* 071-828 1960

Case sales only   **Open** Mon–Fri 9.30–6   **Closed** Sat, Sun, public holidays
Credit cards None accepted; personal and business accounts   **Discounts** Variable (min 10 cases)   **Delivery** At cost; mail order available   **Glass hire** Free with suitable case order   **Tastings and talks** Regular tastings and dinners; to groups on request   **Cellarage** £3.45 per case per year

Farr Vintners, run by ex-Harrods salesman Lindsay Hamilton and ex-van delivery driver Stephen Browett, has come steaming into the top of the fine wine world from almost nowhere, almost overnight. If you are very rich and after something very special (particularly if it's from Bordeaux and in a big bottle), then you should certainly contact Farr; even if they haven't got what you want (the range is wide), they will almost certainly succeed in convincing you, in the gentlest possible way, that what you really want is something that they have got. Astonishingly for a fine wine specialist, they have no retail licence, so all sales are in wholesale quantities – generally by unsplit cases, though if you plump for a melchior of Château Tayac Cuvée Prestige 1982 or 1985, you will have doubled the minimum 9-litre sale and still have bought just one bottle. But the wholesale licence does mean that you will need £100 or so to begin shopping here with any element of choice.

Farr parachuted into the *en primeur* market this year with a 1989 Bordeaux offer whose prices made it seem as if everyone else playing that game had signed a cartel agreement. 'Was there a catch?' we asked Lindsay Hamilton. He assured us there wasn't; the head-turning prices were the outcome of heavy buying and wafer-thin margins, together with a certain amount of goodwill from Bordeaux merchants, many of whom buy back older Bordeaux vintages from Farr. There was no minimum sale, either, other than the statutory one case. If 1990 Bordeaux proves en primeurable, make sure that Farr are at the top of your list of offers to look at. Another recent headline-winning coup was the sale of the Aspinall Curzon Club Cellar from top (an imperial of Pétrus 1970 at £3,150) to bottom (four bottles of Mosaic Medium at £1.50 each).

The company now has a shop, though the two partners stress that it's a talking shop rather than a browsing shop, and that it's best to phone first to check that at least one of them will be there and not in Geneva or Paris picking up auction bargains for recycling. It has an ex-VAT list, too, though 'most wines never make it' there due to the speed of operations. Bordeaux, as mentioned above, is the biggest presence, but growers' Burgundy and Rhône, and Vintage Port and Madeira, are also impressive. Finally, rest assured that there is nothing pin-striped or haughty about Farr; neither partner would look out of place in Oddbins, and they are very friendly and helpful to deal with.

Best buys

Château la Lagune 1984, Haut-Médoc (case), £98.90
Crozes-Hermitage Domaine de Thalabert 1985, Jaboulet (case), £104.65
Château de Beaucastel 1985, Châteauneuf-du-Pape (case), £127.65

Farthinghoe Fine Wine and Food

The Old Rectory, Farthinghoe, Brackley, *Tel* (0295) 710018
Northamptonshire NN13 5NZ

Open Mon–Fri 9–1, 2–5; Sat, Sun, public holidays by arrangement
Credit cards None accepted; personal and business accounts
Discounts Collection discount of £3 per case; 5–10 cases £1.50 per case, 11+ cases £2.50 per case **Delivery** Free on UK mainland (min 3 case) – extra tariff for Highlands; otherwise 1 case £6, 2 cases £3 per case; mail order available
Glass hire Available with charge (£2 for 48 glasses)
Tastings and talks Occasional customer tastings **Cellarage** £4 per case per year (in bond only)

Simon Cox – ex Regular Soldier, and MBE as well as MW – runs the wine side of Farthinghoe, while his wife Nicola runs a cookery school attracting around 2,000 'guests' per year. The two enterprises dovetail very happily, and doubtless many of the guests leave having made wine purchases.

The list is not a long one but, says Simon Cox, 'we sell

nothing we are not absolutely confident about.' And nothing, presumably, customers are not absolutely confident about: the last year has seen Germany, Italy and USA wiped from the Farthinghoe world wine map as they didn't 'sell enough to justify listing and stocking', the newsletter tells us. (It also tells us of the MD's 'very mixed feelings' about having to say farewell to these three ranges, though in truth Italy never really got a foothold in the list.) Champagne, Alsace and Bordeaux are three areas of evident enthusiasm, and Burgundy, the Loire and the Rhône barely less so. A pair of Chileans and a pair of Australians represent the southern hemisphere, and a pair of Cavas the sparkling alternative to the ever-more-costly champagne. Small selections of sherry, port, Madeira, dessert wines and spirits stimulate and then settle the stomach. It's a balanced range, but it is a much smaller one than was the case several years ago.

The list claims that prices include delivery, but this is true only if you buy three cases or more; one or two case orders are garnished with £3 and £6 surcharges respectively. Farthinghoe holds a retail licence, but we are not sure as to how extensively or willingly it is used; certainly neither the list nor the order form offers any encouragement to buy in anything less than unmixed half-dozens or dozens. Vintage Port and Bordeaux are both offered *en primeur* when the occasion warrants, as it did with the latter's 1989. We invite readers to report with their impressions of Farthinghoe's range and service.

Best buys

Savennières 1986, Domaine Baumard, £6.48
Château Saint-Jacques 1986, Bordeaux Supérieur, £5.99
Saint-Véran 1988, Domaine Corsin, £7.69

Ferrers le Mesurier

Turnsloe, North Street, Titchmarsh,   *Tel* (08012) 2660
Kettering, Northamptonshire NN14 3DH

Case sales only   Open (Best to telephone before calling) Mon–Fri 8–8; Sat, Sun, public holidays by arrangement **Credit cards** None accepted; personal and business accounts **Discounts** By arrangement (min 1 case) **Delivery** Free in London, Cambridge and within 50-mile radius of Titchmarsh (min 1 case); elsewhere at cost **Glass hire** Not available **Tastings and talks** Annual Cambridge college tasting; to groups on request possible **Cellarage** Free for up to two years if wine purchased from premises

Ferrers le Mesurier runs a small wholesale business under his own name, selling in the main to companies, colleges and restaurants, but private customers are also encouraged. The list is short and explores eastern France: the Upper Loire, Burgundy, one or two Rhône wines and even an Apremont from Savoie. There is Muscadet, too, and six inexpensive clarets, but Burgundy provides the main nugget of interest; most of the growers are little known in this country, but the proprietor is proud of the quality he has found and is happy to discuss the wines with clients. More reports, please.

Best buys

Sauvignon de Touraine 1989, Domaine de la Presle, £4.49
Château la Rèze 1988, Minervois, £3.34
Apremont 1989, Domaine Jean Perrier, £4.49

Alex Findlater

1991

Vauxhall Cellars, 72 Goding Street, London SE11 5AW
Tel 071-587 1644/1302

Office
Heveningham High House, Halesworth, Suffolk IP19 0EA
Tel (0986 83) 274

Case sales only **Open** (SE11) Mon–Sat 10–8; Sun 10–6; (Suffolk) Mon–Fri 9.30–5.30 **Closed** Sat, Sun (Suffolk), public holidays **Credit cards** Access, Visa; personal and business accounts **Discounts** Available **Delivery** Free locally (min 1 case) and nationwide (min 3 cases); mail order available **Glass hire** Free with 5-case order **Tastings and talks** To groups on request **Cellarage** £4.50 per case per year (duty paid)

The first Alexander Findlater was a Scotsman who founded a business in Dublin in 1823, and it is back to this man and this concern that the four different companies still in operation under the Findlater name can be traced. Only this company, and Findlater (Wine Merchants) Ltd. of Dublin, are still run by members of the Findlater family.

The pioneering spirit that can presumably be attributed to the primordial Findlater emerges strongly in today's Alex, and in his uncompromising, highly committed list. It is uncompromising in its depth and complexity: there are no areas that Alex Findlater turns his back on, though a few obviously fail to arouse much enthusiasm, like Eastern Europe, which seems to be drifting out of reach here at a time when everyone else is hauling it in as fast as they can. But the high degree of commitment is obvious wherever enthusiasm is aroused, as it most spectacularly is for Australasia (which gets a separate list of its own, with an index by grape variety as well as an index by region), but as it also is for Alsace, Champagne, Germany (especially the drier wines), Italy and sherries. These are campaigning selections, aided by the scholarly and closely argued introductions, and anyone wishing to explore the gustatory byways of these continents, countries, regions and genres should make contact via the Suffolk address or via the Emporium at Vauxhall.

Connoisseurs of other regions should not dismiss Findlater, either. There is a lovely range of Bordeaux '85s, almost all drinking beautifully already, and Burgundy, the Rhône and the Loire could furnish several attractive mixed cases. Spain, Portugal and America have been bought open-mindedly, with the palate tuned for quality and character rather than price. But it's those specialist areas that invite the plunge: 64 Australian and New Zealand Chardonnays, with 96 Cabernet Sauvignons or Cab-something blends; 18 German trockens or halbtrockens, 9 Charta wines, and Lingenfelder's Spätburgunder among much else German and new; Capezzana and Le Ragose leading the Italian team; the works, sherry-wise, from Barbadillo, with Valdespino, Gonzalez Byass and Sandeman thrown in for luck; Turckheim, Schlumberger, Kuentz-Bas, Mure and Trimbach from Alsace; almost 30 Champagnes . . . Prepare to be converted; there'll be no turning back.

Best buys

Rosso di Montalcino 1987, La Magia, £5.85
Seppelt Moyston Shiraz-Cabernet 1987, Victoria, £4.07
Dos Cortados, Williams & Humbert, Dry Palo Cortado/Oloroso Sherry, £8.07

Findlater Mackie Todd

Deer Park Road, Merton Abbey, London SW19 3TU   *Tel* 081-543 7528

Open Mon–Fri 9–6; Sat only during December   **Closed** Sun, public holidays
Credit cards All accepted; personal and business accounts   **Discounts** Available
Delivery Free on UK mainland (min 1 case); Northern Ireland and offshore islands £3.50 per case; mail order available   **Glass hire** Available
Tastings and talks Annual tastings in Oxford, Cambridge and City of London; to groups on request   **Cellarage** £4.15 per case per year

During the last year, Findlater's charming old shop in London's Queen Street has closed and operations have been concentrated at Merton Abbey, confirming the company's largely mail-order destiny. Or the companies', for Findlater has, since November 1988, included the migrant Henry Townsend & Co and its Chief Executive, John Casson. Both names are still used, but the identities seem to be liquid, with only one annual list for retail customers (which will bear either the Henry Townsend or Findlater name on it, depending on whose mailing list you are on) and with the multitudinous mailings going out bearing both company names. This programme of mailings is almost as assiduous as that of Bordeaux Direct or the Sunday Times Wine Club, though the sales pitches are very different; if you like to buy wine via breakfast-time proposals in which 'the elegance of the Side-Saddle Racing at Polesden Lacey last summer' (Findlater-sponsored) is discussed, together with the contents of some well-thought-out mixed cases, then you should take steps to put yourself on the Findlater/Townsend mailing list. *En primeur* offers are included in the mailings, and this is a game for which Henry Townsend, in particular, has always enjoyed a good reputation. This is partly due to John Casson's palate – no saturation bombing here, but offers full of opinion and selection from one of 1990's new Masters of Wine – and partly due to his energy. The Editor remembers personal 7 am deliveries by John Casson to darkest inner London (from Buckinghamshire) in an estate car packed with fine young claret. Lest you should assume that this was a strategy to curry favour with the influential, be assured that the the Editor edited nothing at that time, and his influence extended only to five immediate and often sceptical family members.

The list continues much as old Townsend customers will remember it: stiff, thick and classical. It contains a 'finest and rarest' section, printed on grey paper in the centre and called 'The Inner Cellar'. Most of us will be sticking to the outer bits, and enjoying the wide selection of clarets, burgundies, Rhônes and German wines. These are the areas, together with champagne, where the list's depth lies; but John Casson and Findlater's Christopher Rowe evidently have fun wading around in the shallows and fishing for tasty Australians or communicative Italians. The only area neither seems to have developed a taste for is Portugal, whose table wines are unlisted (though ports are sound). Chile and New Zealand are enthusiasms, and North America, too, is deftly covered. Annual tastings are organised for customers in Oxford, Cambridge and London, and half-bottles are something of a speciality, with an annual half-bottle offer being made every year ('one of the most exciting and eagerly-awaited events in wine calendar' – and you never knew about it!).

Best buys

Chardonnay 1989, Vin de Pays des Comptes Rhodaniens, Producteurs Réunis, £5.45
Château Perenne 1985, Premières Côtes de Blaye, £5.52
La Borderie 1987, Côtes de Francs, Berlaere, £5.20

Fine English Wine Company

Ashfield Grange, 2 Station Road,   *Tel* (0904) 706386
Copmanthorpe, York, North Yorkshire
YO2 3SX

Case sales only   Open Mon–Sat 9–5 (other times by appointment)
Credit cards None accepted; business accounts   **Discounts** Not available
Delivery Free within 20-mile radius of York (min 1 case); otherwise at cost; mail
order available   **Glass hire** Not available   **Tastings and talks** To groups on
request   **Cellarage** Not available

This year would be a good one to try a mixed case from the
Fine English Wine Company, as the 1989 harvest of English
wines was probably the best of the decade. There are 28 wines
on the list, though the vintages available are still not specified,
and prices are quoted for unmixed cases on an ex-VAT basis
only, neither of which is very helpful for non-trade customers
like you or me. Some of England's best growers mean that these
problems are worth surmounting: Breaky Bottom, Three Choirs,
Penshurst and Wootton would provide a four-county guide to
Europe's newest wine region, and would help convince
drinking Thomases that the enterprise is worthwhile.

Best buys

Breaky Bottom Seyval Blanc 1989, Sussex, £5.46
Penshurst Ehrenfelser, Kent, no vintage specified, oak-aged,
£4.67
Three Choirs Bacchus, Gloucestershire, no vintage specified,
£6.42

Fine Vintage Wines

3/5 Hythe Bridge Street, Oxford, Oxfordshire   *Tel* (0865) 791313/724866
OX1 2EW
Associated outlet
Grape Ideas Fine Vintage Wine Warehouse,   *Tel* 071-328 7317
2a Canfield Gardens, London NW6 3BS

Open Mon–Sat 11–7   **Closed** Public holidays   **Credit cards** Access, Visa;
personal and business accounts   **Discounts** Large orders negotiable
Delivery Free locally (min 1 case); elsewhere negotiable; mail order available
Glass hire Free with 1-case order   **Tastings and talks** Large annual tasting; to
groups on request   **Cellarage** £5 per case per year

Fine Vintage Wines is, as its name suggests, a fine wine
merchant, operating in tandem with Grape Ideas Wine
Warehouse (q.v.) in Oxford and London. The largest range is
held at Oxford, though it is always best to telephone in advance
to make sure that a particular wine from the list is ready for

you, as a number are held in bond. Others, however, are unlisted, so it's worth dropping in to have a look at what's there, too. You can buy wines from this list on a retail basis at either outlet, though for mail order the minimum sale is 12 mixed bottles. When we visited the Oxford branch the sun was browsing through some of the floor-sited wines at the same time as we were, and we felt that blinds would be a worthwhile investment for this part of the warehouse. Other stocks, we understand, are actually held above the warehouse, which might suit Madeira but is unlikely to suit Krug. Perhaps it's best to favour those wines that you can see for yourself have been dozing in a quiet, dark corner, like elderly dons at evensong – or those that are actually held in bond.

The selection is wide, and 'fine' is charitably defined to include wines from Lazio and Sardinia as well as Pomerol and Pommard. Vintage Port and Madeira, and claret, burgundy and Rhône wines are all thoroughly stocked, though do compare prices with other fine wine merchants before making purchases above the £50 mark. A range of water-milled snuffs, with names like Tom Buck, Irish High Toast and Crumbs of Comfort, adds Oxonian tone to the list.

Best buys

Vintage Port 1983, Gould Campbell, £13.50
Château de Fieuzal 1985, Graves, £12
Vintage Port 1983, Smith Woodhouse, £13.75

John Ford Wines

8 Richardson Road, Hove, East Sussex   *Tel* (0273) 735891
BN3 5RB

Open Mon–Sat 9–7; Sun 12–2   **Closed** Chr Day, Boxing Day, Good Friday, Easter Sunday   **Credit cards** Access, Visa; personal and business accounts
Discounts 5% on 1 case   **Delivery** Free locally (min £25 order); mail order available   **Glass hire** Free with case order   **Tastings and talks** 40 Friday evening tutored tastings; to groups on request   **Cellarage** £5.75 per case per year

---

We have had several enthusiastic reports from readers of the service and range offered by Hove-based John Ford Wines, run by ex-university administrator John Ford with help from his sons Patrick and Robert. 'John Ford invites you to enjoy the Wine Experience' announces a tall printed card, and the experience is defined as 'a combination of customer service, selection, lay-out, atmosphere and ideas'. There is a newsletter, Friday-evening wine tastings, connoisseur evenings, gourmet evenings, wine tours: regular participants must barely get home to turn on their televisions and feed their cats.

The shop itself is sited in the old mews of the Brighton and Hove Horse Bus Company, and comprises three separate units: an attractive, wood-finished 'off-licence' at ground level, with the wines presented in both racks and shelves; and, downstairs, a fine wine cellar and a tasting area, decorated with the Regency prints that John Ford and his wife Jill have researched and written about. 'We like to run the place as a kind of club,' says John Ford.

The list is catholic, with particularly strong representations from Italy and Australia, and with no region or country being overlooked or forgotten. Within each section, wines have been sourced as widely as possible, small growers showing up alongside the larger producers and négociants. There are even two wines from the Massandra Collection on sale: Gurzuf Rose Muscat 1939 at £150 and Ai Danil Tokay 1917 (not a good year for the original owners of these estates, the Russian Royal Family) at £350. These are, by some margin, the most expensive wines on the list; most fall into the £3.50–£8 range. Whatever your tastes, you will certainly find wines to match them here, and you can rely on the communicative skills of the Ford family to help you refine your choice – and bring you back again later.

Best buys

Gran Colegiata 1985, Tinto de Crianza, Toro, Bodegas Fariña, £4.49
Sauvignon de Saint-Bris 1988, Luc Sorin, £4.69
Il Falcone Reserva 1986, Castel del Monte, Puglia, £7.19

Fortnum & Mason

181 Piccadilly, London W1A 1ER   *Tel* 071-734 8040

Open Mon–Sat 9.30–6 **Closed** Sun, public holidays **Credit cards** Access, American Express, Visa; personal and business accounts **Discounts** 5–10% (min 1 case) **Delivery** Free in Greater London (min £30 order except account holders); otherwise at cost; mail order available **Glass hire** Not available
Tastings and talks Promotional tastings of champagne and port; regular tastings of sherry, Italian and Spanish wines; tastings and talks given only by private arrangement **Cellarage** £3.45 per case per year

---

When you push your way through the heavy, gilded, swing doors of Fortnum & Mason, you may be looking for a number of things, but bargains will not be among them. The prices here are as stiff as the doormen's collars; though fairness compels us to mention that we did once get a bargain from F&M, a delicious Manzanilla from a company called Gil de León (about which subsequent enquiries in Spain have revealed nothing), priced £1.95 in a January 1988 sale.

What you will always find at Fortnum & Mason is an extensive range of well-chosen wines – more extensive, in fact, than the rather modest display area suggests. Ask for a list; there are some good things on it, particularly from the classic areas (Bordeaux, Burgundy, German wines, sherry, port). Burrowing into the specialities further still, you will find one of London's best collections of Premier and Grand Cru Chablis (mostly Long-Depaquit), good support for 1982 Burgundy (well thought-of by buyer Alun Griffiths), and ports from small-scale but high-quality producers like Burmester and Martinez – as well as from the bigger names. The attempt to provide 'exemplary service and quality' has seen the offering of wines *en primeur* to Fortnum's customers of late. Fortnum & Mason's 'own label' range is the subject of considerable endeavour on the buying team's part, and none of these wines should disappoint (if they do, let Fortnum's – and us – know). Strength in the classic areas does not mean weakness in the new ones, and Australia, California, New Zealand and England all stand proud on the shelves. It's good to see Tokaj given the support it deserves here, with four Museum wines offered as well as five from the Wine Trust's main range. There is a very fine range of spirits, too. What we would not recommend you buy here is anything widely available elsewhere, unless you are happy to subsidise the doorman's laundry bills.

Best buys

Fortnum & Mason Sauternes 1986 (Château de la Chartreuse), £10.95
Fortnum & Mason Margaux 1986 (second wine of Château Palmer), £12.50
Principe Old Dry Amontillado, Barbadillo, £9.50

Friarwood

26 New Kings Road, London SW6 4ST   *Tel* 071-736 2628

Case sales only   Open Mon–Fri 8.30–6.30; Sat 10–1   **Closed** Sun, public holidays   **Credit cards** All accepted; personal and business accounts
Discounts Available on application   **Delivery** Free in London (min 3 cases); charges elsewhere in application; mail order available   **Glass hire** Free with 1-case order   **Tastings and talks** Tastings every Saturday in the Vinotheque; to groups on request   **Cellarage** 10p per case per week

Friarwood are large stockholders of fine wines: 45,000 cases of cru classé claret and 10,000 cases of fine red burgundy are held, the company claims. That, indeed, is the main reason for contacting Peter and Isabelle Bowen – claret and burgundy. There are a few Loire wines, some Beaujolais, a little Côtes du

Rhône, champagne, port, one Alsace Gewürztraminer, six German wines and three from Franciscan Vineyards in the Napa Valley, as well as some fancy Cognac and Armagnac, but claret and burgundy is the main draw.

The list is rather a frightening one for ordinary folk like you or me, as all the prices are ex-VAT and per case. Where wines are lying in France, the minimum order is ten cases and shipment is at our expense. All this makes it seem like a trade-only operation, yet Friarwood assures us that it is possible to compile mixed cases of wines held in the UK for private customers (have a calculator handy to work out the prices), and that the majority of its business is to the public. Would London claret and burgundy addicts who patronise Friarwood write to us with their impressions?

Best buys

Château Grand Chemin 1985, Côtes de Bourg, £4.69
Château Broustet 1986, Barsac, £9.48
Château Franc-Grâce-Dieu 1985, Saint-Emilion, £7.76

The Fulham Road Wine Centre

899/901 Fulham Road, London SW6 5HU   *Tel* 071-736 7009

Open Mon–Sat 10–9; Sun 12–3 during December   **Closed** Sun (except as above), public holidays   **Credit cards** Access, Visa; personal and business accounts **Discounts** 5% on 1 case   **Delivery** Free in west and central London and parts of Surrey (min 1 case); mail order possible   **Glass hire** Free with 1-case order **Tastings and talks** Wine school in purpose-built tasting room; to groups on request   **Cellarage** Not available

---

Call in at 899–901 Fulham Road if you're thirsty for knowledge, thirsty for art, or simply thirsty for good wines. In addition to being a wine merchant of distinction, the Centre hosts the Fulham Road Wine School, which runs a full programme of straightforward and inexpensive wine courses starting at 7pm on weekday evenings, as well as blind tasting workshops (plus 'post-mortem') during the day on Saturdays. These can enrich your drinking considerably, as well as giving your pride a salutary bruising. Wine Arts, a company specialising in prints, posters, maps and cards inspired by the world of wine, use the Centre as a gallery, so you can take home intoxicating images as well as liquids. There are also all manner of wine accessories for sale.

It's the liquids that will interest most of us, though. Pre-purchase is in the hands of Angela Muir MW and James Rogers, four of the safest in London; shop manager Neil Tully's assertion that 'Within our general selection, a randomly mixed dozen bottles would probably yield a lower rate of disappointment than in most places!' is thus convincing. The list opens with 16 Australian white wines, and it continues equally freshly through 12 pages of well-balanced, open-minded buying. The balance makes it hard to seize on areas of strength or rub salt into areas of weakness, but like its informal associate The Barnes Wine Shop (*q.v.*) it has a particularly good range of what are listed as 'pudding wines', and if you want to taste your way around a series of clear varietals from different patches in the global vineyard, this is as good a place as any to come and get stocked up. The clever Barnes Wine Shop Wine and Food Code is used throughout the list to give you an indication of taste and food matches without the need to write and print a full note (though you do need to think a bit).

There are separate lists for fine and rare wines, and devotees of small bottles or organic wines will be confronted by choice rather than incomprehension. Service and advice here are very good, as one would expect from a shop with a school underneath it. Prices are fair.

Best buys

Cuvée de l'Arjolle 1988, Vin de Pays des Côtes de Thongue, Cabernet/Merlot, £3.99
Rioja Remelluri 1985, £7.25
Les Hauts de Bergelle 1989, Côtes de Saint-Mont (oak-aged), £3.95

Fullers (Fuller, Smith & Turner)

Head office
Griffin Brewery, London W4 2QB   *Tel* 081-994 3691
56 shops in West London and Thames Valley

Open (Usually) Mon–Sat 9–9; Sun 12–3, 7–9 **Closed** Christmas Day, Boxing Day **Credit cards** Access, Visa; personal and business accounts
Discounts Available **Delivery** Free locally; charges elsewhere negotiable
Glass hire Free **Tastings and talks** 2 major tastings at Griffin Brewery annually; regular tastings in selected shops; to groups on request (min 25 people)
Cellarage Not available

The steady improvements we have noted in recent years at Fullers continue, and this year we are happy to report that Piat d'Or, Mouton Cadet and Black Tower have all been shown the door. A range of sound, carefully sourced, and modestly priced wines remain. The shops continue to improve in appearance; cigarettes are 'never promoted'; and the staff are all encouraged to follow the Wine & Spirit Education Trust examination path. We feel that the Fullers package is an attractive one at present, but we would like to hear readers' opinions, too. If you use Fullers from time to time, let us have your views on the range, service and advice available there.

The Bordeaux selection looks good on paper, with finer wines mostly from the 1983 vintage, and petits châteaux from 1986 and 1988. Head of Wine Mark Dally seems keen on the 'second wine' trend, and there are three or four on offer; Le Carillon de l'Angélus 1987 is a Fullers' exclusivity, and it looks good value at £7.72. Burgundy, like Bordeaux, is carefully chosen, with bottles to suit every wallet. There are some rewarding French country wines on offer as well as lovely Loire wines (try the Château Gaudrelle 1986 Vouvray); Alsace, by contrast, has been cut back to two rather lonely bottles.

The German selection is beginning to wake up as customers realise there are better ways to pass a summer afternoon than with one-and-a-half litres of Liebfraumilch; while Fullers is already an excellent place to look for alternatives to champagne – there are fifteen to chose from on the list (as well as many champagnes if you decide to chicken out and pay up). Italy is moving in the right direction; and Spain has already moved, with some exciting wines from Almansa, Priorato, Navarra, Ribera del Duero and Valdepeñas as well as a small party of Riojan nobles. Australia, New Zealand and Eastern Europe are well represented; Portugal isn't – yet. The sherry range could be a deal dryer and more exciting too. There is room for more improvement, and every reason to believe we will see it.

Best buys

Cartoixa Reserva 1982, Priorato, Cellers de Scala Dei, £5.07
Mâcon-Viré 1986, Domaine André Bonhomme, £6.49
Verjus 1988, Navarra, Cenalsa, £3.25

Garrards Wine Merchants ☞

Mayo House, 49 Main Street, Cockermouth, Cumbria CA13 9JS   *Tel* (0900) 823592

Open Mon 10–5.30; Tue–Sat 9.30–8 **Closed** Sun, Thur 1–5.30 during Nov, Jan, Feb, March and April (except on any public holiday week), Boxing Day, 1 Jan, Easter Monday, May Day **Credit cards** Access, Visa; personal and business accounts **Discounts** 5% on 1 case **Delivery** Free within 20-mile radius (min 1 case); elsewhere charges negotiable; mail order available **Glass hire** Free with suitable case order **Tastings and talks** Tastings held for invited groups of customers twice a year; talks and tastings for groups possible **Cellarage** Not available

In the three years since opening their small but attractively laid-out Cockermouth wine shop, ex-Harveys sales representative Christopher Garrard and his wife Joyce have built up an attractive and steadily improving list. 'Why buy from a Wine Merchant?' this list begins; instead of the usual (and misguided) tirade against supermarkets and chains, we are given a short but inspiring enumeration of wine's role in British culture, its benefits to health and the pleasure to be taken in its infinite variety. This would cheer Robert Mondavi, were he ever to find himself in Cockermouth, for it echoes the campaign Mondavi himself is fighting against the neo-Prohibitionist movement in the United States. Let's hope neo-Prohibitionists haven't gained too much ground in Cumbria yet.

Bordeaux is the French area most extensively stocked here, but other parts keep their heads above water – there are Loire reds as well as whites, for example; there is a wine from the Côte Chalonnaise; there are five different Alsace varietals and a choice of four Châteauneufs, including one white. Perhaps the French country wine section is the one that merits most research in the coming twelve months: there are now so many exciting estate wines on offer that the need to buy Bergerac from Cordier, Vin de Table Rouge from Duboeuf, and Vin de Pays du Gard from Stowells of Chelsea is greatly diminished. Plenty of work seems to have gone into the German section, and even the most finicky customer would find something of interest here, from Trockens and Novums through to two 1976 Beerenauslesen. Italy has yet to attain this degree of refinement; again, the moment has never been better for the innovative buying of Italian wines, so perhaps the next 12 months will see expansion in this area. Spain, Portugal and Australia are stocked with generally sound wines, while a sense of adventure is in the air among the ten New Zealanders. Cumbrians are obviously great sherry quaffers, as there are no fewer than 20 on offer, nearly as many as at the Cumbrian Cellar over in Penrith; long may the tradition last. The fine whisky selection, finally, is a reminder that Islay is considerably nearer to Cockermouth than is Isleworth or Islington.

Best buys

Banda Azul Rioja 1986, Paternina, £4.45
Sauvignon Blanc 1989, Nobilo, New Zealand, £6.49
St Hugo Cabernet Sauvignon 1985, Orlando, South Australia, £8.99

Gauntleys of Nottingham

4 High Street, Exchange Arcade,   *Tel* (0602) 417973
Nottingham, Nottinghamshire NG1 2ET

Open Mon–Sat 8.30–5.30 **Closed** Sun, public holidays **Credit cards** Access,
Visa; personal and business accounts **Discounts** 10% on 1 mixed case
Delivery Free locally (min 1 case) and nationally (min 3 cases); mail order
available **Glass hire** Free with 1-case order **Tastings and talks** Regular
bi-monthly tastings; one major charity tasting every year; to groups on request
Cellarage Free for wine purchased from premises

What do you do if it's your turn to take over the family
business, with 100 proud years of trading behind it, yet the
product that you're selling diminishes in appeal every year, and
this decline looks irreversible? That was the problem that faced
John Gauntley, of cigar and tobacco merchants Gauntleys of
Nottingham, in the mid-1980s. John Gauntley's hobby was
wine, so he made the eminently sensible move into wine
trading. Without, of course, abandoning the tobacco business –
indeed, our copy of the Gauntley list came beautifully tobacco
scented.

Since the beginning of 1988, John Gauntley has built up an
impressive range of wines of character and quality – indeed it's
almost a fine wine list, with few bottles under £5 and most over
£10. The only wine from Languedoc-Roussillon, for example, is
Mas de Daumas Gassac 1986 Cabernet Sauvignon red; the kind
of thing that those in the market for a box of 49 gauge double
coronas might wish to wash down their steak with. It also
indicates Mr Gauntley's seriousness of intent in finding the best
from each region; he draws on the published help of one
R Parker in this search, so duff bottles, at the very least, should
not feature here. It isn't a long list, but it's well written and
designed, and very fair to worlds both old and new. Only
Italians have any cause to feel hard done by at present, and Italy
is an area John Gauntley is researching and expanding as we
write. We have had glowing reports from readers of the service
provided by Gauntleys of Nottingham, one of whom cited the
decision to purchase additional cellar space rather than
expanding the retail space as evidence of this merchant's
dedication. 'Wine was originally a hobby,' says John Gauntley;
'now it's a passion.' We await further developments with
interest.

If your favourite wine merchant is not in this section, write and tell us
about him or her. There are report forms at the back of the book.

Best buys

Rouge Homme Shiraz/Cabernet 1984, Coonawarra (South
Australia), £5.35
Vouvray Clos Naudin Sec 1986, Foreau, £7.50
Pinot Noir 1985, Hamilton Russell, £9.10

Matthew Gloag & Son

Bordeaux House, 33 Kinnoull Street, Perth,   *Tel* (0738) 21101
Perthshire PH1 5EU

Open Mon–Fri 9–5   **Closed** Sat, Sun, some public holidays   **Credit cards** Access,
Visa; personal and business accounts   **Discounts** Available for Club members
only   **Delivery** Free on mainland Scotland (min 1 case); otherwise £3.45 per case;
mail order available   **Glass hire** Available   **Tastings and talks** Gloag's Fine
Wines Club holds a large tasting at least twice a year; occasionally to groups on
request   **Cellarage** £3.45 per case or part-case per year

Where, in 1990, could you have gone to a tasting of New
Zealand wines at which 'casual clothing and sensible footwear'
were advised? The answer is Perth; the tutor was the
campaigning Margaret Harvey ('a New Zealander with strong
Scottish connections'); the reason was that the tasting was
followed by a 'guided tour of St Johnstone Football Club's
magnificent new stadium and its impressive facilities'. It is
heartening to see a wine merchant serving the local community
in unusual ways.

Matthew Gloag serves its community in the more usual ways,
too, with a sound selection of wines bundled into a charming
little list. Most of these have a clarety flavour but Rhônes are
there in comparative strength; Margaret Harvey and St
Johnstone Football Club doubtless stimulated sales of the seven
up-market New Zealand wines, and three from Washington
State shows that wine manager Marilyn Brown has a taste for
adventure that is fitting in one who runs marathons for charity
in her spare time. It's a long way from Sanlúcar de Barrameda to
the Firth of Tay, but Barbadillo's sherries make the journey
regularly; a good selection of ports is available, too, though we
would recommend asking for the promised 'youthful'
alternatives to the four 1975s, when these cost between £25 and
£32.50. You will probably wend your way back to claret, finally,
secure in Gloag's 1906 assurance that it 'is at once safe,
wholesome and appetising. As a stimulant it causes no heating
or inconvenience, and, being perfectly free from unfermented
sugar, no acidity. It is probably as near the Ideal Beverage as
can be taken with any pleasure by people who exercise mind
and body . . .' With tasting notes of this calibre, Gloag's Reserve
Claret (sourced from the much-admired Château Cissac) must

waltz off the shelf. Joining Gloag's Fine Wines Club brings you discounts on list prices, as well as giving you access to the tastings that Scottish licensing laws forbid in-store.

Best buys

Gloag's Reserve Claret, Haut-Médoc, £4.75
Corbières Blanc de Blancs 1988, Resplandy, £3.35
Château Lanessan 1985, Haut-Médoc, £10.80

Goedhuis & Co

101 Albert Bridge Road, London SW11 4PF   *Tel* 071-223 6057

Open Mon–Fri 9.30–5.30 **Closed** Sat, Sun, public holidays **Credit cards** Access, Visa; personal and business accounts **Discounts** Not available **Delivery** Free in London (min 3 cases) and UK (exc Scotland) (min 5 cases); otherwise at cost; mail order available **Glass hire** Free with 1-case order **Tastings and talks** Two major annual tastings in May and November to promote new wine lists; to groups on request **Cellarage** £5 per case per year

Jonathan Goedhuis is rather sparing in the information he has given us about himself and his aims, and the lists he issues are invariably modest and sober in appearance. This year's example reminds the browser, from the outside, of the annual report of a small accountancy partnership; last summer's was actually black, and looked like the sort of thing an undertaker hands you when it's time to choose a gravestone for Great Aunt Ethel. 'Hype' is a word we are unlikely to have to use in connection with Goedhuis & Co.

But if you're a claret man or a burgundy woman, you have every reason to obtain one of these cool, calm and collected documents. The selection in both cases is remarkably good: nearly 30 1985 clarets, for example, and thirty-three 1988s, all in bond London already, and all offered by the bottle if required. Look at the names for 1988 at under £10 per bottle (in-bond price; retail around £2 more): d'Issan, Léoville-Barton, Larmande, La Lagune, Haut Batailley, Langoa Barton and so on down. Some of these may have moved up above £10 by the time you read this, but you should be here when it comes to future vintages. Burgundy is every bit as good, with around 30 different growers/domains to chose from. Not much under £10, sadly, but plenty worth having at under £15, especially from the underrated 1987 vintage. This is unquestionably a fine burgundy selection, intelligently discussed in the list.

You will also find good wines from the Loire, Alsace (Turckheim and Rolly Gassmann), champagne, Rhône/Provence (including Beaucastel, Guigal and Chave) and Australia (a dozen boutique-y wines). Churchill and Fonseca provide value in port, and you can have your wines stored in 'the perfect bond . . . an old underground ammunition store' in Wiltshire. And that's it.

Best buys

Château d'Arches 1985, Haut-Médoc, £8.66
Château Lalande-Borie 1985, Saint-Julien, £11
Volnay Premier Cru les Caillerets 1987, Domaine Bouley, £13.35

Gordon & MacPhail

58–60 South Street, Elgin, Moray IV30 1JY   *Tel* (0343) 545111

Open Mon–Fri 9–5.15 Sat 9–5 **Closed** Wed pm (Jan, Feb, March, April, May, Oct to mid-Nov), Sun, public holidays **Credit cards** Access, Visa; personal and business accounts **Discounts** 5% on 6 bottles, 10% on 12 bottles **Delivery** Free within 20-mile radius (min 1 bottle) and elsewhere (min 1 case); mail order available **Glass hire** Free with 1-case order **Tastings and talks**, **Cellarage** Not available

Of course the real reason for journeying to Elgin's South Street is to take advantage of Gordon & MacPhail's superb malt whisky collection, including many 'own bottlings' from less well-known distilleries. Cask strength and dated distillation whiskies are also available in hordes, making this a place of pilgrimage for the malt faithful.

This old-established merchant, now run by the third generation of the Urquhart family, also operates as a wine wholesaler and retailer. The retail list is rather short, and certainly nothing like as interesting or as varied as the wholesale list, with its fine collection of clarets and good German wines, among others. The wholesale side of the business, though, is resolutely just that, with only unbroken cases being sold – which rules out most consumers wishing to explore what's on offer. It would be good to see more of the wholesale range being made available to retail customers on a by-the-bottle basis. Would someone in the Elgin area regularly using Gordon & MacPhail's shop write with their impressions of the range on offer and the service provided to wine drinkers?

Best buys

Domaine des Anges, Côtes du Ventoux (no vintage specified), £3.55
Château de Montrabech 1988, Corbières, £3.70
Cape Mentelle, Semillon 1989, Western Australia, £8.91

Send us your views on the report forms at the back of the book.

Richard Granger

West Jesmond Station, Lyndhurst Avenue,　　　　*Tel* 091-281 5000
Newcastle upon Tyne, Tyne & Wear
NE2 3HH

Case sales only　Open Mon–Fri 8.30–6.30; Sat 8.30–1　**Closed** Sun, public
holidays　**Credit cards** Access, Visa; personal and business accounts
Discounts Not available　**Delivery** Free within 30-mile radius (min 1 case);
otherwise negotiable; mail order available　**Glass hire** Available with charge
(69p/dozen)　**Tastings and talks** Tastings organised and conducted for customers
Cellarage Free but space limited

This Newcastle merchant offers, like some of its competitors in
that city, rather a short list; it is, furthermore, one in which
producers' names are not always cited, and one where you may
not realise that the prices quoted are ex-VAT. There would be
enough to mix a case with on one visit, but the curious might
find themselves short of things to experiment with by the third
or fourth trip. Not so, of course, if you know what you like, and
you've found it here.

Most of the wines are French, and it is certainly in France that
proprietorial interest seems most fully engaged. The Loire
selection is worth dallying over, there are half a dozen good
burgundies from Faiveley and Chanson, and a range of petits
châteaux clarets at between £5 and £10. The mini-portfolio of
Duboeuf Beaujolais, listed for many years, has gone under the
axe this year in favour of 'specialist small growers' offering
'better quality and equal price'. Outside France, Deinhard lends
the German section distinction, Italy looks rather glum, and
everywhere else is swept into 'Other Red Wines' and 'Other
White Wines'. It would be nice to see a little list-expansion by
next year: the long, low, ex-British Rail station from which
Richard Granger and Alastair Stewart run the business looks
large enough to accommodate more stock.

We are very keen to hear from Richard Granger customers,
and to listen to their opinions as to the range on offer, and the
'good service' ('advice, time to discuss requirements,
suggestions, flexibility') that the directors state that they offer.

Best buys

Fleurie 1988, Cuvée Présidente Marguerite, Cave Coopérative de
Fleurie en Beaujolais, £7.42
Saumur Brut, Bouvet Ladubay, £6.84
Penfolds, Koonunga Hill Shiraz-Cabernet 1987, South Australia,
£5.80

Grape Ideas Wine Warehouse ◁▷ ☞

3/5 Hythe Bridge Street, Oxford, Oxfordshire OX1 2EW	*Tel* (0865) 722137
Associated outlet	
2A Canfield Gardens, Swiss Cottage, London NW6 3BS	*Tel* 071-328 7317

Open Mon–Sat 10–7; Sun 12–2 **Closed** Public holidays **Credit cards** Access, Visa; personal and business accounts **Discounts** Approximately 5% per case **Delivery** Free in Oxford (min 1 case); otherwise London £5, England and Wales £10, Scotland £15; mail order available **Glass hire** Free with case order **Tastings and talks** To groups on request **Cellarage** Not available

Grape Ideas is, in style and conception, a wine warehouse. Yet it has a retail licence, and by-the-bottle sales are also permitted during retail hours (i.e. not for long on Sundays, but all the time during the week). On the day of our visit, a Saturday, this was not made clear to us, and we left with the impression that the 'warehouse' part (as opposed to the Fine Vintage Wines area – see separate entry) was by-the-case only; the list clearly states that this is not so, so don't feel you have to buy 12 bottles if you only want two or three. Further complications ensue with pricing: the list quotes a 'wholesale per bottle' price, for unmixed cases only, and a 'bottle price', for retail sales; if you mix a case, you can knock £1.20 off the final price (i.e. 10p per bottle off the retail 'bottle price'). Got it?

The selection is quite a good one, so it's worth untangling the conditions of sale and the subtleties of pricing; and any warehouse-style operation also prepared to sell by the bottle is worth supporting. Grape Ideas has good selections of claret, Loire wines, Chilean wines and Argentinian wines, and the Burgundy, Rhône and Portuguese ranges are numerically strong, too. So is that of Spain, though only two or three producers (one of them being the ubiquitous Torres) provide nearly all the wines. Indeed, this is a general characteristic of the stock, the Portuguese wines being a typical example: of fifteen different wines 14 come from the giant Sogrape. Giants in Portugal, as in Australia, are on the whole a good thing, so perhaps this doesn't matter too much.

There are no fewer than six vintages of Château Musar from the Lebanon available here, and José de Soto's jazzily labelled sherries brighten their little corner of the warehouse (though there are no alternatives if you don't feel like a José de Soto sherry). The list borrows Vintage Ports from Fine Vintage Wines, and includes attractively priced 1983s and 1982s; the non-Vintage Ports, apart from Warre's Traditional LBV '76, are a pretty dull bunch. Eastern Europe means Bulgaria here (a choice of eight); California is slimline, though it does feature the little-seen Schafer and Preston Vineyards; while Italy, Germany and Australia furnish modest but not dull selections. You can hunt for obscure varietal character in Berri Estates' Crouchen-Trebbiano blend, for example; while dessert wine connoisseurs will find two Beerenauslesen and one Eiswein here – minus producers, unfortunately, on the list.

Best buys

Crémant de Loire Extra Brut, Domaine Girault Artois, £6.60
Wyndhams Oak Cask Chardonnay 1986, New South Wales, £4.99
Mâcon-Viré 1987, Domaine André Bonhomme, £6.95

Great Northern Wine Company

Dark Arches, Leeds Canal Basin, Leeds,   *Tel* (0532) 461200/461209
West Yorkshire LS1 4BR

Open Mon–Fri 9–6.30; Sat, public holidays 9–5.30   **Closed** Sun, 25 & 26 Dec,
1 Jan   **Credit cards** Access, Visa; personal and business accounts
Discounts Variable (min 1 case)   **Delivery** Free within 30-mile radius of Leeds
(min 1 case); otherwise at cost; mail order available   **Glass hire** Free with order
Tastings and talks Major annual tasting; regular monthly tastings; to groups on
request   **Cellarage** £2.75 per case per year

Any wine shop whose address is 'Dark Arches, Leeds Canal Basin' – it sounds like the kind of place from which you don't expect to return alive – should offer some lively attractions to tempt customers in, and the Great Northern Wine Company manages to do that. Monthly tutored tastings on board a restaurant barge are one of them, and the atmospheric warehouse/shop is another (the sign outside says Wine Warehouse, and if you buy at least 12 bottles you'll get the lowest prices; the lads hold a retail licence, though, so you can buy single bottles, too). Leeds Canal Basin may have been sinister once, but it becomes less so by the day: this is another of the docklands-style developments that are reclaiming the watery parts of large cities up and down Britain at present. Credit cards will be more use to you than flick knives here now. The Hilton lies just across the River Aire.

The list is not a long one, but it is well balanced, the New World being explored with as much enthusiasm and energy as the Old. You'll find claret and burgundy here, but you'll also come upon plenty of French country wines, including examples from Jura and Savoie as well as the more regularly encountered Gaillacs and Corbières and Bergeracs. Top producers are favoured: Jean Cros, Château de Lastours and Château la Jaubertie in those last three cases, for example. Spain, Portugal,

Italy and Germany are all treated with equal respect, with up to two dozen bottles from each country save Portugal, which warrants more than half a dozen, but that's six more wines than some merchants offer. Chile, Peru and Argentina balance the page of North American wines, while Australia gets two to itself, with fine bottles from the hot continent on sale alongside the usual £4 to £8 solid-value varietals (Brown Brothers, Rosemount and Lindemans provide most, but are seasoned with Cape Mentelle, Moss Wood, Peter Lehmann, Petaluma and Yarra Yering). There are a dozen varied dessert wines from all around the world, enough half-bottles to give you a choice rather than a disappointment, and world beers, while vintage armagnacs put fire in the spirits.

Best buys

Gamay 1989, Gaillac, Domaine Jean Cros, £3.99
Corbières 1988, Cuvée Simone Descamps, Château de Lastours, £4.68
Muscadet du Sèvre et Maine sur lie 1988, Clos des Bourguignons, £4.99

Great Western Wines

Mail order only
254 Kentwood Hill, Tilehurst, Reading,   *Tel* (0734) 451958
Berkshire RG3 6DP
also
Freepost (RG786), 254 Kentwood Hill, Reading, Berkshire RG3 1BR

Open 24-hour service   **Credit cards** Access, Visa; business accounts
Discounts 10% (approx) on case sales   **Delivery** Free for postcodes RG1-RG4 (min 1 bottle); elsewhere at cost   **Glass hire** Not available   **Tastings and talks** Individual private tastings by appointment; to groups on request
Cellarage Free if order paid for in advance

Anyone keen to explore the delights of English (and Welsh) wine should make Great Western Wines, who specialise exclusively in 'home-grown products', one of the first merchants they get in touch with. This Tilehurst company, run by ex-social worker Maurice Moore with help from his French-born wife Annie, has an excellent selection, drawn from vineyards 'roughly approximate to the Great Western Railway area'.

Thirty-eight growers are represented on the list, some of them – like Thames Valley or nearby Westbury – with up to seven or eight wines of different types and vintages. The list also includes wines from organic producers Sedlescombe in Sussex, as well as organic cider from Avalon in Somerset. There is a small highlighted range at under £3, while a guide to the grape varieties commonly grown in England and Wales prefaces the selection of wines. The hesitant might be tempted by the 'taste before you buy' service (phone Maurice Moore for details), as well as by the 'satisfaction guarantee', which gives you the chance to swop any wine that you've bought in case quantities for other wines, if you find that the original purchase is not to your taste. We have had glowing reports from readers of efficient service, and of the quality of the advice offered by Mr Moore. By the time you read this, almost all the 1989s should be in stock, providing the ideal opportunity for you to ditch your prejudices about English wines.

Best buys

Pilton Manor Dry Reserve 1987, Somerset, £4.59
Chalkhill Bacchus 1984, Wiltshire, £4.49
Meon Valley Meonwara 1987 (red), Hampshire, £4.25

Peter Green

37a/b Warrender Park Road, Edinburgh
EH9 1HJ

Tel 031-229 5925

Open Mon–Fri 9.30–6.30; Sat 9.30–7 **Closed** Sun, public holidays
Credit cards None accepted; personal and business accounts **Discounts** 5% off most wines (min 1 case) **Delivery** 50p per trip in Edinburgh; mail order available **Glass hire** Free **Tastings and talks** Annual tasting in November by invitation; to groups on request **Cellarage** Not available

There are probably people living in Edinburgh's Marchmont who pop into Peter Green & Co to buy a bottle of this or a bottle of that, and think that every neighbourhood has somewhere similar. But every neighbourhood doesn't. In fact, there are very few neighbourhoods of the British Isles where you can find as catholic a range of wines as this, or as many half-bottles, or half as much enthusiasm. It's almost a reason for moving to EH9.

The range is what impresses so. One of Michael Romer's aims (he runs the shop with his brother Douglas, Peter Green having been lost to history) is 'never to drink the same wine twice'; another is 'to keep a few thousand items on our shortlist of possible new wines'. There is already something from just about everywhere (including, say, Franconia, Switzerland, Canada and Zimbabwe – though we weren't able to locate any bottles from Savoie and there's only a single Château-Chalon from the Jura). The areas that others ignore or float through, but that the Romers explore thoroughly, are Portugal (the best range in the country?), Italy (serious competition for Valvona & Crolla), Greece (a mixed case) and New Zealand (eight different

Sauvignon Blancs, six Chardonnays, two Gewürztraminers and a Rhine Riesling, as well as seven reds). Australia and South America are nearly as good – does anyone else know of a merchant where you can try 12 different Argentinian wines? – and Bulgaria, Spain and Germany will have you stroking your beard and ransacking your brain for half-remembered recommendations that will help you make your way up the wall of alternatives. Chenin Blanc nutters like us sigh approval at the eleven offered from the Loire (including four from the exemplary Baumard), and look at Alsace, too: over a dozen Gewürztraminers with other varietals in diminishing proportions. Burgundy is adequate; only classed-growth claret addicts have any reason to complain about the range offered, and even then it isn't a very good reason, as there's all sorts of Ducru-Beaucaillou and Gruaud Larose and Margaux and Montrose and so on listed. Whisky? Vintage Port and Madeira (the latter attractively priced)? Fine sherry? Yes, yes and yes. We could plaster the next two pages with some of the names you'll find here, but what's the point? Go, simply, if you have the chance. No reader of this book will fail to find the selection rewarding (and the prices generally match the large chains for those wines common to both). Peter Green is a vital part of Edinburgh's extraordinary year-round wine festival.

Best buys

Dolcetto d'Acqui 1988, Viticoltori d'Acquese, £3.95
Quarts de Chaume 1983, Baumard, £11.25
Antiguas Reservas Cabernet Sauvignon 1984, Cousiño Macul, Chile, £4.99

Green's

Head office
47–51 Great Suffolk Street, London SE1 0BS   *Tel* 071-633 0936

Case sales only   Open Mon–Fri 9–5.30   **Closed** Sat, Sun, public holidays
Credit cards All accepted; personal and business accounts
Discounts Negotiable   **Delivery** Free in London postal districts (min 2 cases); elsewhere at cost; mail order available   **Glass hire** Free with any case order
Tastings and talks To groups on request   **Cellarage** £8.05 per case per year

---

A strange remark prefaces Green's Summer 1990 list. 'Producing a wine list is a source of pride as well as regret; pride in the quality of our selections, and regret that it is too often taken to be a limitation as to the range that is available from us.' To what end does a merchant produce a list, if not to indicate the range he or she offers? And are customers wrong to assume a list is an accurate indication of the range offered? 'We are constantly making new discoveries,' says Green's. So put them on the next list. 'Moreover, we will always put ourselves out to obtain any item not shown on our lists.' Good; though this is a service offered by many merchants. (Apropos, readers: do you ever take merchants – Green's or otherwise – up on this offer? And is there a successful outcome? Write and tell us about the experience.)

Perhaps all this regretfulness is a way of excusing the fact that there still isn't any great depth to the Green's list (or those wines that the company cares to list, at any rate). Three reds, two whites and a rosé comprise the French country wine section, and four of those are from the same property in Hérault. Claret follows, and the selection improves markedly, with a full flush of 1985s providing the most exciting moment in the document.

The Burgundy range isn't as closely textured as that of Bordeaux, though it's good to see a variety of growers' names being featured (Maume, Georges Clerget, René Leclerc and Bernard Moreau are some of those you will find here). Green's Bibendum-linked past haunts it in the choice Rhône selection, and if the Loire is to be reduced to nine bottles, then Green's nine present as good a summary as you could hope for of that enormous river's variety. France ends with Willy Gisselbrecht's five Alsace wines.

After France, it's cigars (mainly Havana) that are available in the most plentiful choice. Germany, Italy, Spain and Australia are all timidly listed; only 'California' has been selected at all ambitiously, with five rarely seen vineyards on offer including a Merlot from Long Island (not exactly California, but never mind). Ports are present in relative strength (mostly Vintage); not so sparkling wines and sherries. Regrettable.

Best buys

Rully Blanc 'La Chaume' 1987, Jacques Dury, £7.90
Château la Croix de Gay 1985, Pomerol, £12.80
Cornas 1986, Noël Verset, £9.95

The Wine Standards Board is the trade's disciplinary department and wine watchdog. Their inspectors are responsible for rooting out any malpractices – but they are concerned largely with labelling irregularities. If you have genuine reason to suspect that the wine in a bottle is not what the label claims it is, contact the Board at: 68½ Upper Thames Street, London EC4V 3BJ; *Tel* 071-236 9512; or contact your local Trading Standards Officer.

A O L Grilli Wines

Not a shop
Little Knoxbridge, Cranbrook Road,   *Tel* (0580) 891472
Staplehurst, Kent TN12 0EU

Case sales only   **Open** Office open daily from 9-midnight (if unattended then
answering machine will be in operation)   **Credit cards** None accepted; personal
and business accounts   **Discounts** 5% on 1 case for business accounts
Delivery For orders to addresses on UK mainland the cost of delivery is included
in the listed prices; mail order available   **Glass hire** Free with 1-case order
Tastings and talks To groups on request   **Cellarage** Not available

A O L Grilli Wines is hardly a mainstream merchant, with its
wholesale licence, its lack of a shop or warehouse, and its small
range. There is a main list, from which you may compile mixed
cases, and a fine wine list, with sales by unmixed case only. It
merits inclusion primarily on the basis that there is a good
range of Portuguese wines here, including three vinhos verdes
(one red, hard to find in Britain), some fine Caves São João
Porta dos Cavaleiros Dão, a Real Vinicola Colares ('Big, rough
and tough' the note in the list says, and it can say that
again . . .) and the good-to-excellent Reguengos de Monsaraz.
You will find other wines (French, Italian, Spanish, German,
English) to aid you in mixing a case, but make sure that it's at
least half full of Portuguese excellence.

Best buys

Dão Porta dos Cavaleiros 1983, Caves São João, £3.43
Reguengos de Monsaraz Reserva 1979, Alentejo, £5.90
Jean Perico Cava, £5.86

Grogblossom

66 Notting Hill Gate, London NW11 3HT   *Tel* 071-792 3834
253 West End Lane, West Hampstead,   *Tel* 071-794 7808
London NW6 1XN
160 High Road, East Finchley, London   *Tel* 081-883 3588
N2 9AS

Open Mon–Fri 11–10; Sat 10–10; Sun 12–3, 7–10; public holidays 12–10
Credit cards Access, Visa   **Discounts** 5% on 1 mixed case   **Delivery** Free locally
(min 1 case)   **Glass hire** Free with party order   **Tastings and talks** Wine of the
week every week in-store   **Cellarage** Not available

London's three Grogblossom shops (Grogblossom means 'red
nose' in Australian) are worth visiting for their relaxed
atmosphere, a steadily improving range of wines and an
excellent selection of world beers. The company has difficulty in
committing the wine range to paper, and the lack of a

photographic memory amongst our own editorial staff means that we are unable to reel off its glories after a single visit, but Australia, New Zealand and France's less classical wines are all present in strength, and the selection seems, in general, an unblinkered one. We hope to have more details from Director Paul O'Connor by next year; readers' reports, too?

Best buys

Planalto Reserva 1986, Douro, Sogrape, £3.49
Bourgogne Rouge (non-vintage), Moillard, £4.99
Brajkovich, Sauvignon Blanc 1989, New Zealand, £5.99

Guildford Wine Market

216 London Road, Burpham, Guildford,   *Tel* (0483) 575933
Surrey GU4 7JS

Open Mon–Sat 10–9; Sun, public holidays 12–2, 7–9 **Closed** Chr Day, 1 Jan,
Easter **Credit cards** All accepted **Discounts** 10% on 1 case of wine
Delivery Free locally **Glass hire** Free with suitable case order
Tastings and talks 4–5 tastings annually in-store on Saturdays; to group on
request **Cellarage** Not available

'Absolutely no conning the public into buying branded overpriced wines because they are what they've heard of,' replies partner Nicholas Brougham in response to our customary request for a bit of self-profiling. 'We don't and won't stock them.' We applaud this resolute stance against the characterless and the bland.

It would be worth nothing, of course, if what is put on the shelves in place of those branded and overpriced bottles fails to excite and intrigue. No danger of that at the Guildford Wine Market; this is an excellent selection. There is plenty in the 'intriguing' category: the Maréchal Foch from Inniskillin in Canada, for example, or the Muscat Cannelli from Chateau Ste Michelle in Washington, Schlumberger's Alsace Pinot Noir, a pair of Zimbabwean Flame Lilies or a Soviet sparkler. Excitement is provided by the wide range of Australian and New Zealand wines (small estates as well as monstrous factory producers, though the qualitative differences between the two are of startling insignificance in the antipodes); a good American choice, from North and South; fair clarets; a serious response to the challenge of French country wines; a better-than-usual German selection; good Hungarian wines, founded on Tokaj; a sound start on Portugal; fine champagnes and sparkling wines; and an unusually broad selection of ports. There's also a good selection of lagers and beers. All wines, we are assured, have a shelf description, which must have given someone a lot of work but will certainly be worthwhile when it comes to those 'intriguing' options. What do customers feel about the Guildford Wine Market? Write and tell us.

Best buys

Siklósi Chardonnay 1988, Hungary, £2.95
Reserva 904 1978, La Rioja Alta, Rioja, £13.30
Niepoort 10 Years Old Tawny Port, £11.45

Hadleigh Wine Cellars

46 Burlington Road, Ipswich, Suffolk   *Tel* (0473) 250242
IP1 2HS

Hadleigh Wine Cellars used to be in Bury St Edmunds but as from September 1990 will be sharing premises with Burlington Wines (*q.v.*), whose phone number is given here as the new one together with their current details are not available as we go to press. They stress the friendliness and lack of pomposity in their approach to selling wine: 'to help people enjoy themselves' is the primary aim. The list is mid-length, with around 200 wines, chosen with care and described with straightforwardness and skill.

Value for money is obviously something that Jonathan Hare and his two fellow directors prize, and the top half of the Bordeaux section, and Champagne, are the only areas where prices rise with any consistency above £10. The £3.50 to £8.50 band is the one where Hadleigh are strongest, and you'll have a reasonable choice from most of the world at around this level. Bordeaux, the Rhône, French country wines and Australian wines are the most exciting and the most widely stocked areas; the commitment to Germany, Italy and Portugal seems tenuous (though ports are admired). America, previously represented only by Quady's Essensia, has disappeared altogether: a new Columbus is awaited.

Best buys

Chardonnay 1988, Vin de Pays de Franche-Comté, Guillaume, £5.09
Syrah 1988, Vins de Pays de l'Ardèche, Les Caves de la Cévenne Ardèchoise, £2.93
Pinot Noir 1987, Vin de Pays de Franche-Comté, Guillaume, £5.09

Half Yard Wines

Fern Cottage, High Street, Barcombe, *Tel* (0273) 400990
nr Lewes, East Sussex BN8 5DH

Case sales only **Open** (Generally) Mon–Fri 9–5; Sat 9–6; occasionally on
Sundays **Closed** Some Sundays **Credit cards** None accepted; personal and
business accounts **Discounts** 5% on 5 cases **Delivery** Free in Sussex, parts of
Kent and London (min 1 case) **Glass hire** Free with 1-case order
Tastings and talks Two annual tastings; to groups on request **Cellarage** Not
available

British Airways purser Maggie Richardson runs this 'cottage
industry' in her spare time. In the two years since setting up
business, she has built a small but attractive list of between
three and seven wines from most of the better-known wine-
producing regions and countries; the aim for the future, she
tells us, is 'to specialise in little-known wines', particularly from
Spain, Chile and Southern France. Prices are attractive, thanks
to 'no overheads': Fern Cottage is home as well as office, and
cellared friends kindly help out with storage. 'Total commitment
to the interested customer' is promised, as well as 'free tastings
on request on the spot!'; we suspect that buying wine here
would be fun as well as rewarding. Can customers confirm?

Best buys

Domaine de St Roch, Cabardès, £2.99
Château Gressier-Grand-Poujeaux 1982, Moulis, £8.97
Concha y Toro Cabernet Sauvignon 1985, Chile, £3.38

Harcourt Fine Wine

3 Harcourt Street, London W1H 1DS *Tel* 071-723 7202

Open Mon–Fri 9–7; Sat 10.30–5 **Closed** Sun, public holidays
Credit cards Access, American Express, Visa; personal and business accounts
Discounts 5% on 1 case **Delivery** Free in City of London and West End (min 1
case); elsewhere at cost; mail order available **Glass hire** Free with case order
Tastings and talks Two annual tastings (Christmas and summer); to groups on
request **Cellarage** Not available

What used to be known as The English Wine Shop has
resurfaced under new ownership as Harcourt Fine Wine – but
English wine is still very much a reason for travelling here. The
range of home-grown wines has in fact doubled in the last year,
and partners Carl Koenen and Neil Mathieson had the wit to
organise one of the first comprehensive tastings of the 1989
vintage in the spring of 1990, showing not only that 1989 was a
terrific year for English wines, but also that English wine had
come of age, with a series of dryish, serious, grown-up wines

from producers all over the country. Everyone who went to that tasting left in a state of high excitement; make your own way to the tiny shop in Harcourt Street to find out why.

When you get there, you'll see that there are plenty of other interesting bottles as well as those containing English wine – curiosities from France, Italy, Germany (Carl Koenen's speciality) as well as fine brandies and spirits, especially Calvados and Armagnac (Neil Mathieson's speciality). Most of these are bin-ends from Harcourt's other business as an importer and trade wholesaler, so they are not listed; 'the range changes all the time so it would be too much hassle to type it all out,' says Neil Matheson, but we think you'll be impressed by what you see there (it includes a good range of half-bottles). You'll also find knowledgable, committed help in making your choice. We wish Harcourt Fine Wine success, and we urge Londoners to drop in and try, at the very least, one of the three English wines listed below.

Best buys

Nutbourne Manor Bacchus 1989, Sussex, £5.25
Breaky Bottom Müller-Thurgau 1989, Sussex, £5.95
Sharpham Vineyards Madeleine Angevine/Huxelrebe 1988, Devon, £5.60

Harpenden Wines

68 High Street, Harpenden, Hertfordshire   *Tel* (0582) 765605
AL5 2SP

Open Mon–Fri 10–10; Sat 9–10; Sun, Good Friday, Boxing Day 12–3, 7–9
Closed Chr Day, 1 Jan   **Credit cards** All accepted; personal and business
accounts   **Discounts** 5% on 1 case for credit card or 7.5% for cheque or cash
Delivery Free locally (min 1 case – except for special circumstances); otherwise at
cost   **Glass hire** Free   **Tastings and talks** Bottles available in-store at weekends;
one summer and one winter tasting at the local hotel   **Cellarage** Possible by
arrangement

A new entry for this well organised and enthusiastically run Harpenden off-licence. It is a first retail outlet for wholesaler Paul Beaton, and another one is planned for summer 1990. The range is not a large one, but it tries hard to do justice to wine-making endeavour in most parts of the world, and it includes some unusual wines (a nobly rotted Orvieto Classico 1986, for example) as well as more popular ranges from Bordeaux and elsewhere in France. Come Christmas, there is a good selection of Vintage Port and malt whisky. If you find yourself visiting 'Harpenden's only independent wine merchant', let us have your impressions of the range and service.

Best buys

Château Haut-Piquat 1986, Lussac-Saint-Emilion, £5.65
Chablis 1988, Domaine de l'Eglantière, Jean Durup, £7.29
Chinon 1988, Domaine des Bouqueries, £5.45

Gerard Harris

2 Green End Street, Aston Clinton,   *Tel* (0296) 631041
Buckinghamshire HP22 5HP

Open Tue–Sat 9.30–8 **Closed** Mon, Sun, public holidays **Credit cards** Access,
Visa; personal and business accounts **Discounts** 10% for 1 case (does not apply
for fine wines) **Delivery** Free within 20-mile radius (min 1 case); otherwise at
cost (min £5.75); mail order available **Glass hire** Free with 1-case order
Tastings and talks Two major tastings annually in May and November; Bell Inn
Fine Wine Society now has over 50 members; to groups on request
Cellarage Not available

Gerard Harris Fine Wines is situated in a small village shop
opposite the Bell restaurant in Aston Clinton, and the two are
under the same ownership. A visit to the wine shop will explain
exactly why the wine list at the Bell is so good, for evident
devotion and enthusiasm has gone into building a list of depth
and breadth. This was over a quarter of a century's work for
Florence Pike (see Philip Eyres Wine Merchant); her assistant
Norman Terrace has now taken over, helped by Dee Blackstock
and Guy Porter.

The transition seems, from the outside, to have been a smooth
one, and claret, champagne, burgundy and German wines
remain as distinguished as ever in their quality and variety. It
should be noted that wines are offered here only when
considered ready for drinking (*en primeur* sales excepted) so, for
example, the biggest selection of Bordeaux at present on the list
is from 1982, supplies of which are already dwindling at some
other merchants. Given the fact that Gerard Harris has cellared
the wines for you, prices are reasonable: Château Fourcas-
Hosten '82 at £9.50, for example, or Château Meyney '82 at
£15.50 at the time of writing. The average age of the burgundies
is well into adolescence here, rather than the earliest infancy of
most other merchants: 1982, 1983 and 1985 are all well
represented, and there are even one or two 1978s left hiding in
the list. The burgundies are sourced from a healthy variety of
growers and négociants, and we hope they will stay that way.

Once away from the classic regions, there are good examples
of most of the world's wine-making, with the emphasis
throughout on top quality (there are, therefore, very few wines
at under £3 per bottle). Three wines from the Jura, two from
Switzerland and five from England show a readiness to take

risks in the interests of providing educative and palate-expanding wines for customers. Alsace, Provence and Languedoc-Roussillon have been explored particularly thoroughly, and the sherries are good, too – especially if you are a manzanilla enthusiast.

Life membership of the Bell Fine Wine Society costs only £15, and gives you access to tutored tastings; a full range of special offers and bin-end sales is also available to customers on the mailing list. The 1982 Fronsac of Château de la Rivière was well worth the £6.90 asked for it in the January 1990 sale.

Best buys

Bairrada Montanha Garrafeira 1982, Portugal, £3.95
Berri Estates, Semillon 1987, South Australia, £3.99
Château Gruaud-Larose 1982, Saint-Julien, £19.90

Roger Harris

Loke Farm, West Longville, Norfolk   *Tel* (0603) 880171
NR9 5LG

Case sales only   Open Mon–Fri 9–5   **Closed** Sat, Sun, public holidays
Credit cards All accepted; personal and business accounts   **Discounts** 2 cases £1 per case, 5 cases £1.50 per case   **Delivery** Free on UK mainland (min 1 case); otherwise at cost; mail order available   **Glass hire** Not available
Tastings and talks To groups on request   **Cellarage** Not available

Of all Britain's specialist merchants, Norfolk-based Roger Harris is perhaps the most thoroughgoing and rigorous in exploring what his chosen region has to offer. And in putting this information across to customers via a calm, rational, systematic and beautifully illustrated list. The only surprising thing in all this is the choice of region itself: Beaujolais. In place of rational explanation and black-and-white photographs, one would expect a list of Yapp-like effusion from a Beaujolais specialist, full of wild sketches of plumpy bacchants and scantily dressed maenads. Exactly why this ex-Peugeot and Lotus engineer chose Beaujolais you can discover in the list; here's a tantalising glimpse of how Alsace and Burgundy failed to secure his attentions. 'Alsace was the closest, and to this day I love the grapiness of their wine but I found the people austere. Burgundy was more distant but within reach and again I loved the wine, but now for its majestic elegance. I found the sense of self importance in the wine appealing but less so the same trait in the people.'

Their loss was Beaujolais' gain. Rather than enumerate exactly who is in the list (lots of small growers) and who isn't (lots of big négociants), we would just say that if Beaujolais holds any attraction at all for you, write for a copy: no document available in Britain, including those that can be bought in bookshops, will be more useful to you. In addition to Beaujolais of every shape and size, you will also find wines from the nearby Coteaux du Lyonnais and a good Mâconnais selection. Champagne and marc complete the list; and it is worth emphasising that prices include free UK delivery. It's case-only, but mixing is encouraged. A first-class operation, and an admirable example of everything that the specialist merchant should be.

Best buys

Beaujolais 1989, Jean Garlon, £5.60
Côte de Brouilly 1989, Château Thivin, £7.20
Moulin-à-Vent 1989, Château de Moulin-à-Vent, £9.65

Harrods

Knightsbridge, London SW1X 7XL   *Tel* 071-730 1234

Open Mon, Tue, Thur–Sat 9–6; Wed 9.30–7; open most public holidays
Closed Sun   **Credit cards** All accepted; personal and business accounts
Discounts Available on full cases (on most wines) – 12 bottles for price of 11
Delivery Free in inner London and within 25-mile radius of M25 (min £50 order);
£5 charge for orders under £50; mail order available   **Glass hire** Not available
Tastings and talks Regular in-store tastings   **Cellarage** Not available

---

Harrods has one of the most complete wine selections available in London: almost every wine-producing country is represented within its range, although some to the tune of a bottle or two only. Hugh Cochrane MW, the Wine Buyer, can afford to favour quality, as most suppliers would stand on their heads to be stocked by Harrods, and price seems to be little object to either merchant or customer. Both fine wines (older vintages are unlisted, but enquiries are welcome) and everyday drinking wines are treated equally seriously; the sense of responsibility stretches on into the spirits and the liqueurs. (If you prefer a sense of adventure to one of responsibility, you may be better served by Selfridges.)

Whatever your tastes, you will find something of quality at Harrods. It is perhaps harder to isolate areas in which the Harrods range is particularly distinguished, though English wines, Italian wines, wines from New Zealand and the United States, and sherry and port all surprise by their extent of their presence. Bordeaux and Burgundy are as good as one would expect, with the halo of Bordeaux first growths being the Wine Department's equivalent of the Fish Department's display of prancing red snapper and frolicsome mackerel that everybody has their photograph taken next to.

And prices . . . high, certainly. No one comes here to save money, though a wine like Valdespino's Coliseo is a bargain even at the Harrods price of £17.50. You pay Harrods prices in order to take your bottles away in a Harrods bag, of course, or have some delivery man climb out of a dark green 1920s-style delivery van with your case or two. (Unmixed cases, note, for the price of eleven bottles, which would bring the more obviously overpriced wines down towards everybody else's price.)

Best buys

Harrods Claret, Sélection Louis Vialard, non-vintage, £3.75
Givry 1986, Clos Salomon, Du Gardin, £8.85
Coliseo, Very Finest Old Amontillado (dry), Valdespino, £17.50

John Harvey & Sons

Order office

31 Denmark Street, Bristol, Avon BS1 5DQ	*Tel* (0272) 268882
5 The Hard, Portsmouth, Hampshire PO1 3DT	*Tel* (0705) 825567

Open Mon–Fri 9.30–6 (Bristol), 9–5 (Portsmouth); Sat 9.30 1 (Bristol)
Closed Sat (Portsmouth), Sun, public holidays **Credit cards** All accepted; personal and business accounts **Discounts** 5–9 cases £1 per case; 10+ cases £1.50 **Delivery** Free on UK mainland (min 2 case); elsewhere £5 per delivery; mail order available **Glass hire** Not available **Tastings and talks** Regular in-store tastings; occasional tastings for invited customers; tasting workshops in summer and winter for limited numbers; to groups on request **Cellarage** £4.37 per case per year

---

The closure of Harvey's Pall Mall shop in April 1990 may make Allied Lyons' balance sheet marginally more attractive, but it was still a sad day for the Royal Warrant holders, as 'business requirements' triumphed over 'the strength of our traditions in St James's'. Business continues to work hand-in-hand with tradition in Portsmouth and Bristol, though, and the Queen will no doubt be taking advantage of Harvey's mail-order facilities in future – free delivery anywhere in the UK for two cases or more (which may be mixed).

Harvey's 88-page list has a very civilised feel to it. Its cover is usually illustrated with some enchanting nonsense from the company's Wine Museum displays; 'personalities' (Roald Dahl, Richard Baker) provide Forewords; there are competitions, essays, illustrations, maps, even book reviews – just the thing to while away a couple of hours by the fireside with. The wine selections themselves are as solid and comfortable as a well-loved armchair: good wines from good properties. Sherry and port are particular strengths, with Harvey-owned Palomino y Vergara's fino Tio Mateo looking appealing at £4.97; at the other end of the sweetness scale are Harvey's fine Old Bottled sherries, unknown in Jerez, almost forgotten in Britain – enjoy them while you can, before they are banned or abandoned. Port features the Cockburn and Martinez ranges, these two houses being sited within Allied Lyons' walled city; but foreigners are given list-space, too, with Churchill, Delaforce, Offley, Noval, Fonseca, Warre, Graham, Smith Woodhouse and Quarles Harris all getting a look in. Harvey certainly offers one of the best ranges of Vintage Port available in Britain today, and prices for these are very fair. Lay down Cockburn 1983 (£18) or Graham 1980 (18.35); drink Martinez 1963 (£34) or Graham 1970 (£32.50).

The other area of excitement is Château Latour, the most prestigious Harvey stablemate: there are 12 vintages on sale from the last two decades, as well as Les Forts de Latour (the château's second wine) back to 1970, with 1984 perhaps offering best value at £11.67 and the 1979 best drinking (at £17.50). Latour is kept company by plenty of other good clarets, and the informative tasting notes should steer you towards what you need in this area. The Burgundy picture is patchier, though the variety it contains indicates endeavour – favour the Clerget and Jadot wines to those from Viénot and Boisset; the Loire and Rhône, meanwhile, seem pitfall-free. Joël Gigou's Jasnières Clos Saint-Jacques Vieilles Vignes 1986 is particularly recommended, and rightly so (£6.97): it's a fine, complex wine at a very reasonable price. The rest of France is well represented, and so is Germany and the New World; but the character and value of Iberian wines, and the excitement of those from Italy, have still to be reflected in the Harvey list. Tastings, *en primeur* offers, bin-end sales and a 'very sophisticated individual cellar planning service by one of our Masters of Wine' are also offered, and Harvey is noteworthy for being one of the few places in Britain to sell that essential fortified-wine tasting tool, the copita glass (£3 each from the shops; also available by mail order in packs of six, plus post and packing).

Best buys

Jasnières, Clos Saint-Jacques Vieilles Vignes 1986, Joël Gigou, £6.97
El Abuelo Old Bottled Oloroso (bottled 1974), £9
Mercurey 1985, Raoul Clerget, £9.97

Richard Harvey Wines   ☞

Not a shop
Home Farm, Morden, Wareham, Dorset   *Tel* (092 945) 224
BH20 7DW
Mainly telephone and mail order

Case sales only   **Open** Callers by appointment; 24-hour answering machine
Credit cards None accepted; personal and business accounts   **Discounts** 2.5% for
1 unmixed case, 5% for 6 unmixed cases   **Delivery** Free within 30-mile radius
(min 3 cases); otherwise 3–5 cases £3.45 per case, 1–2 cases £5.75 per case; mail
order available   **Glass hire** Free with reasonable case order
Tastings and talks Major annual tasting; special producer tasting or dinner 2–3
times annually; to groups on request   **Cellarage** £4.60 per case per year (plus
insurance)

During the last year, Master of Wine Richard Harvey has bought
back the business that bears his name, from Coopers of Wessex.
At present there is no shop, but collections and visits can be
made by appointment, and the list provides all the information
you need to decide whether or not this company can offer you
the mixed case you are looking for.

The range is a broad and balanced one. France is explored
most systematically, with the Rhône section looking particularly
eye-catching; Burgundy, Bordeaux and French country wines are
scarcely less appealing, and the new list, we understand, will
feature France to a still greater extent. Italy, Germany, Spain and
Australia offer less choice, but those producers selected (Castello
di Volpaia, Friedrich Wilhelm Gymnasium, La Rioja Alta,
Bodegas Fariña and Basedow, to pick out a few examples) are all
reliable quality-wine producers. Champagne, sherry (from
Barbadillo) and port (Churchill and others) provide a finishing
flourish.

Best buys

Château Cayla 1986, Premières Côtes de Bordeaux (red), £3.95
Saint-Aubin Blanc, 1988, Henri Prudhon, £8.37
Domaine de Ribonnet Chardonnay 1988, Vin de Pays de la
Haute Garonne (barrel fermented), £5.25

The Wine & Spirit Education Trust is the body in charge of educating
those in and on the fringes of the wine trade. They offer a series of
courses right up to Master of Wine level, the more basic of which are
open to non-trade members who can convince the Trust of their
intention to enter the wine trade. Contact them at: Five Kings House,
Kennet Wharf Lane, Upper Thames Street, London EC4V 3AJ; *Tel* 071-
236 3551.

Haughton Fine Wines

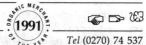

Row's Ground, Chorley Green Lane,
Chorley, Nantwich, Cheshire CW5 8JR

Tel (0270) 74 537

Case sales only **Open** Mon–Fri 9.5.30; Sat 9–1 **Closed** Sun, public holidays
Credit cards Access, Visa; personal and business accounts **Discounts** 5% on 10
cases **Delivery** Free within 30-mile radius and nationwide for 6+ cases;
otherwise 1 case £4, 2 cases £6, 3–5 cases £2.50 per case; mail order available
Glass hire Free **Tastings and talks** To groups on request **Cellarage** Available

Wine-list collectors should under no circumstances omit to send
for Haughton Fine Wines' 'Year Book', an irresistible 180-page
ring-bound . . . well, book. It is beautifully designed and
produced by Crewe-based Computers at Work, which sounds
like a desktop publishing operation; if so, this one is more
publishing and less desktop than most. The quality, depth and
thoroughness of the information it contains rivals that provided
by the country's top three or four mail-order specialists; while
the design puts it ahead of all of them for clarity and style. Take
a look at the Burgundy pyramid on page 67 if you don't believe
us: why hasn't anyone else thought of that? (Our only criticism,
and a carping one in the light of so much that is praiseworthy,
would be to point out that Côte is a feminine noun unhappily
partnered by adjectives in the masculine form.)

An irresistible list is not the only reason for writing or
phoning Nantwich, though. If you're interested in drinking
organic, then Haughton Fine Wines will prove invaluable: you
can furnish a serious cellar from among the 135-strong range the
company offers (printed in green in the list). The Year Book
provides a two-page description of what 'organic' means in the
wine context. Bruce and Judy Kendrick are both ex-ICI
employees, interestingly enough, though Bruce was a software
rather than a chemical man and Judy was PA to one of the
directors. And they stress that it's the quality of the wine that
counts first and foremost rather than its supposed wholeness;
they have no hesitation in listing non-organic finds – if they
taste good.

Pages 43 to 132 of the Year Book are devoted to France, and
this is the most distinguished section of the list. The Kendricks
have reached the parts, like Collioure, Coteaux du Giennois or
Banyuls, that only specialists normally reach, and the selection
from South-West France is one of Britain's best. Australia has
been well-explored (in person, as well as by sample); New
Zealand, too. The rest of the world is briefly though
thoughtfully treated. There are some excellent mixed tasting
cases, and the Haughton Herald (a newsletter) goes out to
everyone on the mailing list during the year. Haughton Fine
Wines would seem to be so admirably poised to make a killing

in the mail-order area, with its nifty list and organic heart, that we are surprised that nationwide delivery charges (£4 and up for under six cases) are not just a little bit more attractive. As it is, only locals have no excuse for not buying here.

Best buys

Château Flotis 1988, Côtes de Frontonnais, £3.96
Mas de Gourgonnier 1986, Réserve du Mas, Coteaux d'Aix-en-Provence-les-Baux, £5.39
Chardonnay 1989, Mountadam, Adelaide Hills, £10.99

Haynes Hanson & Clark

Head office and wholesale warehouse
17 Lettice Street, London SW6 4EH   *Tel* 071-736 7878
Retail
36 Kensington Church Street, London   *Tel* 071-937 4650
W8 4BX

Open Mon–Thur 9–7, Fri 9–6 (SW6); Mon–Sat 9.30–7 (W8) **Closed** Sat (SW6), Sun, public holidays **Credit cards** None accepted; personal and business accounts **Discounts** 10% on 1 unmixed case **Delivery** Free in central London and on regular van-delivery runs (Thames Valley and East Anglia) (min 1 case) and on UK mainland (min 5 cases); otherwise 1 case £4.70, 2 cases £3.20 per case, 3–4 cases £1.80 per case; mail order available **Glass hire** Free with 1-case order **Tastings and talks** Regular in-store tastings for customers (in SW6, SW1, City, Thames Valley/Gloucestershire or East Anglia); to customers on their premises by arrangement **Cellarage** Can arrange on customers' behalf

This is a first-class merchant to buy from, if you have the money for it. We don't mean to suggest that there is systematic overpricing on the Haynes Hanson & Clark list, because there isn't; prices are within the market band for most wines stocked (albeit the top half of that band). But much of the list is occupied by good-to-great Bordeaux and Burgundy, and when the list moves away from these areas it is always the best producers that are sought out. Net result: very little under £5. If you are able to buy wines whose average price is perhaps £7.50 or £8, then we repeat: Haynes Hanson & Clark is first-class.

The partner with the highest profile is Hanson, Anthony (MW), a Burgundy specialist, and the six pages filled by wines from this area (and from Beaujolais) on the summer list looked very good indeed: 1988, 1987 and 1986, with a little 1985 and earlier, from growers of talent or pedigree (pedigree, of course, does not exclude talent): Simon Bize, Philippe Rossignol, Hubert de Montille, Domaine Méo-Camuzet, Jacqueline Jayer, Michel Lafarge, Domaine Gagnard-Delagrange, and wines sourced by Olivier Leflaive Frères. Bordeaux presents less of a buying problem, and the selection is just as good. Both Bordeaux and

Burgundy *en primeur* offers are made, the open-mindedness and quality consciousness of the H H & C team being indicated by the fact that they went to Bordeaux for 1989s and ended by offering second-helpings of the 1988 vintage as well as 1989s, because the value for money of 1988 was so good in comparison with 1989.

The Loire selection is almost exclusively dry, but that is its only failing; wines from the Rhône, Alsace and Champagne are all varied, high in quality and in price. Haynes Hanson & Clark are great believers in the potential of Californian wines to rival France's best, and they have bought accordingly ('Think Meursault, taste Kistler, then compare the prices'). Even among the Australians, H H & C seem to skim the heights rather than rummage around in the depths. Germany and Spain are over rather quickly, and Italy scarcely less so; sherry and port are thorough and workmanlike. The quest at the heart of the list is for fine Pinot Noir, Chardonnay, Cabernet Sauvignon and Merlot, from all the ends of the earth.

Best buys

Mâcon-Viré 1988, Domaine Emilian Gillet, £8.15
Pinot Noir 1988, Saintsbury, Carneros (Napa), £9.49
Château l'Etoile 1986, Graves, £5.90

The Heath Street Wine Co

29 Heath Street, London NW3 6TR   *Tel* 071-435 6845

Open Mon–Sat 10–8 **Closed** Sun, public holidays **Credit cards** Access, Visa; personal and business accounts **Discounts** Negotiable **Delivery** Free in London (min 1 case); elsewhere at cost; mail order available **Glass hire** Free with wine order **Tastings and talks** Quarterly in-store tastings for customers on mailing list; tutored tastings at hotel and club venues; to groups on request **Cellarage** £4 per case per year

---

Hampstead's Heath Street Wine Company has moved orbits in the last year, while remaining at its old address. From being an H Allen Smith outlet, it has now become part of the La Réserve (*q.v.*) group, so from an Iberian orientation one would now expect a move towards France, and finer, older bottles. Yet one would be wrong; retailer Geoff Merrick has stayed in charge, and apart from a core or so of 20 'shipping wines' sourced from La Réserve, he still has a more or less free hand as to what he buys and stocks. The range of fine and unusual wines, he tells us, is set to increase in future, but there are unlikely ever to be as many of these here as you'll find in Walton Street; what Heath Street is aiming to provide, however, is a really wide spread of wines, and it is already well on its way to achieving that.

You won't find anything from Canada, Texas or Switzerland here yet, but you will find half a dozen or more wines from most of the wine regions of the world. Those parts of the list that seem to have been the most fun to put together are French country wines and Italy (old DOCs and new vins de table), and it would be worth making your way up to the heights of Hampstead to look through each of these selections. Champagne and sparkling wines, Portuguese wines, Alsace, the Loire and the Rhône are also amply stocked, and the older vintages of Caves São João's Reserva Particular would be worth a punt. Germany is the only country with cause to feel hard done by. The 'designer' beers and the fancy spirits deserve a sweep of the spotlight, too. Most wines on the list are above £5; but allow yourself a ceiling of £10 and you will have a great number of interesting bottles to chose from. Enthusiastic advice is on tap.

Best buys

Château la Renaudie 1986, Pécharmant (oak aged), £4.25
Jurançon Sec 1988, Grain Sauvage, Caves des Producteurs de Jurançon, £3.95
Georges Gardet Vintage Champagne 1979, £17.95

Hedley Wright

| 10–11 The Twyford Centre, London Road, | *Tel* (0279) 506512 |
| Bishop's Stortford, Hertfordshire CM23 3YT | |

Case sales only **Open** Mon–Thur 9–6; Fri 9–8; Sat 10–6 **Closed** Sun, public holidays **Credit cards** Access, Visa; personal and business accounts
Discounts By arrangement **Delivery** Free within 20-mile radius of cellars and central London (min 1 case); elsewhere at cost; mail order available
Glass hire Free with 1-case order **Tastings and talks** Selection of wines always available in-store; to groups on request **Cellarage** £3.95 per case per year

---

Martin Wright learned about wine trading at the Tony Laithwaite/Bordeaux Direct school in the 1970s, and its lessons have not been wasted on him. Like Tony Laithwaite, he is an assiduous and skilled communicator, and his special offers and lists are copiously informative. We have looked at plenty of 1989 *en primeur* offers this year, including a number more extensive than Martin Wright's; his, though, stood out as being one of the most appealingly written, and his selections some of the most convincingly argued. And, as he never tires of reiterating, 'I am here at the end of the telephone 0279 506512 if you would like more advice . . .'

Unlike Bordeaux Direct, Hedley Wright is a call-in, wholesale operation (though mail-order facilities are available, too); also unlike Bordeaux Direct, it does not spurn 'mainstream' wines, and fishes in the same pool as most other merchants. What it pulls out of that pool is a fine Chilean selection, some excellent claret, and German wines of modest distinction, with good back-up from Burgundy, the Loire, the Rhône, Beaujolais and Australia. Italy and Iberia provide some safe alternatives, but in general the selection from these countries lacks aspiration.

Hedley Wright enjoys an exclusivity on the Chilean wines of Villa Montes; we have not tried these, but Martin Wright is very proud of them, and tells us that his own enthusiasm for them is matched by that of customers. 'Aurelio Montes is recognised as Chile's foremost winemaker,' we learn. The Chilean wines of Santa Helena are also stocked; these we have tried; these, we agree, are good, especially the reds. Another reason for contacting Hedley Wright are the sherries of Manuel de Argüeso; they are normally only seen in Britain dressed up as one of Lustau's almacenistas, though this small company sells its wines like anyone else locally in Spain. Hedley Wright carry a range of eight and, as usual with sherry, the ones that cost £2 more than the cheapest are worth at least £5 more when tasted. Of course these were 'tucked away in some dark part of their cellars' and are 'normally reserved for the family'. 'Rather reluctantly they have released to us a small parcel of their exquisite . . .' and so on: the Laithwaite school, as ever was. But it's all good clean fun, and wines taste better when the imagination as well as the taste buds are engaged.

Best buys

Palo Cortado del Carrascal, Manuel de Argüeso, £6.85
Villa Montes Sauvignon Blanc 1990, Chile, £3.49
Coldstream Hills Pinot Noir 1988, Victoria, £9.99

Douglas Henn-Macrae

Not a shop
81 Mackenders Lane, Eccles, Maidstone, Kent   *Tel* (0622) 710952
ME20 7JA

Case sales only   Open Telephone enquiries welcome Mon–Sat up to 10pm
Closed Sun, Chr & Easter   **Credit cards** Access, Visa   **Discounts** Occasionally available   **Delivery** Free on UK mainland (min 5 cases); otherwise £5.75 per order; mail order available   **Glass hire** Not available   **Tastings and talks** To groups on request   **Cellarage** Not available

The Great British tradition of individuality carried to the point of eccentricity is represented, within these covers, by Douglas Henn-Macrae, ex-schoolmaster and registrar, musician, and specialist wine merchant. Specialist indeed: his wines come from five Texan vineyards, two from Oregon and one from Washington, with the balance being provided by the obscurer sorts of German, like the red sort, or the sort from Hessische Bergstrasse and Württemberg. A further eccentricity is the coding, on the list, of medal-winning wines by an accretion of exclamation marks and asterisks. Until you've cracked the system, it looks like all the tasting notes are unprintable. 'Grünstadter Höllenpfad Portugieser Auslese TROCKEN !!!*' 'Too !!!*ing right,' is the ineluctable response.

There are, though, many good things about this otherwise well-written list. First of all, the accents of the German names and French grape varieties are printed; this is, astonishingly, unusual, most wine merchants simply giving up and pretending accents on foreign words don't exist. Next year we will pay greater attention to merchant-illiteracy of this sort; in the meantime, well done to D H-M for proving that it is possible to run a German list and respect German orthography. Another thing is honesty; the list tells you exactly what stocks of a particular wine are held, down to the last bottle – or, in the case of the Great Texas Vineyards Bankruptcy Purchase – up to the very top of the mountain. 'We made history in the summer of 1988 when we bought up their entire inventory – over 6,000 cases of it – from the bank which closed them down,' writes Mr Henn-Macrae. Anyone for 913 cases of Ivanhoe Blush 1986?

You'd be unwise to dismiss this selection as merely eccentric: Germany can produce some terrific red wines, just as Texas can produce some remarkably good whites, and those of Elk Cove in Oregon and Covey Run in Washington already bask in the sunshine of international repute. For classicists, there are some fine Mosel Rieslings. PhD-level wine buffs and rusty MWs would also find much to wrap their tongues around here: how about comparing two varietal Lembergers (aka Blaüfrankisch), one from Württemberg and one from Washington? Or Rheinpfalz Portugieser Weissherbst with four different Texan Blushes? 'Dallas' historians, finally, should take the opportunity to stock up on Sanchez Creek wines, where Larry Hagman helps pick grapes as his contribution to Real Life. We need our Henn-Macraes, our *franc-tireurs*.

Best buys

Fall Creek Sauvignon Blanc 1988, Texas, £7.58
Grünstadter Höllenpfad Riesling Spätlese 1971, Winzerkeller Leiningerland, Rheinpfalz, £5.51
Texas Vineyards Gewürztraminer 1986, Texas, £3.29

Hicks & Don

Head office
Park House, North Elmham, Dereham,   *Tel* (036 281) 571
Norfolk NR20 5JY
Order office
4 The Market Place, Westbury, Wiltshire   *Tel* (0373) 864723
BA13 3EA
Mainly mail order

Case sales only   **Open** Mon–Fri 9–5.30; Sat by appointment   **Closed** Sun, public
holidays   **Credit cards** Access, Visa; personal and business accounts
Discounts Available on certain items   **Delivery** Free on UK mainland (min 3
cases); charges to off-shore islands are negotiable; mail order available
Glass hire Free with order   **Tastings and talks** To groups on request
Cellarage £2.90 per case per year

If you are interested in buying wines – all manner of wines, not
just Bordeaux – on an *en primeur* basis, then you should make
sure that you are on Hicks & Don's mailing list. At the time of
writing, you could buy 1989 Bordeaux, 1988 and 1989 German
wines, 1988 Rhône, 1989 Beaujolais, 1988 Alsace and 1988
Chablis and Red Burgundy, plus a few snippets from the Loire,
on this basis – though Robin Don MW refers to the method as
'ex-cellars' selling, feeling that 'en primeur' has Beaujolais
connotations (we feel it would only connote this to a French
speaker). Similar offers are made following declared port
vintages, and after exceptional years in Provence, South-West
France and Tuscany. The tasting experience of two well-
seasoned Masters of Wine who have been buying and selling in
this way since 1966 is worth capitalising on; the passage of
three or four years will generally reveal you have acquired
bargains – as well as fine wines. The only drawback, and it is a
major one, is that these offers are for a minimum of three cases.
No problem if you belong to a wine club and can form a small
buying syndicate, but a major disincentive if you are a lone
collector of comparatively modest means. (Remember, in
glancing through the best buys below, that you should add £15
shipping and duty, plus 15 per cent VAT on to the total, before
dividing by twelve to arrive at a per bottle price in your wine
rack.)
　　Lone collectors would normally sidle over towards the general
list and hope to pick up some of the fruits of skilled, early
buying there, but again disincentives lie in wait. It's unmixed
cases only, with the exception of some (but not all) of the
fortified wines, and this targets the list squarely at syndicates,
institutions or private buyers of means prepared to make a
complete commitment to Hicks & Don. The wines, particularly
those from French classic regions, are well chosen, but whereas

one to three bottles of Maurice Chapuits' Corton 1985, Acacia's Pinor Noir 1987, or even Robin Don's own Elmham Park white wine would make an attractive buy, 12 is too many for most of us. Though we would encourage Hicks & Don's customers to write in disagreement.

Best buys

Alsace Riesling 1988, Louis Gisselbrecht (ex-cellars) (case), £36.72
Châteauneuf-du-Pape 1988, Cuvée Prestige, Roger Salon et Fils (ex-cellars) (case), £68
Château Charmail 1989, Haut-Médoc (ex-cellars) (case), £48

High Breck Vintners

Cellars

Spats Lane, Headley, nr Bordon, Hampshire	*Tel* (0428) 713689
GU35 8SY	*Tel* (office) 081-946 6372

Associated outlets

Harbottle Wines, 27 Perrymead Street, London SW6 3SN	*Tel* 071-731 1972
Sir Ronald Preston, Beeston Hall Cellars, Beeston St Lawrence, nr Norwich, Norfolk NR12 8YS	*Tel* (0692) 630771
Col G P Pease, Milverton Cottage, Whitchurch, Pangbourne, Berkshire RG8 7HA	*Tel* (07357) 2624

Case sales only **Open** Mon–Fri 9.30–6; Sat 9.30–12 noon; Sun, public holidays by arrangement **Credit cards** None accepted; personal and business accounts **Discounts** Not available **Delivery** Free locally (no min) and elsewhere (min 3 cases); otherwise £6.90; mail order available **Glass hire** Free with case order **Tastings and talks** 8 tastings annually at High Breck and 3 at each agent; to groups on request **Cellarage** Not available

During 1989 Tom Johnson, High Breck's founder, sold the business to a long-standing customer, Howard Baveystock. In addition to being a 'keen follower of the turf', Mr Baveystock is also devoted to 'the better things in life', one of them, presumably, being High Breck's small but comely list of wines and spirits, chiefly from French growers. The purchasing philosophy remains the same: 'all wines are chosen for themselves rather than their names or labels. We always look for wines of character, and try not to run with the pack.' Sporting metaphors are obviously prized in Headley, Beeston, Pangbourne and SW6.

You can unearth a full range of Alsace wines from Henri Wiederhirn at High Breck, and almost as many Sancerres and Pouilly-Fumés from Gitton Père et Fils. Neither grower is well known in this country, but Wilf Nelson and Tom Johnson are convinced that the quality of their wines is seldom matched elsewhere. There is a further range of central and lower Loire wines from Jean-Paul Tijou (the Chaume is recommended for elevenses), Bergerac from the now-famous Jaubertie, a good selection of clarets (especially the lovely 1985s and the promising 1988s), Beaujolais from the Éventail, and a number of other bits and pieces, often worth a closer look. It's not easy to find Rancio Rivesaltes in Britain; here you do (£6.03). Sherries from Emilio Lustau and his portfolio of almacenistas are always worth trying, and there is plenty of champagne with which to celebrate the victories of outsiders. Growers' names mysteriously go missing in the German section. Red Burgundy and Australia are muscling their way on to the list at present. Prices are reasonable. A 'personable service' is promised. Could we ask readers to report?

Best buys

Alsace 1988, Pinot Gris, Henri Wiederhirn, £5.36
Anjou Blanc Sec, Cuvée Prestige, Château de Bellevue (Jean-Pierre Tijou), £4.16
Coteaux du Layon-Chaume 1985, Jean-Paul Tijou, £5.17

Hilbre Wine Company ☞

Gibraltar Row, Pierhead, Liverpool L3 7HJ   *Tel* 051-236 8800

Open Mon–Fri 8.30–5.30; Sat 9–12.30 **Closed** Sun, public holidays
Credit cards Access, American Express, Visa; personal and business accounts
Discounts Available **Delivery** Free within Merseyside, Wirral, north Cheshire and south Lancashire (min 1 case); elsewhere at cost; mail order available
Glass hire Free with 3-case order **Tastings and talks** Tastings given for wine clubs and societies **Cellarage** Not available

Liverpudlians: do you shop here? If so, we would be keen to hear about the experience. Hilbre has a retail licence, yet only a small proportion of its business is direct to the public, and we would like to know how easy or difficult it is for ordinary customers to buy wine here. Sales Manager John Butcher tells us he is 'always ready to spend time with our A/Cs' (though less ready to spend time filling in our questionnaire); does a one-bottle customer count as an A/C, we wonder?

The (ex-VAT) list is of moderate interest only, with quite a lot of branded wines and négociant selections on it. The large range of Robert Mondavi wines is probably the main reason for making your way to Gibraltar Row; Loire wines, the Chilean wines of Santa Helena and the Australian wines of Orlando and Lindemans would also be worth testing the retail licence on.

Best buys

Robert Mondavi Oakville Cabernet Sauvignon 1985 (half-bottle), Napa, £5.68
Robert Mondavi Reserve Pinot Noir 1985, Napa, £11.52
Jacobs Creek Dry White 1988, Orlando, South Australia, £3.83

J E Hogg

61 Cumberland Street, Edinburgh EH3 6RA   *Tel* 031-556 4025

Open Mon, Tue, Thur, Fri 9–1, 2.30–6; Wed, Sat 9–1 **Closed** Sun, public holidays **Credit cards** None accepted **Discounts** Not available **Delivery** Free in Edinburgh (min 1 case); otherwise at cost; mail order available **Glass hire** Free with reasonable order **Tastings and talks** To groups on request **Cellarage** Not available

There is nothing particularly impressive about J E Hogg's shop in Cumberland Street viewed from the outside, though queuing customers might suggest to you that there is something here that merits investigation. Join the queue, reach the counter, and you may be served by a man in grey grocers' overalls: Mr Hogg himself. Ask for a bottle of Château Grand-Pontet 1986 and walk away with change from a tenner, or ask for a bottle of Penfold's Koonunga Hill and take 70p home from a fiver, or ask for advice – or all three, and you'll have taken full advantage of the J E Hogg service. 'Our core business is in supplying good quality at reasonable prices,' says James Hogg. 'I am happy drinking anything on our shelves.'

The list, it should be said, is shorter than it used to be three or four years ago, mainly due to 'a relative decline in the number of wines over £10 that we stock'. Second-growth clarets and-single vineyard burgundies are no longer within reach of most of Mr Hogg's customers, so these have been left to others to sell. In their place are more wines from Italy, the Loire, Rhône and Alsace and, to a lesser extent, Spain, Australia and California. The range of sherries and ports (especially Vintage Ports) continues to be splendid. 'Although the list may look less impressive to some,' says the proprietor, 'we consider that it has not affected our standing as good wine merchants.' And of course the door has not been slammed on claret and burgundy, by any means; what remains is a good choice of those wines from these areas offering excellent value for money. Around 80 half-bottles should be added to the list of attractions worth queuing for, even in a city as well-endowed as Edinburgh is with wine merchants.

Best buys

Coliseo, Very Old Dry Amontillado, Valdespino, £14.39
Savennières 1988, Clos du Papillon, £5.51
Rouge d'Alsace (Pinot Noir), Dopff et Irion, £4.89

Holland Park Wine Co ☞

12 Portland Road, London W11 4LA   *Tel* 071-221 9614

Open Mon–Fri 10–9; Sat 10–7.30 **Closed** Sun, public holidays
Credit cards Access, American Express, Visa; personal and business accounts
Discounts 5% on 1 case **Delivery** Free locally (min 1 case); otherwise at cost;
mail order available **Glass hire** Free with case order **Tastings and talks** Regular
in-store tastings; to groups on request **Cellarage** £4.75 per case per year

The Holland Park Wine Company has rather a grand ring to its
name, and one might assume that it would be all crusty claret
and double-chinned burgundy here. The assumption would be
false; ex-Bordeaux Direct worker James Handford certainly
stocks clarets in number, and burgundies, too (particularly the
white sort), but wines from the Rhône, Alsace and the Loire
occupy as much space as French classics on the list. There are
five well-contrasted German wines, and Hambledon's excellent
English white for a further perspective on north European
raciness; there are some carefully chosen Italian wines; and the
same stealthy and thoughtful approach to purchasing is evident
in the Spanish, Chilean and New World selections. It is very
much a wine-growers' list, rather than an appellation/
denomination list, with plenty of offerings from those who are
going it alone, planting against the run of tradition, getting
called names by their fellow growers, and producing new,
unusual and striking wines at the end of it all. Nothing double-
chinned about the service, either, and the clearly written list is
full of interesting and entertaining notes. This is a retail shop
that would certainly repay a visit.

Best buys

Sauvignon de Touraine 1989, Domaine de Gabillière, £3.99
Château Guionne 1985, Côtes de Bourg, £4.95
Crichton Hall Chardonnay 1987, Napa, £10.75

---

*Thou dost cause the grass to grow for the cattle, and plants for man to
cultivate, that he may bring forth food from the earth, and wine to gladden
the heart of man, oil to make his face shine, and bread to strengthen man's
heart.*
Psalm 104

Hollingsworth of York

The Granary, Pear Tree Farm, Askham   *Tel* (0904) 702362
Bryan, York, North Yorkshire YO2 3QS

Open 'All hours' (24-hour answering machine)   **Credit cards** None accepted;
personal and business accounts   **Discounts** Available   **Delivery** Free in Yorkshire
and Humberside (min 1 case); otherwise at cost; mail order available
Glass hire Free with 2-case order   **Tastings and talks** To groups on request;
monthly wine club organised at York Technical College   **Cellarage** £3.45 per case
per year

It's by-the-case only from this merchant, and the list is an ex-
VAT one, suggesting that most sales are to other traders rather
than to the general public. However the list does quote bottle
prices, so presumably it is possible for the likes of you or me to
roll up at Pear Tree Farm and mix a case. The main attraction
here is a wide range of wines from Duboeuf; there are also a
number of worthwhile wines from California and Australia, the
Loire and Bordeaux. The rest of the list, by contrast, looks rather
plain, suggesting no great depth of research. More reports,
please.

Best buys

Viña Undurraga Cabernet Sauvignon 1987, Chile, £3.68
Merlot 1987, Franciscan Winery, Napa, £9.03
Principe Old Dry Amontillado Sherry, Barbadillo, £8.97

Hopton Wines   ❧

Hopton Court, Cleobury Mortimer,   *Tel* (0299) 270482
Kidderminster, Hereford & Worcester
DY14 0HH
Shop
13 Teme Street, Tenbury Wells, Hereford &   *Tel* (0584) 810355
Worcester WR15 8BB
Credit cards accepted only in the shop

Open Mon–Sat 9–5.30   **Closed** Sun, public holidays   **Credit cards** Access, Visa;
personal and business accounts   **Discounts** Available   **Delivery** 1 case £9.78,
2 cases £8.63 per case, 3+ cases free   **Glass hire** Free with 1-case order
Tastings and talks Regular tastings at Hopton Court; to groups on request
Cellarage Available; charges negotiable

'Hopton Wines is based at Hopton Court which is situated in
the charming Shropshire village of Hopton Wafers at the foot of
the Titterstone Clee Hill.' With names as pretty as those, it
would be hard for anyone passing through to resist a visit. The
business was begun ten years ago by Farmer Woodward and
has steadily grown since then – so much so that the farm is

now let to a tenant, and Mr Woodward is now a full-time wine merchant with a staff of 12.

The list is a substantial one, broad and balanced, and Shropshire wine enthusiasts will find much to feed their enthusiasm with here. 'It is said that if you really want to find out if your wine merchant is doing his job or not, you should look into the Burgundy section of his list,' we read; and scrutiny is invited. The Hopton version is extensive, with wines from a wide variety of sources, both négociants and growers; a deal of work has certainly gone into it, and there is choice at every level, from generic Bourgogne up as far as Grands Crus. Job done, and well done.

Bordeaux is as good, which it has to be at most country wine merchants; good, too, on the historical side, with vintages back to 1961 available. The Loire, the Rhône and Alsace are treated with respectful seriousness – Alsace particularly so, with a choice of 14 wines from the Cave d'Obernai, Domaine Marcel Deiss, Schlumberger and a Jean Hugel-selected Vendange Tardive Gewürztraminer. The country wines show steady improvement, though one senses that local customers are still perhaps reluctant to buy wines with names that would have meant nothing to their parents.

The approaches to Germany, Italy and Spain are also serious and systematic, with the best from traditional zones like Rioja, Barolo, Barbaresco and Valpolicella slowly being permeated by novel excellencies like Marco de Bartoli's extraordinary Bukkuram or Jean León's Cabernet Sauvignon. In the New World, most excellencies are novel, and Hopton provides a courageous selection with tastes of Canada, Idaho, Oregon and Washington State, as well as an enthusiastic response to the delights of New Zealand (six reds, including two Pinot Noirs, is unusual at a single merchant, even in London). California and Australia bear the Hopton hallmark of thoroughness, with Round Hill red, blush and white leading all the way up to Opus One and Dominus, and Grange topping an Australian section that begins with Canowindra Hill White (Muscat) and Penfold's Dalwood Shiraz/Cabernet. Sherry and port are good, Vintage Port especially so, with bottles from Taylor '24 through to six '85s. There seems little likelihood that Mr Woodward will ever have to take to his plough again.

Best buys

Château Rousset 1985, Bordeaux, £4.22
Durkheimer Feuerberg Gewürztraminer Spätlese 1986, Schloss Koblenz, Rheinpfalz, £4.36
Bourgogne Rouge (non-vintage), Comte de Jeanly, £5.28

House of Townend

See J Townend & Sons.

Ian G Howe

35 Appleton Gate, Newark, Nottinghamshire   *Tel* (0636) 704366
NG24 1JR

Open Mon–Sat 9.30–7; Good Friday 12–3, 7–9 **Closed** Sun, public holidays
except Good Friday **Credit cards** Access, Visa; personal and business accounts
Discounts 2.5% for 1–2 cases (may be mixed), 3.5% for 3+ cases **Delivery** Free
locally (min 1 case) and within 20-mile radius (min 2 cases); elsewhere by
arrangement **Glass hire** Free with 1-case order **Tastings and talks** Regional
tastings; to groups on request **Cellarage** Not available

Francophile Ian Howe and his wife Sylvia have had unusually
bad luck during the last year. 'Both partners have developed
two hernias each. Although this remark is intended to be light
hearted it is in fact a very serious matter for a husband-and-
wife team.' We believe it; and we wish the Howes all the best
for a speedy recovery and better luck during the coming year.

From the customers' point of view, what Ian Howe describes
with understatement as 'this very restricting situation' does not
seem to have affected the high level of service provided. If you
borrow glasses for your party, they will have been hand-
polished rather than blown over by an asthmatic dishwasher,
and the shop itself is immaculately organised, the dark walls
and carpets, and white cloth on the table, giving it the air of an
exclusive nightclub rather than a neighbourhood wine
merchant.

The list itself is equally well organised and, except for ports, a
very small German section and a little cava, exclusively French.
France, of course, is a world of its own, and all of it – not just
the classic bits – is toured by the list, with particularly good
overnight stops in the Loire (there are Demi-Secs and Moelleux
wines from seven different appellations), the Southern Rhône
(Ian Howe is a great Châteauneuf-du-Papist – and has trawled
widely through the Côtes du Rhône and its villages), and South-
West France. Here is the place to come and get that Rosette
Moelleux you have been searching for all these years; there is
Bandol and Collioure; there is Coteaux du Quercy to compare
with the two Cahors.

Newark seems to call less for the greats, though there are fine
burgundies from Armand Rousseau, Pousse d'Or and others
should you be ready for them, and the list has its share of
Northern Rhône asteroids. The emphasis in Bordeaux is firmly
on *petits châteaux*. Champagnes are sumptuous, with
competition (at around half the price) from the Loire sparklers

of Bouvet-Ladubay and the Diane de Poitiers wines from the
Haut-Poitou co-operative. The list of half-bottles is not
enormous, but it is sensibly compiled, with examples from most
parts of France.

Best buys

Minervois 1988, Domaine de Campan, £3.25
Muscadet du Sèvre et Maine sur lie 1989, Domaine de la
Goulbaudière, £4.25
Quarts de Chaume 1985, Domaine du Petit Metris (Joseph
Renou), £10.95

Victor Hugo Wines

Head office

Tregear House, Longueville, St Saviour,	*Tel* (0534) 78173
Jersey	(order office)
8B Quennevais Precinct, St Brelade, Jersey	*Tel* (0534) 44519
3 Stopford Road, St Helier, Jersey	*Tel* (0534) 23421

Open Mon–Fri 8–6; Sat 9–5.30 **Closed** Sun, public holidays
Credit cards Access, American Express, Visa; personal and business accounts
Discounts Available (min 1 case) **Delivery** Free in Jersey (min 1 case)
Glass hire Free with 5-case order **Tastings and talks** Regular promotions on new
products; to groups on request **Cellarage** Free

Jersey's Victor Hugo Wines has continued its expansion during
the last year, with a new case sales department opening at
St Brelade and a new retail shop in St Helier. On the list, the
proximity of France continues to be felt, with a wonderful range
of clarets, Loire wines and Beaujolais, and good wines from
most of the other French regions. A company aim, however, is
to 'cater for all tastes', and you will also find an excellent choice
of Chilean and Portuguese wines, with Spain, Australia and
America also providing bottles of interest.

Italy and Germany occupy more than three pages on the list,
but the range from these two countries is less imaginative than
those of the countries mentioned above, with larger producers
and 'easy' wines of the Frascati/Lambrusco Bianco/Crown of
Crowns type taking up much of the shelf space. Doubtless
Managing Director Mr Flageul would say that this is part of
'catering for all tastes'. Prices, to the taxed British eye, seem
very attractive for the cheaper wines, yet the prestigious wines
appear, if anything, more expensive than in London or
Edinburgh. Victor Hugo's many restaurant clients mean a fine
range of half-bottles is available.

Best buys

Menetou-Salon 1989, Domaine de Montalouise, £4.90
Concha y Toro, Cabernet-Merlot 1987, Chile, £2.52
Clos la Fleur Figeac 1985, Saint-Emilion, £5.25

Hungerford Wine Company ☞

Head office
Unit 3, Station Yard, Hungerford, Berkshire   *Tel* (0488) 683238
RG17 0DY
Shop
24 High Street, Hungerford, Berkshire   *Tel* as above
RG17 0NF

Open Mon–Fri 9–5.30; Sat 9.30–5 **Closed** Sun, public holidays **Credit cards** All
accepted; personal and business accounts **Discounts** 5% on 1 unmixed case;
larger quantities negotiable **Delivery** Free within 15-mile radius of Hungerford
(min 1 case) and on UK mainland (min 5 cases); otherwise £7 per consignment;
mail order available **Glass hire** Free with 1-case order
Tastings and talks Regular tastings on Monday evenings at The Galloping
Crayfish Wine Bar; to groups on request **Cellarage** £3.91 per case per year
(including insurance)

'Undoubtedly good at public relations,' we read, '- but they tire
you out!' Invoicing, according to this reader, is 'slapdash', and
pricing idiosyncratic; an irritant at the best of times but
particularly so in the face of Hungerford's brand of
salesmanship. 'I've bought things from them and would do so
again...but only after serious checking.' That's one reader's
view; we invite others.

What you can be sure of from Hungerford is energy, sheaves
of word-splattered paper and a kind of manic, Filofax
enthusiasm – basically aimed at shifting quantities of claret and
burgundy. If you're a telephone addict, you can ring the special
Wine Line number (0898 446851 – try doing this from a phone
box to see clearly what an expensive pastime it is) which gives
you 'updates' on the latest *en primeur* news, a general vintage
report, prices and tasting notes by commune, or Nick Davies'
latest notes on the situation in Bordeaux. In every way
preferable is the normal phone number which, in addition to
costing less, gives you a real human being to talk to rather than
a tape recording endlessly rewinding and repeating itself. When
it comes to *en primeur*, which Hungerford push as hard as
anyone in Britain, there are 'offer quality guarantees' and 'price
guarantees' and a 'prior commitment scheme' and a bewildering
amount of information; even if, as the reader quoted above
suggests, the quality of the service may not always be up to the
promises and blandishments, this is still a company which
anyone serious about buying in this way should contact. It is

very quick off the mark, with a big spread of Burgundy 1989 being offered at the same time as Bordeaux 1989 (most merchants will offer a small range of Burgundy some months after Bordeaux).

After the *en primeur* onslaught, the normal list is almost an anticlimax, and it comes with riders about this being 'just a small selection of our stocks' and 'we welcome the chance to quote for anything not listed' and 'we also have small stocks of numerous older wines'. Apart from all the claret and all the burgundy, stacked up to the ceiling and in bottles of every conceivable size (impériales – eight bottles in one – a speciality), there is a little from the Loire, Alsace, Champagne, the Rhône, Beaujolais, Spain, Portugal, Australia, New Zealand and California. But really a little; one or two wines only in some cases. All are 'stunning', 'fabulous value and quality', 'potentially a blockbuster' – exhaustion quickly sets in after a broadsheet full of this, especially as the print is usually blue or red or burgundy-coloured. Yet the wines are by-and-large good; the energy and effort praiseworthy; and there's certainly nothing stuffy or snooty about Hungerford. You just need a high hype threshold.

Best buys

Clos du Marquis 1985, Saint-Julien, £9.90
Auxey-Duresses 1988, Javelin, £9.99
Toro Gran Colegiata 1986, Bodegas Fariñas, £4.55

Hunter & Oliver

Head office
Astra House, Edinburgh Way, Harlow, Essex   *Tel* (0279) 453409
CM20 2BE
41 outlets in London, Bristol, Cambridge, Berkshire, Buckinghamshire, Essex, Hertfordshire, Kent, Middlesex, Oxfordshire and Surrey

Open Mon–Sat 9.30–9; Sun 12–3, 7–9; public holidays as appropriate
Credit cards Access, American Express, Grand Metropolitan Shareholders Card, Visa; personal and business accounts   **Discounts** 5% on full cases of wines, beers and minerals   **Delivery** Free locally to each store   **Glass hire** Free with case order   **Tastings and talks** Occasional in-store tastings for selected customers; two comparable wines run on weekly basis for all customers; to groups on request
Cellarage Not available

October 1989 saw the 'launch' of Hunter & Oliver: 40 off-licences belonging to the Dominic Group (Peter Dominic and Bottoms Up) fitted out to appeal to the wealthier shopper, the sort that cruises London's Kings Road, Little Chalfont's Chenies Parade, or Newbury's Broadway. The aim is to grow to 60 shops by the end of 1990, though that, no doubt, will depend on the success of the first 40. 'Mixed' is the current grapevine verdict.

If Hunter & Oliver hasn't been a roaring success so far, it's because its metamorphosis from frog into prince has been inadequately realised. Many parts of the list still have a plodding, Dominic feel; prices look unappealingly bloated in high street terms; and most of the work seems to have been in the hands of designers and marketing manicurists rather than demon wine-buyers and long-haired shop-floor wine nuts. The clothes look princely, but the bloke inside has suspiciously slimy skin and protruding eyes.

But maybe it's your local, so you want to know what's worth a try. Australia, New Zealand, North and South America, Spain and Portugal are where the excitement is, together with Château Musar, Algeria's Red Infuriator and the trio of Israelis. The same areas, in other words, as at Bottoms Up and Peter Dominic. To be fair, they are real strengths, with a choice of eight bottles upwards in each case save the last three, and only the zanier South American offerings need approaching with caution. The French regional wines offer scope for exploration, too, as do Eastern Europe and Italy, but pick your way very carefully through these last two. Germany still feels tacky and uncared-for.

Two wines are 'usually' open for tasting: this is a real step forward, and we urge you to take advantage of the facility. Let us know, too, about the quality of the advice you are given here: princely or toadying? There is a designer-led, fold-out, full-colour list for you to contemplate at home as the cat purrs on your lap: it's clear, it's attractive, but it's low on vintages, terse on producers, sloppy on spelling, and offers zero information on anything other than names and prices. But at least it exists; and at least one reader has written to say that he welcomes this (also that he was impressed by the atmosphere and appearance of the Barnet branch).

Best buys

Señorio de Los Llanos Gran Reserva (vintage not specified), Valdepeñas, £4.89

Lindemans, Semillon-Chardonnay (vintage not specified), New South Wales, £3.99

Goyenechea Syrah (vintage not specified), Villa Atuel San Rafael, Argentina, £3.09

Most wine merchants will supply wine for parties on a sale or return basis.

Ingletons Wines ⌒⊃

Cash & carry

Station Road, Maldon, Essex CM9 7LF	*Tel* (0621) 852433
Maldon No 1 Bond, Beckingham Business	*Tel* (0621) 869474
Park, Tolleshunt Major, Maldon, Essex	
CM9 8NF	

Open (Cash & Carry) Tue–Sat 9–5 **Closed** Mon, Sun, public holidays
Credit cards None accepted; personal and business accounts **Discounts** Not
available **Delivery** Free within 150-mile radius of Maldon (min 6 cases);
elsewhere charges on request; mail order available **Glass hire** Available
Tastings and talks To groups on request **Cellarage** Not available

Anyone with a serious interest in Burgundy should be aware of
the existence of Ingletons: the list includes well over a hundred
different domain-bottled, growers' burgundies, and prices for
these are keen. Mongeard-Mugneret's Fixin '86 at £6.44 or '87
at £7.02, Nuits, Beaune and Volnay *premiers crus* for around £10,
Marc Colin's and Jean-Marc Morey's white Chassagne *premiers*
for under £15 . . . the recitation could continue. There are wines
from other regions, too, with a particularly sound collection of
clarets, but burgundy will be why you come here.

But do you come here? Only ten per cent of Ingletons'
business is with the public, and the list – although admirably
clear and specific about details of producer, *appellation*, year and
ex-VAT price – is bald in every other respect. There are no
tasting notes, no atmosphere-building, no cosseting into
purchase. It seems, in other words, that Ingletons' primary
market is restaurateurs and other traders. We would very much
like ordinary readers who make use of Ingletons' service to
write in with their impressions as to how easy and accessible
they find this company to be.

Best buys

Chassagne-Montrachet Premier Cru Les Chevenottes 1987, Jean-Marc Morey (white), £14.80
Fixin 1987, Mongeard-Mugneret, £7.02
Corton Clos des Meix 1982, Daniel Senard, £14.10

Best buys – in most cases, these are the Editor's choice of three out of a
range of ten wines selected by the merchant in question as being
distinguished in terms of value for money, or offering very fine
quality regardless of price.

Jacqueline's Wines

12a Florence Road, Sutton Coldfield, West   *Tel* 021-373 5949
Midlands B73 5NG

Case sales only   Open Mon–Fri 9–6   **Closed** Sat, Sun, public holidays, day
following public holidays (answering machine outside normal hours)
Credit cards None accepted; personal and business accounts   **Discounts** 5% on 5
cases   **Delivery** Free in Birmingham and within 30-mile radius of Sutton Coldfield
(min 1 case); elsewhere £10 per case; mail order available   **Glass hire** Free with
1-case order   **Tastings and talks** To groups on request   **Cellarage** £1.68 per case
per year

Jacqueline's Wines was founded in 1983 by twin sisters Deborah
and Jacqueline Thompson, whose wine background began with
teenage enthusiasm, developed via the in-depth study of
fermentation at Leicester University, and has flowered with a
wholesale business based at home in Sutton Coldfield.

The list is short, but every wine has been thoroughly
researched and tasted before inclusion, with visits being made
to suppliers wherever possible. The fact that there is more from
California than from Germany or Spain indicates open-
mindedness and a willingness to experiment. All wines are
available by prior arrangement for tasting; urgent deliveries can
be made within an hour if need be; and the twins undertake to
obtain any wine specifically requested by a customer from other
UK shippers. But we remain sceptical that a minimum order of
four cases is convenient and useful for ordinary wine
purchasers. More reports, please.

Best buys

Coteaux du Layon 1985, A Besombes, £3.75
Cape Mentelle Semillon-Sauvignon 1989, £7.06
Rio Viejo, Old Dry Oloroso Sherry, Domecq, £5.73

Tony Jeffries Wines

69 Edith Street, Northampton,   *Tel* (0604) 22375
Northamptonshire NN1 5EP

Open Tue–Fri 10–3; Sat 9–5; Good Friday 12–3   **Closed** Mon, Sun
Credit cards Access, Visa; personal and business accounts   **Discounts** 10% on 1
case   **Delivery** Free within 20-mile radius of Northampton town centre (min 5
cases)   **Glass hire** Free with 1-case order   **Tastings and talks** In-store tastings
held on alternate Sundays from May-September; to groups on request
Cellarage £2.50 per case per year

Ex-army officer Tony Jeffries has run this pleasant and well-
organised wine shop in Northampton since 1982, and readers
have quite properly chastised us for failing to include it in
previous editions. Like a number of the country's very best

high-street independents, this outlet began life with a franchise from Sherston; the legacy of the Sherston époque is a very strong Spanish list, with 50 or so Riojas and a pack of pacesetters from Penedés sharing shelf space with wines from Navarra, Cariñena and Valdepeñas. A large selection of ports at under £10 would be worth asking Mr Jeffries' advice about, and the Australian and New Zealand sections have also been put together with an eye to value for money. Germany, here, is over twice the size of Italy, but France dwarfs both, with customers' affections clearly favouring Bordeaux. There is a better selection of classed growth second wines than you will find on most high streets (or Edith Streets), with the list making it clear to customers that 'second wines' does not mean 'second-rate wines'. Absolutely not.

Sunday mornings in Northampton appear to offer few alternative attractions to Tony Jeffries' fortnightly May-to-September tastings, which we understand are heavily over-subscribed; 'matrimonial negotiations' are at present underway with a view to doubling these into weekly happenings.

Best buys

Château Destieux Berger 1982, Saint-Emilion, £7.45
Marqués de Murrieta 1984, Rioja (white), £7.99
Hungarian Gewürztraminer 1988, £2.45

Jeroboams ⇨

| 51 Elizabeth Street, London SW1W 9PP | *Tel* 071-823 5623 |
| 24 Bute Street, London SW7 3EX | *Tel* 071-225 2232 |

Open Mon–Fri 9–7; Sat 9–6 (Bute Street), 9–2 (Elizabeth Street) **Closed** Sun, public holidays **Credit cards** Access, American Express, Visa; personal and business accounts **Discounts** 5% on 1 case **Delivery** Free in inner London (min 1 case); elsewhere at cost; mail order available **Glass hire** Free with 1-case order **Tastings and talks** Series of three spring tastings of wines and cheeses; to groups on request **Cellarage** Normal bonded warehouse rates

---

Proprietor Juliet Harbutt is a Master of Cheese, and it will probably be something unpasteurised, oozing and bloomy that will draw you into one of the two London shops. Once inside, you will find a small but choice range of wines, mostly over £5, including a good range of half-bottles and large bottles (yes, Jeroboams included). This company holds the agency for Georges Vesselle's fine Champagne, so there's plenty of that lying artfully around (including a Bouzy Rouge); there are also the rather variable burgundies of the négociant and domain-owner Pierre André; and some nice Saint-Emilions. After that, it's South-West France to the fore, with the fine Jurançon of Clos

Guirouilh (both Sec and Moelleux), Pacherenc from Domaine Bouscassé, two different Cahors and a clutch of Bergeracs. There is enough here for some interesting wine and cheese combinations, and the small New Zealand, Swiss and Italian sections may also be worth a dip (though we haven't seen that part of the list).

Best buys

Jurançon Moelleux 1987, Clos Guirouilh (half-bottle), £3.10
Cahors 1982, Domaine du Bru, £5.45
Château Rahoul 1985, Graves, £9.40

S H Jones

Shop

27 High Street, Banbury, Oxfordshire   *Tel* (0295) 251179
OX16 8EW

Open Mon–Fri 8.30–5.30; Sat 9–5 **Closed** Sun, public holidays
Credit cards Access, Visa; personal and business accounts **Discounts** 5% on 1
case, 7.5% on 10+ cases **Delivery** Free within approximately 40-mile radius of
Banbury (min 2 cases); otherwise 1–5 cases £8, 6–12 cases £12 per consignment;
mail order available **Glass hire** Free **Tastings and talks** Continuous in-store
tastings; annual wine tasting (Nov); regular tutored tastings; to groups on
request **Cellarage** £3.20 per case per year

S H Jones must occupy one of the most appealing of any merchants' premises in England. It isn't quite as grand as the castle in which Vessel du Vin live, nor quite as antique as Berry Bros & Rudd's extraordinary St James's shop and cellar, but the double-fronted, gabled 'Old Wine House', plus rear addition in honeyed Cotswold stone, are most attractive. It is the sort of place that brewers like to buy up, fit out in plastic wood and plastic brass, and then drape externally with plastic banners advertising Australian lager. You won't catch S H Jones & Co doing that. Their respect for the environment even extends to a list printed on recycled paper.

The inside of the shop is as attractive as the outside, with extensive use made of both wooden racks and wooden bins to display the wide range of wines. Wines for tasting are available on a little shelf in one corner, and everything is very orderly and clearly labelled. France, as so often, provides the heart of the list, with Bordeaux (including Sauternes) and the Rhône looking particularly splendid, and with the Loire, Burgundy and French country wines not far behind. This is a merchant belonging to the Merchant Vintners buying group, so you'll find growers here that you may know already from lists like those of Adnams or Tanners: the Blanck Frères from Alsace, for example, or Marc Ryckwaert's fine Château du Grand Moulas and the

Châteauneuf of Domaine du Vieux Télégraphe in the Rhône, or Château Feytit-Clinet from Pomerol. Vieux Télégraphe fans will be delighted to find nine red and two white vintages on sale.

There is a serious German list too, including a range of 11 Rheingau wines and 16 from the Mosel-Saar-Ruwer, drawn from a greater variety of growers than that offered by many other merchants. Italy and Iberia are less adventurous; the selections from Australia and New Zealand, and California and Chile, are also cautious, though no doubt many of the wines raise eyebrows in Banbury when suggested as alternatives to familiar Old World names. None of these sections is restricted, and indeed both Australia and California have seen a 50 per cent increase in the number of wines listed during the last year. Port is stocked with enthusiasm; sherry and Madeira less so. You'll find more than 100 half-bottles here, as well as books, glasses, corkscrews, gift packs, wine racks and all manner of ancillary items. And you can look back with pleasure as you leave.

Best buys

Vacqueyras 1985, Trésor du Poète, Roger Combe, £6.10
Chardonnay 1987, J Tiefenbrunner, Alto Adige, £5.05
Chianti Rufina 1987, Villa Vetrice, £3.60

Justerini & Brooks

61 St James's Street, London SW1A 1LZ	*Tel* 071-493 8721
39 George Street, Edinburgh EH2 2HN	*Tel* 031-226 4202

Open (London) Mon–Fri 9–5.30 (6 in Edinburgh); Sat 9.30–1 (Edinburgh only) **Closed** Sun, public holidays **Credit cards** All accepted; personal and business accounts **Discounts** 2–4 cases £1 per case; 5–7 cases £2 per case; 8+ cases £3 per case **Delivery** Free in London (min 2 cases) and in country areas (min 5 cases); mail order available **Glass hire** Free **Tastings and talks** To groups on request and existing customers by invitation **Cellarage** £4.15 per case per year (including insurance)

J&B have a most attractive list, very sober in appearance, with the Royal Warrant, the name and the St James's address embossed in gold. 'FINE WINES', it proclaims, and so many of them are. The section introductions are well written, all the information you need to make informed choices is there, clearly presented, and the list doesn't snap and turn loose-leaf if you open it wide. Bedside reading in clubland, one imagines.

Yet it's not all nobby wine for the wealthy. The central section, tinted a pale mint green, selects wines at £5 and under, as well as presenting a discussion of French country wines and a tasting case. In fact, tasting cases are something J&B try very hard over: they are constantly lancing offers at their customers spiked with ready-mixed cases. The Celebration Case, The Three Bottle Case, The Summer Evenings Case, The Glyndebourne Case, The Inexpensive German Case . . . we expect they'll offer The Case of the Dancing Men or The Case of the Solitary Cyclist one of these days. *En primeur* is another strong area, too; Justerini & Brooks generally weigh in with some of the higher prices of the moment, but at least you can be reasonably sure that the business will still be there in three years' time (it's been there for 200 so far). If you are interested in building up a cellar of fine wine which you are unable to store yourself, then J&B's Personal Cellar Plan will interest you; if you want to do the same sort of thing with a wide range of wines, not just the 'fine' ones, then enquire about the Selected Cellar Plan. This won't be the cheapest way to achieve these ends, but it may well be the most convenient and reliable. You will qualify for free delivery, among other things, and free delivery is not something that this merchant offers lightly.

What of the wines? There are excellent bottles from Bordeaux and Burgundy, as one would expect. Fine clarets are matched by fine Sauternes; in Burgundy, devotees will find many of this region's Parker-lauded, benchmark bottles, and doubtless they will not be so naïve as to gasp at the prices. It is a broad selection from rather a narrow, sought-after region, and thus, in relative terms, superior to the claret range. The Rhône is treated a mite more seriously than the Loire, but neglect is not at issue; while Alsace, Champagne and Germany are up to St James's standards. Everything else is listed with restraint and good taste, with Australia the only zone showing signs of wanting to rise above its station. You would, finally, march into 61 St James's Street expecting to find plenty of Vintage Port, and you would not be disappointed. In Edinburgh, the same goes for whiskies.

Best buys

Cuvée les Peterelles 1989, Domaine Brunier ('in effect de-classified Châteauneuf-du-Pape'), £3.50
Mâcon-Uchizy 1989, Domaine Talmard, £5.70
Clos René 1985, Pomerol, half-bottle, £7.75

If all be true that I do think
There are five reasons why we should drink;
Good wine – a friend – or being dry –
Or lest we should be by and by –
Or any other reason why.
Latin saying, versified by Henry Aldrich

Kiwifruits

25 Bedfordbury, Covent Garden, London *Tel* 071-240 1423
WC2N 4BL

Open Mon–Fri 10–6.30; Sat 10–6 **Closed** Sun, public holidays **Credit cards** All
accepted **Discounts** Not available **Delivery** Free in London (min 10 cases);
otherwise at cost **Glass hire**, **Tastings and talks**, **Cellarage** Not available

'A wide range of New Zealand boutique wines,' is what
Kiwifruits claims that it offers, in addition to other New
Zealand products that a city of London's stature should not have
to do without. There are 25 wines on the latest list, and the
producers include Redwood Valley from the Nelson area; Matua
Valley and Waikoukou from Auckland; Ngatarawa, Vidal's and
Brookfield's from Hawkes Bay; Giesen Wine Estate from
Canterbury and Dry River from Martinborough; as well as reds
from St Nesbit (South Auckland), St Helena (Christchurch) and
Stonyridge (Waiheke Island). This selection gives you a chance
to try New Zealand's efforts with Pinot Gris, Semillon and
Gewürztraminer as well as the more frequently encountered
Chardonnays and Sauvignon Blancs; there are three late-harvest
wines; and two of New Zealand's finest reds (Vidal's Reserve
Cabernet-Merlot and Stonyridge's Cabernet Larose). All within a
bottle's throw of Covent Garden.

Best buys

Waikoukou Haupai Semillon 1985, Auckland, £5.20
Brookfield's Cabernet Sauvignon 1988, Hawkes Bay, £7.75
Matua Valley Pinot Noir Blanc 1989 (blush), Auckland, £6.05

Kurtz & Chan Wines

47–51 Great Suffolk Street, London SE1 0BS *Tel* 071-928 9985

Case sales only **Open** Mon–Fri 8.30–7 **Closed** Sat, Sun, public holidays
Credit cards None accepted; personal and business accounts
Discounts Available **Delivery** Free in London postal area (min 5 cases);
elsewhere 1–4 cases £16, 5+ cases £4 per case; mail order available
Glass hire Free with 5-case order **Tastings and talks** Occasional tastings in-store;
to groups on request **Cellarage** £5 per case per year depending on quantity

Kurtz & Chan is not a Soho-based private detection agency, but
a Southwark-based fine wine merchant. And when we say fine,
we mean . . . Pétrus 1987 back to 1978 inclusive, then 1976, 1975,
1974, 1973, 1971, 1970, 1969, 1966, 1964, 1961, 1950, 1947, 1945
and 1943: some collection. You'll find other clarets to match, and
Sauternes, too (Yquem-heavy); you'll find burgundy, with more
white than red; you'll find most of the big Rhône names
(though Chave in white only); and you'll find a firm underbelly

of Vintage Port (with a good choice of 1970s, drinking well now). There are two Noval Nacionals ('75 and '78) for the thoroughbred collector. The list provides no information on condition, level or taste (supposing you should actually want to go as far as drinking these blue chips); Tinsey Chan or sales director Clare Burke should be able to give you advice on these matters. Prices are claimed to be 'competitive'; if you're in the market for this sort of wine, you will doubtless phone around getting quotations first and be able to verify this for yourself, as hundreds of pounds could be saved or squandered on large or important purchases. It may be, by contrast, that Kurtz & Chan are the only merchants with the wine you want, in which case everything depends on how much you want it.

Best buys

Côte Rôtie Brune & Blonde 1985, Guigal, case price in bond, £100
Warre Vintage Port 1983, case price in bond, £125
Château Pétrus 1982, Pomerol, case price in bond, £3,150

Lay & Wheeler

Head office and wine shop

Culver Street West, Colchester, Essex CO1 1JA	*Tel* (0206) 764446
Wine Market, Gosbecks Road, Colchester, Essex CO2 9JT	*Tel* as above

Open (Wine Shop) Mon–Sat 8.30–5.30; (Wine Market) Mon–Sat 8–8 **Closed** Sun, public holidays **Credit cards** Access, Visa; personal and business accounts **Discounts** 1.5% on 4–12 cases, 3% on 12+ cases **Delivery** Free in Essex and south Suffolk and parts of Cambridgeshire and Hertfordshire (min 1 case) and on UK mainland (min 2) cases); otherwise £4.95 per delivery; mail order available **Glass hire** Free with order **Tastings and talks** Regular tastings held (all customers invited); 8–9 Wine Workshops held monthly at Wine Market; major tutored Workshops held quarterly; to private parties on request **Cellarage** £4.45 per case per year (under review)

'The Magnificent Obsession' is a phrase that has haunted the editorial eardrum during summer 1990. This is, in origin, down to the World Cup, as one of the television football commentators mentioned that it was the title of Peter Shilton's autobiography. Ever since then, we have been daydreaming about obsessions that could reasonably be described as 'magnificent' – and the obsession with wine is certainly one of these. If, furthermore, we had to chose one merchant's list which merits a subtitle identical to that of the great goalkeeper's autobiography, it would be Lay & Wheeler's. Its depth, range, variety and informativeness approaches the obsessional, and leaves you with a heady sense of the magnificence of wine. The photographs, imperfectly focussed and, in places, apparently hand-tinted, make a suggestive contribution (though the collection found in the Adnams list is technically superior). Every detail of every wine is noted; many have tasting notes. It is a benchmark list.

We would need several pages and considerable indulgence on your part to enumerate every wine of interest found in the list. So we will summarise by saying that it is strong across the board, but particularly in the classic areas. Bordeaux, Burgundy, Beaujolais, the Rhône, Alsace, the Loire, Alsace, Germany, Australia and New Zealand are all magnificent; Italy and California are merely very good indeed. If one had to pick holes in this stout document, it would be after putting the magnifying glass on Portugal and Eastern Europe – which are skimpily stocked by comparison with other areas – and perhaps on Spain and sherry, which are good but not obsessionally so. No one's going to argue about the port (buffs will enjoy the collection of four quinta wines, and it would be good to see this expand further; it's an area that no one seems to have specialised in yet). This list, finally, deserves more and better Madeiras, with a handful of vintage wines: perhaps next year?

You could drink from nothing but half-bottles for a year from Lay & Wheeler's list, and then celebrate your abstemiousness by drinking from nothing but magnums the following year. There are special offers galore (including most things *en primeur*), and a series of intelligently conceived 'wine workshops' in Colchester. Indeed, Lay & Wheeler must be one of the country's leading wine educators: nearly a hundred tutored tastings were organised by the company during 1989; and staff education is taken equally seriously. But above all, it is the huge range that should draw you to Lay & Wheeler (and that makes the selection of three 'best buys' more than usually difficult). With over a thousand wines on offer, no wonder the Regency roué used as the company logo has a palpable corporation. That's something else you could easily acquire here.

Best buys

Réserve du Général 1985, Margaux (second wine of Château Palmer), £11.35
Sunnycliff, Chardonnay 1989, Victoria, £5.85
Marsannay 1987, Joseph Roty, £8.56

> *The juice of the grape is the liquid quintessence of concentrated sunbeams.*
> Thomas Love Peacock

Laymont & Shaw

The Old Chapel, Millpool, Truro, Cornwall   *Tel* (0872) 70545
TR1 1EX

Case sales only   **Open** Mon–Fri 9–5   **Closed** Sat, Sun, public holidays
Credit cards None accepted; personal and business accounts   **Discounts** Available
for 2+ cases   **Delivery** Free on UK mainland (min 1 case); mail order available
Glass hire Free   **Tastings and talks** To groups on request   **Cellarage** £2.50 per
case per year

'Brought up "on the bottle" by hotelier father,' says John
Hawes, Managing Director of Laymont & Shaw. It's obviously a
tradition now; the cover of the latest list features a pleasingly
surreal logo by John Hawes' 13-year-old son, 'virtually weaned'
on the wines of La Rioja Alta, the text tells us. This bodega
rather than another, because Laymont & Shaw are its UK
agents, so it made financial sense to use it for weaning purposes
(and then selling what was left over afterwards).

John Hawes studied Spanish and French at Oxford, but it will
have been the Spanish that has served him best in his
professional life. For this is an exclusively Spanish list, well
written and attractively illustrated with maps and drawings. It is
rich in Rioja: La Rioja Alta forms the centrepiece (and never
more so than in 1990, its centenary year), but there are also
wines from López de Heredia, Muga, Murrieta, Riscal,
Remelluri, Beronia, El Coto, Montecillo and Cáceres with which
to measure up the agency range. There is a fine span of sherries,
and – hurrah! – some top quality Montillas, probably the only
ones in Britain. Bodegas Los Llanos represent Valdepeñas, and
none better; Jean León, Masia Bach and Torres are the well-
known Penedés names, and you can taste your way through
what must almost be the complete ranges in each case. From
among Spain's less well-known regions, John Hawes has picked
out wines from Rias Baixas, Priorato, Toro (Bodegas Fariñas' sin
crianza Colegiata rather than the Gran Colegiata), Jumilla ('I
shall get into trouble for writing it but when I drink a bottle of
Altos de Pío I want to say "Spanish Beaujolais"'), Majorca,
Rueda, Costers del Segre and Cariñena. Five fine Málagas from
Scholtz Hermanos provide some bargain dessert drinking, and
much the same could be said at the other end of the meal about
the cavas of Juvé y Camps and Codorníu. John Hawes' list note
on cava describes their attraction perfectly: 'They are essentially
clean, soft and refreshing – the antithesis of expensive BOB
Champagne from a poor vintage.' Truro is an ideal spot from
which to start exploring Spain.

Best buys

Altos de Pío 1988, Vitivino, Jumilla, £4.12
Rioja Viña Ardanza 1983 Reserva, La Rioja Alta, £8.03
Amontillado Carlos VII, Alvear, Montilla, £6.45

Laytons ☞

20 Midland Road, London NW1 2AD   *Tel* 071-388 5081

Open Mon–Fri 9.30–6; Sat 9.30–4.30 **Closed** Sun, public holidays
Credit cards Access, American Express, Visa; personal and business accounts
Discounts Not available **Delivery** Free on UK mainland (min £115 order); mail
order available **Glass hire** Free with 5-case order **Tastings and talks** Tastings
held twice annually by invitation **Cellarage** £4.60 per case per year

Laytons, whose Wine Vaults are sited next to St Pancras, issues
an entertaining, burgundy-flavoured list, full of mementoes
from the past and exhortations for the coming year ('YOUR
VISITS ARE ESSENTIAL TO OUR CONTINUED SUCCESS!').

The burgundy section contains some very fine wines indeed –
two or three Montrachets from '85 and '87, for example, at
around £90 per bottle. Who will buy them? 'Our message is –
don't ignore BOURGOGNE ROUGE,' say Laytons. 'In the right
hands it can be better than many famous village wines from the
less caring fraternity.' You can buy a full case of four of the five
Bourgogne Rouges offered for less than one bottle of those
Montrachets, so it's our message, too. In between comes a fine
collection of Premiers and Grands Crus from Fontaine Gagnard,
Gagnard Delagrange, Comte Armand, Baron Thenard, Chartron
& Trébuchet, J J Confuron and others; and a good collection of
Côte Chalonnaise wines from Alain Roy at Montagny, Chartron
& Trébuchet (Rully and Mercurey) and Baron Thénard at Givry,
and of Mâconnais wines from Guffens-Heynen, Manciat Poncet
and others. So the joint message is: there is burgundy for all
pockets here. Only Chablis disappoints.

There are plenty of clarets, too, from the non-vintage Jolly
Good Claret ('Our title is accurate') up to the loftiest of the lofty
– presumably jolly good too, but also a jolly sight more
expensive. Indeed, classified growths motor out on a
supplementary list, as they are 'bought and sold far quicker
than our main list', despite the prices. *En primeur* offers are
produced for both Bordeaux and Burgundy, as well as themed
offers; Laytons pushed out an offer of the unjustly unloved
1987s under the title HAPPY CLARETS (capital letters and
original thinking are favoured here). There are also some good
sale offers, despite Graham Chidgey's fastidiousness about this
word (he resorted to reproducing a Thesaurus entry for 'stock
up' to head the July 1990 sale).

In Bordeaux and Burgundy you have most of the list, but there are also pages given over to Champagne (Deutz and Krug); to the Loire, Rhône and Alsace (Zind-Humbrecht for this last); a small Australian section, including Len Evans Family Chardonnay ('Chardonnay like an old fashioned barmaid – nothing wrong with that'); California wines from Newton, including the modestly named Epic Merlot; and small sections from Italy and Spain. Vintage Ports stretch back to 1945, and the list contains a reproduction of Laytons' 1966 offer of '1963 Vintage Port as an Investment' ('... we can also reommend this offer for christening presents and for personal consumption when the port matures').

Were you born after 1960? If so, and if you live in London, Laytons are reviving 'The Circle of Wine Tasters' which, despite its rather grand name, is basically an educative initiative for the under-30s for those 'beginning from zero knowledge'. Ring for details.

Best buys

Château Cazebonne 1986, Graves, £5.85
Quincy 1988, Pierre et Jean Mardon, £5.46
Bourgogne Rouge 'En L'Orme' 1986, Domaine Chartron, £6.04

Lea & Sandeman Company   ☞

301 Fulham Road, London SW10 9QH   *Tel* 071-376 4767

Open Mon–Sat 9.30–8.30 **Closed** Sun, public holidays, Easter Saturday
Credit cards Access, Visa; personal and business accounts **Discounts** 5% on 1 case **Delivery** Free in central London (min £100 order); elsewhere at cost; mail order available **Glass hire** Free with suitable order **Tastings and talks** Bottles frequently open in-store; regular customers invited to small tastings of fine wines; to groups on request **Cellarage** Wines bought from premises stored free for 1 year

---

Charles Lea and Patrick Sandeman have a lot of experience to draw on: both worked in the past for Laytons and Caves de la Madeleine; Charles Lea spent time as a manager for Majestic as well as working at Willi's much-admired wine bar in Paris, while Patrick Sandeman worked for five years for Seagrams in Bordeaux, Paris, Oporto and London. Now they have settled down in London's Fulham Road, and put together a worthwhile list full of French growers' wines (many of whom they represent on an agency basis) as well as some unusual wines from other countries. They hunt for quality, which presumably the Fulham Road understands; it does mean, though, that there are few wines on the list at under £5, and you need to be prepared to spend £8.95 on a bottle to give yourself choice from among most of the range.

There are comparatively few French country wines; two Chardonnays from Bugey are among them, though, and you won't often find those elsewhere. It's a shame that Bugey doesn't also supply some Roussette, Jacquère or Mondeuse – its authentic regional wines, in other words – but the list is dismissive of these, and this dismissal sets the tone for the wines that follow: classic flavours (and the grape varieties that produce them) are prized above the off-beat and unusual. No doubt that's what the Fulham Road wants.

Lots of burgundy, therefore, with whites outnumbering reds by around two to one: L&S have researched hard, it would seem, in the Mâconnais and the Côte Chalonnaise, and there are 15 white wines from these areas alone (though only one red: the widely seen and admired '87 Givry from Gérard Mouton). Nor is the Côte d'Or ignored; a choice of ten Meursaults (mostly from Domaine Charles Jobard) is a draw. There is a worthwhile range of white Loire wines (dry only, mainly Sauvignon); and the Champagne section is full and varied. The Alsace wines of Domaine Marcel Deiss are not well known yet in Britain, but are fine; expensive with it. Bordeaux, the Rhône and Beaujolais are present but not extensive (though the separate Fine Wine list contains a quantity of classed-growth claret and Sauternes). There is an avowedly eccentric Italian list, and short but classic peeks at Spanish and Portuguese reds. A fine New Zealand range (15 wines) precedes more restrained performances from California and Australia: as throughout, we note the emphasis on white rather than red wine. Churchill and Sandeman provide a small range of ports for immediate drinking, and Valdespino the same for sherries (and don't leave the best vinegar in town unbought). There is Vintage Port on the Fine Wine list.

Best buys

Rully Premier Cru les Raclots 1987 (Blanc), Domaine Georges Duvernay, £8.35
Pais Colle Manora 1988, Vino da Tavola, Piedmont (mainly Barbera), £6.95
Sancerre Les Monts Damnés 1988, Domaine Claude Thomas, £6.95

Prices were current in summer 1990 to the best of our knowledge but can only be a rough indication of prices throughout 1991.

Liquid Gifts

8 Coronation Parade, Hamble, Southampton,	*Tel* (0703) 452288
Hampshire SO3 5JT	*Tel* Freephone 0800–272121

Open Mon–Sat 9.30–9.30 **Closed** Sun **Credit cards** All accepted; personal and business accounts **Discounts** Available **Delivery** Free UK and worldwide; mail order available **Glass hire**, **Tastings and talks**, **Cellarage** Not available

This is a highly specialised wine merchant, but one that we thought it would be useful for readers to know about. Brian Rowlands' Liquid Gifts is, as the name suggests, a service enabling you to send presents of wines and spirits (gourmet foods, too) to friends or relatives elsewhere in Britain, or around the world. If you want to send an Old Saint Andrews Golf Ball Whisky Miniature to your uncle in Augusta, Liquid Gifts will get it there. Should it arrive broken, they guarantee to replace it promptly and free of charge.

There are over 500 gifts, most of them liquid, so you should be able to find something that is to the taste of whoever it is you wish to treat (alcohol-free wine to reprobates, 'The Romance Pack' to inamoratas, the Macallan 10-year-old to Kingsley Amis). The selection of wines is a serious and extensive one: Geoff Merrill's Coonawarra Cabernet 1986, Beaulieu Vineyard's Georges de Latour Private Reserve Cabernet 1983, Mouton-Rothschild 1985 and Fonseca Guimaraens 1974 Vintage Port would all please birthday boys who have almost everything in their cellars already. You can freephone your order through to Liquid Gifts, messages are included, and same-day dispatch is promised. It all sounds very good. Is it? If you use the service, please let us know how you find it. The prices for the best buys below include delivery throughout the UK (including islands).

Best buys

Château Grand Pontet 1985, Saint-Emilion, £20.99
Seaview Australian Sparkling Wine, £14.59
Armagnac 1975, Domaine de Mouchac, Janneau, £55.99

In writing the entries for merchants included in the *Guide*, the Editor relies on readers' reports, particularly when it comes to the awarding of service symbols. We are concerned that good service may not always be adequately recompensed at present, so please write and let us know whenever you feel you have received particularly good service (or, of course, if you feel the service you have received has been inadequate in any way). Use the forms at the back of the book, or write on a separate sheet of paper if you prefer. Our Freepost facility means that no stamp is required.

London Wine ⌓

Chelsea Wharf, 15 Lots Road, London   *Tel* 071-351 6856
SW10 0QF

Case sales only   **Open** Mon–Fri 9.30–9; Sat 10–7; Sun 10.30–5.30   **Closed** Public
holiday Mondays   **Credit cards** All accepted; personal and business accounts
Discounts Not available   **Delivery** Free in SW1, SW3, SW5–8, SW10–11 (min 1
case); elsewhere at cost; mail order available   **Glass hire** Free
Tastings and talks Regular tastings held; to groups on request   **Cellarage** Not
available

London Wine claims to be the capital's 'oldest wine warehouse
under original ownership', and its aim is to ship in large
quantities for selling on in the trade, while simultaneously
offering the same range 'to the "by-the-case" customer at ultra-
keen prices'. All very sound.

The ramifications of this are that the list is quite a short one,
as this is primarily the retail showcase of an importer; most
wine warehouses would buy widely from a variety of sources
rather than base the range on self-imported wines to be sold on.
But mixing a dozen would be no problem at all: for value we
would recommend choosing from among the Turckheim co-
operative's Alsace wines, Rhônes from Pascal, Beaujolais from
Duboeuf, the Trentino reds and whites from Càvit, a choice of
three New Zealand Sauvignon Blancs and a few bottles of
Romania's easy, stylish reds. Prices are attractive rather than
irresistible: one wine for which a trade price of £29 per case was
quoted at a fair in February 1990 appears in the summer list at
£59.88 per case. Even at the doubled price, it should be added,
the wine is good value for money: it is Càvit's Quattro Vicariati,
a deeply coloured, minty fresh Cabernet-Merlot blend.

En primeur offers are also made: choice is not wide, but prices
are good. And the same comment applies to the short fine wine
list: you can buy Sandeman 1977 here for under £5 more than
Delaforce 1975 from Harvey (£19.55 compared to £15), and
Sandeman '82 at £10.64 on London Wine's Fine Wine list is
infinitely better value than the Gould Campbell Crusted Port on
London Wine's ordinary price list at £9.49. In fact, it is one of
the best bargains in London. What a shame only eight bottles
are available.

Best buys

Quattro Vicariati 1986, Càvit, £4.99
Côtes du Rhône Cuvée Personnelle 1985, Pascal, £4.29
Tokay-Pinot Gris 1988/9, Cave Vinicole de Turckheim, £3.99

Lorne House Vintners ⌒?

Unit 5, Hewitts Industrial Estate, Elmbridge   *Tel* (0483) 271445
Road, Cranleigh, Surrey GU6 8LW

Case sales only   Open Mon–Fri 9–5; Sat 9–1   **Closed** Sun, public holidays
Credit cards None accepted; personal and business accounts
Discounts Available   **Delivery** Free within 25-mile radius of Cranleigh (min 2
cases, 1 case for locals); otherwise £5 per consignment; mail order available
Glass hire Free   **Tastings and talks** Monthly open house tastings; to groups on
request request   **Cellarage** Not available

It was while cruising with the Sunday Times Wine Club that
Dirk Collingwood won a tasting competition; this triumph
resolved him to move out of the motor trade and into that of
wine. Fifteen years on, Lorne House Vintners has grown into a
medium-sized wholesale merchant importing direct from small-
scale growers, primarily in France. The only speciality the
company owns to is 'the quality/price ratio', but Muscadet and
the Loire have always been well researched here, and this
continues to be the case: eight different domain-bottled
Muscadets should set enthusiasts' tongues tingling. Other parts
of France, especially Bordeaux, give range and depth to the list,
and there are between ten and twenty wines each from Italy,
Germany and Spain, most of them with a good reason for being
there. Australia, New Zealand, Chile, California and Lebanon
are offered with a choice of one to six bottles. Garvey's
characterful sherries provide pre-dinner or first-course drinking,
while Churchill's Crusted Port (bottled 1986) would be a good
choice for afterwards. Prices on the list are for unmixed cases,
but mixing is permitted. If you're a regular customer, it would
be well worth joining the 'Shipping Club': a modest first
subscription of £7.50 (£4 annually subsequently) brings you the
chance to 'pre-purchase' selected wines at ten per cent off list
prices.

Best buys

Château de Juge 1989, Bordeaux (white), £3.65
Château Sarail la Guillaumière 1986, Bordeaux Supérieur, £4.70
Prunaio di Viticcio 1986, Lucio Landini (oak-aged
Sangiovese), £8

---

*So far as drinking is concerned, gentlemen, you have my approval. Wine
moistens the soul and lulls our grief to sleep while it also wakens kindly
feelings.*
Socrates

Majestic Wine Warehouses

Head office
421 New Kings Road, London SW6 4RN   *Tel* 071-731 3131
34 branches in London, Birmingham, Amersham, Bristol, Cambridge,
Gloucester, Guildford, Ipswich, Leeds, Maidenhead, Norwich, Oxford,
Poole, Reading, Salisbury, Stockport, Swindon and Taunton

Case sales only   Open (Generally) Mon–Sat 10–8; Sun 10–6   **Closed** Chr Day,
Boxing Day, 1 Jan   **Credit cards** All accepted; personal and business accounts
Discounts Not available   **Delivery** Free locally to branch (min 1 case); mail order
available   **Glass hire** Free with 1-case order   **Tastings and talks** Centrally
organised theme tastings; local tastings organised via manager; occasionally to
groups on request   **Cellarage** Not available

Majestic were Britain's wine warehouse trailblazers. They
bought whatever they could find wherever they could find it,
provided the price was low and quality was good. Obscurity
was no objection – in fact, in the early days, the more obscure a
wine was, the better. The cases were piled up in damp, chilly
caverns such as the celebrated Arch 84 beneath the main line
into Waterloo, and sold by shivering enthusiasts. You could
always be sure of bargains and surprises on a visit to Majestic,
and the success that followed was well deserved.

That was the child. Success meant that Majestic had to grow
up. Adolescence has, as usual, seen expansion in all directions,
the awareness of the need for a new philosophy, but some
difficulty in finding it. The main change between the child
Majestic and the young adult Majestic is that it can no longer be
so carefree and swashbuckling in its buying: with 34 hungry
warehouses to feed, all of whom want the same wines for at
least the duration of a half-yearly list, it has to be more
responsible, sourcing wines of consistent quality and
considerable quantity. That, of course, is the aim of the
supermarkets and big chains, too, which is why the
philosophical problem is posed – how are we different?

After a period in which uncertainty had the upper hand,
Majestic are once again showing the vitality which brought
them to prominence, combined with an assurance in their
buying that suggests adolescence may be nearing its end. The
two key areas for Majestic are avant-garde French country wines
and the New World, and in both the company excels at finding
top-quality, keenly priced wines. The Loire and Rhône valleys
are well explored, and Bulgaria is very definitely Majestic's
favourite part of Eastern Europe. Inexpensive Bordeaux is
another area of strength, and Italy continues to improve. Spain,
Portugal, Germany, Alsace and Burgundy are less exciting, but
there are always two or three wines from each that would be
worth mixing in to your case. Fortified wines are disappointing

at Majestic, however: this area badly needs gingering.
Remember that there is plenty in the warehouses that isn't in
the list, and that includes fine wines, all the way up to the top.
The choice at Majestic is still a big draw.

   Warehouses stand or fall on their pricing, and Majestic
generally stands, particularly in its specialist areas: the three
best buys below each offer astonishing value for money. The
laid-back, sweatshirt style of service, the big packs of offbeat
beer, the oceans of mineral water, the long opening hours and
the usually free local delivery complete what is, after all, an
extremely attractive package.

Best buys

Domaine le Puts Blanc 1989, Vin de Pays des Côtes de
Gascogne, Bordes/Ryman, £2.79
Château Ventenac Rouge 1989, Cabardès, Maurel, £2.89
Australian Semillon 1989, £2.95

Marks & Spencer

Head office
Michael House, 57 Baker Street, London   *Tel* 071-935 4422
W1A 1DN
269 licensed branches nationwide

Open Varies from store to store but generally 9–5.30 (most stores also have late
night shopping once a week); M & S Neighbourhood Food Stores operate longer
hours, generally 8.30–8   **Closed** Sun, public holidays (some stores)
Credit cards Marks & Spencer Chargecard   **Discounts** 12 bottles for the price of
11   **Delivery** £2.95 per order; mail order available   **Glass hire**, **Tastings and talks**,
Cellarage Not available

Marks & Spencer has a well-deserved reputation for quality and
reliability in whatever it sells, and the wine range is no
exception. You have to struggle hard to put together a list of
nearly 200 wines that customers can trust to provide sound,
wholesome flavours year in, year out, and M & S do this as well
as any. Low marks are rarely awarded at Marks & Spencer's
press tastings. The unfortunate side-effect of this kind of success
will be well known to M & S market strategists: it's the 'safety
syndrome'. Customers are loyal to St Michael so long as they are
looking for reliability in a product, but they might be tempted
to go elsewhere for excitement and thrills.

   And the response? An unsaintly selection of ever sexier
underwear is now echoed, down in the food areas, by the wine
department's own growing sense of adventure and abandon.
Marks & Spencer's long-standing relationship with La
Chablisienne (a co-operative rather than a *petite copine*)
continues to bear fruit, and a tasting tour from Jeunes Vignes

(declassified Chablis from young vines) through the lemony, edgy AOC Chablis, the lean, deep, unoaked Premier Cru Beauroy and on up to the rich, complex, oaked Premier Cru Fourchaume would be as good an introduction as any to this comparatively inexpensive (£3.99–£10.99) northern Burgundy region. Cross France to Bordeaux, and you'll find Marks & Spencer has laid on another introduction for the curious consumer – this time to illustrate the differences between three of the Médoc's four top communes, Saint-Julien (£7.99), Margaux (£6.50) and Pauillac (£8.99), via the incognito 'second wines' of some classed-growth châteaux (Léoville-Barton, Brane-Cantenac and Pichon-Baron). More formally dressed second wines are available in the 'Connoisseur Collection' (from certain stores only) – ten further examples up to and including the junior versions of three first growths: Pavillon Rouge (Château Margaux), Les Forts de Latour (Latour) and Carruades de Lafite (Lafite). There's plenty to thrill claret lovers in that selection.

French country wines have been extensively researched this year by the M & S buying team, who have come back with two exciting oak-aged Côtes de Saint-Mont wines, one white and one red, as well as a terrific Gamay Vins de Pays des Coteaux de l'Ardèche (all at £2.99 at time of going to press). The Morgon from Duboeuf (£5.99) has the depth that is becoming increasingly hard to find in many Beaujolais cru wines, while the Beaujolais Blanc (£4.49) is sourced from near Saint-Véran, and charms with the soft Chardonnay fruit of a good Mâcon-Villages. As well as the Saint-Gall Champagnes that have won Marks & Spencer friends in the past, you can find the fine, mature 1980 Vintage Cuvée Orpale Blanc de Blancs here (£17), while the Blanc de Noirs at £12.99 is a beautifully fruity example of white champagne made from undressed Pinot Noir grapes (they leave the colour behind in their skins). The two Settesoli wines from Sicily are full of character, keenly priced (£2.99 each) and beautifully labelled, and the Shiraz-Cabernet 1987 (£4.50) from Australia is another celebrity travelling incognito, this time Penfolds' Koonunga Hill. Twelve bottles for the price of eleven is a temptation worth succumbing to once you have found a wine that suits you, while M & S have done much for the moderate drinker with their range of over a dozen two-glass bottles.

Best buys

Côtes de Saint-Mont 1987 (red, oak-aged), £2.99
Chablis Premier Cru Beauroy 1986, £9.99
Margaux 1987, £6.50

Marske Mill House

London Road, Sunninghill, Ascot, Berkshire *Tel* (0990) 22790
SL5 0PN

Case sales only **Open** Telephone enquiries or orders 7 days per week – open all hours **Credit cards** None accepted; personal and business accounts **Discounts** Available **Delivery** Free on UK mainland (min 3 cases); otherwise 1 case £3, 2 cases £1 per case; mail order available **Glass hire** Not available **Tastings and talks** To groups on request **Cellarage** Not available

Physicist Harry Faulkner has spent most of his working life teaching, as a Senior Lecturer at London University. The community of scholarship being what it is, he found himself spending periods at Rome and Parma Universities, and giving papers at conferences held in Italy, which enabled him to get to know the country well. He says he has 'always (well, 35 years at least) been a wine enthusiast,' and he has now exchanged teaching for selling Italian wine on a wholesale basis.

The list is tiny; don't contact Harry Faulkner if you want a large choice of wines from the length and breadth of the country. But if you'd like to talk about and try the wines of half a dozen or so estates in central and northern Italy with someone who knows them well and visits them regularly, then this Ascot number is worth noting.

Best buys

Sagrantino di Montefalco 1986, Val di Maggio (Arnaldo Caprai), £6.08
Rubino Reserva 1983, Colle di Sole (Carlo Polidori), £4.92
Grechetto dell'Umbria 1988, Val di Maggio (Arnaldo Caprai), £4.63

Master Cellar Wine Warehouse

5 Aberdeen Road, Croydon, Surrey CR0 1EQ *Tel* 081-686 9989
Associated with Davisons Wine Merchants

Case sales only **Open** Tue–Fri 10–8; Sat 10–6; Sun 10–2 **Closed** Mon, public holidays **Credit cards** Access, Visa **Discounts** 2.5% on 10 cases **Delivery** Free locally (min 1 case) and elsewhere (min 10 cases); otherwise charges by arrangement; mail order available **Glass hire** Free with order **Tastings and talks** Tutored tastings in-store and to wine clubs on request **Cellarage** Not available

There are doubtless many attractions to living in Croydon, and one of them is found in Aberdeen Road. The Master Cellar Wine Warehouse, owned by the Davisons chain of off-licences, offers a superb collection of clarets to by-the-case customers (mixed cases are permitted), with the choice from other classic

French regions being nearly as good. There are wines from the rest of the world, too, with the Spanish selection, and the ports, distinguishing themselves in range and variety.

But claret is certainly the main draw. Davisons are among the country's leading hoarders of fine wines, offering them to us only after they come to resemble wine rather than ink. More unusually still, the mark-up charged for this ageing on our behalf is not grasping. Take the delicious Château Roquetaillade-la-Grange 1985 red Graves, for example. You could have bought this from Henry Townsend *en primeur* in May 1986 at the very reasonable price of £36 per case, paid £19.80 shipping, duty and VAT, taken delivery of it in August 1988 and have stored it for two years yourself. Bottle price: £4.65. Or Davisons could have done all that for you for exactly 30p per bottle, the Master Cellar price in August 1990 being £4.95. All the leading vintages from 1966 to 1986 are here, at very good prices: buy Latour 1981 here rather than at T & W Wines and you'll save £21.65 per bottle (£41.60 rather than £63.25); La Lagune 1982 is £3.10 cheaper than at Selfridges (£19.90 as opposed to £22). This, of course, is a warehouse whereas those are retail outlets, but it is a warehouse from which you could stock a fine wine cellar inexpensively, and that is not common.

An exciting range of Sauternes, and lovely red Burgundies, should not pass without comment. It's not all fine wine, either; you could happily mix cases here for under £60. Themed, tutored tastings are organised from time to time to fill in your knowledge of the world beyond Croydon.

Best buys

Château la Tour Saint-Bonnet 1985, Médoc, £4.95
Priorato Extra 1986, Masia Barril (Spain), £5.95
Grahams Vintage Port 1980, £16.75

Mayor Sworder & Co

21 Duke Street Hill, London SE1 2SW　　　　　　*Tel* 071-407 5111

Open Mon–Fri 9–5 **Closed** Sat, Sun, public holidays **Credit cards** None accepted; personal and business accounts **Discounts** Negotiable **Delivery** Free within radius of M25; otherwise £4 per consignment; mail order available **Glass hire** Free **Tastings and talks** Annual tasting for customers; to groups on request **Cellarage** £3.75 per case per year

If you are reading this book on the train from work in Central London to home in Orpington or Tunbridge Wells, you may be rolling over Mayor Sworder's 17,000 square feet of cellars at the moment. They lie under London Bridge, and are Dickensian in scale and obscurity. 'Last summer,' they mailed customers, 'we concentrated on clearing out our main working cellar, and this year we decided to investigate some of the deeper recesses in the labyrinth.' The vision of a pin-striped, grimy-faced wine merchant with a pit helmet strapped to his forehead is an appealing one. Martin Everett and his fearless colleagues unearthed some good things with damaged labels, and the result was a summer bin-end sale in which six magnums of Nuits Saint-Georges les Damodes 1970 could have been yours for £55.77, with 1980 Côtes du Rhône at £20 a case and Château Talbot 1975 at £172.50. Mayor Sworder produce an intriguing range of special offers of which this was just one.

'We specialise in not specialising,' they claim, though the key sector of sales must surely lie in traditional French wines to corporate City clients. The stiff-covered, breast-pocket-sized list contains a range of one or two wines from most places, and plenty from France, with small growers sought out and cultivated wherever possible. Prices are ex-VAT, and the company's several thousand private customers are valued: 'We pride ourselves,' says Martin Everett (an MW), 'on dealing at a personal level with everybody.' There is free delivery within the M25 ring, and cellarage is available. Customers are invited to an annual tasting in the cellars, while the trains roll by overhead. Could we have reports from at least a few of Mayor Sworder's private clients during the next six months, please?

Best buys

Bourgogne Blanc 'La Grande Vigne' 1988, Domaine Brenot, £6.80
Domaine de la Serre 1986, Vin de Pays des Côtes de Thongue, Merlot, £3.32
Ladoix 'Les Grechons' Blanc 1988, Domaine François Capitain, £11.80

Mi Casa Wines

77 West Road, Buxton, Derbyshire SK17 6HQ   *Tel* (0298) 23952

Open Mon–Fri 3–10; Sat 11–10; Sun, Good Friday 12–2, 7–10; Chr Day 12–1 (other public holidays as normal days) **Credit cards** None accepted; business accounts **Discounts** 5% on 1 case **Delivery** Free within 10-mile radius of Buxton (min 1 case) **Glass hire** Free with 1-case order **Tastings and talks** To groups on request **Cellarage** Not available

Anthony Moores' small list of mainly Spanish wines makes Mi Casa worth a call if you live in or near Buxton, or find yourself passing through, and it is complemented by a range of 'world beers' for those who can't take another drop of domestic canned tedium. As usual, and as one would expect, Rioja provides the cornerstone of the range, but there are wines from Jumilla, Priorato, Alella, Ribera del Duero and other smaller areas, including the mysterious 'Cambados' – a part of Spain to which we can find no reference. Osborne's Bailen Oloroso rarely migrates to this country, but can be spotted nesting at Buxton, and there are Austrian dessert wines, Portuguese table wines, Kopke's good 1970 Vintage Port, and a range of Spanish brandies lurking in the rather miscellaneous collection best summarised as 'other'. Could we have a report or two, please?

Best buys

Viña Monty 1981, Rioja, Bodegas Montecillo, £7.95
Condestable (no vintage cited), Jumilla, £2.95
T E Garrafeira 1982, J M Da Fonseca Successores, £6.40

Millevini

3 Middlewood Road, High Lane, Stockport,   *Tel* (0663) 64366
Cheshire SK6 8AU

Case sales only   **Open** Mon–Fri 9.30–3.30 (answering service outside these times   **Credit cards** None accepted; business accounts   **Discounts** 4% on 3 cases **Delivery** Free within 20-mile radius of shop (min 1 case) and elsewhere (min 4 cases); otherwise £5.50; mail order available   **Glass hire** Free with 1-case order **Tastings and talks** To groups on request   **Cellarage** Not available

This mail-order business run by Richard Lever from his Cheshire home specialises exclusively in Italian wines, though the range comes nowhere near the thousand promised by the company name. The list is, rather, medium-sized; it is well annotated, containing both a glossary and bibliography to fuel the enthusiasm stirring within you as you contemplate the names or sample the wines. Most of Italy's important wine-producing regions are covered to the tune of at least a bottle or two, with almost 20 available from Piedmont and good selections, too, from Tuscany, Friuli, the Veneto and Trentino-Alto Adige. Only Sicily is disappointing, with the standard red and white Corvo hardly doing justice to the vitality and endeavour of the island's viticulture at present.

One would have no difficulty in mixing a case or two from the list, though four might be a problem – and four cases is the number needed to qualify for free delivery outside a 20-mile radius of Stockport. Otherwise add £5.50 per order. In the £4 to £8 range, however, there is so much at present that is good value from Italy (and from Millevini) that the 46p extra per bottle on a single mixed-case order would still be worth paying.

Best buys

Montepulciano d'Abruzzo 1985, Barone Cornacchia, £3.41
Trebbiano d'Abruzzo 1985, Valentini, £8.25
Prosecco Brut Spumante, Conti Loredan (Veneto), £4.98

Mitchell & Son ☞

21 Kildare Street, Dublin 2, Republic of   *Tel* (0001) 760766
Ireland

Open Mon–Fri 10.30–5.30; Sat 10.30–1   **Closed** Sun, public holidays
Credit cards All accepted; personal and business accounts   **Discounts** 5% on 1
case   **Delivery** Free countrywide (min 2 cases – may be mixed); otherwise 1 case
£3.80, 2 cases £4.20, 3 cases £5.40, 4 cases £6.80 (rates quoted in Irish punts); 5+
cases free; mail order available   **Glass hire** Free with 2-case order
Tastings and talks Tastings of new wines for customers   **Cellarage** Not available

Mitchells occupies a beautiful, cream-coloured house in the
centre of Dublin, and 21 Kildare Street is an address from which
this family-owned company has traded for over 100 years. The
cellars are now a wine bar/restaurant, with the wine shop
occupying a charming series of rooms on the ground floor. In
the second inside room, a clock ticks on the mantelpiece over
the fireplace: it is housed in a tiny barrel. The lamp at the end
of the mantelpiece is a retired Laurent Perrier bottle. Claret
boxes provide much of the display shelving.

The list is long enough to provide choice, but not so long that
it bemuses. A few names tend to dominate each area, and in
each case Mitchells are the Republic of Ireland agents for these
wines, so the display of rock-solid loyalty should not surprise
us. Ports from Fonseca, sherries from Lustau's Almacenista
range, German wines from Deinhard, Portuguese wines from
José Maria da Fonseca, Champagne from Laurent Perrier, the
Alsace wines of Dopff au Moulin (what a shame there are only
three of them) and Chianti from Vicchiomaggio are all reliable
and often outstanding. Proceed with more caution through
Mommessin's Burgundies and Beaujolais, and Aubert Frères
Loire valley wines. The fact that all the Rhône valley wines are
sourced from the two main Burgundy négociants listed by
Mitchells looks uncommonly like laziness.

English eyes will be smiling when they light upon the prices,
which are almost as high as in Scandinavia; this is not
rapaciousness on the part of Mitchells but a combination of
higher duty rates and 23 per cent VAT obtaining in the
Republic. In-store tasting facilities are available, and special
tastings can be arranged for groups on request.

We would dearly love to hear from readers about other wine
shops, within Dublin or without, that may be of general

interest, as well as with any comments about the range or
service offered by Mitchell & Son.

Best buys

Tinto Velho 1983, Reguengos de Monsaraz, £6.90 (punts)
Hochheim 1987, Deinhard Heritage, £8.50 (punts)
Dry Oloroso sherry, Lustau Almacenista, £12.40 (punts)

Mitchells Wine Merchants

Head office and main outlet
354 Meadowhead, Sheffield, South Yorkshire   *Tel* (0742) 740311/745587
S8 7UJ
Branches
148 Derbyshire Lane, Sheffield, South   *Tel* (0742) 583989
Yorkshire S8 8SE
25 Townhead Road, Dore, Sheffield, South   *Tel* (0742) 366131
Yorkshire S17 3GD

Open Mon–Sat 9–10; Sun, public holidays 12–2, 7–9   **Closed** Chr Day, 1 Jan
Credit cards Access, Visa; personal and business accounts   **Discounts** 10% on 1
unmixed case   **Delivery** Free in Sheffield, parts of South Yorkshire and North
Derbyshire; elsewhere at cost; mail order available   **Glass hire** Free
Tastings and talks Currently building a tasting room over the shop (completion
date Aug 1990); in-store tastings for all new product launches; to groups on
request   **Cellarage** £2.50 per case per year (under bond only)

Three Sheffield outlets for Mitchells Wine Merchants give you
access to a 600-line wine list, with over 100 malt whiskies and a
splendid repertoire of spirits and liqueurs providing a
distracting side-show. The main branch in Meadowhead is
undergoing considerable expansion at the moment, including
the addition of a tasting room, and John Mitchell plans to start a
wine club once this has been completed, offering discounts,
tastings, talks and trips. All wines new to the list are already
given in-store tasting launches, but the room upstairs should
make themed and tutored tastings possible.

The range is a broad one, from Château Margaux '61 at just
under £300 to enough British sherry to launch a thousand trifles.
Spain, where real sherry comes from (there's plenty of that on
the list, too), is the main specialist area, and you can organise a
mini-tour of Rioja for yourself by trying the wines of the 16
different bodegas stocked by Mitchells. John Mitchell (whose
father Dennis began the business in 1935) and his fellow
director David Marriott, together with manageress Pauline
Mountney, provide helpful and lighthearted advice to guide you
through the rest of the range, not all of which may be actually
in front of you on the shelves. Free local delivery is a further
plus. Could readers in Sheffield and environs report back on

their experience of Mitchells, and on the developments at 534
Meadowhead?

Best buys

Nuits-Saint-Georges 1984, Henri Gouges, £9.95
Valdepeñas 1988, El Principe, Bodegas Las Gloria, £2.59
Muscat de Beaumes-de-Venise, Domaine de Coyeux (half-
bottle), £4.95

Moffat Wine Shop

8 Well Street, Moffat, Dumfriesshire   *Tel* (0683) 20554
DG10 9DP

Open Mon–Sat 9–5.30 **Closed** Sun, Wed pm in Jan and Feb
Credit cards Access, Visa **Discounts** 5% on 1 case (may be mixed)
Delivery Free in Dumfriesshire (min 1 case); elsewhere at cost; mail order
available **Glass hire** Free **Tastings and talks** Monthly tastings at a local hotel
from September to March; to groups on request **Cellarage** Free

This shop, run by former financial analyst A K McIlwrick in
partnership with his hotel-owning parents, offers 'plenty of
gossip about life in Moffat' in addition to a medium-sized range
of wines and a good range of whiskies. To put your finger on
the pulse of this small town of 2,000 people, visit 8 Well Street.
   Doubtless there will be a surprising amount to discover about
what seemed, when you drove into it, to be a quiet little place;
what you will discover on the shelves, meanwhile, will be a
choice of wines from Chile, Australia and New Zealand as well
as from Europe. Within the European selection, Italy, Spain and
Portugal rival France for variety; the selections are deep enough
to provide interesting drinking, but not so deep that wine buffs
will be detained for hours. The McIlwricks have collected at
least 20 worthwhile half-bottles, and you can buy some fine, old
wines here for a celebratory evening as well as selecting from
the youthful majority. And you will leave wiser than when you
arrived.

Best buys

Santa Helena Fumé Blanc 1988, Chile, £3.99
Côtes du Ventoux 1988, Jaboulet, £3.82
Château Pigoudet 1985, Coteaux d'Aix-en-Provence, £4.84

Please write to tell us about any ideas for features you would like to
see in next year's edition or in *Which? Wine Monthly*.

Moreno Wines

11 Marylands Road, London W9 2DU   *Tel* 071-286 0678
2 Norfolk Place, London W2 1QN   *Tel* 071-723 6897 (trade)/
706 3055 (retail)

Open Mon–Fri 9–9; Sat 10–9; Sun 12–2   **Closed** Public holidays
Credit cards Access, Visa   **Discounts** 5% on 1 case   **Delivery** Free in UK (min 4
cases if outside London); mail order available   **Glass hire** Free with 1-case order
Tastings and talks Monthly tutored tastings through Moreno Wine Club; to
groups on request possible   **Cellarage** Not available

Moreno's list isn't exclusively Spanish, but it is almost so –
Chilean and Portuguese reds, and New Zealand's whites,
provide the main excursions, with two of Peru's Tacama wines
lending an exotic note.

As with all the Spanish specialists in this *Guide*, Moreno's
range is founded on the rock of Rioja, with the wines of 16
different bodegas reaching Londoners via W2 and W9: a
wonderful range. Prices vary from £3.09 to £28.59; and yet more
Riojas, held in smaller quantities, appear on the Special Reserva
list (fine wines and bin-ends). The only difficulty would be in
chosing between them, and in this respect Moreno are able to
offer you 'good knowledge of the wines and honesty'. Who
would want more?

Penedés is, as usual, dominated by the skilled and assured
wine-making of Jean León and Torres; fans of the latter will find
three different vintages of Black Label to consider ('83, '76 and
'71). Moreno are keeping abreast of developments in Navarra
via the wines of a trio of bodegas, while from Toro the company
brings us two alternatives to the widely seen Colegiata and
Gran Colegiata of Bodegas Fariña: a Novissimo and a Crianza
from José Fermoselle and two Crianzas and a Reserva from
Bodegas Luis Mateos. A range of five Galician wines would be
hard to find anywhere else in London at present. Priorato,
Cariñena, Somontano, Jumilla, León, Alella, Tierra de Barros,
Rueda, Mentrida and Valdepeñas are all represented with
between one and six bottles. From Ribera del Duero there is a
wide range of the Cooperativa's wines (including seven vintages
of Protos) to compare with those of Vega Sicilia (four vintages,
plus a great string of Valbuenas on the Special Reserva list).
Cavas come from five different houses; sherries, meanwhile, are
perhaps a little disappointing by comparison with the wealth of
table wines, though there are still half a dozen of the finest to
chose from.

A lot of energy and effort during the last year has gone into
the development of the Moreno Wine Club, which organises a
series of themed, tutored tastings on different aspects of
Spanish wine. Hispanophiles would do well to ask for details.

Best buys

Condestable Tinto 1988, Señorio de Condestable, Jumilla, £2.69
Masia Barril Extra Tinto 1986, Priorato, £5.96
Viña Real Tinto Gran Reserva 1975, CVNE, Rioja, £9.35

Morris & Verdin

28 Churton Street, London SW1V 2LP   *Tel* 071-630 8888

Case sales only   Open Mon–Fri 9–5.30; Sat 10–3 **Closed** Sun, public holidays
Credit cards None accepted; personal and business accounts **Discounts** Available
on 10+ cases **Delivery** Free in central London and Oxford (min 1 case);
otherwise £6.90 per consignment of less than 5 cases; mail order available
Glass hire Free with 1-case order **Tastings and talks** To groups on request
Cellarage £4.60 per case per year (inc insurance)

Morris & Verdin's primary role in life is as an importer
'searching out the best from France and, in the last few years,
California' – and selling it on to the trade. By-the-case
customers are welcomed, however, and a retail, VAT-inclusive,
bottle-priced list is produced as well as a separate ex-VAT trade
list. If you are interested in 'the best from France' – and there
can't be many of us who aren't – then it's worth asking Jasper
Morris or one of his team for a copy. Remember, of course, that
the best doesn't often cost below £5.

This tall, red-headed and comparatively youthful Master of
Wine must be readily recognisable at 200 yards to most of his
Gallic growers, and they seem to regard him with affection, if
his burgundy allotments are anything to go by. Morris buys
broadly and imaginatively: four different Aligotés, for example,
open the white burgundy section and each, the list assures us,
'has its own distinct style'. Six Meursaults would furnish the
wherewithal for a pricier comparative tasting. Red burgundy
outnumbers white on the Morris & Verdin list (this balance is
often reversed on competitors' shelves), with Rion (for whom
Morris & Verdin is UK agent), Girard Vollot, Capron Manieux,
Comte Lafon, Ponsot, Bachelet and Trapet being the main
growers listed. There are burgundies here under £10 (from the
Hautes Côtes, Monthelie and Savigny, plus Rion's Côte de
Nuits-Villages), though a number of these are poised at around
the £9.90 mark and may have moved over the edge by the time
you read this.

Alsace is another area of Morrisonian enthusiasm; the entire
range comes from an M & V agency, Domaine Ostertag, but is
generally high in quality and full of interest. This domain is one
of the few in Alsace experimenting seriously with barrique-
ageing, and individual vineyard wines, from both AOC Alsace
and AOC Alsace Grand Cru sites, are produced wherever

possible. Twenty-two different Ostertag wines are listed at present. The Loire presents a splendid balance between fresh-and-dry, and old-and-sweet, with historical Chenin from Bourillon Dorléans in Vouvray, J P Chéné in Coteaux du Layon, and Château de Fesles in Bonnezeaux. Sweet wines, in general, receive a sympathetic ear in Churton Street; there's also a good range of Sauternes (including Gilette), and during 1990 Jasper Morris produced an *en primeur* offer called The Great Sweet Wines of France – an excellent idea, bringing Jurançon and the Loire into the fold with Alsace and Sauternes.

The Rhône section of the list breaks no new ground, but everyone on it is either good or great; and Bordeaux is abbreviated, unless you wish to buy ex-cellars. An extensive 1989 Bordeaux *en primeur* offer was made. The list of French country wines is short but choice, and apart from a solitary brace of Riojas the rest of Europe is elsewhere. The wines from Australia, New Zealand and California are cream rather than milk, and so mostly £8 and up. 'We bought these excellent wines,' the list reassures us, 'confident that they are finer than their French counterparts at the same prices.' There's the incentive.

Best buys

Au Bon Climat, Pinot Noir 1988, Santa Maria (California), £11.50
Alsace Sylvaner Vieilles Vignes 1988, Domaine Ostertag, £5.20
Bourgogne Rouge 1986, Domaine Rion, £5.90

Morrisons   ⊂⊃ ⬥

Offices/warehouse
Wakefield 41 Industrial Estate, Wakefield,   *Tel* (0924) 870000
West Yorkshire WF2 0XF
45 branches in Cumbria, Derbyshire, Lancashire, Lincolnshire,
Staffordshire, Teesside and Yorkshire

Open (Generally) Mon, Tue, Wed, Sat 8.30–6; Thur, Fri 8.30–8 **Closed** Sun, some public holidays **Credit cards** Access, Visa **Discounts**, **Delivery** Not available **Glass hire** Free with 1-case order **Tastings and talks**, **Cellarage** Not available

---

The potential range of wines available from Morrisons' 45 supermarkets is very good, though how many of the 45 carry anything approaching the full list is difficult to gauge. If, having read this entry, you feel we are describing a store very different to any of the Morrisons you know, write and tell us. If, on the other hand, all of the wines we mention regularly find themselves nestling up to the baked beans in your trolley, let us know, too. As – collectively – we now buy so many of our wines from supermarkets, we would like readers to monitor and report back to us on these as well as on individual merchants and high-street chains.

The claret section, to start with, has been well assembled, with the red and white wines of the two fast-improving Graves châteaux Smith-Haut-Lafitte and Roquetaillade-la-Grange proving as mouthfilling as their names. Morrisons offer a wide range of inexpensive Burgundies and Beaujolais, with the Marsannay 1987 from Chénu and the Bourgogne Pinot Noir 1985 from Faiveley providing value at £6.29 and £5.75 respectively. The Domaine des Rochettes Anjou Rouge (£2.39), Côtes du Ventoux from La Vieille Ferme (£2.89) and the range of Listel wines would all be good routes into the French countryside, and sweet white wine enthusiasts should try Château de Berbec from the Premières Côtes de Bordeaux (£3.39). The German section, with a wide selection of Riesling Kabinett, Spätlese and Auslese wines, offers little excuse for sticking to Liebfraumilch, and there is exciting variety from Italy, Australia, Greece and Chile, too. It's not often Inferno from the Valtellina (mountain Nebbiolo made, here, by Nino Negri) or Concha y Toro's Casillero del Diablo (a fine Chilean Cabernet Sauvignon) find their way on to supermarket shelves: well done to Morrisons for getting this Satanic pair there. If they are. The full range, we repeat, is very impressive; we hope it is available to a full range of customers.

Best buys

Marqués de Murrieta Rioja Blanco 1985, £5.79
Casillero del Diablo Cabernet Sauvignon 1983, Concha y Toro (Chile), £3.79
Bairrada Reserva 1982, Frei João (Caves São João), £4.29

Nadder Wine Company   ☞

Manor Farmhouse, Sandhills Road, Dinton,   *Tel* (0722) 76734
nr Salisbury, Wiltshire SP3 5ER

Case sales only   **Open** Mon–Fri 9–5.30; Sat 10–5   **Closed** Sun, public holidays
Credit cards Access, Visa; personal and business accounts   **Discounts** 2.5% for
cash with order (min 1 case)   **Delivery** Free within M25 and within 50-radius of
Salisbury (min 1 mixed case) and UK mainland (min 5 cases); otherwise 1–5 cases
at cost; mail order available   **Glass hire** Free with 1-case order
Tastings and talks To groups on request   **Cellarage** Not available

After five years' trading, the Nadder Wine Company, run from the centre of a 1000-acre South Wiltshire farm by Chris Gilbey (of the ex-gin family), offers a mid-length list, 'no hype, no fuss' and a '*very* personal service'. Sales are by-the-case only, but mixing is encouraged; at present, the majority of sales are to the trade, but private customers are actively sought, and as we write a national mail-order distribution service is being instituted.

The claret selection is good, particularly in the petits châteaux/crus bourgeois area; burgundy is less exciting, due to its heavy reliance on the wines of one supplier only, Misserey, for whom Nadder are now English agents. The Rhône section fails to sparkle at present, with Jaboulet-Vercherre's Crozes probably the lowest point; the Loire is better, with Henri Pelle's Menetou-Salon and the Balland-Chapuis Coteaux du Giennois providing two good-value Sauvignon wines to compare with the more expensive offerings from Sancerre (Mellot's is good). Schlumberger's Alsace wines are expensive but high in quality.

Chris Gilbey is very proud of his Franciacorta find, Castello Bornato: the red is a sort of bottled Franco-Italian entente cordiale, with equal parts of Cabernet Franc, Merlot, Nebbiolo and Barbera; the white is a Pinot-Chardonnay blend, though we're not sure if the Pinot is Grigio or Bianco or both. Sadly there is no Franciacorta sparkling wine – or not yet, at least. There are a few other Italian wines, but the Franciacorta looks the most exciting. Spain is exclusively Riojan (Montecillo and CVNE); there is a little more choice from Australia and California. Champagnes are comparatively plentiful, and we are pleased to see Osborne's Quinta among the sherries and a Burmester Colheita 1970 among the ports.

Could readers report on their experiences of buying from Nadder?

Best buys

Alsace Gewürztraminer 1986, Réserve des Princes Abbés, Schlumberger, £6.96
Château Gouvran 1985, Premières Côtes de Bordeaux, £4.82
Franciacorta 1986 (red), Castello Bornato, £5.15

Le Nez Rouge

12 Brewery Road, London N7 9NH	*Tel* 071-609 4711
Associated outlets	
Pagendam Pratt & Partners, Unit 5B1, Street	*Tel* (0937) 844711
7, Thorp Arch Trading Estate, Wetherby,	
West Yorkshire LS23 7BJ	
K F Butler & Co, 19b The Birches Estate, East	*Tel* (0342) 313955
Grinstead, West Sussex RH19 1XZ	

Open Mon–Fri 9–5.30; Sat 10–2 **Closed** Sun, public holidays
Credit cards Access, Visa; personal and business accounts **Discounts** Collection discount on full cases (£2) **Delivery** Free in London (min 1 case); elsewhere 1 case £4.50, 2 cases £2.50 per case, 3 cases £1.50 per case, 3–4 cases £1.50 per case, 5+ cases free; mail order available **Glass hire** Free with 2-case order

Tastings and talks Regular monthly tastings held in shop on Saturdays; annual grand tastings held at outside venues; tutored tastings at London Business School; to groups on request **Cellarage** £3.75 per case per year or part year (unmixed cases purchased through Le Nez Rouge club only)

Le Nez Rouge, with its distinctive logo and unforgettable name, has ceased being a club in any formal sense during the last year, and is now simply the retail outlet of the shipping and importing business Berkmann Wine Cellars. In addition to the London shop just north of Kings Cross, the wines are now available via K F Butler in East Grinstead (acquired by Berkmann Wine Cellars during 1989), and via Pagendam Pratt in Wetherby, West Yorkshire.

Joseph Berkmann has built up a selection of valuable agencies over the years, and it is worth putting your nose round the Nez Rouge door just to get a sniff of these on a retail basis. Beaujolais from Georges Duboeuf (including fine domain bottlings such as Dr Darroze's Quatre Vents Fleurie or the Comte de Sparre's Tour du Bief Moulin-à-Vent) is the foundation stone, but there are also some lovely burgundies from Domaines Albert Morey et Fils, fine Muscadet from Sauvion, Bruno Paillard's silvery champagnes and the elegant, stylish and undervalued ports of Ramos-Pinto. The Provence wines of Les Maîtres Vignerons at Saint-Tropez are sound rather than exciting, and the same goes for the beautifully labelled Alsace wines of Gaston Beck.

That's for the agency turns. But there is much else, including one of the country's very best burgundy lists, with a wide range of small growers' wines through every vintage of the 1980s. Two or three ten-pound notes won't buy you much, unfortunately, but what you take away will be worth having. Claret, too, is wide-ranging, and there are some fine Loire and Rhône wines. With K F Butler have come a promising gang of young Corsicans; and vintage Armagnac collectors will find much to render themselves insolvent with. Half-bottles are plentiful, doubtless thanks to demand from Berkmann's restaurant clients.

Tastings have always been a key element in Berkmann's sales philosophy, and there is plenty of opportunity for Nez Rouge clients to colour their noses in this manner. There are regular themed tastings in the shop every month on Saturdays, occasional tastings at the Berkmann-owned 'Au Jardin des Gourmets' restaurant in Soho, and tutored tastings held at the London Business School. If you like to taste before you buy, then this is a merchant you should most definitely contact. Mail order is available, too, on a by-the-case basis, with free London delivery.

Best buys

Gamay, Vins de Pays de l'Ardèche 1989, Georges Duboeuf, £3.53
Chablis Premier Cru Vau Ligneau 1988, Thierry Hamelin, £8.75
Château Roquetaillade-la-Grange 1985, Graves (red), £5.73

James Nicholson Wine Merchant ☞

27a Killyleagh Street, Crossgar, Co Down, *Tel* (0396) 830091
Northern Ireland BT30 9DG

Open Mon–Sat 10–7 **Closed** Sun, Chr Day, 12–13 July **Credit cards** Access,
Diners Club, Visa; business accounts **Discounts** 5–10% (min 1 case)
Delivery Free in Northern Ireland (min 1 case); elsewhere nominal postal charges;
mail order available **Glass hire** Free with 1-case order **Tastings and
talks** Various tastings and dinners held in-store and at Roscoff's Restaurant
Cellarage £1.75 per case per year

We have long been aware that good wine merchants are as
thinly spread in Northern Ireland as the butter in a cucumber
sandwich, so it is with some relief that we welcome this new
entry to the *Guide*. James Nicholson is an ex-restaurateur who
has been wine importing and wholesaling since 1982. At the
beginning of 1990 he opened a retail shop at Crossgar in County
Down, and list prices include free delivery throughout Northern
Ireland for one case or more. The retail and mail-order side of
the business has been brisk since its inception, we are told.
Ninety-five per cent of the stock is imported direct to Northern
Ireland.

The shop is smart and well appointed; indeed, the interior
would not look out of place on London's Kings Road, though
the building in which it is sited is an architecturally
unimaginative one. The range runs a good middle distance, and
contains a number of the most talked-about wines of the day.
Five from La Jaubertie in Bergerac, for example, or Balland-
Chapuis' Côtes du Giennois, or Bellevue-la-Forêt from the Côtes
du Frontonnais, or Château Vannières from Bandol, or
Vouvray's Château Moncontour – while the price of Cauhapé's
Jurançon here suggests either that the owner has a soft spot for
the Irish, or that mainland British merchants are taking
walloping profits from the wine's celebrity. The entire Beaujolais
and Mâconnais is handed over to Duboeuf and Drouhin, while
Drouhin gets the Côte d'Or and Chablis to himself. Good
producers both, but we feel customers deserve a little more
choice than this. The Rhône is split four ways: Jaboulet, Guigal,
Duboeuf again, and Pierre Dorvin; while Alsace goes to
Gisselbrecht. There seems to be a little more fresh air in the
Bordeaux section.

Outside France there are short ranges from most places, with

Toro's Gran Colegiata, Ceretto's Baroli, the Portuguese Quinta do Carmo and Chilean wines from both Concha y Toro and Cousiño Macul providing value and authenticity. Australian wines are exclusively from Rosemount – good wines, but as with Drouhin and Duboeuf, they offer only one angle on a very complex scene, and we would hope to see them joined by others in the future. There is a little more variety from New Zealand, with Matua Valley and Morton Estate offerings, and from California, where Clos du Bois, Ridge and Sanford meet Robert Mondavi, not for the first time. No one could complain about a choice between Piper Heidsieck, Bruno Paillard and Roederer when it comes to champagne; Hidalgo's subtle Sanlúcar sherries and Grahams stentorian ports are both worth exploring, too. The shop stocks up to 40 half-bottles, though only half of these are listed. Tastings are organised and offers (including *en primeur*) are made as part of the effort 'to attain a level of service and quality which is unrivalled' in Northern Ireland. Readers, please give us the benefit of your judgment as to how far this aim is being achieved.

Best buys

Côtes du Roussillon 1988, Domaine Guittard Rodor, £3.79
Jurançon 1988, Domaine Cauhapé, £5.98
Montagny 1986, Drouhin, £6.69

Nickolls & Perks   ☞

37 High Street, Stourbridge, West Midlands DY8 1TA	*Tel* (0384) 394518/377211
Associated company	
Greenwood & Co, 178 High Street, Lye, West Midlands DY9 8LH	*Tel* (0384) 422217

Open Mon–Sat 9–10 **Closed** Sun, public holidays **Credit cards** Access, American Express, Visa; personal and business accounts **Discounts** 5–10% on 1 case **Delivery** Free within West Midlands area (min 2 cases); otherwise at cost; mail order available **Glass hire** Free with 2-case order **Tastings and talks** Regular tastings through Stourbridge Wine Society; to groups on request **Cellarage** Available

---

Nickolls & Perks have two main specialisms. The first is *en primeur* offers, which are regularly issued for port and Bordeaux wines; the second is port and Bordeaux wines in early, middle and late maturity, joined by Burgundy and Champagne at the same stages of life. These form the basis for a wide range of 'anniversary' bottles that the company dispatches to Japan, Norway, Australia, Holland . . . anywhere where there are anniversaries to celebrate and the desire to do the celebrating with wine.

If you want Bordeaux, Burgundy, port and champagne in a younger and fresher state, you will find good selections here. Clarets of vintages throughout the 1980s, including 1982, are well stocked, and Sauternes from 1983 and 1985 are offered with more choice than usual. This is one of the best Vintage Port lists in the country, with a range of twelve 1963s, for example, and a choice of half a dozen or so ports for every major declared vintage back to 1955; there are plenty of 1970s, 1975s, 1977s, 1980s, 1983s and 1985s. Colheita ports are also offered among the vintages, though all are glossed '(matured in wood)', sensibly avoiding any risk of confusion with Vintage Port. A good range of different shippers' 10, 20, 30 and over 40 years old tawny ports is also worth signalling. Burgundy is less strong, with a majority négociant presence; champagne, however, is splendidly assembled. There are some fine dessert sherries from Sandeman and Gonzalez Byass, and a small range of vintage and solera madeiras. Wines from other regions are stocked but not listed, and these provide alternatives for everyday drinking.

Prices here are generally high, and you are unlikely to unearth any bargains other than in the younger petit-château clarets (where the bargain will be constituted by over-achievement for the appellation rather than notably keen prices). Nickolls & Perks may well have the special bottle you are looking for, though, and unlike some other fine wine merchants they are well geared up to helping the one-bottle purchaser unfamiliar with the heady world of fine wine trading.

Best buys

Château Batailley 1985, Pauillac (half-bottle), £5.40
Royal Corregidor Rich Rare Oloroso, Sandeman, £10.75
Dow's Vintage Port 1985, half-bottle, £10.95

Nicolas   ⇨

157 Great Portland Street, London W1N 5FB	*Tel* 071-580 1622
98 Holland Park Avenue, London W11 3RB	*Tel* 071-243 0571
6 Fulham Road, London SW3 6HG	*Tel* 071-584 1450
282 Old Brompton Road, London SW5 9HR	*Tel* 071-370 4402
71 Abingdon Road, London W8 6AW	*Tel* 071-937 3996

Open (W1) Mon–Sat 10–9; Sun 12–2, 7–9; public holidays 10–5; (SW3)
Mon–Sat 10–9; Sun 12–3, 7–9, public holidays 10–5; (W8) Tue–Sat 11–8.30; (SW5)

Mon–Sat 11–9 **Closed** (W1) Chr Day, Easter Day; (SW3) Chr Day; (W8) Mon, Sun, public holidays; (SW5) Sun, public holidays **Credit cards** Access, Visa; personal and business accounts **Discounts** 5% on 1 mixed case **Delivery** Free locally (min 1 bottle); elsewhere £2; mail order available **Glass hire** Free with suitable case order **Tastings and talks** Promotional tastings; to groups on request **Cellarage** £5 per case per year

As reported in last year's *Guide*, the old Buckingham chain of London merchants has now metamorphosed into a five-taloned English foothold for the French merchants Nicolas (who have 300 shops in the Paris area alone). These *succursales anglaises* are still settling down, with refurbishment of the Holland Park branch 'in the style of the Nicolas shops in Paris' scheduled for completion by the time you read this, and with staff attending five-week Nicolas training courses in Paris.

You'd expect the list – sorry, Carte des Vins – to be strong in French wines, and it is, with good ranges of *petits châteaux* clarets and French country wines from areas largely ignored by British merchants, such as Corsica, Roussillon, Savoie or the Jura. Champagnes are also profuse and splendid. What is more surprising is the number of old clarets and burgundies in stock – we all thought the French drank them up almost as soon as they were bottled, didn't we? But no: 'Nicolas knows how to age these masterpieces. They lie undisturbed in the dark, only to be awakened by our devoted care. Being masterpieces, they are only available in limited quantities.' So for those '76 burgundies and '59 clarets (in limited quantities), make your way here.

Another surprise is the number of non-French wines available in the five shops, particularly Italian, Portuguese and Australian wines. How much this is due to freelance buying at the British end we don't know – but you'll find stimulating wines from most places (even Peru and Zimbabwe) stocked. More disappointing is the fact that, as in Buckingham days, prices are rather high – higher even than Berry Bros, in some cases.

We'll continue to watch developments here with interest (please assist with reports); what we hope will happen is that Nicolas will realise that what they can really offer the British is an unparalleled wealth of wines from every last little corner of France, and major on that, rather than on trendy bottles from the four corners of the globe that everyone else is already working themselves into a lather trying to sell. The time, after all, has never been riper for a really top-flight French country wine specialist.

See page 306 for an explanation of the symbols used in the *Guide*.

Best buys

Château La Vieille Cure 1983, Fronsac, £4.25
Chardonnay, Vin de Pays de l'Ile de Beauté (Corsica) (producer
and vintage not specified), £3.75
Rully Blanc 1988, Domaine de l'Hermitage, £9.50

The Nobody Inn

Doddiscombsleigh, nr Exeter, Devon   *Tel* (0647) 52394
EX6 7PS

Open Mon–Sat 11–11; Sun 12–3 **Closed** Chr Day **Credit cards** Access, Visa;
personal and business accounts **Discounts** 5% for 1 case **Delivery** Free within
10-mile radius (min 1 case); otherwise at cost; mail order available
Glass hire Free with 1-case order **Tastings and talks** Small specialist tastings for
regular customers (by invitations); series of lectures from October to March; to
groups on request **Cellarage** Not available

The Nobody Inn is very definitely Somebody in the world of
British wine retailing. Like all of our favourite merchants, large
or small, chained or unchained, mail-ordered or locally followed,
Nick Borst-Smith's list is *mousseux* with enthusiasm. 'The
continual search for the perfect wine' is his avowed aim, though
the use of 'continual' shows that he knows the search is endless
and possibly cyclical, more of a vocation than an aim. But there
are plenty of leading contenders for perfection gathered together
in Doddiscombsleigh, particularly among the wonderful range
of sweet wines. Interestingly, Nick Borst-Smith says that he has
built up such a good range of these because they go so well
with the 52 different Devon cheeses also sold here. New Worlds
and Old Worlds alike are explored with the same zest for
original, striking tastes. The only areas not explored thoroughly
are those that Sainsburys or Tesco in Exeter have scoured on
your behalf: the less expensive wines from Eastern Europe, the
French countryside, and try-harder co-operatives everywhere.

Other reasons to be cheerful when reflecting on The Nobody
Inn include the list's extensive tasting notes, full of robust
opinions and a strong sense of fun. Examples: 'I shall ignore all
but the best traditional white Rioja. All that cold-fermented
wishy-washy stuff. Ugh!!' Cue for Murrieta. Or of Angas Brut
Rosé: 'Crocodile Dundee would not be seen dead drinking this.
Not only is it fizzy, it's also pink. Of course, unlike British
Fosters, it has flavour.' Or of the fine sweet white Loire
selection: 'I wish the wine press would stop referring to these
sweet Loires as under-rated and excellent value, because some
people are starting to believe it and the prices are not as good
as they were. However, let me say that these wines are underrated and excellent value!'

The malt whisky selection here takes enthusiasm up to the boundaries of fanaticism, and in addition to a huge range of malts that can be purchased by the bottle you can also enjoy tots of cask-strength whisky, many of them from the excellent Scotch Malt Whisky Society. Lovers of the exotic should bring 40 rupees to spend on a tot of 'Snow-Lands, Ye Grand Earl' from Nepal, obviously twice as good (because twice as expensive) as Binnie's Aristocrat Pure Malt from Jagatjil Industries in India. The half-bottle selection is superb, too, and the list of lecturers who have been down to tutor tastings at The Nobody Inn reads like a *Who's Who* of the British wine trade. And of course this is a lovely oak-beamed pub when it's not being one of the region's liveliest wine merchants; in addition to good beer you can enjoy good wine here. Ten to 15 are available by the glass, with further tasting samples usually open (under nitrogen, rather than the more usual pub atmosphere of second-hand cigarette smoke) – just ask what's available.

Best buys

Tinto da Anfora 1988, João Pires, Portugal, £4.28
Côtes du Rhône Blanc 1988, pure Marsanne, Clape, £6.99
Muscat Vin de Liqueur, Cuvée José Sala, half-bottle, £2.23

Oddbins

Head office
31–33 Weir Road, London SW19 8UG   *Tel* 081-879 1199
145 branches

Open (Generally) Mon–Sat 9–9; Sun, public holidays 12–2, 7–9 (not all shops open on Sun) **Closed** Chr Day **Credit cards** Access, American Express, Oddbins Credit Card, Visa; personal and business accounts **Discounts** 5% on unmixed cases; 'seven for the price of six' on all champagne **Delivery** Free within locality of shop (min 1 case) **Glass hire** Free **Tastings and talks** Regular in-store tastings on Saturdays; quarterly customer tastings in Scotland; to groups on request **Cellarage** Not available

1990: Oddbins stays in front. Why?

Because it has a superb wine list: high in quality, as varied as any in the country (though some are more extensive), and priced to compete with warehouses and supermarkets. And because of service, generally assumed to be the preserve of 'the traditional wine merchant'. The traditional wine merchant will certainly give first-class service to a long-standing client of means, buying privately and perhaps corporately, too; Oddbins' distinction lies in giving first-class service to anyone who walks into the shop. The traditional wine merchant, if he or she is worth inclusion in the *Guide*, will match this – and so they should, with one or two shops only to keep up to scratch;

Oddbins have nearly 150 shops. 'The Oddbins staff nationally deserve far more than *one* service symbol,' writes a reader from Birkenhead. 'In my opinion they provide the best service of any wine merchant with their help and advice. Let's hope they keep it up!' 'Superlatively helpful and friendly,' we hear from another reader who uses the Sheffield branch. 'They searched the country for a case of '85 Côte Rôtie for me, and kept it inviolate for months . . . they'll get what you want if there's any possibility of it being available. Terrific.' The Oddbins mix of innovative buying, great attention to service, and a relaxed, casual style of presentation continues to be unique in high-street terms; only the warehouses offer anything similar, but the 12-bottle requirement inevitably acts as a check on appeal. Oddbins' appeal seems to be universal; indeed, we would be mildly relieved to hear from anyone (other than rival merchants) who isn't happy with the Oddbins package.

Such imperfections as there are are generally a consequence of Oddbins' boldness – in stocking the finest wines at keen prices (from Gaja or Guigal, say), regardless of the fact that quantities are limited. This would normally frighten off managers and buyers with 145 branches to feed; not so the Oddbins team. It does mean that customers are disappointed on occasion, when supplies run out (and wines like this generally have to be ordered rather than simply plucked off the shelf). As the reader quoted above testifies, however, strenuous efforts are made to find what is wanted, wherever it may lie.

To concentrate on the fine wines stocked by Oddbins, and its attention-grabbing offers of the great and the greater still, would be to do an injustice to the list, for its real strength lies in the under-£10 range. To see for yourself how good this is, pick out two or three 'mushroom' areas of the wine world, areas where things are changing rapidly, and look at what is on the latest Oddbins list. White Bordeaux, for example, now better than at any moment in any reader's lifetime. Oddbins are in the thick of it, with a range of 20, ranging in price from £2.59 to a bin-end of Smith-Haut-Lafitte '88 at £10.99. The 1988 Château Roquefort Cuvée Spéciale, yours for a five-pound note, will show you what all the fuss is about. Or look at Italy, currently fomenting a renaissance which far too few merchants have even begun to come to terms with yet. The Oddbins summer 1990 list celebrates Italy via a Ralph Steadman study tour (the fact that Oddbins go to Steadman rather than to some soothing design consultancy in order to give a visual charge to the lists is also symptomatic of the imagination and boldness that has put them ahead of the field). In the north-east, three Reciotos (one of Soave; two of Valpolicella) and two Amarones match five Maculan creations. The north-west brings a Spanna, two

Barberas and three Dolcettos (including one from Giacomo Conterno) as part of the necessary context for ten Barolos and the seven Gaja wines. Central Italy is only marginally less distinguished, with the traditional Tuscan denominations balanced by truly worthwhile vini da tavola (including Oddbins' custom-built Ginestro from Villa Banfi at £4.99). The two Montepulciano d'Abruzzo wines, and the Rosso Cònero from the Marches, provide excellent value. The choice from the south is restricted, but it does contain the magnificent Rosso del Conte from Regaleali, as well as its white counterpart Nozze d'Oro, and Marco de Bartoli's fine Marsala and extraordinary Bukkuram. Two broadsheet-sized pages, and barely a dud among them; even the Lambrusco is one of the best, from Cavicchioli. That's the way to do it.

What else? Australia, of course: Oddbins are better than most avowed specialists, both on price and range. 'In 1990 our message is clear: buy and experiment. There has never been a better time to restore your faith in the land of the dingo.' Who lost their faith in the land of the dingo, anyway? Not Oddbins' customers, surely. Another test zone for most merchants is Portugal: Oddbins sail through with flying colours. Eighteen are listed, and every one is worth trying. Spain looks as if it is in need of a Steadman study tour (he takes a few wine buyers in tow, and they find exciting bottles while he reimagines the landscape); wines like the Gran Colegiata, the inexpensive Riojas from Palacio and, of course, Pesquera will tide us over until then. New Zealand and America are very good, with a fine range from Washington – don't fail to try the Kiona wines. Sherry and other fortified wines are also first-rate, though they are generally stranded behind the counter with the spirits, and require some peering at. Oddbins' port selection has improved dramatically in the last twelve months (there was a Steadman study tour during the winter of '89/90): here is the place to catch up on the 1980s you missed until now; here is the place to tour a range of eight different quintas, from the bargain Foz, up past Eira Velha, Bomfim and Roeda to Malvedos and finally Vargellas. Boa Vista and Corte are off the river route, but in no way inferior; indeed the Boa Vista '82 is one of the real successes of the year.

There's France, too. An exciting range of French country wines at under £4 is what we would explore first, and the Rhône would follow: Oddbins are leading specialists for each. The South of France, in particular, is a playground of innovation, and that is what draws the best performances from the buying team. Alsace, the Loire and Beaujolais are more fully stocked than at most addresses in the Guide; what you get from Bordeaux and Burgundy, meanwhile, is a raider's portfolio: big names when they could bring them home at the right price; little names when they could bring home the right quality. Sauternes is not ignored, and Oddbins even stole a march on the *en primeur* specialists by making an offer of Jaffelin's '88s (this négociant-éleveur is much improved since Robert Drouhin, its owner, put the youthful Bernard Repolt in charge) with the wines already sitting in the warehouse, so you could buy in less than case quantities and pay on receipt of bottle. Oddbins' antics with champagne scarcely need repetition here; we would only point out that in terms of alternatives to champagne, Oddbins are again ahead of the field, with a range of over 40 to choose from. The malt whiskies have always been superb, and the Cognacs and Armagnacs good; there are now seven Irish whiskeys and an expanding line in bourbons. There aren't many world beers you won't find here, either.

The half-bottle range has increased in the last year, though most of these are dessert wines. Tastings are on Saturdays (except in Scotland, where the law requires them to be organised differently; they are held every quarter). Do remember to get hold of a copy of the list, as not all branches are the same size and you may not realise the extent of what's available just by looking around the shelves. And keep reporting back: Oddbins may not be the best for ever, even if it looks that way in 1990.

Best buys

Cabernet Sauvignon Prestige 1988, Caves Ramadaire, Vin de Pays d'Oc (Skalli), £3.99
Nutbourne Manor Bacchus 1989, England, £4.99
Bukkuram Moscato di Pantelleria, De Bartoli (half-bottle), £6.99

Old Street Wine Company

309 Old Street, London EC1V 6LE　　　　　　　*Tel* 071-729 1768

Open Mon–Fri 10–7; Sat 11–2　**Closed** Sun, public holidays
Credit cards Access, Visa; personal and business accounts　**Discounts** 5% on 1 case (cash & carry)　**Delivery** Free in EC1, EC2, EC4, N1 (min 1 case or £75 order); elsewhere at cost; mail order available　**Glass hire** Free with suitable order
Tastings and talks Monthly tastings available through The Nearly Private Wine Club; to groups on request　**Cellarage** Not available

The Old Street Wine Company, sited in the London street of the same name (in fact there are two; this is the City one), offers what is described as 'a treasure trove of rare, interesting and unusual wines'. Wines of the Loire are the chief speciality: just over a dozen are listed, but this is 'a selection from our large range'. If you particularly like red Loire wines, as we do, this is a good place to begin exploring them from.

The Loire aside, Old Street's list has a City feel to it: John Corliss is the local agent for Charles Viénot, so this Boisset-owned négociant's burgundies dominate that part of the shop; port, sherry, claret and champagne will fill the rest of your shopping basket. Each of these sections is sourced from a variety of producers, raising the interest level, save in the case of sherry. There, though, the sole supplier is Valdespino, whose wines are interesting enough even without competition, and none of the sherries listed is anything but inspiring. Among the ports, 1970 and 1966 are in good supply, and drink beautifully at present if you have £30–£50 to spare. Bordeaux is sound, though the range is not large. There are wines from other regions available too, but these are not listed, rather disappointingly. Special offers (including *en primeur*) are made from time to time, when John Corliss chances upon something exciting, and the Nearly Private Wine Club lays on some worthwhile monthly tastings with food. Finally, make your way to 309 Old Street on the third Thursday of November, Beaujolais Nouveau day: we don't know what this year's Nouveau will be like, but you can enjoy the proprietor's 'truly superb ham cooked in Guinness'.

Best buys

St-Nicolas de Bourgueil 1988, Domaine du Bourg, J-P Mabileau, £5.75
Menetou-Salon Blanc 1989, Domaine du Chatenoy, £6.59
Chinon 1986, Clos de l'Echo, £7.50

Organic Wine Company

P O Box 81, High Wycombe, Buckinghamshire HP13 5QN	*Tel* (0494) 446557

Associated outlet

Lincolnshire Wine Company, Chapel Lane, Ludborough, nr Grimsby, Lincolnshire DN36 5SJ	*Tel* (0472) 840858

Case sales only Open Mon–Sat 9–6; Sun, public holidays by arrangement **Closed** Chr Day, Boxing Day **Credit cards** Access, Visa; personal and business accounts **Discounts** Negotiable (min 6 cases) **Delivery** Free within 12-mile radius of High Wycombe or Ludborough (min 1 case); otherwise £3.70 within 40-mile radius of High Wycombe and all London postal districts; elsewhere £5 for 1 case, £6.50 for 2–3 cases; mail order available **Glass hire** Free with 3-case order (locally only) **Tastings and talks** Regular tastings in different regional centres in the south-east and London; in-store tastings by arrangement; to groups by arrangement **Cellarage** £4 per case per year

The Organic Wine Company seems to have had another bullish year. Following 1989's takeover of the Lincolnshire Wine Company, 1990 has seen it acquire West Heath Wine's mail-order customers (Andrew Williams having decided to supply trade only in future), as well as opening a 'subsidiary in Canada' and initiating a 'join venture distribution operation in the USA'. Meanwhile, back in High Wycombe, Tony Mason continues to consolidate the list, and continues to let fly with exclamatory newsletters.

Like most organic wine lists, this one is strongest in French and German wines, France and Germany being the two countries where organic farming principles seem to be taken most seriously by wine growers. As well as familiar names like Guy Bossard from the Loire, Château Vieux Georget from Bordeaux, or Mas de Gourgonnier from Provence, there are also large ranges from less well known organic pacesetters, such as Alain Verdet in Burgundy (producer of the first ever organic burgundy to be *tasteviné* – awarded the messy and hideous label of the Confrérie des Chevaliers du Tastevin) or Robert Armoreau of Château du Puy in AOC Bordeaux (whose wines are drunk at the French Assemblée Nationale). It isn't often that you get the chance to pay £20 for a plain Bordeaux Supérieur, but you can here on Château du Puy's 1970 ('now a little fragile'). Most of the German wines come from the prodigious Konrad Knodel, who must give up sleeping entirely during the harvest period in order to produce so many different wines from so many different areas. His wife Andrea is equally frantic designing all the bottle labels which, as the chatty list assures us and the reproduced example would seem to confirm, 'are always a talking point'. Other German wines include three from R & H Christ (what wonderful names organic growers have) in Franconia. Hungary, New York Finger Lakes, Sicily, Trentino-Alto Adige, New Zealand: in their twos and threes they come. You would have no difficulty, and probably a lot of fun, in mixing the obligatory case.

Best buys

Muscadet du Sèvre-et-Maine sur lie 1989, Guy Bossard, £3.99
Bacchus Brut, Bordeaux, bottle-fermented, £5.49
Hautes Côtes de Nuits 1986, Alain Verdet, Tasteviné, £10.95

For merchants who sell a minimum of twelve bottles, we say 'Case sales only' in the details at the head of an entry.

Pallant Wines ⛴

Apuldram Manor Farm, Appledram Lane, Chichester, West Sussex PO20 7PE	*Tel* (0243) 788475

Case sales only **Open** Mon–Sat 9.30–5; Sun, public holidays 10.30–1
Closed Chr Day, Boxing Day, 1 Jan **Credit cards** Access, Visa; personal and
business accounts **Discounts** Available **Delivery** Free within 15-mile radius of
Chichester (min 3 cases normally); elsewhere by arrangement **Glass hire** Free
with 1-case order **Tastings and talks** Saturday tastings throughout summer
season; to groups on request **Cellarage** Not available

If you're touring the countryside near Chichester in search of
Pallant Wines, look for the Spitfire parked outside. It forms part
of the 'Museum of D-Day Aviation' (open summer months only)
which faces the warehouse in which Pallant is housed, itself a
converted cowshed.

The list is not a large one, nor is it particularly adventurous. It
is, however, balanced, and the wines well chosen. The emphasis
is on France, with no one region looking particularly like a
speciality, but none inadequately represented either; the Loire
and Bordeaux offer best value. Germany and Italy have slightly
larger ranges than Spain, but don't overlook the wines from
Jumilla, Toro and Priorato in the latter. In Germany favour the
more expensive wines (especially the Nahe Rieslings of Paul
Anheuser), and in Italy the less well known names (the two
Umani Ronchi wines, for example, in preference to the Chianti
or the Frascati) . Bulgaria and Romania represent Eastern Europe
at Apuldram Manor Farm, and do so well; there are four
Chilean wines, and small but enjoyable selections from
Australia and New Zealand. Separate selections of organic and
dessert wines conclude the list. Mixing a case should not be
difficult, and you can indulge in an aeronautical fantasy or two
as you leave.

Best buys

Altos de Pio 1988, Jumilla, £3.74
Kreuznacher St Martin Halbtrocken 1988, Paul Anheuser, Nahe,
£4.56
Bourgueil 1988, Clos de la Henry, Morin, £4.25

We have tried to make the *1991 Which? Wine Guide* as comprehensive
as possible, but we should love to hear from you about any other wine
merchants you feel deserve an entry, or your comments on existing
entries. Write to us either by letter or using the report forms supplied
at the back of the book.

Pavilion Wine Company

Finsbury Circus Gardens, Finsbury Circus,   *Tel* 071-628 8224
London EC2M 7AB

Case sales only   **Open** Mon–Fri 9–8   **Closed** Sat, Sun, public holidays
Credit cards Access, American Express, Visa; personal and business accounts
Discounts 2.5% for 6–11 cases; 3.5% for 12–25 cases   **Delivery** Free on UK
mainland (min 3 cases); otherwise 1 case £6.90, 2 cases £3.45; mail order available
Glass hire Free with reasonable case order   **Tastings and talks** Not available
Cellarage £5.75 per case per year (inc insurance)

The managing director of the Pavilion Wine Company, David
Gilmour, began his career in the wine trade as cellarman for
Gerald Asher, and followed this with seventeen years' work as
managing director of Bow Wine Vaults, before making the move
to Finsbury Circus Gardens. Pavilion runs two wine bar/
restaurants in addition to the wholesale wine merchant
business, this last being aimed primarily at sales within the
trade rather than to the general public, to judge by the ex-VAT
list. Mixing cases is not permitted.

For most readers, therefore, the Pavilion Wine Company will
not be of great interest. The few readers who may be interested
are those who know they like any of the following:
Zind-Humbrecht's fine Alsace wines (David Gilmour was the
first UK importer of the single vineyard examples of these);
burgundies from a range of good growers in modest areas, such
as Hubert Lamy, Aubert and Patricia de Villaine or Philippe
Joliet; Rhône classics like Jaboulet's Cornas, Vieux Télégraphe's
or Beaucastel's Châteauneuf, or Guigal's Brune et Blonde Côte
Rôtie; fine dry white wines from the Loire; or Mas de Daumas
Gassac (again, David Gilmour claims to have been the first UK
importer of these). Prices for these wines are competitive –
providing you are prepared to buy twelve bottles of each. There
is also a small range of wines from California, Australia, Italy
and Spain, as well as a number of Vintage Ports, but the non-
mixing rule excludes experimental purchases of any of these.

Best buys

Alsace 'Marée' Edelzwicker 1988, Domaine Zind-Humbrecht
(case), £50.26
Bourgogne La Fortune 1986, A & P de Villaine (case), £75.50
Jasnières Clos Saint-Jacques 1986, Joël Gigou (case), £69.81

Why not club together with friends to enjoy volume discounts and
free delivery?

Thos Peatling

Head office
Westgate House, Bury St Edmunds, Suffolk   *Tel* (0284) 755948
IP33 1QS
33 branches throughout East Anglia (including Peatlings at Ostlers in London)

Open Hours vary from branch to branch   **Credit cards** Access, American Express, Visa; personal and business accounts   **Discounts** 5% on 1 case   **Delivery** Free in East Anglia (min 1 bottle); elsewhere 1 case £3.80, 2 cases £7.60, 3 cases £11, 4 cases £14.50, 5+ cases free; mail order available   **Glass hire** Free with appropriate case order   **Tastings and talks** Vary from shop to shop; to groups on request   **Cellarage** Free (under review as we went to press)

The Thos Peatling range continues to go from strength to strength – and we would include the range of shops as well as the range of wines in that statement. Many consumers regretted the disappearance of Ostlers, the Clerkenwell Australian/New World specialist, and the news that the premises had been acquired by a brewer would normally have been greeted with dismay. When it became known that the brewer was Greene King, owner of Thos Peatling, dismay turned into relief. And in this case relief became excitement when Peatling unveiled its plan to maintain the Ostler New World tradition by converting the premises into 'Peatlings Wine Centre', and by keeping on ex-Ostler Tony Keys as a part-time consultant. 'Peatlings Wine Centre' has got off to a good start, giving Londoners access both to Peatling's attractive list and to much of the best from Australia and California.

Mostly, of course, it's East Anglians who benefit from Peatling's range. The clarets are terrific, especially those *petits châteaux* imported and bottled by Peatling in Bury, climbing on the shelves in a state of maturity at under £10. But you'll also find plenty of classed growths, up to eagle's-nest heights: every first growth's 1984 is on this year's list, at between £29.99 and £39.95. Burgundy is a match for claret chez Peatling, most of it top small growers' wines. Hidden away in the Burgundy section of the list is a wonderful old photograph with a caption that will tell you what a velinche and a flogger were once used for under the quays of Kings Lynn.

Nearly every merchant in this *Guide* is proud of his or her 'own' champagne, and Peatling really have cause to be: the Brusson non-vintage is excellent, biscuity and concentrated. If you feel safer with a 'name', though, there are plenty to choose from. Other regions of France, Germany, Italy, Spain, Portugal and Eastern Europe are all given space to show what they can do; there are no conspicuous absentees here. The New World selection is already good, and looks set to improve further under traction from Clerkenwell.

Anyone who has visited Peatling's key shops will know that the standard of design, lighting and layout is as high as that achieved by any of Britain's chains; in this respect, for example, Peatling is far ahead of Oddbins, though Oddbins would probably retort that their customers like it chaotic. Peatling's list design reflects the contemporary, spacious elegance of the shops; like them, though, it proves to be well filled on close inspection. Free delivery of as little as one bottle within the delivery area is unusually attractive (though the list says that this is only for a minimum sale of £25); perhaps a natural development for Peatling would be to make the mail-order side of the service more attractive by providing free national delivery for somewhat less than the minimum five cases specified at present. But let's not hurry them: they've done very well so far.

Best buys

Château Le Monge 1985, Médoc, £4.29
Peatling's Australian White, non-vintage, £4.15
Château Meyney 1982, Saint-Estèphe, £11.29

Le Picoleur ☞

47 Kendal Street, London W2 2BU   *Tel* 071-402 6920

Open Mon–Fri 10–8; Sat 10–6 **Closed** Sun, public holidays
Credit cards Access, Visa; personal and business accounts **Discounts** 5–10% on 1 case **Delivery** Free in London (min 1 case); mail order available **Glass hire** Free with case order **Tastings and talks** To groups on request **Cellarage** Not available

This Bayswater shop, allied with Knightsbridge-sited La Réserve (*q.v.*), Fulham's Le Sac à Vin and Hampstead's Heath Street Wine Company (*q.v*), offers a choice range of good-to-fine wines. Bottles under £5 are very definitely in a minority here; a twenty-pound note, on the other hand, will buy you one or two well-chosen examples of European classicism or New Worldly endeavour.

The shop itself is good-looking, with its pine bins and racks, its banks of claret boxes displaying everything but claret, its neat price labels and its stuffed dog pretending to be a security camera. Just the sort of place to tempt a futures dealer, home from the City harvest, into parting with £105 for a magnum of Roederer Cristal 1982. Classed growth clarets from '82, '78 and '70, well-signed Burgundies from the generally generous '80s and a few lofty Rhônes might follow, while the fine selection of Sauternes would be hard to resist for dessert. If your daily toil has rewarded you less prodigiously, there are half a dozen good *petits châteaux* from 1986, 1985 and 1983, French country wines from La Vieille Ferme on the Rhône-Provence axis and from Domaine Sarda-Mallet way down west in Roussillon among others, a small selection from Italy, Spanish Riojas, and welcome representations from Germany, California, Australia and New Zealand vying for your custom. It would be hard to imagine 11 better sherries than those that shop manager Richard Brazier offers, while malt whisky, Armagnac, Cognac and Poland's fine vodkas will all help recycle further twenty-pound notes. Tasting facilities are not offered (though they are at La Réserve), but reductions on certain wines or certain regions are always in operation 'to encourage customers'. Encouraged? Write and tell us.

Best buys

Cépage Sauvignon 1989, Guy Saget, £3.25
Montepulciano d'Abruzzo 1988, Ronchi, £3.50
Château Musar 1981, Serge Hochar (Lebanon), £5.95

Pimlico Dozen

46 Tachbrook Street, London SW1V 2LX	*Tel* 071-834 3647
Associated outlets	
Cork Talk, 186 Trinity Road, London SW17 7HR	*Tel* 081-682 0054
Cork Talk, 519 Old York Road, London SW18 1TF	*Tel* 081-877 1908

Case sales only Open (Pimlico Dozen) Mon–Fri 10–7; Sat 10–6 (Cork Talk); Mon–Sat 11–9; Sun 12–3 **Closed** Sun, public holidays **Credit cards** Access, Visa; business accounts **Discounts** Not available **Delivery** Free in inner London (min 1 case); elsewhere charges variable **Glass hire** Free with 1-case order **Tastings and talks** Annual in-store tasting **Cellarage** £4.50 per case per year (min 3 cases)

Pimlico Dozen continues as a warehouse selling in 12-bottle quantities in Tachbrook Street, but during the last year two retail outlets have been opened in Wandsworth, both called Cork Talk (wine merchants are beginning to show the same desperation as hairdressers to find memorably meaningless names for their businesses). We assume the Cork Talks draw on the Dozen's list.

Which is a sound but unexciting one. Look at French country wines, for example: there are about 18, where one would want at least two dozen from a warehouse. Many producers' names are missing. There are good wines like Domaine Saint-André from Gascogne, the K de Krevel Montravel (though at £6.60 this isn't really a country wine in price) or the Caves Berticot wines from the Côtes de Duras; but in other places – Provence, for example – a single and rather dull offering fails its region.

This is Pimlico, however, so perhaps we should have looked at the clarets first. There are around eight listed from 1986 and 1985, trailing away through earlier vintages (though that is where most of the classed growths are, should you want to mix those into your dozen). Burgundy has been the subject of some effort, too, with a good spread of producers; and there are champagnes for all tastes (with the very lovely Henriot Blanc de Blancs at over £1.50 less than at Victoria Wine as we write). The Rhône, the Loire and – especially – Alsace are rather abbreviated.

The Spanish section is sound, though it breaks no new ground; Italian wines, by contrast, seem to excite manager Richard Veale and his colleagues, or whoever does the buying for the Dozen, into a little modest innovation (Bucci's oak-aged Verdicchio; the inexpensive Cabernet/Sangiovese Rugo; a Rosso di Montalcino – though we don't know whose; and Torre Ercolana, a Cesanese-Cabernet-Merlot blend from Bruno Colacicchi in Lazio). German wines look terrible; the fact that the list describes Bairrada as being a 'Firm cedary red from the Douro' doesn't inspire confidence; and the New World sections again seem shorter than a warehouse's premises would warrant, Chile excepted. More reports, please, on both Dozen and Cork Talk.

Best buys

Cousiño Macul Antiguas Reservas 1982 Cabernet Sauvignon, Chile, £5.25
Château Cayla 1987, Bordeaux Blanc (oak-aged), £4.25
Côtes de Duras Merlot 1989, Caves Berticot, £3.20

Christopher Piper Wines

1 Silver Street, Ottery St Mary, Devon   *Tel* (0404) 814139/812197
EX11 1DB

Open Mon–Fri 9–1, 2–6; Sat 9–1, 2.30–6 **Closed** Sun, public holidays
Credit cards Access, Visa; personal and business accounts **Discounts** 5% on 1 mixed case, 10% on 3 mixed cases **Delivery** Free in South-West (min 4 cases) and rest of UK (min 6 cases); otherwise £6.90 per consignment; mail order available
Glass hire Free **Tastings and talks** In-store tastings three times a month; three main tastings annually; to groups on request **Cellarage** £3.60 per case per year

---

Quite a number of merchants in this *Guide* have Masters of Wine on their staff, but there aren't many whose chairman has a degree in oenology from Bordeaux University. Yet such is the case with Chris Piper, and he still keeps his hand in by making

529

the wine every year at Château des Tours in Brouilly (you can buy the results in half-bottles, bottles, magnums, jeroboams and salmanazars). Furthermore, we are told, 'Chris Piper's experience as an oenologist and grower in France gives the company entrées which others might not have.'

Entrées or no entrées, this is certainly a very fine merchant for Burgundy and Beaujolais, for Bordeaux (white as well as red), for the Rhône, for the Loire and for French country wines. If we had to pick out just one of these areas for distinction, it would be Burgundy and Beaujolais combined, where this is one of the best lists in the country. Wines from everywhere else – Germany, Italy, Spain, Portugal, Australia, New Zealand and North America – are sourced, let's say, responsibly: the ranges are not large or original, but all the producers have proven reputations, and you are unlikely to take home a duff bottle with Prüm or Bürklin-Wolf or Tollo or CVNE or Tyrrells or Mondavi on the label.

If you are a half-bottle hunter, you won't know where to begin here: there are enough to furnish a respectable cellar on their own. And Piper faithfuls are given plenty more to do than simply lug home purchases: in addition to tastings and wine weekends, there is also an annual French jaunt (for a maximum of 40 persons) to go and see some of the company's suppliers.

Best buys

Morgon, Domaine Jean Descombes, £6.77
Mainzer Domherr Bacchus Kabinett 1989, Louis Guntrum, Rheinhessen, £4.16
Côtes du Rhône 1988, Château de Saint-Georges, £3.99

Premier Wine Warehouse

3 Heathmans Road, London SW6 4TJ   *Tel* 071-736 9073

Case sales only **Open** Mon–Fri 11–8; Sat 10–6; Sun 11–4 **Closed** Public holidays **Credit cards** Access, Visa; business accounts **Discounts** Negotiable **Delivery** Free within 3-mile radius (min 1 case); elsewhere at cost; mail order available **Glass hire** Free with 1-case order **Tastings and talks** Tasting held in-store every two months (20–30 wines); to groups on request **Cellarage** Not available

This solo wine warehouse at Fulham's Parsons Green has French and Spanish sections that offer you plenty of choice, and that include many good well-known and less well-known wines. Australia comes third, in terms of seriousness of treatment, and Italy fourth, by which time the range is down to ten bottles – though each, it should be said, is well chosen, and each has a story to tell. Portugal is inadequate, with two bottles only, even if they are good 'uns; and Germany woefully so, with a Niersteiner Gutes Domtal and a Piesporter Michelsberg trying to represent their country like beer-heavy football fans panting around the field, five minutes behind the ball, in an international eleven. North America is altogether elsewhere, though there are four wines from Chile. The small fine-wine range, too, sticks to France and Spain.

Within France and Spain, at least half the wines are under £5, though there are glamour bottles (notably Guigal's Rhônes, big old Rioja from Muga and Lopez de Heredia, and Pesquera and Vega Sicilia) at well over that. Toro, Jumilla, Almansa, petit château claret and the fine sherries of Valdespino, Williams & Humbert and Barbadillo provide the best value. Make your party a tapas party, and serve chilled fino throughout: with Pando, Solear and Inocente to hand, you have three of incomparable quality. Mixed cases ask to be larded with big Australians from Rosemount and Lindemans; Yarra Yering, too, if you can afford it. And Coopers Creek offers a new twist to the magnificent (and still unfolding) tale of New Zealand's Sauvignon Blancs. Good beers, as well. The proprietors claim 'over 50 years of wine knowledge and trade experience between them – and neither approaching senility!' Test this by asking 'Which wine in your warehouse stands head and shoulders above all the rest for concentration of flavour?' If the answer is anything but 'Coliseo', treat their claim with suspicion.

Best buys

Colegiata 1985, Toro, Bodegas Fariñas, £3.49
Domaine de Montmarin 1989, Vin de Pays des Côtes de Thongue (white, Marsanne variety), £2.99
Coliseo, Very Old Amontillado, Valdespino, £16

Pugsons Food and Wine

Cliff House, 6 Terrace Road, Buxton,   *Tel* (0298) 77696
Derbyshire SK17 6DR

Open Mon–Sat 9–5.30; Sun 11–5 **Closed** Chr Day, Boxing Day, Sun from 1 Jan to 1 April **Credit cards** Access, Visa; personal and business accounts
Discounts 5% on 1 case **Delivery** Free locally (min 1 case or with groceries); otherwise at cost; mail order available **Glass hire** Free with 1-case order
Tastings and talks Series of tastings during Buxton Festival, annual tasting and through Buxton Gastronomes; to groups on request **Cellarage** £5.60 per case per year

---

This enterprising Buxton shop specialises in both wine and cheese – and carries a range of other food items, too. The list covers all of these, from House Plonque at £2.25 a bottle to 1 oz

Pugsons

packets of sea salt with basil from Provence for pasta, by way of
honey, oil, mustard, vinegar, coffee, ox tongue in jelly, Fourme
d'Ambert, Morbier, Reblochon, Cornish Yarg, Mrs Kirkham's
Farmhouse Lancashire . . . and some wonderful old photographs
and woodcuts. What a shame that wine is not seen more often
in this, its natural context. The list has a wholeness to it; it is
also enormously informative and entertaining, with almost
every item annotated and with interesting section introductions.
Highly recommended.

The wine selection is not large, but it is intelligent. Most of it
is French; there are then two or three wines from other wine-
producing countries, with Chile – seven wines – the largest
after France. There are wines in each price bracket, from £3 to
£30 or more; a mini-collection of 'second wines', too, with the
seldom-seen Château la Candale from d'Issan and Domaine de
Fontarney from Brane-Cantenac rubbing shoulders with
Connétable Talbot, Bahans Haut Brion and Clos du Marquis. In
Burgundy, there is Marsannay in three colours, and Pommard
Clos des Epenaux from Comte Armand's domain, where partner
Peter Pugson helped harvest the grapes in 1971 (the vintage at

present on sale is 1982). Saget provides most of the Loire section, and there is a good range of champagnes, from 'House' and de Hostomme through De Castellane, Clicquot and Roederer to Krug. Whether you're hungry or thirsty – or simply curious – this shop would be well worth a visit.

Best buys

Château Pitray 1986, Côtes du Castillon, £5.75
Villa Montes, Sauvignon Blanc 1988, Chile, £4.20
Domaine de Fontarney 1983, Margaux, £9.50

Arthur Purchase & Son

31 North Street, Chichester, West Sussex   *Tel* (0243) 783144
PO19 1LY

Open Mon–Sat 9–5.30 **Closed** Sun, public holidays **Credit cards** Access, Visa; personal and business accounts **Discounts** 5% on 1 mixed case of wine **Delivery** Free within 60-mile radius of Chichester (wholesale only); otherwise 75p within Chichester, £1.50 outside Chichester; mail order available **Glass hire** Free with reasonable case order **Tastings and talks** Regular wine of the week tastings; to groups on request **Cellarage** £2.88 per case per year

Arthur Purchase & Son believes that it is 'the oldest surviving wine merchants in the country with an unbroken family history of control'. The first Purchase made the first sale in 1780 (he was Stephen; Arthur came later), and this Chichester business is now run by Christopher Purchase, a sixth-generation descendant.

A sense of history is probably one of the main draws here, for the list is neither long nor ambitious. However, there are good bottles to be had: the five fino sherries are among the best of those available; Saget's Loire wines are always a pleasure, while the Muscat José Sala is one of the cheapest of wine treats, wherever it is stocked; the modest claret range contains bottles for every pocket, with a welcome emphasis on Saint-Emilion and Côtes de Castillon; Nutbourne Manor (is it the Bacchus?) has produced lovely wines in the past: the vineyard is for sale as we write, but we hope it will continue in the same vein. The wonderful but expensive Penfolds Bin 707 is a bolder offering. The list is spare with producers' names, and this makes the Burgundy and German sections, in particular, difficult to gauge. Would Chichester readers write with their impressions of the Purchase service?

Send us your views on the report forms at the back of the book.

Best buys

Château de Fayolle 1986, Bergerac, £4.05
Pinot Grigio 1989, Cavit, £3.97
Fino Inocente, Valdespino, £5.82

Arthur Rackhams

Head office and cellars

Winefare House, 5 High Road, Byfleet,	*Tel* (09323) 51585
Surrey KT14 7QF	
The Vintner, 66 Kensington Church Street,	*Tel* 071-229 2629
London W8 4BY	
Le Viticulteur, 391 King's Road, London	*Tel* 071-352 6340
SW10 0LP	

12 branches in London and Surrey

Open Some outlets Mon–Sat 10–6; Sun, public holidays 12–2; other outlets
Mon–Sat 10–10; Sun, public holidays 7–9 **Credit cards** Access, Visa; personal and
business accounts **Discounts** Members' Club discount (The Vintner Wine Club)
Delivery Free on UK mainland (min 5 cases) for wine club; mail order available
for wine club **Glass hire** Free **Tastings and talks** Tastings in-store every
weekend; tastings through club; to groups on request **Cellarage** Not available

This unusual wine merchant defies categorisation. At first
glance, it appears to be a chain of 14 superior off-licences
scattered around the wealthier pockets of London and Surrey.
Look a little closer, and you discover a nascent specialist in
growers' wines from France and Spain. Look closer still, and
you find a wine club ostensibly aimed at mail-order customers
all over mainland Britain. If trade customers and restaurateurs
take a look, they'll discover an expanding agency business
based on the products of those small growers. A final piece of
trend-bucking lies in the Rackham family's continuing
ownership of the company that bears their name.

The off-licences are called Arthur Rackhams, and they carry a
well-balanced range of wines from most of the world's wine-
producing countries. The most exciting area is France, and
within France the champagne range, with which Arthur
Rackham has always been associated, is as wide as ever. You
will also notice shelves bearing the legend 'Viticulteur': this
marks a collection of wines researched for Arthur Rackhams by
Stanislas Rynkowski, a French teacher of Polish extraction who
complements work in a London comprehensive with perhaps
more rewarding cultural exchanges on France's wine routes. The
resulting collection of growers' wines from all the leading
French regions is high in quality, and well worth browsing
through, though we hope James Rackham will let
Mr Rynkowski provide the Viticulteur list with its accents for

future editions: Pouilly Fume and Macon Fuisse will not help francophile Anglophones sound intelligible in France.

Viticulteur has been joined during the last year by Bodega, a similar initiative using the Spanish skills and experience of Sarah McWatters: Loxarel Cavas, Bodegas Valduero from Ribera del Duero, Bodegas Parxet from little Alella, Bodegas Vicente Malumbres from Navarra, and some of the most ambitious wines yet seen in the UK from two leading La Mancha bodegas feature in the initial collection. Will 1991 bring us Fattoria at Rackhams?

Then comes The Vintner Wine Club. There is a sizeable membership fee of £14, 'payable by continuous credit card authority', and if you buy fewer than five cases at a time you will have to pay £3.50 per case delivery charges for the mail-order service. These conditions must be something of a deterrent to most potential mail-order customers. However, membership does entitle you to approximately seven per cent off the (fairly steep) list prices, even if you just stroll into a shop and buy one bottle; it also gives you the chance to attend two tasting festivals and an annual dinner, suggesting that the club is probably aimed at shop regulars. If you're not a regular, finally, but you have a Rackhams near you, go in and ask for as much advice as you feel you might need. Arthur Rackhams was the first wine merchant ever to receive the government-sponsored National Training Award for excellence in training, so sound advice should be something you can count on here. Write and let us know how you get on.

Best buys

Alsace Grand Cru Bruderthal 1988/9, Gewürztraminer, Domaine Gérard Neumeyer, £6.65
Côte de Nuits-Villages 1985, Domaine Gérard Julien, £10.45
Brut Champagne, Jacky Charpentier, £11.89

Raeburn Fine Wines and Foods

23 Comely Bank Road, Edinburgh EH4 1DS   *Tel* 031-332 5166

Open Mon–Sat 9–7; Sun 10–6 (not open for alcoholic drinks on Sun)
Credit cards None accepted; business accounts   **Discounts** 5% on unmixed cases,
2.5% on mixed cases; large quantities negotiable   **Delivery** Free in Edinburgh
(min 1 case); elsewhere negotiable; mail order available   **Glass hire** Free with
wine order   **Tastings and talks** To groups on request   **Cellarage** £3.95 per case
per year (under bond only)

What with Peter Green, Valvona & Crolla, J E Hogg, Justerini & Brooks – and the extraordinary Raeburn Fine Wines and Foods, as well as Oddbins and most of the big supermarkets and chains, Edinburgh must be the best place in Britain to buy wine. We would include London in the runners-up because, although you can buy just about everything somewhere in the capital, it would take days to research and command or collect it, thanks to the distances involved, lamentable public transport and traffic-choked roads. Edinburgh has the virtue of being considerably smaller. Some would argue for Bristol's supremacy, but our own view is that Bristol's merchants trade rather heavily on the past, whereas Edinburgh's leading independents – and Zubair Mohamed of Raeburn is a perfect example – trade on an enthusiasm that will blow your spectacles off at fifty paces.

If they haven't been knocked off already, that is, by the jungle of wines and wine boxes, often topped by the parental line in floristry, that packs this tiny grocery shop in the irresistibly named Comely Bank Road. Couldn't some bibulous Edinburgh benefactor provide the wherewithal to set Zubair Mohamed up in the retailing style which he deserves? At present, this must be the most unpromisingly housed of Britain's leading wine merchants (much of its stock isn't on the premises), while anyone who is serious about wanting to get at the pet foods or cereals may need to spend the best part of an hour playing weightlifter's draughts with cases of wine and whisky on what remains of the floor space.

Never mind the premises, look at the list. Zubair Mohamed seems to keep his ear close to the ground – or nose in the wind, we're not sure what the best metaphor would be – and every producer listed is one that bottles exciting wines. The list isn't as extensive as Peter Green's or D Byrne's, to take two of the most outstanding examples in the *Guide*, but it is very well researched and targeted. Twelve Vouvrays from Huet, for example: that's the kind of coverage that a producer of his calibre deserves, and Zubair Mohamed isn't afraid to list something as extraordinary as Huet's 1969 Pétillant if he thinks it merits it (as an 'amazing drinking experience'). *Ibid.* for Rolly Gassmann in Rorschwihr: Raeburn stocks 21 examples. The principle is the same in Bordeaux, Burgundy and the Rhône, though the number of producers listed is wider as there is more to chose from; and the same throughout France, which forms the core of the list. Of the range outside France, Germany and Australia seem to have aroused the most proprietorial curiosity – or the greatest customer demand. Zubair Mohamed has worked hard at unearthing treasures from the smaller Australian wineries (Moss Wood, Cape Mentelle, Redgate, Seville Estate, Balgownie, Brokenwood) rather than taking easy options from the big fellows – easier than ever with Australia as the general standard is so high. Germany looks classic and firmly anchored in quality, with almost everything selling at between £4.95 and

£7.95 – the price zone in which this country has so much to offer.

When Raeburn is able to get its teeth firmly into Italy, the results will be superb; a good start has been made, with seven Quintarellis, Monsanto's Chianti and Il Poggione's Brunello and Rosso di Montalcino. Spain, California and New Zealand are bell-sound, but cautious (or unaccommodatable); and there's nothing yet from Portugal. As Raeburn has increased its proportion of directly imported wines, it is building up a fine range of half-bottles, and this must be the only florist in the country making *en primeur* offers, let alone *en primeur* offers of depth. The direct importing results in some good prices, too. Don't leave Edinburgh without making your way (it may be circuitously) here.

Best buys

Château les Ollieux 1988, Corbières, £4.35
Alsace Sylvaner Réserve 1987, Rolly Gassmann, £4.95
Saint-Joseph, Clos de l'Arbalestrier 1985, Emile Florentin (red), £8.95

Ravensbourne Wine Co

6.1.13 Bell House, 49 Greenwich High Road, London SE10 8JL

Tel 081-692 9655

Case sales only **Open** Mon–Fri 9–5; Sat 10–2 **Closed** Sun, public holidays **Credit cards** None accepted; business accounts **Discounts** Variable **Delivery** Free in Greater London and surrounding boroughs (min 1 case); elsewhere charges negotiable; mail order available **Glass hire** Free with 1-case order **Tastings and talks** Spring-summer/winter tasting by invitation to launch new list; to groups on request **Cellarage** Not available

---

Terence Short and Stephen Williams founded the Ravensbourne Wine Company on Christmas Eve 1986, which made its first two days of existence days off, and the first month of trading, we'd imagine, pretty slow. However, they have been gathering speed ever since, and they now offer Londoners, particularly the neglected ones living in the south-east quarter of the metropolis, an enterprising and unusual range of wines to chose from. Many are organic; all are presented with pride and enthusiasm, two qualities that shine out of the discursive (both directors are from South Wales) list. Eighteen years of combined experience with Oddbins has given them a nose for the unusual, especially when it's inexpensive as well, and the Greenwich premises have the chaotic, recently unpacked look familiar to all Oddbins regulars.

Sales are, however, by-the-case. There is enough variety on

the list to make mixing one unproblematic, and the 'free London doorstep delivery service' means that cyclists and the car-less are in no manner discriminated against. There are wines from most parts of France, with perhaps the most interesting selections coming from Provence, Languedoc-Roussillon and the South-West, described by Williams and Short as 'the "Rip Van Winkle" section of the list' ('sleepy backwaters . . . previously ignored . . . sadly neglected . . .THE TRANQUIL RUSTIC MAGIC THAT IS RURAL FRANCE'). The Provençal wines of Domaine du Jas d'Esclans are justly crowed over; there is something from Tursan, an appellation still seldom seen in Britain; and the fine Jurançon Sec of Domaine Cauhapé is by now a magic name for many.

Italy, Spain and Portugal are each enthusiastically stocked; Germany at present is a disappointment. Consolation comes in the form of a big Bulgarian range, from the party-fodder country wines up to the serious reserve, premium and controliran wines. America, Chile, Australia and New Zealand are each present with between six and twelve wines. English wines enjoy support from Ravensbourne, and Wales's three vineyards are all patriotically listed, albeit on a bin-end basis. Barbadillo's sherries, Feuerheerd's ports and Henriques & Henriques' Madeiras complete the list, though the recurrent invitation to lob a request at Short and Williams is repeated with more than usual insistence concerning other houses' Vintage Ports. Schutz Jubilator, Rolling Rock, Gambrinus, Pitfield Dark Star and friends form a beery epilogue.

A 'genuine, caring, personal service that only a bespoke, independent vintner can provide' is claimed, and we read that all wines 'are regularly presented to a large number of customer tasting groups for evaluation and critical appraisal'. This sounds admirable: could readers confirm?

Best buys

Domaine de Luch Merlot 1989, Vin de Pays de l'Hérault, £2.79
Château Belair 1989, Bergerac, £2.89
Peter Lehmann, Shiraz 1986, Barossa, £4.75

Wine in bag-in-box ages and spoils quicker than in bottle. If you buy boxes, buy and drink up one box before you buy the next. Boxes in the storecupboard will lose their freshness. Used or unopened, a wine box will keep better if you store it tap downwards, keeping wine, not air, in the valve.

Reid Wines

| The Mill, Marsh Lane, Hallatrow, Nr Bristol, Avon BS18 5EB | *Tel* (0761) 52645 |
| Reid Wines Warehouse, Unit 2, Block 3, Vestry Trading Estate, Otford Road, Sevenoaks, Kent TN14 5EL | *Tel* (0732) 458533 |

Open (Hallatrow) Mon–Fri 9.30–5.30; (Sevenoaks – credit cards only accepted here)) Mon–Fri 10–6; Sat 10–1 **Closed** Sun and public holidays (Sevenoaks) **Credit cards** Access, Visa; personal and business accounts **Discounts** 5% (min £250) at Sevenoaks only **Delivery** Free in central London and within 25 miles of Hallatrow and Sevenoaks (min 1 case); elsewhere at cost; mail order available **Glass hire** Free with 1-case order **Tastings and talks** Monthly tastings at Sevenoaks; to groups on request **Cellarage** 15.50 per case per year

Reid Wines' list is the oenophile's equivalent of the antiquarian bookseller's list: much that is curious and much that is fine is noted down carefully and accurately, even if stocks run to one half-bottle only; the whole is larded with quotations that divert your attention from the rather high ex-VAT prices; and almost anything that a buff might require to satisfy the highways and byways of an exotic palate are here.

We applaud the candid approach of the notes. 'Latour is rather weak, due to over-production,' we read of a bottle of the 1953, price £138. 'Still no one has bought Michael Broadbent's desert-island magnum of Romanée-Conti 1966. Can it be too expensive?' It costs £747.50: you decide. 'Still here, regrettably' is noted of the 1977 Château Grillet at £32.78. And if you're 37 in 1991, you will hardly want to celebrate with the bottle of Nicolas Meursault of your birth year (£51.75). 'Very little of any merit came out of 1954,' is the mortifying verdict. Honesty of this sort inclines us to believe Messrs Reid when, with evident reluctance, they finally get round to noting 'Extremely fine' or 'Outstanding'.

The list isn't just of interest to connoisseurs of the fine and the rare. Bill Baker and Simon Wood have explored Italy, California, Australia and New Zealand with thoroughness, and their trophies are all worth bringing home and hanging in the list. Sherry, port and Madeira are done justice, and among the less classic regions of France, Alsace is mouthwatering. It would be nice to see more from Germany, and more fine old Chenin Blanc from the Loire, but no doubt such wines are absent in quantity because Reid's customers don't request them as often as they might. Spirits, too, are fine, with plenty of venerable Cognacs and a fistful of Armagnacs; Reid is probably the only merchant in the country who can supply a *tour de France* of marcs, though the offer of a magnum only for the Rhône's is puzzling. And if Reid really want to offer the best of everything, we recommend the replacement of the (good) Sandeman sherry vinegar with the (fine) Valdespino version.

Best buys

Puligny-Montrachet les Perrières 1986, Carillon, £25.58
Cornas Coteau 1985, Michel, £9.77
Redwood Valley Late Harvest Rhine Riesling (New Zealand, half-bottle), £6.26

La Reserva Wines

SPANISH SPECIALIST OF THE YEAR **1991**

Unit 6, Spring Grove Mills, Manchester Road, Linthwaite, Huddersfield, West Yorkshire HD7 5QG	*Tel* (0484) 846732
Associated outlet	
Grapehop, 17 Imperial Arcade, Huddersfield, West Yorkshire HD1 2BR	*Tel* (0484) 533509

Open Mon–Fri 9–5.30; Sat 9–6 **Closed** Sun, Chr and New Year
Credit cards Access, Visa; personal and business accounts **Discounts** 10% on 1 mixed case **Delivery** Free within 25-mile radius (min 1 case locally); elsewhere 3–5 cases £6; mail order available **Glass hire** Free with 1-case order
Tastings and talks Regular tastings by invitation; to groups on request
Cellarage Not available

In Huddersfield, a homage to Spain. Travel to La Reserva's shop and tasting room and not only will you find one of Britain's best selections of Spanish wines, but also white walls, dark wood and stone flags – premises that look like nothing so much as a quiet bar between Seville and Jerez. 'I'm always happy to talk about Spain and the Spanish scene,' says Keith Gomersall. Only the understatement is British here.

The list talks for hours about Spain. There are Riojas of all ages from no fewer than 26 different bodegas, and the Navarra and Penedés selections are proportionately exhaustive. The three Galician whites put La Reserva firmly in the avant-garde; indeed, there are few DOs that La Reserva doesn't represent, which is quite an achievement, given the speed with which Spain has minted these over the last few years. If you can't afford the Ribera del Duero wines of either Vega Sicilia or Pesquera (prices start at £11.99 for Pesquera's Tinto Especial 1987), then there are options to consider from Peñalba Lopez, Ismael Arroyo and Valduero, with the latter's Tinto '87 setting you back only £4.99. Seven different cava producers provide both cause and means for celebration, and the selection of sherries is superb, with only Valdespino and Gonzalez Byass conspicuous by their absence. The Victoria Regina and Fino Imperial from Diez Hermanos will raise West Yorkshire eyebrows for their prices (£20.40 and £19.99 respectively), but if you try them you'll find they are worth every penny, and are concentrated enough to raise the dead, eyebrows included.

The Spanish selection is so good that you'd forgive La Reserva even if they stocked nothing else; but they also have truly impressive ranges from Australia, New Zealand, Chile and Portugal, while Italy and Germany are very sound, too. And France? There is a well-selected range from Bordeaux and adequate choice from the other regions, with nine wines from the Jura making a welcome appearance. Call in on Saturdays and you'll always have something to taste. And plenty to talk about.

Best buys

Marius 1982, Bodegas Piqueras, Almansa, £3.99
Montesinos 1982, Bodegas Bleda, Jumilla, £2.99
Moss Wood 1987 Cabernet Sauvignon, Margaret River, £10.99

La Réserve

56 Walton Street, London SW3 1RB	*Tel* 071-589 2020
Le Picoleur, 47 Kendal Street, London W2 2BU	*Tel* 071-402 6920
Le Sac à Vin, 203 Munster Road, London SW6 6BX	*Tel* 071-381 6930
The Heath Street Wine Co, 29 Heath Street, London NW3 6TR	*Tel* 071-435 6845

Open Mon–Fri (SW3) 9.30–8, (W2) 10–8, (SW6) 12–9.30, (NW3) 10–8; Sat (SW3) 9.30–6, (W2) 10–6, (SW6) 12–9.30, (NW3) 10–8; Sun (SW6) 12–2, 7–9
Closed Sun (SW3, W2, NW3), public holidays **Credit cards** Access, Visa; personal and business accounts **Discounts** 5% on 1 case **Delivery** Free in London (min 1 bottle); otherwise £6.50 per case; mail order available
Glass hire Free with order **Tastings and talks** Regular programme of tastings; to groups on request **Cellarage** Not available

---

This shop, in one of the Knightsbridge/South Kensington area's prettiest streets, seems to be the senior member of Mark Reynier Fine Wines' team of four London shops (the other three are Le Picoleur *q.v.*, Le Sac à Vin and The Heath Street Wine Company *q.v.*). In addition to furnishing locals with smart wines at £3.50 and up, La Réserve also doubles as a fine wine merchant, with a 'Rare and Unique Selection' approaching 200 bottles. The wines on both lists are well chosen and, while you will probably be able to better the prices by hunting high and low, nothing is well in excess of market levels, and there aren't so many places, even in London, where you can nip out and buy a bottle of 1961 Yquem at 7.45 on a Thursday evening.

Taking the two lists together, Burgundy is a major strength, and an opening offer of the 1988 wines of Rousseau, de Vogüé and Bonneau du Martray was made during 1990. Bordeaux and Sauternes, and champagne, are certainly up to the neighbourhood's requirements; other areas of France, California, Australia and New Zealand will tempt local young Turks with £5 to £15 to spend. Directors Simon Coughlin and Mark Reynier also offer cleverly themed, tutored tastings: you could have attempted to answer the question 'Which is the best château in Saint-Julien?' with Brian Chadwick on 21 March 1990 for £30, while £45 would have taken you up the north face of Dom Pérignon on 2 May, via a vertical tasting with the rope tied to Don Hewitson. Don Gonzalo, Tio Diego and Inocente – all sherries from Valdespino – offer more intensity of flavour per penny than anything else in La Réserve.

Best buys

Don Gonzalo Old Dry Oloroso, Valdespino, £7.10
Givry 1987, Gérard Mouton, £7.95
Savennières 1988, Clos Saint-Yves, Jean Baumard, £6.50

Reynier Wine Library

See Eldridge Pope. *Tel* 071-435 6845

Richmond Wine Warehouse

138C Lower Mortlake Road, Richmond, *Tel* 081-948 4196
Surrey TW9 2JZ

Case sales only Open Mon–Sat 10–7 **Closed** Sun, public holidays
Credit cards Access, Visa; personal and business accounts
Discounts Negotiable **Delivery** Free locally (min 1 case); otherwise at cost
Glass hire Free with 1-case order **Tastings and talks** Every Saturday in-store; to groups on request **Cellarage** Available

The last year has seen a move across the car park for Richmond Wine Warehouse, to a larger, lighter building, but otherwise everything is much as before. A journey to Lower Mortlake Road puts you in touch with a French-based list of wines of a quality (and price) level a notch or two above that of most wine warehouses, with a particularly good selection of classed-growth and *cru bourgeois* clarets. There is plenty of burgundy, too, though this area is primarily sourced through négociants rather than growers, and deft selections from the French regions, and from Italy, Spain, Australia and California, provide infantry support.

Portugal is weak, though, and Germany is weaker: this part of the warehouse most definitely needs a clean sweep for next year. It would be nice, too, to see a more ambitious range of sherries. The De Souza ports (from the Barros Almeida group) are worth trying, though experiment with the two colheitas (listed as 'wood port': 1978 at £8.90, 1967 at £13.75) before the marginally overpriced LBV and Vintage Ports.

En primeur offers are made when Stephen Addy feels the time is right (as he did with 1989 Bordeaux); and there are tastings every Saturday based on a regional theme, with suppliers present whenever possible.

Best buys

Château Puyfromage 1986, Bordeaux Supérieur, £4.15
Château de la Coustarelle 1986, Cahors, £3.99
Domaine de Richard, Saussignac, £5.76

Howard Ripley

35 Eversley Crescent, London N21 1EL   *Tel* 081-360 8904
Mainly mail order

Case sales only   **Open** Mon–Sat 9–10; Sun, public holidays 9–12
Credit cards None accepted; business accounts   **Discounts** Not available
Delivery Free in London postal districts (min 4 cases); otherwise at cost; mail order available   **Glass hire** Free with 4-case order   **Tastings and talks** Every Wednesday lunchtime (by invitation only); to groups on request   **Cellarage** Not available

---

Howard Ripley is a practising dentist with a long-standing, high-profile addiction to burgundy. In 1983 he made the transition from enthusiast to merchant – without, it should be added, losing any of his enthusiasm along the way. A cellar fire left him undeterred, and his list increases in strength from year to year.

Burgundy, more than any other of the world's wine regions, needs Ripleys. It needs, in other words, passionate, persistent specialists prepared to return obsessively to the temple, to search high and low there for the sapid and the authentic, and then to return to their own lands to preach, prophesy and convert the sceptical and the agnostic.

Take novelist Julian Barnes, for example. 'I've drunk so much junk trying to crack burgundy that I've given up,' he wrote last year, and many would echo that. Contact Ripley. Arrange a visit to 35 Eversley Crescent (don't forget to bring £200). Enjoy a glass or two of wine, cheese and biscuits, and an unhurried discussion with the prophet. Return home with your purchases, drink them, and only then pass final judgment on the region. If the wines of Ampeau, Sauzet, Bize, Dujac, Lafarge, Mugnier, Bonneau du Martray and a re-nascent Domaine René Engel fail

543

to move you, then – burgundy-wise – you are a lost soul, beyond redemption.

Best buys

Hautes Côtes de Beaune 1986, Cornu, £6.90
Volnay Premier Cru 1987, Michel Lafarge, £18.40
Corton-Charlemagne 1985, Bonneau du Martray, £36.80

Rodgers Fine Wines ⚐

Not a shop
37 Ben Bank Road, Silkstone Common,   *Tel* (0226) 790794
Barnsley, South Yorkshire S75 4PE

Case sales only   Open By appointment (answerphone available for orders)
Credit cards Access; personal and business accounts   **Discounts** Not available
Delivery Free nationwide (min 1 case); mail order available   **Glass hire** Available
with charge   **Tastings and talks** To groups on request   **Cellarage** Not available

David Rodgers is an ex-British Coal surface superintendent, and not the only merchant in this *Guide* whose change of profession came about through back injury. A commitment to fine German wines, indeed, is almost more unusual, and is certainly more welcome.

The business is still a young one; its aim is to seek out fine wines from small domains in Germany not otherwise or seldom imported to Britain; four, including the strictly organic wines of Weingut Haus Thiel in the Rheinhessen, have been gathered into the Rodgers fold so far. Quite sensibly, Mr Rodgers has realised that the market for such a specialised business must be nationwide rather than Barnsleywide, and so free delivery anywhere in the UK is offered (cases only, but they may be mixed). Mr Rodgers is also prepared to give tastings and talks anywhere in Britain, on any day of the week, at any time of day. There is commitment and enthusiasm here! Wines from a wide range of grape varieties made in a wide variety of styles mean that an interesting tasting case could be assembled without any difficulty, and connoisseurs should note that the rarer dessert wines are well represented, including a red Eiswein and a Trockenbeerenauslese Riesling Strohwein. We hope to read reports from customers of Rodgers Fine Wines over the next twelve months.

See the back of the Guide if you would like to help the Wine
Development Board with their Wine in Pubs campaign.

Best buys

Uffhofer Pfaffenberg Silvaner 1986, Kabinett Trocken, Weingut
Haus Thiel, Rheinhessen, £5.13
Horrweiler Gewürzgartchen Spätburgunder Weissherbst 1987,
Halbtrocken, Weingut Herbert Polzer & Sohn, Rheinhessen
(rosé), £4.99
Windesheimer Rosenberg Kerner 1986, Spätlese, Weingut
Schmidt Kunz, Nahe, £7.79

C A Rookes

Unit 7, Western Road Industrial Estate,   *Tel* (0789) 297777
Stratford upon Avon, Warwickshire
CV37 0AH

Open Mon–Fri 9–6; Sat 9–2 **Closed** Sun, public holidays **Credit cards** Access,
Visa; personal and business accounts **Discounts** Not available **Delivery** Free
within van delivery area (no min); elsewhere at cost; mail order available
Glass hire Free with order **Tastings and talks** Wines always available in-store
for tasting; also tastings in-store and at local venues for customers on mailing list
several times a year; plans for a new wine club starting autumn 1990; to groups on
request **Cellarage** £3.45 per case per year (inc handling, transport and insurance)

'I suppose,' writes proprietor John Freeland, 'you could say that
I am a true, traditional, independent, privately owned wine
merchant, having been in the trade now for over 22 years,
having started at the bottom washing bottles and making
cardboard boxes, progressing to driving the van and now
running my own business, continuing the personal involvement
with the producers of the wines that I supply and introducing
them to the consumer when they are here in England so that
they can meet the man who makes the product they enjoy so
much . . .' And, in support of this traditional image, the April
'Budget Beaters and Bin Ends' list shows a photograph of the
original Mr Rookes, complete with bowler, waistcoat and pocket
watch, standing next to a 1904 Peugeot outside the shop, itself
signposted by several large bunches of hanging grapes. As the
address is now Unit 7, Western Road Industrial Estate, the
photograph marks a fond farewell to old premises.

Tradition certainly marks the list, though there is enough
balance from Australia, New Zealand and California to ensure
that the mark is not a blemish. The range is not large, though it
is not small either, and the selections are comparatively
cautious. When a producer has been found that meets
Mr Freeland's requirements (Jean Cros/Château Larroze in
Gaillac; Château Val-Joanis in Lubéron; Château de la Rivière in
Fronsac; Ellner, Gosset and Laurent-Perrier in Champagne;
Champy and Charles Gruber in Burgundy, and Chanut in

Beaujolais), they are given considerable loyalty. Outside France, the buying seems to be a bit pickier, with more producers' names jostling for list space – though the overall selections are smaller. The quality of the information given in the list, we should point out, is first-rate: modestly but lengthily informative, with exclamation marks (the bane of most wine lists) completely excised. This feat merits some kind of award – let's call it the Golden Full Stop – and we urge other merchants to follow suit. (Strangely enough the April circular mentioned above is not exclamation-mark-free; indeed double exclamation marks are occasionally used.) The overall range is broad enough to satisfy most tastes, and includes a port under the extraordinary name of J B Bairisford-Ffarquhar Bin 58, sadly one of the unglossed wines.

Best buys

Château Lamothe 1986, Premières Côtes de Bordeaux (red), £4.85
Muscadet du Sèvre et Maine sur lie 1988, Château de la Touche, £4.85
Stoneleigh Sauvignon Blanc 1988, Corban Estate, Marlborough, New Zealand, £6.80

William Rush

Tecklewood, Uplands Close, Gerrards Cross,   *Tel* (0753) 882659
Buckinghamshire SL9 7JH

Case sales only   Open Mon–Sun 9.30–7.30   **Closed** Chr Day
Credit cards Access   **Discounts** 5% on unmixed cases (cash payment)
Delivery Free within 10-mile radius of Gerrards Cross (min 1 case); otherwise at cost; mail order available   **Glass hire** Free with minimum case order
Tastings and talks Regular tastings throughout the year; to groups on request
Cellarage Not available

William Rush is what one might term a 'campaigning wine merchant'. He writes to us to express his 'belief that all of the media including yourselves are very much too concerned to beat the drum for the multiples. I will offer an example. Settesoli Bianco di Menfi has been on my list (and no doubt many other small operators') for two years at a price of £2.55, then £2.65 and only just now £3.05. It is only when the mighty Marks & Spencers decide at last to stock it . . . that it becomes eligible to be *Which? Wine Monthly* Wine of the Month! The factor is not the wine, but the retail source? . . . This is a little 'cri de coeur' on behalf of myself and also my many friends in the Wine Trade who do much the same thing as myself, and feel much as I do.' Indeed, many other small merchants do feel this and write to us to express similar views, so we will take this opportunity to express our position on this general question. (On the specific question of Settesoli Bianco di Menfi, it should be made clear that any wine on sale in Britain is eligible to be a *Which? Wine Monthly* Wine of the Month.)

Journalists in general serve the public, and Consumers' Association serves the consumer. Our responsibility is to provide the maximum amount of help and guidance to the maximum number of consumers. If half a dozen small independent merchants up and down the country stock a particular wine, that wine will only ever reach a tiny minority of consumers, no matter how vociferously it is recommended. If a large multiple stocks it, the number of consumers that the wine may reach is increased, in most cases, thousandfold or more. We therefore have a responsibility to look at the offerings of large chains and multiples particularly closely, because every recommendation made will provide guidance to a very large number of consumers. We also, of course, have a responsibility to small independent merchants, and we try not to fail in this. If any merchant feels we do fail to do justice to his or her business, we would invite them to get in touch with us as soon as possible, and express the grounds for discontent. But we would have to reject as irresponsible and unrealistic any calls for us to pay less attention to those retailers who sell most wine to most people.

We also feel that Mr Rush is taking rather a negative approach. If he stole a two-year march on Marks & Spencer, what better sales pitch could he wish for? 'What sounder recommendation,' he might wish to claim, 'of my buying skills could there be?' We do not intend to criticise him for having only one branch instead of 300, and we would be happy to convey his pride at the scoop to readers.

William Rush's list is a small one, but he draws customers' attention to the fact that he has sourced it from a number of different suppliers. There may, therefore, be more real choice here than at merchants with a larger number of wines, most of which have been sourced from big foreign merchants' portfolios, he implies. Burgundy, Bordeaux (with a Cordier emphasis here), the Loire and the Rhône are all represented with between six and twelve wines, and Italy, too; five French country wines, a few from Beaujolais, Alsace, Champagne, and five dessert and table wines pave the way for a small selection of ports, Cognacs and one or two other spirits. The wines have obviously been chosen with care, and each selection is lengthily argued in the list.

Send us your views on the report forms at the back of the book.

Best buys

Coteaux du Giennois 1989, Sauvignon Blanc, Balland-Chapuis, £4.90

Saint-Joseph Rouge 1988, Louis Chèze, £8.75

Vouvray Demi-Sec 1985, Poniatowski, £6.75

Russell & McIver

Office

The Rectory, St Mary-at-Hill, London   *Tel* 071-283 3575
EC3R 8EE

Cellars

Arch 73, St Thomas Street, London SE1 3QX   *Tel* 071-403 2240

Customers may collect wine from the office if they telephone in advance

Open Mon–Fri 9–5.30 (office); 8–4 (cellar) **Closed** Sat, Sun, public holidays
Credit cards None accepted; personal and business accounts **Discounts** Not
available **Delivery** Free on UK mainland (min 1 case in London, 4 cases
elsewhere); otherwise £4.60 per consignment; mail order available
Glass hire Free with 1-case order **Tastings and talks** Annual 3-day autumn
tasting in the City and regional tastings by invitation; to groups on request
Cellarage £3.45 per case per year

Russell & McIver has no shop, just an office in a rectory next to
a twelfth-century church rebuilt by Wren after the Great Fire of
1666. The church is St Mary-at-Hill, within stone-throwing
distance of the Thames or of Eastcheap, in the heart of the City
of London. You may suppose, therefore, that Russell & McIver
represents an archetype of the traditional besuited merchant,
and you're right. Indeed, it's the last of its line, having outlived
all its other old Square Mile rivals.

Yet there is also a kind of comfortable, open-necked
informality about the service. 'Everyone answers the phone –
from Chairman down!' says director Christopher Davey, and the
list is clearly designed, accessible and informative. Each wine is
accompanied by a tasting note and optimal drinking date, and
there are photographs and label reproductions to soothe and
comfort the eye while the questing brain decides what most
exactly meets its requirements. The range is not enormous, but
plenty of choice is spread before that organ; the strengths of the
list are traditional, but not ultra-so (England, California,
Australia and New Zealand have all made their way into the
rectory); prices are rather better than an EC3 address and 125
years of history would lead us to expect.

Russell & McIver buy and ship direct wherever possible, and
the result is a particularly strong range of *cru bourgeois* clarets,
growers' burgundies, French country wines and German wines.
The team is very proud of its 'own-label' wines (including port
and Cognac); there is a fine selection of cigars; and this is one

of the few places where you can find the magnificently labelled Lomelino Madeiras (a range of four 10-year-old Special Reserves). As befits a traditional merchant, Russell & McIver are accommodating whenever a customer requests the opportunity to taste before purchase, and sample bottles are unhesitatingly dispatched to those whose interest is serious. 'Mr Sample is our biggest salesman,' says joint Managing Director 'Budge' Baverstock Brooks, and this speaks well for the quality of this independent company's wine-buying.

Best buys

Savigny-lès-Beaune Premier Cru Lavières 1981, Domaine Boillot, £10.58
Bourgogne Blanc 1987, Domaine Michelot-Buisson, £8.80
Côtes du Rhône 1985, Domaine du Grand Tinel, E Jeune, £4.95

Safeway   ⌷ ⬤ 🏠

Head office
Safeway House, 6 Millington Road, Hayes,   *Tel* 081-848 8744
Middlesex UB3 4AY
Approximately 290 branches

Open Varies from store to store, generally Mon–Fri 8–8; Sat 8–6; Sun 10–5 (Scotland only)   **Closed** Sun, public holidays   **Credit cards** Access, Visa
Discounts, **Delivery** Not available   **Glass hire** Available   **Tastings and talks**, **Cellarage** Not available

---

Safeway has, during the last year, continued the improvements that were put in hand after this supermarket's wine range explored the depths of mediocrity in 1987/88. It's now hard to find mediocrity anywhere on the Safeway list, and excellence, as often as not, peers brightly out at you from behind the ranks of green glass.

If you're the sort of customer that hunts for organic mushrooms, unwaxed oranges and the chance to recycle your plastic carrier bags, then you will probably shop at Safeway anyway, and you will have noted the comparatively wide range of organic wines on sale here. Indeed, Safeway sponsors Britain's only organic wine fair, and its commitment to this area (powered, of course, by your commitment to it) is firm. Doubters as to the value of the exercise should try the Domaine Anthea Merlot, Vins de Pays d'Oc (£3.09).

In other respects, the Safeway policy has been to 'refresh' the list with purchases of quality wines from wherever the buying team finds them, and this has led to some laudably adventurous selections for a supermarket. Spain is an exciting area, with Navarra, Ribera del Duero and Utiel Requena all covered; the range of Labouré-Roi burgundies is bold; French country wines and Italian wines are done justice; and listen out for a requested price check for Errazuriz Panquehue Chilean Cabernet Sauvignon over the intercom (the answer is a lot easier to pronounce than the question: good value, at £3.79). Bravo for the half-bottles of Carta Blanca fino sherry from Blazquez with a 'best before' date on; bravo, too, for tawny port in half-bottles. Safeway's 'own-label' Californian Petite Syrah (£3.59), though, is a repellent example, should you require one, of the excesses of technological wine-making: blackcurrant aroma and flavour and an inky depth of colour are packed in like muscle on a steroid-happy body-builder, but vinosity or 'wininess' – that most essential part of any wine – is completely missing. Fascinating stuff.

Liz Robertson MW leads the buying, and deserves great credit for having made Safeway one of the more stimulating of British supermarkets for the wine consumer.

Best buys

Safeway Bordeaux Cabernet Sauvignon (oak-aged), £3.49
Trocken Silvaner 1988, Ihringer Vulkanfelsen, Kaiserstuhler Winzergenossenschaft, £2.55
Viña Pedrosa 1986, Ribera del Duero, £6.95

Sainsbury Bros ⇨

3 Edgar Buildings, George Street, Bath, Avon   *Tel* (0225) 460481
BA1 2EG

Open Mon–Fri 10–6; Sat 10–5.30   **Closed** Sun, public holidays
Credit cards Access, Visa; personal and business accounts   **Discounts** Available
Delivery Free within 30-mile radius of Bath (min 1 case); otherwise £8 per case throughout UK   **Glass hire** Free with 1-case order   **Tastings and talks** In-store tastings most Saturdays; tastings held in cellars every 3 months by invitation; to groups on request   **Cellarage** £2.88 per case per year

---

A thigh-slapping Georgian toper has been chosen as the logo for Bath's Sainsbury Brothers, and late twentieth-century topers will find a small range of wines in George Street's Edgar Buildings that might incite them to slap thighs of their own. Ports and sherries, Australian wines and Loire wines are chief among these, and there is quite a good selection of clarets. Beaujolais is mainly from Loron, and Burgundy mainly from Chanson and Mommessin, which makes the ranges a little dull and uniform. Four wines from the Vincent family's Château de Fuissé will, however, show you what the Mâconnais is capable of. Chile is explored with a degree of enthusiasm here; Italy and Spain with more of a sense of duty, though there are a few worthwhile bottles in both areas. Fontanafredda's 1978 Barolo should be memorable, and the two reds from Torres are sound, reliable wines. As in Burgundy, we feel that there is too great a readiness to source all wines from large merchant portfolios – all Tuscan/Umbrian wines from Melini, for example, or all Veneto wines from Bolla. This is not the best way to find excellence; it's often the easy way out. Portugal is a different case: Periquita and Pasmados, and the two João Pires wines, are among the country's best.

The list is methodically organised, though until you work out the method it looks like madness: in fact it's alphabetical, by region or by country or by genre, all depending. And the prices are ex-VAT, though you might be forgiven for thinking otherwise. What do customers think of Sainsbury Bros? Write and let us know if you feel we're being unfair.

Best buys

Periquita 1987, J M da Fonseca Successores, £3.81
Seppelt's Chardonnay 1988, South Australia, £6.71
Colheita Port 1977, Vieira da Souza, £9.35

J Sainsbury

Head office
Stamford House, Stamford Street, London SE1 9LL   *Tel* 071-921 6000
291 licensed branches; 8 licensed SavaCentres

Open Generally Mon–Sat 8.30–6 (late night trading Thur/Fri until 9)
Closed Sun   **Credit cards** None accepted   **Discounts**, **Delivery**, **Glass hire** Not available   **Tastings and talks** Tastings and talks on request very occasionally
Cellarage Not available

Discuss buying wine in supermarkets with most people, and Sainsbury is the name that will be heard time after time; it is the magnetic north of the subject. Sainsbury was the first large chain to realise the potential of wine as a supermarketable commodity of unique character. Unlike keenly priced lavatory-pan cleaning fluids or bargain multipacks of cat food, an enterprising line in wines can add lustre and excitement to customers' perceptions of the shops themselves, at the same time as large sales help profitability. Sainsbury was the first chain to get the wine package right: a range wide enough to stimulate but not so wide that it left shoppers bewildered; and, inside the bottles, sound wines at keen prices. The Sainsbury own-label range, launched in 1973, was a highly successful lever in forcing open the supermarket share of the wine market: 'Sainsbury' in effect became a trustworthy brand of wines from here, there or wherever, it didn't really matter much. You simply followed the one that you liked best, or that seemed best value. Buying it was a great relief: no one humiliated you because you confused Saint-Estèphe with Saint-Emilion; you never felt ripped off; it was extravagantly convenient.

Times change, of course. Ten years later, in 1983, Sainsbury's 'Vintage Selection' was launched: a step up-market, and a step away from the emphasis on own-label wines. This has been a great success. On one Saturday afternoon visit to a branch of Sainsbury before this entry was written, the Vintage Selection wines had almost all been bought, with at least eight lines completely missing; whereas the 'own-label' range was still looking solid on the shelves. This may be a consequence of stacking or supply vagaries, but we suspect that it simply indicates popularity, and that the Vintage Selection wines are the pointer to the future. Indeed, the Sainsbury 'own-label' range is looking increasingly tired now, though the wines inside the bottles are as reliable as ever; the tame watercolours of the French own-label selection, and the comparative monotony of the Italian own-label designs, must surely have almost run their course. We note that increasing use is now made of suppliers' labels when they are suitably decorative (the Côtes du Brulhois, the Frontonnais from Bellevue-la-Forêt, the Château la Bouysses Cahors); and 'new' own-label designs, like that of the Chilean Sauvignon Blanc, have a much more contemporary feel to them – though Sainsbury still lag far behind Asda in this respect. If there is another ten-year change at around the 1993 mark, we would predict that it will be a goodbye to any uniform style of own-brand labelling.

As far as the list is concerned, Sainsbury is still the supermarket to beat. It never stops dusting down its laurels: bringing in new lines but at the same time hanging on to the old ones that no one wants to lose; trying this half-bottle or that sparkling wine innovation, but never losing a sense of control, coherence or identity over the whole range. Tesco seems a little chaotic and haphazard by comparison, though of late a worthy competitor; Asda stylish but less virtuoso in its buying skills; Waitrose rather eclectic, and already halfway to being a wine merchant; Safeway industrious, but still looking for a clear profile; Marks & Spencer safer still, more firmly attached to classic names, and less willing to compete on price (and give over floor space to wine).

Strengths and weaknesses? In terms of range, we feel there are no major weaknesses, though it would be a relief, for example, to see some of the French, Italian, German and Spanish own-label wines step out briskly from behind their dull own-label uniforms and assume the character that the wines merit. The red Sainsbury's Cannonau del Parteolla, for example, or the Sainsbury's Toro, or the Sainsbury's Baden Dry: these are all excellent wines at bargain prices, but they just don't look as exciting as they should. Other of the own-label wines worth singling out are the white Vin de Pays des Côtes du Tarn, the Alsace Pinot Blanc and Gewürztraminer, the much-loved Retsina (Britain's best and cheapest), the Washington State Sauvignon Blanc, the Frontonnais and Cahors, the Syrah Vin de Pays de Vaucluse from Domaine Chancel, the Valpolicella Classico Negarine, the red Bairrada from Caves Aliança, the Romanian Pinot Noir and the three fine own-label sherries in half-bottles.

Take in the Vintage Selection, and all the other interlopers on the list, and there are a good three or four cases of exciting wines to take home. An abridged litany would intone half-bottles of Osborne's fine Fino Quinta, Romeira's Garrafeira 1980 (or 1974 in magnum – a coup), the long-standing Portuguese stalwart Quinta da Bacalhôa and the new arrival Herdade de Santa Marta, Berberana's 1975 Gran Reserva, the Chianti Classico Riserva of Castello di San Polo in Rosso, the fine red Chinon of Domaine du Colombier, all of the clarets (don't worry too much about the vintages: the 1984s have been made by those well able to cope with a less than usually splendid summer), any of the Kabinett and Spätlese wines in the vintage selection, the Quincy, the sweet Clos Saint-Georges and Château Mayne des Carmes (Rieussec's second wine), and, for those who think that Sainsbury aren't adventurous enough, the beautifully packaged white from Château d'Arlay in the Jura. You may, of course, have your own favourites, or think that the wines we have cited are unpleasant; write and let us know. Write, too, if you are less enthusiastic than we are about Sainsbury, and tell us why. (As always, remember that our judgment is based on the full range; we, too, lament the fact that not all stores carry the full range, but this problem is universal in the supermarket sphere.)

Best buys

Sainsbury's Toro 1986, £3.85
Fino Quinta, Osborne, half-bottle, £2.79
Domaine du Colombier 1989, Chinon, £4.45

We have tried to make the *1991 Which? Wine Guide* as comprehensive as possible, but we should love to hear from you about any other wine merchants you feel deserve an entry, or your comments on existing entries. Write to us either by letter or using the report forms supplied at the back of the book.

Sandiway Wine Co

Chester Road, Sandiway, nr Northwich, *Tel* (0606) 882101
Cheshire CW8 2NH

Open Mon, Tue, Thur, Fri, Sat 9–1, 2–5.30, 6.30–10; Wed 9–1, 6.30–10; Sun 11–2, 7–10; public holidays variable   **Credit cards** Access, Visa; personal and business accounts   **Discounts** 5% on 1 case   **Delivery** Free within 10-mile radius (min 1 case)   **Glass hire** Free with 1-case order   **Tastings and talks** In-store tastings; occasional tutored tastings in local hotel; to groups on request   **Cellarage** Not available

Graham Wharmby's Cheshire 'village offy' has a lot more to offer than most of its kind. 'We're stupid enough to stock a certain number of completely unconventional wines like a range of Jura wines, £11 fizzy Frascatis, 1964 Piesporter etc., so there's almost always something of interest . . .' he tells us, and the list confirms this. It contains 'a core selection of wines which we anticipate stocking throughout the year', but others come and go, rather like customers. 'We try to keep a modest selection of older champagne,' the list confesses us at one point, 'but with this week's sale of a case of Taittinger Comtes de Champagne '75 we are currently out of stock. Oddments should be located shortly.'

French country wines, Italian wines and New World wines seem to form the core of the core; Bordeaux looks good, too, and there are some fine sherries from Valdespino and Barbadillo. For other regions, you'll have to take your chance on the carousel, but those wines listed suggest that an open mind and a taste for the unusual is the guiding principle throughout.

Best buys

Viña Undurraga Cabernet Sauvignon 1987, Chile, £3.45
Côtes de Jura Savagnin 1986, Luc et Sylvie Boilly, £6.75
Barolo Sori Ginestra 1985, Conterno e Fantino, £10.95

Sapsford Wines

33 Musley Lane, Ware, Hertfordshire *Tel* (0920) 467040
SG12 7EW

Case sales only   **Open** 'All hours'   **Closed** Easter, Chr   **Credit cards** None accepted   **Discounts** 5% on 5 cases collected   **Delivery** Free within 10-mile radius of Ware (min 1 case) and elsewhere (min 5 cases); otherwise £3.50 per case; mail order available   **Glass hire** Free with 2-case order   **Tastings and talks** 6–8 tastings annually in Ware; to groups on request   **Cellarage** £3 per case per year

Mary and Barry Sapsford are primarily Loire Valley specialists: a selection of 60 wines from this region are offered, all of them bought direct from growers or co-operatives. The emphasis is on the dryer styles of wine, and the Loire's excellent red-wine potential has not been neglected by the Sapsfords. (There can't be many places in Hertfordshire where you can purchase a varietal Côt, known elsewhere in France as Malbec or Auxerrois. Barbeillon's 1988 version is £3.80.) A small selection of superb sweet Chenins from Coteaux du Layon is offered, with Sorin's 1986 looking very attractive at £6.95; further development in this area would be welcome. A selection of 11 different Loire sparkling wines is another big draw, with the most expensive of these barely half the price of most champagnes.

The list contains tasting notes of occasionally surreal exuberance; trying to ascertain the appellation and grower for each wine, however, is not always easy. The Loire selection is complemented by wines from Bordeaux, Burgundy, the Rhône, Italy and Iberian fortifieds. If you're going to furnish a Burgundy selection from a single négociant, then Jaffelin is as good a choice as any; and a preference for organic where practice does not betray theory is evident in the selections from Guy Bossard, Les Terres Blanches, Cru du Coudoulet, and the Guerrieri-Rizzardi family in the Veneto. Tastings and suppers are organised, and the Sapsfords seem to carry out their self-appointed mission to act as 'the link between grower and drinker' with enthusiasm and modesty.

Best buys

Cheverny 1988, Sec, Gendrier, £3.50
Anjou Villages 1987, A Sorin, £3.75
Coteaux du Layon-Rochefort 1976, A Sorin, £6.95

SavaCentre

See J Sainsbury.

Ashley Scott

P O Box 28, The Highway, Hawarden,   *Tel* (0244) 520655
Deeside, Clwyd CH5 3RY   (answering machine)

Case sales only **Open** 24-hour answering service (orders delivered although collection may be arranged from warehouse) **Credit cards** None accepted; personal and business accounts **Discounts** 5% on 1 unmixed case **Delivery** Free in North Wales, Cheshire, Merseyside (min 1 case); elsewhere at cost; mail order available **Glass hire** Free with 1-case order **Tastings and talks** Annual tasting in November by invitation (available on request); talks and tastings provided for local organisations **Cellarage** Available

This exclusively mail-order operation run by Michael Scott and his wife Jean offers a short but carefully chosen list, with the vast majority of wines retailing (in a mixed case of 12 bottles) at under £10. A real effort has been made to find something from almost everywhere at the best price possible, which would explain why the Luxembourgeois and Moroccan sections, at two bottles each, are 100 per cent larger than the American section. And the fact that Château Ramage-la-Batisse 1982 is sold 65p cheaper than the 1987 betokens a laudable lack of avarice.

As the operation is mail order only, though, there is little excuse for not typing out the producer's name in every case rather than some only: anyone who has tasted a range of Dão or Bairrada wines will know that the difference in palatability between producers can be considerable. And on the Burgundy-Beaujolais axis, the names Thorin and Viénot appear and reappear rather more regularly than one might wish. More reports, please.

Best buys

Château Ramage-la-Batisse 1982 (Haut-Médoc), £6.50
Viña Irache Tinto 1987 (Navarra), £3.30
Inocente Macharnudo Fino, Valdespino, £5.95

Sebastopol Wines   ⚖

Sebastopol Barn, London Road, Blewbury,   *Tel* (0235) 850471
Oxfordshire OX11 9HB

Case sales only   Open Tue–Sat 10.30–5.30   **Closed** Sun, Mon
Credit cards Access, Visa   **Discounts** 5% on 1 unmixed case and selected cases; collection discount of £1 on unmixed case   **Delivery** Free within 10-mile radius from Blewbury (min 1 case); elsewhere at cost; mail order available
Glass hire Free with 1-case order   **Tastings and talks** At least once a month on Saturdays   **Cellarage** Not available

---

Sebastopol Wines offers a short, rather unambitious list. The most startling thing about it, in fact, is the complete absence of any Italian or German wines; Oxford's linguists may find the uniform rejection of the accent, the circumflex and the cedilla surprising, too. This is a wholesale operation, so you will have to buy at least 12 bottles, which means that the absence of any Italian or German options puzzles still further.

There are good wines, of course, from solid producers like Jaboulet and the Perrin family (Château de Beaucastel and La Vieille Ferme) in the Rhône; from Brédif and Poniatowski in the Loire; Chasse-Spleen in Bordeaux; Dujac and Tollot-Beaut in Burgundy; Torres, León and Fernandez in Spain; J M da Fonseca in Portugal; Penfolds in Australia. There is a satisfying selection of southern France's organic whoppers: Domaine de Trévallon, Domaine Richeaume and Mas De Daumas Gassac. Free tastings are given once a month on Saturdays. Prices are fair. But it would be nice to see just a little evidence of Dionysiac eccentricity, intoxication and risk-taking. More reports, please.

Best buys

Côtes du Rhône 1988, La Vieille Ferme gold label, £4.47
Saumur Mousseux, Brut Rosé, Gratien & Meyer, £6.25
Côtes de Provence 1982, Cépage Cabernet, Domaine Richeaume, £7.86

Seckford Wines

2 Betts Avenue, Martlesham Heath, Ipswich,   *Tel* (0473) 626072
Suffolk IP5 7RH

Case sales only   **Open** Mon–Sat 10–6   **Closed** Sun, public holidays
Credit cards Access, Visa; personal and business accounts
Discounts Negotiable   **Delivery** Free within 25-mile radius (min 1 case);
elsewhere negotiable; mail order available   **Glass hire** Free with 1-case order
Tastings and talks 4–5 weekend tastings annually by invitation; tastings and talks
by arrangement   **Cellarage** Available

Managing Director Richard Harvey-Jones has been economical in the information he has supplied us with and, finding ourselves without readers' reports on this East Coast company, we are unable to pass on any background details about Seckford Wines.

The list's strengths are in France and Australia. Within France, the usual balance is struck: clarets and white Bordeaux outnumber Burgundies, which in turn outnumber the Rhône, the Loire, Alsace, Champagne, Beaujolais and French country wines; almost all these areas, however, present you with a choice of at least a dozen bottles from which to mix your own dozen. The buying is safe and sound, even in danger zones like Burgundy: the once-bitten have no need to be shy of names like Faiveley, Jaffelin, Dujac, Leflaive or Pousse d'Or. The Australian section, too, respects the balance of power between the various wine-producing states, as it does that between large producers like Brown Brothers or Orlando and smaller wineries such as Moss Wood and Cape Mentelle. Between the two fall eight Spanish wines, with the Viña Magana 1980 from Navarra being the only wine not widely available elsewhere; Italy and Germany offer slightly more choice, with a flutter of sweeter and older German wines lending a little excitement (two 1959 Spätlesen are listed). There are eight wines from New Zealand, with Cloudy Bays at the right time of year (ask in November about the Sauvignon); small selections, too, from the Americas. The interior of Seckford's premises are most attractive, with neat pine bins and clever use of claret boxes in the centre of the shop; wayward tendrils of the vine, meanwhile, romp across the ceiling and walls in mural form. Good, sound buying would seem to make this a secure as well as a pleasant place to buy wine, though we would invite confirmation of this from Ipswich readers.

Best buys

Mâcon-La Roche Vineuse 1987/8, Domaine du Vieux Saint-Sorlin, £5.79
Cru du Coudoulet 1986, Côtes du Rhône, Pierre Perrin, £5.30
Château Puyguéraud 1986, Côtes des Francs, £5.45

Selfridges

400 Oxford Street, London W1A 1AB   *Tel* 071-629 1234

Open Mon–Wed, Fri, Sat 9.30–6; Thur 9.30–8   **Closed** Sun, Chr Day
Credit cards All accepted, Sears Gold Card; personal and business accounts
Discounts 5% on 1 case   **Delivery** Free in central London (min £10 order); otherwise at cost; mail order available   **Glass hire** Not available
Tastings and talks In-store promotional tastings (108 tastings days planned for 1991)   **Cellarage** Not available

Back in 1986 or so, Selfridges used to have a wine list. 'The best cellars in Oxford Street,' it said across the front, in bright red letters. The 'cellars' are even better now than they were then, having moved out of a cubbyhole behind tobacco and eaten up cameras, telescopes and clocks, but the neat little A5 wine list has disappeared. The stock is now told in longhand, apparently by a clerk seated at a high, tallow-stained desk. Surely Sears could afford to print a list?

The lack of a list is no problem, of course, if you are just dropping in to take refuge from Oxford Street's horrible taxi, car and bus fumes, as many will be, or if you're en route from perfume to petits fours. But with a range of wines as extensive and as fine as Selfridges', it seems strange not to be able to take home with you some means of documentation, so that those without photographic memories (and plenty of film spooled up) will be able to return with a clear idea as to what they wish to buy. Prices are generally but not uniformly expensive, and a list would also be helpful in isolating areas in which Selfridges offers good value as well as good choice.

Fine clarets, burgundies, ports and champagnes are extensively stocked, many of them in temperature-controlled cabinets in a little attic gallery above the main wine sales area, accessible via some stairs. A distinguished and serious German selection deserves applause and purchase, and the Italian section does justice to that country's enormous fine-wine potential. Spain and Portugal are less adventurous, but there is still plenty of choice available within these areas. You'd have to travel south to the Strand to find a better Australian selection, and 14 different New Zealand wines may be worth risking lungfuls of hydrocarbons for. The American zone is stimulating, and the Gallo range at Selfridges will give you a chance to gauge whether the publicity onslaught the world's largest wine producer threw at Britain during 1990 was justified or not. Buyer John McLaren also deserves credit for his belief in sherry: Selfridges has one of London's best selections of this shockingly undervalued wine. Israeli wines from Yarden, and the Special Reserve Cabernet Sauvignon from Carmel, should be tried by every serious wine lover, Jewish or Gentile, and Selfridges is one of the places that gives you the chance to do that. The beer selection is terrific, and so is the range of spirits, from Polish vodka to a glenful of malts, via Condom and Jarnac. And if you want a can of white Lambrusco, you'll find it here, too. But not a list.

Best buys

Vouvray 1986, Clos de Nouys, £5.25
Gigondas 1986, Domaine Raspail-Ay, £7.50
Nobilo, Gewürztraminer 1985 (New Zealand), £5.50

Edward Sheldon   ➦

New Street, Shipston-on-Stour,   *Tel* (0608) 61409/61639/62210
Warwickshire CV36 4EN

Open Mon–Fri 8.30–1, 2–5.30; Sat 8.30–1 **Closed** Sun, public holidays
Credit cards Access, Visa; personal and business accounts **Discounts** 5% on 1 case, 10% on 6 cases **Delivery** Free within 50-mile radius (min 1 case); otherwise 2–5 cases £3 per case, 6–10 cases £2 per case, 11+ cases free; mail order available
Glass hire Available with 1-case order **Tastings and talks** Annual summer and autumn tastings; tastings through Wine Coaster Wine Club; to groups on request
Cellarage Not available

'Any major changes in the last year?' we asked T N Furnivall, Director of Edward Sheldon. 'Only being taken over,' was the reply. The holding company is now Andrew Weir Vintners; we understand that 'only' indicates that business will continue very much as usual. We await confirmation of this with the 1990 list, still in preparation at the end of July.

Sheldon's profile is very much that of the traditional wine

merchant, with burgundy and claret occupying most of the cellar space. Clarets have a largely Médoc emphasis, and there is a good spread of vintages back as far as 1970; Burgundy is grower-sourced (Pousse d'Or, Ponsot, Parent, Rousseau, Clerc, Lamy, Voarick, Dujac et al.), with négociants just topping up the range where necessary. Magnums and half-bottles of both are plentiful. There is a lot of grand and frighteningly expensive champagne; Vintage Ports are extensively stocked, but this is another of those infuriating merchants who bleats about 'the volatile market in Vintage Ports' (there is nothing remotely volatile about it; most specialists complain that it moves too slowly) and refuses to print prices. We suggest you reward this feebleness and timidity by buying elsewhere, unless Sheldon is the only merchant to stock what you are looking for.

There is nothing exceptional about the rest of the list: company policy seems to be to aim for the best suppliers in every field, which means that most of the wines are reliable, costly and widely available elsewhere. The list contains four prices: even the highest (VAT inclusive) is for unmixed cases only, so if you wish to buy fewer than 12 bottles, or even mix a case, you will have to add a further 5 per cent to that price. If 40 per cent of trade is with the general public, as Edward Sheldon claims, does that not justify including a true retail price per bottle in the list?

Best buys

Quinta de Camarate 1984, J M da Fonseca Successores, £5.12
Coopers Creek Sauvignon Blanc 1989, New Zealand, £7.15
Volnay Premier Cru Les Fremiets 1985, Domaine Parent, £15.03

Sherborne Vintners

The Old Vicarage, Leigh, Sherborne, Dorset   *Tel* (0935) 872222
DT9 6HL   (orders)

Case sales only   Open Mon–Fri 9–6; Sat 9–2; Sun, public holidays by appointment   **Credit cards** None accepted; personal and business accounts **Discounts** 6–10 cases £1 per case, 11+ cases £2 per case   **Delivery** Free within 20-mile radius of Sherborne (min 2 cases) and UK mainland (min 3 cases); elsewhere £5 per case; mail order available   **Glass hire** Free with 2-case order (locally)   **Tastings and talks** To groups on request   **Cellarage** £4.20 per case per year

Sherborne Vinters offer two lists to their customers, most of whom are the mail-order kind. One is an extensive list of Spanish wines; the other is an equally large list of medal-winning and commended wines from *WINE* magazine's annual marathon tasting, 'The WINE International Challenge'. (Happily for Sherborne, there is some overlap between the two.)

This approach seems an eminently sensible one. If you are an adventurous customer, with a taste for Iberian originality, you will find much to explore in the Spanish list. Ian Sinnot has found wines from Extremadura (Bodegas Inviosa, within the Tierra de Barros zone), as well as from Alella, Priorato and Ampurdan-Costa Brava. There is plenty of Rioja, and Navarra gets its due, too. If, on the other hand, you are a customer who likes sound, well-made, panel-pleasing wines from all over the world, pick from the 'Challenge' list, which as *WINE* readers will know ranges far and wide in its search for excellence. Prices are average in both cases, and the choice thrown up by the combined lists is good.

Best buys

Matusalem Old Sweet Oloroso, Gonzalez Byass, £12.83
Lar de Barros Reserva 1986, Bodegas Inviosa (Extremadura), £4.43
Raimat Chardonnay Brut (sparkling wine), £7.28

André Simon

50/52 Elizabeth Street, London SW1W 9PB	*Tel* 071-730 8108
21 Motcomb Street, London SW1X 8LB	*Tel* 071-235 3723
14 Davies Street, London W1Y 1LJ	*Tel* 071-499 9144

Open Mon–Fri 9.30–7; (Elizabeth St) 9.30–8.30; Sat (Davies St) 9.30–1, (Motcomb St) 9.30–4.30, (Elizabeth St) 9.30–7.30 **Closed** Sun, public holidays
Credit cards Access, American Express, Visa; personal and business accounts
Discounts 5% on 1 case **Delivery** Free in central London (min 1 case); elsewhere at cost **Glass hire** Free with 1-case order **Tastings and talks** Not available
Cellarage £3.50 per case per year (available on a small scale)

André Simon managed to produce one of the most half-hearted of this year's responses to our appeal for information, with most of our questionnaire left uncompleted and no up-to-date list supplied. The introduction to the out-of-date list we did receive is full of bluster about the selections, service and expertise of the independent wine merchant; we view this with a little scepticism. Do you receive better service than *Which? Wine Guide* does from André Simon? Write and let us know if you think you do.

The only reason André Simon remains in the *Guide* is because its wines are generally well chosen and high in quality. For this, and for the 'smart' sites in which the three shops are situated, you pay high prices. Laytons is the parent company, so the burgundies and clarets are particularly worthwhile; Alsace and the Loire offer much less choice, but quality is still good. The Italian range is the only one outside France that offers much of interest.

Best buys

Bourgogne Rouge 1986, Domaine Machard de Gramont, £6.85
Montagny Premier Cru Bonnevaux 1988, Domaine Arnoux, £8.05
Alsace Gewürztraminer 1987, Domaine Zind-Humbrecht, £7.20

Smedley Vintners

Rectory Cottage, Lilley, Luton, Bedfordshire   *Tel* (046 276) 214
LU2 8LU

Case sales only   **Open** Mon–Fri 8.30–9; Sat 9–5; Sun, public holidays 10–5
Credit cards None accepted; personal and business accounts
Discounts Available   **Delivery** Free within 50-mile radius of Lilley (min 1 case); otherwise £10 per delivery; mail order available   **Glass hire** Free
Tastings and talks 2 main tastings annually; occasional smaller tastings; 2–3 tutored dinners annually; courses at North Herts College; to groups on request
Cellarage Available

Following over 20 years in a number of key wine trade positions, Master of Wine Derek Smedley now distils his experience into a succinct list of the world's wines, available on a by-the-case basis ('mixed cases are encouraged') from his base at Lilley, near Luton. Free delivery is available within a 50-mile radius of Rectory Cottage. French country wines and Italian wines seem to be enthusiasms, but the overall balance is good, with only non-fortified wines from Portugal conspicuously elsewhere. The range is not wide, but even the buffiest of customers would find a dozen bottles of interest here. A small wholesale merchant serving the local community with sound advice and reliable wines? We'd like confirmation of this from Smedley customers, please.

Best buys

Domaine de San de Guilhem 1989, Vin de Pays des Côtes de Gascogne (white), £3.48
Domaine de Limbardie 1988, Vin de Pays des Coteaux de Murviel, Merlot, £3.56
Cabernet Sauvignon 1987, Santa Helena (Chile), £3.56

> *Wine is a friend, wine is a joy; and, like sunshine, wine is the birthright of all.*
> André Simon

Snowdonia Wine Warehouse ☞

Old Abattoir, Unit 3, Builder Street,   *Tel* (0492) 870567
Llandudno, Gwynedd LL30 1DR

Open Mon–Fri 9–5; Sat 9–1 **Closed** Sun, public holidays **Credit cards** None
accepted; personal and business accounts **Discounts** Available **Delivery** Free in
north Wales (min 1 case); otherwise at cost **Glass hire** Free with 2-case order
Tastings and talks To groups on request **Cellarage** Not available

A first appearance in the *Guide* for this lively wine warehouse,
run with crusading zeal and commendable lack of pomposity by
Harry and Veronica Pinkerton and Paul Richards. Wales appears
to be something of a wine-buying desert at present, so the more
crusading the trio can manage, the better. The setting for the
crusade is an ex-abattoir coaxed into the suggestion of a
Spanish bodega, with ideal temperature and humidity
conditions for wine storage – and a lot of four-legged ghosts.

It has to be said at the outset that the list needs improving:
growers/producers only appear to be mentioned if there's room

Snowdonia Wine Warehouse

for their names on one line, and this makes any long-distance assessment of the wines impossible. Spelling is cavalier. Most wines on the list can be identified by one means or another, however, and the selection seems to be governed by a desire to find positive, characterful bottles from as many different sources as possible.

There's an appealing, well-priced range of Bordeaux '82s and '83s; Faiveley and Latour are two names short enough to fit on the line in the Burgundy section, and ditto for Duboeuf in Beaujolais; the long Rhône appellation names and the innate wordiness of German wine description, however, have chased most of these growers into oblivion. Italy, Spain and Portugal are lively, while there is obvious enthusiasm for the wines of Australia, New Zealand, Chile and Romania. Within the capacious Champagne zone, Musical Happy Birthday Champagne (£18.63) rubs shoulders with a balthasar of Pol Roger (£286.50 – well, it is 16 bottles' worth). Vintage Port, too, is extensively listed, with an infrequently seen range from the Royal Oporto *sous-marque* Hoopers offering an inexpensive route into the splendours of the Upper Douro.

All this, and 'No Pretentious Waffle!'

Best buys

Romanian Pinot Noir (presumably Dealul Mare 1984/6), £2.59
Stoneleigh Sauvignon Blanc 1988/9, Marlborough (New Zealand), £6.24
Quinta de Santa Amaro 1986, João Pires (Portugal), £3.75

Frank E Stainton

3 Berry's Yard, Finkle Street, Kendal,   *Tel* (0539) 731886
Cumbria LA9 4AB

Open Mon–Sat 8.30–6   **Closed** Sun, public holidays   **Credit cards** Access, Visa; personal and business accounts   **Discounts** 5% on 1 case (mixed)   **Delivery** Free in south Cumbria and north Lancashire (min 1 mixed case); otherwise 1 case £7, 2 cases £9, 3–4 cases £12, 5 cases free; mail order available   **Glass hire** Available with charge   **Tastings and talks** Tasting room on premises available for tastings; private tastings organised for groups of 12–25 people on request   **Cellarage** Not available

In this attractive shop in Kendal, in which most wines rest on inclined shelving with the remainder neatly binned behind them, you will find a medium-sized range of wines. The balance struck between different areas is largely traditional, with France the most important supplier. Within France, it is Bordeaux and Burgundy that dominate, with most of Burgundy being sourced from the more reputable négociants-éleveurs rather than growers; there is also a good selection of Sauternes, with steady support for Château Rieussec. The Rhône and Alsace follow the Burgundy pattern, with the wines of Hugel and Jaboulet Aîné dominating selections. The Loire is too large a region for one concern to impose itself in the same way, but producers of consistency – Brédif in Vouvray, for example, or de Ladoucette in Pouilly Fumé – are those favoured by Frank Stainton. The French country wine collection, however, is very poor: seven wines only, though it does include a seldom-seen pair from the Jura.

Germany is more important than Italy or Spain in Berry's Yard, though none of these sections could be described as deficient. Louis Guntrum-sourced wines provide most of the German selection, with other producers occupying guest spots on the shelves and, among them, you'll find two Franken wines worth trying, one red and one white, both from Fürstlich Castell'sches Domänenamt. A single-vineyard Orvieto (Vigneto Torricella), three Venegazzù wines, Umani Ronchi's Cumaro and Jermann's Vintage Tunina show that Italian developments are not passing Kendal by; while Spain is represented by a series of risk-free classics from Torres, CVNE and Ochoa. Portugal is not ignored, either, with Caves São João being the nearest local equivalent to a Hugel or a Jaboulet.

The New World, champagne and sparkling wines bring the list to a close (port and sherry opened it), and the selections share the Stainton hallmark of caution and surefootedness, keeping up with what's happening in each area without attempting to occupy the vanguard. Which probably goes down quite well in Kendal.

Best buys

Wehlener Sonnenuhr Riesling Kabinett 1986, S A Prüm, Mosel, £6.95
Hill-Smith, Cabernet Sauvignon-Malbec 1988, South Australia, £4.45
Cumaro Rosso del Marche, Umani Ronchi (pure Montepulciano Vino da Tavola), £10.35

The Wine & Spirit Education Trust is the body in charge of educating those in and on the fringes of the wine trade. They offer a series of courses right up to Master of Wine level, the more basic of which are open to non-trade members who can convince the Trust of their intention to enter the wine trade. Contact them at: Five Kings House, Kennet Wharf Lane, Upper Thames Street, London EC4V 3AJ; *Tel* 071-236 3551.

Stapylton Fletcher ☞

3 Haslemere, Sutton Road, Maidstone, Kent   *Tel* (0622) 691188
ME15 9NE

Case sales only   Open Mon–Fri 8–6; Sat 8.30–12.30 **Closed** Sun, public
holidays **Credit cards** Access, Visa; personal and business accounts
Discounts £1.15 per case on 6–11 cases, £2.30 on 12+ cases **Delivery** Flat rate of
£1.15 for all deliveries; mail order available **Glass hire** Free
Tastings and talks Annual tastings in Tunbridge Wells, London and Camberley;
to groups on request **Cellarage** £3.45 per case per year

In response to our question 'What do you offer that none of
your competitors do?', Stapylton Fletcher's managing director
R S Fletcher wrote: 'It would be highly presumptuous to answer
this in the affirmative.' The affirmative would be no answer,
and we deplore this misplaced coyness. What can be
presumptuous about a little self-analysis? Why refuse the chance
to communicate something about your business? This sort of
pompous soggy-mindedness does not help the *Guide* or the
company in question and is completely British in its wearisome
amateurishness.

Enough of coyness. This is a wholesale merchant, the majority
of whose custom is with the trade, but which also seems to
encourage the public to buy from it (by providing VAT-
inclusive lists and by stressing 'mixed cases available'). There
are plenty of half-bottles, so we would guess that most of the
trade customers are restaurateurs. The prices of the wines are
generally moderate; this has as its cause, or as one of its causes,
the fact that the producers of the wines are little-known – so
take advantage of any tasting facilities you may be offered
before buying. (R S Fletcher says that at least three tastings are
organised annually, though we don't know if these are primarily
for trade or private customers, or if both are welcomed). Of
course there are producers of wide repute on the list, too: from
the Loire, from Haut-Poitou, from Gaillac and Cahors, from
Champagne and Bordeaux, from Penedés and from the New
World. The strengths of the list appear to lie in French country
wines, including Beaujolais; in the Chilean range; in the 11
wines from Washington State; in the nine English wines and in
the six flavoured Polish vodkas (try the fine honey-flavoured
Krupnik or the heroic pepper-charged Pieprzówka). There are
six interesting-looking Portuguese wines whose names mean
nothing to us (they are described in the list as 'very typical ones
which will at least appeal to those who like Portuguese wines' –
which sounds vaguely threatening). The Italian and German
sections look dull, and Burgundy looks curate's egg-like. You
will find good wines, though, in each section: from André
Delorme and Domaine des Varoilles, for example, in Burgundy;

from the Friedrich Wilhelm Gymnasium in Germany; or from
Antinori or Altesino in Italy. More reports, please.

Best buys

Domaine de l'Arjolle 1988, Vin de Pays des Côtes de Thongue,
Prosper Teisserenc (red), £3
Manzanilla la Gitana, Hidalgo (fino sherry), £4.55
Château de la Chaize 1988, Brouilly, £5.70

Summerlee Wines   ⟨₪⟩

64 High Street, Earls Barton,   *Tel* (0604) 810488
Northamptonshire NN6 0JG
London office
Freddy Price, 48 Castlebar Road, London   *Tel* 081-997 7889
W5 2DD

Open (Summerlee Wines) Mon–Fri 9–6 **Closed** Sat, Sun, public holidays
Credit cards None accepted; personal and business accounts **Discounts** Not
available **Delivery** Free within area of London, Oxford and Cambridge, also East
Midlands (min 2 cases); otherwise £6.32 per consignment; mail order available
Glass hire Free with 2-case order **Tastings and talks** Occasional in-store tastings;
monthly tastings held by Freddy Price through The Winetasters Wine Society; to
groups on request **Cellarage** £5.75 per case per year

Freddy Price, consultant and buyer for Summerlee Wines, has
over 30 years' wine trade experience, and the Summerlee list
reflects this with some glorious German wines, fine Bordeaux
and Burgundy selections, and pretty good everything else –
although once we leave the specialist areas the choice drops
away to half a dozen wines or fewer.

Germany would perhaps be the main reason for making one's
way to Earl's Barton, if only because so many other merchants'
lists are weak and emaciated in this area. Summerlee's selection
does justice to the variety of German wine flavours: you'll find
graceful, Bonsai beauty in Schloss Saarstein's Rieslings,
masterful balance and delicacy in Max Ferd Richter's Mosels,
perfumed earthiness from Paul Anheuser in the Nahe, rich and
suggestive complexities from the Rheingau wines of
Johannishof, and searching depth and breadth from the
Franconian wines of Juliusspital. These last are unbeaten as
wines-for-food, the Holy Grail of today's wine-making Parsifals;
and they've always done it like that in Franconia.

Freddy Price is equally skilled at nosing out top *petit-château*
Bordeaux, and the Summerlee 1989 *en primeur* offer was one of
the best in the field in this respect. Chablis from William Fèvre
(selling here as Domaine Auffray rather than Domaine de la
Maladière: the wines are identical), white Burgundies from
Patrick Javillier, and reds from Georges Clerget, Jean Boillot and

567

Bernard Morey would all reward investment. The Domaine du Comte version of Vin de Pays de Gascogne is a Paris medal-winner, and there's hot competition for that particular gong; another southerner worth trying is the oak-aged, near-organic Faugères Cuvée Spéciale of Gilbert Alquier. Just as sufferers from supermarket Liebfraumilch are directed to Summerlee for Teutonic re-education, so those abused by supermarket Soave are encouraged to test the curative properties of Roberto Anselmi's versions (they include a fine dessert Recioto).

The shop at Earls Barton has a retail licence, and single bottles may be bought there; mail order is by the case only, though mixing is permitted – at no extra cost this year. The free delivery area is a generous one, including London, Oxford and Cambridge.

Best buys

Würzburger Stein Silvaner Kabinett 1989, Juliusspital, Franconia, £6.44

Graacher Himmelreich Riesling Kabinett 1989, Max Ferd Richter, Mosel, £5.58

Château de Gardegan 1986, Côtes de Castillon, £4.13

Sunday Times Wine Club

Mail order wine club

New Aquitaine House, Paddock Road,   *Tel* (0734) 481713
Reading, Berkshire RG4 0JY   (enquiries)
                                  Tel (0734) 472288 (orders)

Open (Mail order phones) Mon–Fri 9–5; answerphone Mon–Fri 5–9, Sat, Sun, public holidays   **Credit cards** All accepted   **Discounts** Available   **Delivery** Free nationwide (min £50 order); otherwise £3.75 per delivery   **Glass hire** Not available   **Tastings and talks** Regular tastings throughout the year all over the country; to groups on request   **Cellarage** Not available

---

The list changes every month at the Sunday Times Wine Club, and anyone who has ever been a member will know that this mail-order club gets more paper (and more of it in full colour) through your letter box than any other. For the 'ordinary' wine drinker (as opposed to the wine buff), these are the most skilful and exciting mailings in the country. Tony Laithwaite, in addition to being a tireless noser-out of the unusual and the intriguing, is a master-communicator, and every sheet in the monthly envelope bubbles with enthusiasm, up-to-the-minute design – and opportunities to save £2, £3.50, £1.50 . . .

The company runs hand-in-hand with two others: Bordeaux Direct (which has six shops, *q.v.*); and the Barclaycard Wine Options continuous buying scheme. The parent company is

Direct Wines (Windsor) Ltd, sourcing a huge number of wines annually, all of which are exclusives. The Sunday Times Wine Club and Bordeaux Direct share some wines, though in the main the lists are different; Wine Options shares no wines with the other two. According to Tony Laithwaite, the wines selected for the Sunday Times Wine Club tend to be more 'classical' than those selected for Bordeaux Direct, where the unusual and the offbeat are favoured.

'Classical', though, still has to be put into context. It does not mean endless *crus bourgeois* and growers' burgundies, though once in a while you get a sniff of those. In May 1990, for example, it meant a mixed case of Alsace wines, ditto of Yugoslavian wines, two English wines, two different mixed cases of French country wines, a Loire-and-Rhône case, a Chilean case, two Australian wines, a 'Flying Winemakers' case (see Bordeaux Direct), and a special offer on a Gamay from Côtes du Forez. Club members also receive the quarterly *Wine Times*, an excellent little magazine edited by Jim Ainsworth and distinguished by contributions from Club President Hugh Johnson and Burton Anderson among others, and everyone has the opportunity to attend the annual Vintage Festival, the largest private wine fair in the country, as well as other regional tastings and tours. Life is never dull with the Sunday Times Wine Club, and there are few better schools for the inquisitive beginner than this. It is probably not so attractive for drinkers who have already found their feet, know their enthusiasms, and want to pursue these as far as they lead. Bargain-hunters, too, may find the Sunday Times Wine Club less than satisfactory, because all those extras have to be paid for somehow . . . The fact that the wines are exclusives makes it difficult to make objective remarks about their pricing, but the wines in that Yugoslavian mixed case, for example, worked out at £3.83 each, and there weren't many other merchants in Britain selling Yugoslavian wines at any average of £3.83 per bottle in May 1990. (According to the mailing, they are 'six of the finest wines of Eastern Europe', and the Laithwaite-led expedition into Yugoslavia revealed that the country 'has more to offer than we ever dared hope for'. The labelling – not Yugoslavian, we suspect – is superb.)

A more-or-less constantly changing list makes the precise specification of 'best buys' of doubtful value, though we've tried anyway; if you like what you've heard so far, we suggest you take advantage of one of the attractive introductory offers the Club offers from time to time.

Best buys

Vin de Pays de Tourgon 1989, Épervier selection, £3.60
Alpi Juliani Merlot 1988, Yugoslavia, £3.80
Canepa Estates Gewürztraminer 1990, Chile (Flying
Winemakers), £4.50

Supergrape ☞

81 Replingham Road, Southfields, London   *Tel* 081-874 5963
SW18 5LU

Open Mon–Fri 10–2, 5–9.30; Sat 10–9.30; Sun 12–2, 7–9   **Closed** Public holidays
Credit cards Access, Visa; business accounts   **Discounts** 5% on 1 case
Delivery Free in central London (min 1 case); elsewhere at cost   **Glass hire** Free
with 1-case order   **Tastings and talks** Six tastings annually for wine club
members; to groups on request (min 25 people)   **Cellarage** Not available

---

Southfield's Supergrape changed hands in August 1989, and
new owner Michael Hall – formerly a wine wholesaler – intends
to ensure that the shop lives up to its former slogan 'the best
little wine shop south of the river'. A 'rebuilding programme' is
planned for this year, 'to increase space'. Will the shop then
cease to be little?

The list is a varied one, especially if the shop is still little, and
the number of fine wines (chiefly from Bordeaux and Burgundy,
but also including four vintages of Mas de Daumas Gassac and
five of Beaucastel, as well as Martha's Vineyard 1982, Opus One,
and Grange 1980) is higher than we would have guessed. France
and the New World get the biggest listings; there is also a good
selection of champagnes and other sparkling wines. Port is a lot
better than sherry which, like Italian whites, is a weak area. But
Supergrape looks a good shop to drop in to, whether you want
something special for a present or a big night, or something
simple but interesting to take home to lighten a dull, dark
evening. Join the Wine Club and, in addition to six tastings a
year, you get discounts of around 50p for every £10 spent.

Best buys

Château de Parenchère 1986, Bordeaux Supérieur, £4.95
Cru du Coudoulet 1986, Côtes du Rhône, Perrin, £5.95
Cloudy Bay Chardonnay 1988, New Zealand, £10.50

---

*. . . Sir W. Pen . . . and I to the Dolphin, where we found Sir W. Batten,
who is seldom a night from hence, and there we did drink a great quantity
of sack and did tell many merry stories . . .*
Samuel Pepys 14.11.1660

Tanners Wines

26 Wyle Cop, Shrewsbury, Shropshire SY1 1XD	*Tel* (0743) 232400
	Tel (0743) 232007
	(sales order office)
72 Mardol, Shrewsbury, Shropshire SY1 1PZ	*Tel* (0743) 66389
39 Mytton Oak Road, Shrewsbury, Shropshire SY3 8UG	*Tel* (0743) 66387
36 High Street, Bridgnorth, Shropshire WV6 4DB	*Tel* (0746) 763148
4 St Peter's Square, Hereford, Hereford & Worcester	*Tel* (0432) 272044
The Old Brewery, Brook Street, Welshpool, Powys SY21 7LF	*Tel* (0938) 552542

Open Mon–Sat 9–5.30 **Closed** Sun, public holidays **Credit cards** Access, American Express, Visa; personal and business accounts **Discounts** Available **Delivery** Free on UK mainland (min £75 order); free in Cheshire, Gloucestershire, Hereford & Worcester, Staffordshire, Shropshire, mid and parts of north Wales (min 1 case); mail order available **Glass hire** Free if wine purchased from shop **Tastings and talks** Wine always available in all shops; tutored tastings for customers 5–6 times a year; to groups on request **Cellarage** Not available

'None of our competitors can beat our service,' claims Tanners, and anyone who has bought from this, the most industrious of British mail-order merchants, is likely to substantiate the assertion.

The list is typical of the whole operation: no grandiose A4 all-colour production here, but a workaday A5, stocky and thick-set, its every page bearing the evidence of research, effort and thoroughness. It is one of the most complete lists in the country; there are almost no areas of weakness or resonant absence, and only Eastern Europe looks as if it needs further development work. The range offered in each sub-area reflects, with almost mathematical precision, the status of that sub-area in the British wine-buying consciousness, and when you get down to the minutiae of producer and vintage Tanners is once again hard to fault. Consider the burgundies: Henri Germain, Machard de Gramont, Lafon, Pousse d'Or, Domaine des Varoilles, Georges Roumier, Domaine Dujac and Armand Rousseau, with 1985, 1987 and 1988 explored at length: the wine-buying is as near watertight as it is possible to be. Does it play safe, though? Not really. How many other merchant competitors have a go at moving wines from Switzerland, the Jura and Savoie? How many others offer four Greek wines? How many others go looking for a Spanish rosé and come back with one from Somontano? How many others offer a range of five early landed vintage Cognacs and four vintage Armagnacs? And the hard work and thoroughness go beyond the range of wines, on into the malt whiskies, the Hereford gin, the extensive library of books and range of glasses. Intelligently composed special offer cases and *en primeur* offers are made from time to time, and if you miss an *en primeur* offer, Tanners are one of the merchants who list young fine wines from the start – 1988s in 1990, for example.

A newsletter – *Talking Tanners* – goes out to customers on the mailing list, and tastings are organised in all the shops. Prices are fair, taking the level of service into account, and considering the quality of the 136-page list, with its attractive sepia drawings, splendidly clear maps, and informative, unpretentious text. An innovation for this year is the wine-resistant, wipe-clean cover.

This is one of our few essential merchants. Anyone beginning to explore wine would be well advised to entrust themselves to Tanners – for clarity, classicism and completeness.

Best buys

Château de Sabazan 1987, Côtes de Saint-Mont (red), Producteurs Plaimont, £5.18
Alsace Pinot Blanc 1988, Rolly Gassmann, £6.96
Tanners Claret, Bordeaux (selected and blended by Peter Sichel), £3.67

Tesco

Head office
New Tesco House, P O Box 18, Delamare Road, Cheshunt, Hertfordshire EN8 9SL
For wine enquiries write to: Head office
Bentley House, Pegs Lane, Hertford, Hertfordshire SG13 8EG
362 licensed branches

Tel (0992) 32222

Tel as above

Open Varies from branch to branch **Closed** Sun **Credit cards** Access, Visa **Discounts, Delivery, Glass hire** Not available **Tastings and talks** Regular in-store tastings **Cellarage** Not available

---

Tesco's profile as a wine retailer is more merchant-like than many of its supermarket competitors. This is partly a question of packaging: Tesco do sell a wide range of own-label wines as well as producer-labelled wines, but these are designed in a varied manner to fit the product rather than any particular house style or uniform. Tesco, moreover, are aiming wherever possible to provide customers with superstores rather than supermarkets; the result of this is that the wine sections are often large areas, with a variety of different styles of shelving, and the wines are stacked (insofar as the branch most visited by the Editor is concerned, anyway) without the maniacal, quarter-inch precision favoured by some of its rivals. The overall impression is unusually rambling and easy-going for a supermarket, and the fact that wines are occasionally offered on a bin-end or sale basis adds further to the sense of this being a medium-sized wine merchant with unusually low prices sited within a supermarket.

The range itself – wide, perhaps inconsistent but always stimulating, with real specialisms – also adds to the 'merchant' impression, and so too did Tesco's association with a number of semi-promotional, semi-educative reference brochures issued free last year via *WINE* magazine. What destroys the impression, as always, is the staff problem: no one ever seems to have any idea about the wines when you ask them. We receive many letters every year complaining about this (the problem, we should make clear, is by no means confined to Tesco). The scenario is nearly always the same: a customer has heard about a wine stocked by the supermarket, but it is generally not stocked in his or her branch. The (usually junior) assistant stacking the shelves is asked about it, doesn't really catch the name properly, and doesn't have the faintest idea about whether it should be there or shouldn't be. He or she will generally spend ten minutes valiantly looking up and down the shelves, and another ten wandering around in some stockroom labyrinth, before coming back to confirm that it can't be found. Ordering the wine never seems to be easy, and is generally best done by telephoning afterwards and asking for someone important, like the manager. But things can still go wrong, even then; one Tesco customer wrote to us to say that he had got this far, but when he went to collect the wine it was a different one again from the one he wanted (and at a very different price). Supermarkets are going to have to tackle this problem sooner or later if they want to stay ahead in the wine-selling business; the obvious solution would seem to be to nominate some sort of 'wine liaison manager' for each store who would be available to give advice whenever needed, and who would really know one end of the list from the other. Superstores such as Tesco, presumably, would be the perfect places to begin such a system and to see if it improves wine sales significantly. Our own view – based on the mail we receive – is that such a system would be greatly welcomed by customers, and may indeed improve sales. We would be interested to hear supermarkets' views on this – some may already have piloted such a system.

Back to the list. Those specialisms we mentioned earlier are in Italian and German wines, where Tesco seem to have tried consistently harder than their rivals over the last few years. Of course you can buy white Lambrusco and Liebfraumilch in large bottles here, but the fact that the German range doesn't peter out half a dozen bottles later but climbs on up to fine Riesling Kabinett, Spätlese and Auslese wines, even an '85 Mosel Eiswein, with serious wines from all of this country's major wine-producing regions, is encouraging. Similarly in Italy: quality Italian wine isn't just represented by a bottle or two from Antinori, but by two Piedmontese organic vini da tavola (the strikingly labelled Rosso and Bianco dell'Uccellina from Piedmont), by a real range of fine Chiantis (try the elegant Selvapiana), by two Montepulciano d'Abruzzo wines, by Rosso Cònero, by Franciacorta, by Tiefenbrunner's Pinot Grigio, and by a fine Lugana from Ca dei Frati . . . among others.

France is good, too, particularly clarets and French country wines – notably the old favourite Domaine d'Escoubes and a good Côtes du Lubéron, Domaine des Baumelles. There's a dazzling range of champagne; sound and largely inexpensive Spanish wines (Don Darias also strides firmly into the 'old favourite' category); and a really promising range of nine Portuguese reds, all of which – save perhaps the less exciting Tesco Dão and Tesco Bairrada – should be tried. Quinta da Santa Amaro is a lovely, supple wine, very attractively priced, while the Tinto Velho Reguengos de Monsaraz 1983, the widely seen Caves Velhas Garrafeira 1976, and the T E Garrafeira 1982 are all made of sterner stuff.

With its New World range Tesco keep up rather than push ahead, though it's good to see support for Israel's new wines. You'll find one of these among the rosés – and while we're on the subject, notice how seriously Tesco (or its customers) take rosé. More seriously than the rest, for sure. This supermarket has tried hard with sherry, but hasn't yet found the right wines or packaging to inspire great enthusiasm; and the ports are rather variable, with tawnies probably looking most attractive. 'Competent and wide ranging' was one reader's verdict on Tesco, and it's one with which we would concur.

Best buys

Tinto Velho Reguengos de Monsaraz 1983, Alentejo, £4.05
La Grange Neuve de Figeac 1985 (second wine of Château Figeac), Saint-Emilion, £8.49
Ca dei Frati 1988, Lugana, £4.45

Cellarage is generally provided at the rates quoted only when the wines have been bought from the merchant concerned.

Thresher and Wine Rack

Head office
Sefton House, 42 Church Road, Welwyn   *Tel* (0707) 328244
Garden City, Hertfordshire AL8 6PJ
Approximately 1,000 branches nationwide and 40 branches as Wine
Rack

Open Hours vary from branch to branch but generally Mon–Sat 10–10; Sun, Good
Friday permitted hours   **Closed** Chr Day   **Credit cards** Access, Visa
Discounts Available   **Delivery** Free within 10-mile radius of each branch (min 1
case)   **Glass hire** Free   **Tastings and talks** Regular tasting programme at Wine
Rack stores   **Cellarage** Not available

There are almost a thousand Thresher shops in Britain and
upwards of 40 Wine Rack shops, the latter being a more
glamorous version of the former, catering specifically for 'the
wine-aware enthusiast' – you and me, in other words.

You have sent in mixed reports, as is often the case with
chains – one branch in Leicester is 'unimaginative and dull –
nothing at all to tempt or interest' while a second is 'far better
laid out . . . Haut-Bages-Avérous was indeed there at the
recommended price . . .' The overall verdict is positive: most
shops now seem to be bright and pleasant places to buy wine
in, and the range of wines on offer from this Whitbread-owned
chain continues to improve steadily. The mnemonic
exhortations to staff pinned behind the counter at one branch
we visited were full of admirable strategies and practices, and
most were followed.

It has not been made clear to us exactly how the lists of
Thresher and Wine Rack differ; a certain amount of cross-
referring suggests that Wine Rack's list has everything that
Thresher's does, plus more, so we will regard Wine Rack's as
the master list. Not every Wine Rack will stock the full range;
and not every Thresher will stock a large proportion of the Wine
Rack list – indeed, some will stock only a small proportion. As
always, much depends on what the marketing analysts think of
your area: you may drink nothing but Echézeaux and Krug, but
if all your neighbours prefer Hofmeister or Newcastle Brown, or
if the only people that bother to shop locally – rather than
driving off in company cars to shop elsewhere – are Guinness
drinkers, then it will be them that your local branch will serve.

Clarets are an area of strength. Threshers are among those
who think that 'second wines' are a good idea, and they are
doing their utmost to pursuade customers to share this view,
with a range of seven listed. In some cases, the real thing
(Figeac, Léoville-Las-Cases, Lynch-Bages) is there to compare
with junior (Grange Neuve de Figeac, Clos du Marquis, Haut-
Bages-Avérous). Dry Bordeaux whites are good, too, with La

575

Louvière, de la Rouergue and Bonnet leading the team; Sauternes, by contrast, is a disappointment. The excursion into red Burgundy seems more hesitant than that into claret, perhaps inevitably, given Burgundy prices: the Mercureys and the Givry are worthwhile attempts to circumvent this problem, while two Pousse d'Or Volnays are the lure for those with £25 to spare. White burgundy ranges more deeply, with the top wines coming from Jadot, while the Mâconnais and the Côte Chalonnaise provide most of the bottles under £10. The Loire and the Rhône are adequate, just; Alsace, by contrast, is terrific, and it is at around this point that you begin to suspect that Thresher is a good place to shop for white wines in general. The Zind-Humbrecht range is the reason why Alsace is so worthwhile here; the wines are more expensive than the widely stocked Turckheim co-operative's, for example, but very good. And more is in the offing: 'we will be extending our Alsace range to specialist status', the Thresher PR department tells us, presumably during the next 12 months. French country wines complete a generally positive picture, with Domaine Sainte-Eulalie from Minervois and two of the excellent Corbières of Château de Lastours amid around 18 reds (we exclude Piat d'Or, which has more to do with technology and marketing than the countryside); whites are a match for reds, with Gascogne three ways (one in oak), a half of Pacherenc, and an aspiring Chardonnay from the Jardin de la France all beaming brightly.

There are a few notables from the rest of Europe, like Antinori's Orvieto Classico Abboccato Campogrande, three or four fine German Rieslings, and the famous Barca Velha from Portugal's Douro Valley (Ferreira), but basically it's fast forward from France to the New World. An earnest selection from California is worth exploring, and Australia and New Zealand are both regions that have set the Thresher imagination into harvesting mode: try the fine pair of Stoneleigh whites from New Zealand. And keep reporting.

Best buys

Alsace Gewürztraminer Herrenweg 1988, Zind-Humbrecht, £7.99
Château Bonnet 1988, Entre-Deux-Mers, £4.99
Scharzhofberger Riesling Kabinett 1986, Weingut von Hövel, Saar, £5.59

Most wine merchants will hire out glasses free of charge, provided they are collected and returned clean, and that you are buying enough wine to fill them! In most cases, it's first come, first served, so get your order in early to ensure supply.

Topsham Wines

36 High Street, Topsham, nr Exeter, Devon   *Tel* (0392) 874501
EX3 0DU

Open Mon–Sat 9.30–1, 2.15–7.30; Sun 12–1; public holidays mornings only
Credit cards Access, Visa; personal and business accounts **Discounts** 10% on 1
case **Delivery** Free for Exeter postal districts (min 1 case); elsewhere delivery
£7.50 **Glass hire** Free **Tastings and talks** Charity wine tasting for customers; to
groups on request **Cellarage** £3 per case per year

Andrew Tarry's Topsham Wines does not have a large range,
but the wine-buying net is cast widely – as far as Zimbabwe
and Chile. The list is balanced, with Spain, Portugal and New
Zealand looking enthusiastically researched, and North America
the only section failing to yield up to half a dozen bottles of
interest. Andrew Tarry's career began in Fortnum & Mason's
wine department, and the good selection of clarets, port and
sherries (including Domecq's top-of-the-line 51–1A, Sibarita and
Venerable) may draw on the experience of those years and the
tastes formed during them. The list has a clean, smart look to it,
and the company symbol – a ship in a bottle, woodcut-style – is
most appealing. Could Exeter readers give us their impressions
of the range and service offered?

Best buys

Periquita 1978, J M da Fonseca Successores, Portugal, £4.50
Gewürztraminer 1988, Nobilo, New Zealand, £5.75
Château Pontoise Cabarrus 1985, Haut-Médoc, £5.95

J Townend & Sons

Head office
Red Duster House, 101 York Street, Hull,   *Tel* (0482) 26891
Humberside HU2 0QX
The Wine Cellars, Oxford Street, Hull,   *Tel* as above
Humberside HU2 0QX
Willerby Manor Wine Market, Well Lane,   *Tel* (0482) 656475
Willerby, Humberside HU10 6ER
8 branches (House of Townend) and 4 branches (Wine Markets) in
Humberside and Yorkshire

Open (Retail) Mon–Sat 10–10, Sun 10–9 **Credit cards** Access, Visa; personal and
business accounts **Discounts** 10% (minimum quantity negotiable)
Delivery Free within 60-mile radius of Hull (min 2 cases); otherwise £4.60 per
case; mail order available **Glass hire** Free with case order
Tastings and talks Monthly wine club tasting; to groups on request
Cellarage £3.10 per case per year

The Hull-based 'House of Townend' is now starting to draw on
the fourth generation of the Townend family, and claims to be

'the only old established private wine merchant still remaining in the county' – Humberside being meant, presumably. You can read Alderman Jack Townend's story on page 5 of the list: as well as founding the company, he was 'reputed to be the only man who played for Hull and Hull Kingston Rovers on the same day'. To find out how he did it, ask for a copy of the list.

The range of wines offered at Townend shops varies, with the Wine Market at Willerby Manor Hotel carrying the largest range (600 wines). The list is clear and well designed, and membership of the Wine Market Wine Club brings you the opportunity to attend tutored tastings and an annual tasting, as well as a 5 per cent discount on 'any six bottles of wine not already on special offer'. The Humberside taste in wine seems to be a conservative one: claret for reds, German wines for whites. Those, at least, are the largest parts of the list. The Rhône, however, rivals Burgundy, indicating a canniness on Humbersiders' part, and the theory that value for money is an important consideration here is borne out by the large Australian and New Zealand ranges. The buying is safe rather than imaginative, and there is a strong Merchant Vintners cast to it (Merchant Vintners is a buying consortium working on behalf of the country's 'independent' wine merchants).

Best buys

Sauvignon Blanc 1988, Stoneleigh (New Zealand), £9.69
Châteauneuf-du-Pape 1987, Domaine du Vieux Télégraphe, £7.99
Copitas (sherry and port glasses; box of 6), £9

Madeleine Trehearne Partners

20 New End Square, London NW3 1LN   *Tel* 071-435 6310

Case sales only   Open '24 hours, 7 days a week'   **Credit cards** None accepted; personal and business accounts   **Discounts** 5% on 5 cases   **Delivery** Free in Greater London; elsewhere at cost; mail order available   **Glass hire** Free with 1-case order   **Tastings and talks** 4 tastings a year; to groups on request **Cellarage** Available

From a beautiful four-storey, wistaria-festooned house in Hampstead, English lecturer Madeleine Trehearne ('Owner. Drayswoman') runs a small, friendly wine business. All the wines are French, with the accent on Burgundy and the Loire; the wines are carefully chosen, and prices are good, with only champagne and a fine old Quarts de Chaume exceeding £10 at the time of writing. Fine foods are increasingly stocked, and recipe ideas freely given. Our only reservation is that it is an extremely short list for a merchant without a retail licence; two dozen or so wines only. Buying them, though, sounds fun.

Best buys

Menetou-Salon 1988, Domaine de Chatenoy, Bernard Clément,
£5.75
Givry Premier Cru Clos de la Servoisine (Rouge) 1987, Domaine
Joblot, £6.65
Bourgogne Blanc 1987, Robert De France, £5.95

Turville Valley Wines

The Firs, Potter Row, Great Missenden,   *Tel* (02406) 8818
Buckinghamshire HP16 9LT

Case sales only **Open** Mon–Fri 9–5.30 **Closed** Sat, Sun, public holidays
Credit cards None accepted; personal and business accounts **Discounts** Available
occasionally **Delivery** Free locally and in London (min 5 cases); elsewhere at cost;
mail order available **Glass hire, Tastings and talks** Not available
Cellarage £4.03 per case per year

'With a constantly changing inventory, Turville Valley Wines
encourage their customers to let them know the sort of wines
they require, rather than waiting for their list, so that they can
be offered such wines as soon as they become available.' So
there you are. If you're looking for a particular vintage of
classed growth claret, *premier* or *grand cru* burgundy, Rhône
from the big names, port, madeira or maybe some venerable old
Krug, put Michael Raffety and his team on to it.

There is a list, of course, and there are also plans afoot to raise
the profile of the company with fine wine tastings and fine wine
and food dinners during the coming months. Remember, as you
look through the list, that VAT still has to be added, and note
also that, as Turville Valley Wines is as yet unlicensed, you will
have to buy at least 12 bottles, which means considerable outlay
as there isn't much here below £30 per bottle. Yet prices, given
that we're up in the stratosphere here, are competitive: buy a
case of Pétrus '83 from Turville rather than from Fine Vintage
Wines and you will save over £300, even if you are £1,735
poorer.

Best buys

White burgundy from Ramonet-Prudhon
Graham's Vintage Port
Vintage Madeira

For merchants who sell a minimum of twelve bottles, we say 'Case
sales only' in the details at the head of an entry.

T & W Wines

51 King Street, Thetford, Norfolk IP24 2AU   *Tel* (0842) 765646

Open Mon–Fri 9.30–5.30; Sat 9.30–2.30 **Closed** Sun, public holidays
Credit cards All accepted; personal and business accounts **Discounts** Not
available **Delivery** Free within 15-mile radius of Thetford (min 1 case) and
elsewhere (min 4 cases); otherwise 1–3 cases £9.76; mail order available
Glass hire Free with 1-case order **Tastings and talks** Not available
Cellarage £4.70 per case per year

Everything about T & W Wines is characterised by
thoroughness, neatness and efficiency. From a charming shop in
a quiet East Anglian country town comes probably the biggest
range of wines in Britain, 3,000 in total (though only 600 are
actually stored on the premises, and by no means all are listed).
T & W is unquestionably the leading specialist in the country
for large and small bottles (there are over 300 half-bottles, and
they get a listing of their own). The list, like the shop, is
clearly laid out and unfussy, though be warned that the prices
are all ex-VAT. The selection is impeccable. 'Quality of wines
and service is of the utmost importance to us,' says Trevor
Hughes, an ex-hotelier. 'All wines are guaranteed, even rare old
wines. In general we do not buy from other importers in
England, but only direct from the producer. Our philosophy is
never to buy wine on price; only on quality. The same goes for
delivery: we dispatch wine normally within 24 hours of receipt
of order, and we use express carriers.'

For this, expect to pay. You can get almost anything from
T & W – even that Jeroboam of Romanée-Conti 1985, 'probably
one of the greatest burgundies ever produced', at £2,300 – and
the customers that T & W can best serve are those for whom
money is of little object. There is no point in reciting all the
glories of the list, and no space to do it anyway. Suffice it to say
that everything you would expect to find there is there, and
among the treasures that you might not expect is a wonderful
range of Tokaj from vintages between 1947 and 1983, a good
collection of small-grower champagnes as well as no fewer than
ten Krug vintages back to 1952, a lovely range of back vintages
of white Marqués de Murrieta at not too knee-trembling a price,
the legendary Sauternes of Château Gilette, and fine Californian
wines from Flora Springs, Dunn, Far Niente, St Clement, Silver
Oak, Duckhorn and Costello. If it's your father's seventieth
birthday next year, or your own twenty-fifth wedding
anniversary, you'll find one page in the list devoted to
'Anniversary Years' and what T & W can supply you with to
lubricate the occasion fittingly. Rapid delivery guaranteed.

Best buys

Margaux Private Reserve 1985 (second wine of Château Kirwan),
£10.29
Chardonnay 1986, Flora Springs (Napa Valley), £10.23
Tokaj Aszú Essencia 1957 (Hungary) (50cl), £69.00

Ubiquitous Chip Wine Shop   ⌇ 🕮 ⟹

12 Ashton Lane, Glasgow G12 8SJ   *Tel* 041-334 5007

Open Mon–Fri 12–10; Sat 10–10   **Closed** Sun   **Credit cards** All accepted;
personal and business accounts   **Discounts** 5% on 1 case   **Delivery** Free in
greater Glasgow (min 3 cases); mail order available   **Glass hire** Free with 1-case
order   **Tastings and talks** Regular informal tastings on Sundays in the restaurant;
to groups on request   **Cellarage** Available

The Ubiquitous Chip is a restaurant, just completing the second
decade of existence; you might think, therefore, that it does not
live up to its name, and you'd be right. The name is a kind of
challenge on Ron Clydesdale's part, only possible in a country
where irony and understatement furnish the rivets of everyday
speech.

Challenges are obviously relished here: the restaurant was
originally an unlicensed one. To build up a head-turning wine
list from nothing, and then – when customers start to ask if
they can buy bottles to take home – to rise to that challenge and
go on to make yourself into one of Glasgow's leading wine
merchants, shows bristle-chinned determination. Prices
throughout are very fair (and even better than that in restaurant
terms), and the list is admirably balanced. The temptation to go
for the showy bottles is resisted; good-value wines from try-
harder producers are the order of the list. New Zealand, Eastern
Europe, Spain and Portugal are all better than you might
imagine, even given the generally high standard; and how
many restaurants give you a choice of two Cahors, or Sardinian
or Sicilian reds with your haunch of venison and clapshot? Fine
sherries from Valdespino, Domecq and Garvey are well worth
roaming through; even Coliseo is here, at the appealingly low
price of £13.95. Sceptical? Try it; only try it. The malt whiskies,
finally, are breathtaking: three pages of 'em, including bottles
from distilleries that no longer exist.

As this is Scotland, in-store tastings are not yet permitted, but
informal Sunday-morning tastings in the restaurant are
organised for customers on the mailing list. Bin-end clearances,
we are told, offer slow-moving wines to customers at cost prices
– a claim that rings true from the Chip.

Best buys

Quinta do Côtto 1985, Douro, Montez Champalimaud (Portugal), £3.95

Donnafugata Rosso 1985, Tenuta di Donnafugata (Sicily), £5.25

St Magdalene Single Malt Whisky, distilled 1964, Lowland, £22.25

Unwins Wine Merchants

Head office

Birchwood House, Victoria Road, Dartford,   *Tel* (0322) 72711
Kent DA1 5AJ

Approximately 300 branches in South-East England

Open Mon–Sat 10–2, 4–10; Sun, public holidays 12–2, 7–9.30   **Closed** Chr Day
Credit cards All accepted; personal and business accounts   **Discounts** 10% on
case lots   **Delivery** Free in South-East England (min 1 case); mail order available
Glass hire Free   **Tastings and talks** Occasional branch tastings; to groups on
request   **Cellarage** Not available

Unwins, unlike a number of other high-street chains, is independent: it is owned by the Wetz family, who originally came from Alsace. Not being part of a large group means that Unwins shops operate 'without the constraints of having to push parent company lines,' as wine buyer William Rolfe puts it. They can buy whatever they want from whomever they want.

This is all well and good, but it's only part of the equation. The other, and probably more important part, is Unwins' aspirations as a wine retailer, reflected in the position, size and look of their shops, and how much of the list each one stocks. Here, the news is not so good: many of the shops are cast in a very traditional off-licence mould, with the emphasis on beer, Piat d'Or, and Lambrusco in large party bottles. The more interesting wines, if they are there at all, have to fend for themselves, with little back-up other than a plastic shelf price tag clipped into a plastic shelf. There is, as yet, no evidence of any of the re-presentation or fresh thinking towards wine-selling seen in some of the shops of some of the other big chains.

Yet there are good things on the list, chiefly a fine selection of classed-growth clarets. (Ordering these through the branch manager will almost certainly be necessary, and we suspect that at least 95 per cent of Unwins' customers are unaware of their existence.) Most of the burgundy, depressingly, seems to come from Bichot – this may not be 'a parent company line', but it's pretty constrained nonetheless. There are some good Loire wines, and Châteauneuf-du-Pape fans get four to choose from; the rest of the Rhône is largely sourced from a négociant called

Mousset, the owner of one of the Châteauneuf-du-Pape
properties listed. There are a few good wines from South-West
France, but the French countryside here is mostly vins de pays
in litre or three-litre bottles. Germany and Italy present a pretty
bleak picture; Rioja, one Portuguese garrafeira, three New
Zealanders and a small clutch of Australian reds are the straws
to be clutched outside France. Unwins, at present, cannot be
said to be an exciting place to buy wine.

Best buys

Sancerre 1988, Clos des Roches, Vacheron, £6.95
Châteauneuf-du-Pape 1987, Château des Fines Roches, £8.45
Sauvignon Blanc 1986, E & J Gallo (California), £3.49

The Upper Crust

3–4 Bishopsmead Parade, East Horsley,   *Tel* (04865) 3280
Surrey KT24 6RT

Open Mon–Sat 9–9; Sun 12–2, 7–9; public holidays 11–1, 6–8 **Closed** Chr Day
Credit cards Access, Visa; personal and business accounts **Discounts** 5% for 1
case **Delivery** Free within 30-mile radius (min 1 case); elsewhere at cost; mail
order available **Glass hire** Free with 1-case order **Tastings and talks** Regular
tastings every Saturday 11–4 from April-August and October-December; to groups
on request **Cellarage** £3.50 per case per year

East Horsley's Upper Crust, 'open 364 days a year', is one of
Britain's most stimulating independent merchants. Fanatical
enthusiasm is the first requirement for entry to the small club of
half-a-dozen or so who qualify for consideration as Independent
Merchant of the Year, and that is a quality Barry Ralph has in
plenty. The range of wines is huge, and most are annotated on
the list. For those who are used to the rather chaotic,
exclamation-mark-bespattered, laugh-a-minute style of this
document, invariably issued two months or more behind
schedule due to the torrent of new arrivals, the neatness and
orderliness of the shop comes as a surprise. During the spring
and autumn, tastings are held on Saturdays. Not only does The
Upper Crust make it worth finding out where East Horsley is, it
also makes a visit appealing.

Barry Ralph's latest enthusiasm is Italy. 'I will send you the
best ever list produced in June 1990,' he promised us. 'Watch
out for Italy!' June came; no list arrived. The Editor met Barry at
a tasting of Alsace wines and he said he was now producing a
special Italian supplement, which we would have within a few
days. Another month passed, and eventually a draft copy
reached us, bulging at the seams as usual. 'Unfortunately the
shop is not big enough physically to stock all these tremendous

wines, but they are always available with a little notice. I apologise for this wine guide getting out of control, but that's how it is. The greatest list I have ever produced, and I never did know where to stop . . . JUST WAIT TILL NEXT YEAR . . .!!!'

Well, it was worth the wait for fans of Northern and Central Italian wines (the South and the Islands are covered only sketchily). There is a wonderful range of Barolo and Barbaresco, including a page of fine wines of vintages back to 1961 from almost a dozen producers, and Super Tuscans have also fired the Ralph palate into extensive buying. Allegrini and Pieropan restore faith in the names Valpolicella and Soave, and there are Chiantis from Grati, Isole e Olena, Berardenga, Castello di Cacchiano, the La Canonica co-operative, Vicchiomaggio, Villa di Vetrice and Antinori. Altesino provides the Brunello and Rosso di Montalcino. No doubt East Horsley has been ringing to cries of 'Ciao, Barry!' this summer.

Don't, of course, forget the rest of the list – not that anyone at The Upper Crust is liable to let you forget it. The selections from Alsace, Burgundy, Chablis, Beaujolais, Australia and New Zealand are superb, while from everywhere else they are simply very good. As always with a first-rate merchant, you'll find that a wide range of suppliers contribute wines to the list, often in just one- or two-bottle quantities; complete ranges from a single source always imply laziness, and you won't find any of that here. The only time when wide ranges of wines from a single source are carried is when (as with Schlumberger in Alsace) the wines really merit it. Even there, you will find hot competition from the co-operative at Turckheim, from Trimbach, from Willm and from Hugel. Something else that Barry Ralph is prepared to do, and that is actually quite uncommon among many independent merchants, is travel: the fine selections from New Zealand and Australia, certainly among the best in the country, are based on thorough visits, as the notes make clear.

So there you are. Out with the map, and off to East Horsley. Or pick up the phone: mail-order is offered, and the list certainly justifies it when you wish to try the more exotic items. For bottles more easily available elsewhere, the £6 minimum delivery charge is something of a disincentive.

Best buys

Soave Classico 1989, Pieropan, £5.65
Dolcetto d'Alba 1988, 'Gagliassi', Mascarello, £6.69
Bourgogne Blanc 1987, Vallet Frères ('declassified Meursault'), £8.95

Valvona & Crolla ᝊ ⤳ 🦞

19 Elm Row, Edinburgh EH7 4AA *Tel* 031-556 6066

Open Mon–Sat 8.30–6 **Closed** Sun, 1–7 January **Credit cards** Access, Visa;
business accounts **Discounts** 5% on 1 case **Delivery** Free on UK mainland (min
£20 order for Edinburgh, £100 for UK mainland); otherwise £5.90 per consignment;
mail order available **Glass hire** Free with any reasonable order
Tastings and talks Regular in-store tastings planned for the end of 1990; quarterly
tastings annually; to groups on request **Cellarage** Not available

Philip Contini's list of Italian wines includes much of the best
that this most versatile of wine-producing countries has to offer,
from the highlands of the Alto Adige to the islands of Sicily and
Sardinia. A range of champagnes is also listed, together with a
pageful of ports ('The Port of Leith' is for sale at only £6.99,
while Dow 1980 looks terrific value at £13.89).

The 23 pages of Italian wines strike the necessary balance
between producers for whom innovation is paramount, like
Maurizio Zanella or Marco de Bartoli, and those working within
DOC-sanctioned traditions, like Giacomo Conterno, Borgogno or
Pio Cesare. There is balance, too, between selections from the
stars (over 20 wines from Gaja, and Biondi-Santini's Brunello in
eight different vintages) and selections of less prized producers
or denominations (a choice of eight different Montepulcianos
d'Abruzzo is an excellent idea, and there is no sweeping
dismissal of wines from Emilia-Romagna, or of Valpolicella).
The list is basically a non-annotated one, though enthusiastic
endorsements burst through from time to time; and there is
sound philosophy underlying the advice Philip Contini gives to
his customers: '... only your palate can decide what is good and
pleasing to you. In other words, do not take all you read as
"gospel" – have a bit of fun, taste for yourself, and make up
your own mind about a wine.' That's good advice at any time,
and never more so than with Italian wines, which often seem
shockingly frank and characterful to palates nurtured on the
tasteful urbanities of claret. If this festival of Italian wine can't
cure you of blinkered francophilia, nothing will. It's a
magnificent selection.

Best buys

Montepulciano d'Abruzzo 1988, Bianchi, £3.19
Ser Gioveto (Sangiovese) 1987, Rocca delle Macie (Tuscany),
£7.39
Rosso del Conte 1984, Regaleali, Conte Tasca d'Almerita (Sicily),
£11.39

Helen Verdcourt Wines ▭?

Spring Cottage, Kimbers Lane, Maidenhead,   *Tel* (0628) 25577
Berkshire SL6 2QP

Case sales only   **Open** All hours (24-hour answering machine)
Credit cards None accepted; personal and business accounts   **Discounts** 5% for
order of more than 12 cases   **Delivery** Free in central London, Berkshire,
Buckinghamshire and Surrey (min 1 case); elsewhere mail order delivery service at
cost (except Ireland)   **Glass hire** Free with wine order
Tastings and talks Tastings through various clubs; to groups on request
Cellarage Not available

Helen Verdcourt is in the middle of her third career at the
moment, as a distinctive solo wine merchant with a surprisingly
lengthy list. Evidence of the first career – as a biologist – can be
found in the list, with its illustrations of grape-guzzling
caterpillars and wine-bibbing moths. The second career, as a
mushroom-grower, seems to have had less impact – unless it is
in the inclusion of four or five botrytis-affected wines. And all
those years spent breeding and judging Siamese cats is traceable
only in her stealth and sure-footedness in finding the best
bottles from wherever the list pauses.

It pauses most memorably in the Rhône, where you'll find
fine red and white wines from the Perrins of Beaucastel, from
Jaboulet, Meffre, Guigal, Dervieux, Sorrel, Vallouit – and
Château Rayas 1985. Bordeaux and Burgundy are shorter, but
careful and varied, too (Bordeaux is full of ripe '85s from
Graves and Pomerol at present, though a number of these carry
the 'bin-end' tag). Southern France is dominated by Château de
Lastours, Château Vignelaure and Mas de Daumas Gassac, so
the people of Maidenhead and environs are obviously prepared
to pay for quality.

Germany is over almost before it begins, but Helen Verdcourt
seems to enjoy hunting around in Italy, Spain and Portugal. The
New World means the Antipodes at Spring Cottage, with Cape
Mentelle, Moss Wood and Cloudy Bay providing the icing on a
Rosemount/Wynns/Hill Smith cake. Helen Verdcourt spends
three or four nights a week tutoring tastings for wine clubs and
charities – with energy like that, she's probably got at least two
more careers ahead.

Best buys

Château la Courançonne 1985, Côtes du Rhône Villages-Seguret,
Gabriel Meffre, £4.20
Cape Mentelle Semillon-Sauvignon 1989, Western Australia, £7
Cru du Coudoulet 1986, Côtes du Rhône, Pierre Perrin, £5.25

Vessel du Vin ☞

Warehouse and office
Thurland Castle, Tunstall, via Carnforth,   *Tel* (046 834) 360
Lancashire LA6 2QR
Associated outlet
73 Penrhyn Road, Kingston upon Thames,   *Tel* 081-541 5753
Surrey KT1 3EQ

Case sales only   **Open** Office hours Mon–Fri 9–5   **Closed** Sat, Sun, public
holidays   **Credit cards** None accepted; personal and business accounts
Discounts 2% on £500 order   **Delivery** Free on mainland UK (min 1 case); mail
order available   **Glass hire** Not available   **Tastings and talks** Planned monthly
tastings in Kingston; to groups by arrangement   **Cellarage** £3.95 per case per year

This company has quite a complicated family tree. If the names
Redpath & Thackray or Hein Wines mean anything to you, then
stick with this entry: all three have been mixed into Vessel du
Vin. It is the only merchant in the *Guide* based in a *château*, and
quite a handsome one at that: Lancashire's solid and serene
Thurland Castle. And its list is as photographically
distinguished as John Armit's is pictorially distinguished. We
don't know who's taken the photos, but they are superb – and
beautifully printed. The background information the list
contains is good, but nothing like as compelling as the
photographs. One shows a sad-looking Piedmontese producer
called Luigi Artusio standing, in his suit, in a cold cellar. Like
all good photographs, it is enormously yet mysteriously
suggestive. Photography, by its nature, tells everything, so it is
only when it seems to hide things that it moves beyond itself –
as here.

The avowed aim of Vessel du Vin is 'to provide an
imaginative and highly selective choice of quality wines', and it
succeeds, though perhaps better at being highly selective than
at being imaginative. The range from Northern and Central Italy
(including the wines of the gloomy Signor Artusio and his
Cantina della Porta Rossa) is strong; there is nothing from
Southern Italy or the islands. This may well be the best listing
of wines from Provence in Britain, and the Southern Rhône is
well covered; there is nothing from the Northern Rhône.
Burgundy is almost all Bouchard Père et Fils; there is a short
Bordeaux section; and one or two wines (literally) from Alsace,
Spain and England. The champagnes of the small seven-grower
co-operative Champagne Palmer find a home here, together
with Marie-Pierre Palmer-Bécret, 'a charismatic French woman'
as the list puts it. In addition to being charismatic (something,
admittedly, she is good at), she also acts on behalf of the
Champagne Palmer agency. And there you have it: selective
throughout, and imaginative in its championing of Provence,

the Southern Rhône and some less well-known Northern Italians
– and in its photographer and list printer.

Best buys

Côtes du Rhône Villages-Cairanne 1985, Domaine de l'Oratoire
Saint-Martin, £4.95
Château Simone 1985, Palette (red), £8.80
Moscato d'Asti 1988, Cantina del Parroco di Neive, £6.35

Victoria Wine

Head office
Brook House, Chertsey Road, Woking,   *Tel* (0483) 715066
Surrey GU21 5BE
Over 850 branches nationwide; also approx 140 branches of Haddows

Open Hours vary from branch to branch   **Credit cards** All accepted; personal and
business accounts   **Discounts** 5% on 1 case of wine, 3% on any 5 bottles of wine
Delivery Mail order available   **Glass hire** Free   **Tastings and talks** Promotional
tastings in-store from time to time; to groups on request (apply to Head Office)
Cellarage Not available

Victoria Wine (which includes the Scottish Haddows chain) was
for many years the slumbering giant of the British wine scene.
'Is it in a coma, or just sleeping?' we Lilliputian doctors
muttered, as we prodded and poked its doughy form. We
thought we could hear a heartbeat, but it could just have been
wishful hearing. Time passed; nothing much happened.

Last year, though, the giant began to stir; this year, amid the
clapping of tiny hands, it staggered up on to its feet. It shows
every sign of wanting to run about a bit next year, and as for
the year after that . . .

The changes that have brought about this reawakening at
Victoria Wine are twofold. First, there has been an
organisational overhaul. The Gare du Vin and South of the
Bordeaux experiments are over: all have reverted to being
Victoria Wines outlets. But the shops are firmly divided up into
one of four 'Family Groups', and the group in which each finds
itself governs the number of different wines it carries. The 155
different Family Group One shops, for example, must stock at
least 335 wines of the total 550 wines available. The 202 Family
Group Four shops, by contrast, need carry only 85 wines, filling
up the rest of their shelf space with cans of Skol and Mackeson.
Most shops (398) are in Family Group Two; least (68) are in
Family Group Three. If you live near a Family Group Four shop,
move. Preferably to somewhere just off London's Kings Road,
where the flagship Group One branch is, at number 123 (lots of
numbers, but at least that one is easy to remember). The interior

design of the shops is slowly being changed, too, with ash wood replacing plastic, and the wines of different regions being divided from one another to make it easier for customers to make sense of the battalion on display. Eventually, shelf tickets will contain mini-notes on each wine, and this will be very helpful for those of us who don't carry wine encyclopedias around in our heads.

The other important element in getting the giant vertical again has been a much livelier approach to wine-buying than heretofore. Victoria Wine now stocks – shout it from the rooftops – a number of Exciting Wines. At least three have already been mentioned in the Editor's Choice section, and there are others: a very competitively priced Vins de Pays des Côtes de Gascogne, as nettley fresh as any; a beautifully fragrant Vin de Pays des Côtes Catalanes; a fat, nutty, white Côtes du Rhône; a fine, concentrated Chardonnay and a lushly blackcurranty Cabernet Sauvignon from Errazuriz Panquehue in Chile; the minty red Côtes du Brulhois; a stunning Coteaux du Languedoc from Domaine de Pradel, balanced and deep; and the characterful red Côtes de Saint-Mont (Val de Sensac), full of rich herbiness. Of these wines, only the Chilean Chardonnay is over £4. If you have more money to spend, there are plenty more good wines to buy: clarets; burgundies; fine German wines; exciting Australian extroverts like Wolf Blass and his whopping, super-oaked Chardonnay; sparkling wines and champagnes (the Henriot Blanc de Blancs is horribly expensive, yet hard to fault in its tongue-turning, creamy complexity). Italy ain't bad, but it's scheduled to get better this autumn; perhaps it will be Spain and Portugal's turn next year. Victoria Wine are already very good for South American wines, with Chile, Brazil and Argentina all listed; and we were pleased to find that, on calling at one of the Oxford branches, the assistant had tasted, and was able to talk encouragingly about, the intriguing Torrontes from Argentina. Well done, too, to Victoria Wines for hauling in half-bottles of the outstanding Redwood Valley Late Harvest Rhine Riesling – one of the finest New Zealand dessert wines to reach Britain to date.

Before you put your house-next-to-a-Group-Four-shop up for sale, know that Victoria Wine produce a list, and that it's a good one. Not only is it accurate, but it's also intelligent; it's even honest. 'Sauternes is a difficult area to find inexpensive wines of interest [in] so it is worth snapping up any remaining stock of our Victoria Wine Sauternes in half-bottles. Unfortunately, once this limited supply of halves has finished it will not be replaced as there really isn't a comparable wine at the price.' You don't need to sell up, because when you have the list, you can use it to order wines from your local branch. And, we repeat, this is really a list worth exploring. Put your name down for the Wine Club (it costs nothing), and you will be sent leaflets with special offers as well as being kept up to date with new lists. Victoria Wine also offer a drinks gift service called Post Haste – if you use this, let us know how efficient it is. And please report back to us, too, on your own experience of the woken giant.

Best buys

Vin de Pays des Côtes Catalanes 1989 (white), £2.69
Domaine de Pradel 1988, Coteaux du Languedoc (red), £3.29
Redwood Valley Late Harvest Rhine Riesling 1988, New Zealand (half-bottle), £5.89

La Vigneronne

105 Old Brompton Road, London SW7 3LE   *Tel* 071-589 6113

Open Mon–Fri 10–9; Sat 10–8; Sun 12–2.30 **Closed** Public holidays
Credit cards All accepted **Discounts** 5% on 1 case **Delivery** Free locally (min 1 case); otherwise at cost; mail order available **Glass hire** Not available
Tastings and talks To groups on request **Cellarage** £6 per case per year (inc insurance)

La Vigneronne, about ten minutes' walk from South Kensington tube station, looks from the outside like any of the other smallish off-licences that lie so thickly on the ground in West London. Go inside, and you notice that there are rather a lot of bottles there, so you start to browse. And the more you browse, the more astonished you become – at the range, eclecticism and depth of the stock. If you see wines that you know already, you'll notice that they are more expensive at La Vigneronne. But mostly you just notice bottles that you have never seen before, or that you read about somewhere two years ago but have never found, or that you dreamed of once, sleeping your way through an afternoon in a hotel in Narbonne, or that baffle you completely. Like?

Like seven fortified solera wines from De Muller in Priorato, cask-aged antiques, at £45 to £50 each; like 20 vins doux naturels from Banyuls, Maury and Rivesaltes, including three nineteenth-century examples; like seven different mistelles, including Pineau des Charentes, Floc de Gascogne, the Jura's Macvin and Ratafia from Champagne; like a wide range of Provence's wines, including Bellet and Palette and different cuvées of the organic Terres Blanches; like the widest selection of Alsace wines you're likely to find anywhere, including grands crus galore; like six Bourgueils and four vins jaunes; like Alsace eaux-de-vie made from everything from the usual plums and cherries to quince, holly berries and elder; like eight grappas;

like 34 sherries; like a real range of old solera and vintage Madeiras . . . and so on, and so on. We've just cited the wackier wines, but there are plenty of gorgeous aristos from Bordeaux and Burgundy, too. And while you are wondering how much of this exotica you have the money to buy and the strength to lug home, plumbers are dropping in for cans of Coke and British Telecom engineers for Seven-Up, just like in any small neighbourhood shop.

To get hold of the fat little list, you need to become a subscriber, at present for £10 per year. However, each issue (it's called 'The Wine Journal') brings you at least £20's worth of money-off offers and tasting tickets, as well as the chance to buy a range of discounted 'Subscribers' Case Offers'. La Vigneronne runs one of London's best programmes of tastings, and its *en primeur* offers make everyone else's look wooden-headed: at the time of writing you could buy 1989 Beaujolais, Mâcon, Loire and Alsace wines, as well as a selection of Antinori's top 1986 cuvées on a first-bite basis, and some Château Coutet '89 too. Nothing stands still at La Vigneronne; Liz and Mike Berry's shop is one of Britain's most constantly stimulating wine merchants.

Best buys

Mas Jullien 1987, Les Cailloutis, Coteaux du Languedoc, £5.50
Brauneberger Juffer Sonnenuhr Riesling Kabinett 1986, Wilhelm Haag, Mosel, £7.95
Alsace Grand Cru Wiebelsberg Riesling 1985, Marc Kreydenweiss, £11.95

Villeneuve Wines

27 Northgate, Peebles, Peeblesshire   *Tel* (0721) 22500
EH45 8RX

Open Mon–Wed 10–6; Thur, Fri 10–8; Sat 9–10   **Closed** Sun
Credit cards Access, Visa; personal and business accounts   **Discounts** 5% on 1 case   **Delivery** Free in Edinburgh, Borders, Glasgow (min 1 case); otherwise at cost; mail order available   **Glass hire** Free   **Tastings and talks** To groups on request   **Cellarage** Not available

Villeneuve Wines in Peebles is not a big shop, but maximum use is made of the available space in order to accommodate as many bottles as possible. Despite this, the overall look is not cluttered; the bottles are shelved neatly and tidily, each with its own descriptive price tag. It looks like an agreeable spot to do 10 or 15 minutes' browsing in.

The list is mid-length, with the emphasis on France, but also with an evident commitment to try to find something from most countries and for all tastes. Merchants can be divided into cats and magpies: the cats are those who stick with a single supplier once they have found what they want, and take a range from that supplier; magpies are those who pick a bottle from here and a bottle from there until they have a list that brings together as many growers as wines. Villeneuve is a catmerchant; having found Jaboulet's Rhône wines, the burgundies of Faiveley and Bouchard (Père et Fils), the Loire wines of Saget and Langlois Château, the Bergeracs of Jaubertie, the Barolos of Borgogno, the New Zealand wines of Montana and Stoneleigh or the Provençal wines of Domaines Ott and Domaine de Trévallon, Director Kenneth Vannan sticks with them, and puts a range on display. As these producers are good ones, the system is a match for that of the magpies; it is a disaster, of course, if the producers are indifferent ones. Only the most relentlessly curious customer would fail to get about six months' worth of useful wine shopping from Villeneuve – and more, of course, as the list evolves. The single and the temperate will be pleased by the range of half-bottles; and we understand that knowledgeable advice is enthusiastically offered here.

Best buys

Domaine de Trévallon 1986, Coteaux d'Aix-en-Provence-les-Baux, Eloi Dürrbach, £8.99
Alsace Pinot Blanc 1988, Cave Coopérative de Ribeauvillé, £3.69
Beronia Reserva 1982, Rioja, £4.49

Vinature

16 Cotton Lane, Moseley, Birmingham
B13 9SA

Tel 021-449 1781/7472

Case sales only **Open** Mon–Fri 9–6; Sat 10–4 **Closed** Sun, public holidays **Credit cards** None accepted; personal and business accounts **Discounts** 5% on 2–5 cases, 10% on 6–11 cases, 12.5% on 12+ cases **Delivery** Free within Greater Birmingham and elsewhere (min 6 cases); otherwise £5.45 per case; mail order available **Glass hire** Free **Tastings and talks** Regular talks and tastings to various groups **Cellarage** Not available

---

Birmingham-based Vinature have a range of almost one hundred organic wines from most of the world's major wine-producing countries. Ex-environmental researcher and teacher Clive Gilbert also claims the largest range of guaranteed vegan wines in the UK, with plenty on the list for vegetarians, too. (Many of the traditional finings used for clarifying wines are based on animal or dairy products, which is why this issue arises in the wine context.)

You'll find unusual as well as familiar names here; Vinature have actually gone out and hunted down organic producers for themselves, and are the exclusive stockists of Domaine des Cèdres from the Côtes du Rhône, Domaine de Matens from the Gaillac region, Domaine l'Ametlier from near Pézenas, Mas Madagascar from Gard, Christian Georget from Bourgueil, Olson Vineyards from California and 'the legendary Simone Couderc' from Coteaux du Languedoc. (Perhaps next year's list will relate the legend.)

Not many merchants stock any Côtes du Jura wines, let alone organic, but Vinature have found one; while the Bordeaux red and Entre-Deux-Mers white of Château La Blanquerie, the Côtes de Provence white of Connesson and the sweet Sainte-Croix-du-Mont of Château Lousteau-Vieil have all won plaudits from fairs, guides and gurus (of the neatly turned-out American rather than the hirsute Indian sort). And here is some interesting news: 'Lenz Moser [see Editor's Choice], Austria's most celebrated oenologist, is going organic. Moser hopes to convert all of his vineyards by the turn of the century. His first ecological wine is delightfully perfumed, dry and clean with excellent body and length.' Buy it here.

Best buys

Château La Blanquerie 1986, Bordeaux Supérieur (suitable for vegans), £3.29
Fumé Blanc (Sauvignon Blanc) 1989, Olson Vineyards, California (suitable for vegans), £5.43
Corbières 1989, La Romanissa (suitable for vegetarians), £3.33

Vinceremos Wines

Unit 10, Ashley Industrial Estate, Wakefield   *Tel* (0924) 276393
Road, Ossett, West Yorkshire WF5 9JD

Case sales only   Open Mon–Fri 9–6; Sat 10–4   **Closed** Sun, public holidays
Credit cards Access, Visa; personal and business accounts   **Discounts** £1 for 10+ cases; £2.50 for 20 cases   **Delivery** Free withing 25-mile radius of Leeds (min 1 case); otherwise 1–5 cases 75p per order; 6+ cases free; mail order available
Glass hire Free with order   **Tastings and talks** Tri-annual public tastings; to groups on request   **Cellarage** Not available

Confirmation that organic wine sales are booming in Britain at present comes from Vinceremos who, since publication of the last *Guide*, have been forced to leave their old mansion house in 'rural inner Leeds' and move to an 'ergonically [ergonomically?] practical light industrial warehouse half a mile from junction 40 of the M1' in order to increase storage space. The Vinceremos list also confirms the French lead in organic wine production, with an excellent choice of French country wines as well as a producer or two in most of the classic regions. Some of the

Vinceremos growers are widely seen elsewhere, like Guy Bossard; others are near-exclusives. Jerry Lockspeiser's Provence pair, Domaine du Jas d'Esclans and Domaine Richeaume, are far better than many of the non-organic wines of the region, and the same could be said of the Vins de Pays de l'Hérault of Domaine de Clairac. Organic champagne from José Ardinat and Jean Bliard is joined by organic Clairette de Die, sparkling Saumur and Blanquette de Limoux. There are a few organics from Spain, Italy, Germany, Hungary, Australia, New Zealand, California and England, as well as organic spirits, beers and juices.

Then off comes the organic hat, and on goes the pith helmet (or whatever explorers wear nowadays): Soviet wines and beers, Brazilian beer ('Every bottle sold sends a donation to save the rain forests of Brazil'), Greek wines from Calliga on Cephalonia, Omar Khayyam from India, Peruvian wines from Tacama and a range of six Flame Lilies from Zimbabwe join eighteen bottles from three wineries in Australia (Montrose, Peter Lehmann and Baileys of Glenrowan – try the two fortified dessert wines from this last producer). Drink to future elections in Nicaragua, and any sort of elections in Cuba, with the Flor de Caña and Havana Club rums. The list, of course, is printed on recycled paper.

Best buys

Côtes du Rhône 1988, Vignoble de la Jasse, £3.95
Côtes de Provence 1986, Domaine du Jas d'Esclans, £3.95
Côtes de Provence Cabernet Sauvignon 1988, Domaine Richeaume, £8.69

Vineyards Wine Warehouse

Vine House, London Road, Ashington, West Sussex RH20 3DD   *Tel* (0903) 892933

Case sales only   Open Mon–Sat 10–6; Sun, Good Friday 10–4
Credit cards Access, Visa **Discounts** 2.5% on 3 cases, 5% on 6+ cases
Delivery Free in West Sussex (min 1 case); otherwise £3 per case in Hampshire, Surrey and East Sussex and £6 per case nationwide **Glass hire** Free with 1-case order **Tastings and talks** Approx every 3 months to regular customers by invitation; to groups on request **Cellarage** Not available

---

A good selection of Loire wines, a promising exploration of *petit-château* claret under £10, the beginnings of a good Spanish and Portuguese range (including two fine Kopke colheita ports) and plenty of sparkling wines (champagne included) have won Vineyards Wine Warehouse a place in this year's *Guide*. Australia, New Zealand and Chile are good as far as they go, while Germany and Italy need a little polishing. So does the list:

producer information is very erratic and vintages almost uniformly absent. While we applaud the intent to provide brief tasting notes on wines, comments like 'Incomparably delightful' leave the questing purchaser no wiser. Could we ask readers in the West Sussex area to report?

Best buys

Château Poyanne 1986, Côtes de Bourg, £5.35
Montlouis Cristal Chenin Brut (sparkling wine), £5.25
Kopke Colheita 1977 (tawny port), £11.75

El Vino

47 Fleet Street, London EC4Y 1BJ	*Tel* 071-353 6786
New El Vino, 30 New Bridge Street, London EC4V 6BJ	*Tel* 071-236 4534
The Olde Wine Shades, 6 Martin Lane, Cannon Street, London EC4R 0DP	*Tel* 071-626 6876

Open (Off-sales) Mon–Fri 9–7.45 **Closed** Sat, Sun, public holidays
Credit cards Access, American Express, Visa; personal and business accounts
Discounts Available on payment of order (min £50 order) **Delivery** Free locally (no min) and elsewhere on UK mainland (min 2 cases); otherwise £4.80 for 1–2 cases; mail order available **Glass hire** Free with order **Tastings and talks** Twice yearly tutored tastings by invitation to regular customers; lunchtime tastings in wine bars; to groups on request **Cellarage** £2 per case per year

After a four-year absence from the *Guide*, El Vino returns, thanks to a much-improved list, and to a sense that tradition alone will no longer suffice as an incentive to customers. Greater emphasis, we understand, is to be given to staff training and to wine sales services (including a mail-order and gift operation, special offers and tastings); and the wine shops are to be refitted. We hope that *Guide*-reading City workers will monitor these improvements, and report back.

El Vino's strengths lie in own-label fortified wines, and French and German wines; indeed apart from a nod at Rioja, the rest of the world might as well not exist. Within France, you won't be surprised to hear that claret is particularly good, with a tempting range of older, mature vintages, attractively priced. Lafite '70 costs £85 from El Vino compared with £122 from Fine Vintage Wines; while Ducru-Beaucaillou of the same year can be had for £49 from El Vino compared with £64.50 from Christchurch Fine Wines. Differentials are reduced with more recent vintages, but El Vino's £15.80 for Château Batailley 1982 still beats the Averys price of £17.39. Burgundy is up to scratch, and the Rhône selection is rather better than one might expect, with El Vino actually taking the trouble to age its Hermitage and Châteauneuf before selling it: thanks. But unless we know whose Hermitage or Châteauneuf it is, we have no idea whether it's a bargain or a disaster, and the list does not tell us. Nor does it let us into the secret of whose Santenay '78 we are offered at £10.20, or Clos Vougeot '78 at £30, or Morey-St-Denis '82 at £8.40 . . . Unless producers are specified in future, it will be hard to take 'The Armchair Wine Buyer's Guide' seriously as the mail-order document it is intended to be: you will simply have to go to the shops to taste first.

That, in truth, has always been El Vino's special appeal. It has a chain of three 'tasting houses': wine bars/informal restaurants where you can try selections from the list with food, and then buy them for drinking at home if you like what you find. For the moment, that would seem to be the best course to continue to take. Sir David Mitchell, MP, and his brother Christopher, the two directors of this family-owned company, promise '*no* hard sell'. An innovation since El Vino's last inclusion is that women are now served at the bar.

Best buys

Petit Chablis 1987/88 (Domaine de l'Eglantière, though the list doesn't tell you), £6.65
Château Cissac 1975, Haut-Médoc, £14.95
El Vino No 3 Fino Sherry, £4.25

Vintage Roots   ⠛⠃

Not a shop
25 Manchester Road, Reading, Berkshire   *Tel* (0734) 662569
RG1 3QE

Case sales only   **Open** Mon–Fri 9–6; Sat by appointment (24-hour answering service)   **Closed** Sun, public holidays   **Credit cards** Access, Visa; personal and business accounts   **Discounts** Available   **Delivery** Free within 30-mile radius of Reading; otherwise 1 case £3.95, 2 cases £5, 3+ cases £6; mail order available   **Glass hire** Free with 5-case order   **Tastings and talks** Annual London tasting; in-store tastings on request; to groups on request   **Cellarage** Not available

This Reading-based wholesale company, run from home, sells only organic wines. The list is short and friendly, with a useful first page that explains exactly what 'organic' does and doesn't mean in the wine context. Then it's on to the wines, and a range that goes some way beyond the usual heavy-sediment Rhônes and wholemeal Vins de Pays d'Ocs. There are smart white burgundies from Jean Javillier (Meursault 1987, £8.99) and Jean-Claude Rateau (Puligny-Montrachet 1988, £12.70), champagnes from Jean Bliard, Serge Faust and Régis Poirrier, Californian wines from Frey and New Zealand wines from James Millton, two Australian wines from Botobolar, plenty from Italy, two Hungarian reds and a white, a red Valdepeñas – even Muscat de Rivesaltes, and a brace of Cognacs. Organic drinking can be catholic, too. The tasting notes accompanying each wine are thorough and well written, and include serving suggestions and mention of whether decanting is needed or not.

Prices are generally fair, given that organic farming is always more expensive than the other sort. If you live more than 30 miles from Reading, though, delivery costs can add 33p per bottle on a single mixed case.

Best buys

Vin de Pays des Collines de la Moure, Merlot 1987/88, Domaine de Farlet, £3.15
Saint-Gilbert 1986/7, Shiraz/Cabernet, Mudgee, Botobolar Vineyard, £5.99
Blanquette de Limoux, Cuvée Malvina-Buoro, Domaine de Mayrac, £5.99

The Vintner/Viticulteur

See Arthur Rackhams.

A L Vose   ☞

Town House, Main Street, Grange-over-Sands, Cumbria LA11 6DY   *Tel* (05395) 33328

Open Mon–Sat 9–6; public holidays 9–6 or permitted hours   **Closed** Sun
Credit cards Access, Visa; personal and business accounts   **Discounts** 10% on 1 case   **Delivery** Free in Cumbria and north Lancashire (min 1 case); elsewhere at cost; mail order available   **Glass hire** Free with case order
Tastings and talks Annual tasting by invitation; monthly club meetings; to groups on request   **Cellarage** £1.50 per case per year

If you are an Austrian and your wife or husband is a Brazilian, Cumbria's fearless and exotic A L Vose is the merchant from whom you should buy home tastes while abroad. Don't worry if you live in Kent: 'We like to think that we are rather good on delivery,' the Vose family tell us. The Austrian range (26 wines and seven fruit brandies and liqueurs, all with tasting notes) is longer than the Brazilian (eight varietals from Palomas); their rarity value in a British wine merchant's shop is about the same at present.

The German section is also good: five pages of wines, with a welcome readiness to stock wines made from grapes other than the Riesling (though fine Rieslings are here, too, especially from the Mosel). Two reds from the Ahr and a range of eight from Franken confirm that this is a merchant whose courage is not in

question. There are good, fighting selections from North
America and Australia; while Chile, a surprisingly lengthy
French range, Italy, Portugal and Spain all contain wines to
intrigue, lending the list as a whole good depth and balance.
We are pleased to see a range of Vintage Ports from Cálem,
especially the front-ranking 1985, but why are none of the ports,
not even the rubies and whites, priced? Normally merchants
bleat about 'speculators' at this point, but we have yet to meet
anyone who felt it was worth their while speculating on Dom
José Ruby from Royal Oporto or Cálem's Fine Dry White. You'd
be better off betting on next month's weather.

Best buys

Kremser Hauerinnung Grüner Veltliner Spätlese 1985, Winzer
Krems, Austria, £6.80
Château Dallau 1986, Bordeaux Supérieur, £5.40
Pinot Noir 1985, Palomas, Brazil, £4.10

Waitrose

Head office
Doncastle Road, Southern Industrial Area,   *Tel* (0344) 424680
Bracknell, Berkshire RG12 4YA
92 licensed branches in London, Midlands and the Home Counties

Open Varies from store to store but generally Mon, Tue 9–6; Wed 9–8; Thur 8.30–
8; Fri 8.30–9; Sat 8.30–5 **Closed** Sun, public holidays **Credit cards** None
accepted **Discounts** 5% on £100 expenditure or full cases **Delivery** Not
available **Glass hire** Free **Tastings and talks** Occasional evening tastings for
customers **Cellarage** Not available

We mentioned, in discussing Tesco's wine areas, that they
contrived to look less supermarket-like and more wine
merchant-like than those of some of their rivals, but the master
of this art is, of course, Waitrose. Not only does the company
reject the 'own-label' principle almost completely, with the vast
majority of the wines selling in the producer's own packaging
as at any ordinary wine merchant, but it also creates dedicated
wine areas with their own entrances and exits, and their own
tills, wherever possible. You can use Waitrose exactly like a
wine merchant, therefore; and it would be a wine merchant
with a good, varied range and some extremely attractive prices.
There is a clear, unfussy and very John-Lewis-like list (never
knowingly stylish) to take home and look through, and it
includes straightforward information on wine storage and
serving. The only discrepancy between Waitrose and a good
wine merchant, as usual, would be in terms of advice from the
assistants – if you do try asking questions, let us know how you

get on. And an innovation for this year is, as it happens, greater integration of wine into the rest of the shop, in that you will be able to pay for your wines at any till rather than having to pay for them separately in the wine area as previously. This facility has been instituted in response to customers' requests.

Balance has always been the hallmark of the Waitrose list under Julian Brind MW and his team, and it continues to be so. France leads and Italy follows, though Spain, Portugal, Italy and the New World are not far behind. There is less from Eastern Europe here than at most supermarkets, reflecting, we suppose, the geographical concentration of Waitroses in the more prosperous parts of southern Britain. Most of the regional ranges begin at under £3 and are topped by fine wines that approach or exceed £10.

If we examine the most recent new arrivals on the list, they have the look of finishing touches to a picture already largely painted, rather than massive, slashing revisions to sections misconceived from the outset, or scrambling attempts to line the shelves with the trendy and the talked-about. In come one or two new burgundies at the lower end of the price scale, taking advantage of three good vintages in a row; in come a Cahors and a Dão, because the team have found examples that taste better than most (at just under £4.50, neither are particularly cheap); in comes a crisp Saumur Brut with the Waitrose name on it, because the non-champagne sparkling sector is about to become the focus of considerably more interest to customers than previously (thanks to Champagne's policy of rationing by price); in come two new white Bordeaux, to reflect the extraordinary quality and value that whites from this region now offer; in comes a Jacquère from Savoie, to add a little further variety to French white country wines. Waitrose always manages to spike its list with a number of singular wines, like the pleasingly aromatic Wagner Barrel-Fermented Seyval Blanc from New York State, the delicious Moscato d'Asti from Michele Chiarlo, or the big, mallowy Verdelho from Houghton in Western Australia – but it never bellows its own originality at you; you'll just have to nose your way around the display and un-niche them for yourself. The overall impression is perfectly summed up by the reader who described it as 'A lovely quiet selection'. Careful, thoughtful, varied and unshowy: Waitrose's contribution to our high streets is a valuable one.

Best buys

Don Hugo, Alto Ebro (non-vintage; red), £2.59
Domaine du Petit Clocher 1988, Anjou Rouge, £2.99
Château de Berbec 1986, Premières Côtes de Bordeaux, £3.95

Peter Watts Wines

Wisdom's Barn, Colne Road, Coggeshall, *Tel* (0376) 561130
Essex CO6 1TD

Case sales only **Open** Mon–Fri 9–1, 2–5.30; Sat 9–1 (2–5.30 prior to Christmas)
Closed Sun, public holidays **Credit cards** Access, Visa; personal and business
accounts **Discounts** Not available **Delivery** Free in England (min 2 cases);
otherwise at cost; mail order available **Glass hire** Free with 1-case order
Tastings and talks Tastings held twice annually **Cellarage** Not available

Peter Watts is an importer and wholesaler who seeks out small
producers of quality wines, chiefly in France and Germany. If
your palate is jaded by the wines of the worthy and the famous,
make your way to Wisdom's Barn at Coggeshall in Essex where
there are always a few bottles open for tasting; the selection is
wide, so mixing a case shouldn't be a problem. The Watts
approach seems to work particularly well in Burgundy, where
Robert Ampeau and Domaine de Mazilly lead a varied field.
Petit-château Bordeaux is extensive, too. The champagnes of the
Joly family have been a great success for their importer, and
these are now joined by a range from Nominé-Renard, about
which Mr Watts is equally confident.

The New World and South America are represented on the
list, with Undurraga's Chilean wines proving a safer bet than
the wacky Palomas trio from Brazil. Spain is sound, though
Torres hardly qualifies as a small or little-known producer, and
the same could be said of Italy, where Santa Sofia takes centre
stage.

A quarter of trade at present is with the public; if that
includes you, please write and let us know your opinion of the
range and the service provided by Peter Watts Wines.

Best buys

Vin de Pays des Coteaux de Fontcaude 1985, Domaine de
Mallemort (Cabernet/Merlot), £3.50
Mosel 1988, J & H Selbach, £3.10
Alsace Grand Cru Praelatenberg 1986, Gewürztraminer, Louis
Siffert, £5.55

The Wine Standards Board is the trade's disciplinary department and
wine watchdog. Their inspectors are responsible for rooting out any
malpractices – but they are concerned largely with labelling
irregularities. If you have genuine reason to suspect that the wine in a
bottle is not what the label claims it is, contact the Board at: 68½ Upper
Thames Street, London EC4V 3BJ; *Tel* 071-236 9512; or contact your
local Trading Standards Officer.

Weavers of Nottingham

1 Castle Gate, Nottingham, Nottinghamshire   *Tel* (0602) 580922
NG1 7AQ
17 Castle Gate (tasting room)

Open Mon–Sat 9–5.45   **Closed** Sun, public holidays   **Credit cards** All accepted;
personal and business accounts   **Discounts** 10% on 1 case   **Delivery** Free within
25-mile radius of Nottingham City centre (min 1 case); otherwise £5 for first case,
thereafter £1.50 per case; mail order available   **Glass hire** 10 pence per dozen
Tastings and talks Tastings by invitation; to groups on request   **Cellarage** Not
available

A 'personal, relaxed and unsnobbish service' is claimed by
Weavers of Nottingham, and reports from local readers seem to
bear this out: 'a welcome oasis in a desert of brash commercial
indifference,' writes one contented customer. The company is
approaching its 150th anniversary, while Alan Trease, the
Managing Director, is the third generation of his family to run
Weavers, which is based in two attractive Georgian buildings in
Castle Gate. The shop is in No 1, while wines can be tasted, or
wine-related items bought, in No 17.

The A4 list has a Georgian stateliness to its design, and the
wines are clearly and unambiguously specified. An extensive
champagne selection gets it under way, with Krug and Roederer
present in startling strength; there is also a range of a dozen or
so sparkling alternatives to champagne. Chablis from William
Fèvre, Long Depaquit, Laroche and the co-operative La
Chablisienne presumably indicates another Trease enthusiasm;
Patriarche and Bouchard Père et Fils dominate burgundies from
further south. There is sterling support from Weavers for the
Vintners Pride of Germany group of producers, and Castle Gate
would be a good place to begin a reassessment of fine Rhine
wines. Bordeaux needs no reassessment, just investment, and
there is lots here to invest in. The Spanish section is sound but
unambitious, propped up by Rioja from two or three large
bodegas plus a selection of Torres wines; Italy needs more
research. The rest of the list contains but one surprise: four
Cypriot wines compared with only two from Portugal (one of
those being Mateus Rosé). A long list of ports cannot really
compensate for the lack of some of the country's superb red
table wines, though it tries. The range of sherries is fine: 11
finos to chose from! Is there an Andalusian community in
Nottingham?

Best buys

Château la Brande 1979, Fronsac, £5
Pando, Williams & Humbert (fino sherry), £4.95
Château Kirwan 1985, Margaux (half-bottle), £7.20

Wessex Wines

197 St Andrews Road, Bridport, Dorset *Tel* (0308) 23400
DT6 3BT

Case sales only **Open** Mon–Sun 8.30–9 **Closed** Occasional holidays
Credit cards None accepted; personal and business accounts **Discounts** 5% on
minimum of 6 bottles (unmixed) **Delivery** Free within 20-mile radius of Bridport
(min 1 case); elsewhere at cost; mail order available **Glass hire** Free with 1-case
order **Tastings and talks** Two large general tastings annually; to groups on
request **Cellarage** Not available

Wessex Wines' owner, Michael Farmer, is a merchant with
broader horizons than many. He began work in the wine trade
with Christophers in 1964, and subsequently spent a number of
years in vineyards in Burgundy and Switzerland, as well as
working for wine importers in California. Wessex Wines is now
in its twelfth year of existence, and Michael Farmer has been
back in the UK for fifteen years, but the list still has a well-
travelled look, with labels from Canada, Zimbabwe, Argentina
and Washington State among those affixed to it.

Throughout, the emphasis is on inexpensive wines; indeed,
you have to look quite hard to find bottles costing over £7 or £8.
The French regions furnish most of the list, with modest
contributions from Italy and Germany, and appealing selections
from Spain and Bulgaria. Given the broad horizons and the
emphasis on inexpensive wines, it is hard to account for
Portugal's table-wine absence from the list. Australia and New
Zealand provide nearly two dozen bottles, with Rosemount and
Cooks respectively dominant. A sighting of four ports from
Niepoort is welcome; couldn't Michael Farmer be pursuaded to
add some of the excellent Niepoort vintages of the 1980s (such
as 1980, 1982, 1985 or 1987) to keep the solitary Graham's 1970
company?

Best buys

Château du Cros 1985, Loupiac (sweet white), £5.89
Merlot del Trentino 1987, Cavit, £3.99
Château Musar 1982, Lebanon, £5.36

Best buys – in most cases, these are the Editor's choice of three out of a
range of ten wines selected by the merchant in question as being
distinguished in terms of value for money, or offering very fine
quality regardless of price.

Whiclar & Gordon Wines ✒

Glebelands, Vincent Lane, Dorking, Surrey RH4 3YZ	*Tel* (0306) 885711 (24-hour answering service) *Tel* (0306) 885686/888161 (orders/queries)
Mill Lane, Bridge, Canterbury, Kent CT4 5LM	*Tel* (0227) 830439

Case sales only **Open** Mon–Fri 9–5.30; Sat 9–4 (Dorking), 9–1 (Bridge)
Closed Sun, public holidays **Credit cards** Access, Visa; personal and business
accounts **Discounts** Not available **Delivery** Free in Surrey, Kent and London
(min 1 case); elsewhere 1–11 cases £1.50 per case; mail order available
Glass hire Free with 1-case order **Tastings and talks** 2 major in-store tastings in
Dorking; 2 day tasting at Dorking Halls; to groups on request **Cellarage** Not
available

This is a new name in the *Guide* – composed of two old ones. In
January 1990 Andrew Gordon of Andrew Gordon Wines joined
forces with Ian Whigham of Whiclar Wines to form Whiclar &
Gordon. Interestingly, Thomas Hardy & Son (Australia's second
largest wine producers) are a major shareholder in the new
company. The two warehouses are sited at Dorking in Surrey
and at Bridge in Kent.

Whiclar & Gordon have produced an original list, tall in
format and bound using three-quarter sized sheets – so that full
pages (containing the listing of the wines) are interleaved with
half-width pages containing label reproductions, background
information and wine descriptions. It's a clever idea, and it
works well. The list is medium length, with Andrew Gordon
bringing an extensive French range to the partnership and Ian
Whigham a host of New World wines. In between come two
pages of Italian wines (dominated by the Hardy-owned Brolio/
Ricasoli portfolio), one of German wines, and nibbles from
Spain, Portugal, Greece, Hungary and England (including
Nutbourne Manor's excellent Bacchus).

Hardy, of course, dominates the Australian selection, with its
Earlybird, Bird Series, Stamp Collection, Eileen Hardy Selection
and Nottage Hill wines, but Lindemans, Rosemount, Penfolds
and Yarra Yering also get a look in. Masson, Franciscan and
Mondavi provide Californian wines, as do Montana and Nobilo
for New Zealand, and Caliterra for Chile. But in fact it is in
France that the greatest variety is to be found, with fine
Bordeaux and burgundies and good French country wines.
Claret-lovers might be interested in the wide selection of 1981
crus classés, many of them reasonably priced; within Burgundy,
perhaps the focus of attention will fall on wines from less well
known villages and from the Côte Chalonnaise, giving a good

range of authentic tastes for under £10 (and more authenticity for over £10, if you want Premiers and Grands Crus). The country tour takes in Gaillac and Apremont, and most areas between. You can even lease a row of vines in a Côtes de Duras vineyard through the 'Wineshare' scheme. Wellington boots and a car full of demijohns are not necessary: it will be turned into 30 cases of wine a year on your behalf.

Best buys

Domaine Tapie 1989, Vin de Pays des Côtes de Gascogne (white), £2.75
Domaine du Puget 1988, Merlot, Vin de Pays de l'Aude, £2.45
Bourgogne Rouge 1987, oak-aged, Cave de Buxy, £4.75

Whighams of Ayr ☞

8 Academy Street, Ayr, Ayrshire KA7 1HT   *Tel* (0292) 267000
Whighams Young & Saunders at Jenners,   *Tel* 031-225 2442
48 Princes Street, Edinburgh EH2 2YJ

Open Mon–Sat 9.30–5.30 **Closed** Sun, public holidays **Credit cards** Access, American Express, Visa; personal and business accounts **Discounts** 15% on 1 case **Delivery** Free in Scotland (min 3 cases); mail order available
Glass hire Free **Tastings and talks** Major tastings held twice annually; to groups on request **Cellarage** £3.45 per case per year

There aren't many merchants in this *Guide* that have been waiting for a shipment of wine for over 200 years. Whighams' 15 pipes of Madeira were, unfortunately, deposited on a West Indies sea bed by the good ship Nelly in 1767, the year after the company was founded (as Alexander Oliphant & Co). It must have been a blow at the time; today it's just one of a number of evocative anecdotes in the brochure produced by the company to celebrate its long history.

A terrible quantity of claret has made its way past Ailsa Craig and round the Heads of Ayr during those two centuries if today's selection is anything to go by, for this is certainly the deepest stratum of the list. The Whigham philosophy is one of firm relationships with long-standing suppliers (in many cases with Whighams acting as Scottish agents), and the long-standers here are Château Puyfromage, a Bordeaux Supérieur shipped by the company since 1967 (the irresistibly named Fromage Blanc from Entre-Deux-Mers has recently been added to the list), and the fourth-growth Château Beychevelle. The maritime associations of this Saint-Julien property doubtless strike a chord with Ayr's old sea dogs; there are plenty of other growths available, classed or not, with which to compare this pair.

Burgundy is long on Chanson and short on Bichot, but a

Whighams

choice from two négociants-éleveurs is better than a choice from one. Plenty of champagne, some Loire, a trio of Rhône wines and a handful of Beaujolais bring France to an end. There is a good selection of Mosels and Rheinhessens from Dr Willkomm; and Orsola in Piedmont has recently joined Pasqua's Veneto wines and Castell'in Villa's Chiantis. There isn't much else; though the Swiss wines from the Vaud are unusual and welcome. Nearly everything on the list costs over £5. The port selection is of interest, though we deplore the mysterious refusal to price these wines in the list: what possible justification can there be for leaving us in the dark about how much is to be asked for a bottle of Fonseca's Bin No 27 or Siroco white port – or Taylor 1970, come to that? This is one tradition that should be scuttled as soon as possible.

See page 306 for an explanation of the symbols used in the *Guide*.

605

Best buys

Château Puyfromage 1986, Bordeaux Supérieur, £5.80
Graacher Abtsberg Riesling Kabinett 1988, Dr Willkomm
(Mosel), £6
Young & Saunders Champagne (non-vintage), £11.11

Whitesides Wine Merchants   ✷ ☞

Shawbridge Street, Clitheroe, Lancashire   *Tel* (0200) 22281
BB7 1NA

Open Mon–Sat 9–5.30 **Closed** Sun, public holidays **Credit cards** Access, Visa;
personal and business accounts **Discounts** 5% on 1 unmixed case **Delivery** Free
within 50-mile radius (min 1 case); elsewhere at cost; mail order available
Glass hire Free **Tastings and talks** Regular tastings for invited customers; to
groups on request **Cellarage** Not available

Clitheroe, twinned with Rivesaltes in France, could count itself
fortunate if it just had D Byrne & Co to draw on as a wine
merchant; the fact that it has Whitesides as well leads us to
classify it as one of the most thoroughly spoilt towns in Britain.
    Whitesides produces a well-organised and informative list, in
which Parker's scores, Webster's recommendations,
International Wine Challenge medals, and *Which? Wine Monthly*
selections all egg you on to purchase. The range has a slightly
neater, more contained and rational feel to it than does
D Byrne's, where a baroque prodigality seems to be the guiding
principle. But don't be misled: there are plenty of highways and
byways here, too, with Greece, Cyprus and Lebanon providing
a mixed case; with four pages of Australian wines and over two
dozen from New Zealand; and with a wide range from
California led by thirteen from Robert Mondavi (Blush Zin to
Opus One).
    The only part of France inadequately listed is the South, from
Provence through the Midi to the South-West; all the classic
regions are generously stocked, with Burgundy, Beaujolais and
the Rhône present in depth (Duboeuf and Jaboulet dominating
in the last two cases). The emphasis in the Loire is on dry wine,
with four Sancerres and another four Pouilly-Fumés for
Sauvignon Blanc fiends. The German section will please
traditional tastes, with most of the wines listed being of
Kabinett grade and up, and Trocken wines almost completely
absent. Italy and Spain are equally conformist, with familiar
names (Chianti, Barolo, Frascati, Orvieto, Rioja – and Torres)
offered most widely. Throughout the list, table wines, branded
wines and bulk wines are as prominent as those of individuality
and character; better both, of course, than just the former.

Spirits and beers are as widely stocked as wines, and the range of half-bottles is extensive.

Best buys

Fitou 1986, Cave Pilote, £3.59
Bernkasteler Badstube Riesling 1989 Qualitätswein, Friedrich Wilhelm Gymnasium, £4.84
Pernand-Vergelesses 1987, Domaine Besancenot-Mathouillet, £9.49

Whittalls Wines

Château Pleck, Darlaston Road, Walsall, West   *Tel* (0922) 36161
Midlands WS2 9SQ

Case sales only   Open Mon–Fri 9.15–5.30   **Closed** Sat, Sun, public holidays
Credit cards None accepted; personal and business accounts   **Discounts** Not
available   **Delivery** Free within 8-mile radius; elsewhere 1–3 cases £5, 4–5 cases
£7.50, 5+ cases free; mail order available   **Glass hire** Free with 4-case order
Tastings and talks Not available   **Cellarage** £1.15 per case per year

Living in Walsall? Fancy a mixed case of fine wines? Some classed growth claret from 1982, 1985 and 1986 would fill half the case nicely (the Cordier properties Talbot and Meyney are well represented here, and produce lovely wines); for the rest, try a bottle of Rodet's burgundy, Jaboulet or Guigal's Rhône (Hermitage if you can afford it, Crozes if you can't), Etienne Daulny's Sancerre, a Schloss Vollrads Kabinett, the Marius Tinto from Almansa and a Hungarian Tokaj Aszú 5 puttonyos for dessert. It'll cost between £100 and £150 depending on exactly what you choose, and the place to go for all this is the Darlaston Road. Just look for Château Pleck.

Château Pleck? That's what it's called. The name of Whittalls' base is in fact rather more imaginative than the choice of (mainly fine) wines on its list, but then if you're shelling out £100 or more for a case of wine you don't necessarily want to take risks. Most producers listed have very sound reputations. The range is wide enough to mean that you should set aside a good half-hour for choosing exactly what goes into your case; prices are reasonable, though not quite as good as the ex-VAT list makes you think at first. (Prices of the Best Buys do include VAT.) If you're a Château Pleck regular, or if you make your first journey there during the next twelve months, write and let us know your experiences.

If your favourite wine merchant is not in this section, write and tell us about him or her. There are report forms at the back of the book.

Best buys

Sancerre 1988, Etienne Daulny, £6.27
Crozes-Hermitage 1988, Domaine de Thalabert, Jaboulet, £6.40
Château Paveil-de-Luze 1986, Margaux, £6.73

Willoughbys

53 Cross Street, Manchester M2 4JP	*Tel* 061-834 6850
100 Broadway, Chadderton, Oldham, Greater Manchester OL9 0AA	*Tel* 061-620 1374
1 Springfield House, Water Lane, Wilmslow, Cheshire SK9 5AE	*Tel* (0625) 533068
Associated outlets	
George Dutton & Son, Godstall Lane, St Werburgh Street, Chester, Cheshire CH1 1LN	*Tel* (0244) 321488
Thomas Baty & Sons, 37–41 North John Street, Liverpool L2 6SN	*Tel* 051-236 1601

Open Mon–Sat 9–6 **Closed** Sun, public holidays **Credit cards** Access, Visa; personal and business accounts **Discounts** 5% on 1 case **Delivery** Free in Greater Manchester, Merseyside, Cheshire and Lake District (min 1 case) **Glass hire** Free with 1-case order **Tastings and talks** Regular weekend tastings held in-store; specific tastings for regular customers; to groups on request **Cellarage** £4.02 per case per year

If you have anything to celebrate, make a note of Willoughbys' address: in addition to one of the widest ranges of champagne in the country (between one and seven champagnes each from no fewer than 22 producers), this old-established Manchester merchant also has an excellent range of sparkling wines. The claret section makes you tipsy just looking at all that closely typed nomenclature: there are 79 1986s listed, from the wonderfully named 'Willoughbys Daily Claret' up to Château Margaux, and 78 1985s; with lorryloads of 1987, 1984 and 1983 (no nonsense about 'off years' here); with more 1982 than most merchants have managed to hang on to; and with smaller quantities of earlier vintages. This is a real collectors' collection, with great châteaux and unknown châteaux and well-loved châteaux and châteaux that Uncle Raymond always used to buy; and prices are reasonable. If you are not vintage-obsessed, tuck into the 'super seconds' from 1987 at under £15 (Pichon-Lalande at £14.05, and Ducru-Beaucaillou and Cos d'Estournel at £13.05 as we write). The Sauternes is as good, very good. Is Bordeaux twinned with Manchester, by any chance?

To say that the burgundy selection does not match up to the clarets is not to dismiss it: on anyone else's list, it would look impressive. Textile millionaires will enjoy the seven Domaine de la Romanée-Conti wines, while the rest of us will derive as much pleasure from exploring the ranges from Rodet and Parent. The Jura and Haut-Poitou are taken seriously here, and so is Corsica; the Rhône is a bit of a disappointment, but Willoughbys' buyer has taken a good look around Languedoc-Roussillon. Outside France, the list dissipates slowly, like a vapour trail; there is no shortage of choice in the German, Italian and Spanish sections, but the buyer seems to have searched for sound wines with familiar names rather than outstanding wines regardless of their names. Willoughbys do have good selections from England and New Zealand, though, and at no point do the offerings look inadequate.

Perhaps there is there a Scottish community near Cross Street? The whiskies are superb – as good as the clarets in terms of choice; and other spirits and liqueurs are not far behind. We suspect there may be good Vintage Ports here, too, to match the fine range of tawnies, LBVs and brands; this, though, is another merchant who is drearily coy about Vintage Port: not only do we not know what the prices are like, but we don't even know what may or may not be available, as the main list goes glassy-eyed at this point. Maybe we'll be able to tell you next year. The weekend tastings held in the shops look worth taking part in, and note the good range of half-bottles available.

Best buys

Château Léoville-Barton 1987, Saint-Julien, £9.75
Château Graville-Lacoste 1988, Graves (dry white), £5.19
Château de Rully 1988, Rully, Rodet, £9.99

Winchcombe Wine Merchants

21 North Street, Winchcombe,   *Tel* (0242) 604313
Gloucestershire GL54 5LH

Open Mon–Sat 9–10; Sun 12–2, 7–9; Good Friday 12–3, 7–10 **Closed** Chr Day, Boxing Day, 1 Jan **Credit cards** Access, Visa; personal and business accounts **Discounts** 5% up to £50, 7.5% on £50+ (wine only), 5% on sparkling wines **Delivery** Free within 20-mile radius; elsewhere at cost; mail order available **Glass hire** Free with case order **Tastings and talks** To local groups on request **Cellarage** Not available

Several recommendations have reached us during the last year for this small and neatly organised shop in Gloucester. Ted Adlard used to farm, but retired early for health reasons; with the help of his wife Sue, he has now turned a hobby into a second career. The stated aim is to provide a range of interesting and relatively unusual wines, with a particular emphasis on those of Spain. The range of wines has increased from 140 when the Adlards took over to 250 or more at the time of writing, and expansion of the list is to continue.

There is a good Spanish selection, mainly drawn from Rioja and Navarra, and France is well covered, too, with a solid hike around the vins de pays and an enthusiast's ramble through the different regions of Bordeaux. Most other countries are represented to the tune of a bottle or two, and the local Three Choirs wines put in a welcome appearance – they are among England's best.

Best buys

Gran Feudo 1986, Chivite (Navarra), £3.71
Marqués de Griñon Blanco 1988 (Rueda Superior), £6.01
Château des Annereaux 1985, Lalande de Pomerol, £7.82

Windrush Wines

Wholesale outlet
The Barracks, Cecily Hill, Cirencester,   *Tel* (0285) 650466
Gloucestershire GL7 2EF
Retail outlet
3 Market Place, Cirencester, Gloucestershire   *Tel* (0285) 657807
GL7 2PE

Open Mon–Fri 9–6; Sat 9–6 (Market Place only) **Closed** Sun, public holidays
Credit cards Access, Visa; personal and business accounts **Discounts** By
arrangement **Delivery** Free on mainland UK (min 1 case); mail order available
Glass hire Free with 1-case order **Tastings and talks** Occasional tutored tastings;
to groups on request **Cellarage** £4.60 per case per year (min 5 cases)

Master of Wine Mark Savage has, over the last decade and a half, made Windrush Wines one of the country's most stimulating merchants. Not by dint of exclamatory advertising and publicity-seeking media interventions; strategems of this sort would be completely uncongenial to the quietly spoken, thoughtful Mr Savage. But by building a most unusual list in which the wines, and particularly the Pinot Noirs, of North America are matched to the most authentic and distinctive wines of the Old World, with Pinot Noir again the point of reference.

'If there is one single word in the wine writer's vocabulary that I most dislike, it is the word 'best', for it implies that there is one correct answer to a question which is an amusing one precisely by virtue of the variety of answers that it offers . . .' writes Mark Savage in this year's list. This stress on the relativity of wine appreciation is fitting in one who specialises in Pinot Noir, for no other grape produces such a wide range of flavours and styles, often 'difficult', in the wines produced from it. Any reader exploring red burgundy and ready to go beyond, into Oregon and Washington, should certainly frequent the Windrush list. Other pleasures lie in Mark Savage's devotion to Saint-Emilion, in the fine Bandol of Domaine Tempier and the Collioure of Mas Blanc, and in a collection of individualists from Germany, Tuscany and Piedmont. You would guess that, if anyone was going to include Tasmania in their Australian selection, it would be Mark Savage – and you'd be right. The monstrous Lagavulin is among the four malt whiskies stocked, and the spirits list includes pear and apple brandies from Oregon. Windrush, home of the brave. If you enjoy wines of character, make for Cirencester's Market Place, or take advantage of Windrush's free nationwide delivery.

Apologies to Mark Savage for 'Best Buys' below: here, as elsewhere throughout the *Guide*, these three wines are a selection from ten or so that the merchant concerned – who should know everything on the list intimately – has put forward as offering particularly distinguished quality and value.

Best buys

Hautes Côtes de Nuits 1985, Domaine Michel Gros, £7.95
Snoqualmie Fumé Blanc 1988 (Washington), £4.98
Ponzi Pinot Noir Reserve 1987 (Oregon), £12.95

The Wine Emporium

7 Devon Place, Haymarket, Edinburgh   *Tel* 031-346 1113
EH12 5HJ

Case sales only   Open Mon–Sat 10–7; Sun 11–5   **Closed** Chr Day, Boxing Day, 1 & 2 Jan   **Credit cards** Access, Visa; personal and business accounts **Discounts** Not available   **Delivery** Free in central Scotland (min 1 case); elsewhere charges on application; mail order available   **Glass hire** Free with 1-case order   **Tastings and talks** Monthly tutored tastings; to groups on request **Cellarage** £2.76 per case per year

There are two main reasons for shopping by the case at The Wine Emporium rather than shopping by the bottle at one of Edinburgh's superb retail merchants: you want to taste before you buy, or you want to buy wine on a Sunday. Scottish law rather creakily denies either option to retail-licence holders.

The cover of the Emporium's list, by Jan Gray, is stylish and youthful in feel, and this is echoed by the warehouse itself – which houses contemporary art exhibitions as well as wine. The Wine Emporium has been unable to supply us with an up-to-date version of the list, however, and we are in any case unsure as to what proportion of the wines stocked are actually listed – if it's a high proportion then the range is not wide, nor would

the warehouse deserve to be called an Emporium. Could we
have more reports on the range and choice available here,
please? The only useful conclusions we can draw in the interim
is that Italy and Spain are treated as seriously as France (Spain
is due to expand further this year), and that French country
wines are as important as the classic regions. And it would
seem to be a good place to come and talk whisky: 'Although our
malt whisky range is not large, we have one of the world's
foremost experts on the subject on the staff,' general manager
John Lamond tells us.

Best buys

Salice Salentino 1983 (producer not specified), Puglia, £3.99
Cousiño Macul Chardonnay 1989, Chile, £3.99
Marius Reserva 1982, Almansa, £3.79

Wine Growers Association   ⇨

Mail order only
430 High Road, Willesden, London   *Tel* 081-451 0981/1135
NW10 2HA
or
Freepost, London NW10 1YA

Credit cards Access, Diners Club, American Express, THF Goldcard, Visa;
business accounts **Discounts** Possible **Delivery** Free within M25 (min 3 cases)
and on UK mainland (min 6 cases); otherwise £3.75 in London and £4.25 on UK
mainland **Glass hire**, **Tastings and talks**, **Cellarage** Not available

It is strange to note how much better the Wine Growers
Association list is now that the company has slimmed down to
a mail-order-only operation than it used to be when it had a
chain of shops. It is distinctly specialised today, too: claret on
the one hand, and Italian wines on the other. A third speciality
is being developed as we write, in 'top-quality estates in south
and south-western France'.

The claret range is wide, covering vintages back to 1978 with
good choice from among both petits châteaux and classed
growths. Burgundy is also widely stocked, much of it emanating
from négociants (chiefly Reine Pédauque) rather than growers.
These négociants climb all over the Rhône section, too,
distressingly.

No, it's Italy you would want to turn to next, and you'll find
an excellent selection there. Tedeschi's superb Veneto range
would be worth filling an unadulterated case or two from; these
are wonderful wines. The Piedmont selection is excellent:
Borgogno, Brugo, Conterno e Fantino, Giuseppe Cortese,
Marchesi di Gresy, Arione and Fratelli Alessandria provide a

fine choice of Barolos, Barbarescos and other Nebbiolo-based wines. Trentino-Alto Adige and Friuli-Venezia Giulia supply most of the Italian white-wine interest, and there are representative selections from Lombardy, Umbria, the Marches and Latium, though not Emilia-Romagna (Cavicchioli's Lambrusco will, however, be found with the sparkling wines). The fine Tuscan range is sourced from Tenuta Caparzo, Castellare, Pagliarese, Cerro and Fattoria dell'Ugo, and contains all the big DOCs as well as bargain vini da tavola like Fattoria dell'Ugo's Rugo and prestige versions like I Sodi di San Niccolo from Castellare. Southern Italy, in Willesden, is dominated by Sardinia and the Sella & Mosca range, strong on variety and value, and there are outstanding wines from Abruzzo, Calabria, Apulia and Basilicata (including Fratelli d'Angelo's Caneto d'Angelo). There are a couple of vini da tavola from Sicily.

A page and half of Portuguese and Spanish wines must remain undescribed as we have yet to be shown that part of the list. Enterprising Australian, New Zealand and Californian selections steer the list towards a close, and Cálem's worthy port range is a final asset. Delivery terms, for a mail-order-only company, are not particularly attractive, particularly for customers outside the M25 boundary: you have to order six cases before you qualify for free delivery.

Best buys

Valpolicella Classico Superiore 1987, Vigneto Valverde, Tedeschi, £4.40
Torbato di Alghero 1988, Terre Bianche, Sella & Mosca, £4.40
Spanna del Piemonte 1987, Agostino Brugo, £3.75

The Wine House

10 Stafford Road, Wallington, Surrey   *Tel* 081-669 6661
SM6 9AD

Open Tue–Sat 10–6; Sun 12–2; public holidays variable   **Closed** Mon
Credit cards Access, Visa; personal and business accounts   **Discounts** To members of Wine Circle only   **Delivery** Free within 5-mile radius (min 1 case); elsewhere at cost; mail order available   **Glass hire** Free
Tastings and talks Occasional all-ticket tastings; to groups on request
Cellarage Not available

This is the kind of wine merchant that every neighbourhood dreams of: a small shop bulging with bottles, an enthusiastic and well-informed owner, and fair prices.

The Wine House has a list that would shame some mail-order specialists by its appearance, thoroughness and accuracy. Almost all the entries are annotated, and the notes reveal that

Morvin Rodker has tasted many of the wines thoughtfully and repeatedly, gauging their development. A glance around the shelves, or through the list, shows that the temptation to pick a sole supplier in a particular area, and source a complete range from that supplier, is resisted – one senses an appealing inability to let matters rest, a perfectionist's desire to find something better for every category, and for every new vintage. And there are few categories to fault. Maybe a Greek wine or two for next year, or something red from Sicily? It's as hard as that to find holes in this range.

The strengths are manifold. Spain is very fine, with a great swathe of Riojas, including three of this region's excellent rosés, and a dozen or so Reservas and Gran Reservas; The Wine House is also one of the few places in Britain where you can try wines from León, Somontano, Ampurdan-Costa Brava and Priorato. Red Bordeaux is nearly as good, with some nifty *petits châteaux* to balance the big guns, and a lot of open-minded work has gone into the burgundy section. (It requires an open mind to list, and champion, sparkling red Bourgogne Mousseux, £6.20.) Morvin Rodker's Italian section is soundly constructed, with the generally underrated wines of the Veneto splendidly prominent. And the Australian zone is rich enough to satisfy the most insatiable enthusiast, with many of the big names present, and a number of smaller producers represented, too. Yugoslavia, Portugal and Washington State are all particularly well researched, and the selection of over 25 sherries forms a much-needed defence of this fine but beleaguered wine.

An annual fee of £3 brings you into the Wine Circle. Once inside, you'll receive occasional mailings and updates of the list; more importantly, though, it entitles you to the discounted list price (usually about ten per cent less), provided you buy at least 12 bottles (which may be mixed) at any time.

Best buys

Château Sarail-La Guillaumière 1986, Bordeaux Supérieur, £4.95
Granato 1986, Trentino, Foradori, £12.95
Milion Pinot Noir 1986, £2.65

Prices were correct to the best of our knowledge as we went to press. They, and ranges of wines stocked, are likely to change during the course of 1991 and are intended only as rough indication of an establishment's range and prices.

Wine Raks

21 Springfield Road, Aberdeen AB1 7RJ	*Tel* (0224) 311460
1 Urquhart Road, Aberdeen AB2 1LU	*Tel* (0224) 641189

Open Mon–Sat 10–10 **Closed** Sun, Chr Day, Boxing Day, 1 Jan
Credit cards Access, Visa; personal and business accounts **Discounts** Available
Delivery Free locally (min 1 case); otherwise at cost; mail order available
Glass hire Free with 1-case order **Tastings and talks** To groups on request
Cellarage £4.99 per case per year

Electronics graduate Tariq Mahmood saw wine turn from a hobby into a profession about seven years ago, with his founding of Wine Raks in Aberdeen. There are now two branches, and in addition to wine you'll find a wonderful range of beers and an enterprising tea and coffee list. Cigars, too; even chocolates: 'On occasion we have been requested by beautiful ladies "when are you going to purvey some decent chocolates?". And we replied "as from now!"' The informative list is full of delightful turns of phrase.

There is a range of over 1,000 wines, enthusiastically if rather chaotically noted, with an enormously complex and thoroughgoing wine-and-food matching system to help you plan tonight's dinner. If you find the codes too much, 'just tell our staff what you're eating and we will put a wine to match,' Tariq Mahmood assures us. As much buying at source as possible is done (Mr Mahmood estimates that 80 per cent of stock is directly imported), and the range is full of variety. France provides much of the richness (a huge Alsace span from the fine Turckheim co-operative is worth citing); port and Portuguese table wines have also obviously fired proprietorial enthusiasm. The Springfield Road branch is pleasant and spacious, with the wines more clearly organised on the shelves than in the list itself.

We feel that Wine Raks would be a stimulating and enjoyable place to buy wine, particularly as many bottles in the range are not widely seen elsewhere. For the same reason, we are keen that Aberdeen readers should report back to us on how successful they feel the buying is, and with their general opinions of this 'small, diligently run local company'.

Best buys

Beauvolage Blanc de Blancs Brut, Touraine Mousseux, £6.20
Dão 1985, Rittos, £3.39
Château Milon 1985, Saint-Emilion, £8.95

The Wine Schoppen

1 Abbeydale Road South, Sheffield, South Yorkshire S7 2QL	*Tel* (0742) 365684/368617

Associated outlets

Wine Schoppen (Kidderminster), 131 Stourbridge Road, Broadwaters, Kidderminster, Hereford & Worcester DY10 2UH	*Tel* (0562) 823060
Pennine Wines, 5/7 Station Street, Huddersfield, West Yorkshire HD1 1LS	*Tel* (0484) 25747
R T Wines, Unit 11a, The Springboard Centre, Manth Lane, Coalville, Leicestershire LE6 4DR	*Tel* (0530) 39531 Ext 235
Barrels & Bottles, 1 Walker Street, Sheffield, South Yorkshire S3 8GZ	*Tel* (0742) 769666

Open Mon–Fri 9.30–6 Sat 9–5 **Closed** Sun, public holidays **Credit cards** Access, Visa; personal and business accounts **Discounts** 2.5% (min 3 cases) **Delivery** Free within 15-mile radius of any branch (min 1 case); elsewhere £3.95 per consignment; mail order available **Glass hire** Free with 1-case order **Tastings and talks** In-store tastings held every first Saturday of the month; tastings by invitation 4 times per year; wines always available for tasting in-store; monthly tastings through wine tasting club; to groups on request **Cellarage** £2.50 per case per year

Eddie and Anne Coghlan's neat, well-organised Sheffield shop is very popular with readers of the *Guide*, and not only for the wines they can buy there. Tastings for customers are laid on and, in addition, members of 'The Wine Circle' get a monthly tutored tasting. Circle members set off for Europe on Wine Study Tours two or three times a year, and great pride is taken in providing customers with knowledgeable and helpful advice. Commercial services include a range of hampers and giftpacks, wine accessories, books and gift tokens.

As the company name suggests, the emphasis in the 500-wine list is on Germany, and specifically the Mosel, Rheinhessen, Rheingau, the Ahr valley and Franconia. If you like fine German wine but find the nomenclature and detail confusing, put yourself in the Coghlans' hands; the selection is large enough to guarantee, for once, something for all tastes. If you prefer beefy reds, however, don't think that you have to go elsewhere to buy: Portugal is well covered, and the Spanish and Australian selections are adequate. There is a good range of claret for those who look for elegance in red wines, while Brazil, Chile and Greece will satisfy the adventurous. Nineteen ports, most of them from one of the leading Portuguese houses, Cálem, bring the clearly marshalled and designed list to a close. Everything about The Wine Schoppen suggests careful and thoroughgoing efficiency. (Pennine Wines of Huddersfield, R T Wines of

Coalville in Leicestershire and the new Barrels & Bottles in Sheffield carry limited ranges from this list but can order anything not in stock.)

Best buys

Westhofener Steingrube Silvaner Spätlese 1986, Weingut Meiser (Rheinhessen), £3.75

Nussdorfer Bischofskreuz 1988 (Nagel Hoffbaur), Rheinpfalz, £2.99

Sommerhauser Steinbach Silvaner Trockenbeerenauslese 1976, Ernst Gebhardt (Franken) (half bottle), £19.20

The Wine Society

Registered office (Mail order only)

Gunnels Wood Road, Stevenage, Hertfordshire SG1 2BG

Tel (0438) 741177 (enquiries)
Tel (0438) 740222 (24-hour answering service)

Open Mon–Fri 9–5; Sat 9–1 (showroom open all year for collections) **Credit cards** Access, Visa; personal and business accounts **Discounts** £1.20 on 1 unmixed case **Delivery** Free in UK (min 1 case or for orders of over £75); otherwise £3 **Glass hire** Free with 1-case order **Tastings and talks** Series of tutored tastings for members at Stevenage; regular tastings for members around the country; to groups on request **Cellarage** £3.60 per case per year (including insurance)

'The Wine Society' has rather a haughty ring to it, and some readers may still be under the impression that you have to be recommended by a member before you can join, as was the case a few years ago. (Officially you do have to be proposed by another member, but if you do not known any, the Company Secretary will be able to propose you without any problems.) Rather than being a bastion of crusty exclusivity, the Wine Society is in fact a co-operative – and a vintage one, at that, having been founded in 1874. No recommendations are needed any more: all you have to do to join is pay £20 for a lifetime share in the co-operative, and even this – joy unbounded – 'attracts credited dividends repayable on death'. The fact that the Wine Society is a co-operative means that all the profits go back into the Society itself, apart from the dividends paid out to dead members, and how useful that can be was proved conclusively by an unfortunate incident which took place during the last year. The Bordeaux firm of négociants J Meyniac et Cie defaulted during the autumn, and the Wine Society was one of its largest creditors. A large proportion of the debt owed by Meyniac to the Society was in the form of members' *en primeur* claret purchases. After what the annual report described as 'a careful but hectic interlude', Sebastian Payne, the Chief Wine Buyer, succeeded in rebuying every single case lost through the Meyniac default, and the Society has announced that it is easily able to sustain its probable £628,864 loss (though legal procedings are under way in Bordeaux to recover as much as possible). Whether a private company would have been able to do the same in similar circumstances is open to question; much would have depended on the profits taken out of the company by its owners.

And the list? Objectively speaking, it has to be one of the country's top fifteen, and we know from the response from Member readers that for many of you it is in the top five. It isn't one of that 'splendid cornucopia' breed of lists where enthusiasm runs riot and so many wines are stocked that nobody knows, literally or metaphorically, which way to turn. Instead it has a sort of Whitehall feel to it: highly organised, neat and efficient, filled with an elegently trimmed selection of over-achieving, dome-headed wines. You won't find a single 'obvious' entry in the whole document: every bottle has had to work hard in competitive examination to argue its way in. They are still wines like any others, of course, and we don't want to overplay this cranial card; a lot of them will taste bloody good, full stop. But we do feel that the Society probably best suits highly organised, serious and scholarly drinkers rather than the hirsute and hedonistic; that is the tone of the list, the appeal of the selection. Prices are not cheap, though the buyers obviously work hard to find the best in every category, and to fill every category down to £2.95 or so. A large number of ready-mixed cases is available.

The list is organised into sparkling, white, red and fortified, rather than country-by-country; last year's Editor liked this, this year's doesn't, but it probably does not make much difference either way once you get used to it. No one will be surprised to hear that most of the wines are French; nor, given the profile sketched above, should they be surprised to find that the Wine Society are just as good at hunting out curious and diverting bottles from *la France profonde* as they are at bringing home the bacon (sooner or later) from Burgundy and Bordeaux. Only the Wine Society would sell five vins jaunes; only the Wine Society would actually have to ration them; only the Wine Society would get the serving instructions right (though we still think the analogy with sherry, while tempting, is misleading). The Loire looks particularly good, but no Francophile will be disappointed by what he or she finds here.

Outside France, Germany – producer of Europe's most intellectually stimulating wines? – is well served; Italy, Spain and Portugal (mainly reds), too. Eastern Europe seems to have failed all the entrance exams so far, one Tokaj and partner excepted; the New World, meanwhile, is full of the sort of wines that send you lurching for your pocket guides: Wirra Wirra Church Block 1987, say, or Pyrus Coonawarra Red 1985. The sherries are very good, and the Wine Society is one of the last companies to import sherry in cask to bottle themselves. The casks are then dispatched to Scotland, where they receive the Society's 'fillings' – young whiskies that are cask-aged into The Society's Highland Blend. (Apropos, the list is full of The Society's Generics, printed in green in the list and evidently – we suspect the *hauteur* of this name on the label plays a part here – popular with members. You can even have The Society's Plum Pudding stuffed into your case. It must be a fat little thing: 'Please note that this occupies two compartments in a wine case', members are told with characteristic exactitude.) There are some good historical Vintage Ports, but only four ports under £10 – of which The Society's Crusted looks the best value. The spirit section is comparatively short and wine-buffy, with lots of Cognac and a Grappa Montagliari di Chianti Classico; there are glasses, cigars, and all sorts of other kit, like Decanter Driers and Foil Cutters. When it comes to buying Replacement Title Pages for The Society's Cellar Book, you have a choice between Blank Replacement Title Pages and Ready-Printed Replacement Title Pages. These people think of everything!

Society tastings are organised up and down the country, and every year there are Open Days at the Stevenage headquarters. You may go in person to the Stevenage showroom to collect your wine if you wish, but the delivery service has a very high reputation. Offers (including *en primeur*) and communications of all sorts are copious; and when *Which? Wine Monthly* asked its readers which of the merchants they used were they most pleased with, the winner was the Wine Society.

Best buys

Domaine de la Gardie 1988, Marsanne, Vin de Pays de l'Hérault (white), £3.85
Côt de Touraine 1988, Oisly-et-Thésée (red), £4.30
Château Pique-Caillou 1985, Graves (red), £8.45

Find the best new wine bargains all year round with our newsletter, *Which? Wine Monthly*, available for just £19 a year from: Dept WG91, Consumers' Association, Freepost, Hertford SG14 1YB – no stamp is needed if posted within the UK. (Price valid until 31.12.90.)

Winecellars

153/155 Wandsworth High Street, London   *Tel* 081-871 2668/3979
SW18 4JB
Associated outlet
The Market, 213–215 Upper Street, London   *Tel* 071-359 5386
N1 1RL

Open Mon–Fri 10.30–8.30; Sat 10–8.30   **Closed** Sun, Chr Day, Boxing Day, Easter
Day   **Credit cards** Access, Visa; personal and business accounts
Discounts Collection and quantity discounts available (min 1 case)   **Delivery** Free
within M25 (min 1 case); elsewhere £3 for less than 2 cases, 2+ cases free; mail
order available   **Glass hire** Free with 1-case order   **Tastings and talks** Series of
tutored tastings offered to the public throughout the year (excluding the summer
months); to groups on request   **Cellarage** Not available

Ever since Winecellars began to assume its present configuration
in the mid-1980s, it has offered a well-researched, well-written,
but rather serious and sometimes almost forbiddingly
informative list. The considerable wine scholarship of its two
MWs, Nicolas Belfrage and David Gleave, took over last year's
offering almost completely, with the wines seemingly relegated
to italicised footnotes at the end of the essays. Wonderful for
buffs like us, but perhaps not ideal for marching out into
Wandsworth High Street and winning new converts.

This year's list should relish that missionary role. The cover is
now in full colour, and features the staff, every one of whom is
kitted out with a winning smile or shapely legs, or both
(Mr Belfrage is the only staff member finding it hard to supply
either, but he manages to convey a kind of fatherly wisdom in
their place). The back cover shows the two MWs happily setting
about the product. There are recipes on tinted paper in the
middle of the list, while the balance between listings,
information and breathing space is ideal on all the other pages.
Competent and often atmospheric illustrations of producers and
winescapes add to the friendly feel. The list begins with The
Nicolas Belfrage Personal Selection (a mixed all-Italian case for
£77.10) and The David Gleave Personal Selection (a mixed
mostly-Italian case for £75.15), accompanied by third sightings
of the Selectors, this time realised with a little illustrator's
licence. Maps, finally, help focus our attention on the
whereabouts of the regions whose wines we are considering. It
is an enormous improvement on last year's list.

The wines, of course, were already pretty good, and there has
been no slippage on that front. Both Gleave and Belfrage are
Italian specialists; both have a book and a beltful of articles to
their names; and the wines, naturally enough, reflect their
Italian skills. The first 17 pages are given over to Italy, and the
recipes are Italian, too – supplied by the wine-growers

themselves. The selection of Northern and Central Italian wines is superb, with wonderful Barolo, Barbaresco and Chianti Classico from growers like Aldo Conterno, Fratelli Monchiero, Mauro Mascarello, Badia a Coltibuono, Isole e Olena and Castello di Volpaia. It is equally heartening, though, to see nine different Barberas and eight Dolcettos, to see real Soave (from Pieropan and Anselmi) and real Valpolicella (Allegrini, Quintarelli, Masi), to see Chianti Rufina match Chianti Classico, to see a big range of white varietals from Collio and Trentino-Alto Adige, to see four vin santo wines alongside Sassicaia, Tignanello and Cepparello. South of Abruzzi and Lazio, the selection is relatively disappointing, though there are still 20 or so good wines to chose from. Messrs B and G are disappointed, too: 'The South of Italy remains something of an unhappy hunting ground. During a visit there last autumn, I only came across two producers who had anything to offer in the way of quality. One had no wine to sell, while the other sold all he produced to local customers at prices which were, in my view, prohibitive.'

Winecellars may be an Italian specialist, but it also stocks a large and well-chosen range of other wines. Most are French; there is a fine span of country wines, including examples from the Jura; and the Rhône and the Loire offer something over a dozen wines each. Wandsworth residents doubtless demand that claret and burgundy are kept up to scratch; in each case, the level of variety is good, with a wide number of producers contributing a wine or two each. The German and Spanish selections are restrained but adequate, with the German wines listed by grape variety – a sensible innovation that merits imitation by other merchants. There are nearly a dozen Portuguese wines; sadly 'our customers do not seem to be very interested in them'. Wake up, folks!

The New World selection is composed of 'challenging' wines, such as Redbank's Mountain Creek Shiraz: 'I want to drink it because it stamps its character on my palate, not because it is a safe bet.' This quest for character would account for the fact that sherries are sourced from Valdespino, and it sets us up for the page of sweet wines, mainly from Italy: strange, exotic and stimulating. How good Italy is getting at sparkling-wine production can be gauged by trying a bottle of Mompiano Spumante Brut, and there are others from Italy, France and Spain to compare with the various champagnes. Look out, finally, for the special offers on wines like '85 Barolo and Tuscan wines: these would enable you to build the kind of collection that most merchants can furnish you with in claret and burgundy alone.

(The Market in Islington's Upper Street carries some of the list and can order anything not stocked.)

Best buys

Dolcetto d'Acqui 1989, Viticoltori dell'Acquese, £3.75
Montepulciano d'Abruzzo 1989, Miglianico, £3.69
Chianti Classico Riserva 1985, Vigneto Rancia, Felsina
Berardegna, £10.89

Wines from Paris ☞

The Vaults, 4 Giles Street, Leith, Edinburgh   *Tel* 031-554 2652
EH6 6DJ

Case sales only   **Open** Mon–Sat 10–6; Sun 11–6 during Edinburgh International Festival and during Dec   **Closed** Sun (except as above), Christmas, New Year and Easter   **Credit cards** Access, Visa; personal and business accounts **Discounts** Quantity discounts; £1 off per case collected   **Delivery** Free on mainland Scotland (min 1 case); mail order available   **Glass hire** Free **Tastings and talks** Various tastings organised during the year; to groups on request   **Cellarage** Not available

---

The Paris in question is not the one with the vineyard in Montmartre, but ex-journalist and press officer Judith Paris. Her wine warehouse is sited in Leith, in the severe, granitic and deeply historical surroundings of The Vaults, parts of which have been used to store wine for nine centuries. Neighbours today include The Scotch Malt Whisky Society, a predominantly mail-order supplier of fine cask-strength malt whisky, and The Vintners' Rooms, an elegant restaurant and wine bar. 'An uncommon alliance,' they claim.

The interior of Wines from Paris is a contrast to the exterior: it is as light, bright and white as that is grey and craggy. The list and associated typography are contemporary in feel, designer-led, and the logo appears to borrow that strange hermaphrodite the Prudential have chosen for their symbol, dunking him/her in a (Paris) goblet filled with red wine. At which point the hermaphrodite throws a pose, and the glass begins to topple.

The wines listed are well up to the extraordinarily high standards set by competition in Edinburgh. France and Australia are the two most extensively stocked sections, but it is a list without palpable absences. The Italian, German and Spanish sections are not long, but they contain both classics and curiosities, and are low on pap and filler. There are nine wines from Portugal, and they all merit a home in The Vaults. It's good to see a range of six Tokajs – we hope they receive the support they deserve – and the generally stylish tone is heightened by Ramos-Pinto ports and José de Soto sherries, both among the avant-garde of their regions in labelling terms.

In France, most parts attain parity with each other, though Bordeaux – well catered for elsewhere in town – is less widely stocked than Burgundy and Beaujolais. Nick Ryman's Château la Jaubertie, Rhône wines from the Perrin family, Mas de Daumas Gassac, Ostertag's Alsace wines, Saget's Loire portfolio, Chablis from Durup and Burgundy from Comtes Lafon, Daniel Rion and Girard Vollot are some of the names you will find here. Australia sees more unusual wineries come to Edinburgh : Leo Buring, Elderton, Tim Adams, Peel Estate, Evans & Tate, Schinus Mole and Longleat, for example, with Yarra Yering and Vasse Felix. There are five New Zealand wines, too, from Matua Valley and Delegats. Tutored tastings, as often as possible led by the producer in question, are organised at McKirdy's restaurant in Leith; during 1990 you could have met André Ostertag and Nick Ryman, for example. And if you only have a bike, or you're on a one-day coach trip from Inverness, don't be dissuaded from a visit: prices include free Scottish delivery.

Best buys

Château de Chasseloir 1987, Muscadet de Sèvre et Maine sur lie, vinifié en fûts de chêne neufs, Chéreau Carré, £7.89
Château Mayne-Blanc 1986, Lussac Saint-Emilion, £7.65
Old Triangle Rhine Riesling 1989, Hill-Smith, Barossa Valley, £2.99

Wines Galore

161–165 Greenwich High Road, London   *Tel* 071-858 6014
SE10 8JA

Open Mon–Fri 10–7; Sat 10–5 **Closed** Sun, public holidays **Credit cards** All accepted **Discounts** Approx 10% per case **Delivery** Not available **Glass hire** Free with appropriate case order **Tastings and talks** Monthly tastings in wine bar; to groups on request **Cellarage** Not available

Wines Galore, next to Greenwich railway station, is the larger of Davy's two retail shops (the company is best known for its wine bars); there is also a Davy's Wine Shop in Borough High Street, carrying more or less the same range.

The chief delight of Davy's is linguistic. The wine bars are uniformly spendid in name (Boot & Flogger, Chopper Lump, Colonel Jaspers, Crusting Pipe, Guinea Butt, Gyngleboy, Lees Bag, Skinkers, Tappit-Hen, Truckles of Pied Bull Yard, Udder Place Wine Rooms, to intone but a few), and this kind of verbal Georgiana conditions everything about the Davy's operation. Wines Galore, for example, is 'Hard by Davys Wine Vaults' in

Greenwich High Road, and the cover of the list is decorated with a recently unrolled parchment map showing you how to get there. Many of the wines are Davy's own, as sold in the bars, and their curlicued labels tells you that Davy's are 'Purveyors of Wine by the Glass, Bottle, Hogshead, Pipe and Butt' (though prices are not given for Hogsheads, Pipes or Butts in the list), that what you have bought is 'Fine <u>Foreign</u> Wine' and that it is 'All <u>Neat</u> as <u>Imported</u>'. Bare boards are prized more highly by Davy's than any quantity of deep-pile burgundy carpet and suede-finished wallpaper. Some of us find this kind of thing hard to resist.

If you are not of our number, you will be looking for more: top wines at good prices. Your success at the Davy's outlets will be moderate only. The list is short; adequate, but little more. Prices tend to be high, even for the own-label wines. Warre's and Smith Woodhouse's Late Bottled Vintage are the best there are, for example, but at £14.30 you can buy true Vintage Port (some of the attractive but not great 1982s) for less. The range offered is balanced, with wines from all the wine-producing countries of consequence save Portugal and North and South America: you'll have a choice of between six and twelve bottles in most cases, and good wines are often to be found. But this would not seem to be enough, given the upper-echelon prices, to justify the existence of the shops, unless they serve some obscure function in relation to the wine bars. Readers, what do you think? Please report your views.

Best buys

Coteaux de Murviel 1989, Domaine de Limbardie (Cabernet Sauvignon), £4.45

Davy's Blanc de Blancs sparkling wine (méthode traditionnelle), Varichon & Clerc, £5.70

Château de Terrefort-Quancard 1986, Bordeaux Supérieur, £5.65

Wines of Interest

46 Burlington Road, Ipswich, Suffolk IP1 2HS   *Tel* (0473) 215752
Burlington Wines, at above address
Hadleigh Wines, at above address

Open Mon–Fri 9–6; Sat 9–1 **Closed** Sun, public holidays **Credit cards** None accepted; personal and business accounts **Discounts** Not available **Delivery** Free in City of London, Ipswich and central Norwich (min 1 case) and elsewhere (min 6 cases); otherwise at cost; mail order available **Glass hire** Free with suitable order **Tastings and talks** Regular series of tastings in London, Ipswich and Norwich; to groups on request **Cellarage** £2.50 per case per year

See Burlington Wines.

Wines of Westhorpe   ▱

Field House Cottage, Birch Cross,   *Tel* (0283) 820285
Marchington, Staffordshire ST14 8NX

Bond address for collections
Cargo Bonding Ltd, Derby Turn, Derby   *Tel* (0283) 64622
Road, Burton on Trent, Staffordshire
DE14 2QD

Case sales only   **Open** (Warehouse) Mon–Fri 8.30–4.30; (office) Mon–Fri 9–5.30
Closed Sat, Sun, public holidays   **Credit cards** Access, Visa
Discounts Available   **Delivery** Free on UK mainland, Isle of Man, Isle of Wight
and Ireland (min 1 case); mail order available   **Glass hire** Not available
Tastings and talks Occasionally to groups on request   **Cellarage** Not available

Wines of Westhorpe have always been known for stocking just
about everything from Bulgaria – 40 different wines in the
summer list – and the company tackles Hungary seriously, too
(16 wines and 7 Tokajs, including the Aszú Essencias of 1976
and 1957). Both countries are beginning to produce top-quality
wines now, and Wines of Westhorpe stocks a number of these
as well as lakes of party lubricant.

Chile is the next country in Director Alan Ponting's sights,
and the range is being built on a base of Peteroa. There are
nearly 20 French wines, too, half of which are distinguished by
their subterranean prices, and half of which aren't distinguished
by anything much, adequate though they may be. It is still very
much the Balkan-Danube axis that draws you to Westhorpe.
Sales are by the case, and mixing is possible only by drawing
on ready-mixed cases; as there are 24 of these and the list itself
isn't a long one, this should not be a problem. Price, of course,
is a great draw: £100 will buy you four bottles at some
merchants in this *Guide*; here it will buy you nearly four dozen.

Best buys

Svichtov Cabernet Sauvignon 1986 Controliran, Bulgaria, £3.32
Peteroa Sauvignon Blanc 1989, Chile, £2.89
Tokaj Aszú 4 puttonyos 1984, Hungary, £5.16

---

*Telemachus let them talk, and went along to his father's storeroom, a big
and lofty chamber stacked with gold and bronze, and with chests full of
clothing, and stores of fragrant oil. There, too, shoulder to shoulder along
the wall, stood jars of mellow vintage wine, full of the true unblended juice,
waiting for the day when Odysseus, for all he had suffered, should find his
home again.*
Homer *The Odyssey*

Wizard Wine Warehouses

Head office
6 Theobold Court, Theobold Street,   *Tel* 081-207 4455
Borehamwood, Hertfordshire WD6 4RN
12 outlets in London, Surrey, Buckinghamshire, Berkshire and Kent

Open Opening hours vary from branch to branch **Closed** Sun (Surbiton,
Reading and Bletchley branches only) **Credit cards** Access, American Express,
Visa; business accounts **Discounts** 5% for 10 mixed cases **Delivery** Free within
20-mile radius of each branch (min £100 order) **Glass hire** Free with 1-case
order **Tastings and talks** Regular tastings for existing customer by invitation;
theme-tastings at weekends in all branches; to groups on request **Cellarage** Not
available

If you live in London or the South-East, it's worth checking to
find out if you have one of the 12 or so Wizards near you. There
are two very good things about this warehouse chain.

The first is that its buying policy closely reflects what we all
liked so much about the wine warehouse movement when it
first germinated under the familiar inner city railway arches;
let's call it the Jolly Roger approach. Swoop, grab, sell off, move
on. Lists never stood still; there was always a new heap of this
or stack of that whenever you dropped in, and as likely as not it
had 'bargain' written all over it. Nobody on the staff came over
all stiff and timid when it was time to shift thirty pallets of
Gewürztraminer from Honolulu, or a warehouse full of some
mysterious and antique Portuguese red with a label like a Polish
bus ticket; they simply opened bottles, made a fuss over it, cut
the price to the bone, and off it went. Warehouses took off like
hot air balloons because they were exciting places for wine
enthusiasts to visit. As some of the chains got bigger, and solo
warehouses got set in their ways, they became less exciting and
more institutional, but Wizard seem to have managed to keep
the Jolly Roger flying as well as any.

The second reason is that – despite the typical warehouse
locations and the wide, cheap range – it is not company policy
to sell exclusively by the case. Wherever the local licensing
magistrates are prepared to grant a retail licence, Wizard will
sell by the bottle – and that means at most of the warehouses
(check first, though, if you know that you don't want a whole
case). This policy seems to have developed during the years that
Wizard were Bejam-owned; now the company is back on its
own, but sensibly it has decided not to get strict about being
by-the-case-only again.

There's the list, too, of course. It's pretty good for everything
except German wine, which has never been adopted or fostered
by any warehouse or warehouse chain; it is very strong for
French regional and country wines, non-champagne sparkling

wines and Bulgarians. At the time of writing, there are still a remarkable number of wines at under £3, while the majority of the list is under £5; there are fine wines in stock, too, if you want them, with a range of Bordeaux 'second wines' performing their usual role of tone-raising and lustre-adding for under a tenner. And don't forget the unlisted wines, the bankrupt stock, the auction bargains. Specific tastings are at weekends, but you'll always find bottles open to try whenever you drop in.

Best buys

Delegat's Sauvignon Blanc 1989, New Zealand, £5.49
Moulins de Citran 1987, Haut-Médoc (second wine of Château Citran), £5.89
Herdade de Santa Marta 1988, João Pires, Alentejo (white), £3.99

Woodhouse Wines

Hall & Woodhouse, Blandford Forum, Dorset   *Tel* (0258) 452141
DT11 9LS

Open Mon–Fri 10–5; Sat 9.30–1 **Closed** Sun, public holidays
Credit cards Access, Visa; personal and business accounts **Discounts** 5% on 1 bottle cash & carry **Delivery** Free in Taunton, Bristol along M4 to London and southwards to the coast (min 1 case); elsewhere 1–2 cases £5 per case, 3–5 cases £3 per case, 6–10 cases £2.50 per case, 10+ case negotiable; mail order available
Glass hire Free with 1-case order **Tastings and talks** Two annual tastings; to groups on request **Cellarage** £2.30 per case per year

The attractive green logo for Woodhouse Wines contains the date 1777; perhaps this was the year in which the company was founded, in which case it is a very old one by any standards, or perhaps it is a date of significance for Blandford Forum, where it is situated.

This is a late entrant to the Guide, but one which deserves its three paragraphs. Deserves them, first of all, for making an opening offer of 22 different 1989 clarets in which the minimum order was six bottles rather than a case: an excellent idea for the lone buyer of comparatively modest means. Deserves them, too, for its clear, mid-length and open-minded list, with its emphasis on quality wines in the £3 to £8 range.

Most of the wines are from France, with a choice of a dozen or so from most regions and considerably more than that from Bordeaux. Spain, Italy and Australia are the biggest contributors outside France, but Portugal, Eastern Europe, New Zealand, California and Germany all offer small but thoughtful ranges. There is plenty of port, sherry and champagne, with over a dozen sparkling wines from various countries. Manager Angus Avery tells us that the shop is being 'enlarged and greatly improved' at the moment, and we hope to be able to give you an impression of this next year, together with the explanation for 1777.

Best buys

Château Bel Air Clairet 1989, Bordeaux Rosé, £3.88
Castillo de Almansa 1982, Bodegas Piqueras, Almansa, £3.39
Solear, Manzanilla Pasada, Barbadillo, £5.98

Wright Wine Co

The Old Smithy, Raikes Road, Skipton,   *Tel* (0756) 794175/700886
North Yorkshire BD23 1NP

Open Mon–Sat 9–6; public holidays 10–4 **Closed** Sun **Credit cards** None accepted; personal and business accounts **Discounts** 5% on mixed cases
Delivery Free within 30-mile radius of Skipton; elsewhere at cost
Glass hire Free **Tastings and talks** Monthly wine club meetings (evenings)
Cellarage Not available

This Skipton-based merchant has an extensive and varied list – as well as a knowledgeable delivery man. 'Our van driver, who holds a distinction for the [Wine and Spirit Education Trust] higher certificate, is currently studying for the diploma.' Perhaps Wright Wine Co will end up with Britain's first van-driving MW in a year or two.

A great curiosity about wine is also evident in the list, which gives considerable space to wines from less well known parts of the world such as Brazil (a range of four), Israel (another four) and England (six to chose from). Countries whose credentials are more firmly established like New Zealand and Chile get between eight to twelve spaces on the shelves, and so on up the scale until France is reached, with the ranges from Alsace, the Loire, Beaujolais and champagne forming a French quartet of unusual excellence. But balance and harmony prevail throughout, and whatever you come looking for – a fine Mosel Spätlese, a choice of Chablis premiers crus and growers, a top Bairrada, Sassicaia or Château Musar – Bob Wright or general manager Paul Finney will be able to fish off the shelves for you. Indeed, the commitment to a first-class range goes beyond wine into malt whisky, cognac, sake, goldwasser, ouzo . . . and Brontë Yorkshire Liqueur in half-litre stone jars. Into half-bottles, too: there are over 50 of these, together with magnums of claret and champagne up to nebuchadnezzar size.

Best buys

Domaine de Valmagne 1988, Vin de Pays des Collines de la
Moure, £3.39
Alsace Gewürztraminer 1985, Willm, £5.50
Marius Reserva 1982, Almansa, £4.20

Peter Wylie Fine Wines

Plymtree Manor, Plymtree, Cullompton, Devon EX15 2LE	*Tel* (088 47) 555

Open Mon–Fri 9–6; Sat (only by appointment) **Closed** Sun, public holidays
Credit cards None accepted; personal and business accounts **Discounts** £20–£200
on unmixed cases (min 1 case) **Delivery** Free in central London (min 3 cases);
mail order available **Glass hire, Tastings and talks** Not available
Cellarage £4.60 per case per year

Plymtree Manor is a graceful yet imposing William and Mary
house with an extensive cellar, and that cellar is filled with some
very exciting wines indeed. Peter Wylie's business has come a
long way from its modest beginnings in Streatham, and
Cullompton must provide a striking contrast to Soho's Greek
Street, where this merchant learned his trade while working for
and with Wallace Milroy for ten years.

Claret and Sauternes form the backbone of the extensive 'fine
and rare' wine list, and some bone it is, too. The Lafites and the
Montoses and the Palmers and the Moutons spin before your
eyes, changing vintages more quickly than models can change
outfits. Burgundy, champagne and port are the supporting acts,
with good case quantities available of Vintage Port from 1955
onwards, and of burgundy of the 1980s. Six Vintage Madeiras
are available, though £155.25 for a Cossart Gordon 1950 Sercial
is well above other merchants' prices for a youthful 40 year old.
Perhaps prices don't matter much to the majority of Peter
Wylie's customers: the wine, the maker, the year, the condition
will be the crucial factors. Should you require 1890 Lafite, there
are two bottles on offer: the one with lower shoulder level will
cost £1,006.25; the one with very high shoulder level will cost
£1,351.25. Such is the price of shoulders in the fine wine
business.

Peter Wylie has also offered a small range of 1989 clarets *en
primeur*; and cellar planning, valuations and purchase from
customers, investment advice and a 'winesearch' facility are
some of the other services offered.

Best buys

Taylor 1980, £16.10
Château Cos d'Estournel 1985, Saint-Estèphe, half-bottle, £11.50
Château Rieussec 1986, Sauternes, half-bottle, £11.50

Yapp Brothers

The Old Brewery, Mere, Wiltshire BA12 6DY   *Tel* (0747) 860423

Open Mon–Fri 9–5; Sat 9–1 **Closed** Sun, public holidays **Credit cards** Access,
Visa; personal and business accounts **Discounts** Quantity and collection
discounts available **Delivery** Free on UK mainland (min 2 cases); otherwise 1
case £2.50; mail order available **Glass hire** Free with 1-case order
Tastings and talks A variety of tastings held on Saturdays and some evenings,
cost £4 per person in 1990; to groups on request **Cellarage** £4 per case per year or
part-year

After last year's splendid 20th anniversary list, complete with
growers in full colour and reproduction manuscript scores for
celebratory drinking songs by five composer friends (including
Harrison Birtwistle and Peter Maxwell Davies – don't tell us you
threw it away!), it's back to black-and-white and A5 this year.
Continuity is provided by the wines, and by Robin Yapp's own
richly upholstered prose: he is the only writer on wine whose
style can be traced back in an unbroken line to Henry Vizetelly.
Willie Rushton's drawings provide delightful leaven.

'Rhône, Loire, Yapp' reads the copy for the advertisements;
this is one of the few specialist wine merchants with the
courage to stick rigorously to the specialisms in question.
Champagne, Alsace and a little fish soup prove too much to
resist and infiltrate the list's nether regions, while 'Rhône' is
stretched down into Provence, but basically France's two great
wine rivers are what is on offer, and France's two great wine
rivers are what you will get. Ancenis commands a page to itself;
so does Thouarsais; so does Azay-le-Rideau. No other merchant
will offer you a range of eight wines from the Orléanais, four
from Saint-Pourçain-sur-Sioule, another eight from Bandol,
another four from Lirac. Robin Yapp has even discovered a lost
wine region called Brézème, concealed in the crevice between
the Northern and Southern Rhônes. As for all the big names,
the Chaves and Clapes, these were stocked here long before Mr
Parker switched on the American collecting market to their
quality; indeed 'Parker' is a name that Yapp sometimes must
wish he'd never heard, for sudden upswings in demand (and
price) must have picked uncomfortable holes in the Rhône/
Provence section on more than one occasion. But the Yapps
(Robin works in partnership with his wife Judith, despite the
'Bros' bit) return almost obsessively to their sampling grounds,

and always succeed in stitching up the holes with new discoveries for which their enthusiasm is by and large unbridled.

Indeed, almost everything about the Yapps is unbridled: enjoyment, commitment, the spirit of celebration, perhaps prices, certainly the desire to be more than just traders. One is left with the impression that the Yapps themselves are their own best customers or, put another way, that customers are joint-merchants on an annual voyage of discovery. Walk into the yard at the Old Brewery with its tables and chairs, its fountain, and its salvaged cellar equipment; or walk into the shop with its comfortable sofa, its portraits of growers and its litter of corkscrews; and you will know you are somewhere between Britain and France, somewhere between lunch and dinner, somewhere between the last bottle and the next. As good a place as any for a wine enthusiast to be.

Best buys

Sancerre Clos les Perriers 1989, André Vatan, £6.95
Gigondas 1985, Domaine Saint-Gayan, Roger et Jean-Pierre Meffre, £7.25
Domaine de Trévallon, Coteaux d'Aix-en-Provence les Baux 1988, Eloi Dürrbach, £10.25

Yorkshire Fine Wines Company   ◁▷ ☞

Sweethills, Nun Monkton, York, North   *Tel* (0423) 330131
Yorkshire YO5 8ET

Case sales only   Open Mon–Fri 8–5 **Closed** Sat, Sun, public holidays
Credit cards Access, Visa; personal and business accounts **Discounts** 4% on 1
case **Delivery** Free in north of England; otherwise 1 case £9.20, 2 cases £6.90 per
case, 3 cases £5.75 per case, 4 cases £4.60 per case, 5+ cases free; mail order
available **Glass hire** Free **Tastings and talks** In-store tastings and to groups on
request **Cellarage** £5.75 per case per year

During 1990, the Yorkshire Fine Wines Company continued up the path it has been cutting for itself since 1974: that of a first-class trade wholesaler. We include the company in the *Guide* because private customers are also encouraged; the only obstacle standing in your way is the fact that all the prices on the list are ex-VAT, something that a calculator should help you over without much difficulty. Mixed cases are not a problem, and delivery in Northern England is free. If you fail to establish your address as being in Northern England, however, you should prepare yourself for fairly steep delivery charges unless you can compile an order of five cases or more.

The list is an excellent one, both in terms of fireside appeal and in the wines it puts on display. The fireside appeal is accounted for by pleasing design and a series of entertaining features by many hands: suppliers like Javier Hidalgo, agents like Geoffrey Roberts, importers like Neil Sommerfelt, even rival merchants like David Gleave of Winecellars or Jasper Morris of Morris & Verdin, as well as by Yorkshire Fine Wines buyer David Bywater. Photographs and clean, graphic maps add further appeal.

The choice of wines is extensive. As with most trade wholesalers (whose customers require more continuity than the general public), much of the list is occupied by full ranges from a single supplier, rather than many different bottles from a crowd of small growers. Yet there are enough suppliers to ensure that tedium is kept well at bay, and in some areas – champagne, for example, or burgundy – the range is splendidly multiple. The main champagne suppliers are Krug, Mumm and Charles Heidsieck, but there are few grandes marques that do not find a niche somewhere on pages 14–15, and rosé champagne as well as cuvées de prestige are present in force. Burgundy is an area in which no list can excel without variety, and while Latour certainly provides more wines than any other, there are also growers in plenty (Machard de Gramont, Raoul Clerget, Domaine de la Pousse d'Or, Domaine Dujac, Daniel Rion and Etienne Sauzet all feature). Beaujolais and the Rhône offer considerable choice, and the Loire and Bordeaux still more. Many of the Alsace wines come from Domaine Marcel Deiss at Bergheim, for whom Yorkshire Fine Wines is North of England agent; they merit exploration. The French country wine selection is less impressive; doubtless Corbières and Vin de Pays de l'Hérault are names that still sit uncomfortably in many hotel wine lists, though this must change before long.

Wines from Germany, Italy and Spain are all stocked with respect but a degree of caution. The North American selection, by contrast, is adventurous: Inniskillin from Canada, Rose Creek from Idaho, Ponzi from Oregon and four Washington State Wineries share list space with a big range of Californian wines (Mondavi-dominated). Australia and New Zealand have a firm foothold at Nun Monkton, too. Ports are present in fortifying quantities, with everything from Graham joined by a certain amount from Fonseca and others; the vintages go back to 1924.

Restaurant and hotel customers may hold back list development in areas like the Midi, but they account for a range of over 200 half-bottles – one of the best in Britain. Regular bin-end offers go out to customers on the mailing list, and presumably ordinary (non-trade) customers like us are able to take advantage of the four per cent discount on list prices (which are in general rather high) offered to those who pay cash/cheque on delivery. There's another reason for having your calculator handy as you look through the list.

Best buys

Alsace Riesling 'Engelgarten' 1986, Domaine Deiss, £7.89
Bourgueil Réserve 1986, Domaine Druet, £7.88
Quinta de Santa Amaro 1986, João Pires, Portugal, £5.21

Part IV

Find out more about wine

wine tours

Find out more about wine

There is more activity than ever before for those who want to find out more about wine. You can join wine clubs and wine societies, you can go on wine courses, or you can travel to the vineyards in the company of like-minded enthusiasts. In this section we list a wide variety of what's available.

Some of these activities are organised by wine merchants themselves – and in the listings that follow this is plainly indicated by a reference back to the **Where to buy** section of the *Guide*. Many merchants in addition to those listed below offer informal 'club' facilities, details of which will usually be found on the merchant's list. Other activities are run independently or (in the case of some wine courses) in conjunction with auction houses or cookery schools.

WINE CLUBS

Alba Wine Society
Leet Street, Coldstream, Borders TD12 4BJ **Tel** (0890) 3166
Membership of this Scottish mail order wine society is by an initial fee of £10. Thereafter, membership is free so long as you buy at least one case of wine each year. In addition, members are offered a variety of tutorial events and tastings including the annual Alba Wine Society Tasting. (See also the **Where to buy** section.)

Les Amis du Vin
19 Charlotte Street, London W1P 1HB **Tel** 071-636 4020
Life membership £15. Discounts: five per cent off all wines, ten per cent off unmixed cases, free delivery for 2+ cases or over £75. Priority booking for tastings. Regular newsletter and special offers including *en primeur*. (See also the **Where to buy** section.)

Averys Bin Club
7 Park Street, Bristol, Avon BS1 5NG **Tel** (0272) 214141
Members join the Club by committing themselves to subscribing a minimum monthly amount of £30 by banker's order. Members may use the Club for buying wines for everyday drinking and *en primeur* for future drinking; Averys will also assist in the selection

of wines for laying down when the opportunity arises. Members may purchase wines at a discount of five per cent off prices in Averys' current wine list, and receive a regular newsletter, special offers at discounted prices, tastings and *en primeur* offers and tasting notes by Master of Wine John Avery. New members receive a Bin Club Cellar Book and membership certificate. (See also the **Where to buy** section.)

Christchurch Fine Wine Co
1-3 Vine Lane, High Street, Christchurch, Dorset BH23 1AE
Tel (0202) 473255
Membership costs £5, which is refunded upon the purchase of one case of wine. Members receive a monthly newsletter, invitations to tutored tastings (nine are held between April and December) and five per cent discount off the basic wine list. In 1990, for the first time, there was a trip to the Loire in September lasting nine days (approximate cost £300). (See also **Where to buy** section.)

Coonawarra Club
Mark Gibson (secretary), 9B Hornsey Lane Gardens, London N6 5NX **Tel** 071-480 6907 Membership £5, renewal £2 per annum. Tastings of Australian wines, sometimes tutored. Occasional dinners with appropriate wines.

Howells of Bristol Limited Bin Club
The Old Brewery, Station Road, Wickwar, Gloucestershire GL12 8NB **Tel** (0454) 294085 **Telex** 444729 (**Cres Ho**) **Fax** (0454) 294090
This club specialises in laying down fine wines for future enjoyment. Members build up their individual cellar through a regular monthly subscription (recommended minimum £40). Howells says that this avoids lump sum payments and allows members to develop their cellar at their own financial pace, acquiring wines at opening prices and enjoying them when they are properly mature. Wines are stored in Howells' historic cellars. Twice a year, in spring and autumn, members are offered a broad selection of wines, and when merited, an *en primeur* offer. Tasting notes and 'ready for drinking' dates are included for each wine. On joining (once-only membership fee of £15), a cellar book is provided and cellar cards follow each purchase of wine.

The International Wine & Food Society
108 Old Brompton Road, London SW7 3RA **Tel** 071-370 0909
President Michael Broadbent MW. Director Hugo Dunn-Meynell. Enrolment fee £10. Membership terms on application; special rates

for members under 25. The London headquarters has a library, club and hotel facilities; worldwide contacts. Nearly 200 regional branches organise dinners, tastings, lectures and visits. The journal, quarterly newsletters and annual vintage guide to wine-buying are free of charge to members.

Lay & Wheeler
6 Culver Street West, Colchester, Essex CO1 1JA **Tel** (0206) 764446
Fax (0206) 564488
A series of popular wine workshops are held in the Colchester Garrison Officer's Club: during 1990 Zelma Long, President of Simi Winery in California and one of the world's foremost oenologists, presented ten of Simi's premium wines. Monthly workshops are also held at Lay & Wheeler's Wine Market in Colchester. These workshops are presented by members of Lay & Wheeler's buying team. Topics in 1990 included Australia v California, Northern Rhône and the Upper Loire, and Chablis and the Mâconnais. (See also the **Where to buy** section.)

Lincoln Wine Society
8 Green Lane, North Hykeham, Lincoln, Lincolnshire LN6 8NL
Tel (0522) 680388
Chairman Norman Tate. Monthly talk and tasting sessions, sometimes with guest speakers. Fine wine evenings held three times a year, regular newsletters and an annual trip to a wine region. Membership £5 annually (£8 joint membership).

Methuselah's
29 Victoria Street, London SW1H 0EU **Tel** 071-222 0424/3550
Annual subscription £20. Tutored tastings are usually held every second Monday of the month. A two-course dinner with coffee at £10.50 a head is available after tastings.

Martin Mistlin's Fine Wine Dining Club
41 Kingsend, Ruislip HA4 7DD **Tel** 081-427 9944 (day)
The Club specialises in wine and food events such as tastings, dinners and wine tours. The subscription for 1991 is approximately £9.50.

Le Nez Rouge Wine Club
Berkmann Wine Cellars, 12 Brewery Road, London N7 9NH
Tel 071-609 4711
Club Secretary Debby McCleary. Advantages to members are reduced prices, regular special offers, monthly tastings, dinners, etc. The club list is sent out twice a year. (See also the **Where to buy** section.)

North East Wine Tasting Society
Nigel Ellam (Secretary), 1 East View, High Heworth, Gateshead,
Tyne & Wear NE10 9AR **Tel** 091-438 4107
Monthly meetings are held in Newcastle. Most members are
'enthusiastic amateurs' and the tastings are aimed at improving
knowledge of wine-producing areas, grape varieties and the wines
themselves. Annual membership is £10.

The **University of Newcastle** also runs numerous wine courses
and tours under the guidance of Rev M Savage. Information is
available from the Centre for Continuing Education at the
University (**Tel** 091-222 6000).

Northern Wine Appreciation Group
D M Hunter, 21 Dartmouth Avenue, Almondbury, Huddersfield,
West Yorkshire HD5 8UR **Tel** (0484) 531228
Weekly meetings are held in West Yorkshire from September to
June 'to taste, assess and extend the members' experience of wine
and food'. The relationship between food and wine leads to the
planning of the meals which form part of the group's activities.
Graded tutored tastings and special events are held for new
members to help them integrate.

Ordre Mondial des Gourmets Dégustateurs
Details from: Martin Mistlin, 41 Kingsend, Ruislip HA4 7DD
Tel 081-427 9944 (day)
This is a French wine guild with a British chapter (the
headquarters are in Paris). Its aims are the promotion of the
knowledge of fine wines and spirits. Varied regular tastings and
dinners are held with access to meetings abroad. The subscription
in 1989 was £65 for professionals, £45 for amateurs. Subscriptions
may be increased for 1991, but this was undecided as we went to
press.

Private Wine Club
309 Old Street, London EC1V 6LE **Tel** 071-729 1768
This is a 'non-profit-making wine club consisting entirely of wine
lovers' run by John Corliss. Membership is by contribution to
Capital Radio's Help a London Child Appeal (minimum £5). This
brings a quarterly newsletter, an invitation to the Grand Annual
Tasting in November and to the Great Beaujolais Breakfast. Other
tastings in 1990 included the 1981 vintage Cabernet Sauvignons
from Australia, the wines of Fronsac and the 1989 vintage of the
Rhône and Loire. (See also Old Street Wine Co.)

The Sunday Times Wine Club

New Aquitaine House, Paddock Road, Reading, Berkshire
RG4 0JY **Tel** (0734) 481713

Also known as The Wine Club. Mail order only. President Hugh
Johnson, Club Secretary Jillian Cole. There are various levels of
membership: the most basic (£5 for the first year, £3 for
subsequent years) brings an annotated wine list, tastings, tours,
entry to the Annual London Vintage Festival and a lively quarterly
magazine edited by Jim Ainsworth. Tastings are arranged around
the country and tours around the wine-making regions. (See also
the **Where to buy** section.)

Tanglewood Wine Society

'Tanglewood', Mayfield Avenue, New Haw, Weybridge, Surrey
KT15 3AG **Tel** (09323) 48720

This club, with over 100 members, is now in its sixth year.
Membership costs £6 per person or £10 for a couple at the same
address. A charge is made for each tasting, averaging £7.50 per
head.

Helen Verdcourt Wines

Spring Cottage, Kimbers Lane, Maidenhead, Berkshire SL6 2QP
Tel (0628) 25577

Two local clubs (which have now been running regularly for ten
years) meet monthly, one in Maidenhead, the other in Englefield
Green, for tastings tutored by Helen Verdcourt. No membership
fees; tastings are charged at cost. Helen Verdcourt also tutors for
two terms of Adult Education at Beaconsfield College in Wine
Appreciation, where other clubs meet occasionally. (See also the
Where to buy section and **Wine tours**.)

La Vigneronne

105 Old Brompton Road, London SW7 3LE **Tel** 071-589 6113

The tutored tastings of fine and rare wines held twice a week
(usually Monday and Thursday) are very popular. No membership
fee. However, subscribers to La Vigneronne, who pay £10
annually, receive a wine journal twice a year. This includes details
and tasting notes of all wines and special offers. Subscribers are
also offered wines *en primeur* and import tastings, which are held
three times a year. (See also the **Where to buy** section.)

Vintner Wine Club

Winefare House, 5 High Road, Byfleet, Surrey KT14 7QF
Tel (09323) 51585

Initial enrolment fee and annual membership £14. The Vintner:

James Rackham. Quarterly newsletter. Comprehensive list of 300 wines and individual tasting notes. Members can get a discount on single bottles at every branch of Arthur Rackhams. Gastronomic programme of monthly tutored tastings and dinners in West End and Surrey restaurants. La Grande Taste – weekend members' tastings at Arthur Rackhams. The Vintner Festival held at a London venue every October. (See also Arthur Rackhams in the **Where to buy** section.)

The Wine & Dine Society
96 Ramsden Road, London SW12 8QZ **Tel** 081-673 4439
Weekly tastings of wines from all over the world, including fine and rare bottles. Guest speakers. Dinners in London follow an ethnic theme.

Wine and Gastronomic Societies (WAGS)
Martin Mistlin, 41 Kingsend, Ruislip HA4 7DD
Tel 081-427 9944 (day)
This society comprises the Alsace Club of Great Britain (President Hugh Johnson), the Cofradia Riojana and the Gallo Nero Club of Great Britain (President The Hon Rocco Forte). A joining fee of £12 allows members to attend tastings and dinners featuring wines from these regions plus occasional events based on other wine regions. (No annual subscription.) Wine tours abroad and wine weekends in the UK will feature in the clubs' activities.

The Winetasters
P B Beardwood (Secretary), 44 Claremont Road, London W13 0DG
Tel 081-997 1252
Annual subscription £5 (£1.50 if you live more than 50 miles from London). Non-profit-making club which organises tastings, seminars, dinners and tours (the major tour in 1989 was to Northern Italy – the next major tour, in 1991, will be to the Rhône). The club grew out of the Schoolmasters' Wine Club.

Winewise
Michael Schuster, 107 Culford Road, London N1 4HL
Tel 071-254 9734
Promotes all aspects of tasting, understanding and appreciating wines and spirits. Regular tastings include two wine courses: a Beginners' Course (£85 for six evenings) and an Intermediate Course (£125 for six evenings). Each course is limited to 18 participants. Other tastings are held to examine the wines of individual properties ('vertical') and vintages ('horizontal'), and to compare fine wines from round the world. There are blind tastings

each spring, workshops on Saturday mornings and many fine
wine tastings late on Sunday afternoons. A brochure of tasting
details is mailed regularly on request.

Zinfandel Club
Spenser Hilliard (Secretary), 22 Risley Avenue, London N17 7EU
Tel 071-353 0774 (work), 081-801 1617 (home)
Membership fee £5. Sporadic meetings to taste California wines,
sometimes tutored. Occasional dinners with appropriate wines.

WINE COURSES

David Baillie Vintners School of Wine
The Sign of the Lucky Horseshoe, 86 Longbrook Street, Exeter,
Devon EX4 6AP **Tel** (0392) 221345
This West Country wine merchant plans to repeat his School of
Wine course in 1991. The course is run once a year at the Imperial
Hotel, Exeter, and comprises seven three-hour evening sessions of
tastings and lectures given by experienced members of the wine
trade, with an optional exam at the end, leading (for those who
pass) to a Certificate from the David Baillie School of Wine. Cost in
1990 was £120. (See also the **Where to buy** section.)

Christie's Wine Course
63 Old Brompton Road, London SW7 3JS **Tel** 071-581 3933
Principals Michael Broadbent MW and Steven Spurrier, Secretary
Caroline de Lane Lea. Christie's holds an Introduction to Wine
Tasting course, concentrating on the principal wines of France.
The course runs on five consecutive Tuesday evenings, lasting
approximately two hours, six times a year. Cost £125. Starting in
September 1990 Christie's will be offering Master Classes,
specialist tastings of top-quality wines. Places for between 15-30
people, cost £30-£50. Discussion and tasting are conducted by top
wine experts (in 1990 the roll included Michael Broadbent MW,
Serena Sutcliffe MW, David Peppercorn MW, Pamela Vandyke
Price and Steven Spurrier).

Corney & Barrow's Wine Course
12 Helmet Row, London EC1V 3QJ **Tel** 071-251 4051
Aimed particularly at Corney & Barrow's younger customers and
those within the hotel/restaurant trade, the cost of the four-session
course – £20 per session or £75 for all four – covers the cost of
wines, tuition, information sheets, maps and glasses. Numbers are
restricted to a maximum of 20. Further details from Judy Emerson
at the above address. (See also the **Where to buy** section.)

Ecole du Vin, Château Loudenne, Bordeaux

Ecole du Vin, Château Loudenne, St-Yzans-de-Médoc, 33340
Lesparre, France **Tel** 010 33 (56) 090503 **Fax** 010 33 (56) 090287
Six-day courses (starting on Monday) are held for a dozen students
five times a year at Gilbey's Château Loudenne, under the
direction of Charles Eve MW. Accommodation and cuisine of very
high standard in the château. Aimed at the public and
professionals in the trade, the lectures and tastings cover all
aspects of viticulture and vinification. Visits are arranged to other
Bordeaux areas and châteaux. Cost, which includes all meals and
drinks, in 1991 is 11,900 francs, plus travel to France.

The Fulham Road Wine School

The Fulham Road Wine Centre, 899-901 Fulham Road, London
SW6 5HU **Tel** 071-384 2588
A selection of courses, from a straightforward introduction to
identifying flavours and styles of wine through to tastings
covering grape types and classic wine regions in greater detail.
Also how to match food and wine, and Saturday workshops from
January to May. (See also the **Where to buy** section.)

German Wine Academy

P O Box 1705, 6500 Mainz, Federal Republic of Germany
A 12th-century monastery is the setting for courses (delivered in
English), which include lectures by wine experts, vineyard visits
and tastings. The basic seven-day course is run throughout the
year (DM 1640 per person) and is supplemented by more advanced
courses and an extended, culturally oriented course conducted at a
more relaxed pace. Further information from the German Wine
Information Service, Chelsea Chambers, 262a Fulham Road,
London SW10 9EL **Tel** 071-376 3329.

Leith's School of Food and Wine

21 St Alban's Grove, London W8 5BP **Tel** 071-229 0177
Some of Leith's wine courses are for students of the School only, as
part of their food and wine studies. However, at least two courses
are available to outsiders: five two-hour evening sessions starting
in January 1991, leading to the award of Leith's Certificate (if you
pass the exam); and ten two-hour evening sessions starting in
October, leading to Leith's Advanced Certificate of Wine,
examined by Leith's Master of Wine, Richard Harvey. This is
roughly analogous to the Wine and Spirit Education Trust's
Higher Certificate, without the sessions on licensing and labelling
laws, and with particular stress on tasting. Cost £145 and £275
respectively. Other courses are also sometimes available.

The Lincoln Wine Course
Norman Tate, 8 Green Lane, North Hykeham, Lincoln,
Lincolnshire LN6 8NL **Tel** (0522) 680388
Wine course offered at Yarborough Adult Education Centre,
Lincoln, starting in September each year. This is a two-term course
(two hours a week) with the emphasis on tasting as well as gaining
a good general knowledge of wine. Cost is approximately £42 per
term. Specialist evenings are sometimes held.

Sotheby's
Wine Evenings with Sotheby's, 34-35 New Bond Street, London
W1A 2AA **Tel** 071-408 5272; Wine Department now at Unit 5,
Albion Wharf, London SW11 4AN **Tel** 071-924 3287
Sotheby's are planning to launch a new series of wine evenings
towards the end of 1990. Enquiries to the Wine Department at the
above address.

Tante Marie School of Cookery
Woodham House, Carlton Road, Woking, Surrey GU21 4HF
Tel (0483) 726957
Conal Gregory MW, MP, organises wine appreciation courses,
generally during the autumn and winter, on three weekday
evenings (lasting two hours), aimed at those with modest
knowledge and including extensive tutored tastings.

WINE TOURS

Arblaster & Clarke Wine Tours
104 Church Road, Steep, Petersfield, Hampshire GU32 2DD
Tel (0730) 66883
This is a small family-run specialist tour operator in its fifth year.
Tours in 1991 will include eight Champagne weekends (from
£169), four- and five-day tours to all the other major vineyard areas
in France (from £249), plus Portugal, Spain, Germany, California
and Italy. The tours are accompanied by a wine guide and tour
manageress and visits are to leading domaines, many of whom do
not normally receive visitors. For those who prefer self-drive,
individual itineraries are also organised.

Allez France
27 West Street, Storrington, West Sussex RH20 4DZ
Tel (0903) 745793; VINEscapes Bespoke Wine Holidays **Tel** (0903)
742345

The Allez France 'VINEscapes' wine holidays are for the independent-minded traveller to France, and are based on hotels chosen for their setting, cuisine, character and comfort – in Alsace, Champagne, Burgundy, Chablis, Rhône/Provence, Bordeaux and the Loire. These include a 'unique' selection of hotels with their own vineyards. Bookings include information on the wine regions. Travel arrangements are flexible but inclusive.

Australian Tourist Commission
Gemini House, 10-18 Putney Hill, London SW15 6AA
The Tourist Commission can provide information on tours and holidays available through Australian travel firms. For more specific information on wine tours, contact South Australia House, 50 Strand, London WC2N 5LW **Tel** 071-930 7471, and see also Victour below.

Blackheath Wine Trails
13 Blackheath Village, London SE3 9LA **Tel** 081-463 0012
In 1990, thirteen wine tours were offered: Bordeaux & Cognac, Champagne, the Loire, Lisbon Coast, Alsace, Madrid and Rioja, northern Portugal and the Douro, Jerez, Tuscany, Burgundy and Madeira. Tours vary from four to eight days and prices range from £312 to £700. All are air/coach except Champagne, which is ferry/coach.

DER Travel Service
18 Conduit Street, London W1R 9TD **Tel** 071-408 0111
As well as Rhine cruises, DER arranges air and rail holidays in German and Austrian hotels, guest houses or apartments, many of them in wine-growing areas: with your own car you can tour the wine-growing areas of the Rhine and Mosel on the 'Wine Regions Tour'. An eight-night tour in 1990 cost from £193 (for five adults travelling) to £232 (for two adults travelling).

English Vineyards
Many English vineyards are open to the public offering guided tours, tastings and sales. For further information contact The English Vineyards Association, 38 West Park, London SE9 4RH **Tel** 081-857 0452

Eurocamp
Edmundson House, Tatton Street, Knutsford, Cheshire WA16 6BG
Tel (0565) 3844
(Reservations only: 28 Princess Street, Knutsford, Cheshire WA16 6BG)

Eurocamp arranges self-drive camping and mobile-home holidays at 200 sites in Europe, many of which are 'almost among the grapes – and the more well-known grapes at that'. These include the Gironde, Saumur, Meursault, Bergerac, Cahors, Mosel, Bordeaux and Rhineland.

Eurocamp Independent (at the above address) **Tel** (0565) 55399 offers a ferry/pitch reservations 'package' for campers and touring caravan owners to over 250 sites in Europe.

Francophiles

Ron and Jenny Farmer, 66 Great Brockeridge, Westbury-on-Trym, Bristol, Avon BS9 3UA **Tel** (0272) 621975
The Farmers offer France 'lovingly packaged' on their personally escorted holidays of discovery in the regional heartlands. Their clients are 'not usual coach holiday travellers but ones who appreciate in-depth, unhurried visits and structured tastings'. In 1991 they offer Alsace, Provence, Cévennes, Auvergne, Savoy, Charentes, the Dordogne and the Jura. Also 'Bonnes Tables de France', gourmet short breaks in spring and autumn.

Hide-a-Way Wine Holiday in Burgundy

Maureen and Ken Deeming, Oak Lodge, Ambleside Road, Keswick, Cumbria CA12 4DL **Tel** (07687) 72522
Vacancies in Maureen and Ken Deeming's 'small, renovated 200-year-old Burgundian cottage' are available for certain weeks between July and September. The price is 2,150 francs per person per week (maximum 6 double rooms) and consists of bed and continental breakfast and four evening meals with house wine. Visitors are taken to selected vineyards of the Côte de Nuits, the Côte de Beaune, the Côte Chalonnaise, the Mâconnais and Beaujolais for tastings on three days (Monday, Wednesday, Friday) starting at approximately 9.30 and returning at approximately 5.30.

KD German Rhine Line

G A Clubb Rhine Cruise Agency, 28 South Street, Epsom, Surrey KT18 7PF **Tel** (0372) 742033
In 1990, a week-long cruise left from Cologne, visited vineyards on the Rhine, the Mosel and in Alsace, and included lectures and tutored tastings. This 'floating wine seminar' ended in Basle.

Moswin Tours

P O Box 8, 52b London Road, Oadby, Leicestershire LE2 5WX
Tel (0533) 719922/714982 **Fax** (0533) 716016

Fully inclusive tours, by air or coach, to the Mosel Valley and its wine festivals with sightseeing excursions, wine tastings and visits to vineyards in the autumn. These range from 4 to 11 days. Also available are independent tailor-made wine tours to the Mosel Valley (budget to luxury) with an option of staying with a wine grower (May to October), wine seminars, and visits to other wine-growing regions of Germany and France.

Premier Wine Tours
4 Elms Crescent, London SW4 8RB **Tel** 071-498 1459
For 1991 Premier Wine Tours are planning two 'Circle Tours' of France. Each tour will begin and end in Paris and last approximately 32-35 days. The tour will run through all the major wine regions of France and participants may join and leave the tour at any time (minimum stay three days). The aim is to provide a totally flexible wine-tasting holiday with a relaxed, informal atmosphere.

Sonata Travel
227 Umberslade Road, Selly Oak, Birmingham B29 7SG
Tel 021-472 8636
This company (which recently took over Special Interest Tours of Leicester), offers group coach tours to French wine regions for 4-7 days. Joining points are at Birmingham, Leicester and London.

Tanglewood Wine Tours
'Tanglewood', Mayfield Avenue, New Haw, Weybridge, Surrey KT15 3AG **Tel** (09323) 48720
In 1990, tours were offered of four nights in Burgundy and the Loire Valley. Travel was by luxury coach with accommodation in comfortable hotels situated centrally in Beaune and Saumur respectively. There was also an additional Champagne weekend based in the centre of Reims. (See also **Wine clubs**.)

Helen Verdcourt Wine Tours
Spring Cottage, Kimbers Lane, Maidenhead, Berkshire SL6 2QP
Tel (0628) 25577
During 1990 a short 4-day tour to the Champagne area was being planned for October. (See also the **Where to buy** section and **Wine clubs**.)

Victour
Tourist Office, Victoria House, Melbourne Place, Strand, London WC2B 4LG **Tel** 071-240 3974 or 071-836 2656

The Victoria Tourism Commission produce a good wine and food guide to Victoria with helpful notes on wineries and ideas for self-drive visits. They also have details of various rail and coach tours including brochures for Australian Wine Tours, Peter Heath's Unique Winery Tours, Winery Walkabout and Bogong Jack Cycling Winery Tours. The Commission will also assist in planning group tours around the state's 140 public wineries.

Vintage Wine Tours
8 Belmont, Lansdown Road, Bath, Avon BA1 5DZ
Tel (0225) 315834/315659/480306
Concentrates on designing tours for groups (10-40 people) by air and coach, and will arrange tours to any destination, including gourmet meals, sightseeing excursions and any special requirements. In 1990 the major destinations were Germany, Spain and France. Weekend breaks to the Champagne area are also offered.

Wine Tours by Helen Gillespie-Peck Travel Services
103 Queen Street, Newton Abbot, Devon TQ12 3BG **Tel** (0626) 65373
Helen Gillespie-Peck has been teaching about wines for the last 16 years. On offer in 1991 are tours to Bordeaux/Bergerac, Burgundy, Rioja/Barcelona, northern Portugal, Italy and Vienna (including Hungarian wines). Main tours are of 10-12 days' duration. Also gastronomic weekends in Normandy, Brittany, Bordeaux and Provence. Tours are by ferry and luxury coach. Numbers are limited to a maximum of 32 per departure.

World Wine Tours
4 Dorchester Road, Drayton St Leonard, Oxfordshire OX9 8BH
Tel (0865) 891919
World Wine Tours, run by Liz and Martin Holliss, offer a wide range of quality wine tours for the novice and connoisseur alike, each lasting from four to eight days. All tours are led by wine experts, most of whom are Masters of Wine. A maximum of 30 bookings are accepted on to any one tour (the average is 20 clients per tour). In 1991 over 25 tours have been planned, visiting top wine estate and châteaux in Alsace, Austria, Bordeaux, Burgundy, Chablis, Champagne, Germany, Loire Valley, Madeira, Penedés, Portual, Rhône Valley, Rioja, Tuscany and Umbria. Inclusive prices range from £475-£950 per person. Specially tailored tours can be arranged both for private groups of wine enthusiasts and as corporate incentives/hospitality. Also on offer: stays in historic

private châteaux throughout France, cruises in luxury hotel barges in Alsace, Burgundy or the Midi, self-catering at Castello Vicchiomaggio in Tuscany and a series of wine weekends in the UK.

If readers have any comments to make, or experiences to pass on, concerning the services offered by any of the clubs or wine tour operators listed, please write to the Editor using the Freepost address given at the back of the book (use the report forms if wished).

Index

The index covers the regional section only and includes the principal wines produced there, grape varieties, a selection of producers and Taste Boxes. See also the Glossary on page 83.

INDEX

INDEX

Wine in Pubs

Research shows that wine-drinking in Britain is increasing and a more discriminating consumer is emerging who looks for value-for-money, good-quality wines. What are the pubs doing about it?

A *Which?* survey conducted in 1987 found that wine in pubs was generally poor quality, in poor condition, expensive and served in a variety of quantities. Following these dismal results, the Wine Development Board embarked on a campaign aimed at improving the overall standard of wines served in Britain's pubs.

The Wine Development Board's Wine in Pubs campaign, launched at a London seminar in April 1988, has a two-fold strategy – education, through its manual, *Profit from Wine*, and incentive, through its awards for Wine Pubs. The Wine Development Board believes that the standard of wine in pubs is improving. Predictions are that even more interest will develop as a result of the breaking of the tied house system, liberating publicans to buy whatever they want from the source of their choice.

Would you help the Wine Development Board assess the success of their Wine in Pubs campaign by answering the questions opposite for your favourite wine pub?

Questionnaire: Wine in Pubs

Name of Pub
_____

Address of Pub
_____

1 Does the pub serve wine in a plain or marked glass, and, if so, of what capacity?

_____

2 How many different types of red and white wines are available?

_____

3 Does the pub sell wine by the bottle? _____

4 Are white wines served properly chilled? _____

5 Are you offered a wine list to choose from? _____

6 Are the wines promoted or prominently displayed?

_____

7 What do you consider the quality of the wine to be like?
   (a) Excellent
   (b) Reasonable
   (c) Awful

8 Did you think the wine was stale? _____

9 Did you think the wine was good value for money?

_____

10 Did you see anyone else drinking wine when you were there?

_____

Your name
_____

Your address

_____

Please send the completed questionnaire to the Wine Development Board, Five Kings House, 1 Queen Street Place, London EC4R 1QS

Report to the Editor *Which? Wine Guide*

This report is

a new recommendation ☐

a comment on existing entry ☐

please tick as appropriate

name of establishment _____

address _____

tel no: _____

please continue overleaf

date of most recent visit

signed

I am not connected directly or indirectly with the management or proprietors

name   *in block letters, please*

address

Send to: Which? Wine Guide, Freepost, London NW1 4DX
(please note: no postage required within UK)

Report to the Editor *Which? Wine Guide*

This report is

a new recommendation ☐ *please tick as appropriate*

a comment on existing entry ☐

name of establishment

address

tel no:

please continue overleaf

date of most recent visit
_____

signed
_____

I am not connected directly or indirectly with the management or proprietors

name   *in block letters, please*
_____

address
_____
_____

Send to: Which? Wine Guide, Freepost, London NW1 4DX
(please note: no postage required within UK)

Report to the Editor *Which? Wine Guide*

This report is

a new recommendation ☐   *please tick as appropriate*

a comment on existing entry ☐

name of establishment
_____

address
_____

tel no:

_____

please continue overleaf

date of most recent visit
_____

signed
_____

I am not connected directly or indirectly with the management or
proprietors

name   *in block letters, please*
_____

address
_____
_____

Send to: Which? Wine Guide, Freepost, London NW1 4DX
(please note: no postage required within UK)

Report to the Editor *Which? Wine Guide*

This report is

a new recommendation ☐   *please tick as appropriate*

a comment on existing entry ☐

name of establishment

_____

address

_____

tel no:

_____

please continue overleaf

date of most recent visit
_____

signed
_____

I am not connected directly or indirectly with the management or proprietors

name   *in block letters, please*
_____

address
_____
_____

Send to: Which? Wine Guide, Freepost, London NW1 4DX
(please note: no postage required within UK)

Report to the Editor *Which? Wine Guide*

This report is

a new recommendation   ☐   *please tick as appropriate*

a comment on existing entry   ☐

name of establishment

address

tel no:

please continue overleaf

date of most recent visit
_____

signed
_____

I am not connected directly or indirectly with the management or
proprietors

name   *in block letters, please*
_____

address
_____

_____

Send to: Which? Wine Guide, Freepost, London NW1 4DX
(please note: no postage required within UK)

Report to the Editor *Which? Wine Guide*

This report is

a new recommendation   ☐   *please tick as appropriate*

a comment on existing entry   ☐

name of establishment

address

tel no:

please continue overleaf

date of most recent visit
_____

signed
_____

I am not connected directly or indirectly with the management or
proprietors

name   *in block letters, please*
_____

address
_____

Send to: Which? Wine Guide, Freepost, London NW1 4DX
(please note: no postage required within UK)

Report to the Editor *Which? Wine Guide*

This report is

a new recommendation   ☐   *please tick as appropriate*

a comment on existing entry   ☐

name of establishment

address

tel no:

please continue overleaf

date of most recent visit
_____

signed
_____

I am not connected directly or indirectly with the management or
proprietors

name   *in block letters, please*
_____

address
_____
_____

Send to: Which? Wine Guide, Freepost, London NW1 4DX
(please note: no postage required within UK)